THE ROUTLEDGE COMPANION TO SEXUALITY AND COLONIALISM

Unique in its global and interdisciplinary scope, this collection brings together comparative insights across European, Ottoman, Japanese, and US imperial contexts while spanning colonized spaces in Latin America, the Caribbean, Africa, the Indian Ocean, the Middle East, and East and Southeast Asia. Drawing on interdisciplinary perspectives from cultural, intellectual and political history, anthropology, law, gender and sexuality studies, and literary criticism, *The Routledge Companion to Sexuality and Colonialism* combines regional and historiographic overviews with detailed case studies, making it the key reference for up-to-date scholarship on the intimate dimensions of colonial rule. Comprising more than 30 chapters by a team of international contributors, the *Companion* is divided into five parts:

- Directions in the study of sexuality and colonialism
- Constructing race, controlling reproduction
- Sexuality in law
- Subjects, souls, and selfhood
- Pleasure and violence.

The Routledge Companion to Sexuality and Colonialism is essential reading for students and researchers in gender, sexuality, race, global studies, world history, Indigeneity, and settler colonialism.

Chelsea Schields is Assistant Professor of History at the University of California, Irvine. Her scholarship explores the histories of sexuality, race, and the politics of oil and empire in modern Europe and the Caribbean. Her current book project examines how the age of oil and the end of empire brought renewed intervention in Caribbean intimate life. Recent articles have appeared in *Historical Reflections/Réflexions Historiques* (2019), *Gender & History* (2019), and *Radical History Review* (2020).

Dagmar Herzog is Distinguished Professor of History at the Graduate Center, City University of New York. She is the author of *Sex after Fascism: Memory and Morality in Twentieth-Century Germany* (2005), *Sexuality in Europe: A Twentieth-Century History* (2011), *Cold War Freud: Psychoanalysis in an Age of Catastrophes* (2017), and *Unlearning Eugenics: Sexuality, Reproduction, and Disability in Post-Nazi Europe* (2018). She is currently researching the theology and history of disability in Germany, 1900–2020.

THE ROUTLEDGE COMPANION TO SEXUALITY AND COLONIALISM

Edited by Chelsea Schields and Dagmar Herzog

LONDON AND NEW YORK

First published 2021
by Routledge
2 Park Square, Milton Park, Abingdon, Oxon OX14 4RN

and by Routledge
52 Vanderbilt Avenue, New York, NY 10017

Routledge is an imprint of the Taylor & Francis Group, an informa business

British Library Cataloguing-in-Publication Data
A catalogue record for this book is available from the British Library

Library of Congress Cataloging-in-Publication Data
Names: Herzog, Dagmar, 1961- editor. | Schields, Chelsea, editor.
Title: The Routledge companion to sexuality and colonialism / edited by
Chelsea Schields and Dagmar Herzog.
Description: Milton Park, Abingdon, Oxon; New York, NY: Routledge, 2021. |
Includes bibliographical references and index. |
Identifiers: LCCN 2020053275 (print) | LCCN 2020053276 (ebook) |
ISBN 9781138581395 (hardback) | ISBN 9780429505447 (ebook) |
ISBN 9780429999925 (adobe pdf) | ISBN 9780429999918 (epub) |
ISBN 9780429999901 (mobi)
Subjects: LCSH: Sex. | Imperialism.
Classification: LCC HQ21 .R874 2021 (print) | LCC HQ21 (ebook) | DDC 306.7--dc23
LC record available at https://lccn.loc.gov/2020053275
LC ebook record available at https://lccn.loc.gov/2020053276

ISBN: 978-1-138-58139-5 (hbk)
ISBN: 978-0-367-77185-0 (pbk)
ISBN: 978-0-429-50544-7 (ebk)

Typeset in Bembo
by Taylor & Francis Books

CONTENTS

Contents

Contents

FIGURES

CONTRIBUTORS

Gülhan Balsoy is Associate Professor of History at İstanbul Bilgi University. She received her Ph.D. at Binghamton University, New York. She spent a year in Berlin as a post-doctoral researcher at the "Europe in the Middle East-The Middle East in Europe" (EUME) program. She is the author of *The Politics of Reproduction in Ottoman Society, 1838–1900* (Routledge, 2013). The Turkish translation of this book, *Kahraman Doktor İhtiyar Acuzeye Karşı*, won the 2016 Yunus Nadi Social Sciences and Research Award. She took part in the "(Over)medicalization of Childbirth as a Public Problem" project funded by Agence Nationale de la Recherche. Currently she is working on a book project that explores the urban experiences of destitute women and discusses the links between gender and poverty in late nineteenth-century Ottoman Istanbul.

Chad Thomas Black is Associate Professor of Latin American History at the University of Tennessee, Knoxville. He is the author of *The Limits of Gender Domination: Women, the Law and Political Crisis in Quito, 1765–1830*, as well as other work on gender and sexuality under late colonial Spanish rule.

Nicole Bourbonnais is Associate Professor of International History and Co-Director of the Gender Centre at the Graduate Institute of International and Development Studies in Geneva, Switzerland. Her work explores the themes of sex, gender, and reproductive politics; decolonization and transnational activism in the twentieth century; and the history of health and medicine. She is the author of the book *Birth Control in the Decolonizing Caribbean: Reproductive Politics and Practices on Four Islands, 1930–1970* (Cambridge University Press, 2016). Her current research projects explore the history of global family planning activism and the development of the maternal and child health paradigm.

Esther Captain is Senior Researcher and staff member at the Royal Netherlands Institute of Southeast Asian and Caribbean Studies (KITLV) in Leiden, the Netherlands. At KITLV she is currently developing a new research line on postcolonial Netherlands, with links to Indonesia and the Caribbean. Moreover, she is a researcher at the "Independence, Decolonization, Violence and War in Indonesia, 1945–1950" program at the same institute. She has been combining university functions at Utrecht University and the University of Amsterdam with policy and grassroots work at Amsterdam University of Applied Sciences, the National Committee for Remembrance and Liberation Day, the Heritage of the War program at the Ministry of Health, Welfare and Sports, and the Indo-European Remembrance Center in The Hague. She has been a visiting fellow at Rutgers Center for Historical Analysis of Rutgers University (USA).

Howard Chiang is Associate Professor of History at the University of California, Davis. He is the author of *After Eunuchs: Science, Medicine, and the Transformation of Sex in Modern China* (Columbia University Press, 2018), which received the 2019 International Convention of Asia Scholars Best Book in the Humanities Prize and the Bonnie and Vern L. Bullough Book Award from the Society for the Scientific Study of Sexuality, and *Transtopia in the Sinophone Pacific* (Columbia University Press, 2021). He is the Founding Chair of the Society of Sinophone Studies.

Santanu Das is Senior Research Fellow at All Souls College and Professor of Modern Literature and Culture at the University of Oxford. He is the author of *Touch and Intimacy in First World War Literature* (Cambridge, 2006) and the editor of *Race, Empire and First World War Writing* (Cambridge, 2012) and the *Cambridge Companion to First World War Poetry* (2013). His book *India, Empire and First World War Culture: Writings, Images, and Songs* (Cambridge, 2018) was awarded the Hindu Non-Fiction Prize in India, the Ananda Coomaraswamy Prize in the US, and the European Society of Study of English Book Prize. He is currently working on the experience and aesthetics of sea voyages, from Victorian times to now.

Corrie Decker is Associate Professor of History at the University of California, Davis. Her first book, *Mobilizing Zanzibari Women: The Struggle for Respectability and Self-Reliance in Colonial East Africa* (Palgrave Macmillan, 2014), investigates Muslim girls' education and women's professionalization in twentieth-century Zanzibar. Her second book, co-authored with Elisabeth McMahon, is *The Idea of Development in Africa: A History* (Cambridge University Press, 2021). Her work also appears in the *American Historical Review, Past & Present*, the *Journal of Women's History*, and other journals and edited volumes. Decker is currently researching the history of puberty and maturity in twentieth-century East Africa.

Susanna Ferguson is a historian of women, gender, and sex in the Arab world and Assistant Professor of Middle East Studies at Smith College. Her research focuses on how questions about women, gender, and sex shaped political thought in the nineteenth- and twentieth-century Arab world. She is working on a book manuscript tracing the history of the concept of upbringing (in Arabic, *tarbiya*) through journals written and edited by women. Highlighting the analytic potential of an Arabic concept theorized by women, the study reframes histories of gender, progress, and democracy in the Arab world and beyond. Other research interests include histories of representative politics in the Arab world; histories of education and schooling; and histories of science and the sexed body. Ferguson is also a longtime host at the Ottoman History Podcast.

Christina Firpo is Professor of Southeast Asian History at California Polytechnic State University in San Luis Obispo, California. Her research focuses on women in Vietnam. She is the author of more than a dozen articles and book chapters on colonial Vietnamese history. She is also the author of *Black Market Business: Selling Sex in Northern Vietnam* (Cornell University Press, 2020) and *The Uprooted: Race, Children, and Imperialism in French Indochina*

(University of Hawai'i Press, 2016), which was shortlisted for the 2017 book award from the International Convention of Asia Scholars, and was awarded the 2017 Colleagues Choice Book Award from the International Convention of Asia Scholars.

Diana Garvin is Assistant Professor of Italian Studies, specializing in Mediterranean Studies. She works in the Department of Romance Languages at the University of Oregon. Prior to this she conducted her postdoctoral research at the American Academy in Rome as the 2017–2018 Rome Prize winner for Modern Italian Studies. Her book, *Feeding Fascism: The Politics of Women's Food Work,* is forthcoming with the University of Toronto in 2021. She has also published articles with *Critical Inquiry, Signs, Journal of Modern European History, Journal of Modern Italian Studies, Annali d'italianistica,* and *Design Issues.* Garvin's research has been supported by the Fulbright Global Scholar award, Getty Library Research grant, Oxford Cherwell award, CLIR Mellon Fellowship, and University of Oregon Presidential Fellowship.

Nicole von Germeten's publications include books and essays on Afro-descended populations in Spanish America, focusing on Catholic brotherhoods and Jesuit proselytization. She has also explored transactional sex, honor, the history of emotions, violence, witchcraft, sodomy, and suicide. She received her Ph.D. in history from the University of California at Berkeley. Her research has taken her to more than 30 historic archives in Colombia, Spain, and Mexico. She held a post-doctoral fellowship at Princeton University and was a visiting scholar at Stanford University. While teaching as a Professor of History at Oregon State University in Corvallis, Dr von Germeten is currently writing a book on the origins of law enforcement in Mexico City and an English translation of the Inquisition case file of Paula de Eguiluz, an Afro-Caribbean freedwoman accused of witchcraft and sorcery.

Kate Imy is Assistant Professor of History at the University of North Texas. Her first book, *Faithful Fighters: Identity and Power in the British Indian Army* (Stanford, 2019) examines anti-colonialism, faith, and the body in the colonial Indian army. It won award citations from the American Historical Association (Pacific Coast Branch) and the American Political Science Association (International Security Branch). Her work has appeared in *Gender & History*, the *Journal of British Studies*, and *Twentieth Century British History*. She is a two-time recipient of the Critical Language Scholarship program (Hindi and Urdu) and held previous fellowships in India (Fulbright) and the United Kingdom (Institute of Historical Research). Her second book project examines the colonial origins of the "hearts and minds" idea of war in Singapore and Malaya. In 2021 she is the Lee Kong Chian NUS-Stanford Fellow on Southeast Asia.

Wigbertson Julian Isenia is a Ph.D. candidate of cultural analysis at the University of Amsterdam. His project, "Sexual Citizenship in the Dutch Caribbean" in collaboration with the University of Curaçao, centers on the concepts of gendered and sexual citizenship beyond their legal conceptualization in Curaçao and Bonaire through an analysis of cultural articulations and practices such as archival collections, literature, theater, and cultural performance. He co-curated the exhibition "Nos Tei" (Papiamentu/o for we are here or we exist) at IHLIA LGBT Heritage (2019), a response and addition to the exhibition 'With Pride' by IHLIA (2018–2019). He co-edited the special issue "Sexual politics between the Netherlands and the Caribbean: Imperial entanglements and archival desires" (*Tijdschrift voor Genderstudies*, 2019). His latest article, "Looking for Kambrada: Sexuality and social anxieties in the Dutch colonial archive, 1882–1923," received an honorable mention for the Gregory Sprague Prize.

Nora Jaffary teaches Latin American history at Concordia University in Montreal. Her research focuses on social and gender history in colonial and nineteenth-century Mexico. Her book *Reproduction and Its Discontents in Mexico: Childbirth and Contraception from 1750 to 1905* (UNC-Chapel Hill, 2016), examining midwifery, monstrous births, infanticide, abortion, and the emergence of Mexican obstetrics, won the Canadian Historical Association's Wallace K. Ferguson Prize in 2017, and Honorable Mention for the Latin American Studies Association's Howard F. Cline Book Prize in Mexican History in 2018. She is currently at work on a book on the history of abortion in Mexico from the early colonial period to the present.

Rachel Jean-Baptiste is Associate Professor of History at the University of California, Davis whose research and publications focus on French-speaking Africa, gender and sexuality, history of race and multiracial identities, and citizenship. She received her B.A. from Bryn Mawr College and a Ph.D. from Stanford University in history. She has published a book, *Conjugal Rights: Marriage, Sexuality, and Urban Life in Colonial Libreville, Gabon* (Ohio University Press, 2014), and articles that have appeared in edited volumes and journals such as *The Journal of Women's History*, *The Journal of African History*, and *The Journal of The History of Sexuality*.

Elisa von Joeden-Forgey is the Endowed Chair in Holocaust and Genocide Studies at Keene State College. Before this she was the Marsha Raticoff Grossman Associate Professor of Holocaust and Genocide Studies at Stockton University in New Jersey, where she also directed the master's program in Holocaust and Genocide Studies and founded the world's first academic, graduate-level Genocide Prevention Certificate Program. She is former President of Genocide Watch, former First Vice President of the International Association of Genocide Scholars, and founder of the Iraq Project in Genocide Prevention and Accountability. She received her M.A. and Ph.D. in history from the University of Pennsylvania and her B.A. from Columbia University. She has received fellowships from the Social Science Research Council, the Ford Foundation, and the MacArthur Foundation. Her most recent publication is the edited volume *The Cultural History of Genocide, Vol. 5: The Era of Total War*, forthcoming from Bloomsbury Press.

Susanne M. Klausen is Brill Professor in Women, Gender, and Sexuality Studies at Penn State University. Her research focus is the politics of fertility. She has written on these topics in modern South Africa and transnationally, mainly in studies of eugenics and birth-control movements, and women's struggles to access safe abortion. She is currently writing a monograph on the Immorality (Amendment) Act (1950) that criminalized interracial sexual relationships between whites and people of color in South Africa during apartheid.

Liat Kozma is Associate Professor in the Department of Islamic and Middle Eastern Studies and the Harry Friedenwald Chair of History of Medicine at the Hebrew University of Jerusalem. Since 2017 she has been the head of the research team, "A Regional History of Medicine in the Middle East," funded by the European Research Council. Her publications include *Global Women, Colonial Ports: Prostitution in the Interwar Middle East* (SUNY Press, 2017) and *Policing Egyptian Women: Sex, Law, and Medicine in Khedival Egypt* (Syracuse University Press, 2011). She is also the co-editor, with Magaly Rodriguez Garcia and Davide Rodogno, of *The League of Nations' Work on Social Issues: Visions, Endeavours and Experiments* (UN Press, 2016) and, with Avner Wishnitzer and Cyrus Schayegh, of *A Global Middle East: Mobility, Materiality and Culture in the Modern Age, 1880–1940* (IB Tauris, 2014).

Laura C.L. Landertinger is Visiting Assistant Professor in the Department of Sociology at Hartwick College in New York. Before joining the faculty at Hartwick she taught in the School of Public Administration at the University of Victoria. There she also held the position of a Social Sciences and Humanities Research Council Postdoctoral Fellow in Sociology. Dr Landertinger's scholarship is located at the intersections of race, gender, and settler colonialism. Broadly social justice oriented, her research examines how power and inequality are reproduced and resisted in and through institutional contexts. Of particular interest to her are the fields of law, education, and child welfare.

Amandine Lauro is Research Associate of the Belgian National Fund for Scientific Research (FNRS) at the Free University of Brussels (ULB), where she teaches African and gender history. Her research focuses on gender, race, and security in colonial Africa and more specifically in the Belgian Congo. She has published a book and several contributions on these issues. She is currently working on a research project on the history of gender-based and sexual violence in the Belgian empire.

Brianna Leavitt-Alcántara received her Ph.D. in history from the University of California, Berkeley. She is currently an Associate Professor of History and Director of Latin American, Caribbean, and Latinx Studies at the University of Cincinnati. Her research focuses on gender and religion in colonial and nineteenth-century Central America. Her first book, *Alone at the Altar: Single Women and Devotion in Guatemala, 1670–1870* (Stanford University Press, 2018), considers how non-elite single women forged complex alliances with the Catholic Church in Guatemala's colonial capital, and how those alliances significantly shaped local religion and the spiritual economy, late colonial reform efforts, and post-independence politics. Her new book project, *The Virgin's Wrath: Gender, Religion, and Violence*, examines gender relations, Mayan Catholicism, and violence in eighteenth-century Chiapas.

Martin Nesvig is a Mexicanist and Hispanist whose research has focused on the religious and cultural history of New Spain, the Inquisition, and debates about contact and conquest in colonial Mexico. He has published five books on topics ranging from inquisitional censorship, religious sociology, and local religion. His most recent book, *Promiscuous Power: An Unorthodox History of New Spain* (University of Texas Press, 2018), examines the local-centric and often raunchy history of imperial power on the ground level in post-contact Michoacán. The book received honorable mention for the 2020 Howard F. Cline Award from the Latin American Studies Association. He is currently completing a book, *The Xolotl Orgy*, which relates the cultural influence of Mesoamerican/Nahua culture—in cosmology, the use of hallucinogens such as peyote, and the introduction of Nahuatl loanwords into Mexican Spanish. This collection's essay is drawn from that research project. He is Professor of History at the University of Miami.

Brooke N. Newman is Associate Professor of History at Virginia Commonwealth University. She specializes in the history of early modern Britain and the British Atlantic world, with a particular focus on the colonial Caribbean, gender and sexuality, slavery, race, and imperial citizenship. She is the author of *A Dark Inheritance: Blood, Race, and Sex in Colonial Jamaica* (Yale University Press, 2018) and the co-editor of *Native Diasporas: Indigenous Identities and Settler Colonialism in the Americas* (University of Nebraska Press, 2014). Her current book project traces the evolving policies and attitudes of the British Crown and prominent members of the royal family toward imperial rule, slavery, and the transatlantic trade in enslaved Africans, and abolition between 1660 and 1860.

Sara Pursley is Assistant Professor in the Departments of Middle Eastern and Islamic Studies and of History at New York University. She is the author of *Familiar Futures: Time, Selfhood, and Sovereignty in Iraq* (Stanford University Press, 2019) and numerous articles, including "Ali al-Wardi and the Miracles of the Unconscious," *Psychoanalysis & History* (2018); "The Stage of Adolescence: Anticolonial Time, Youth Insurgency, and the Marriage Crisis in Hashimite Iraq," *History of the Present* (2013); and "'Lines Drawn on an Empty Map': Iraq's Borders and the Legend of the Artificial State," *Jadaliyya* (2015). From 2009–2014 she served as Associate Editor of the *International Journal of Middle East Studies*.

Tracy Robinson is a Senior Lecturer and Deputy Dean (Graduate Studies and Research) in the Faculty of Law at the University of the West Indies (UWI), Mona Campus, Jamaica. Her research and publications focus on constitutional law, family law, and gender, sexuality and law in the Anglophone Caribbean. She is a co-founder and co-coordinator of the Faculty of Law UWI Rights Advocacy Project that led strategic litigation in Belize and Guyana challenging the criminalization of LGBTQ persons. Robinson was a member of the Inter-American Commission (IACHR) between 2012 and 2015 and she was its Inaugural Rapporteur of the Rights of LGBTI Persons and the Rapporteur on the Rights of Women.

Katherine Schweighofer is Assistant Professor of Gender Studies at Lawrence University. She holds a Ph.D. in Gender Studies from Indiana University alongside degrees from New York University and Princeton University. Her interdisciplinary research interests include histories of gender and sexuality, critical geographies of rurality, ecofeminism, feminisms and counterculture movements of the 1970s, and LGBTQ sports history. Her current manuscript engages contemporary Rural Queer Studies scholarship in a re-examination of the women's land movement during the 1970s and early 1980s as a point of resistance to heteropatriarchal systems of colonialism, capitalism, and community. She regularly teaches courses on histories of gender and sexuality, feminist and queer theories, and gender and sports cultures.

Caroline Séquin is Assistant Professor of Modern European History at Lafayette College (Easton, PA). She completed her Ph.D. in Modern European History at the University of Chicago. She has since published "The Moving Contours of Colonial Prostitution (Fort-de-France, Martinique, 1940–1947)," *Clio. Femmes, Genre, Histoire* (2019) and is currently at work on a book that examines the articulation between prostitution regulation and racial politics in so-called "colorblind" France and in the French empire in the century following the abolition of slavery. Her work has been supported by the Western Society for French History, the French Colonial Historical Society, and the Society for French Historical Studies.

Gregory D. Smithers is Professor of History at Virginia Commonwealth University and a British Academy Global Professor at the University of Hull, United Kingdom. He is the author of numerous books and articles, the most recent being *The Cherokee Diaspora* (2015) and *Native Southerners* (2019). His forthcoming book, *Reclaiming Two-Spirits: Sexuality, Spiritual Renewal, & Sovereignty in Native America*, is forthcoming from Beacon Press.

Judith Surkis is Professor of History at Rutgers, where she specializes in the history of Modern France and French empire and intellectual, legal, and gender history. She is the author of *Sexing the Citizen: Morality and Masculinity in France, 1870–1920* (2006) and *Sex, Law, and Sovereignty in French Algeria, 1830–1930* (2019).

Aiko Takeuchi-Demirci (Ph.D. American Studies, Brown University) is Assistant Professor of Sociology in the College of Social Sciences and Humanities at Koç University and Co-Director of the Koç University Center for Asian Studies (KUASIA). She is author of *Contraceptive Diplomacy: Reproductive Politics and Imperial Ambitions in the United States and Japan* (Stanford University Press, 2018), which won the 2020 John Whitney Hall Prize from the Association for Asian Studies. She is also editor of the *Journal of Transnational American Studies* and NOTCHES: (Re)marks on the History of Sexuality.

Françoise Vergès (Ph.D. Berkeley), from Reunion Island, is a political theorist, a decolonial and antiracist feminist, and a public educator. Recent publications include *The Wombs of Women: Race, Capitalism, Feminism* (Duke University Press, 2020), *Resolutely Black: Conversations with Aimé Césaire* (Polity, 2020), *Une théorie féministe de la violence. Pour une politique antiraciste de la protection* (La Fabrique, 2020), and a forthcoming book, *A Decolonial Feminism* (Pluto, 2021).

Seçil Yılmaz is a historian of gender, sexuality, and medicine in the Ottoman empire and modern Middle East. She is currently working on a book manuscript concentrating on the social and political implications of venereal diseases in the late Ottoman empire by tracing the questions of colonialism, modern governance, biopolitics, and sexuality. Her other projects include research on the relationship between religion, history of emotions, and contagious diseases in the late Ottoman empire as well as the history of reproductive health technologies and humanitarianism in the modern Middle East. Her research appeared in the *Journal of Middle East Women's Studies* and she is the co-curator of the podcast series on Women, Gender, and Sex in the Ottoman World at Ottoman History Podcast. Yilmaz is an Assistant Professor of History at Franklin and Marshall College.

ACKNOWLEDGMENTS

All books are feats of collectivity. This is especially so for an edited volume of this scope and size. Our first debt is to this volume's contributors, who explored colonial sexuality with extraordinary rigor and nuance. Numerous people offered direction to important resources and scholarship, including Yousuf Al-Bulushi, Sharon Block, Long Bui, Sarah Carter, Katherine Ellinghaus, Sheldon Garon, Tadashi Ishikawa, Margaret Jacobs, Stephen Sheehi, Brianna Theobald, Sasha Turner, Tessa Ong Winkelmann, Seçil Yılmaz, and Ran Zwigenberg. At Routledge, Alexandra McGregor supported the project and offered valuable guidance from beginning to end. For indispensable and outstanding research and editing assistance, we warmly thank Arinn Amer, Miranda Brethour, Kate Kelley, and Julián Gonzáles de León Heiblum. We are grateful to Jaune Quick-to-See Smith and the Garth Greenan Gallery for permission to reprint the book's stunning cover image, which powerfully evokes many of the themes explored herein. Students in our classes Gender & Empire at Goucher College, Decolonization and the Global Imaginary at UCI, and Geopoliticization of Sex at the Graduate Center have reminded us of the political stakes of knowledge production, inspiring ideas and commitments in this volume.

At the time of writing, unrelenting and entangled global crises have brought some of this volume's themes into stark relief. These crises have also spurred deeper appreciation for—and ever greater reliance on—the wider webs of interconnection in which all loves are sustained. With endless admiration for their ethical ways of being in the world, and with gratitude for their love and patience, we thank Yousuf Al-Bulushi and Michael Staub.

Cover image: Jaune Quick-to-See Smith, "Fear" (2004–2005). Courtesy the artist and Garth Greenan Gallery, New York.

INTRODUCTION

Sex, intimacy, and power in colonial studies

Chelsea Schields and Dagmar Herzog

Among a profusion of historical "turns," perhaps none has enjoyed such lasting influence as that of the imperial turn: the recognition that imperial networks and relations shaped the modern world and the constitution of modernity itself. In the 1980s and 1990s, scholars working across multiple disciplines—from history to anthropology to literary criticism—powerfully attuned students of colonialism to its transformative role in shaping metropolitan and colonial cultures alike. Often dubbed the "new imperial history," this scholarship challenged the containerized view of nation-state histories and spotlighted instead the relational developments that knit together metropoles and colonies, often across vast global expanses.[1]

As the chronological and geographical scales of historical accounts expanded to include "metropole and colony in a single analytic field,"[2] they simultaneously telescoped *inward*. Ever more private domains—from the surveillance and regulation of nonmarital sex to the corporeal intimacies of childrearing, and from the fantasies buttressing racialized rule to the organization of domestic space—were revealed to be central matters of colonial preoccupation. Meditating on the syncopated patterns in the evolution of European empires, Ann Laura Stoler showed how widespread practices of concubinage were not incidental relations that followed the movement of colonists overseas. Joint-stock companies and colonial authorities calculatingly coordinated relationships between European men and colonized women in an effort to out-source the nurturing and care of the former. Yet, by the nineteenth century, shifting definitions of white prestige eventually demanded the movement of "full blooded" European wives and children to the colonies, which corresponded with tightening legal prohibitions on interracial sex, marriage, and citizenship.[3] Following Michel Foucault, Stoler subsequently reconceived colonial intimacies as key vectors of power, inspiring an abundance of consequent scholarship. While colonial sexual relations had previously been viewed more through a Freudian lens—in which individual desires were understood as repressed, regulated, or released—Stoler called attention to the ways colonial contexts were sites for the manufacture of desire itself.[4]

Scholars across a wide range of regional fields soon agreed that colonial hierarchies were not ready-made, as efforts to shore up the division between colonizer and colonized required enormous amounts of labor and often violent intervention. A now voluminous body of scholarship has shown, in a luxuriant plethora of variations, how "the very categories of 'colonizer' and 'colonized' were secured through forms of sexual control."[5] Informed further by the work of Edward Said, scholars entering the field in the 1990s also elaborated the erotic dimensions of the "colonial gaze" and its resonance in the literary, visual, and material cultures of empire.[6] At the same time, scholars investigated domesticity and conjugality as raced and classed projects, and many showed how domestic ideals centered on bourgeois respectability and the nuclear household were constantly threatened by intimate traversing of the color line.[7] Relatedly, scholars explored the extraordinary attention devoted by colonial regimes to a eugenic conception of the social body, linking the concurrently emerging anxieties about venereal disease and the biological "degeneration" of the working class in the metropole to fears of both racial and environmental–atmospheric ruin in the colonies.[8] The simultaneous rise of women's and gender history brought additional topics into focus, opening up nuanced research on women as both agents and antagonists of empire—as mothers, wives, educators, missionaries, healers, sex workers, and political actors in their own right.[9] The pioneering work of Antoinette Burton revealed that even seemingly progressive feminist movements functioned within and sought legitimacy through the racial logics of empire.[10] Others highlighted how debates on sexual politics saturated nearly all politics in the colonies—from rationalizing legitimations of the civilizing mission to later nationalist ripostes—making sex a central register for discussing colonial and anti-colonial politics more broadly.[11]

Each of these interventions required new ways of reading and reflecting on colonial archives. The now widely accepted but not therefore any less profound insight that archives are expressive and constitutive of power owes a great deal to the careful reflections of colonial studies scholars.[12] Reading *along* the archival grain for pronounced anxieties about sex, race, and class has fundamentally changed scholarly approaches to colonial studies as a whole. This approach has likewise compelled scholars to reckon with how colonialism (but also at times opposition to it) inaugurated new ways of defining and categorizing sex itself—initiating novel epistemic frameworks that could displace existing definitions of erotic matters or occlude possibilities for organizing life otherwise.[13] This insight has been especially important in theorizing practices of same-sex eroticism and gender expression beyond Western binaries.[14]

Part of what has given the "imperial turn" its enduring critical purchase over the past 30 years is the field's consistent foregrounding of the interconnections of race, sexuality, gender, and class. Building on the ground prepared by anti-imperial, Third World, and Black feminists, scholars since the 1980s have advanced the case for the mutual constitution of these categories.[15] It was not without assigning sexual deviance to Blackness, for example, that race could be cohered as a marker of difference that legitimated Black unfreedom while simultaneously producing whiteness as a system of sexual rightness.[16] Scholars of settler colonial societies and Indigenous Studies have likewise shown how precolonial understandings of kinship and gender expression were weaponized by white settler regimes across North America and Oceania to underwrite projects of dispossession and extermination, processes that simultaneously cast settlers as arbiters of proper sexual morality.[17] As such, sexuality and sexual control have not been ancillary matters for the construction of race and the policing of racial boundaries in colonial societies; they have proven central to the reproduction of social hierarchies and the material inequities that they sustain. Following from this, recent studies of sexuality and colonialism have returned to political economy—to the broader political and economic projects that bodily intimacies uphold—while maintaining nuanced attention to affect, desire, and emotion.[18]

If attention to the intimate workings of racialized power remains essential in scholarship today, it is not least because our present necessitates confrontation with this unfinished past. Returning to historical sites where difference was produced and solidified has served as a powerful reminder of the instability of those categories. Yet ample attention to the porousness of racial–sexual demarcations has not succeeded in dislodging the political and economic disparities that they legitimize, as many entries in this volume attest.[19] The maintenance of colonial hierarchies in an ostensibly decolonized world has, in the past decade, generated new scholarly and activist responses. Whereas scholars of the 1990s and early 2000s were especially concerned with the fungibility of racial categories and the construction of colonial power in all its raced, sexed, and classed dimensions, today this focus has given way to an emphasis on colonized experiences and evasions of power and the imaginaries and practices of selfhood, care, kinship, survival, and eroticism that persisted nonetheless—what Neferti X.M. Tadiar has called forms of "remaindered life."[20] Moving beyond Foucault-inspired efforts to document myriad constellations of power-knowledge and catalyzed by the tremendous interventions of Black, Indigenous, and Decolonial Studies, this focus has required new approaches to archival sources focused not only on their prolix volubility but also on their gaps—and to the lives that persist in the margins.[21]

In view of the sustained importance of studies of sexuality and colonialism over the past three decades and the ongoing urgency to dislodge the most tenacious and pernicious legacies of this history, this volume offers both an overview and a contribution to this rich interdisciplinary field. It covers both terrains by joining critical historiographic surveys organized by world regions with original case studies that advance the field in new directions. In defining "colonialism," we heed the call of Frederick Cooper to take a longer view of the colonial that decenters Europe's colonial experiences.[22] The volume's coverage ranges from the rise of the Spanish empire in the sixteenth century to the growing management of difference in the Ottoman empire by the late nineteenth century, and from Japanese rule in East and Southeast Asia in the twentieth century to the durability of colonial projects in the Caribbean and settler colonial societies today. This expansive view of colonialism allows us to think both comparatively and relationally about the management of sex and intimacy across different imperial contexts.

If "colonialism" remains a disputed concept among those who believe in its diffuse effects and enduring potency and those who endorse a more precise, bounded definition of specific forms of foreign rule and expansion,[23] then attention to sexuality may well be one way to study what made empires "colonial," as Gülhan Balsoy argues in this volume. Comparison also points out how forms of sexual and reproductive regulation attended differing political and economic projects in the colonies. For example, in post-slavery colonies in the Caribbean and even in Japan's colonial holdings in East Asia, incitements for colonized women to reproduce attended efforts to bolster colonial economies in different periods of transition.[24] At the same time, however, increasingly violent and masculinist forms of conquest attended the expansion of predominantly Anglo settler colonies. In these environments, settlers brutally restricted Indigenous fertility in a bid to accelerate the dispossession of land and its reimagination as white space.[25] Yet both forms of reproductive control were central to the creation of colonial societies and often worked in terrifying tandem, as the decimation of Indigenous populations in North and South America was followed by heightened reliance on African slavery. According to Tiffany Lethabo King, these modes of displacement and racial terror move "as one"; they are "distinct yet edgeless" forms of violence.[26] Reading the entries in this volume with and against each other, comparison can highlight not only specificities but also connections across seemingly distinct predations.

If comparison helps us to think more precisely about the role of sexual and reproductive regulation in colonial societies, other entries in this volume remind us that empires never learned in isolation. In at times disjointed and contrapuntal ways, the management of sexuality in one empire could inform its treatment in another, necessitating a relational view of trans-imperial exchange. Roman and Iberian law on the heritable condition of slavery, for example, influenced the emerging empires of the seventeenth- and eighteen-century Atlantic World.[27] Western eugenic science traveled to imperial Japan, although it would take on new meanings and significance in that process.[28] Knowledge traversed imperial boundaries on the backs of soldiers, functionaries, and administrators whose movements exceeded the neatly defined routes between metropole and colony. Restoring to view these wider networks of exchange and movement, some entries in this volume call into question the very primacy of colonialism in defining intimate relationships, instead placing colonial considerations along-side a constellation of other interests.[29] If this question cannot be settled once and for all, it is not least because empires—their forms of rule and theft, their temporal and geographic reach—differed in concrete ways; a fact laid bare not least through attention to their varied prohibitions and incitements to sex.

Boundaries unbound

Scholars of sexuality and colonialism have not only pointed out the porosity of social categories of difference and their historical evolution, they have also rightly highlighted the permeability of geographic space. Thus, as Kate Imy argues in this volume, studying sexuality on the basis of geographic areas influences the very concepts under discussion, potentially flattening the diversity of those regions and "erasing those who transcended or transgressed multiple identity categories simultaneously."[30] In part to mitigate this, we have organized historiographic overviews according to two principles. Where possible, we have embraced broad geographic regions that often encompassed multiple or overlapping imperial powers. In other cases—for example, in the treatment of settler colonialism or the early empires of Spain and Portugal—the separate development of these historiographies has necessitated a different approach focused on colonizing powers and modes of colonialism itself. Bringing together these historiographies yields two surprising insights.

The first concerns the tremendous possibilities and constraints of various source bases. In most cases, "official knowledge"—administrative reports, court proceedings and litigation, legal or medical knowledge—has been more bountiful than personal reflections and desires, a problem that has generated innovative scholarly responses. As Nicole von Germeten documents in this volume, in the Spanish Americas the voluminous records of the Holy Inquisition ironically preserved thousands of cubic feet of records about the very erotic practices and preferences that it attempted to eradicate. Using these sources to explore pleasure in its many varied forms—a focus that unsettles once more top-down views on the workings of power—has been one of the fruitful new directions of scholarship in this area. Similarly, as Nicole Bourbonnais shows in her entry on the Caribbean, the perceived absence of marginalized voices in Caribbean archives has prompted some scholars and activists to read sources not strictly for the voices they represent but for the kinds of acts or praxis of which they might contain traces.[31] Working-class Afro-Caribbean refusal to conform to Western standards of household organization and conjugality in the post-slavery Caribbean, a practice widely documented and endlessly discussed in state records, can be read also as a practice of refusal; it signals the incomplete penetration of the colonial state into the erotic lives of its subjects. Imy's entry on South and Southeast Asia powerfully calls into question whether what we classify as sex is itself a product of colonialism. Imy explores the intimate practices and ritual performances to which colonial authorities ascribed erotic meaning, forming an epistemological legacy of colonialism that lives on in the classificatory schemes of archives and the documentary record.[32]

A second insight that resonates across entries is the unstable meaning of colonialism itself. As Corrie Decker as well as Susanna Ferguson and Seçil Yılmaz point out, the definition of colonialism is doubly vexed in regions characterized by multiple and often overlapping forms of incursion. Does Oman count as a colonial power in East Africa, where until the nineteenth century it controlled large parts of the Swahili coast? Should Egypt be regarded as a colonized state or precisely as the initial colonizer of twice-colonized Sudan? Was the Ottoman empire, whose imperial longevity saw that polity's transformation from an early modern power into an imperial state ruled along ever stricter axes of difference, "colonial"? And as Gregory Smithers' contribution on settler colonialism explores, the presumptive historicity of colonialism is not past at all; rather, it is an ongoing relation in the white settler states of the United States, Canada, Australia, and New Zealand. Questions about the slipperiness and variability of colonialism resonate across the Japanese empire in East and Southeast Asia, where Japan "liberated" former European colonies in order to introduce new forms of rule based on the "co-prosperity" of the Asian region and peoples. Yet even in this effort, as Aiko Takeuchi-Demirci argues, Japanese imperial expansion relied in part on ideas of scientific racism and reproductive control heavily indebted to (and simultaneously always seeking to overcome dependence on) European contributions. If these insights disrupt the "fantasy of sovereignty"[33] for any one imperial state, highlighting instead their many mutual connections and fuzzy demarcations, they also point up the troublesome question of exactly how *unique* the colonial treatment of sexuality may have been. As each of the contributions in this section point out, sovereign nation-states, like the empires that preceded them, were no less active in "adopt[ing] sexuality, family, and reproduction as key arenas for intervention."[34]

The race–sex nexus

Questions about the durability and distinctiveness of colonial ideologies and systems of sexual control likewise span the entries in this volume, in particular as they concern the colonial preoccupation with reproduction. Perhaps no area has received more attention in the history of sexuality in and under colonialism than its most visible and dramatic effects: sex across the color line and the puzzles apparently presented by offspring of mixed descent.[35] The meanings ascribed to both the relationships and the ensuing progeny varied greatly across time and space. Yet, taking a broader view both of the colonial period and of reproductive policies and practices across empires, the essays assembled in this section raise new questions about when, where, and whether race became an organizing principle in the regulation of reproductive sexuality and, indeed, about the specifically "colonial" dimensions of these concerns.

These essays lay bare that the construction of race—a hierarchic way of organizing humanity—relied on multiple techniques beyond the strict policing of interracial sex, a phenomenon that Bourbonnais terms the "race–sex nexus." Brooke Newman's essay on the eighteenth-century British Atlantic shows how notions of racial heritability, in particular those concerning the imparting of enslaved status from a woman's womb to her offspring, relied not only on scrutiny of women's reproductive capacity but also, crucially, on *legal* innovation. Françoise Vergès' contribution links the wombs of women to racial capitalism; in a sweeping analysis, Vergès exposes racial capitalism as a global and long-lasting enterprise that relied on racialized valuations of women's reproductive labor from the era of trans-Atlantic slavery through to the present day. Diana Garvin provocatively casts interracial wet-nursing in Italian East Africa as a foodway—a process of consumption believed by the Fascist regime to imperil racial purity. Moving to nineteenth-century Canada, Laura Landertinger shows that different forms of reproductive control prevailed in the settler colony. Longstanding practices of

Indigenous child removal and child theft sought to break the survival of Indigenous communities, dissolving not only connections of culture and kinship but also claims to land. Together these essays compel us to think about the multivalent techniques of race-making exceeding reproductive sexuality while also pointing out how reproduction has concretely attended different kinds of colonial and economic projects.

Further essays invite us to reconsider from yet other angles the assumptions of a uniquely colonial preoccupation with reproductive politics and practice. Nora Jaffary's entry on New Spain (present-day Mexico) reveals the seemingly routine occurrence of abortion and infanticide, practices neglected by religious and colonial authorities in the Spanish colonies. Indeed, such findings challenge standard assumptions about religion and sexuality, showing that religious authorities were not strictly prohibitive—some practices were overlooked entirely.[36] Balsoy's contribution, by contrast, shows how the late-nineteenth century Ottoman empire took renewed interest in the reproductive politics of its core and peripheral territories, unequally distributing material and medical support for pregnant women. Interestingly, Ottoman interventions into reproductive life occurred at precisely the same time as the newly independent Mexican state began to police those practices once overlooked by colonial authorities. This convergence in the nineteenth century suggests that pro-natalist politics spanned nation-states and empires alike.

Sex and the law

For the scholar of sexuality and colonialism, legal sources have offered a singularly rich trove of discussion on sexuality and its surveillance. But these sources are not without obvious limitations. As Anjali Arondekar has observed of the colonial archive more broadly, the intellectual challenge is to "juxtapose productively the archive's fiction-effects (the archive as a system of representation) alongside its truth-effects (the archive as material with 'real' consequences)."[37] Similarly, laws in colonial settings are often inventive and not reactive—they create rather than respond to perceived problems of sexual deviance or dangerous unions. And they are, perhaps more perniciously, occlusive. They reflect the ambitions of people in power and relay often only in filtered form the voices of colonized subjects. Given the prohibitive orientation of laws, these sources attend frequently to what may *not* be done without explicit attention to tacit areas of acceptance. Such omissions are indeed telling, for in many cases routine violations—sexual or otherwise—constituted the core of colonial common sense.[38]

But as recent scholarship has pointed out, in their garrulous denunciations and shifting strategies these sources also concede evidence of colonial failure or else offer signs of defiance, subterfuge, or dismissal. Chad Black's chapter shows how plebeian Quiteños in the late eighteenth century leveraged colonial policing powers to mediate social conflicts with friends, neighbors, and former lovers. As Quiteños cleverly wielded the law to serve their own ends, they also became accomplices in the expansion of colonial surveillance. Their encounters with authorities, however, revealed a separate moral economy from that privileged by colonial elites. Turning to French Indochina in the twentieth century, Christina Firpo analyzes the spectacular failure of colonial regulations on prostitution. The patchy extension of French law allowed sex workers in Tonkin to move their businesses into non-regulated jurisdictions under the control of Vietnamese officials, where they subsequently operated as "singing houses" and "dance halls." Innovatively reading legal sources against the grain, Rachel Jean-Baptiste argues that official sources compel historians to exercise greater historical imagination to place those marginalized at their center. Reviewing a drawn-out custody battle for a *métis* child in French West Africa in the 1930s, Jean-Baptiste reads the case files for their intense passions and rivalries—emotions that reveal maternal love, loss, and longing as heretofore underappreciated but vital dynamics in the colonial story.

Laws did, of course, have concrete and significant consequences for people in the colonies. And often the "fiction-effects" of colonial representations and racialized assumptions structured the "truth-effects" of the law. Liat Kozma shows how the nascent efforts of the League of Nations to produce international law to contain the traffic of women and children reflected colonial interests and muddled (but no less consequential) racial ideologies. According to European officials tasked with studying traffic in the Middle East, Muslim men prevented women from becoming prostitutes and yet, paradoxically, the officials also alleged that brothels in the Middle East served as safe havens protecting Muslim women from honor killings. Tinted with colonial fantasies of Muslim sexuality, these incoherencies found their way into the frameworks adopted by emerging supranational bodies and into laws on international trafficking in the twentieth century. Continuing the investigation of international laws and norms,[39] Sara Pursley challenges longstanding assertions that religious jurisdiction over family matters in the Middle East emerged out of local religious traditions. Instead, Pursley argues that British and international interventions actively transformed legal practices in Iraq during World War I and the mandate period (1920–1932), hardening communitarian boundaries by confining Iraqi subjects to certain religious courts. Susanne Klausen's entry examines a series of legislative acts in apartheid South Africa that prohibited sex, including even the intention to have sex, between whites and "non-whites." As Klausen powerfully demonstrates, these laws and the harms to lives and loves they caused were an indispensable feature of the apartheid project, its significance missed in studies more typically focused on labor exploitation and spatial segregation.

Subjects, souls, selfhood

Since the insurgent writings of Frantz Fanon, postcolonial theorists have persuasively elucidated how colonialism altered one's sense of self, inaugurating new subjectivities formed along the axes of race, class, sexuality, and gender.[40] Following on this insight, the authors in this volume consider the intricate interiority of life under colonialism, including notions of desire and sexual selfhood.

Unexpected sources have furnished profound truths about intimate personhood. Through an analysis of testamentary wills, Brianna Leavitt-Alcántara shows how mixed-race single women reworked official discourses of gender, sexual mores, and religiosity in seventeenth-century Guatemala. Leavitt-Alcántara's analysis, too, confounds reductive assumptions about the relationship of religion to sexuality. Women who bore children out of wedlock might still gain recognition in religious networks, and even clerical authorities recognized different gradations of so-called "illegitimacy." Building on Kozma's invitation to mine the reports of League of Nations anti-trafficking initiatives, Caroline Séquin uses these documents to access the voices of white French women traveling to sell sex. Like so many others in the age of empire, white French women hoped to increase their wealth by relocating to colonial Dakar—at just the moment that prostitution was becoming restricted in new ways in the metropole. Like Séquin's expansive chapter that moves from metropole to colony and back, recent scholarship has begun to relocate studies of colonial sexuality from the outposts of empire to their metropolitan centers.[41]

In the flows of people, goods, and ideas that colonialism initiated, categories, identities, and bodies were also redefined. Judith Surkis's analysis of nineteenth- and twentieth-century French juridical approaches to mixed marriages in Algeria shows how jurists increasingly fixed notions of religion to bodies. Although putatively referring to religious difference, French jurists represented Muslim law and legal difference as a matter of corporeality, elaborating on fantasies of Muslim law as bound to men's sexual rights and women's degradation while casting so-called "secular" French civil law as sexually and civilizationally superior. Katherine Schweighofer shows how even radical efforts to combat patriarchy and capitalism often ended up reproducing its more destructive dynamics. Turning to the lesbian land movement in the United States in the 1970s and 1980s—a rural "back to the land" effort with a DIY ethos—Schweighofer shows how lesbian landers utilized settler colonialist power structures, including land acquisition and access to financial and legal resources, to achieve their own liberation while compromising the access of Native and other women of color to the same forms of freedom.

Sites of more ambiguously colonial status present alternate puzzles about identities, alliances, and commitments. Howard Chiang's reflection on the emergence of transsexuality as a concept in postwar Taiwan calls into question core assumptions of postcolonial studies, including the hegemony of the West and even imperial Japan as forces initiating sexual modernity. Such a "transing" of flows of sexual knowledge serves, as Chiang writes, to "denaturalize the West, provincialize China, Asia and the rest." Thinking from another quasi-colonial space, the Caribbean island of Curaçao—an overseas territory of the Netherlands—Wigbertson Julian Isenia asks how spaces that defy normative definitions of "colony" or "nation-state" might open new intellectual and political possibilities for conceiving of sexuality and citizenship alike. Through a close reading of the life and works of Fridi Martina (1950–2014), a Curaçaoan playwright, Isenia shows how Martina shunned the identitarian logics of dominant Euro-American LGBTQ politics in much the same way that Dutch citizens from the Caribbean have shunned national independence. Martina's non-identitarian view of sexual praxis highlights the mobility and survival of notions of sexual selfhood that do not map neatly onto Euro-American understandings.

Pleasure and violence

As many entries in this volume attest, pleasure and violence formed two sides of the same colonial coin. The pursuit of sexual pleasure was inescapably bound up with other investments: in times of war, a common occurrence in phases of colonial military conquest and in an age of unrelenting global warfare, men's virility was proven in the bedroom as on the battlefield. The routine appearance of sexual violence in many colonial societies not only served the appetites of desire; it was also a strategy to subdue and humiliate colonized communities by signaling that women could not be protected.[42] The blurred boundaries between pleasure and violence, desire and terror raise questions about the perilously close relationship between these dynamics.

In the highly overdetermined colonial context, scholars have recently begun to ask whether colonial subjects and enslaved people experienced forms of sexual pleasure[43] and whether the contrast between "coercion" and "consent" even provides the most useful framework for understanding intimacies in environments already defined by the usurpation of self-determination.[44] Martin Nesvig's contribution in this volume offers a meditation on these very questions, turning to the rural outposts of sixteenth-century New Spain to examine how Nahua women navigated the advance of Spanish authority. In a 1573 Inquisitorial investigation into alleged religious idolatry of a Spanish official in Colima, numerous Nahua women plainly recounted their own and others' sexual experiences with the Spanish notary, indicative of tacit acceptance and even, perhaps, individual erotic expression. Santanu Das examines the life worlds of Indian troops sent to the Western Front in World War I. Das mines photographs, postcards, novels, songs, and paintings, unearthing a vibrant landscape of male friendship, homosociality, and tactility beyond strictly sexual liaisons. Proximity to death and the overwhelming violence of trench warfare spurred moments of intense emotional depth and bodily contact among Indian sepoys and also with European women who hosted and nurtured them.

The brute violence of colonialism paired uneasily with its overarching emphasis on the so-called "civilizing mission." Tracy Robinson's chapter reveals that the creation of a Jamaican counterpart to Britain's already existing anti-sodomy statute emerged primarily as a means to discipline the Black male subject—both corporeally and spiritually—after the abolition of slavery. In Jamaica, legislators attempted to introduce new bodily punishments that were absent in the metropolitan version of the law. In the Dutch East Indies, as Esther Captain demonstrates, the intense violence of World War II and Japanese occupation of the colony triggered distinct sexual responses. Confined to internment camps, some white Dutch colonists held fast to performances of sexual propriety that had long been associated with the superior position of whites. Other Dutch men and women, however, rejected these strictures in the carnivalesque violence of the war; in defiance of European norms, some male internees reportedly declared: "We are the homosexuals, we don't care about women anymore!"

If other empires obfuscated the overt and quotidian forms of violence that shored up colonial rule, King Leopold's "private colony" of the Congo presented an additional opportunity for rival imperial regimes to tout their purportedly more humanitarian legacies. Amandine Lauro's contribution shows how the end of Leopold's personal rule and the start of Belgian national administration resulted in intensified efforts to "clean up" Belgium's violent reputation by condemning and managing interracial liaisons. Yet this renewed attention to interracial sex appeared to be as much an outcome of colonial anxieties about the legitimacy of Belgian rule as about fears of mass rebellions and uprisings if white sexual prerogatives were to remain unchecked. Indeed, as Elisa von Joeden-Forgey's powerful study reveals, threats of rebellions and uprisings in response to European sexual behavior appeared in other colonies, too. Rape actually played a central role not only in the forms of violence meted out by Germans during the Herero genocide; it had also been an immediate precipitant of the Herero anticolonial rebellions of 1904 that, in turn, in the minds of German colonists, prompted the genocidal response.

Conclusion: new directions

Collectively, the contributions in this volume catalyze yet further areas for study in the infinite entanglements of sexuality and colonialism. There is, it seems, little dispute that empire was a pornographic project—as Pumla Dineo Gqola has recently written.[45] Nonetheless, scholars equipped with a wide range of visual, literary, medical, administrative, and legal sources have brought nuanced attention to the ways subjects were able to navigate the "machine of desire" in colonial societies.[46] Of course, we must be cautious in emphasizing strategies of survival, creativity, and persistence without adequate attention to the violence against which such strategies were deployed. Yet to speak only of annihilation or hegemonic forms of power produces additional dangers and historical inaccuracies. The entries in this volume grapple with the many disparities and contradictory logics of colonialism while also—without romance or fetishization—restoring to view both the alterity of the past (the distinct ways that people conceived of selves, kin, and community, as well as issues of age, maturity, and agency)[47] and the complex acts of negotiation, collusion, and defiance that conditioned the possibilities for survival in colonial societies.

This approach does not only flip the "fiction-effects" of the archive; it does not simply return the gaze of colonial representations or add voices once missing or silenced. It also offers transformative accounts of what counts as sex and intimacy itself. From the actions of single women in Guatemala to claim pious personas to the survival of Caribbean understandings of sexuality as praxis and not identity, new realms emerge as sites of theorizing and experiencing selfhood in all its myriad dimensions. If students of colonialism have long established that domains once previously ignored comprised the "intimacy" of colonialism—including acts, longings, beliefs, dress, and the spatial organization of homes and cities—then this same multiplicity also characterized how colonized subjects themselves conceived of the intimate. Their views expand our definitions beyond sexual liaisons or encounters to include also the deliberate construction of kinship, friendship, and fluid and multiple identities. In these efforts, the history of emotions appears with stunning vibrancy. Indian sepoys yearn for embrace in the final fleeting moments of life and African mothers implore colonial authorities with righteous indignation to confirm their right to parental care. These at once expansive and profound perspectives on the interiority of personhood, of what makes the self, often diverged from colonial understandings—and as such these notions persist in traces in the bureaucratic hum of archives, undetected by parties potentially unaware of their subversive potential.

Finally, bodies emerge here as locations of ambivalent investments—as sites of desire, punishment, and sensory and tactile indulgence. They variously mete out and receive violence, just as they transmit and imperil life. Entries in this volume not only think productively from the vantage of the bodily; they also show how disparate understandings of corporeality itself emerged in dialogue with different colonial regimes.[48]

If centering the intricate crossings of gender, class, sexuality, and race in analyses of colonialism remains a relevant focus for research and critical reflection, it is not least because the structures and ideologies that summoned and solidified such assemblages remain active today, necessitating ongoing engagements with the colonial past that keeps on, in ever new ways, "haunting" the present. Yet recent social movements—from the Movement for Black Lives to Indigenous uprisings against renewed encroachment—have also reminded us of the urgency of imagination to inspire ways of living, being, and loving more capacious and radical than our current inherited categories.[49] The entries in this volume attend to both of these indispensable, at once intellectual and political projects: they think through the historically specific creation of colonial societies and the inequities that defined them, as well as the alternative possibilities and imaginaries that arose at their margins and in their fissures and interstices.

Notes

1 Burton, *After the Imperial Turn*; Howe, *The New Imperial Histories*; Ghosh, "Another Set of Imperial Turns?"
2 Stoler and Cooper, "Between Metropole and Colony," 4.
3 Stoler, "Making Empire Respectable."
4 Stoler, *Race and the Education of Desire*, 167; Gilman, *Difference and Pathology*; Nandy, *The Intimate Enemy*; Young, *Colonial Desire*. For an early and controversial view of imperial sexuality that regarded interracial sex as a natural and in fact liberal expression of male desire in the colonies, see Hyam, *Empire and Sexuality*.
5 Stoler, "Making Empire Respectable," 635.
6 Pratt, *Imperial Eyes*; Sharpley-Whiting, *Black Venus*; Bleys, *The Geography of Perversion*; Alloula, *The Colonial Harem*; Boone, *The Homoerotics of Orientalism*; Mitchell, *Vénus Noire*.
7 Clancy-Smith and Gouda, *Domesticating the Empire*; Ghosh, *Sex and the Family*; McClintock, *Imperial Leather*; Hunt, "Domesticity and Colonialism"; Chaudhuri, "Memsahibs and Motherhood"; Carter, *The Importance of Being Monogamous*; Burton, *Dwelling in the Archive*; Rafael, "Colonial Domesticity";

Summers, "Intimate Colonialism"; Wanhalla, *Matters of the Heart;* Hodes, *White Women;* White, *The Comforts of Home;* Ellinghaus, *Taking Assimilation to Heart;* Haskins, "Domesticating Colonizers"; Barrera, "Sex, Citizenship and the State."

8 Ballhatchet, *Race, Sex and Class;* Levine, *Prostitution, Race, and Politics;* Stoler, *Carnal Knowledge;* Frühstück, *Colonizing Sex;* Salesa, *Racial Crossings;* Smithers, *Science, Sexuality, and Race;* Martínez, *Genealogical Fictions;* Ray, *Crossing the Color Line;* Bland, "British Eugenics and 'Race Crossing'"; Vaughan, *Curing Their Ills.*

9 On the somewhat separate trajectory of studies of gender and empire, see Camiscioli, "Women, Gender, Intimacy, and Empire." For pioneering and representative works, see Silverblatt, *Moon, Sun, and Witches;* Seed, *To Love, Honor, and Obey;* Warren, *Ah Ku;* Pierce, *The Imperial Harem;* Curtis, *Civilizing Habits.* On colonial masculinity, see Sinha, *Colonial Masculinity.*

10 Burton, *Burdens of History.* See also, Chaudhuri and Strobel, eds., *Western Women and Imperialism.*

11 Pedersen; "National Bodies"; Scully, "Rape, Race, and Colonial Culture"; Briggs, *Reproducing Empire.*

12 Stoler, *Along the Archival Grain;* Burton, *Archive Stories;* Trouillot, *Silencing the Past;* Glissant, *Caribbean Discourse;* Said, *Culture and Imperialism;* Fuentes, *Dispossessed Lives.*

13 Mitra, *Indian Sex Life.*

14 Arondekar, *For the Record;* Manderson and Jolly, *Sites of Desire;* Proschan, "Eunuch Mandarins"; Oyěwùmí, *The Invention of Women;* Wekker, *The Politics of Passion;* Hoad, *African Intimacies,* ch. 1; Lugones, "Heterosexualism"; Rifkin, *When did Indians Become Straight?;* Morgensen, "Theorising Gender"; Tortorici, *Sins against Nature;* Tamale, *African Sexualities;* Aldrich, *Colonialism and Homosexuality;* Shah, *Stranger Intimacy;* Newell, *The Forger's Tale.*

15 On activist knowledge, see hooks, *Ain't I a Woman;* Davis, *Women, Race and Class;* Combahee River Collective, *The Combahee River Collective Statement;* Taylor, *How We Get Free;* Mohanty, "Under Western Eyes"; Alexander, *Pedagogies of Crossing;* Morgensen, *Spaces between Us;* Trinh, *Woman, Native, Other;* Sandoval, *Methodology of the Oppressed.*

16 Morgan, *Laboring Women,* ch. 1; Carter, *The Heart of Whiteness.*

17 Rifkin, *When Did Indians Become Straight?;* Kauanui, *Hawaiian Blood;* Arvin, *Possessing Polynesians.* More recently, settler claims to sexual progressivism in places like the United States, Canada, and Israel have featured in justifications for expanding imperialism and ongoing domination. See Elia, "Gay Rights with a Side of Apartheid"; Morgensen, "Queer Settler Colonialism"; Puar, *Terrorist Assemblages.*

18 Recent works have combined attention to the political economy of sex and affect. See especially, Jean-Baptiste, *Conjugal Rights;* Ray, *Crossing the Color Line;* Vergès, *The Wombs of Women;* Cole and Thomas, *Love in Africa;* Germeten, *Profit and Passion.* For a different take on "intimacy" as entanglements of seemingly disparate places, economies, and peoples, see Lowe, *The Intimacies of Four Continents;* Carby, *Imperial Intimacies.*

19 See especially Bourbonnais; Ferguson and Yılmaz; Decker; Vergès; Isenia; Landertinger.

20 Tadiar, "Decolonization, 'Race,'" 151.

21 See for example, Rifkin, *The Erotics of Sovereignty;* Driskill, et al., *Queer Indigenous Studies;* Hartman, *Wayward Lives;* Shah, *Stranger Intimacy;* Agard-Jones, "What the Sands Remember"; Turner, *Contested Bodies;* Johnson, *Wicked Flesh;* Ambaras, *Japan's Imperial Underworlds.* In this volume, see especially Imy; Germeten; Bourbonnais; Leavitt-Alcántara; Isenia; Das; Schweighofer.

22 Cooper, *Colonialism in Question,* 27.

23 On "coloniality" as a system of enduring ideological and political force, see Quijano, "Coloniality of Power"; Wynter, "Unsettling the Coloniality of Being"; Mignolo, *The Darker Side;* Lugones, "Heterosexualism." For a counterargument, see Cooper, *Colonialism in Question,* 27–32.

24 De Barros, *Reproducing the British Caribbean;* Park "Bodies for Empire."

25 Jacobs, *White Mother.* In this volume, see Smithers; Landertinger.

26 King, *The Black Shoals,* x.

27 See Newman in this volume.

28 See Takeuchi-Demirci in this volume.

29 For a parallel argument, see Bashford, *Global Population.*

30 See Imy in this volume and Loos, "Histories of Sexuality."

31 See especially Wekker, *The Politics of Passion;* Sheller, *Citizenship from Below.*

32 See especially Arondekar, *For the Record.*

33 Berlant and Edelman, *Sex, or the Unbearable,* viii.

34 Ferguson and Yılmaz in this volume.

35 Stoler, *Carnal Knowledge;* Garraway, *The Libertine Colony;* Saada, *Empire's Children;* White, *Children of the French Empire;* Firpo, *The Uprooted;* Ray, *Crossing the Color Line;* Lee, *Unreasonable Histories;* Vergès,

Monsters and Revolutionaries; Newman, *A Dark Inheritance*; Livesay, *Children of Uncertain Fortune*; Hahm, "Family Matters."
36 See also in this volume, Pursley; Leavitt-Alcántara.
37 Arondekar, "Without a Trace," 12.
38 For similar arguments, see Bailkin, "The Boot and the Spleen"; Hartman, "Venus in Two Acts."
39 On sexuality, empire, and international bodies and laws, see especially Kozma, *Global Women*; Ishikawa, "Human Trafficking."
40 Fanon, *Black Skin*; Spivak, "Can the Subaltern Speak"; Bhaba, *The Location of Culture*.
41 See Matera, *Black London*, ch. 5; Ray, *Crossing the Color Line*; Shepard, *Sex, France, and Arab Men*. On race, gender, and metropolitan cultures, see Boittin, *Colonial Metropolis*; Joseph-Gabriel, *Reimagining Liberation*.
42 On the relationship between pleasure and brutality, see Herzog, *Brutality and Desire*; Branche, "Sexual Violence," 252–253; Elkins, *Imperial Reckoning*, 208–209; Hartman, *Scenes of Subjection*; Marshall, "The Bleaching Carceral"; Westermann, *Drunk on Genocide*.
43 Lindsey and Johnson, "Searching for Climax."
44 Ray, *Crossing the Color Line*; Thornberry, *Colonizing Consent*; Block, *Rape and Sexual Power*. In this volume, see Decker; Nesvig; Lauro; Captain.
45 Gqola, *Rape*, 37.
46 Young, *Colonial Desire*, 181.
47 On age and maturity, see Aderinto, *When Sex Threatened the State*; Pande, *Sex, Law, and the Politics of Age*; Decker, "A Feminist Methodology of Age-Grading"; Shah, *Stranger Intimacy*. In this volume, see Decker; Kozma; Captain.
48 For a lucid meditation on bodies and empire, see Burton and Ballantyne, *Bodies in Contact*. In this volume, see Surkis; Robinson; Imy.
49 Kelley, *Freedom Dreams*.

Bibliography

Aderinto, Saheed. *When Sex Threatened the State: Illicit Sexuality, Nationalism, and Politics in Colonial Nigeria, 1900–1958*. Champaign, IL: University of Illinois Press, 2015.

Agard-Jones, Vanessa. "What the Sands Remember." *GLQ: A Journal of Gay and Lesbian Studies* 18, no. 2 (2012): 325–346. doi:10.1215/10642684-1472917.

Aldrich, Robert. *Colonialism and Homosexuality*. London: Routledge, 2003.

Alexander, M. Jacqui. *Pedagogies of Crossing: Meditations on Feminism, Sexual Politics, Memory and the Sacred*. Durham, NC: Duke University Press, 2005. doi:10.1215/9780822386988.

Alloula, Malek. *The Colonial Harem*. Translated by Myrna Gozich and Wlad Godzich. Manchester, UK: Manchester University Press, 1996.

Ambaras, David. *Japan's Imperial Underworlds: Intimate Encounters at the Borders of Empire*. Cambridge, UK: Cambridge University Press, 2018.

Arondekar, Anjali. "Without a Trace: Sexuality and the Colonial Archive." *Journal of the History of Sexuality* 14, no. 1/2 (2005): 10–27. doi:10.1353/sex.2006.0001.

Arondekar, Anjali. *For the Record: Sexuality and the Colonial Archive in India*. Durham, NC: Duke University Press, 2009.

Arvin, Maile. *Possessing Polynesians: The Science of Settler Colonial Whiteness in Hawai'i and Oceania*. Durham, NC: Duke University Press, 2019.

Bailkin, Jordanna. "The Boot and the Spleen: When Was Murder Possible in British India?" *Comparative Studies in Society and History* 48, no. 2 (2006): 462–493. doi:10.1017/S001041750600017X.

Ballhatchet, Kenneth. *Race, Sex and Class under the Raj: Imperial Attitudes and Policies and their Critics*. New York: Saint Martin's Press, 1980.

Barrera, Giulia. "Sex, Citizenship and the State: The Construction of the Public and Private Sphere in Colonial Eritrea." In *Gender, Family and Sexuality: The Private Sphere in Italy 1860–1945*, edited by Perry Wilson, 76–92. New York: Palgrave Macmillan, 2004.

Bashford, Alison. *Global Population: History, Geopolitics, and Life on Earth*. New York: Columbia University Press, 2014.

Berlant, Lauren and Lee Edelman. *Sex, or the Unbearable*. Durham, NC: Duke University Press, 2013.

Bhabha, Homi. *The Location of Culture*. New York: Routledge, 1994.

Bland, Lucy. "British Eugenics and 'Race Crossing': A Study of an Interwar Investigation." *New Formations*, no. 60 (2007): 66–78.

Bleys, Rudi. *The Geography of Perversion: Male-to-Male Sexual Behavior Outside the West and the Ethnographic Imagination, 1750–1918*. New York: New York University Press, 1995.

Block, Sharon. *Rape and Sexual Power in Early America*. Chapel Hill, NC: University of North Carolina Press, 2006.

Boittin, Jennifer Ann. *Colonial Metropolis: The Urban Grounds of Anti-Imperialism and Feminism in Interwar Paris*. Lincoln, NE: University of Nebraska Press, 2010.

Boone, Joseph. *The Homoerotics of Orientalism*. New York: Columbia University Press, 2014.

Branche, Raphaëlle. "Sexual Violence in the Algerian War." In *Brutality and Desire: War and Sexuality in Europe's Twentieth Century*, edited by Dagmar Herzog, 247–260. London: Palgrave, 2009.

Briggs, Laura. *Reproducing Empire: Race, Sex, Science, and US Imperialism in Puerto Rico*. Berkeley, CA: University of California Press, 2002.

Burton, Antoinette. *Burdens of History: British Feminists, Indian Women, and Imperial Culture, 1865–1915*. Chapel Hill, NC: University of North Carolina Press, 2000.

Burton, Antoinette, ed. *After the Imperial Turn: Thinking with and through Nation*. Durham, NC: Duke University Press, 2003.

Burton, Antoinette. *Dwelling in the Archive: Women Writing House, Home, and History in Late Colonial India*. Oxford, UK: Oxford University Press, 2003.

Burton, Antoinette, ed. *Archive Stories: Facts, Fictions, and the Writings of History*. Durham, NC: Duke University Press, 2006.

Burton, Antoinette and Tony Ballantyne, eds. *Bodies in Contact: Rethinking Colonial Encounters in World History*. Durham, NC: Duke University Press, 2005.

Camiscioli, Elisa. "Women, Gender, Intimacy, and Empire." *Journal of Women's History* 25, no. 4 (2013): 138–148. doi:10.1353/jowh.2013.0056.

Carby, Hazel V. *Imperial Intimacies: A Tale of Two Islands*. London: Verso, 2019.

Carter, Julian. *The Heart of Whiteness: Normal Sexuality and Race in America, 1800–1940*. Durham, NC: Duke University Press, 2007.

Carter, Sarah. *The Importance of Being Monogamous: Marriage and Nation Building in Western Canada in 1915*. Edmonton: University of Alberta Press, 2008.

Chaudhuri, Nupur. "Memsahibs and Motherhood in Nineteenth-Century Colonial India." *Victorian Studies* 13, no. 4 (1981): 517–536.

Chaudhuri, Nupur and Margaret Strobel, eds. *Western Women and Imperialism: Complicity and Resistance*. Bloomington, IN: Indiana University Press, 1992.

Clancy-Smith, Julia and Frances Gouda. *Domesticating the Empire: Race, Gender, and Family Life in French and Dutch Colonialism*. Charlottesville, VA: University of Virginia Press, 1998.

Cole, Jennifer and Lynn Thomas, eds. *Love in Africa*. Chicago, IL: University of Chicago Press, 2009.

Combahee River Collective. The Combahee River Collective Statement. (1977).

Cooper, Frederick. *Colonialism in Question: Theory, Knowledge, History*. Berkeley, CA: University of California Press, 2005.

Curtis, Sarah. *Civilizing Habits: Women Missionaries and the Revival of French Empire*. Oxford, UK: Oxford University Press, 2010.

Davis, Angela. *Women, Race, and Class*. New York: Vintage, 1983.

De Barros, Juanita. *Reproducing the British Caribbean: Sex, Gender, and Population Politics after Slavery*. Chapel Hill, NC: University of North Carolina Press, 2014.

Decker, Corrie. "A Feminist Methodology of Age-Grading and History in Africa." *American Historical Review*. 125, no. 2 (2020): 418–426. doi:10.1093/ahr/rhaa170.

Driskill, Qwo-Li, Chris Finley, Brian Joseph Gilley, Scott Lauria Morgensen. *Queer Indigenous Studies: Critical Interventions in Theory, Politics, and Literature*. Tucson, AZ: University of Arizona Press, 2019.

Elia, Nada. "Gay Rights with a Side of Apartheid." *Settler Colonial Studies* 2, no. 2 (2012): 49–68. doi:10.1080/2201473X.2012.10648841.

Elkins, Caroline. *Imperial Reckoning: The Untold Story of Britain's Gulag in Kenya*. New York: Henry Holt, 2005.

Ellinghaus, Katherine. *Taking Assimilation to Heart: Marriages of White Women and Indigenous Men in the United States & Australia, 1887–1937*. Lincoln, NE: University of Nebraska Press, 2006.

Fanon, Frantz. *Black Skin, White Masks*. Translated by Richard Philcox. New York: Grove Press, 1952.

Firpo, Christina. *The Uprooted: Race, Children and Imperialism in French Indochina, 1890–1980*. Honolulu: University of Hawai'i Press. 2016.

Frühstück, Sabine. *Colonizing Sex: Sexology and Social Control in Modern Japan*. Berkeley, CA: University of California Press, 2003.

Fuentes, Marisa. *Dispossessed Lives: Enslaved Women, Violence, and the Archive*. Philadelphia, PA: University of Pennsylvania Press, 2016.

Garraway, Doris. *The Libertine Colony: Creolization in the Early French Caribbean*. Durham, NC: Duke University Press, 2005.

Germeten, Nicole von. *Profit and Passion: Transactional Sex in Colonial Mexico*. Berkeley, CA: University of California Press, 2018.

Ghosh, Durba. "Another Set of Imperial Turns?" *The American Historical Review* 117, no. 3 (2012): 772–793. doi:10.1086/ahr.117.3.772. Gilman, Sander. *Difference and Pathology: Stereotypes of Sexuality, Race, and Madness*. Ithaca, NY: Cornell University Press, 1985.

Ghosh, Durba. *Sex and the Family in Colonial India: The Making of Empire*. Cambridge, UK: Cambridge University Press, 2006.

Glissant, Édouard. *Caribbean Discourse: Selected Essays*. Charlottesville, VA: University Press of Virginia, 1989.

Gqola, Pumla Dineo. *Rape: A South African Nightmare*. Johannesburg: MF Books, 2015.

Hahm, Jooyeon. "Family Matters: Concubines and Illegitimate Children in the Japanese Empire, 1868–1945." Ph.D. diss., University of Pennsylvania, 2019.

Hartman, Saidiya. *Scenes of Subjection: Terror, Slavery, and Self-Making in Nineteenth-Century America*. Oxford, UK: Oxford University Press, 1997.

Hartman, Saidiya. "Venus in Two Acts." *Small Axe* 12, no. 2 (2008): 1–14. doi:10. 1215/-12–12-1.

Hartman, Saidiya. *Wayward Lives, Beautiful Experiments: Intimate Histories of Riotous Black Girls, Troublesome Women and Queer Radicals*. New York: W.W. Norton, 2019.

Haskins, Victoria. "Domesticating Colonizers: Domesticity, Indigenous Domestic Labor, and the Modern Settler Colonial Nation." *American Historical Review* 124, no. 4 (2019): 1290–1301. doi:10.1093/ahr/rhz647.

Herzog, Dagmar, ed. *Brutality and Desire: War and Sexuality in Europe's Twentieth Century*. London: Palgrave, 2009.

Hoad, Neville. *African Intimacies: Race, Homosexuality, and Globalization*. Minneapolis, MN: University of Minnesota Press, 2006.

Hodes, Martha. *White Women, Black Men: Illicit Sex in the Nineteenth-Century South*. New Haven, CT: Yale University Press, 1999.

hooks, bell. *Ain't I a Woman: Black Women and Feminism*. Boston, MA: South End Press, 1981.

Howe, Stephen. *The New Imperial Histories Reader*. New York: Routledge, 2010.

Hunt, Nancy Rose. "Domesticity and Colonialism in Belgian Africa: Usumbra's *Foyer Social*, 1946–1960." *Signs* 15, no. 3 (1990): 447–474. doi:10.1086/494605.

Hyam, Ronald. *Empire and Sexuality: The British Experience*. Manchester, UK: Manchester University Press, 1990.

Ishikawa, Tadashi. "Human Trafficking and Intra-Imperial Knowledge: Adopted Daughters, Households, and Law in Imperial Japan and Colonial Taiwan." *Journal of Women's History* 29, no. 3 (2017): 37–60. doi:10.1353/jowh.2017.0032.

Jacobs, Margaret. *White Mother to a Dark Race: Settler Colonialism, Maternalism, and the Removal of Indigenous Children in the American West and Australia, 1880–1940*. Lincoln, NE: University of Nebraska Press, 2009.

Jean-Baptiste, Rachel. *Conjugal Rights: Marriage, Sexuality, and Urban Life in Colonial Libreville, Gabon*. Athens, OH: Ohio University Press, 2014.

Johnson, Jessica Marie. *Wicked Flesh: Black Women, Intimacy, and Freedom in the Atlantic World*. Philadelphia, PA: University of Pennsylvania Press, 2020.

Joseph-Gabriel, Annette. *Reimagining Liberation: How Black Women Transformed Citizenship in the French Empire*. Urbana-Champaign, IL: University of Illinois Press, 2020.

Kauanui, J. Kēhaulani. *Hawaiian Blood: Colonialism and the Politics of Sovereignty and Indigeneity*. Durham, NC: Duke University Press, 2008.

Kelley, Robin D.G. *Freedom Dreams: The Black Radical Imagination*. Boston, MA: Beacon Press, 2002.

King, Tiffany Lethabo. *The Black Shoals: Offshore Formations of Black and Native Studies*. Durham, NC: Duke University Press, 2019. doi:10.1215/9781478005681.

Kozma, Liat. *Global Women, Colonial Ports: Prostitution in the Interwar Middle East*. Albany, NY: SUNY Press, 2017.

Lee, Christopher J. *Unreasonable Histories: Nativism, Multiracial Lives, and the Genealogical Imagination in British Africa*. Durham, NC: Duke University Press, 2015. doi:10.1215/9780822376378.

Lim, Sungyun. *Rules of the House: Family Law and Domestic Disputes in Colonial Korea*. Berkeley, CA: University of California Press, 2018.

Lindsey, Treva and Jessica Marie Johnson. "Searching for Climax: Black Erotic Lives in Slavery and Freedom." *Meridians* 12, no. 2 (2014): 169–195. doi:10.2979/meridians.12.2.169.

Livesay, Daniel. *Children of Uncertain Fortune: Mixed-Race Jamaicans in Britain and the Atlantic Family, 1733–1833.* Chapel Hill, NC: University of North Carolina Press, 2017.

Loos, Tamara. "Transnational Histories of Sexuality in Asia." *American Historical Review* 114, no. 5 (2009): 1309–1324. doi:10.1086/ahr.114.5.1309.

Lowe, Lisa. *The Intimacies of Four Continents.* Durham, NC: Duke University Press, 2015.

Lugones, María. "Heterosexualism and the Colonial/Modern Gender System." *Hypatia* 22, no. 1 (2007): 186–209. doi:10.1111/j.1527-2001.2007.tb01156.x.

Manderson, Leonore and Margaret Jolly, eds. *Sites of Desire, Economies of Pleasure: Sexualities in Asia and the Pacific.* Chicago, IL: University of Chicago Press, 1997.

Marshall, Yannick. "The Bleaching Carceral: Police, Native and Location in Nairobi, 1844–1906." Ph.D. diss., Columbia University, 1997.

Martínez, Maria Elena. *Genealogical Fictions: Limpieza de Sangre, Religion, and Gender in Colonial Mexico.* Stanford, CA: Stanford University Press, 2008.

Matera, Marc. *Black London: The Imperial Metropolis and Decolonization in the Twentieth Century.* Berkeley, CA: University of California Press, 2015.

McClintock, Anne. *Imperial Leather: Race, Gender, and Sexuality in the Colonial Contest.* London: Routledge, 1995.

Mignolo, Walter. *The Darker Side of Western Modernity.* Durham, NC: Duke University Press, 2011.

Minh-ha, Trinh T. *Woman, Native, Other: Writing Postcoloniality and Feminism.* Bloomington, IN: Indiana University Press, 1989.

Mitchell, Robin. *Vénus Noire: Black Women and Colonial Fantasies in Nineteenth-Century France.* Athens, GA: University of Georgia Press, 2020.

Mitra, Durba. *Indian Sex Life: Sexuality and the Colonial Origins of Modern Social Thought.* Princeton, NJ: Princeton University Press, 2020.

Mohanty, Chandra Talpade. "Under Western Eyes: Feminist Scholarship and Colonial Discourses." *Boundary 2* 12/13, no. 3/1 (1984): 333–358.

Morgan, Jennifer. *Laboring Women: Reproduction and Gender in New World Slavery.* Philadelphia, PA: University of Pennsylvania Press, 2004.

Morgensen, Scott Lauria. *Spaces between Us: Queer Settler Colonialism and Indigenous Decolonization.* Minneapolis, MN: University of Minnesota Press, 2011.

Morgensen, Scott Lauria. "Queer Settler Colonialism in Canada and Israel: Articulating Two-Spirit and Palestinian Queer Critiques." *Settler Colonial Studies* 2, no. 2 (2012): 167–190. doi:10.1080/2201473X.2012.10648848.

Morgensen, Scott Lauria. "Theorising Gender, Sexuality and Settler Colonialism: An Introduction." *Settler Colonial Studies* 2, no. 2 (2013): 2–22. doi:10.1080/2201473X.2012.10648839.

Nandy, Ashis. *The Intimate Enemy: Loss and Recovery of Self Under Colonialism.* Delhi, Oxford University Press, 1983.

Newell, Stephanie. *The Forger's Tale: The Search for Odeziaku.* Athens, OH: Ohio University Press, 2006.

Newman, Brooke. *A Dark Inheritance: Blood, Race, and Sex in Colonial Jamaica.* New Haven, CT: Yale University Press, 2018.

Oyěwùmí, Oyèrónké. *The Invention of Women: Making an African Sense of Western Gender Discourses.* Minneapolis, MN: University of Minnesota Press, 1997.

Pande, Ishita. *Sex, Law, and the Politics of Age: Child Marriage in India, 1891–1937.* Cambridge, UK: Cambridge University Press, 2020.

Park, Jin-kyung. "Bodies for Empire: Biopolitics, Reproduction, and Sexual Knowledge in Late-Colonial Korea." *Ui Sahak* 23, no. 2 (2014): 203–238. doi:10.13081/kjmh.2014.23.203.

Pedersen, Susan. "National Bodies, Unspeakable Acts: The Sexual Politics of Colonial Policy-Making." *Journal of Modern History* 63 (1991): 647–680. doi:10.1086/244384.

Pierce, Leslie. *The Imperial Harem: Women and Sovereignty in the Ottoman Empire.* Oxford, UK: Oxford University Press, 1993.

Pratt, Mary Louise. *Imperial Eyes: Travel Writing and Transculturation.* London: Routledge, 1992.

Proschan, Frank. "Eunuch Mandarins, Soldat Mamzelles, Effeminate Boys, and Graceless Women: French Colonial Constructions of Vietnamese Genders." *GLQ: A Journal of Gay and Lesbian Studies* 8, no. 4 (2002): 435–467. doi:10.1215/10642684-8-4-435.

Puar, Jasbir. *Terrorist Assemblages: Homonationalism in Queer Times.* Durham, NC: Duke University Press, 2007.

Quijano, Anibal. "Coloniality of Power, Eurocentrism, and Latin America." *Nepantla* 1, no. 3 (2000): 533–580. doi:10.1177%2F0268580900015002005.

Rafael, Vincent. "Colonial Domesticity: White Women and United States Rule in the Philippines." *American Literature* 67, no. 4 (1995): 639–666. doi:10.2307/2927890.

Ray, Carina. *Crossing the Color Line: Race, Sex, and the Contested Politics of Colonialism in Ghana.* Athens, OH: Ohio University Press, 2015.

Rifkin, Mark. *When did Indians Become Straight? Kinship, the History of Sexuality, and Native Sovereignty.* Oxford, UK: Oxford University Press, 2011.

Rifkin, Mark. *The Erotics of Sovereignty: Queer Native Writing in the Era of Self-Determination.* Minneapolis, MN: University of Minnesota Press, 2012.

Saada, Emannuelle. *Empire's Children: Race, Filiation, and Citizenship in the French Colonies.* Translated by Arthur Goldhammer. Chicago, IL: University of Chicago Press, 2011.

Said, Edward. *Culture and Imperialism.* New York: Knopf, 1993.

Salesa, Damon. *Racial Crossings: Race, Intermarriage, and the Victorian British Empire.* Oxford, UK: Oxford University Press, 2011.

Sandoval, Chela. *Methodology of the Oppressed.* Minneapolis, MN: University of Minnesota Press, 2000.

Scully, Pamela. "Rape, Race, and Colonial Culture: The Sexual Politics of Identity in the Nineteenth-Century Cape Colony, South Africa." *American Historical Review* 100 (1995): 335–359. doi:10.1086/ahr/100.2.335.

Seed, Patricia. *To Love, Honor, and Obey in Colonial Mexico: Conflicts Over Marriage Choice, 1574–1821.* Stanford, CA: Stanford University Press, 1988.

Shah, Nayan. *Stranger Intimacy: Contesting Race, Sexuality and the Law in the North American West.* Berkeley, CA: University of California Press, 2012.

Sharpley-Whiting, Tracy Denean. *Black Venus: Sexualized Savages, Primal Fears, and Primitive Narratives in French.* Durham, NC: Duke University Press, 1999.

Sheller, Mimi. *Citizenship from Below: Erotic Agency and Caribbean Freedom.* Durham, NC: Duke University Press, 2012.

Shepard, Todd. *Sex, France, and Arab Men, 1962–1979.* Chicago, IL: University of Chicago Press, 2017.

Silverblatt, Irene. *Moon, Sun, and Witches: Gender Ideologies and Class in Inca and Colonial Peru.* Princeton, NJ: Princeton University Press, 1987.

Sinha, Mrinalini. *Colonial Masculinity: The 'Manly Englishman' and the 'Effeminate Bengali' in the Late Nineteenth Century.* Manchester, UK: Manchester University Press, 1995.

Smithers, Gregory. *Science, Sexuality and Race in the United States and Australia, 1780–1940.* New York: Routledge, 2008.

Spivak, Gayatri. "Can the Subaltern Speak?" In *Marxism and the Interpretation of Culture*, edited by Cary Nelson and Lawrence Grossberg, 271–313. London: Macmillan, 1988.

Stoler, Ann Laura. "Making Empire Respectable: The Politics of Race and Sexual Morality in 20th-century Colonial Cultures." *American Ethnologist* 16, no. 4 (1989): 634–660. doi:10.1525/ae.1989.16.4.02a00030.

Stoler, Ann Laura. *Race and the Education of Desire: Foucault's History of Sexuality and the Colonial Order of Things.* Durham, NC: Duke University Press, 1995.

Stoler, Ann Laura. *Carnal Knowledge and Imperial Power: Race and the Intimate in Colonial Rule.* Berkeley, CA: University of California Press, 2002.

Stoler, Ann Laura. *Along the Archival Grain: Epistemic Anxieties and Colonial Common Sense.* Princeton, NJ: Princeton University Press, 2008.

Stoler, Ann Laura and Frederick Cooper. "Between Metropole and Colony: Rethinking a Research Agenda." In *Tensions of Empire*, edited by Frederick Cooper and Ann Laura Stoler, 1–56. Berkeley, CA: University of California Press, 1997.

Summers, Carole. "Intimate Colonialism: The Imperial Production of Reproduction in Uganda, 1907–1925." *Signs* 16, no. 4 (1991): 787–807. doi:10.1086/494703.

Tadiar, Neferti X.M. "Decolonization, 'Race,' and Remaindered Life under Empire." *Qui Parle* 23, no. 2 (2015): 135–160. doi:10.5250/quiparle.23.2.0135.

Tamale, Sylvia. *African Sexualities: A Reader.* Cape Town: Pambazuka Press, 2011.

Taylor, Keeanga-Yamahtta, ed. *How We Get Free: Black Feminism and the Combahee River Collective.* Chicago, IL: Haymarket Books, 2012.

Thornberry, Elizabeth. *Colonizing Consent: Rape and Governance in South Africa's Eastern Cape.* Cambridge, UK: Cambridge University Press, 2018.

Tortorici, Zeb. *Sins against Nature: Sex and Archives in Colonial New Spain*. Durham, NC: Duke University Press, 2018.

Trouillot, Michel-Rolph. *Silencing the Past: Power and the Production of History*. Boston, MA: Beacon Press, 1995.

Turner, Sasha. *Contested Bodies: Pregnancy, Childrearing, and Slavery in Jamaica*. Philadelphia, PA: University of Pennsylvania Press, 2017.

Vaughan, Megan. *Curing Their Ills: Colonial Power and African Illness*. Stanford, CA: Stanford University Press, 1991.

Vergès, Françoise. *Monsters and Revolutionaries: Colonial Family Romance and Métissage*. Durham, NC: Duke University Press, 1999. doi:10.1215/9780822379096.

Vergès, Françoise. *The Wombs of Women: Race, Capital, Feminism*. Translated by Kaima Glover. Durham, NC: Duke University Press, 2020. doi:10.1215/9781478008866.

Wanhalla, Angela. *Matters of the Heart: A History of Interracial Marriage in New Zealand*. Auckland: Auckland University Press, 2014.

Warren, James. *Ah Kuh and Karayuki-san: Prostitution in Singapore, 1870–1940*. Singapore: National University of Singapore, 2003.

Wekker, Gloria. *The Politics of Passion: Women's Sexual Culture in the Afro-Surinamese Diaspora*. New York: Columbia University Press, 2006.

Westermann, Edward. *Drunk on Genocide: Alcohol and Mass Murder in Nazi Germany*. Ithaca, NY: Cornell University Press, 2021.

White, Luise. *The Comforts of Home: Prostitution in Colonial Nairobi*. Chicago, IL: University of Chicago Press, 1999.

White, Owen. *Children of the French Empire: Miscegenation and Colonial Society in French West Africa, 1895–1960*. Oxford, UK: Clarendon Press, 1999.

Wynter, Sylvia. "Unsettling the Coloniality of Being/Power/Truth/Freedom: Towards the Human, After Man, Its Overrepresentation—An Argument." *CR: The New Centennial Review* 3, no. 3 (2003): 257–337.

Young, Robert. *Colonial Desire: Hybridity in Theory, Culture, and Race*. London: Routledge, 1995.

PART I

Directions in the study of sexuality and colonialism

1

OLD EMPIRES, NEW PERSPECTIVES

Sexuality in the Spanish and Portuguese Americas

Nicole von Germeten

As oceanic crossings began in the fifteenth century between Europe, Africa, Asia, and the Americas, the Spanish and Portuguese crowns oversaw movements of people and, along with their bureaucrats, functionaries, and intellectuals, filed thousands of cubic feet of texts and documents preserving their imperial interpretations of sexuality. The focus here will be on such documentation from areas most affected by Iberian institutions, most importantly in the viceroyalties of New Spain and Peru, and the undertakings of the Catholic Church.[1] These institutions promoted Iberian understandings of gender, justice, and family life, which shaped the unfolding of the history of sexuality as captured in the written record. The intellectual trajectory of the modern disciplines of history, literary studies, and anthropology derives from imperial ways of thinking about sexuality, and therefore early modern approaches and sources continue to affect today's scholarship. Some of the strongest subfields include case studies of non-heteronormative sex and sexual fantasies, as well as analysis of the processes for negotiating illegitimacy and contesting race labels applied at baptism.[2]

Europeans transcribed their visual impressions of indigenous Americans, creating a voyeuristic imperial archive from the very first moment of contact. Take, for example, the letter of Pero Vaz de Caminha, written during a 1500 landing on the coast of Brazil. This missive describes the genitals of girls in what appeared to Europeans as their completely innocent nudity.[3] Europeans wavered between this Edenic interpretation of pre-Fall indigenous purity to an opposing vision of demonically influenced corruption, but both extremes highlight how imperial authorities attempted to dehumanize and exert power over conquered peoples, cataloguing them within biblical referents. The written archive of indigenous sexuality grew as the first priests and friars composed confession manuals that voiced their perspectives on how they envisioned the new populations encountered in highland Mexico and Peru and how other clerics should further shape their verbal interactions with them.[4] The Spanish presence in these heavily populated areas also led to the purposeful creation of knowledge around indigenous civilizations. For example, in Mexico City, Franciscan friar Bernardino de Sahagún collected information from local people, some of whom remembered the times before the Spanish invasion. These informants guided the views of the Florentine Codex, which included a particular interpretation of pre-conquest sexuality.[5] Later on, colonized commentators of indigenous descent trained by Europeans, such as Felipe Guaman Poma de Ayala in the late sixteenth and early seventeenth centuries, wrote their own treatises on their ancestors' history, sometimes bemoaning what they viewed as a decline in sexual morality since the coming of the Spanish.[6]

To contextualize this early creation of various written sources dealing with sexuality, scholars note that medieval and early modern Spaniards used sexual ideologies as essential organizing principles for the strengthening of their monarchs' rule and territorial expansion, understandings of justice, and elite cultural expressions. This Old World framework long predated Castilian conquest and rule of the Americas. One of the most important sections of the *Siete Partidas*, the fundamental Spanish medieval law code, deals with inheritance laws, which were highly complex in this non-monogamous culture.[7] Spanish literary classics obsessively dramatized sexual matters, from the fourteenth-century *Libro de Buen Amor* (focusing on a cleric's numerous love affairs, often arranged by his *alcahueta*, or go-between) to the *Tragicomedia de Calisto y Melibea*, better known as *La Celestina*, in honor of the unforgettable central character of a murdered bawd.[8] Later, in the era of Iberian expansion, dramas about honor killings drew popular audiences to the *corrales de comedias*. But these works of fiction perhaps represent sexual fantasy more than popular understandings of sex within daily life, especially for the poor majority of the population.[9] Historians of early modern Spain have aptly noted that "women's propensity to engage in non-marital relationships and bear illegitimate children strongly challenges the two major frameworks for understanding early modern Spanish sexuality: the Mediterranean honour code and the Catholic Reformation."[10]

While this quote refers to peasant women in remote Galicia, these tensions between the Christian ideal of chastity and the complexity of sexual practice existed at all levels of society and regions under Spanish control. Castile's rise to domination over the Iberian Peninsula emerged out of fifteenth-century rumors of royal impotence. Hapsburg kings in the sixteenth and seventeenth centuries consulted with renowned mystical women to help sustain the sometimes-precarious Hapsburg dynasty in a unified Spain, and asked for their prayers as they arranged multiple marriages that resulted in procreation with their young teenage nieces.[11] Around the same time, the most Spanish of all saints, Teresa de Avila, forever memorialized the sexually suggestive bliss of mystical ecstasy in her evocative descriptions of an arrow deeply piercing her heart. In her more practical observations, Teresa strongly cautioned her peers about the "special friendships" between enclosed nuns.[12] One of the most obvious manifestations of the contrast between clerical projects and Iberian grassroots understandings of sexuality is the popular rejection of the sinfulness of "simple fornication," or sex between consenting, unmarried, lay adults.[13]

In the Americas, nuns, priests, and friars also wrote on sexuality, weaving their pious statements into a web of imperial rhetoric that featured frequent royal decrees regarding what were viewed as women's highly seductive styles of clothing and their tendencies toward constant "pecados publicos," or widely known sins such as adultery, non-monogamy, and transactional sex.[14] Despite the very well documented and researched sexual contradictions obvious in early modern Spain, historians of Latin America often have focused on these proscriptive approaches to sexuality, with an approach to women's history that emphasizes the institutions that enclosed women, especially nunneries, but also houses of voluntary as well as involuntary enclosure, known as *recogimientos*.[15]

One of the most famous of all the early modern commentators is the ever-fascinating poet, dramatist, philosopher, and intellectual leader Sor Juana Ines de la Cruz (1648 to 1695), whose life and work have inspired analyses of viceregal women's sexuality going back at the least to the pseudo-Freudian perspectives of Ludwig Pfandl, published in German in 1942.[16] Octavio Paz popularized Sor Juana's biography in the 1960s, with an emphasis on his interpretation of sexually repressive viceregal society.[17] The 1980s ushered in a new robust era whose productivity flourishes to the present, as ongoing scholarship mines a bountiful treasure of writings by a wide range of religious women.[18] Sor Juana's sexuality continues to fascinate readers, who disagree on labeling her a lesbian or a skilled poet who strategically dedicated love poems to her powerful patronesses.[19]

Around the time of increasing historical and literary studies inspired by Sor Juana, scholars started to produce the works of family and women's history which began to more seriously explore viceregal sexuality. More than 30 years have passed since the publication of *Sexuality and Marriage in Colonial Latin America*, edited by Asunción Lavrin, but this collection of essays (the first of its kind in English) remains an essential source.[20] While providing key insights into marital life, it also pioneered studies of non-normative sexuality for colonial Latin America and set the stage for further exploration of women's sexual agency and complex understandings of laws and traditions. Silvia Arrom and Patricia Seed's masterworks from this era also helped make possible a rather rapid transition from classic women's history to new approaches to the history of gender and sexuality, especially for New Spain.[21]

While the 1980s and early 1990s heralded the beginning of a robust era in literary, ethnographic, and historical studies of sexuality in viceregal Latin America, some rather heated debates also took place during these decades. Despite the immense contributions of Lavrin, Seed, Arrom, and later Ann Twinam, perhaps the most famous and controversial works of history in the 1990s dealing with gender and sexuality were written by men. In contrast to the major publications from the aforementioned women in this era, the sweeping books written by Steve Stern and Ramon Gutiérrez concentrated their analysis on power and violence as related to their views of sexual conquest and gender roles under Spanish rule.[22] Stern's *Secret History of Gender* provided valuable insights into women's resistance and the concept of masculinity in Mexico.[23] However, Stern's view that conflict and resistance within patriarchy should replace the honor–shame framework around gender roles and sexuality did receive firm criticism. Susan Socolow critiqued Stern's emphasis on "power, domination, and struggle" as removing "joy, passion, love, and loyalty" from relationships, a very valid reminder that desire should play a role in analyzing sexuality.[24] Gutierrez's very popular book, *When Jesus Came, the Corn Mothers Went Away*, treating marriage and conquest in seventeenth-century New Mexico, received criticism for its predominant theme of oppression and resistance.[25] Reviewers noted that both of these books did not adequately acknowledge the pioneering work on marriage and sexuality by authors such as Seed, revealing the gendered tensions within academia in this era.[26] A supposition could be made that these large tomes, with their focus on power, and therefore politics, received more recognition among scholars as "important," while pioneers including Lavrin and Arrom focused on newer and less valued topics, marginalized as "women's history."

In response to these classic books, at the advent of the twenty-first century, Karen Vieira Powers criticized the persistent focus in Latin American historiography on "gloryify[ing] male sexual domination and ascrib[ing] to women the constricted role of passive sexual objects." The essay concludes optimistically, observing that the work of current and future scholars will complicate the age-old "discourse of sexual conquest" and the slightly newer "totalizing discourse of rape and victimhood that is equally disempowering," a prediction that has come true in a variety of angles taken by early twenty-first century scholarship.[27]

Fundamental to the history of sexuality in the Iberian empires is the study of honor, a field that can encompass masculinity studies as well as women's history. A traditional, and still popular, understanding conceives of conquest as an expression of Iberian masculinity and an opportunity for men to achieve status according to the violent and rapacious demands of the honor code. Military conquest and imperialism equate to sexual domination of women and indigenous people. In this view, women only possessed honor based on their sexual reclusion and the effectiveness of their male protectors. Historians have complicated this vision of honor as a destructive drive, and now many view it as a varying and utilitarian tool used by a broad range of colonial subjects in order to negotiate their diverse goals both in daily life and in litigation. The possession of elite male honor derives not from rampant sexual violence but from asserting one's noble lineage, wealth, Christian piety, and service to the monarch.[28] Several historians have shown how men, including non-Europeans, defined and exercised honor in their individual lives and how their approaches changed over time and varied according to regional differences. How women claimed honor has caused more debate; was honor just based on a woman's sexual reputation, or did other factors play a role? Gutiérrez's *When Jesus Came* sparked controversy for trapping women between repressive institutions and families and aggressive men. In contrast, Twinam's classic *Public Lives, Private Secrets* finds examples of women with one or more illegitimate children who managed to hold onto a publicly honorable reputation. Men's sexual activity did not threaten their honor, as was usually the case for women, but Twinam argues that a sense of conscience based on ethics and religion did influence men. Therefore, according to Twinam, Spanish men did have moral codes beyond asserting honor through sexual aggression and sincerely desired to pass on their honor to their children, even if they did not fit the strictest definitions of having a "pure" Spanish, legitimate lineage.[29]

Along with honor, ethnographic approaches to indigenous sexuality before and after European contact also complicate the passive view of sexuality critiqued by Vieira Powers. Earlier approaches first conceived of indigenous women suffering significant losses in their status and standards of living under Spanish rule, in contrast to an understanding of gender parallelism of precolonial civilizations.[30] However, historians have challenged this sweeping negative assessment with more intensive research into indigenous language sources and viceregal legal documents.[31]

Iberian imperialism created a racialization of sexuality that lingers in archives; its effects remain powerful to the present day. Scholars have found the words that created this association most obviously in the records of the Holy Offices of both the Spanish and the Portuguese Inquisition Tribunals, most notably in the files relating to witchcraft and sorcery. Especially in the seventeenth century, these cases are saturated in eroticism, racialized sexual tension, and fears of violence and gendered power exchanges. In the late 1980s Ruth Behar's famous article on sexual witchcraft set the tone for much future analysis. Behar interpreted very intimate acts, such as a woman serving a husband or master food ensorcelled with her own bodily fluids in order to *amansar* (tame) or *ligar* (bind) him, as a form of political resistance. In Behar's view, this demonstration of female power overturned gender and racial hierarchies. Joan Cameron Bristol brought sexual witchcraft more into the mainstream of viceregal life, accurately noting its popularity and opportunities for connections across a wide range of women. The inquisitors' efforts to write down women's traditional spells, divinations, potions, and erotic practices do suggest that sex could offer a means to achieve personal desires; not just sexual but also emotional, economic, and social, although the existence of these cases proves that women risked violent reactions from men or prosecution when they acted on their passions. Regardless of debates over agency and sexuality, the documentation of erotic magic and the sometimes coterminous narratives of orgiastic encounters with demons reaffirm an imperial vision of highly sexualized women (especially of African descent) through a link to sorcery and witchcraft.

In terms of the historiography of sexuality in the viceroyalties, what sociologists might call "deviance" remains one of the most vibrant areas of study. Excellent older articles and edited collections have covered male same-sex love and desire, while two recent books by Zeb Tortorici push non-heteronomative sexuality scholarship far beyond these topics.[32] Women who came before the Holy Office presenting their sexual fantasies seemed to have a fully realized erotic imagination and often had taken quite dramatic steps to carry them out.[33] Tortorici's *Sins Against Nature: Sex and Archives in New Spain* challenges readers to consider and question what is secret and hidden, and what is catalogued and labeled in the records we use to explore the history of sexuality—itself a misnomer, as "sexuality" as a concept did not exist until long after the era under discussion. Tortorici's large body of documentation from far-flung archives disproves that "unnatural" acts and beliefs were uncommon or unusual.

The study of non-heteronormative sexuality has experienced a boom in the last several years, although this topic has lurked for decades in studies by Richard Boyer on bigamy, Serge Gruzinski on homosexuality, and of course on the very popular "Lieutenant Nun," the Basque transgender soldier of fortune Catalina de Erauso.[34] Scholars can thank the voluminous records of the Holy Office of the Spanish Inquisition and the diocesan courts in every major population center for archiving a profusion of cases involving "unnatural sexuality." The "Archival Turn" of the last few decades has helped historians to analyze the categorizations and silences of viceregal records which touch on sex acts and beliefs related to sex. Ironically, the large corpus of surviving documentation preserves explicit descriptions of acts perpetrated by clergymen that the viceregal church wished would remain secret for the sake of its own reputation, as well as the heretical words of laypeople whom the authorities hoped to silence so as not to spread their influence, even as the inquisitors' henchmen tortured their physical bodies to produce these words. These contradictions and complexities fit with archival theories that contest the idea that archives have some kind of understandable organization in support of imperialism, or even that archive-creators wanted these files to be clear and organized.

Another area that social scientists label as "deviance," even into recent years, is transactional sex. Historians have skimmed over the prolific documentation of direct exchanges of sex acts for money and gifts, even as they have thoroughly explored the broader transactional nature of sex in the viceregal Americas through traditional institutions such as the dowry.[35] Understanding the transactionality and materiality of sex in their milieu, women in Spain and its empire exercised varying levels of control over the commodification of their sexual and reproductive acts. In the act of sacramental marriage, young women in the viceroyalties converted their sexual capital into economic and social capital, generally within the context of their parents' or guardians' machinations. If they eloped with their own choice of husband they risked losing all or part of their inheritance.[36] Among the elite, women who were ensconced within a family support network brought dowries with them into marriage and received *arras*, or a significant gift of money from their groom, to further bolster their financial stability. Lucky orphan girls who lacked the financial padding of a natal family received charitable donations to fund their dowries, making them more attractive potential wives.[37] In clearer gestures of personal agency, unmarried Spanish American women could more directly convert sexual or erotic capital into money by suing their lovers for defloration.[38] Winning a defloration or "breach of promise" case rewarded women with money that they could use for child support or a dowry to marry another man. Often these women enjoyed family support and advocacy as they litigated their defloration compensation suits.

Litigious material clearly remains one of the best sources for documenting the history of sexuality in the Iberian empires. But more creative sources also exist, which scholars have not fully exploited to this point. For example, along with religious art depicting the Virgin of Guadalupe and paintings of nuns known as *monjas floridas* before taking their vows, the eighteenth-century *pinturas de castas* represent the most famous artwork produced in the Spanish viceroyalties. While clearly about empire, racial categorization, and the exoticizing of colonial subjects, the "casta paintings" also depict dozens of combinations of sexual liaisons and the children born from sex between racially mixed couples. Scholars have not discussed in depth how these images preserve a carefully artistic presentation of flirtation, desire, and even fetishized sexual degradation and violence.[39] The casta paintings may have titillated viewers fascinated by what they viewed as depraved American eroticism.

In conclusion, women's history and gender history have broken exciting new ground in the history of sexuality in Spanish America since the late 1970s. Ethno-history and literary studies have strengthened the field, along with very thoughtful approaches to non-heteronormative sexuality categorized as "unnatural" in the viceregal era. However, this field still struggles with legacies of the power-obsessed discussions of the 1990s, which women's history generally in Spanish America has overcome with bountiful evidence. Agency and desire remain under-studied and confusing topics, and offer opportunities for future scholars to shape the history of sexuality in the Americas.

Notes

1 In the interest of space and cohesiveness, I have generally left out Brazil's colonial era from this essay, despite its great importance in the history of sexuality and imperialism, especially as it relates to the African diaspora and the Atlantic slave trade. An enormous historiography exists for the history of sexuality in Brazil, going back at least as far as Freyre's *Casa Grande e senzala*. Three other essential books on this topic are: Higgins, *"Licentious Liberty"*; Graham, *Caetana Says No*; Furtado, *Chica Da Silva*.

2 On case studies of non-heteronormative sex and sexual fantasies, see Tortorici, ed., *Sexuality and the Unnatural in Colonial Latin America*; Tortorici, *Sins Against Nature*. On negotiating illegitimacy and race, see Twinam, *Public Lives, Private Secrets*; Twinam, *Purchasing Whiteness*.

3 "'There Can Easily Be Stamped Upon Them Whatever Belief We Wish to Give Them,' The First Letter from Brazil (1500)," in *Colonial Latin America*.

4 On confession manuals and indigenous peoples, see Balsera, *The Pyramid Under the Cross*; Harrison, *Sin and Confession in Colonial Peru*.

5 Sigal, *The Flower and the Scorpion*.

6 For a brief overview of Guaman Poma de Ayala, see Mills, Taylor, Graham, *Colonial Latin America*, 173–186.

7 Alfonso and Burns, *Las Siete Partidas*, vol. 5, 72–188.

8 Ruiz, *El libro de buen amor*; Fernando de Rojas, *La Celestina, o tragicomedia de Calisto y Melibea* (Madrid: Imprenta de don León Amarita, 1822).

9 Twinam, *Public Lives, Private Secrets*, 31. On rhetoric and realities of honor killings, see Urán, *Fatal Love*; Yarbro-Bejarano, *Feminism and the Honor Plays of Lope de Vega*; Tylus and Milligan, eds., *The Poetics of Masculinity in Early Modern Italy and Spain*.

10 Poska, *Women and Authority in Early Modern Spain*, 123.

11 Fedewa, *María of Ágreda*, 149, 154–155, 162, 278.

12 Eire, *From Madrid to Purgatory*, 449; Peers, ed. and trans., *The Complete Works of St Teresa of Avila*, vol. 3, 227.

13 Saint-Saëns, "'It Is Not a Sin!'" 15; Schwartz, *All Can Be Saved*, 31.

14 Mannarelli, *Private Passions and Public Sins*, 102–104; Walker, *Shaky Colonialism*, 33.

15 Van Deusen, *Between the Sacred and the Worldly*; Delgado, *Laywomen and the Making of Colonial Catholicism in New Spain*.

16 Pfandl, *Sor Juana Inés de la Cruz*; Pfandl, *Juana Inés de la Cruz*.

17 Paz, *Sor Juana Inés de la Cruz*; Paz, *Sor Juana, or The Traps of Faith*.

18 Important innovators in Sor Juana studies include Bergmann and Schlau, eds., *The Routledge Research Companion to the Works of Sor Juana Inés de la Cruz*; Arenal and Schlau, eds., *Untold Sisters*; Kirk, *Sor Juana Inés de la Cruz*.

19 Velasco, *Lesbians in Early Modern Spain.*

20 For an earlier work more focused on creating the field of women's history, see Lavrin, ed. *Latin American Women.*

21 Arrom, *The Women of Mexico City*; Seed, *To Love, Honor, and Obey in Colonial Mexico.*

22 On power and violence in relation to sexual conquest and gender roles, see Stern, *The Secret History of Gender*; Gutiérrez, *When Jesus Came, the Corn Mothers Went Away.*

23 Burns, "The Secret History of Gender," 559.

24 Socolow, "The Secret History of Gender," 163–165.

25 Seed, "When Jesus Came the Corn Mothers Went Away," 967–968.

26 Kellogg, "When Jesus Came the Corn Mothers Went Away," 429.

27 Powers, "Conquering Discourses of 'Sexual Conquest,'" 7.

28 Johnson and Lipsett-Rivera, eds., *The Faces of Honor.*

29 Twinam, *Public Lives, Private Secrets*, 30–33, 41, 212–215.

30 Trexler, *Sex and Conquest.*

31 Townsend, *Malintzin's Choices*; Restall, *Maya Conquistador*; see also Sigal, "Imagining Cihuacoatl."

32 For older articles and edited collections, see Spurling, "Under Investigation for the Abominable Sin"; Spurling, "Honor, Sexuality, and the Colonial Church"; Berco, *Sexual Hierarchies, Public Status*; Carvajal, *Butterflies Will Burn.*

33 Holler, "The Spiritual and Physical Ecstasies of a Sixteenth-century Beata"; Holler, "The Devil or Nature Itself?"; Jaffary, *False Mystics*; van Deusen, *Embodying the Sacred.*

34 Boyer, *Lives of the Bigamists*; Gruzinski, "The Ashes of Desire"; Velasco, *The Lieutenant Nun.*

35 Rodríguez, *El amor venal*; Powers, *Women in the Crucible of Conquest*; Germeten, *Profit and Passion.*

36 Germeten, *Violent Delights, Violent Ends*, 87–90, for an example of a couple that married for love, risking financial support.

37 Van Deusen, *Between the Sacred and the Worldly*, 105–109; Lavrin, "In Search of Colonial Women in Mexico," 34–35.

38 For numerous examples of men paying in defloration suits, see Barahona, *Sex Crimes*, 4, 6, 35, 44, 82, 130, 151–153.

39 Katzew, *Casta Painting*; Guzauskyte, "Fragmented Borders, Fallen Men, Bestial Women."

Bibliography

Arenal, Electa and Stacey Schlau, eds. *Untold Sisters: Hispanic Nuns in their Own Works.* Albuquerque, NM: University of New Mexico Press, 2010.

Arrom, Silvia Marina. *The Women of Mexico City, 1790–1857.* Stanford, CA: Stanford University Press, 1985.

Atondo Rodríguez, Ana María. *El amor venal y la condición femenina en el México colonial.* México: Instituto Nacional de Antropología e Historia, 1992.

Balsera, Viviana Díaz. *The Pyramid Under the Cross: Franciscan Discourses of Evangelization and the Nahua Christian Subject in Sixteenth-Century Mexico.* Tucson, AZ: University of Arizona Press, 2005.

Barahona, Renato. *Sex Crimes, Honour, and the Law in Early Modern Spain: Vizcaya, 1528–1735.* Toronto: University of Toronto Press, 2003.

Berco, Christian. *Sexual Hierarchies, Public Status: Men, Sodomy, and Society in Spain's Golden Age.* Toronto: University of Toronto Press, 2007.

Boyer, Richard E. *Lives of the Bigamists: Marriage, Family, and Community in Colonial Mexico.* Albuquerque, NM: University of New Mexico Press, 1995.

Boyer, Richard E. and Geoffrey Spurling, eds. *Colonial Lives: Documents on Latin American History, 1550–1850.* New York: Oxford, 2000.

Burns, Kathryn. "The Secret History of Gender: Women, Men, and Power in Late Colonial Mexico by Steve Stern." *American Anthropologist* 100, no. 2 (1998): 559.

Carvajal, Federico Garza. *Butterflies Will Burn: Prosecuting Sodomites in Early Modern Spain and Mexico.* Austin, TX: University of Texas Press, 2003.

Delgado, Jessica. *Laywomen and the Making of Colonial Catholicism in New Spain (1630–1790).* Cambridge, UK: Cambridge University Press, 2018.

Eire, Carlos M.N. *From Madrid to Purgatory: The Art and Craft of Dying in Sixteenth-Century Spain.* Cambridge, UK: Cambridge University Press, 1995.

Fedewa, Marilyn H. *María of Ágreda: Mystical Lady in Blue*. Albuquerque, NM: University of New Mexico Press, 2009.

Freyre, Gilberto. *Casa Grande e senzala*. Rio de Janeiro: Olympio, 1933.

Furtado, Júnia Ferreira. *Chica Da Silva A Brazilian Slave of the Eighteenth Century*. New York: Cambridge University Press, 2009.

Germeten, Nicole von. *Violent Delights, Violent Ends: Sex, Race, and Honor in Colonial Cartagena de Indias*. Albuquerque, NM: University of New Mexico Press, 2013.

Germeten, Nicole von. *Profit and Passion: Transactional Sex in Colonial Mexico*. Oakland, CA: University of California Press, 2018.

Graham, Sandra Lauderdale. *Caetana Says No: Women's Stories from a Brazilian Slave Society*. New York: Cambridge University Press, 2002.

Gruzinski, Serge. "The Ashes of Desire: Homosexuality in Mid-Seventeenth-Century New Spain." Translated by Ignacio López Calvo. In *Infamous Desire: Male Homosexuality in Colonial Latin America*, edited by Pete Sigal, 197–214. Chicago, IL: University of Chicago Press, 2003.

Gutiérrez, Ramón A. *When Jesus Came, The Corn Mothers Went Away: Marriage, Sexuality, and Power in New Mexico, 1500–1846*. Stanford, CA: Stanford University Press, 1991.

Guzauskyte, Evelina. "Fragmented Borders, Fallen Men, Bestial Women: Violence in the Casta Paintings of Eighteenth-century New Spain." *Bulletin of Spanish Studies* 86, no. 2 (2009): 175–204.

Harrison, Regina. *Sin and Confession in Colonial Peru: Spanish-Quechua Penitential Texts, 1560–1650*. Austin, TX: University of Texas Press, 2014.

Higgins, Kathleen J. *"Licentious Liberty" in a Brazilian Gold-Mining Region: Slavery, Gender, and Social Control in Eighteenth-Century Sabarâa, Minas Gerais*. Pennsylvania, PA: Pennsylvania State University Press, 1999.

Holler, Jacqueline. "The Spiritual and Physical Ecstasies of a Sixteenth-century Beata." In *Colonial Lives: Documents on Latin American History, 1550–1850*, edited by Richard Boyer and Geoffrey Spurling, 77–100. Oxford, UK: Oxford University Press, 2000.

Holler, Jacqueline. "The Devil or Nature Itself? Desire, Doubt, and Diabolical Sex among Colonial Mexican Women." In *Sexuality and the Unnatural in Colonial Latin America*, edited by Zeb Tortorici, 58–76. Oakland, CA: University of California Press, 2016.

Jaffary, Nora. *False Mystics: Deviant Orthodoxy in Colonial Mexico*. Lincoln, NE: University of Nebraska Press, 2004.

Johnson, Lyman L. and Sonya Lipsett-Rivera, eds. *The Faces of Honor: Sex, Shame, and Violence in Colonial Latin America*. Albuquerque, NM: University of New Mexico Press, 1998.

Katzew, Ilona. *Casta Painting: Images of Race in Eighteenth-Century Mexico*. New Haven, CT: Yale University Press, 2004.

Kellogg, Susan. "When Jesus Came, The Corn Mothers Went Away: Marriage, Sexuality, and Power in New Mexico, 1500–1846 by Ramón A. Gutiérrez." *Hispanic American Historical Review* 72, no. 3 (1992): 429.

Kirk, Stephanie. *Sor Juana Inés de la Cruz and the Gender Politics of Knowledge in Colonial Mexico*. New York: Routledge, 2016.

Lavrin, Asunción, ed. *Latin American Women: Historical Perspectives*. Westport, CT: Greenwood, 1978.

Mannarelli, María Emma. *Private Passions and Public Sins: Men and Women in Seventeenth-Century Lima*. Translated by Sidney Evans and Meredith Dodge. Albuquerque, NM: University of New Mexico Press, 2007.

Mills, Kenneth B., William B. Taylor, and Sandra Lauderdale Graham, eds. *Colonial Latin America: A Documentary History*. Lanham, MD: Scholarly Resources, 2002.

Paz, Octavio. *Sor Juana Inés de la Cruz, o, Las trampas de la fe*. México: Fondo de Cultura Económica, 1982.

Paz, Octavio. *Sor Juana Inés de la Cruz, or The Traps of Faith*. Translated by Margaret Sayers Peden. Cambridge, MA: Belknap Press of Harvard University Press, 1988.

Peers, E. Allison, ed. and transl. *The Complete Works of St. Teresa of Avila*. Vol. 3. London: Burns and Oates, 2002.

Pfandl, Ludwig. *Juana Inés de la Cruz, die zehnte Muse von Mexiko: Ihr Leben, ihre Dichtung, ihre Psyche*. Munich: H. Rinn, 1946.

Pfandl, Ludwig. *Sor Juana Inés de la Cruz, La décima musa de México: Su vida, su poesía, su psique*. Ciudad México: Universidad Nacional Autónoma de México, 1963.

Poska, Allyson. *Women and Authority in Early Modern Spain: The Peasants of Galicia*. Oxford, UK: Oxford University Press, 2005.

Powers, Karen Vieira. "Conquering Discourses of 'Sexual Conquest': Of Women, Language, and Mestizaje." *Colonial Latin American Review* 11, no. 2 (2002): 7–32.

Powers, Karen Vieira. *Women in the Crucible of Conquest: The Gendered Genesis of Spanish American Society, 1500–1600.* Albuquerque, NM: University of New Mexico Press, 2005.

Restall, Matthew. *Maya Conquistador.* Boston, MA: Beacon Press, 1998.

Saint Saëns, Alain, ed. *Sex and Love in Golden Age Spain.* New Orleans, LA: University Press of the South, 1996.

Schwartz, Stuart B. *All Can Be Saved: Religious Tolerance and Salvation in the Iberian Atlantic World.* New Haven, CT: Yale University Press, 2008.

Seed, Patricia. *To Love, Honor, and Obey in Colonial Mexico: Conflicts Over Marriage Choice, 1574–1821.* Stanford, CA: Stanford University Press, 1988.

Seed, Patricia. "When Jesus Came, The Corn Mothers Went Away: Marriage, Sexuality, and Power in New Mexico, 1500–1846 by Ramón A. Gutiérrez." *American Historical Review* 97, no. 3 (1992): 967–968.

Sigal, Pete, ed. *Infamous Desire: Male Homosexuality in Colonial Latin America.* Chicago, IL: University of Chicago Press, 2003.

Sigal, Pete. "Imagining Cihuacoatl: Masculine Rituals, Nahua Goddesses and the Texts of the Tlacuilos." *Gender and History* 22, no. 3 (2010): 538–563. doi:10.1002/9781444343953.ch1..

Sigal, Pete. *The Flower and the Scorpion: Sexuality and Ritual in Early Nahua Culture.* Durham, NC: Duke University Press, 2011.

Socolow, Susan. "The Secret History of Gender: Women, Men, and Power in Late Colonial Mexico by Steve Stern." *The Americas* 53, no. 1 (1996): 163–165.

Spurling, Geoffrey. "Honor, Sexuality, and the Colonial Church: The Sins of Dr. González, Cathedral Canon." In *The Faces of Honor: Sex, Shame, and Violence in Colonial Latin America*, edited by Lyman Johnson and Sonya Lipsett-Rivera, 45–67. Albuquerque, NM: University of New Mexico Press, 1998.

Spurling, Geoffrey. "Under Investigation for the Abominable Sin: Damián de Morales Stands Accused of Attempting to Seduce Antón de Tierra de Congo (Charcas, 1611)." In *Colonial Lives: Documents on Latin American History, 1550–1850*, edited by Richard Boyer and Geoffrey Spurling, 112–129. New York: Oxford University Press, 2000.

Stern, Steve. *The Secret History of Gender: Women, Men, and Power in Late Colonial Mexico.* Chapel Hill, NC: University of North Carolina Press, 1995.

Tortorici, Zeb, ed. *Sexuality and the Unnatural in Colonial Latin America.* Oakland, CA: University of California Press, 2016.

Tortorici, Zeb. *Sins Against Nature: Sex and Archives in Colonial New Spain.* Durham, NC: Duke University Press, 2018.

Townsend, Camilla. *Malintzin's Choices: An Indian Woman in the Conquest of Mexico.* Albuquerque, NM: University of New Mexico Press, 2006.

Trexler, Richard C. *Sex and Conquest: Gendered Violence, Political Order, and the European Conquest of the Americas.* Ithaca, NY: Cornell University Press, 1995.

Twinam, Ann. *Public Lives, Private Secrets: Gender, Honor, Sexuality, and Illegitimacy in Colonial Spanish America.* Stanford, CA: Stanford University Press, 1999.

Twinam, Ann. *Purchasing Whiteness: Pardos, Mulattos, and the Quest for Social Mobility in the Spanish Indies.* Stanford, CA: Stanford University Press, 2015.

Uribe Uran, Victor. *Fatal Love: Spousal Killers, Law, and Punishment in the Late Colonial Spanish Atlantic.* Stanford, CA: Stanford University Press, 2016.

Van Deusen, Nancy E. *Between the Sacred and the Worldly: The Institutional and Cultural Practice of Recogimiento in Colonial Lima.* Stanford, CA: Stanford University Press, 2001.

Van Deusen, Nancy E. *Embodying the Sacred: Women Mystics in Seventeenth-Century Lima.* Durham, NC: Duke University Press, 2018.

Velasco, Sherry. *The Lieutenant Nun: Transgenderism, Lesbian Desire, and Catalina de Erauso.* Austin, TX: University of Texas Press, 2000.

Velasco, Sherry. *Lesbians in Early Modern Spain.* Nashville, TN: Vanderbilt University Press, 2011.

Walker, Charles. *Shaky Colonialism: The 1746 Earthquake-Tsunami in Lima, Peru, and Its Long Aftermath.* Durham, NC: Duke University Press, 2008.

Yarbro-Bejarano, Yvonne. *Feminism and the Honor Plays of Lope de Vega.* West Lafayette, IN: Purdue University Press, 1994.

2

SEXUAL HIERARCHIES AND EROTIC AUTONOMY

Colonizing and decolonizing sex in the Caribbean

Nicole Bourbonnais

The Caribbean is immensely heterogeneous, the legacy of a long process of imperialism by British, French, Dutch, Spanish, and Danish states from 1492. The original Carib and Arawak communities were decimated by colonial wars and slavery in the region, largely replaced by a mix of white European settlers, enslaved Africans, and indentured Asian laborers. As a result, Caribbean cultures contain elements from multiple traditions and Caribbean peoples speak a range of European and creole languages. Political decolonization has also been an uneven process in the region. Haiti, the Dominican Republic, and Cuba shed their European colonial masters in the nineteenth century but faced repeated American interventions throughout the early twentieth century. Suriname, a Dutch colony, and the majority of British Caribbean islands obtained independence in the 1950s–1970s, but a number of islands remain territories or overseas departments of European countries, or contain ambiguous status (such as Puerto Rico, an "unincorporated territory" of the United States). The region also continues to be economically dominated by foreign interests, exercising a fragile sovereignty in the context of an unequal world system.

The linguistic, cultural, and political diversity of the Caribbean has made it difficult at times to visualize the region as a coherent entity. And yet, when we look to the field of sexuality, we see a remarkable degree of convergence. Below, I explore the rich literature on sexuality in the Caribbean, identifying common themes, interesting departures, and areas for future research. The first section—"Colonizing islands, colonizing bodies"—focuses on the dominant discourses of reproduction and sexuality instilled by the colonial project. "Nationalism and colonial continuities" examines how nationalist movements responded to colonial discourses with their own regimes of sexual control and how the region's dependent position in the world economy continues to reinforce colonial sexual hierarchies. Indeed, in this context, it is nearly impossible to employ a neat analytical separation between the "colonial" and the "postcolonial." Scholars of the present—anthropologists, sociologists, and gender theorists—have had as much to say as historians about the powerful hold of colonial structures, making interdisciplinary exchanges crucial. This scholarship has also illustrated how actors have attempted to adapt, circumvent, or outright refuse colonial hierarchies throughout history. "Sexual practice and agency in a colonial/neo-colonial world" thus moves beyond discourse and politics to highlight sexual practices, as documented by social histories, ethnographies, and cultural studies. These studies provide us with an entry point to envision a more complete form of sexual decolonization, with implications for scholarship and politics far beyond the region.

Colonizing islands, colonizing bodies

One of the most dominant characteristics shared across the Caribbean has been the deep impact of the trans-Atlantic slave trade on the structure of colonial societies. From 1501–1866 an estimated six million enslaved Africans arrived in the Caribbean, where they labored on plantations under the violent control of a small white European elite. As Jennifer Morgan, Sasha Turner, and others have illustrated, this system relied on tight control over the sexual and reproductive bodies of enslaved men and women.[1] The slave system was also justified by claims of European superiority and African inferiority that had a distinct sexual dimension. In colonial documents, missionary records, and travel narratives alike, black men were portrayed as sexually pathological and black women as loose and available, in need of "civilizing" through contact with white Christian sexual morality.[2] At the same time, plantation records illustrate how European men used their position of power to sexually dominate enslaved women. Black women were also hired out for commercial sex by white women, who outnumbered male slaveowners in some Caribbean cities.[3] Although white female sexuality was subject to tight regulation by colonial institutions, white women had the ability to claim protection from non-marital rape and a vitally different relationship to reproduction: white women produced free humans, black women birthed slaves.[4] As a result, patterns of sex and reproduction tightly enforced hierarchies of race, class, and gender across Caribbean societies.[5]

The legacies of the slave system continued well beyond emancipation. Low marriage rates, female-headed households, and the high rates of children born outside of wedlock amongst freed peoples across the region were condemned by colonial officials and Christian missionaries, who saw the sexually restrained nuclear family model as the basis of social order.[6] This anxiety intersected with concerns over low population growth in the late nineteenth- and early twentieth-century English Caribbean to drive a series of state interventions aimed at increasing reproduction.[7] By the 1930s, however, the narrative had shifted starkly: now *high* fertility and "overpopulation" were seen as the problem, in need of containment from Puerto Rico to Barbados and beyond.[8] The 1930s–1950s also saw an outpouring of research by social scientists and colonial states investigating the supposedly "disordered" Caribbean family structure, blamed for everything from poverty to labor rebellion to anti-colonial sentiment.[9] Locating the cause of unrest in the reproductive and familial practices of black women, of course, conveniently directed attention away from the impact of colonial structures and policies.

While the majority of the historiography has focused on the dynamics between white European and Afro-Caribbean populations, some pioneering works have turned their attention to the intimate contours of Asian indentureship, a major source of labor following the abolition of slavery.[10] More than 400,000 Indian (and a lesser number of Chinese and Javanese) laborers arrived in the Caribbean from 1834 to 1920, coming to form significant populations in Trinidad and the Guianas.[11] The preference for male laborers led to a significant gender imbalance within this community; in Trinidad, for example, there were twice as many Indian men than women until the 1930s.[12] Colonial officials, missionaries, and indentured men alike expressed concern over women's supposed "freedom of intercourse," lack of faithfulness, and exercise of polyandry in this context.[13] Colonial officials also replicated discourses from British India, setting up the "feminized" Indian male in contrast to the "hypersexual" African.[14]

If historical scholarship has provided a rich analysis of the formation and evolution of the race–sex nexus from the fifteenth to nineteenth centuries, there are some notable lacunas. Scholars often recognize how maritime culture facilitated sex work in the early colonial period, yet discussions of the actual nature and regulation of prostitution prior to the twentieth century appear only occasionally.[15] In-depth study of the sex trade within particular ports or a consideration of the trans-regional circulation of sex, perhaps using ship records or local law enforcement records, would provide a critical foundation for the in-depth explorations of sex work that exist for later periods (as discussed below). We also know little about the regulation of same-sex sexuality before the late twentieth century. As Robinson points out, although contemporary laws against sodomy and sexual indecency are often seen as a "giant fossil or contemptible relic"[16] of the colonial era, these laws have not been static or consistently applied over time. Tracing the political, economic, and social contexts that shaped legal reforms and the application of law in practice in earlier periods might help us better understand the institutionalization of —and potential fissures in—colonial heterosexual norms that continue to impact the region today.

Nationalism and colonial continuities

Whether currently independent or not, the territories of the Caribbean have experienced both the pull of nationalist sentiment and the limits of sovereignty in an unequal world system. Historical scholarship across the region has carefully tracked how nationalist movements in the nineteenth and twentieth centuries challenged European claims of racial and moral superiority, undermined colonial power, and enhanced the degree of political and economic control at the local level. However, these movements have been widely critiqued for failing to challenge the constrictive hierarchies of sex and gender instilled by colonial rule. As Sheller argues, the revolutionary war in Haiti (1791–1804) further entrenched a militarized, hierarchical masculinity that undermined the egalitarian and democratic values of republicanism.[17] Middle-class nationalist leaders across the twentieth-century Spanish, Dutch, and English Caribbean embraced discourses of "respectability," condemning single motherhood and childbirth outside of wedlock among the working classes in ways often starkly reminiscent of colonial narratives.[18] Even pan-Africanist movements rooted more firmly in the working classes largely replicated conservative sexual discourses, calling on black women to reproduce and defend the purity of the race.[19] The limited scholarship on middle-class Indo-Caribbean activism similarly highlights the efforts of male leaders to construct an image of a delicate, modern Indian woman firmly under patriarchal control.[20] In the face of colonial discourses that justified political rule on the basis of the subjects' supposedly disordered sexuality, nationalist movements responded by attempting to enforce sexual order within their communities.

These nationalist narratives drew on common scapegoats in defining the limits of sexual citizenship. As studies of Puerto Rico, Bahamas, Curaçao, and Aruba alike have shown, middle-class movements particularly targeted sexually "immoral" women and prostitutes.[21] Nationalisms were also constructed in relation to other subordinated communities and other islands: Arubans blamed moral decay on Afro-Curaçaoan prostitutes while Curaçaoans in turn condemned Dominican prostitutes.[22] Same-sex practices have also been frequently invoked by political leaders in the region, portrayed as a form of "deviance" threatening national coherence and/or a sign of the influence of "Westerners" impinging on a supposedly firmly heterosexual native past. As Alexander argues, this narrative seems ironically to forget the colonial roots of *anti*-sodomy legislation (as noted above).[23] Regardless of the internal coherence of these discourses or who is deemed the "other," all accept the underlying (colonial) premise that a community's sexual practices are critical to "the success or failure of political rule."[24]

There have been challenges to these narratives throughout the region: liberal nationalists and black feminist activists on several Anglophone Caribbean islands, for example, called out sexual double standards and demanded recognition of women's reproductive rights as early as the 1930s and 1940s.[25] More historical analysis that moves beyond dominant leaders would help us see the multiple versions of nationalism put forward during decolonization processes and think more critically about why broader visions did not come to fruition. However, it is generally safe to say that those who assumed power in the post-colonial period did not prioritize sexual decolonization. As Kempadoo argues, the new postcolonial elite "privileged heterosexuality and masculine dominance, upheld a modified version of the European monogamous marriage system as the dominant norm, and continued to view African Caribbean working women's sexual behavior as loose yet subordinate to men's needs."[26] Alexander refers to this as a process of "recolonization"[27] in which postcolonial states replaced white colonial heteropatriarchy with black heteropatriarchy, in the process undermining the full "psychic, sexual and material" self-determination of the broader population. As she argues, "the neo-colonial state continues the policing of sexualized bodies … as if the colonial masters were still looking on."[28]

The socialist Cuban Revolution (1953–1959) provides an interesting potential counter-point, promising a more fundamental rupture with colonial political, social, and economic structures. Scholars have shown how revolutionary ideology did, indeed, challenge several aspects of male domination and racial discrimination. Oral histories and anthropological studies of Cuba, however, illustrate the resilience of pre-revolutionary double standards surrounding sexuality, the heteropatriarchal underpinnings of the revolutionary "New Man" ideal, and the continued hypersexualization of black bodies.[29] The regime's program of "rehabilitation" of prostitutes—widely touted as one of the revolution's success stories— also took on conservative tones as female nationalist leaders attempted to remake sex workers into "maternal," desexualized women.[30] Most infamously, the regime undertook an unprecedented crackdown on same-sex practices, purging presumed homosexuals from institutions and sending them to forced labor camps.[31] While recent official policy has shifted to condemning homophobia, oral histories indicate continued trauma surrounding this policy.[32] Sex work in Cuba has also gained renewed visibility in the past few decades as the collapse of the Soviet Union fuelled an economic crisis and the island joined the rest of the region in turning to foreign tourism for survival.[33]

Perhaps nowhere are the continuities between colonial and neo-colonial structures more evident than in the contemporary position of the Caribbean within the structures of global sex tourism. As Kempadoo points out, "territories that once served as sex havens for the colonial elite are today frequented by sex tourists, and several economies now depend upon the region's racialized, sexualized image."[34] Scholars have illustrated how sex tourism across the islands has been fuelled by both colonial narratives of the hypersexualized "native" female body and by continuing global economic inequality.[35] The more recent phenomenon of white tourist women seeking out transactional sexual relationships with black men does little to disrupt sexual and racial hierarchies. As Kempadoo points out, these women's narratives of island "romance" uphold traditional ideas about white femininity, while their underlying desire for sexual experimentation with a racial Other builds on and maintains colonial race structures.[36]

Interestingly, scholars of the region have argued that even more progressive interventions by European actors, such as contemporary LGBTQ activism and the legalization of same-sex marriage in French and Dutch overseas departments, remain mired by the legacy of colonialism. King criticizes a model in which imperial interventionism becomes the basis for expanding the rights of sexual minorities, such that "a particular 'freedom' … depends upon a particular unfreedom."[37] Agard-Jones argues that French activists writing about the islands "unwittingly support the mapping of a development teleology on France's Caribbean territories," labeling them as less "modern" and positioning themselves as "saving" local gay people in a way that invokes colonial narratives.[38] The labeling of the Caribbean as "the most homophobic place on earth" by the international press might also be seen as a neo-colonial, paternalistic narrative.[39] Andil Gosine further criticizes the assumption that the labels and structure of gay activism in the North are the standard by which all forms of sexual activism in the South must be measured. As Trinidadian activist Corey Robinson puts it, "this is sounding a bit like Columbus here, discovering us."[40]

While these critiques challenge the colonial undertones and continued privileging of Northern actors in transnational spaces, they also create an underlying tension. As Smith points out, scholars and activists alike often find themselves trapped, forced to either reinforce narratives that portray the Caribbean as "other," based on its supposedly extreme homophobia, or to deny homophobia exists altogether.[41] Perhaps one way out of this bind is to ensure that analysis of the political realm—which tends to accentuate the most extreme voices on any end of an issue—is accompanied by attention to the daily realities of Caribbean people, so that we can see how these narratives play out, or do not, in practice. In the next section I turn to the rich scholarship from Caribbean social history, anthropology, and cultural studies that has taken us beyond discourse analysis to consider how Caribbean peoples have navigated sexuality under colonial and neo-colonial regimes.

Sexual practice and agency in a colonial/neo-colonial world

It has become something of a truism to remark on the difficulty of accessing marginalized voices within colonial archives, perhaps nowhere more so than in the context of slave societies. And yet scholars of the Caribbean have managed to painstakingly comb sources to provide us with glimpses of the sexual practices of enslaved peoples. Bush-Slimani argues that references in plantation records to abortion methods and late weaning might be read as evidence of enslaved women taking measures to control their reproduction.[42] Turner argues that the *silences* in the archives may also be telling. Planters' ignorance of women's pregnancy and childbirth practices, for example, illustrates their exclusion from this aspect of enslaved life, which may have provided women with a "small measure of autonomy."[43] Planters' complaints about their difficulty controlling enslaved women's "nocturnal wanderings"[44] also hint at the possibility of sexual lives outside of plantation boundaries. And yet scholars have been careful to remind us of the limits to this sexual "agency" within slave societies. Fuentes, for example, argues that we must remain conscious of "the forces of power that bore down on enslaved women, who sometimes survived in ways not typically heroic, and who sometimes succumbed to the violence inflicted on them."[45]

Historians across the region have also debated whether the sexual and conjugal practices of working-class Caribbean peoples after slavery might be seen as a form of resistance to colonial structures. Johnson and Moore, for example, argue that freed Jamaicans' diverging family patterns illustrate their desire to be "the masters of their own lives."[46] Studies from English,

French, and Dutch Caribbean contexts have argued that lower-class women may actually prefer remaining unmarried to retain more independence,[47] and some have suggested that high fertility rates represent an assertion of Afro-Caribbean values.[48] However, other studies—often within the same contexts—argue that working-class women *do* aspire to marriage; their determination to build families outside of wedlock may have been "more a matter of necessity than choice."[49] There is also plenty of evidence of working-class women actively seeking out birth control to challenge the idea that unrestrained fertility is a universal cultural value.[50] The longevity of these debates may point to the difficulty of defining cultural principles and the complex personal imperatives that shape intimate lives, both of which are hard to tease out from limited colonial sources. More oral and life history studies are needed across the region, so we can see how people have reconciled these elements in practice. At the very least, as Barrow notes, the resilience of unique Caribbean kinship structures challenges the colonial assumption that the co-resident nuclear family is "natural, universal and essential."[51]

Scholars have also explored how women's sexual work can provide a path for economic security and upward mobility under both colonial and neo-colonial rule. Studies of twentieth-century archives surrounding the legislation of prostitution and contemporary anthropological research illustrate the diversity of the forms sex work can take, from a structured institution to a temporary, informal arrangement. In contrast to traditional narratives of victimhood, this research suggests that women have frequently entered into relationships of transactional sex consciously and with clear objectives in mind. As Charles notes, poor women in Haiti describe their bodies as "my piece of land … a resource, an asset, a form of capital that can reap profits if well invested."[52] But Sheller reminds us that this form of "agency" also comes at a price: sexual vulnerability and dependence on private relationships.[53] Indeed, while some sex workers are able to achieve levels of financial security or opportunities for migration by appealing to the colonial sexualized fantasies of Northern men, many others do not.[54] Transforming individual acts of sexual agency into a broader overturning of social structures, Kempadoo argues, will likely require the type of collective organization undertaken by the contemporary sex worker movement.[55]

In contrast to the visibility of sex work in the Caribbean, queer relationships and same-sex practices have largely been hidden from view, a "*secreto abierto*" (open secret) unacknowledged by those involved or the broader community. King argues that this is not quite the same as "hiding" or merely internalized homophobia; we might see it rather as a matter of discretion attributed to sexual practice more broadly.[56] Hamilton describes adherence to this silence as a "survival strategy;"[57] for Agard-Jones it is a form of "radical passivity."[58] In any case, it leads to serious gaps in the historical record.[59] Agard-Jones, however, illustrates how careful readings of travel narratives, literature, and popular memory can allow us to construct "an unstable, atomized archive of queer relation"[60] in the colonial Caribbean. Anthropological studies from the 1930s onward have also documented a variety of local terms describing same-sex practice across the region, including: "making zami" in Grenada, Carriacou, Dominica, Trinidad, and Barbados; "antiwoman" in St. Kitts; "malnom and antiwoman" on Dominica; "sodomite" and "man royal" in Jamaica; "kapuchera" or "kambrada" in the Dutch Antilles; "buller man" in Trinidad; and "ma divine" in the French-speaking Caribbean.[61] These popular categories point to a longer history of queer relationality and practice in the Caribbean that demands further research in order to adequately situate it within the social, political, and economic context of the twentieth century.

A fascinating counterpoint to the general silence surrounding same-sex desire in Caribbean communities is presented by Wekker's rich historical and anthropological analysis of the "mati work" in Suriname, a practice in which women have sexual relationships with both men and women, either simultaneously or consecutively.[62] References to mati relationships date back to colonial archives and missionary records from at least the beginning of the twentieth century, and the relationships continue to be relatively widespread and generally accepted amongst the working classes. Wekker argues that the mati work draws on West African grammatical principles that allow for flexible incarnations of gender and a celebration of sex as a normal and healthy part of life. Indeed, in stark contrast to colonial and nationalist discourses of "respectability" and sexual restraint, mati women "unabashedly enjoy sex, are active sexual beings, take sex seriously, can disengage sex from love, and, strikingly, talk about sex openly, using distinct linguistic expressions of their own."[63]

As Wekker herself notes, it can be difficult to talk about this kind of overt sexual expression in a context so over-determined by longstanding colonial narratives linking black women's presumed hypersexuality to inferiority.[64] Indeed, part of the reticence around sexuality in nationalist movements and contemporary middle-class culture may reflect a fear that "any departure from a wholesome, straightforward sexuality would risk a return to the scene of colonial degradation."[65] But these official discourses have never fully managed to quell sexual expression anyway. Cultural studies have identified multiple spaces in which alternative norms of sexuality have survived, from erotic literature,[66] to popular plays and performances,[67] to Caribbean carnivals.[68] Cooper argues that the self-professed "slackness" of Jamaican dancehall culture could be seen as a "radical, underground confrontation"[69] with colonial and nationalist patriarchal ideology, creating a potentially liberating space in which women are able to play out eroticized roles and celebrate a black, full-bodied sensuality that flies in the face of Eurocentric standards. Puri makes a similar case in analysing the calypso song *Lick down me nani* by Indo-Trinidadian singer Drupatee Ramgoonai, whose double entendres barely cover an invocation to oral sex.[70]

Of course, this is not to say that all expressions of popular culture are inherently progressive or liberating. Cross-dressing Carnival characters at times do little more than mock poor black women and/or trans people,[71] and Mohammed reminds us of the long history of misogyny, homophobia, and celebration of violence against women in Caribbean music.[72] Even Cooper acknowledges that the line between celebration and exploitation of the black female body is "as thin as some of the fashionable garments sported by women in the dancehall."[73] In-depth anthropological fieldwork posing these questions to participants themselves provides a fruitful avenue to side-step either/or discussions on female sexual exploitation. Still, this literature reminds us that blatant sexuality does not *have* to be seen as pathological; it can also be empowering and pleasurable. Perhaps these spaces of the "vulgar popular,"[74] where sexuality is portrayed "not as a battle or even a question but as a fact,"[75] might also provide a path out of the narrow confines of colonial and neo-colonial discourses and toward sexual decolonization.

Indeed, as Gosine argues, it is not enough to deconstruct: we must also "construct and refashion."[76] Taking their cues from both scholarly and activist circles, Caribbean cultural critics have envisioned structures of sexuality that might provide for more breathing space. As Alexander argues, "the work of decolonization consists as well in the decolonization of the body";[77] the goal is "erotic autonomy," liberation of the sexual from both colonial and nationalist intervention.[78] For King, we need a world of "women voicing, advocating for, and/or pursuing control of their own sexuality or erotic pleasure on their own terms."[79] But this sexual liberation need not mean a refusal of nationalism altogether or a capitulation to internationalist narratives that (as we have seen) frequently reinforce inequalities of their own. Gosine, for example, argues that the activist organization CAISO mobilizes Caribbean cultural markers to posit same-sex desire as essentially "Trinbagonian," rather than invoking a globalized "sexual identity."[80] The desire is not for the dissolution of the nation but for a "*transformed* nation" advocating a "progressive homonationalism" inclusive and responsive to all.[81] As King argues, "what island bodies look like and which other bodies they desire have been quite varied for an extremely long time; what remains is for Caribbean laws and hierarchies to catch up."[82]

Conclusion

The interdisciplinary scholarship on the Caribbean illustrates the common dynamics of colonial sexual discourses across imperial projects, linguistic divides, and political regimes, as well as the remarkable longevity of colonial race–sex–class hierarchies. It also shows how subjugated peoples have responded in different ways to colonizing, nationalizing, and re-colonizing projects: carving out spaces to live and express their sexuality even when their rights to do so have not been recognized from above. There are several gaps in our understanding: studies of same-sex sexuality and sex work would benefit from reaching farther back in time; we might gain from more exploration of alternative nationalist/activist visions put forth by marginalized actors; and both historical debates and contemporary cultural theories could be enhanced with grounding in oral histories. But, overall, this is a rich literature that pushes us to think about sex and sexuality in all of its facets. Perhaps most exciting of all is the willingness to move beyond critique, to think about what a full decolonization, "imagined simultaneously as political, economic, psychic, discursive, *and* sexual,"[83] might entail.

The methodological techniques, theories, and creativity illustrated in this work have implications for wider scholarship on colonialism and sexuality. The careful reading of sources to explore enslaved lives provides a model for social history methodology in colonial contexts; the delicate rendering of agency–victimhood in studies of sex work might prove valuable to studies of other regions similarly locked in the neo-colonial sex tourism nexus; and the complexities of same-sex practices under heteropatriarchal regimes resonate with other countries living with the legacy of colonial anti-sodomy laws. But this conversation need not be confined to areas formerly colonized by European empires; those in former metropolitan societies might also benefit from the challenges presented by this literature. In her analysis of the transference of "mati work" to the Netherlands by Surinamese female migrants, for example, Wekker questions the assumption that the women will soon adopt the language and practices of "modern" Dutch lesbianism. She asks: why is it so inconceivable that Dutch women instead might adopt some of the (sexually liberating) behavioral repertoire of Surinamese women?[84] Perhaps, by taking the politics and practices of sex in the Caribbean seriously, we might all free ourselves from the constrictive sexual norms and teleological narratives of modernity inherited from our shared colonial past.

Notes

1 Morgan, *Laboring Women*; Turner, *Contested Bodies*.
2 Morgan, *Laboring Women*; Johnson and Moore, *Neither Led Nor Driven*.
3 Fuentes, *Dispossessed Lives*; Jones, "Contesting the Boundaries."
4 Fuentes, *Dispossessed Lives*, 74–79.
5 Matinez-Alier, *Marriage, Class and Colour*; Morgan, *Laboring Women*; Turner, *Contested Bodies*.
6 Johnson and Moore, *Neither Led Nor Driven*; Findley, *Imposing Decency*; Macpherson, *From Colony to Nation*; Wekker, *The Politics of Passion*.
7 De Barros, *Reproducing the British Caribbean*.

8 Briggs, *Reproducing Empire*; Bourbonnais, *Birth Control in the Decolonizing Caribbean*.
9 Barrow, *Family in the Caribbean*; Chamberlain, "Small Worlds."
10 Mohammed, *Gender Negotiations Among Indians in Trinidad*; Puri, *The Caribbean Postcolonial*; Niranjana, "Indian Nationalism and Female Sexuality."
11 De Barros, *Reproducing the Caribbean*, 44.
12 Barrow, *Family in the Caribbean*, 343.
13 Niranjana, "Indian Nationalism and Female Sexuality."
14 Puri, *The Caribbean Postcolonial*, 187.
15 See for example, Fuentes, *Dispossessed Lives*, ch. 2.
16 Robinson, "Authorized Sex," 5.
17 Sheller, *Citizenship from Below*.
18 Briggs, *Reproducing Empire*; Bourbonnais, *Birth Control in the Decolonizing Caribbean*; Wekker, *The Politics of Passion*; Allen, "Contesting Respectability."
19 Macpherson, *From Colony to Nation*; Ford-Smith, "Unruly Virtues of the Spectacular."
20 Niranjana, "Indian Nationalism and Female Sexuality."
21 Findley, *Imposing Decency*; Kempadoo, *Sexing the Caribbean*; Alexander, "Erotic Autonomy"; Schields, "'This is the Soul of Aruba Speaking.'"
22 Kempadoo, *Sexing the Caribbean*; Schields, "'This is the Soul of Aruba Speaking.'"
23 Alexander, "Erotic Autonomy," 83.
24 Smith, "Introduction," in *Sex and the Citizen*, 4.
25 Bourbonnais, *Birth Control in the Decolonizing Caribbean*.
26 Kempadoo, *Sexing the Caribbean*, 19.
27 Alexander, "Erotic Autonomy," 66.
28 Ibid., 83.
29 Hamilton, *Sexual Revolutions in Cuba*; Allen, *¡Venceremos?*
30 Hynson, "'Count, Capture, and Reeducate.'"
31 Guerra, "Gender policing, homosexuality and the new patriarchy."
32 Hamilton, *Sexual Revolutions in Cuba*; Allen, *¡Venceremos?*
33 Hynson, "'Count, Capture and Reeducate.'"
34 Kempadoo, *Sexing the Caribbean*, 1.
35 Ibid.; Brennan, *What's Love Got to Do with It?*
36 Kempadoo, *Sexing the Caribbean*.
37 King, *Island Bodies*, 66.
38 Agard-Jones, "Le Jeu de Qui?"
39 King, *Island Bodies*, 83–85.
40 Quoted in Gosine, "CAISO, CAISO," 871.
41 Smith, "Introduction," 11.
42 Bush-Slimani, "Hard Labour."
43 Turner, *Contested Bodies*, 14.
44 Ibid., 63.
45 Fuentes, *Dispossessed Lives*, 3.
46 Johnson and Moore, *Neither Led Nor Driven*, 136.
47 Ibid.; see also Wekker, *The Politics of* Passion; Charles, "Popular Imageries of Gender and Sexuality."
48 Heuring, "Health and the Politics of 'Improvement' in British Colonial Jamaica."
49 Altink, *Destined for a Life of Service*, 6.
50 Bourbonnais, *Birth Control in the Decolonizing Caribbean*.
51 Barrow, *Family in the Caribbean*, x.
52 Charles, "Popular Imageries of Gender and Sexuality," 170.
53 Sheller, *Citizenship from Below*, 153.
54 Brennan, "Tourism in Transnational Places," 633. For a similarly nuanced analysis of prostitution in the circum-Caribbean, see Putnam, *The Company They Kept*.
55 Kempadoo, *Sexing the Caribbean*.
56 King, *Island Bodies*, 64.
57 Hamilton, *Sexual Revolutions in Cuba*, 162.
58 Agard-Jones, "Le Jeu de Qui?"
59 LaFont, "Very Straight Sex."
60 Agard-Jones, "What the Sands Remember," 331.

61 Wekker, *The Politics of Passion,* 77–78, 214–219.
62 Wekker, *The Politics of Passion.*
63 Ibid., 173.
64 Ibid., 5.
65 Smith, "Introduction," 10.
66 Hamilton, *Sexual Revolutions in Cuba;* Tinsley, *Thiefing Sugar.*
67 Ford-Smith, "Unruly Virtues of the Spectacular."
68 King, *Island Bodies;* Puar, "Global Circuits."
69 Cooper, *Sound Clash,* 4.
70 Puri, *The Caribbean Postcolonial,* 196–205.
71 King, *Island Bodies,* 44–51.
72 Mohammed, "A Blueprint for Gender in Creole Trinidad."
73 Cooper, *Sound Clash,* 245.
74 Ford-Smith, "Unruly Virtues of the Spectacular," 33.
75 King, *Island Bodies,* 124.
76 Gosine, "CAISO, CAISO," 874.
77 Alexander, "Erotic Autonomy," 21.
78 Alexander, "Erotic Autonomy."
79 King, *Island Bodies,* 124.
80 Gosine, "CAISO, CAISO."
81 King, *Island Bodies,* 117.
82 Ibid., 17.
83 Alexander, "Erotic Autonomy," 100.
84 Wekker, *The Politics of Passion,* 239.

Bibliography

Agard-Jones, Vanessa. "Le Jeu de Qui? Sexual Politics at Play in the French Caribbean." In *Sex and the Citizen: Interrogating the Caribbean,* edited by Faith Smith, 181–198. Charlottesville, VA: University of Virginia Press, 2011.

Agard-Jones, Vanessa. "What the Sands Remember." *GLQ: A Journal of Lesbian and Gay Studies* 18, no. 2 (2012): 325–346. doi:10.1215/10642684-1472917.

Alexander, M. Jacqui. "Erotic Autonomy as a Politics of Decolonization: An Anatomy of Feminist and State Practice in the Bahamas Tourist Economy." In *Feminist Genealogies, Colonial Legacies, Democratic Futures,* edited by M. Jacqui Alexander and Chandra Talpade Mohanty, 63–100. New York: Routledge, 1997.

Alexander, M. Jacqui and Chandra Talpade Mohanty, eds. *Feminist Genealogies, Colonial Legacies, Democratic Futures.* New York: Routledge, 1997.

Allen, Jafari S. *¡Venceremos? The erotics of black self-making in Cuba.* Durham, NC, and London: Duke University Press, 2011.

Allen, Rose Mary. "Contesting respectability: Sexual politics in post-emancipation colonial Curaçao." In *Archaeologies of erasures and silences: Recovering othered languages, literatures and cultures in the Dutch Caribbean and beyond,* edited by Nicholas Faraclas, Ronald Severing, Christa Weijer et al., 99–112. Curaçao and Puerto Rico: University of Curaçao and Universidad de Puerto Rico, 2017.

Altink, Henrice. *Destined for a Life of Service: Defining African-Jamaican Womanhood, 1865–1938.* Manchester, UK, and New York: Manchester University Press, 2011.

Barrow, Christine. *Family in the Caribbean: Themes and Perspectives.* Kingston: Ian Randle Publishers, 1996.

Bourbonnais, Nicole C. *Birth Control in the Decolonizing Caribbean: Reproductive Politics and Practices on Four Islands, 1930–1970.* New York: Cambridge University Press, 2016. doi:10.1017/9781316339930.

Brennan, Denise. "Tourism in Transnational Places: Dominican Sex Workers and German Sex Tourists Imagine One Another." *Global Studies in Culture and Power* 7, no. 4 (2001): 621–663. doi:10.1080/1070289X.2001.9962680.

Brennan, Denise. *What's Love Got to Do with It? Transnational Desires and Sex Tourism in the Dominican Republic.* Durham, NC: Duke University Press, 2004.

Briggs, Laura. *Reproducing Empire: Race, Sex, Science and U.S. Imperialism in Puerto Rico.* Berkeley, CA: University of California Press, 2002.

Bush-Slimani, Barbara. "Hard Labour: Women, Childbirth and Resistance in British Caribbean Slave Societies." *History Workshop*, no. 36 (Autumn 1993): 83–99. doi:10.1093/hwj/36.1.83.

Chamberlain, Mary. "Small worlds: childhood and empire." *Journal of Family History*, 27, no. 2 (2002): 186–200. doi:10.1177/036319900202700207.

Charles, Carolle. "Popular Imageries of Gender and Sexuality: Poor and Working-Class Haitian Women's Discourses on the Use of their Bodies." In *The Culture of Gender and Sexuality in the Caribbean*, edited by Linden Lewis, 169–189. Gainesville, FL: University Press of Florida, 2003.

Cooper, Carolyn. *Sound Clash: Jamaican Dancehall Culture at Large*. New York: Palgrave Macmillan, 2004. doi:10.1057/9781403982605.

Crespo-Kebler, Elizabeth. "'The Infamous Crime against Nature': Constructions of Heterosexuality and Lesbian Subversions in Puerto Rico." In *The Culture of Gender and Sexuality in the Caribbean*, edited by Linden Lewis, 190–212. Gainesville, FL: University Press of Florida, 2003.

Crichlow, Welsey E.A. "History, (Re)Memory, Testimony and Biomythography: Charting a Buller Man's Trinidadian Past." In *Interrogating Caribbean Masculinities: Theoretical and Empirical Analysis*, edited by Rhoda E. Reddock, 185–224. Kingston, Jamaica: University of the West Indies Press, 2004.

De Barros, Juanita. *Reproducing the British Caribbean: Sex, Gender, and Population Politics after Slavery*. Chapel Hill, NC: University of North Carolina Press, 2014.

Faraclas, Nicholas, Ronald Severing, Christa Weijer et al., eds. *Archaeologies of erasures and silences: Recovering othered languages, literatures and cultures in the Dutch Caribbean and beyond*. Curaçao and Puerto Rico: University of Curaçao and Universidad de Puerto Rico, 2017.

Findley, Eileen J. Suárez. *Imposing Decency: The Politics of Sexuality and Race in Puerto Rico, 1870–1920*. Durham, NC: Duke University Press, 1999.

Ford-Smith, Honor. "Unruly Virtues of the Spectacular: Performing Engendered Nationalisms in the UNIA in Jamaica." *interventions* 6, no. 1 (2004): 18–44. doi:10.1080/1369801042000185642.

Fuentes, Marisa. *Dispossessed Lives: Enslaved Women, Violence and the Archive*. Philadelphia, PA: University of Pennsylvania Press, 2016.

Gosine, Andil. "CAISO, CAISO: Negotiating sex rights and nationalism in Trinidad and Tobago." *Sexualities* 18, no. 7 (2015): 859–884. doi:10.1177/1363460714550916.

Guerra, Lilian. "Gender policing, homosexuality and the new patriarchy of the Cuban Revolution, 1965–70." *Social History* 35, no. 3 (2010): 268–289. doi:10.1080/03071022.2010.487378.

Hamilton, Carrie. *Sexual Revolutions in Cuba: Passion, Politics and Memory*. Chapel Hill, NC: University of North Carolina Press, 2014.

Heuring, Darcy Hughes. "Health and the Politics of 'Improvement' in British Colonial Jamaica, 1914–1945." Ph.D. diss., Northwestern University, 2011.

Hynson, Rachel. "'Count, Capture, and Reeducate': The Campaign to Rehabilitate Cuba's Female Sex Workers, 1959–1966." *Journal of the History of Sexuality* 24, no. 1 (January 2015): 125–153. doi:10.7560/JHS24106.

Johnson, Michele A. and Brian L. Moore. *Neither Led Nor Driven: Contesting British Cultural Imperialism in Jamaica, 1865–1920*. Mona, Jamaica: University of the West Indies Press, 2004.

Jones, Cecily. "Contesting the Boundaries of Gender, Race and Sexuality in Barbadian Plantation Society." *Women's History Review* 12 no. 2 (2003): 195–232. doi:10.1080/09612020300200355.

Kempadoo, Kamala. *Sexing the Caribbean: Gender, Race, and Sexual Labor*. New York and London: Routledge, 2004.

King, Rosamond S. *Island Bodies: Transgressive Sexualities in the Caribbean Imagination*. Gainesville, FL: University Press of Florida, 2014.

LaFont, Suzanne. "Very Straight Sex: The Development of Sexual Morés in Jamaica." *Journal of Colonialism and Colonial History* 2 no. 3 (Winter 2001): 1–38. doi:10.1353/cch.2001.0051.

Lewis, Linden, ed. *The Culture of Gender and Sexuality in the Caribbean*. Gainesville, FL: University Press of Florida, 2003.

Macpherson, Anne S. *From Colony to Nation: Women Activists and the Gendering of Politics in Belize, 1912–1982*. Lincoln, NE: University of Nebraska Press, 2007.

Matinez-Alier, Verena. *Marriage, Class and Colour in Nineteenth-Century Cuba: A Study of Racial Attitudes and Sexual Values in a Slave Society*. Ann Arbor, MI: University of Michigan Press, 1989.

Mohammed, Patricia. *Gender Negotiations Among Indians in Trinidad, 1917–1947*. Hampshire, UK: Palgrave Macmillan, 2002. doi:10.1057/9781403914163.

Mohammed, Patricia. "A Blueprint for Gender in Creole Trinidad: Exploring Gender Mythology through Calypsos of the 1920s and 1930s." In *The Culture of Gender and Sexuality in the Caribbean*, edited by Linden Lewis, 129–168. Gainesville, FL: University Press of Florida, 2003.

Morgan, Jennifer. *Laboring Women: Reproduction and Gender in New World Slavery*. Philadelphia, PA: University of Pennsylvania Press, 2004.

Niranjana, Tejaswini. "Indian Nationalism and Female Sexuality: A Trinidadian Tale." In *Sex and the Citizen: Interrogating the Caribbean*, edited by Faith Smith, 101–124. Charlottesville, VA, and London: University of Virginia Press, 2011.

Puar, Jasbir Kaur. "Global Circuits: Transnational Sexualities and Trinidad." *Signs* 26, no. 4, (Summer 2001): 1039–1065. doi:10.1086/495647.

Puri, Shalini. *The Caribbean Postcolonial: Social Equality, Post-Nationalism, and Cultural Hybridity*. New York: Palgrave Macmillan, 2004. doi:10.1057/9781403973719.

Putnam, Lara. *The Company They Kept: Migrants and the Politics of Gender in Caribbean Costa Rica, 1870–1960*. Chapel Hill, NC: University of North Carolina Press, 2002.

Reddock, Rhoda, ed. *Interrogating Caribbean Masculinities: Theoretical and Empirical Analyses*. Kingston, Jamaica: University of the West Indies Press, 2004.

Robinson, Tracy. "Authorized Sex: Same-Sex Sexuality and Law in the Caribbean." In *Sexuality, Social Exclusion & Human Rights: Vulnerability in the Caribbean Context of HIV*, edited by Christine Barrow, Marjan de Bruin and Robert Carr, 3–22. Kingston, Jamaica: Ian Randle Publishers, 2009.

Schields, Chelsea. "'This is the Soul of Aruba Speaking': The 1951 Campo Alegre Protest and Insular Identity on Aruba." *New West Indian Guide* 90, no. 3/4 (January 2016): 195–224. doi:10.1163/22134360-09003002.

Sheller, Mimi. *Citizenship from Below: Erotic Agency and Caribbean Freedom*. Durham, NC: Duke University Press, 2012.

Smith, Faith, "Introduction: Sexing the Citizen." In *Sex and the Citizen: Interrogating the Caribbean*, edited by Faith Smith, 1–17. Charlottesville, VA, and London: University of Virginia Press, 2011.

Smith, Faith, ed. *Sex and the Citizen: Interrogating the Caribbean*. Charlottesville, VA, and London: University of Virginia Press, 2011.

Tinsley, Omise'Eke Natasha. *Thiefing Sugar: Eroticism between Women in Caribbean Literature*. Durham, NC: Duke University Press, 2010.

Turner, Sasha. *Contested Bodies: Pregnancy, Childrearing, and Slavery in Jamaica*. Philadelphia, PA: University of Pennsylvania Press, 2017.

Wekker, Gloria. *The Politics of Passion: Women's Sexual Culture in the Afro-Surinamese Diaspora*. New York: Columbia University Press, 2006.

3

SEXUALITY IN COLONIAL AFRICA

Current trends and new directions

Corrie Decker

Scholars examining colonialism and sexuality in Africa face two significant problematics: one, the enduring legacy of colonial racial sexual stereotypes that portray African men and women as hypersexualized; and, two, the political repercussions of doing research on non-heteronormative sexualities, especially in African countries where colonial-era anti-homosexuality laws still exist. These two issues are interconnected historically and methodologically. With some exceptions, historians have done much work to tackle the first problem, while scholars and professionals working in other disciplines have been at the forefront of efforts to address the second one. The debates between history, interdisciplinary sexuality studies, and activism have opened up new avenues for understanding the legacies of colonialism in postcolonial constructs of sexuality and gender in Africa.

Colonial interventions regarding African sexuality have shifted over time, starting with the sexualization of African bodies, particularly those of African women, from at least the sixteenth century, then turning toward concerns about interracial relationships in the late nineteenth and early twentieth centuries during the expansion of European colonization. By the 1910s and 1920s, colonial discourses focused on the role of sexuality in public health and the control of populations, which incited efforts to control women's and girls' sexualities. Since at least World War II, and in some cases earlier, colonial authorities became increasingly alarmed about the sexuality of youth. African history methodologies and approaches—such as gender and women's history, oral history and life history, and ethnography—have opened the door to more nuanced understandings of the history of sexuality in colonial Africa, as some of the contributions to the current volume demonstrate.[1]

The definition of "imperialism" in Africa has likewise shifted over time, and this shift is reflected in the scholarship. Scholarship on the early modern era (fifteenth to the eighteenth centuries) highlights shifting relations of trade and romance between Africans and Portuguese, Spanish, Dutch, and Italian colonizers.[2] There is a rich body of work on the history of sexuality in Ottoman Africa in the period before World War I, which tends to fall under the category of Middle East history.[3] Scholarship on Omani imperialism and slave-trading in nineteenth-century East Africa illuminates the important role of African female slavery and concubinage in shaping Indian Ocean cultures.[4] The bulk of scholarship on the history of sexuality and imperialism in Africa, however, foregrounds British, French, and other European empires that dominated the continent since 1800. Much of this research focuses on the first half of the twentieth century, when European colonial interventions in the everyday life of African people became central to the political and economic goals of the state. The definition of "imperialism" has also taken on new theoretical meaning since at least the 1990s, when African studies scholars began reading "the colonial" as a methodological or ideological framework rather than simply reference to an historical era.

Enduring colonial racial and sexual stereotypes

Whether referring to the beautiful and powerful Senegalese women traders on whom Portuguese men (*lançados*) "threw themselves" in the sixteenth and seventeenth centuries or to the enslaved African women subjected to rape and torture during the Middle Passage, the objectification and sexualization of African female bodies has permeated European imperialist discourses.[5] One of the best-known examples of European colonial constructs of African female sexuality is the case of Saartjie (Sara) Baartman, also known as the "Hottentot Venus." Baartman was a South African woman who was brought to Europe in 1810, where she was put on display and subjected to public voyeurism and ridicule. Historian Sander Gilman contextualized the Baartman case within a Victorian "iconography of female sexuality" that conveyed the slippages between discourses on race, class, and gender in nineteenth-century literature.[6] European portrayals of African women as simultaneously grotesque and erotic contributed to what gender and sexuality studies scholar Anne McClintock referred to as a "porno-tropic tradition" in European imperialism.[7] During the nineteenth century, Europeans employed representations of African female bodies like Baartman's in pseudoscientific studies of racial difference as fodder for Social Darwinist theories that helped to justify further colonization of the African continent.[8] This ambiguous representation of African women's bodies as simultaneously enticing and dangerous exposed European anxieties about interracial sex during the era of conquest in Africa.

Colonial discourses on African male sexuality intensified amidst the spread of white colonization on the continent in the late 1800s and early 1900s and the subsequent rise of "black peril" discourses. "Black peril" generally refers to the moral panics in which whites accused black men of sexually assaulting white women and girls, often without evidentiary basis. Published in the late 1980s, Dane Kennedy's *Islands of White* explained how black peril panics arose in Kenya and Southern Rhodesia (today Zimbabwe) in the early twentieth century along with increasing white immigration, and in particular the arrival of more white women, to these colonies.[9] Jock McCullough's *Black Peril, White Virtue* (2000) urged that these "moral panics" must also be understood in the context of tensions between the colonies and the metropole as well as the gender, race, and class politics (for instance, with the rise of first-wave feminism) within and around white settler communities.[10] The respectability, class, and social status of the white women, as well as the identity of the black men, were on trial in "black peril" cases.

There were "white perils" as well. The phrase "while peril" in the early twentieth century referred to white women who disregarded racial sexual norms of settler society to have sex with indigenous Africans. The other "white peril" was the very realistic fear among Africans of white men raping African women and girls.[11] Anyone who has done research on this topic knows how important it is to remember that white men in colonial Africa rarely, if ever, faced charges for raping African women or girls. Whether enticing, debauched, or dangerous, African sexuality was portrayed in a reductionist, racist framework intertwined with Victorian ideas about gender, sex, class, and civilization.

43

The colonial trope of African hyper(hetero)sexuality has had and continues to have a profound influence over ideas about African sexualities globally. As legal scholar Sylvia Tamale explained, "Beginning with the first contact with African communities, researchers from the Global North maintained a voyeuristic, ethnopornographic obsession with what they perceived as exotic (read perverse) African sexual cultures."[12] Colonial stereotypes about African sexuality have not disappeared. They endure in present-day interventions to control the spread of HIV/AIDS, to govern sex tourism, to prevent sexual violence, and to promote family planning. These are worthy causes, but the development discourses framing them too often reify colonial representations of African women and men as sexually promiscuous and ignorant about putatively superior Western sexual and reproductive norms.[13]

Historians have sought to counter colonial constructs of African sexualities by looking for voices of African women and men in the historical record and by incorporating oral histories into their research.[14] Since the 1970s and 1980s, many historical and anthropological works have featured oral histories and life histories of women in order to center women's experiences of love and sex during the colonial era.[15] Even more than oral histories collected by scholars, the self-expression of African artists, poets, novelists and others has been crucial to challenging colonial and ("post")colonial narratives of African sexualities.[16]

Interracial relationships in conquest and colonialism

W.E.B. DuBois referred to European conquest in Africa as "the rape of a continent already furiously mangled by the slave trade."[17] DuBois intentionally used the word "rape," not only as a metaphor but also as a reminder that "[l]ying treaties, rivers of rum, murder, assassination, mutilation, rape, and torture have marked the progress of Englishmen, German, Frenchmen and Belgian on the dark continent."[18] Without a doubt, rape—both literal and figurative— and other forms of sexual violence against African women and men undergirded European conquest of the continent, but not all interracial sexual relationships were inherently violent. Historian George E. Brooks argued that romantic unions between European men and African women during the era of early European contact in West Africa offered a "mutual advantage" in wealth and status to both the trading "queens" residing along the West African coast, known as *signares,* and the European *lançados.* [19] The fact that these men abided by local Wolof and Lebou customs regarding marriage and familial obligations, Brooks argued, proves that African women held prominent positions in emerging colonial contact and settlement. Historian Hilary Jones explains that during the eighteenth century, when the *signares* predominated, "imperialism operated as much through the private, intimate spheres of marriage, household, and sexuality as it did through French policies and practices enacted in its overseas possessions."[20] Research by another historian, Lorelle Semley, carries the stories of *métis* communities that emerged from these relationships and others into the nineteenth and twentieth centuries to show how they became instrumental in shaping ideas of citizenship and belonging under French colonialism.[21]

Interracial relationships during the colonial era emerged amidst complex emotional and political landscapes that shaped people's understandings of their own and others' love lives.[22] The transition to formal colonial rule in the nineteenth century brought new pressures to interracial romances. Focusing on colonial Gold Coast, present-day Ghana, Carina Ray argues that colonialism did not necessarily represent a shift in the *kinds* of relationships that existed so much as it marked a change in how these relationships were perceived and governed.[23] Diverse unions based on love, concubinage, rape, prostitution, and marriage existed in the precolonial and colonial eras. However, in the context of entrenched segregation policies under colonial rule, both Europeans and Africans began to disparage interracial relationships as immoral and socially destructive. Ray notes that while Gold Coast families took care of the children of interracial unions and welcomed them into their communities, some people believed that children abandoned by their European fathers served as evidence of their parents' debauchery. In twentieth-century francophone Africa, too, many people viewed mixed-race children as a reflection of their mothers' sexual improprieties. Rachel Jean-Baptiste demonstrates how *métis* men in postwar francophone Africa pushed back against this stigma by portraying their mothers and sisters as "honorable women" who contributed "to social and biological reproduction in African societies."[24]

Fertility, disease, and women's sexuality

Rising concerns about the spread of venereal disease and its connection to population decline in the early twentieth century brought women's fertility and sexual behavior into the lime-light.[25] Colonial officials believed Africans were more prone to contracting venereal diseases than other populations because of the colonial trope about African sexual promiscuity. This pathologization of African bodies, Megan Vaughan explains in her 1991 book *Curing Their Ills*, "created a direct, biomedical interest in African sexuality and a discourse on that sexuality which was produced not only 'about', but in dialogue with, certain groups of Africans."[26] For instance, panic over the spread of syphilis among the Baganda people in British colonial Uganda, Vaughan explains, did not derive solely from the imposition of colonial discourses; it also emerged out of Baganda elite men's complaints that colonialism disintegrated indigenous patriarchal control over African women's sexuality. Colonial programs for preventing the spread of venereal diseases and encouraging marriage and maternity reinforced both colonial and African patriarchal authority over women's sexuality.

Colonial authorities in Africa and other regions introduced controversial legal and medical interventions, such as the registration and examination of sex workers and other women, in order to control the spread of venereal diseases.[27] Historian Lynette Jackson researched the *chibheura* ("open up") medical examinations carried out on single women heading to cities in Southern Rhodesia.[28] Luise White's groundbreaking 1990 book *Comforts of Home*, based on oral histories with former sex workers in colonial Nairobi, tells a different story. "In Kenya," White explains, "unrestrained female sexuality was not seen to have the same causal relationship to venereal disease that it was seen to have elsewhere."[29] She argues that the Kenyan colonial government tolerated prostitution in the capital city of Nairobi because sex workers ensured the "reproduction of male labor power."[30] Women's cooking, bathing, sexual acts, and other services provided the "comforts of home" necessary for regenerating male laborers. Female sex workers in colonial Nairobi redefined urban culture, avoided harassment from police and patriarchs, and maintained a degree of financial and social autonomy throughout the colonial era.

Improving African women's health—especially sexual and reproductive health— became a cornerstone of the colonial economic project to ensure a healthy and productive labor force.[31] Debates about maternity and child welfare in colonial Africa contributed to the increase in funding and attention toward female education and women's and child rights movements. Nancy Rose Hunt's research into interventions around birth spacing in the Belgian Congo demonstrates how European women intervened to reduce infant mortality and increase birth rates in Africa.[32] Hunt notes that "assumed association between degeneration and the tropics," which initially discouraged white women from coming to the colonies, became in the 1920s the basis for recruiting European women as a moralizing influence over both European men and African women.[33] Officials understood that women would have more success than men in convincing other women to change their sexual and reproductive norms.

Even where they sought to change local cultures, some interventions to reduce infant mortality and increase fertility had the added bonus of reinforcing the moral and social order of African patriarchal "tradition." Biomedical and social interventions were derived in part from fears that urban migration and too much "westernization" had damaging psychological effects on Africans, especially African women.[34] In colonial parlance, those who ventured outside domestic and reproductive roles were "wicked" women who threatened the social order.[35]

Marriage, gender, religion, and cultural change

Debates about sexuality, marriage, and reproduction in colonial Africa often circled back to questions of whether or not and how to control the behavior of women and girls, and what role religion and custom would play in this endeavor. Historical studies based in Kenya have offered rich analyses of this issue. The "politics of the womb," Lynn Thomas explains, rested on debates about "material and moral issues" that reified "old hierarchies based in gender, generation, and kinship, and contributed to the construction of new ones grounded in racial difference and 'civilized' status."[36] Tabitha Kanogo attributes these conflicts in Kenya to male anxieties over the exchange of daughters and brides through marriage customs that viewed girls and women as "social capital."[37] Similarly, Brett Shadle argues that cultural and economic changes explain the spike in legal battles over adultery, rape, and forced marriage in Kenya during the 1940s and 1950s.[38]

Colonialism exacerbated conflicts between elders and youth and women and men, but it also offered women and young people new options and opportunities regarding love, sex, marriage, and divorce. Many scholars point to the moral campaigns of Christian missionaries against polygyny, bridewealth, initiation rites, and premarital sex—to name just a few of the many issues—but sometimes Christian sexual norms reinforced African patriarchal authority. In late-nineteenth-century Uganda, for example, the governing body of the Buganda Kingdom and Christian missionaries initially collaborated over legal and social reforms designed to prevent married women from having affairs and leaving their husbands.[39] Disagreement arose over the high cost of bridewealth in the following decades, but even then patriarchs and missionaries had the shared goal of stabilizing marriages to reduce the influence of "bad women."

There is a very robust body of scholarship on drastic changes in marriage practices related to issues of sexuality and reproduction.[40] For instance, Rachel Jean-Baptiste notes that efforts in the early twentieth century to codify customary laws around marriage in French colonial Gabon were designed to "buttress the colony's demographic growth."[41] Margot Lovett reveals how women from western Tanzania who threatened local patriarchies by defying their husbands' orders were deemed adulterers and prostitutes.[42] Accusations of sexual transgressions in colonial Africa often point to fears about the disruption of the social order amidst rising economic hardship.

Changing ideas about gender and its relation to sexuality have been another fruitful area of scholarship. Contributing to studies of masculinity, Stephan Miescher's *Making Men in Ghana* (2005) not only traced the multiple and sometimes contradicting subjectivities of men who came of age in colonial Ghana, but also traced how the church shaped young men's ideas about sexuality. Presbyterian male teachers were particularly careful not to engage in "pre- and extramarital sexual relations [because they] could have serious personal and professional consequences."[43] Interdisciplinary studies of gender in Africa have carved out new avenues for thinking about the relationship between gender, sexuality, and colonialism.[44]

Consent, age, and the sexualities of children and youth

One of the more innovative discussions about sex and marriage in recent scholarship has been around the question of consent.[45] In their Introduction to the edited volume *Marriage by Force? Contestation over Consent and Coercion in Africa*, Bunting, Lawrance, and Roberts explain that the issue of forced marriage arose across the continent of Africa out of nineteenth-century antislavery campaigns.[46] While there are strong parallels between slavery and forced marriage with regard to questions of autonomy, Carina Ray warns against investing too much in a "binary opposition between consent and coercion."[47] Research on the history of consent points to the fundamental debate over who had the authority to consent in the cases of marriage or sexual intercourse, a question that often pitted African customary law, which was intended to uphold the authority of local patriarchs or elders, against colonial law, which presumed that all individuals—including girls and women—had what Tabitha Kanogo refers to as "legal personhood."[48]

Historian Elizabeth Thornberry unravels four different discursive threads in the history of consent in the Eastern Cape, South Africa: customary, spiritual, liberal, and racial.[49] Xhosa customs prevalent in the region during the early colonial era framed consent in familial terms, wherein male elders had control over young men's and women's sexuality. The introduction of Christianity in the nineteenth century sought to redefine consent in terms of sin and temptation. Meanwhile, colonial legal interventions around consent drew on British liberal traditions professing rights and protections of the individual subject. Racial segregation and colonial racial and sexual constructs of South African women and men added yet another matrix to these intersecting and often competing forms of consent. All of these ideas informed the adjudication of cases involving sexual assault in South African courts, especially but not only in cases involving interracial sexual assault.

Ambiguities over age and maturity haunted debates about consent everywhere in colonial Africa. Colonial officials found it extremely difficult to pin down exactly how and when African children should be recognized as adults.[50] Historical studies of age in colonial Africa highlight the importance of taking this into consideration along with gender, race, and class. Abosede George's study of girl hawkers in colonial Lagos points out that, while some officials associated hawking with illicit juvenile sexuality, social reformers (mainly elite African women) pressed the government to protect these girls from sexual abuse or forced marriage. Similarly, Saheed Aderinto argued that anxieties over sexuality and maturity were central to campaigns to prevent child prostitution, but "[i]n Nigeria, the idea of the erotic child, or a child as an object of sexual pleasure, emerged alongside the struggle against sexual perversion."[51] This apparent contradiction in representation of children reflects a more pervasive contradiction in European discourses on African sexuality: colonial stereotypes of African sexuality presumed that African children matured faster than European children, and, at the same time, colonial discourses infantilized African adults through the derogatory use of the terms "boy" and "girl" to refer to men and women working in the homes and offices of settlers and colonial officials ("office boy," "houseboy," "housegirl," etc.). Infantilizing language sought to deflate the perceived sexual prowess of African men and women and reinforce the racial hierarchy that maintained social order in the colonies. Starting in the 1920s, international child rights movements pressed colonial officials to implement legal protections against child marriage, child labor, and other forms of child endangerment, but officials, missionaries, patriarchs, and young people sparred over who, exactly, could—and could not—be considered a "child." African girls were often portrayed as precocious sexual insti-gators if they had sexual relations with older men.[52] None of these constructs and discourses adequately conveys how young people perceived themselves and their sexuality. Girls and boys, young women and men were savvy at navigating the gaps between cultural, social, and legal ideas of childhood in order to assert their sexual autonomy or demand state protection.[53]

Anxieties over young people's gender and sexuality intensified during the 1950s and 1960s as African countries prepared for independence from colonial rule.[54] Lynn Thomas's study of pregnant schoolgirls asserting their positionality as "modern" subjects in paternity cases and Laura Fair's analysis of young lovers' secret meetings in Zanzibar's dark movie theaters show how young people began to redefine sexual and gender cultures.[55] African literature from and about the nationalist era also portrays the 1950s and 1960s as a time of drastic reshuffling of ideas about race, sex, and gender globally. Tayeb Salih's *Season of Migration to the North* (1966), published in both English and Arabic, reverses the racial/sexual gaze by exploring a Sudanese man's sexual conquests of white women during his postcolonial stay in Britain, Sudan's former colonizer. In *The Abandoned Baobab: The Autobiography of a Senegalese Woman* (1991), Ken Bugul (pen name of Mariètou M'Baye) navigates the interplay between sex, race, and the (neo-)colonial gaze during the volatile 1960s. The protagonists in both works recognize the power of their sexualized bodies as a "fetish" in Europe, where they struggle to reclaim lost selves and precolonial/decolonial identities. Youth sexuality was so important for nationalism and decolonization because it represented the rebirth of African autonomy and identity. At the same time, young people's sexual behavior reflected shifting subjectivities in late colonial and postcolonial Africa, a period of great uncertainty about the cultural, moral, and economic norms governing sexuality and marriage.

New directions

The biggest trend in recent studies of sexuality and colonialism has focused on the legacies of colonialism in contemporary political conflicts over the criminalization of homosexuality. With few exceptions, this work has been carried out by scholars in disciplines other than history.[56] Productive interdisciplinary engagement on these topics would not have been possible without the publication of Ifi Amadiume's *Male Daughters, Female Husbands* (1987), Oyèrónkẹ Oyèwùmí's *The Invention of Women* (1997), and other works that urged scholars to pay more attention to African epistemologies of gender and sexuality.[57] Over the past two decades, scholarship in the fields of media studies, anthropology, sociology, legal studies, lit-erature, and political science has opened up the debate about what constitutes "African sexuality" or, more appropriately, "African sexualities," and how these ideas have shifted over time.[58] Neville Hoad's *African Intimacies* (2007) juxtaposes several key historical events and debates, starting with the 1886 execution of the Buganda king's pages for refusing to have sex with him and ending with controversial statements against homosexuality by prominent African leaders such as Zimbabwe's President Robert Mugabe in the 1990s. While this was not the first study of homosexuality in African history, this book did open up new ways of thinking about the political and chronological correlations between the emergence of the concept of homosexuality and the expansion of European imperialism in Africa. Marc Epprecht's *Heterosexual Africa?* (2008) provided a more in-depth historical account of how colonial anthropology and ethnopsychology constructed the notion of *an* African sexuality as heterosexual and reproductive, thus contextualizing the contemporary claim among some leaders that homosexuality is "un-African."

Queer studies scholars working on or in Africa are very aware that colonial sexual and racial politics persist. This is precisely why so many queer studies scholars have looked to Africa's colonial past for proof of both Africans' diverse sexual history and the colonial origins of anti-homosexuality laws. The treasure hunt for the magical "queer archive" is part of a global recuperative project.[59] Thérèse Migraine-George and Ashley Currier warn scholars against engaging in the quest for a "queer archive" in Africa as a way to speak back to contemporary tropes that homosexuality is "un-African." The "queer archive" is itself "a moving archive," they explain; the fact that it is constantly in formation means that it produces constantly shifting information. Interpreting Africa's "queer archive" rests on the recognition that historical analysis of homosexuality must always acknowledge the weight of the present on the past and vice versa. Rather than searching for an historical record of queerness, which is usually defined in contemporary neoliberal terms, Migraine-George and Currier urge scholars to embrace queer methodologies in order to discover the "best practices that remain to be invented and implemented across and against disciplinary boundaries."[60]

Conclusion

The legacies of colonialism in contemporary sexual politics in Africa abound well beyond the debate over anti-homosexuality laws. Since the 1980s, international interventions to stop the spread of HIV/AIDS have echoed colonial-era campaigns to diagnose and treat cases of syphilis and gonorrhea. In the same way, historians recognize colonial discourses and practices in postcolonial development programs that promote family planning (i.e., population control), protect girls from becoming "child brides," and teach mothers how to care for their children. In addition to pointing out the ways in which colonialism endures into the present, cutting-edge historical research also shows the other possibilities that existed both within and outside these discourses. What other sexualities or ideas about sexuality shaped people's understanding of themselves and others in particular times and places? When and why did these ideas and practices seem to disappear, or did they? How has the assumption that African epistemologies were destroyed by colonialism prevented scholars from recognizing enduring forms of and ideas about sexuality in Africa? Addressing these questions redirects us away from the project of targeted recovery—whether for the sake of the past or the present—and toward research that engages the imagination necessary for analyzing the intersections between colonialism and sexuality.

Notes

1 In addition to the current essay, see Musisi, "Gender and Sexuality in African History"; Epprecht, "Sexuality, Africa, History."
2 See for example, Brooks, *Eurafricans in Western Africa.*
3 Booth, *Harem Histories*; Pollard, *Nurturing the Nation*; Cuno, *Modernizing Marriage.*
4 Sheriff, "*Suria*: Concubine or Secondary Slave Wife?"; Hopper, "Slavery, Family Life, and the African."
5 Brooks, *Eurafricans in Western Africa*, 50; Mustakeem, *Slavery at Sea.*
6 Gilman, "Black Bodies, White Bodies."
7 McClintock, *Imperial Leather*, 22.
8 Dubow, *Scientific Racism*, 23–24.
9 Kennedy, *Islands of White.*
10 McCullough, *Black Peril, White Virtue.*
11 Phillips, "The 'perils' of sex and the panics of race"; Thornberry, *Colonizing Consent*, 21. See also Mbogoni, *Miscegenation, Identity and Status in Colonial Africa.*

12 Tamale, "Researching and theorising sexualities in Africa," 19. See also Sigal, Tortorici, and Whitehead, *Ethno-Pornography*.
13 Decker and McMahon, *The Idea of Development in Africa*.
14 See for example, White, *Comforts of Home*; Epprecht, *Hungochani*; Ray, *Crossing the Color Line*.
15 See for example, Shostak, *Nisa*; Mirza and Strobel, eds. and transl., *Three Swahili Women*; Marks, *Not Either an Experimental Doll*.
16 See for example, Salih, *Season of Migration to the North*; Bugul, *The Abandoned Baobab*; the poetry of Gabeba Baderoon; and the many personal contributions to Tamale, *African Sexualities*.
17 DuBois, *Africa, Its Geography, People and Products and Africa, 36*.
18 Ibid.
19 Brooks, Jr., "The *Signares* of Saint-Louis and Gorée."
20 Jones, *The Métis of Senegal*, 21.
21 Semley, *To Be Free and French*, 69–111.
22 See Gengenbach, "'What My Heart Wanted'"; White, *Children of the French Empire*; Mbogoni, *Miscegenation, Identity and Status in Colonial Africa*.
23 Ray, *Crossing the Color Line*, 4.
24 Jean-Baptiste, "'Miss Eurafrica,'" 571, 573.
25 Doyle, *Before HIV*.
26 Vaughan, *Curing Their Ills*, 130.
27 Levine, *Prostitution, Race & Politics*; Aderinto, *When Sex Threatened the State*; Walther, *Sex and Control*; Kozma, *Global Women, Colonial Ports*; Saddock, "Government and the Control of Venereal Disease in Colonial Tanzania."
28 Jackson, *Surfacing Up*, 105–106. See also Jackson, "'When in the White Man's Town.'"
29 White, *Comforts of Home*, 176.
30 Ibid., 12.
31 Hunt, *A Colonial Lexicon*; Klausen, *Race, Maternity, and the Politics of Birth Control in South Africa*; Thomas, *The Politics of the Womb*; Turrittin, "Colonial Midwives and Modernizing Childbirth in French West Africa"; McCurdy, "Urban Threats"; Kanogo, *African Womanhood in Colonial Kenya*; Decker, *Mobilizing Zanzibari Women*; Klausen, *Abortion Under Apartheid*.
32 Hunt, "'Le Bebe en Brousse.'"
33 Ibid., 411.
34 Vaughan, *Curing Their Ills*; Jackson, *Surfacing Up*.
35 Hodgson and Curdy, "*Wicked Women*." In this volume, note in particular the following chapters addressing colonial sexuality: Allman, "Rounding Up Spinsters"; Musisi, "Gender and Cultural Construction of 'Bad Women'"; Parpart, "'Wicked Women' and 'Respectable Ladies.'"
36 Thomas, *Politics of the Womb*, 4.
37 Kanogo, *African Womanhood*, 2.
38 Shadle, *"Girl Cases."*
39 Musisi, "Gender and the Cultural Construction of 'Bad Women,'" 176.
40 Cooper, *Marriage in Maradi*; Shadle, *"Girl Cases"*; Jean-Baptise, *Conjugal Rights*; Burrill, *States of Marriage*; Stockreiter, *Islamic Law, Gender, and Social Change*; Jean-Baptiste and Burrill, "Love, Marriage, and Families in Africa"; Byfield, "Women, Marriage, Divorce and the Emerging Colonial State"; Hawkins, "'The Woman in Question'"; Tashjian and Allman, "Marrying and Marriage on a Shifting Terrain."
41 Jean-Baptise, *Conjugal Rights*, 69.
42 Lovett, "'She Thinks She's Like a Man.'"
43 Miescher, *Making Men in Ghana*, 139.
44 See Ouzgane and Morrell, *African Masculinities*; Uchendu, *Masculinities in Contemporary Africa*.
45 Bunting, Lawrance, and Roberts, *Marriage by Force?*; Thornberry, *Colonizing Consent*.
46 See also Razy and Rodet, *Children on the Move in Africa*.
47 Ray, *Crossing the Color Line*, 5.
48 Kanogo, *African Womanhood*, 8.
49 Thornberry, *Colonizing Consent*.
50 George, *Making Modern Girls*; Shadle, "Debating 'Early Marriage' in Colonial Kenya"; Aderinto, *When Sex Threatened the State*; Ocobock, *Uncertain Age*.
51 Aderinto, *When Sex Threatened the State*, 11.
52 See also Decker, "The Elusive Power of Colonial Prey."

53 Thomas, "The Modern Girl and Racial Respectability in 1930s South Africa"; George, *Making Modern Girls*; Ocobock, *Uncertain Age*; Duff, *Changing Childhoods in the Cape Colony*.

54 Mutongi, "'Dear Dolly's' Advice"; Ivaska, *Cultured States*; Plageman, "The African Personality Dances Highlife"; Aderinto, *When Sex Threatened the State*; Doyle, "Premarital Sexuality in Great Lakes Africa"; Klausen, *Abortion Under Apartheid*.

55 Thomas, "Schoolgirl Pregnancies, Letter-Writing, and 'Modern' Persons"; Fair, "Making Love in the Indian Ocean."

56 The exceptions include Epprecht, *Hungochani*; Epprecht, *Heterosexual Africa?*; Schmidt, "Colonial Intimacy." Marc Epprecht's oral history interviews with men working in Zimbabwean mines in *Hungochani* (2004) offered much-needed nuance to the extensive colonial and postcolonial discourse about sexual and social relationships within male migrant labor communities.

57 Amadiume, *Male Daughters, Female Husbands*; Oyèwùmí, *The Invention of Women*.

58 Murray and Roscoe, *Boy-Wives and Female Husbands*; Gaudio, *Allah Made Us*; Tamale, *African Sexualities*; Newell, *The Forger's Tale*; Hoad, *African Intimacies*; Munro, *South Africa and the Dream of Love to Come*; Nyeck and Epprecht, *Sexual Diversity in Africa*; Zabus, *Out in Africa*; Wieringa and Sívori, *The Sexual History of the Global South*; Donham, *The Erotics of History*; M'Baye and Muhonja, *Gender and Sexuality in Senegalese Societies*; Currier, *Politicizing Sex in Contemporary Africa*.

59 See for example, Arondekar, *For the Record*.

60 Migraine-George and Currier, "Querying Queer African Archives," 202.

Bibliography

Aderinto, Saheed. *When Sex Threatened the State: Illicit Sexuality, Nationalism, and Politics in Colonial Nigeria, 1900–1958*. Champaign, IL: University of Illinois Press, 2015.

Amadiume, Ifi. *Male Daughters, Female Husbands: Gender and Sex in an African Society*. London: Zed Books, 1987.

Arondekar, Anjali. *For the Record: On Sexuality and the Colonial Archive in India*. Durham, NC: Duke University Press, 2009.

Booth, Marilyn, ed. *Harem Histories: Envisioning Places and Living Spaces*. Durham, NC: Duke University Press, 2010.

Brooks, George. *Eurafricans in Western Africa: Commerce, Social Status, Gender, and Religious Observance from the Sixteenth to the Eighteenth Century*. Athens, OH: Ohio University Press, 2003.

Brooks, Jr., George E. *The Women in Africa: Studies in Social and Economic Change*, edited by Nancy J. Hafkin and Edna G. Bay, 19–44. Palo Alto, CA: Stanford University Press, 1976.

Bugul, Ken. *The Abandoned Baobab: The Autobiography of a Senegalese Woman*. Charlottesville, VA: University of Virginia Press, 1991.

Bunting, Annie, Benjamin N. Lawrance and Richard Roberts, eds. *Marriage by Force? Contestation over Consent and Coercion in Africa*. Athens, OH: Ohio University Press, 2016.

Burrill, Emily. *States of Marriage: Gender, Justice, and Rights in Colonial Mali*. Athens, OH: Ohio University Press, 2015.

Cooper, Barbara. *Marriage in Maradi: Gender and Culture in a Hausa Society in Niger, 1900–1989*. Portsmouth, UK: Heinemann, 1997.

Cuno, Kenneth. *Modernizing Marriage: Family, Ideology, and Law in Nineteenth- and Early Twentieth-Century Egypt*. Syracuse, NY: Syracuse University Press, 2015.

Currier, Ashley. *Politicizing Sex in Contemporary Africa: Homophobia in Malawi*. Cambridge, UK: Cambridge University Press, 2019. doi:10.1017/9781108551984.

Decker, Corrie. *Mobilizing Zanzibari Women: The Struggle for Respectability and Self-Reliance in Colonial East Africa*. London: Palgrave Macmillan, 2014. doi:10.1057/9781137472632.

Decker, Corrie. "The Elusive Power of Colonial Prey: Sexualizing the Schoolgirl in the Zanzibar Protectorate." *Africa Today* 61, no. 4 (2015): 42–60. doi:10.2979/africatoday.61.4.43.

Decker, Corrie and Elisabeth McMahon. *The Idea of Development in Africa: A History*. Cambridge, UK: Cambridge University Press, 2020.

Donham, Donald. *The Erotics of History: An Atlantic Example*. Oakland, CA: University of California Press, 2018.

Doyle, Shane. "Premarital Sexuality in Great Lakes Africa, 1900–1980." In *Generations Past: Youth in East African History*, edited by Andrew Burton and Hélène Charton-Bigot, 237–261. Athens, OH: Ohio University Press, 2010.

Doyle, Shane. *Before HIV: Sexuality, Fertility, and Mortality in East Africa*. Oxford, UK: Oxford University Press, 2013.

DuBois, W.E.B. *Africa, Its Geography, People and Products and Africa – Its Place in Modern History*. Oxford, UK: Oxford University Press, 2007.

Dubow, Saul. *Scientific Racism in Modern South Africa*. Cambridge, UK: Cambridge University Press, 1995.

Duff, Sarah. *Changing Childhoods in the Cape Colony: Dutch Reformed Church Evangelicalism and Colonial Childhood, 1860–1895*. London: Palgrave Macmillan, 2015.

Epprecht, Marc. *Hungochani; The History of a Dissident Sexuality in Southern Africa*. Montréal: McGill-Queen's University Press, 2004.

Epprecht, Marc. *Heterosexual Africa? The History of an Idea from the Age of Exploration to the Age of AIDS*. Athens, OH: Ohio University Press, 2008.

Epprecht, Marc. "Sexuality, Africa, History." *The American Historical Review* 114, no. 5 (2009): 1258–1272. doi:10.1086/ahr.114.5.1258.

Fair, Laura. "Making Love in the Indian Ocean: Hindi Films, Zanzibari Audiences, and the Construction of Romance in the 1950s and 1960s." In *Love in Africa*, edited by Jennifer Cole and Lynn M. Thomas, 58–82. Chicago, IL: University of Chicago Press, 2009.

Gaudio, Rudolf Pell. *Allah Made Us: Sexual Outlaws in an Islamic African City*. Hoboken, NJ: Wiley-Blackwell, 2009.

Geiger, Susan, Nakanyike Musisi and Jean Marie Allman, eds. *Women in African Colonial Histories*. Bloomington, IN: Indiana University Press, 2002.

George, Abosede. *Making Modern Girls: A History of Girlhood, Labor, and Social Development in Colonial Lagos*. Athens, OH: Ohio University Press, 2014.

Gilman, Sander L. "Black Bodies, White Bodies: Toward an Iconography of Female Sexuality in Late Nineteenth-Century Art, Medicine, and Literature." *Critical Inquiry* 12, no. 1 (1985): 204–242. doi:10.1086/448327.

Hoad, Neville. *African Intimacies: Race, Homosexuality and Globalization*. Minneapolis, MN: University of Minnesota Press, 2007.

Hodgson, Dorothy and Sheryl Curdy, eds. *"Wicked Women" and the Reconfiguration of Gender in Africa*. Portsmouth, UK: Heinemann, 2001.

Hopper, Matthew S. "Slavery, Family Life, and the African Diaspora in the Arabian Gulf, 1880–1940." In *Sex, Power, and Slavery*, edited by Gwyn Campbell and Elizabeth Elbourne, 167–181. Athens, OH: Ohio University Press, 2014.

Hunt, Nancy Rose. "'Le Bebe en Brousse': European Women, African Birth Spacing and Colonial Intervention in Breast Feeding in the Belgian Congo." *The International Journal of African Historical Studies* 21, no. 3 (1988): 401–432.

Hunt, Nancy Rose. *A Colonial Lexicon: Of Birth Ritual, Medicalization, and Mobility in the Congo*. Durham, NC: Duke University Press, 1999.

Ivaska, Andrew. *Cultured States: Youth, Gender, and Modern Style in 1960s Dar es Salaam*. Durham, NC: Duke University Press, 2011.

Jackson, Lynette A. *Surfacing Up: Psychiatry and Social Order in Colonial Zimbabwe, 1908–1968*. Ithaca, NY: Cornell University Press, 2005.

Jean-Baptiste, Rachel. "'Miss Eurafrica': Men, Women's Sexuality, and Métis Identity in Late Colonial French Africa, 1945–1960." *Journal of the History of Sexuality* 20, no. 3 (2011): 568–593. doi:10.1353/sex.2011.0053.

Jean-Baptise, Rachel. *Conjugal Rights: Marriage, Sexuality, and Urban Life in Colonial Libreville*. Athens, OH: Ohio University Press, 2014.

Jean-Baptiste, Rachel and Emily Burrill. "Love, Marriage, and Families in Africa." In *Holding the World Together: African Women in Changing Perspective*, edited by Nwando Achebe and Claire C. Robertson, 275–294. Madison, WI: University of Wisconsin Press, 2019.

Jones, Hilary. *The Métis of Senegal: Urban Life and Politics in French West Africa*. Bloomington, IN: Indiana University Press, 2013.

Kanogo, Tabitha. *African Womanhood in Colonial Kenya, 1900–1950*. Athens, OH: Ohio University Press, 2005.

Kennedy, Dane. *Islands of White: Settler Society and Culture in Kenya and Southern Rhodesia, 1890–1939*. Durham, NC: Duke University Press, 1987.

Klausen, Susanne M. *Race, Maternity, and the Politics of Birth Control in South Africa, 1910–39*. London: Palgrave Macmillan, 2004.

Klausen, Susanne M. *Abortion Under Apartheid: Nationalism, Sexuality, and Women's Reproductive Rights in South Africa*. Oxford, UK: Oxford University Press, 2015.

Kozma, Liat. *Global Women, Colonial Ports: Prostitution in the Interwar Middle East*. Albany, NY: State University of New York Press, 2017.

Levine, Philippa. *Prostitution, Race & Politics: Policing Venereal Disease in the British Empire*. New York: Routledge, 2003.

Marks, Shula, ed. *Not Either an Experimental Doll: The Separate Worlds of Three South African Women*. Bloomington, IN: Indiana University Press, 1987.

M'Baye, Babacar and Besi Brillian Muhonja, eds. *Gender and Sexuality in Senegalese Societies*Lanham, MD: Lexington Books, 2019.

Mbogoni, Lawrence. *Miscegenation, Identity and Status in Colonial Africa: Intimate Colonial Encounters*. Abingdon, UK: Routledge, 2019.

McClintock, Anne. *Imperial Leather: Race, Gender and Sexuality in the Colonial Conquest*. Abingdon, UK: Routledge, 1995.

McCullough, Jock. *Black Peril, White Virtue: Sexual Crime in Southern Rhodesia, 1902–1935*. Bloomington, IN: Indiana University Press, 2000.

Miescher, Stephan F. *Making Men in Ghana*. Bloomington, IN: Indiana University Press, 2005.

Migraine-George, Thérèse and Ashley Currier, "Querying Queer African Archives: Methods and Movements," *WSQ: Women's Studies Quarterly* 44, no. 3/4 (2016): 190–207.

Mirza, Sarah and Margaret Strobel, eds. and transl. *Three Swahili Women: Life Histories from Mombasa, Kenya*. Bloomington, IN: Indiana University Press, 1989.

Munro, Brenna M. *South Africa and the Dream of Love to Come: Queer Sexuality and the Struggle for Freedom*. Minneapolis, MN: University of Minnesota Press, 2012.

Murray, Stephen O. and Will Roscoe, eds. *Boy-Wives and Female Husbands: Studies in African Homosexualities*. New York: Palgrave Macmillan, 1998.

Musisi, Nakanyike. "Gender and Sexuality in African History: A personal reflection." *The Journal of African History* 55 (2014): 303–315. doi:10.1017/S0021853714000589.

Mustakeem, Sowande M. *Slavery at Sea: Terror, Sex, and Sickness in the Middle Passage*. Champaign, IL: University of Illinois Press, 2016.

Newell, Stephanie. *The Forger's Tale: The Search for Odeziaku*. Athens, OH: Ohio University Press, 2006.

Nyeck, S.N. and Marc Epprecht, eds. *Sexual Diversity in Africa: Politics, Theory, Citizenship*Montréal: McGill-Queen's University Press, 2013.

Ocobock, Paul. *Uncertain Age: The Politics of Manhood in Kenya*. Athens, OH: Ohio University Press, 2017.

Ouzgane, Lahoucine and Robert Morrell, eds. *African Masculinities: Men in Africa from the Late Nineteenth Century to the Present*. London: Palgrave Macmillan, 2005.

Oyěwùmí, Oyèrónkẹ́. *The Invention of Women: Making an African Sense of Western Gender Discourses*. Minneapolis, MN: University of Minnesota Press, 1997.

Plageman, Nate. "The African Personality Dances Highlife: Popular Music, Urban Youth, and Cultural Modernization in Nkrumah's Ghana, 1957–1965." In *Modernization as Spectacle in Africa*, edited by Peter J. Bloom, Stephan F. Miescher and Takyiwaa Manuh, 244–267. Bloomington, IN: Indiana University Press, 2014.

Pollard, Lisa. *Nurturing the Nation: The Family Politics of Modernizing, Colonizing, and Liberating Egypt, 1805–1923*. Oakland, CA: University of California Press, 2005.

Ray, Carina. *Crossing the Color Line: Race, Sex, and the Contested Politics of Colonialism in Ghana*. Athens, OH: Ohio University Press, 2015.

Razy, Elodie and Marie Rodet, eds. *Children on the Move in Africa: Past & Present Experiences of Migration*. Melton, UK: James Currey, 2016.

Saddock, Musa. "Government and the Control of Venereal Disease in Colonial Tanzania, 1920–60." In *The Sexual History of the Global South: Sexual Politics in Africa, Asia, and Latin America*, edited by Saskia Wieringa and Horacio Sivori, 83–98. London: Zed Books, 2013.

Schmidt, Heike. "Colonial Intimacy: The Rechenberg Scandal and Homosexuality in German East Africa." *Journal of the History of Sexuality* 17, no. 1 (2008): 25–59. doi:10.1353/sex.2008.0011.

Semley, Lorelle. *To Be Free and French: Citizenship in France's Atlantic Empire*. Cambridge, UK: Cambridge University Press, 2017. doi:10.1017/9781316181669.

Shadle, Brett. *"Girl Cases": Marriage and Colonialism in Gusiiland, Kenya, 1890–1970*. Portsmouth, UK: Heinemann, 2006.

Sheriff, Abdul. "*Suria*: Concubine or Secondary Slave Wife? The Case of Zanzibar in the Nineteenth Century." In *Sex, Power, and Slavery*, edited by Gwyn Campbell and Elizabeth Elbourne, 99–120. Athens, OH: Ohio University Press, 2014.

Shostak, Marjorie. *Nisa: The Life and Words of a !Kung Woman*. Cambridge, MA: Harvard University Press, 1981.

Sigal, Pete, Zeb Tortorici and Neil L. Whitehead, eds. *Ethno-Pornography: Sexuality, Colonialism, and Archival Knowledge*. Durham, NC: Duke University Press, 2020.

Stockreiter, Elke E. *Islamic Law, Gender, and Social Change in Post-Abolition Zanzibar*. Cambridge, UK: Cambridge University Press, 2015. doi:10.1017/CBO9781107261440.

Tamale, Sylvia. *African Sexualities: A Reader*. Nairobi: Pambazuka Press, 2011.

Thomas, Lynn. *The Politics of the Womb: Women, Reproduction and the State in Kenya*. Oakland, CA: University of California Press, 2003.

Thomas, Lynn. "Schoolgirl Pregnancies, Letter-Writing, and 'Modern' Persons in Late Colonial East Africa." In *African Hidden Histories: Everyday Literacy and Making the Self*, edited by Karin Barber, 180–207. Bloomington, IN: Indiana University Press, 2006.

Thomas, Lynn. "The Modern Girl and Racial Respectability in 1930s South Africa," *Journal of African History* 47 (2006): 461–490. doi:10.1017/S0021853706002131.

Thornberry, Elizabeth. *Colonizing Consent: Rape and Governance in South Africa's Eastern Cape*. Cambridge, UK: Cambridge University Press, 2019. doi:10.1017/9781108659284.

Uchendu, Egodi. *Masculinities in Contemporary Africa*. Dakar: Council for the Development of Social Science Research in Africa (CODESRIA), 2008.

Vaughan, Megan. *Curing Their Ills: Colonial Power and African Illness*. Palo Alto, CA: Stanford University Press, 1991.

Walther, Daniel J. *Sex and Control: Venereal Disease, Colonial Physicians, and Indigenous Agency in German Colonialism, 1884–1914*. New York: Berghahn Books, 2015.

White, Luise. *Comforts of Home: Prostitution in Colonial Nairobi*. Chicago, IL: University of Chicago Press, 1990.

White, Owen. *Children of the French Empire: Miscegenation and Colonial Society in French West Africa, 1895–1960*. Oxford, UK: Clarendon Press, 1999.

Wieringa, Saskia and Horacio Sívori, eds. *The Sexual History of the Global South: Sexual Politics in Africa, Asia, and Latin America*. London: Zed Books, 2013.

Zabus, Chantal. *Out in Africa: Same-Sex Desire in Sub-Saharan Literatures & Cultures*. Melton, UK: James Currey, 2013.

4

ON ENDLESS EMPIRES

Sexuality and colonialism in the Middle East and North Africa

Susanna Ferguson and Seçil Yılmaz

The study of sexuality is as vital to understanding governance and power in the Ottoman and other early modern Muslim empires as it is in the nation-states of the modern Middle East. The study of these regions likewise poses important questions for the comparative study of sexuality and empire. Because the Ottomans ruled both as an ascendant early modern Muslim empire and a nineteenth-century colonial power, the Ottoman experience brings continuities and ruptures between these two forms of expansionist governance into stark relief. Likewise, the study of sexuality reveals important continuities between the workings of power under imperial rule and the rule of semi- and postcolonial nation-states. For the Middle East, then, sexuality remains a crucial domain for understanding that imperial and colonial power are by no means things of the past.

Sex and desire in early modern Muslim empires

Beginning in the sixteenth century, Muslim empires—Ottomans, Mughals, and Safavids— governed territories stretching from the Balkans to South Asia. As western European states struggled to survive dynastic rivalries and religious wars, Muslim sovereigns largely maintained religious hegemony and kept their ruling dynasties intact. Until the eighteenth century brought the rise of mercantilist nation-states and an international market economy in western Europe, the early modern Muslim empires stood as examples of enduring imperial sovereignty from "the Balkans to Bengal."[1] The Ottoman empire was the most durable of the early modern Muslim empires, and its success in governing vast territories for more than six centuries poses intellectual and methodological questions for the study of sexuality and empire.

Some scholars have located explanations for the Ottomans' longevity in the sexual politics of the royal palace. Leslie Peirce's seminal study, *The Imperial Harem* (1993), demonstrated that, contrary to Orientalist depictions of the harem as an exotic space of desire and fantasy, the harem was in fact the ultimate royal office, where the power of the Sultan's mother (*valide sultan*) and other women was brought to bear on the all-important politics of reproduction and succession at the Ottoman court.[2] Thus the sexual politics of the Ottoman imperial household, governed by the principle of female seniority, were an essential element of empire-making in the early modern Ottoman world.[3] In the early modern Ottoman empire the enslavement of non-Muslim women as well as men of African descent and their incorporation into royal households as concubines and eunuchs likewise reveals how critical the politics of sex—in this case enmeshed with those of race and religion—were to the making of elite classes and imperial power.[4] Until their abolition in the early twentieth century, practices of enslavement and harem politics helped to regulate imperial succession and bolster imperial power.[5]

By depicting the sexual politics of "the East" as a location of vice, fantasy, and immorality, Orientalist writings from the nineteenth and early twentieth centuries largely obscured not only sexuality's role in empire-making but also its relationship to ethics and morality within the frameworks of Islamic and customary law. There were methodological questions at stake, too. For historians, a lack of primary sources made it difficult to unearth the social characteristics and narratives of sexual lives and led scholars to rely on literary sources.[6] Starting in the 1970s, historical scholarship began to confront these misconceptions and methodological challenges. Historians of sexuality working on early modern Muslim societies developed a broad base of primary sources[7] to overcome stereotypes of sexuality in the region as either wild and uncontrolled, or completely dominated by men and religious authorities.[8] Fatima Mernissi's *Beyond the Veil* (1975), Abdelwahab Bouhdiba's *La sexualité en Islam* (1975), and Edward Said's *Orientalism* (1978) brought new approaches to the history of sexuality in what began to be called "Islamicate" contexts.[9] By examining the spatial boundaries that defined male–female contact (Mernissi), exploring the implications of heterosexual marriage in the foundation of Islam (Bouhdiba), and identifying the construction of an "ontological and epistemological distinction" between "West" and "East" as a technique of imperial power (Said), these authors confronted normative and anachronistic readings of sexuality in the Middle East and the broader Muslim world.[10] Together these works reframed available sources such as religious and legal texts and literary narratives through new tools such as feminist theory and literary criticism.

In the 1990s and 2000s these revisionist approaches, alongside the growing influence of women's and gender studies, inspired scholars to re-examine legal texts such as fatwa collections and court records to shed new light on the history of women, gender, and family in the early modern Islamicate world.[11] While these historians largely worked within the borders of modern nation-states, the legal texts that formed the basis for their analyses also suggested the importance of centuries of innovation and continuity in legal traditions and imperial practices across the Ottoman and broader Islamicate worlds. Feminist approaches to court records of marriages, divorces, custody claims, and sexual violence unearthed a wealth of social–historical insight, not only about women's lives but about femininity, masculinity, and the politics of reproduction and the family. These studies provided striking evidence of the centrality of sex and reproduction in Islamicate societies, illuminating, for example, married women's property rights and instances of divorce due to male impotence. This literature also suggested two concrete problems for writing the history of sexuality through legal sources: first, court records were predominantly partial summaries of cases, offering little opportunity to trace narratives or characters over time[12]; and, second, because the courts used "man" and "woman" as central categories, their records provided scant evidence about non-conforming sexual practices and non-heterosexual forms of life.[13] In response to these challenges, Elyse Semerdjian has argued that same-sex relations do appear in court records under particular historical conditions. Her research shows that Aleppo's *sharia* courts prosecuted same-sex practices among men under the aegis of extra-marital sex (*zina*) after the rise of the conservative Kadızadeli movement in the seventeenth century.[14]

Given the difficulty of locating sexuality in legal sources, others turned to cultural, literary, and aesthetic material to shed light on the non-binary and dynamic characteristics of early modern sexuality. Afsaneh Najamabdi's study of Qajar aesthetics (2005) and Andrews and Kalpakh's work on early modern Ottoman poetry (2005) analyzed genres in which young, beardless men, rather than women, represented the pre-eminent objects of sexual desire within elite literary, artistic, and cultural production.[15] Along similar lines, Khaled el-Rouayheb's *Before Homosexuality in the Arab-Islamic World, 1500–1800* (2005) argued that the term "homosexuality" itself is insufficient to grasp both the nature of sexual expression and the legal implications of same-sex eroticism in early modern Arabic-speaking societies. According to el-Rouayheb, while Islamic legal thinkers between the sixteenth and nineteenth centuries condemned anal intercourse between men (*liwāt*), they regarded affective exchange between male lovers through poetry and artistic expression "as less serious transgressions."[16] While legal and literary studies largely staged elite and middle-class narratives of sexual practice, Dror Ze'evi's *Producing Desire* (2006) demonstrated the potential of reading literary, medical, legal, and performative "scripts" together to assemble a broader history of sexuality.[17] Ze'evi's study used medical texts, Sufi poetry, dream interpretation, shadow theater, and travelogues to shed light on the sexual universes of ordinary inhabitants of early modern Ottoman cities. More recent studies have opened up the social history of same-sex practices by imagining desire as a spatial phenomenon, scrutinizing what "homosociality" entailed and how it shaped queer lives in early modern Muslim societies. For example, Serkan Delice demonstrated that eighteenth-century public baths were a meeting-place for male lovers as well as spaces of male prostitution; the regulation of public baths might suggest an eagerness among Ottoman administrators to constrain and control sexual practices among men.[18]

Delice's work on eighteenth-century bathhouses fruitfully complicates a narrative of European-inspired nineteenth-century transformation established by scholars, including Ze'evi and Najmabadi, who argued that emerging European critiques of homoeroticism, translated into Islamicate contexts by both Orientalists and local reformers, made non-heteronormative desires appear incompatible with modernity. While the reception of European sexual anxieties in the nineteenth-century Islamicate world undoubtedly played a role in the rise of heterosexual norms and state surveillance of sexuality, future research might usefully follow Delice's lead in looking beyond European influence to highlight the roles of local and regional contexts in the emergence of modern regimes of sex and gender.

Writing the history of sexuality in early modern Muslim societies has not merely entailed discovering new sources and challenging Orientalist narratives. It has also often served as the stage for a debate characterizing pre-modern Islamicate sexualities as either "more perverse" or "more liberated" than sexual mores in early modern Europe or in the Middle East today. Indeed, the shift between early modern and modern sexual mores in the Islamicate world, as elsewhere, seems to have silenced a multiplicity of sexual practices and expressions in favor of an increasingly disciplinary and binary modernity.[19] It is to that complex transition that we now turn.

High colonialism (1798–1946)

The eighteenth century brought the rise of mercantilist nation-states and a global market economy in western Europe; these factors, alongside Napoleon's brief but spectacular invasion of Egypt in 1798, inaugurated a shift from the hegemony of the early modern Muslim empires to the era of high colonialism in the Middle East. Between 1798 and the end of World War II, British, French, Italian, and—until 1922—Ottoman empires brought new lands, markets, and domains of life under their control. This age of imperial expansion overlapped with the emergence of nation-making projects, which also sought to capture lands and revenues, organize populations, and remake social and intimate life. As sovereignty began to depend not only on territory but also on population, both modern empires and nation-states adopted sexuality, family, and reproduction as key arenas for intervention.[20]

Scholarship on the modern Middle East and North Africa has produced an expansive understanding of colonialism, arguing that the Ottomans acted as a colonial power alongside the British and the French.[21] But what was Ottoman colonialism? Scholars have identified as "colonial" various aspects of nineteenth-century Ottoman rule, showing that Ottomans—like their European counterparts—sought to expand territorial control over people who didn't want them there,[22] to differentiate center from periphery in temporal, ethnic, or cultural terms,[23] and to justify interventions by promising (however hollowly) to "civilize" those peripheries.[24] Others focused on what differentiated Ottoman from European colonialism, noting that the forms of difference understood to separate Ottoman center from periphery were considered bridgeable over time, rather than innate.[25]

Scholarship on European imperial expansion in the Arab world showed how colonialism entailed not only territorial control and resource extraction but the imposition of systems of power and knowledge based on binary categories: colonizer/colonized, modernity/tradition, secular/religious, and East/West. More recent scholarship has complicated the association between colonial power and binary categories by identifying a "triangular" relationship between British, Ottomans, and Egyptians in the twice-colonized Sudan[26] and emphasizing that colonialism in the Levant involved the "constant negotiation of power relationships and identities" among colonial administrators, subjects, and local elites.[27] Others have focused on colonialism's material aspects; for example, the extraordinary power of a dual (foreign and indigenous) elite over the Egyptian bureaucracy in the late nineteenth century.[28] Another line of inquiry has shown how Middle Eastern state-building projects adopted practices of surveillance, coercion, revenue monopolization, and discipline similar to those wielded by European and Ottoman colonial enterprises.[29] For these states, too, sexuality, family, and gender were central to consolidating power.[30]

Debates about sexuality, intimacy, gender, and desire have enriched the exploration of colonial power in the Middle East. In the 1970s and 1980s, Arab feminists such as Nawal El Saadawi and Fatima Mernissi began to investigate histories of sexuality, gender, and body in the Islamic tradition and the modern Middle East.[31] Starting in the 1980s, social histories like Judith Tucker's *Women in Nineteenth-Century Egypt* (1985) tracked transformations in non-elite women's lives in the colonial period.[32] Challenging the idea that women's oppression results from a monolithic, ahistorical "Islam," Leila Ahmad's *Women, Gender, and Islam* (1992) argued that more careful attention to historical contexts—especially colonial contexts—can help us to understand the resilience of patriarchy in the Middle East, as elsewhere.[33]

In the early 2000s two works connected gender and sexuality more plainly to colonialism in the Middle East. Elizabeth Thompson's *Colonial Citizens* (2000) adopted gender as both analytic tool and object of study to understand the formation of a colonial civic order in mandate Syria and Lebanon in the face of a "crisis of paternity" after World War I. That order was one in which elite, male Syrian and Lebanese intermediaries would manage workers, women, and the pious for the French, in return for keeping their power over other citizens. Eve Troutt Powell's *A Different Shade of Colonialism* (2003) identified sexuality and race as central nodes for the operation of Egyptian colonial power in the Sudan. As Egyptian intellectuals and administrators identified Nubian sexuality as excessive, they helped to create an "other" to define the good Egyptian nation.

In addition to these works, a formidable body of scholarship has demonstrated the ongoing centrality of childrearing and reproduction to the colonial encounter and the emergence of the modern state. Scholars have shown, for example, how both British colonial administrators and Egyptian elites associated Egypt's perceived civilizational backwardness with the status of its women, shared concerns about the invisibility of "the harem," and attempted to reform Egyptian family life to better police the population.[34] Together, as Deniz Kandiyoti has written, these works suggested that "underlying reformers' and polemicists' writings on the modern family, monogamy, and educated mothers and housewives [… was] a new regulatory discourse on sexuality that attempt[ed] to institutionalize monogamous heterosexuality as the normative ideal."[35] The new heterosexual ideal helped to forge emerging national collectives, authorize forms of racial and class difference, and shape the practices of colonial elites as well as anti-colonial and subaltern actors.[36]

What did this ideal replace, and to what effects? Lila Abu-Lughod's edited volume, *Remaking Women: Feminism and Modernity in the Modern Middle East* (1998), provided some clues. Contributors showed, for example, how modern medical training, sometimes administered by force, delegitimized pre-existing networks of midwives[37], and modern norms of domesticity fractured homosocial networks and isolated women within a newly demarcated private sphere.[38] Afsaneh Najmabadi's *Women With Mustaches and Men Without Beards* (2005) pushed still further, showing how the emergence of heterosexuality as the dominant norm in late nineteenth-century Iran erased the figure of the *amrad*, or sexually desirable adolescent male, from public consciousness even as the shadow of that figure haunted understandings of love, homeland, and citizenship long into the twentieth century.[39] Najmabadi subsequently raised key questions for the study of sexuality in the Middle East based on that research: to what extent does posing questions about other times and places in terms of now-stable categories of "gender" (often understood as masculinity/femininity) and "sexuality" (often understood as homo/heterosexual) limit the kinds of answers we can formulate?[40] The implications of this question bear further exploration, although Najmabadi's own subsequent work on the history of transsexuality in twentieth-century Iran offered powerful evidence that "sexuality" is neither a universal nor stable analytic concept.[41]

Published the same year as Najmabadi's *Women With Mustaches*, Joseph Massad's *Desiring Arabs* (2005) questioned the universality of sexual concepts and categories in a more polemical fashion. The book analyzed texts about sex and sexuality by Arab writers of the nineteenth and twentieth centuries, who examined the sexual practices of the Arab classical past to serve a variety of ends. Following Said, Massad showed how the modern study of "sexuality in the Arab world" began as a product of the colonial encounter, as Europeans and Arabs alike came to believe that sexual practices were evidence of "civilizational worth" or lack thereof.[42] Extending this argument into the contemporary period, Massad controversially identified a "Gay International" of mainly Euro-American NGO and activist networks that "both produces homosexuals, as well as gays and lesbians, where they do not exist, and represses same-sex desires and practices that refuse to be assimilated into its sexual epistemology."[43]

New directions

Exciting new directions are emerging in the study of sexuality and colonialism in the Middle East. Hanan Hammad's *Industrial Sexuality* (2016) followed Wilson Chacko Jacob's *Working Out Egypt* (2011) in addressing masculinity. Hammad's study also raised critical questions about the political economy of sexuality and gender, asking how changing regimes of production, labor migration, and urbanization shaped sex, intimacy, family, and reproduction in twentieth-century Egypt.[44] Liat Kozma's *Global Women, Colonial Ports* (2017) traced the history of prostitutes, regulators, and procurers in the Mediterranean to show how colonial power mediated the global mobility of people, practices, and ideas between the two World Wars—and how the problem of prostitution likewise structured international norms and institutions.[45] Kozma's work on the history of sexology in Arabic and Hebrew and Omnia El Shakry's *The Arabic Freud* (2017) have added much to our understanding of the scientific study of sex in the Arab world; future work might further counter arguments about the modern silencing of sex by showing how older forms of sex talk and practice were translated into new registers in the modern period.[46] Taking a different tack, Marie Grace Brown's *Khartoum at Night* (2017) beautifully examined bodily practice to show how women's bodies were sites for fashioning not only sexualities and selves but also communities, institutions, and the experience of empire in Sudan.[47] Jasbir Puar's *Terrorist Assemblages* (2007) posed key questions about the transnational co-constitution of affect, sexuality, and race in the age of American empire.[48] More recently, anthropologist Maya Mikdashi and literary scholar Tarik El-Ariss have proposed that queer and affect studies might allow us to ask new questions about citizenship, colonialism, and sexuality.[49] How, Mikdashi asks, could queer studies' uncoupling of gender and sex challenge other presumed unities, such as that linking sect, faith, and citizenship in modern Lebanon? What would colonialism look like, wonders El-Ariss, if we approached it as a somatic experience? Finally, work on settler colonialism and pinkwashing in Israel/Palestine and on America's relationships with Gulf oil monarchies reminds us that, in the Middle East, colonialism and empire are features not only of the past but of the present: sexual politics, as Gil Hochberg has put it, remain "essential for our understandings of national movements, colonial oppression, new technologies of state surveillance, and new modes of racial/ethnic/religious segregation" today.[50]

Conclusion

Over the past 50 years scholarship on sexuality and empire in the Middle East has developed in conversation with the study of similar questions in other world regions. Thus many of the phenomena charted here may prove familiar to scholars of colonialism elsewhere. Among these commonalities are, for example, the importance of sexuality, governmentality, and population regulation to colonial projects; the role of heterosexuality in shaping modern state power; and the seductive appeal of recovering pre-modern sexual worlds as evidence of a past either "more diverse" or "more perverse" than the modern (hetero)sexual landscape.

The unique temporality of empire in Ottoman and post-Ottoman contexts, however, raises useful questions for the comparative history of sexuality and power. Because the Ottomans were both an early modern and a modern empire, Ottoman history highlights differences and similarities between these two geopolitical moments and governance regimes. Likewise, research on settler colonialism and American interests in the region suggests that empire and colonialism are hardly things of the past—indeed, as contemporary conflicts in Yemen and Syria attest, new actors are entering the field. In light of these observations, it may be fruitful to look for alternative regional and comparative categories. It was nineteenth-century imperial geographies, after all, that produced not only the concept of a "Middle East" but the binary of East and West that still haunts questions about the uniqueness (or lack thereof) of Middle Eastern relationships to sexuality and power in comparison to European counterparts. New turns in the scholarship—toward the transnational circulation of sexual science; the global political economy of sex work; and the role of sexuality and reproduction in contemporary politics—are beginning to look beyond that binary. Instead, they point toward new frameworks for studying sexuality that complicate the explanatory and categorizing potential of old imperial borders.

Notes

1 Ahmed, *What Is Islam?*, 32.
2 Peirce, *The Imperial Harem*.
3 Ibid., 24; Peirce, "Seniority, Sexuality, and Social Order."
4 Fay, *Unveiling the Harem*, 148–149; Hathaway, *The Chief Eunuch of the Ottoman Harem,* 34–38.
5 Toledano, "Ottoman Concepts of Slavery in the Period of Reform, 1830s–1880s."
6 Peirce, "Writing Histories of Sexuality in the Middle East"; Ze'evi, *Producing Desire*.
7 Peirce, "Writing Histories of Sexuality in the Middle East," 1325.
8 Semerdjian, "Rewriting the History of Sexuality in the Islamic World."
9 Said, *Orientalism*; Mernissi, *Beyond the Veil*; Bouhdiba, *La Sexualité en Islam*. On the "Islamicate," see Babayan and Najmabadi, eds., *Islamicate Sexualities*.
10 Said, *Orientalism*, 2–3.
11 Tucker, *In the House of the Law*; Peirce, *Morality Tales*; Semerdjian, *"Off the Straight Path."*
12 Heather Ferguson has argued that court documents are themselves performative and are not straightforward representations of historical reality. See Ferguson, "Property, Language and Law."
13 Semerdjian, "'Because he is so tender.'"
14 Ibid., 177. Sarah Ghabrial has likewise used court records to study marriage, sexuality, medicine, and femininity in colonial Algeria. See Ghabrial, "The Traumas and Truths of the Body."
15 Andrews and Kalpaklı, *The Age of Beloveds*; Stephen Murray refers to these figures as "third gender." See Murray and Roscoe, *Islamic Homosexualities*, 56.
16 El-Rouayheb, *Before Homosexuality in the Arab-Islamic World*.
17 Ze'evi, *Producing Desire*, 12–15.
18 Delice, "The Janissaries and their bedfellows."
19 Ze'evi, *Producing Desire*, 169–170.
20 Foucault, "Governmentality."
21 Minawi, *The Ottoman Scramble for Africa*; Deringil, "'They Live in a State of Nomadism and Savagery'"; Mikhail and Philliou, "The Ottoman Empire and the Imperial Turn," 724–725.
22 Deringil, "'They Live in a State of Nomadism and Savagery.'"
23 Makdisi, "Ottoman Orientalism."
24 Ibid., 782–783; Kuehn, *Empire, Islam, and Politics of Difference*.
25 Kuehn, *Empire, Islam, and Politics of Difference*.
26 Powell, *A Different Shade of Colonialism*.
27 Thompson, *Colonial Citizens*, 1.
28 Cole, *Colonialism & Revolution in the Middle East*.
29 Fahmy, *All the Pasha's Men*.
30 Kozma, *Policing Egyptian Women*.
31 See *inter alia* El Saadawi, *The Hidden Face of Eve*; Mernissi, *Beyond the Veil*.
32 Tucker, *Women in Nineteenth-Century Egypt*; Zilfi, ed., *Women in the Ottoman Empire*; Smith, *Mediterraneans*.
33 Ahmed, *Women and Gender in Islam*.
34 Mitchell, *Colonising Egypt*, esp. 111; Pollard, *Nurturing the Nation*.
35 Kandiyoti, "Some Awkward Questions on Women and Modernity in Turkey," 284. On anti-colonial literary politics that challenged heteronormative nationalisms, see Hayes, *Queer Nations*.
36 Baron, *Egypt as a Woman*.
37 Fahmy, "Women, Medicine, and Power in Nineteenth-Century Egypt." Balsoy has complicated this for the Ottoman case, arguing that midwives also benefited from state recognition. See Balsoy, *The Politics of Reproduction*.
38 Najmabadi, "Crafting an Educated Housewife in Iran." Elsewhere, Najmabadi suggested that the new private sphere sanitized women's erotic expression. See Najmabadi, "Veiled Discourse–Unveiled Bodies."
39 Najmabadi, *Women with Mustaches and Men without Beards*.

40 Najmabadi. "Beyond the Americas."
41 Najmabadi, *Professing Selves.*
42 Massad, *Desiring Arabs*, 49.
43 Ibid., 163.
44 Hammad, *Industrial Sexuality*; Jacob, *Working Out Egypt.*
45 Kozma, *Global Women, Colonial Ports.* Camila Pastor has also written on the history of women prostitutes and performers in mandate Syria and Lebanon. See Pastor, "Performers or Prostitutes?"
46 Kozma, "'We, the Sexologists …'"; Kozma, "Sexology in the Yishuv"; El Shakry, *The Arabic Freud.*
47 Brown, *Khartoum at Night.*
48 Puar, *Terrorist Assemblages.*
49 Mikdashi, "Queering Citizenship, Queering Middle East Studies," 350–352; El-Ariss, *Trials of Arab Modernity.*
50 Vitalis, *America's Kingdom*; Hochberg, "Introduction."

Bibliography

Ahmed, Leila. *Women and Gender in Islam: Historical Roots of a Modern Debate.* New Haven, CT: Yale University Press, 1992.

Ahmed, Shahab. *What Is Islam?: the Importance of Being Islamic.* Princeton, NJ: Princeton University Press, 2015.

Andrews, Walter G. and Mehmet Kalpaklı. *The Age of Beloveds: Love and the Beloved in Early-Modern Ottoman and European Culture and Society.* Durham, NC: Duke University Press, 2005.

Babayan, Kathryn and Afsaneh Najmabadi, eds. *Islamicate Sexualities: Translations across Temporal Geographies of Desire.* Cambridge, MA: Center for Middle Eastern Studies of Harvard University, 2008.

Balsoy, Gülhan. *The Politics of Reproduction in Ottoman Society, 1838–1900.* London: Routledge, 2013.

Baron, Beth. *Egypt as a Woman: Nationalism, Gender, and Politics.* Berkeley, CA: University of California Press, 2007.

Bouhdiba, Abdelwahab. *La Sexualité en Islam.* Paris: Presses universitaires de France, 1975.

Brown, Marie Grace. *Khartoum at Night: Fashion and Body Politics in Imperial Sudan.* Stanford, CA: Stanford University Press, 2017.

Clancy-Smith, Julia Ann. *Mediterraneans: North Africa and Europe in an Age of Migration, c.1800–1900.* Berkeley, CA: University of California Press, 2011.

Cole, Juan. *Colonialism & Revolution in the Middle East: Social and Cultural Origins of Egypt's 'Urabi Movement.* Cairo: American University in Cairo Press, 1999.

Cuno, Kenneth. *Modernizing Marriage: Family, Ideology, and Law in Nineteenth- and Early Twentieth-Century Egypt.* New York: Syracuse University Press, 2015.

De Maria Campos and Camila Pastor. "Performers or Prostitutes? Artistes during the French Mandate over Syria and Lebanon, 1921–1946." *Journal of Middle East Women's Studies* 13, no. 2 (July 2017): 287–311. doi:10.1215/15525864-3861312.

Delice, Serkan. "The Janissaries and their bedfellows: Masculinity and male friendship in eighteenth-century Ottoman Istanbul." In *Gender and Sexuality in Muslim Cultures*, edited by Gul Ozyegin, 115–136. Farnham, UK: Ashgate, 2015.

Demirci, Tuba and Selcuk Somel. "Women's Bodies, Demography, and Public Health: Abortion Policy and Perspectives in the Ottoman Empire of the Nineteenth Century." *Journal of the History of Sexuality* 17, no. 3 (2008): 377–420. doi:10.1353/sex.0.0025.

Deringil, Selim. "'They Live in a State of Nomadism and Savagery': The Late Ottoman Empire and the Post-Colonial Debate." *Comparative Studies in Society and History* 45, no. 2 (2003): 311–342. doi:10.1017/S001041750300015X.

El-Ariss, Tarek. *Trials of Arab Modernity: Literary Affects and the New Political.* New York: Fordham University Press, 2013.

El-Rouayheb, Khaled. *Before Homosexuality in the Arab-Islamic World, 1500–1800.* Chicago, IL: University of Chicago Press, 2005.

El Saadawi, Nawal. *The Hidden Face of Eve: Women in the Arab World*, translated by Sherif Hatata. London: Zed Books, 1982.

El Saadawi, Nawal. *Women at Point Zero*, translated by Sherif Hatata. London: Zed Books, 1983.

El Shakry, Omnia S. *The Great Social Laboratory: Subjects of Knowledge in Colonial and Postcolonial Egypt.* Stanford, CA: Stanford University Press, 2007.

El Shakry, Omnia S. *The Arabic Freud: Psychoanalysis and Islam in Modern Egypt.* Princeton, NJ: Princeton University Press, 2017.

Fahmy, Khaled. *All the Pasha's Men: Mehmed Ali, His Army and the Making of Modern Egypt.* Cairo: The American University in Cairo Press, 2010.

Fahmy, Khaled. "Women, Medicine, and Power in Nineteenth-Century Egypt." In *Remaking Women: Feminism and Modernity in the Middle East*, edited by Lila Abu-Lughod, 35–72. Princeton, NJ: Princeton University Press, 1998.

Fay, Mary Ann. *Unveiling the Harem: Elite Women and the Paradox of Seclusion in Eighteenth-Century Cairo.* Syracuse, NY: Syracuse University Press, 2012.

Ferguson, Heather. "Property, Language and Law: Conventions of a Social Discourse in Seventeenth-Century Tarablus al-Sham." In *Family History in the Middle East: Household, Property, and Gender*, edited by Beshara Doumani, 229–244. Albany, NY: State University of New York Press, 2003.

Foucault, Michel. "Governmentality." In *The Foucault Effect: Studies in Governmentality*, edited by Graham Burchell, Colin Gordon and Peter Miller, 87–104. Chicago, IL: University of Chicago Press, 1991.

Ghabrial, Sarah. "The Traumas and Truths of the Body: Medical Evidence and Divorce in Colonial Algerian Courts." *Journal of Middle East Women's Studies* 11, no. 3 (2015): 283–305. doi:10.1215/15525864-3142438.

Graham-Brown, Sarah. *Images of Women: The Portrayal of Women in Photography of the Middle East, 1860–1950.* New York: Columbia University Press, 1988.

Hammad, Hanan. *Industrial Sexuality: Gender, Urbanization, and Social Transformation in Egypt.* Austin, TX: University of Texas Press, 2016.

Hayes, Jarrod. *Queer Nations: Marginal Sexualities in the Maghreb.* Chicago, IL: University of Chicago Press, 2000.

Hochberg, Gil. "Introduction: Israelis, Palestinians, Queers: Points of Departure." *GLQ: A Journal of Lesbian and Gay Studies* 16, no. 4 (2010): 493–516. doi:10.1215/10642684-2010-001.

Jacob, Wilson Chacko. *Working Out Egypt: Effendi Masculinity and Subject Formation in Colonial Modernity, 1870–1940.* Durham, NC: Duke University Press Books, 2011.

Kallander, Amy Aisen. *Women, Gender, and the Palace Households in Ottoman Tunisia.* Austin, TX: University of Texas Press, 2013.

Kandiyoti, Deniz. "Some Awkward Questions on Women and Modernity in Turkey." In *Remaking Women: Feminism and Modernity in the Middle East*, edited by Lila Abu-Lughod, 270–287. Princeton, NJ: Princeton University Press, 1998.

Khalidi, Rashid. "The 'Middle East' As a Framework of Analysis: Re-Mapping a Region in the Era of Globalization." *Comparative Studies of South Asia, Africa and the Middle East* 18, no. 1 (May 1998): 74–81. doi:10.1215/1089201X-18-1-74.

Kozma, Liat. "Sexology in the Yishuv: The Rise and Decline of Sexual Consultation in Tel Aviv, 1930–39." *International Journal of Middle East Studies* 42, no. 2 (2010): 231–249. doi:10.1017/S002074381000003.

Kozma, Liat. *Policing Egyptian Women: Sex, Law, and Medicine in Khedival Egypt.* Syracuse, NY: Syracuse University Press, 2011.

Kozma, Liat. "'We, the Sexologists …': Arabic Medical Writing on Sexuality, 1879–1943." *Journal of the History of Sexuality* 22, no. 3 (2013): 426–444. doi:10.7560/JHS22303.

Kozma, Liat *Global Women, Colonial Ports: Prostitution in the Interwar Middle East.* Albany, NY: SUNY Press, 2017.

Lockman, Zachary. *Field Notes: The Making of Middle East Studies in the United States.* Stanford, CA: Stanford University Press, 2016.

Makdisi, Ussama "Ottoman Orientalism." *The American Historical Review* 107, no. 3 (2002): 768–796. doi:10.1086/ahr/107.3.768.

Massad, Joseph. *Desiring Arabs.* Chicago, IL: University of Chicago Press, 2005.

Mernissi, Fatima. *Beyond the Veil: Male-Female Dynamics in a Modern Muslim Society.* Cambridge, MA: Schenkman Publishing, 1975.

Mikdashi, Maya. "Queering Citizenship, Queering Middle East Studies." *International Journal of Middle East Studies* 45, no. 2 (2013): 350–352. doi:10.1017/S0020743813000111.

Mikhail, Alan and Christine M. Philliou. "The Ottoman Empire and the Imperial Turn." *Comparative Studies in Society and History.* 54, no. 4 (2012): 721–745. doi:10.1017/S0010417512000394.

Minawi, Mostafa. *The Ottoman Scramble for Africa: Empire and Diplomacy in the Sahara and the Hijaz*. Stanford, CA: Stanford University Press, 2016.

Mitchell, Timothy. *Colonising Egypt*. Berkeley, CA: University of California Press, 1988.

Murray, Stephen O. and Will Roscoe. *Islamic Homosexualities: Culture, History, and Literature*. New York: New York University Press, 1997.

Najmabadi, Afsaneh "Veiled Discourse–Unveiled Bodies." *Feminist Studies* 19, no. 3 (1993): 487–518. doi:10.2307/3178098.

Najmabadi, Afsaneh. "Crafting an Educated Housewife in Iran." In *Remaking Women: Feminism and Modernity in the Middle East*, edited by Lila Abu-Lughod, 91–125. Princeton, NJ: Princeton University Press, 1998.

Najmabadi, Afsaneh. *Women with Mustaches and Men without Beards: Gender and Sexual Anxieties of Iranian Modernity*. Berkeley, CA: University of California Press, 2005.

Najmabadi, Afsaneh. "Beyond the Americas: Are Gender and Sexuality Useful Categories of Historical Analysis?" *Journal of Women's History* 18, no. 1 (2006): 11–21. doi:10.1353/jowh.2006.0022.

Najmabadi, Afsaneh. *Professing Selves: Transsexuality and Same-Sex Desire in Contemporary Iran*. Durham, NC: Duke University Press, 2013.

Peirce, Leslie P. *The Imperial Harem: Women and Sovereignty in the Ottoman Empire*. New York: Oxford University Press, 1993.

Peirce, Leslie P. "Seniority, Sexuality, and Social Order: The Vocabulary of Gender in Early Modern Ottoman Anatolia." In *Women in the Ottoman Empire: Middle Eastern Women in the Early Modern Era*, edited by Madeline Zilfi, 169–196. Leiden: Brill, 1997.

Peirce, Leslie P. *Morality Tales: Law and Gender in the Ottoman Court of Aintab*. Berkeley, CA: University of California Press, 2003.

Peirce, Leslie P. "Writing Histories of Sexuality in the Middle East." *The American Historical Review* 114, no 5 (2009): 1325–1339. doi:10.1086/ahr.114.5.1325.

Pollard, Lisa. *Nurturing the Nation: The Family Politics of Modernizing, Colonizing, and Liberating Egypt, 1805–1923*. Berkeley, CA: University of California Press, 2005.

Powell, Eve Troutt. *A Different Shade of Colonialism: Egypt, Great Britain, and the Mastery of the Sudan*. Berkeley, CA: University of California Press, 2003.

Puar, Jasbir. *Terrorist Assemblages: Homonationalism in Queer Times*. Durham, NC: Duke University Press, 2007.

Said, Edward W. *Orientalism*. New York: Pantheon Books, 1978.

Semerdjian, Elyse. "Rewriting the History of Sexuality in the Islamic World." *Hawwa* 4, no. 2 (2006): 119–130. doi:10.1163/156920806779152309.

Semerdjian, Elyse. *"Off the Straight Path": Illicit Sex, Law, and Community in Ottoman Aleppo*. Syracuse, NY: Syracuse University Press, 2008.

Semerdjian, Elyse. "'Because he is so tender and pretty': sexual deviance and heresy in eighteenth-century Aleppo." *Social Identities* 18, no. 2 (2012): 175–199. doi:10.1080/13504630.2012.652844.

Thomas Kuehn, *Empire, Islam, and Politics of Difference: Ottoman Rule in Yemen, 1849–1919*. Leiden: Brill, 2011.

Thompson, Elizabeth. *Colonial Citizens: Republican Rights, Paternal Privilege, and Gender in French Syria and Lebanon*. New York: Columbia University Press, 2000.

Tucker, Judith E. *Women in Nineteenth-Century Egypt*. Cambridge, UK: Cambridge University Press, 1985.

Tucker, Judith E. *In the House of the Law: Gender and Islamic Law in Ottoman Syria and Palestine*. Berkeley, CA: University of California Press, 1998.

Vitalis, Robert. *America's Kingdom: Mythmaking on the Saudi Oil Frontier*. Stanford, CA: Stanford University Press, 2006.

Ze'evi, Dror. *Producing Desire: Changing Sexual Discourse in the Ottoman Middle East, 1500–1900*. Berkeley, CA: University of California Press, 2006.

Zilfi, Madeline C., ed. *Women in the Ottoman Empire: Middle Eastern Women in the Early Modern Era*. Leiden: Brill, 1997.

5

SEXUALITY AND THE JAPANESE EMPIRE

A contested history

Aiko Takeuchi-Demirci

The history of sexuality in modern Japan represents the country's complex relationship with Western nations on the one hand and its imperialist ambitions in the Asia-Pacific world on the other. With the establishment of a modern nation-state in the late nineteenth century, known as the Meiji Restoration (*Meiji ishin*), a centralized system of defining and regulating sexuality took shape in Japan. The Japanese government modeled the system after those in Western nations and implemented it in their imperialist endeavors in the Asia-Pacific. Following victories in the Sino–Japanese War (1894–1895), the Russo–Japanese War (1904–1905), and World War I (1914–1918), the Empire of Japan (*Dai-Nippon Teikoku*) expanded its colonial rule over Taiwan, Korea, Okinawa, and the South Pacific islands. After the Manchuria Incident of 1931, the Japanese army further invaded into mainland China, as well as other areas in the Asia-Pacific region, triggering intense battles and conflicts with Western imperial powers that ultimately culminated in World War II. The regulation of the bodies of imperial subjects, especially their sexual and reproductive activities, became integral to the development of the Japanese empire.

The central government aimed to elevate the sexual morality and reproductive fitness of Japanese subjects on the mainland as well as in the colonies to the level of Western nations. The influx of new practices and theories of sexuality from the West in the process of modernization also gave the public opportunities and tools to challenge existing gender and sexual norms and create alternative ones. Indeed, the authorities' increased efforts at controlling people's sexual behaviors and practices triggered a growing—and often uncontainable—resistance and yearning for freedom among the masses. Scholarship on sexuality in modern Japan has highlighted the public and popular discourses on non-heteronormative or non-procreative practices and expressions of sexuality—homosexuality, reproductive control, and (to a lesser extent) interracial sexuality—that flourished during the times of relatively liberal regimes, such as the interwar and the postwar periods. Wartime censorship and suppression drove these unsanctioned forms of sexuality underground, but they re-emerged immediately after World War II, although with different meanings and functions in different political and social contexts.

The sexuality of colonial subjects became the focus of state concern when it came to the issue of prostitution. The Japanese military established an elaborate and extensive system of regulated prostitution throughout the empire in order to protect the sexual wellbeing of Japanese soldiers. Over recent decades, oral history has helped fill the gap in traditional scholarship and uncovered the buried voices and stories of those who became victims of state-sanctioned sexual violence, especially the "comfort women." The alternative history that these figures helped reveal continues to attract political controversy and produce competing narratives over wartime, as well as pre- and postwar, sexuality.

Individual studies of Japanese modern history tend to focus either on the prewar or postwar period, but when we piece these stories together we see a continuing trajectory and development in the history of sexuality. The prewar expressions of transgression and homosexuality and demands for non-procreative sexuality re-emerged and flourished after the demise of the empire. Voices and memories of sexual oppression and exploitation continue to challenge official narratives of the Empire of Japan. Indeed, the struggles over sexuality continue as long as the memories and effects of the empire haunt not only Japan but also its former colonies.

Gender ambiguity, same-sex love, and the *ero-guro* culture

Japan's proclaimed status as an imperial power to civilize and rule the Asia-Pacific region required the government to contain any traces of premodern, "barbarian" sexuality in the metropole. In premodern Japan, gender lines were not as clearly demarcated as in medieval Europe.[1] After the Meiji Restoration of 1868, the government attempted to suppress non-heteronormative sexuality along the lines of Victorian norms of respectability. In order to enforce a "civilized morality," as Gregory Pflugfelder illustrates in his work on male homosexuality, the state sought to criminalize "same-sex love" (*dōsei ai*) as a "barbarian" practice of the premodern past. Mainstream culture also helped marginalize "male–male sexuality" by confining it to the Japanese past, the southwestern region, and the world of adolescence.[2]

Whereas Meiji officials and writers sought to bury same-sex love in the historic past, intellectuals in the early twentieth century soon realized that these practices were thriving in the present, especially in the tide of individualism, liberalism, and cosmopolitanism of the Taishō period (1912–1926). A new generation of psychologists and sexologists influenced by the works of Sigmund Freud, Havelock Ellis, and other European scholars avidly explored and enlightened the public about the "truth of sex." Sexologists now associated same-sex love with the "civilized" West, rather than the "barbarian," premodern Japan, and categorized it as a "disease of civilization" (*bunmeibyō*), much like alcoholism and tuberculosis.[3] Sabine Frühstück's *Colonizing Sex* further illustrates how some sexologists invoked the "liberation of sex" as a modernization project against traditional modes and superstitions. Through public lectures, professional journals, and mass magazines, liberal biologists sought to demystify "deviant" sexual acts, including homosexuality and masturbation, as normal developmental processes of adolescence leading toward adult heteronormative sexuality. The number of books and magazine articles on the issues of sex exploded from the late 1910s until the mid-1930s, when the authorities sharpened their censorship on public morality.[4]

Many contemporary critics, however, still attributed the "feminization of males" and "masculinization of females" to the moral depravity caused by Westernization. While some saw the former as a worrisome condition, as Jennifer Robertson demonstrates, many conservatives almost exclusively directed their fearful anger at the latter. The critics would blame women for compromising the masculinity of males, as they believed the two genders were losing their polarity because women were becoming more masculine. Critics also juxtaposed the "Western Masculinized Female"—the embodiment of social instability and social disorder—with the feminine "Good Wife, Wise Mother" (*ryōsai kenbo*), a symbol of social stability and cultural integrity. The media sensationalized stories of female double suicides, especially those between a "mannish lesbian" and a feminine partner. Conservative psychologists vilified these women who did not conform to the ideal of femininity—the "New Woman" (*atarashii onna*) and the "Mannish Lesbian"—as examples of the worst ramifications of Westernization. They explained the lesbian double suicide as a symptom of neurasthenia, a social and psychological maladjustment to modernity.[5]

While most scholarly studies of the history of sexuality in imperial Japan tend to focus on the (male) regulators of sexuality, some scholars have also shed light on women's defiance and agency. Michiko Suzuki finds lesbian women's defiance expressed in their literary works. In her analysis of the early stories of Yoshiya Nobuko,[6] Suzuki describes the lesbian protagonists as "resistant figures" who rejected "society's demands for girls to mature into compliant, heterosexual Good Wives, Wise Mothers." Instead, the stories portrayed adult same-sex love as "legitimate, permanent, and deserving of acceptance," even though, in the end, it was ultimately condemned and censored in mainstream society.[7]

Even when there was no hint of lesbianism, contemporary critics also saw the "Modern Girl" in the 1920s and 1930s as a threat to the heteronormative model of sexuality. As Barbara Sato illustrates, against the backdrop of the post-World War I rise of consumerism, the Modern Girl—with her signature short, bobbed hair and Western clothes—represented defiance against traditional norms about Japanese women.[8] Miriam Silverberg further challenges the media portrayal of the Modern Girl as promiscuous and an apolitical consumer, equivalent to the Western flapper. By placing the Modern Girl as part of the "erotic grotesque and nonsense" (*ero guro nansensu*) culture that colored the prewar decades, Silverberg describes the Modern Girl as defining her own sexuality and deliberately crossing the societal boundaries of class, gender, and culture. While distinct from the New Women in the organized women's movement, it was nonetheless a mass-based movement of resistance.[9]

The images and lifestyles associated with the Modern Girl—defiant sexuality and seductive consumerism—further flowed into the peripheries of the empire, such as Korea, Taiwan, and Okinawa. With its emphasis on female visuality and sexuality, the Modern Girl in Korea—*modeon geol*—also challenged Korean patriarchy and Confucian morality. Inspired by Japanese women's magazines, the image of modern womanhood proliferated in Korean magazines and newspapers in the 1920s and 1930s. By actively consuming goods and lifestyles from Japan, as Yeon Shim Chung demonstrates, the *modeon geol* "inadvertently participated in Korea's colonial subordination to Japan." While Korean male critics condemned the *modeon geol* trend, the colonial Japanese government tolerated this form of sexual decadence to avoid direct political challenges to Japanese hegemony.[10] Furthermore, Japanese pharmaceutical companies frequently used the image of the Modern Girl—and her supposed promiscuity and sexual backwardness—as an icon of venereal disease to advertise their products to Korean consumers. The Japanese medical industry thus claimed to uplift and save Korean women by selling "the empire's medical/scientific modernity."[11] The Modern Girl gained its adherence even in the remote, agrarian island of Okinawa—far from the centers of urban culture, consumerism, and capitalist growth—mainly through the circulation of mass magazines. The Modern Girl in these peripheries of the Japanese empire came to represent a "colonial modernity" and assimilation into Japanese metropolitan culture through consumption.[12]

Wartime censorship and suppression drove expressions of same-sex love and the *ero-guro* culture underground, although not entirely out of existence. Even though public references to male–male sexuality within the ranks of the military were taboo, for example, Pflug-felder notes that wartime authorities held a "relatively benign stance" toward the subject.[13] Similarly, the government did not find the image of Modern Girl—associated with amusement and decadence—worthy of censorship or regulation, unlike the geisha or café waitresses, who were directly associated with prostitution. Nonetheless, by the beginning of the Pacific War the government strictly censored and outlawed any expressions associated with Western decadence. The *ero guro* culture would reappear after the war, although in a more depoliticized and superficial manner.[14]

During the Allied occupation of Japan (1945–1952), constraints and censorship on public representation of sexuality relaxed somewhat, and commercial publications dealing with sexuality proliferated. While occupation-era censorship had driven sexologists into the realm of popular journals rather than scholarly ones, some of them also worked side by side with the state to "free Japan of the militarist suppression" of sex.[15] At the same time, the Japanese government sought to control and contain the newly liberated sexuality with the help of these sex experts. Just as they tried to suppress prewar expressions of sexual transgression and commercialized sexuality, Japanese leaders and critics worried that the influx of American movies and lifestyles after World War II could exacerbate the loosening of sexual morals among Japanese youth. Thus in 1947 the Ministry of Education established the Council for Purity Education (*Junketsu kyōiku iinkai*), publishing a *Basic Outline of Purity Education* (*Junketsu kyōiku kihon yōkō*) two years later. The *Basic Outline* raised social issues such as the decline of morals, youth delinquency, and the spread of venereal disease and aimed to solve them through "the appropriate and thorough spread of purity education."[16] This initiative was initially linked to the state's concern about private prostitution, specifically the "woman of the night" (*yami no onna*). The occupation's General Headquarters (GHQ) was likely involved in the initiative, as Saitō Hikaru demonstrates, shifting its focus from anti-prostitution to a "wholesome sex education" in the face of the nationwide introduction of coeducation.[17] The GHQ sought to avoid dealing with the issue of prostitution for reasons discussed later in this chapter.

(Non-)procreative sexuality and reproductive control

Beginning in the nineteenth century, the Japanese government's efforts to elevate the educational standards of women to the level of their Western counterparts led to the formation of a new generation of educated, professional women in Meiji Japan. Because women were barred from public speaking and political assemblies, journals and newspapers became the primary means for them to express their political and personal thoughts. The influential feminist journal *Seitō* ("Bluestockings"), launched in 1911, became an important arena where the New Women discussed, challenged, and explored societal ideas about gender and sexuality. Subjects considered taboo appeared on the pages of *Seitō*, including discussions of virginity, abortion, and prostitution. By the 1920s intellectuals also started to discuss the matter of reproductive control. Birth control could potentially liberate women's sexuality from the burden of procreation. However, supporters of the birth control movement in early twentieth-century Japan—liberal intellectuals and feminists—discussed the matter of birth control mostly in relation to other Western-imported theories, such as neo-Mathusianism, socialism, and eugenics, as a solution to Japan's pressing population problem.

Nonetheless, birth control was a radical concept, and nationalist pro-natalists and moral conservatives worried that its spread might lead not only to the degeneration of sexual morals among the youth but also to the negligence of women's reproductive duty. When the American birth control advocate Margaret Sanger first visited Japan in 1922 the Japanese public compared the impact of her visit to Matthew Perry's arrival in 1853, which opened Japan to international trade. Although the birth control movement flourished in Japan in the 1920s, the advocates were soon subjected to censorship and suppression as Japan entered the "15-year" war regime with the military's Manchurian invasion.[18] Under the slogan "Bear and Prosper" (*umeyo fuyaseyo*), the wartime government promoted more births among Japanese subjects both on the mainland and in the colonies. Although the colonial governments also promoted pro-motherhood ideologies, such as the concept of the "Good Wife, Wise Mother," the main concern of the central government was the (declining) birth rate of the Japanese, not that of the colonial subjects.[19]

The military government sought not only to increase the Japanese population but also to improve its quality through the regulation of reproduction. Since the Meiji period, national leaders had found it important to equip women with proper scientific knowledge in health so they would produce stronger children, as Sumiko Sitcawich illustrates in her analysis of eugenic education in the Japan Women's College.[20] The elite women's advocacy for eugenic reproduction found its expression in a petition campaign, led by the New Woman's Association (*Shin-fujin kyōkai*), to urge parliament to pass a bill that would prohibit men with venereal disease from marrying.[21] The efforts of nationalist eugenicists to prevent the propagation of the "unfit"—a loose and broad category of those with both hereditary and non-hereditary conditions, including epilepsy, tuberculosis, alcoholism, and "low intelligence"—culminated in the National Eugenic Law of 1940, which was modeled after the 1933 Nazi sterilization law. Unlike the German law, however, the Japanese government did not enforce compulsory sterilization because it went against its overall pro-natalist position.[22]

However, the essence of the wartime eugenic law lived on—and even reinforced its effectiveness—after World War II. The Eugenic Protection Law, enacted in 1948, "liberalized" restrictions on abortion, sterilization, and birth control.[23] But it was essentially based on the same eugenic standpoint with the goal of national/racial fitness in the face of imperialist competitions. National leaders were especially worried about the survival of the race after the empire had lost its overseas colonies and its subjects were suffering from the consequence of war and defeat. In this context, postwar birth control advocates claimed to spread "proper" knowledge about sex and married life among young couples, with the ultimate goal to rebuild the Japanese race.[24] It was nearly half a century later, in 1994, after feminists and disability-rights activists lobbied for the removal of the eugenic philosophy defining the Eugenic Protection Law, that the government finally renamed it the Maternal Protection Law.[25]

Interracial sexuality and eugenics

Even though interracial intimacy and companionship existed in medieval Japan, mostly in or surrounding the treaty ports, it was not until the Meiji period, in 1873, that the law recognized conventional marriages between Japanese and foreigners.[26] After the opening of the country to foreign trade in 1853, Japanese individuals were also permitted to travel abroad, starting in 1866. Kamoto Itsuko analyzes the link between the repeal of the travel ban (*kaikin*) and the approval of international marriages, which officials had already started to discuss before the Meiji Restoration in 1868. According to Kamoto, there were reportedly 265 cases of international marriages in mainland Japan up until 1899.[27] Eighty per cent of those marriages were between a Japanese female and a non-Japanese male, who typically lived in residential areas exclusively for foreigners (mainly British, Chinese, Germans, and Americans); 20 per cent were between a Japanese male and a foreign female, mostly cases in which the couple met while the Japanese man was studying or traveling abroad, usually in Europe.[28]

Western men's sexual attraction toward Japanese women had been documented well before the legalization of international marriage.[29] The romanticized relationship between a Western man and a Japanese woman was further popularized by the tale of *Madame Butterfly*. Around this time, Westerners who traveled or lived in Japan wrote about Japan, and Japanese goods entered the European/American markets, all of which contributed to the cultural and literary imagery of Orientalism.[30] These early accounts helped form the idea of "Oriental women"— childlike, naïve, submissive, and sexually available—who represented "the escapism of sexual fantasy" of Western men in nineteenth-century culture.[31] Even while Japan was expanding its own empire in Asia, it remained subjected to the imperialist gaze of Western powers.

Compared to the rich Western imaginations on Japanese women's sexuality, we know little about Japanese views on interracial intimacy through existing scholarship. Gary Leupp, in his comprehensive work on interracial intimacy before 1900, offers insight into how Japanese women reacted to Western men during the early period of contact, usually describing the encounter as "disgust" or "terror."[32] Note, however, that most of these accounts are based on the writings of Western men (or, sometimes, Japanese men).

Jennifer Robertson provides a Japanese perspective on the crossing of ethnic boundaries as expressed in popular culture during wartime (1931–1945). In her cultural analysis of the all-female Takarazuka Revue, established in 1913, Robertson links the actors' crossing of gender lines with the crossing of ethnic lines in their theater performances. Just as the female actors performed (idealized) male roles, the Japanese revue actors also took on the roles of "imperial peoples" (*kōmin*)—Taiwanese, Koreans, Chinese, and Micronesians—to represent an idealized Japanese empire under the Greater East Asia Co-Prosperity Sphere (*daitōa kyōeiken*). Robertson illustrates how the revue functioned as a technology of Japanese imperialism by representing the doctrine of assimilation (*dōka*).[33] The military government thus established its role as an anti-colonial colonizer by presenting Japan as the leader and liberator of the Asian race threatened by European and American imperialism.

While the Takarazuka Revue represented "imperial fantasies," the "colonial realities" of race/ethnic mixing were quite different.[34] Influenced by Western genetics and eugenics, Japanese intellectuals have discussed the theories of race mixing since the Meiji period. In 1884 Takahashi Yoshio, disciple of Fukuzawa Yukichi, the famous political theorist and founder of Keio University, published *Nihon jinshu kairyō-ron* (*Improvement of the Japanese Race*). In the book, Takahashi encouraged the Japanese people to marry white Westerners to improve the quality of the race. Others, such as Katō Hiroyuki, opposed such theories, claiming that intermarriage would alter the quality of the race and lead to the extinction of the Japanese.[35] After Japan's annexation of the Korean Peninsula in 1910, scholars and officials debated the matter of inter-ethnic marriage between the Japanese and Koreans. The colonial government presented an assimilation policy and encouraged intermarriage.[36] Some eugenicists, such as Unno Kōtoku, supported this idea, claiming that the Japanese race, as the "superior" one, would eventually absorb the Korean race.[37] However, most eugenicists and officials in the mainland opposed intermarriage, based on the concept of "purity" of the Japanese blood. These eugenicists emphasized the deleterious effects of interracial marriage and warned of it as a factor leading to the demise of the empire, citing the example of the Roman empire.[38]

Interracial marriages expanded during the occupation of Japan after World War II, most visibly between Japanese women and American GIs. After the 1947 amendment to the War Brides Act, Japanese spouses of American military personnel were able to immigrate to the United States. While the majority of these women were engaged in office work inside military bases, or worked as domestic helpers or nurses, some of the brides were originally recruited by the regime to serve the GIs.[39] The American media picked up the war bride phenomenon and the theme soon found its way to Hollywood, as represented in films such as *Japanese War Bride* (1952, directed by King Vidor) and *Sayonara* (1957, directed by Joshua Logan, adapted from the 1953 novel by James Michener). These stories represented variations of the classic Orientalist narrative of *Madame Butterfly* as they portrayed the sacrifice and assimilation of Japanese brides into heterosexual marriage and American (white) domesticity.[40] They also reflected America's Cold War cultural imperative of racial tolerance and international reconciliation.[41] The Japanese women in these stories represented an idealized, domestic femininity; in fact, one magazine assured the American audience that these war brides did not include "prostitutes or criminals."[42]

Despite their presence in public imagery, research into the real Japanese war brides was largely overlooked; only recently have scholars started to shed light on the actual voices and experiences of these brides, who survived discrimination and hardships between two cultures/nations.[43] Yasutomi Shigeyoshi's study, in particular, highlights the different perceptions surrounding war brides in the United States and Japan. The Japanese typically associated these war brides with prostitutes catering to GIs (called *pan-pan*), with the media equating the stories of war brides with negative images of betrayal, corruption, and tragedy. The Japanese–American community, especially first-generation Japanese emigrants (*Issei*), held similar negative images about war brides and often treated them with contempt. Many second-generation Japanese Americans, on the other hand, held a more positive view, seeing Japanese war brides as examples of successful assimilation into American mainstream (white) society.[44]

Militarism and sexuality

Prostitution was an integral part of the development and maintenance of the Japanese empire. Impoverished women in rural villages in Japan had been sold and sent abroad since the final years of the Tokugawa regime in the mid-nineteenth century. As Bill Mihalopoulos illustrates, these Japanese sex workers, the so-called *karayuki-san* (meaning "a person traveling to China"), were in fact part of a broader group of peasants who became "free labor" and migrated abroad for opportunities as Japan expanded into the global economy, especially in Southeast Asia. Their number increased rapidly after the Meiji Restoration, especially after the Sino–Japanese War (1894–1895) and the Russo–Japanese War (1904–1905), expanding to a variety of areas including Southeast Asia, the South Pacific, Australian colonies, and the North American northwest. Even while the government promoted the flow of capital and Japanese laborers in the colonial world economy, they simultaneously controlled and stigmatized certain types of female labor, in particular prostitution.[45]

In the decades following the Meiji Restoration the government established a system of regulated prostitution based on the laws and practices in France and Germany. After a series of local regulations, the central government set up a nationwide system for licensed prostitution in 1900 with the Rules Regulating Licensed Prostitutes (*Shōgi torishimari kisoku*). As Sheldon Garon notes, the Japanese system of licensed prostitution went much further than European counterparts in restricting the liberties of prostitutes, making it almost impossible for them to work or live outside brothels. It was a system formed through the cooperation of the state, brothel owners, and parents selling their daughters to escape poverty.[46]

The primary characteristics of the modern system of public prostitution were frequent mandatory health examinations for all registered prostitutes and hospitalization of those affected by venereal disease. The system of medical examinations for prostitutes had existed since Japan opened its doors to foreign trade in the late nineteenth century through treaty ports. Considered as part of the practice of modern, civilized nations, the system soon spread across the country.[47] These inspections were intended to protect Japanese men, especially soldiers, as well as their families from the diseases that prostitutes supposedly carried and transmitted.

With the rise of the public prostitution system, abolitionist campaigns also developed among moral reformers. Japanese abolitionists, mainly Protestants inspired by the international abolitionist and social purity movements that emerged at the end of the nineteenth century, aimed to modernize the sexual norms among Japanese along the lines of British and American contemporaries. Momentum for abolition grew in the 1920s and early 1930s. The state responded to the international abolitionist pressures by ratifying the League of Nation's 1921 Convention for the Suppression of the Traffic in Women and Children. Although bureaucrats did not necessarily favor abolition, they did resolve to implement several reforms that would respect "the liberties of prostitutes."[48] In the end, however, the abolitionist campaigns were no match for the well-organized collusion between bureaucrats and the brothel businesses. In reality, both abolitionists and regulationists worked side by side with the state to defend sexual norms and the "national family" (kokka). Not just prostitutes but other women—waitresses, dancers, and factory workers—whose sexuality was considered uncontrolled and unmanageable also became the target of state regulation. In fact, abolitionists joined forces with licensed brothel owners to press the government to suppress dance halls, cafés, and clandestine prostitution.[49]

By the late 1930s state-sanctioned brothels—"comfort stations"—were well-established across the empire, and Japanese, Chinese, Korean, and other women under Japanese colonial rule were subjected to sexual slavery. With the Manchuria Incident in 1931 and the Shanghai Incident in 1932, the Japanese army embarked on a military invasion into China. Soon after, the imperial Japanese navy and army established the first comfort stations, ostensibly to prevent the raping of local women and to limit the spread of venereal disease.[50] Such a system did not prevent further violence against women, as was most notoriously demonstrated by the Nanking Massacre of 1937, also known as the Rape of Nanking.[51] After this atrocity the military increased the number of comfort stations in China, with the military government's main concern being to protect the wellbeing of the Japanese soldiers and their families, not the local women.

Although the army's initial plan was to use only Japanese professional prostitutes, they soon faced the difficulty of recruiting enough women to satisfy the troops. As a result the military increasingly started to exploit Korean, Taiwanese, Chinese, and other local women for this role.[52] While Japanese prostitutes continued to serve the military abroad, they mainly worked for high-ranking officers and experienced better conditions than the other Asian comfort women. The Japanese eugenic philosophy and prejudice against other Asian people contributed to this tendency to use non-Japanese women; after all, the government aimed to promote the idea of Japanese women as "Good Wife and Wise Mother," while they assigned a lower sexual and moral standard to other Asians.[53]

Soon after the end of World War II the Japanese government, now fearing the possibility of "mass rape" committed by the Allied troops against Japanese women, willingly provided Japanese prostitutes to the GIs. The Allied soldiers continued to use the facilities run by the Recreation and Amusement Association, as well as other brothels in traditional red-light districts, until General Douglas McArthur, head of the occupation force, announced "the abolition of Japan's feudalistic licensed brothels" and "the emancipation of women from the enslaved prostitution business." The ban was actually issued in response to reports the GHQ received stating that the GIs continued to contract venereal disease. The GHQ still allowed "voluntary" prostitution, leading to the increase of so-called "women of the night" (*yami no onna*) and *pan-pan*. [54]

The GHQ, the Japanese government, and even moral reformers were complicit in this organized crime against women. Yoshimi Yoshiaki has revealed that the GHQ was aware of the Japanese military's comfort women system, as they interviewed Japanese soldiers and civilians, as well as some Korean comfort women. Because the Allied soldiers had been using the same system of state-sponsored prostitution, they did not prosecute during war crime trials the Japanese who had been responsible for the sexual exploitation of comfort women. Fujime Yuki criticizes abolitionist women's groups for not only remaining silent on the comfort women issue during the war but for also continuing to blame the "women of the night" for "seducing" American soldiers during the occupation. [55]

Some independent studies, from both the South Korean and Japanese sides, on the subject appeared in the 1970s and 1980s, including Senda Kako's *Jūgun ianfu* [*The Comfort Women*] (1973) and Kim Il-myon's *Tennō no guntai to Chōsen ianfu* [*The Emperor's Forces and Korean Comfort Women*] (1976). [56] The issue, however, was not widely problematized among the public, nor did these studies lead to a wider investigation into the issue. For the most part, the history of sexual violence against comfort women was buried in silence for almost five decades.

The tide finally shifted in the 1990s, when Kim Hak-sun gave testimony about her experience at the Korean Church Women United office in 1991, becoming the first publicly known Korean "comfort woman." Together with two other women, she filed a lawsuit in the Tokyo District Court. Following the lawsuit, in 1992 Yoshimi Yoshiaki uncovered Japanese government documents that revealed the military's involvement in recruiting women and organizing comfort stations. Yoshimi presented and published these documents to make them accessible to the public. In the context of an increasing awareness of women's human rights, the issue attracted the attention of feminists in Japan, South Korea, the Philippines, and other Asian countries, leading to the first Japanese Military "Comfort Women" Asian Solidarity Conference in Seoul in 1992. Following the death of wartime emperor Hirohito and the end of the Cold War, the 1990s saw a surge of public debates over Japan's wartime atrocities and injustices. An increasing number of publications have appeared over the decades featuring the actual testimonies and experiences of comfort women of different nationalities and regions, as well as the transnational redress movements. [57]

Scholars in Japan have also illuminated the Japanese government's response to the comfort women issue, typically characterized by ignorance and denial. After the 1991 testimony of three Korean comfort women, the government conducted two internal investigations between 1991 and 1993. In response to the survey's results, Chief Cabinet Secretary Kōno Yōhei admitted that the imperial army was involved in the establishment and management of the comfort stations and the transfer of comfort women. The so-called Kōno statement also promised to revise the teaching of Japanese history to include some mention of this system. Beginning with Maruyama Tomiichi's administration, from 1995 to 2007, the Japanese government also arranged for "atonement" payments to selected victims through a non-governmental body, the Asian Women's Fund (AWF). However, these state redress initiatives were presented to the public as quasi-private in nature, and the government refused to issue a formal apology and offer surviving victims state-mandated compensation. [58]

Despite mounting international pressure to officially acknowledge and redress wartime sexual slavery, there has been a backlash against the issue in Japan since the 2000s, especially after Abe Shinzō took office in 2006. Conservative politicians, media commentators, and academics have disputed the historical accuracy of sexual slavery and have instead claimed that comfort women were either volunteers or paid "professionals." Affected by these revisionist forces and right-wing demands, publishers of textbooks started to drop references to the comfort station system.[59]

The history of sexuality—especially as it relates to women, militarism, and the empire—remains a contested arena, where various actors present their own visions and narratives about gender, nation, and world politics. Sexuality was often a tool for the central government to control the morality, reproduction, and racial quality of the Japanese and to elevate them to a standard comparable to that of Western powers. The sexuality of colonial subjects was marginalized and only expected to serve the interests of Japanese soldiers. Scholarly and public interest focusing on past issues of sexuality have helped uncover multiple realities and historical narratives, especially those that highlight personal experiences and agency. These studies show us that the empire's regulatory power over sexuality was never complete; the expressions of deviant or non-conforming sexualities have remained and resurfaced—some immediately after the demise of the empire, others more than half a century later. The past has also taught us that, once these stories and voices are revealed, no censorship can fully contain them.[60]

Notes

1 Roden, "Taishō Culture and the Problem of Gender Ambivalence," 42–43.
2 Pflugfelder, *Cartographies of Desire*, 149, 193, 285.
3 Ibid., 285.
4 Frühstück, *Colonizing Sex*, 5, 82, 100, 160.
5 Robertson, "Dying to Tell," 10, 24.
6 I use the Japanese convention of placing surnames before given names for Japanese historical figures as well as for Japanese authors whose work is published in Japanese.
7 Suzuki, *Becoming Modern Women*, 38, 59.
8 Sato, *The New Japanese Woman*, 51–54.
9 Silverberg, *Erotic Grotesque Nonsense*, 47–60.
10 Chung, "The Modern Girl (*Modeon Geol*) as a Contested Symbol in Colonial Korea," 82, 85.
11 Park, "Picturing Empire and Illness," 120, 130.
12 Ito, "The 'Modern Girl' Question in the Periphery of Empire," 242.
13 Pflugfelder, *Cartographies of Desire*, 327.
14 Sato, *The New Japanese Woman*, 69; Silverberg, *Erotic, Grotesque, Nonsense*, 60.
15 Frühstück, *Colonizing Sex*, 180.
16 Koyama, "Junketsu kyōiku no tōjō," 17.
17 Saitō, "Junketsu kyōiku iinkai no kigen to GHQ," 47, 53.
18 For details on Sanger's 1922 visit to Japan and its impact on the birth control movement in Japan, see Takeuchi-Demirci, *Contraceptive Diplomacy*, 35–48.
19 The Governor-General of Korea, for example, launched a health campaign called "A Week for Caring for Infants and Children" in 1931. Park, "Picturing Empire," 122–123. Meanwhile, in the metropole, the Institute of Population Problems (*Jinkō mondai kenkyūjo*), under the jurisdiction of the Ministry of Health and Welfare, presented pro-natalist policies, such as financial incentives and tax reductions for large families as well as stricter regulations against the production and sales of contraceptives. For an American observation on wartime population policies in Japan, see Office of Population Research, "Japanese Population Policy," 264–267.
20 Leading feminists such as Hiratsuka Raichō received eugenic education at the Japan Women's College. See Sitcawich, "Eugenics in Imperial Japan."
21 The petition never passed, however, partly because it targeted only men as disease carriers. Garon, *Molding Japanese Minds*, 725; Fujime, *Sei no rekishigaku*, 320.
22 Frühstück, *Colonizing Sex*, 166; Norgren, *Abortion before Birth Control*, 32.

23 Compared to the wartime National Eugenic Law, the Eugenic Protection Law expanded the target of eugenic sterilization, simplified the procedures for voluntary sterilization, and removed obstructive restrictions on therapeutic abortion. For details, see Matsubara, "The Enactment of Japan's Sterilization Laws," 197.

24 Takeuchi-Demirci, *Contraceptive Diplomacy*, 164–167.

25 Norgren, *Abortion before Birth Control*, 79–81.

26 Leupp, *Interracial Intimacy in Japan*, 196.

27 Kamoto, *Kokusai kekkon no tanjō*, 72, 94.

28 Nakamura, *Kindai teikoku Nihon no sekushuariti*, 184.

29 Leupp, *Interracial Intimacy in Japan*, 78–79, 132.

30 Yoshihara, *Embracing the East*, 9–10.

31 Said, *Orientalism*, 190.

32 Leupp, *Interracial Intimacy in Japan*, 188.

33 Robertson, *Takarazuka*, 92.

34 Ibid., 137.

35 Suzuki, *Nihon no yūseigaku*, 32–40.

36 Takeda Shūko argues that there was a sharp increase in Korean–Japanese intermarriages between 1938 and 1942 in Japan, but comparatively fewer cases in Korea. Takeda, *Kokusai kekkon no shakaigaku*, 62–67.

37 Oguma, *Tanitsu minzoku shinwa no kigen*, 136–137.

38 Ibid., 250; Takeshita, *Kokusai kekkon no shakaigaku*, 56

39 Yasutomi, "America no sensō hanayome," 151; Leupp, *Interracial Intimacy in Japan*, 219.

40 Marchetti, *Romance and the "Yellow Peril,"* 160.

41 See also, Klein, *Cold War Orientalism*.

42 Yasutomi, "America no sensō hanayome," 155.

43 See for example, Glenn, *Issei, Nisei, War Bride*; Crawford et al. eds., *Japanese War Brides in America*.

44 Yasutomi, "America no sensō hanayome," 158–163, 169.

45 Tanaka, *Japan's Comfort Women*, 167; Mihalopoulos, *Sex in Japan's Globalization*, 1, 11.

46 Garon, *Molding Japanese Minds*, 713.

47 Frühstück, *Colonizing Sex*, 42; Fujime, *Sei no rekishigaku*, 90.

48 Garon, *Molding Japanese Minds*, 719, 724.

49 Ibid., 727–728; Frühstück, *Colonizing Sex*, 39.

50 Son, *Embodied Reckonings*, 5.

51 Since the 1970s there has been intense debates over the history and memory of the Nanking Massacre, not just in Japan but also in China and the United States. For details, see Yoshida, *The Making of the "Rape of Nanking."*

52 Around the time of the Russo–Japanese War, some Japanese physicians and military officers claimed that "all Korean and Chinese prostitutes are poisonous." Such a stereotype led to stricter and routine medical examinations of Korean prostitutes, especially after the annexation of Korea in 1910. Park, "Picturing Empire," 117–118.

53 Tanaka, *Japan's Comfort Women*, 18, 31–32.

54 Ibid., 133, 151, 161; Fujime, *Sei no rekishigaku*, 327. Some recent studies have highlighted the presence and "agency"—albeit a limited one—of these Japanese "sex workers" during the Allied occupation period. For example, Kovner, *Occupying Power*.

55 Yoshimi, *Jūgun ianfu shiryōshū*, 84; Fujime, *Sei no rekishigaku*, 326–329.

56 Senda, *Jūgun ianfu*; Kim, *Tennō no guntai to Chōsen ianfu*. For early English-language research on comfort women, see Hicks, *The Comfort Women*.

57 For example, Soh, "The Korean 'Comfort Women'"; Son, *Embodied Reckonings*; Kimura, *Unfolding the 'Comfort Women' Debates*; Nishino et al. eds., *Denying the Comfort Women*.

58 Nishino, *Denying the Comfort Women*, 1–3.

59 Ibid., 3–4; Kimura, *Unfolding the "Comfort Women" Debates*, 16–17.

60 A controversy in Japan erupted in August 2019 over a special exhibit, "Exhibit of Non-Freedom of Expression: A Sequence," which included a statue of a girl representing the "comfort women." The exhibit was part of an international art festival held in Aichi Prefecture, "Aichi Triennale 2019." After protests from politicians and threatening phone calls from anonymous members of the public, the exhibit was cancelled after its third day. The controversy and media coverage, however, drew extraordinary public interest, both domestically and internationally, to the exhibit and the historical representation of comfort women.

Bibliography

Chung, Yeon Shim. "The Modern Girl (*Modeon Geol*) as a Contested Symbol in Colonial Korea." In *Visualizing Beauty: Gender and Ideology in Modern East Asia*, edited by Aida Yuen Wong, 79–90. Hong Kong: Hong Kong University Press, 2012.

Crawford, Miki Ward, Katie Kaori Hayashi and Shizuko Suenaga, eds. *Japanese War Brides in America: An Oral History*. Santa Barbara, CA: ABC-CLIO, 2010.

Frühstück, Sabine. *Colonizing Sex: Sexology and Social Control in Modern Japan*. Berkeley, CA: University of California Press, 2003.

Fujime, Yuki. *Sei no rekishigaku: Kōshō seido, dataizai taisei kara baishun bōshihō, yūsei hogo hō taisei e* [Histography of Sex: From the System of State-Regulated Prostitution and Criminal Abortion to the System of Anti-prostitution Law and Eugenic Protection Law]. Tokyo: Fuji shuppan, 1997.

Garon, Sheldon M. *Molding Japanese Minds: The State in Everyday Life*. Princeton, NJ: Princeton University Press, 1997.

Glenn, Evelyn Nakano. *Issei, Nisei, War Bride: Three Generations of Japanese American Women in Domestic Service*. Philadelphia, PA: Temple University Press, 1986.

Hicks, George. *The Comfort Women: Sex Slaves of the Japanese Imperial Forces*. New York and London: W. W. Norton & Company, 1995.

Ito, Rui. "The 'Modern Girl' Question in the Periphery of Empire: Colonial Modernity and Okinawan Women in the 1920s and 1930s." In *The Modern Girl Around the World: Consumption, Modernity, and Globalization*, edited by Alys Eve Weinbaum et al., 240–262. Durham, NC: Duke University Press, 2008.

Kamoto, Itsuko. *Kokusai kekkon no tanjō: 'Bunmeikoku Nihon' e no michi* [The Emergence of 'Kokusai Kekkon': On Becoming a 'Civilized Nation']. Tokyo: Shinyōsha, 2001.

Kim, Ill-myon. *Tennō no guntai to Chōsen ianfu* [The Emperor's Army and Korean Comfort Women]. Tokyo: Sanichi shobō, 1976.

Kimura, Maki. *Unfolding the 'Comfort Women' Debates: Modernity, Violence, Women's Voices*. New York: Palgrave Macmillan, 2016.

Klein, Christina. *Cold War Orientalism: Asia in the Middlebrow Imagination, 1945–1961*. Berkeley, CA: University of California Press, 2003.

Kovner, Sarah. *Occupying Power: Sex Workers and Servicemen in Postwar Japan*. Stanford, CA: Stanford University Press, 2012.

Koyama, Shizuko. "Junketsu kyōiku no tōjō—Danjo kyōgaku to danjo kōsai" [The Rise of Chastity Education: Coeducation and Courtship]. In *Sekushuariti no sengoshi* [The Postwar History of Sexuality], edited by Shizuko Koyama, Akaeda Kanako and Imada Erika, 15–34. Kyoto: Kyoto daigaku gakujutsu shuppankai, 2014.

Leupp, Gary P. *Interracial Intimacy in Japan: Western Men and Japanese Women, 1543–1900*. New York: Continuum, 2003.

Marchetti, Gina. *Romance and the "Yellow Peril": Race, Sex, and Discursive Strategies in Hollywood Fiction*. Berkeley, CA: University of California Press, 1993.

Matsubara, Yoko. "The Enactment of Japan's Sterilization Laws in the 1940s: A Prelude to Postwar Eugenic Policy." *Historia Scientiarum* 8, no. 2 (1998): 187–201.

Mihalopoulos, Bill. *Sex in Japan's Globalization, 1870–1930*. London: Pickering & Chatto, 2011.

Nakamura, Shigeki. *Kindai teikoku Nihon no sekushuariti* [Sexuality of Modern Empire Japan]. Tokyo: Akashi shoten, 2004.

Nishino, Rumiko, Kim Puja and Onozawa Akane, eds. *Denying the Comfort Women: The Japanese State's Assault on Historical Truth*. New York and London: Routledge, 2018.

Norgren, Christiana A.E. *Abortion before Birth Control: The Politics of Reproduction in Postwar Japan*. Princeton, NJ: Princeton University Press, 2001.

Office of Population Research. "Japanese Population Policy." *Population Index* 7, no. 4 (1941): 264–267.

Oguma, Eiji. *Tanitsu minzoku shinwa no kigen: Nihonjin no jigazō no keihu* [The Myth of the Homogeneous Nation]. Tokyo: Shinyōsha, 1995.

Park, Jin-kyung. "Picturing Empire and Illness: Biomedicine, Venereal Disease and the Modern Girl in Korea under Colonial Rule." *Cultural Studies* 28, no. 1 (2014): 108–141. doi:10.1080/09502386.2013.775319.

Pflugfelder, Gregory. *Cartographies of Desire: Male–Male Sexuality in Japanese Discourse, 1600–1950*. Berkeley, CA: University of California Press, 1999.

Robertson, Jennifer Ellen. *Takarazuka: Sexual Politics and Popular Culture in Modern Japan*. Berkeley, CA: University of California Press, 1998.

Robertson, Jennifer Ellen. "Dying to Tell: Sexuality and Suicide in Imperial Japan." *Signs* 25, no. 1 (1999): 1–35. doi:10.1086/495412.

Roden, Donald. "Taishō Culture and the Problem of Gender Ambivalence." In *Culture and Identity: Japanese during the Interwar Years*, edited by J. Thomas Rimer, 37–55. Princeton, NJ: Princeton University Press, 2014.

Said, Edward W. *Orientalism*. New York: Vintage Books, 1979.

Saitō, Hikaru. "Junketsu kyōiku iinkai no kigen to GHQ" [The Origin of the Committee on Chastity Education and GHQ]. In *Sekushuariti no sengoshi* [The Postwar History of Sexuality], edited by Shizuko Koyama, Akaeda Kanako and Imada Erika, 35–55. Kyoto: Kyoto daigaku gakujutsu shuppankai, 2014.

Sato, Barbara Hamill. *The New Japanese Woman: Modernity, Media, and Women in Interwar Japan*. Durham, NC: Duke University Press, 2003.

Senda, Kako. *Jūgun ianfu* [Comfort Women]. Tokyo: Fitabasha, 1973.

Silverberg, Miriam Rom. *Erotic Grotesque Nonsense: The Mass Culture of Japanese Modern Times*. Berkeley, CA: University of California Press, 2006.

Sitcawich, Sumiko Otsubo. "Eugenics in Imperial Japan: Some Ironies of Modernity, 1883–1945." Ph.D. diss., Ohio State University, 1998.

Soh, Sarah. "The Korean 'Comfort Women': Movement for Redress." *Asian Survey* 36, no. 12 (1996):1226–1240. doi:10.2307/2645577.

Son, Elizabeth W. *Embodied Reckonings: "Comfort Women," Performance, and Transpacific Redress*. Ann Arbor, MI: University of Michigan Press, 2018. doi:10.3998/mpub.8773540.

Suzuki, Michiko. *Becoming Modern Women: Love and Female Identity in Prewar Japanese Literature and Culture*. Stanford, CA: Stanford University Press, 2010.

Suzuki, Zenji. *Nihon no yūseigaku: Sono shisō to undō no kiseki* [Eugenics in Japan: The Trajectory of Its Thoughts and Movement]. Tokyo: Sankyō shuppan kabushiki geisha, 1983.

Takeda, Shūko. *Kokusai kekkon no shakaigaku* [Sociology of International Marriages]. Tokyo: Gakubunsha, 2000.

Takeuchi-Demirci, Aiko. *Contraceptive Diplomacy: Reproductive Politics and Imperial Ambitions in the United States and Japan*. Stanford, CA: Stanford University Press, 2018.

Tanaka, Yuki. *Japan's Comfort Women: Sexual Slavery and Prostitution during World War II and the US Occupation*. New York: Routledge, 2002.

Yasutomi, Shigeyoshi. "America no sensō hanayome e no manazashi" [Views toward War Brides in America]. In *Shashin hanayome, sensō hanayome no tadotta michi: Josei imin shi no hakkutsu* [The New Look at the History of Japanese Picture Brides and War Brides], edited by Shimada Noriko, 151–183. Tokyo: Akashi shoten, 2009.

Yoshida, Takashi. *The Making of the "Rape of Nanking": History and Memory in Japan, China, and the United States*. New York: Oxford University Press, 2006.

Yoshihara, Mari. *Embracing the East: White Women and American Orientalism*. New York: Oxford University Press, 2003.

Yoshimi, Yoshiaki. *Jūgun ianfu shiryōshū* [Compiled Material on Comfort Women]. Tokyo: ōtsuki shoten, 1992.

6

TRANSACTIONS

Sex, power, and resistance in colonial South and Southeast Asia

Kate Imy

This chapter examines the historiography of sex and sexuality in colonial South and Southeast Asia by thinking through the lens of "transactions." It uses the term to reflect the various "trans" realities of how sexed and sexualized bodies shaped and were shaped by colonial rule. Studies of sex in South and Southeast Asia often emphasize the transnational as well as transactional, as people traded or lost a sense of comfort, home, and stability through voluntary, forced, and coerced migrations in the region. Transnational networks of power, meanwhile, often involved the trade of sexual acts for knowledge, wealth, power, or status. Such transactions increasingly reflected the material inequity of colonial rule, linking sexed bodies with material wealth through marriage contracts, concubinage, or prostitution. At the same time, it suggests that "trans-actions" can be understood as acts of individual and collective resistance that transgressed or transcended colonial power by developing or maintaining alternative understandings of the gendered and sexed body. This discussion of "transactions," as a result, emphasizes how the materiality of the body and the material realities of imperial power could both confine and create opportunities for alternative understandings of sexual power. It considers the ambitious and fruitful work of various scholars who think about historical sex and sexuality within and beyond discussions of identities and discourses. At the heart of each "transaction" is the possibility of betrayal, revocation, rejection, or liberation, with tremendous physical and material consequences for the modern world.

The works discussed below are indebted to the profound scholarship of Edward Said and Ann Laura Stoler on sex, race, and colonialism.[1] As many scholars have suggested, however, conversations about sexuality can often limit as much as they elucidate. Tamara Loos has argued that one challenge is studying sex and sexuality "on the basis of geographic areas" because of how local "religions, language groupings, erotic acts" or any other "organizing typology" influence the very concepts of discussion.[2] This is a valid concern. Regional analyses, at times, cannot help but replicate Euro- and US-centric "area studies" methodologies that echo colonial models. They tend to flatten the ethnic, religious, and social diversity while, at times, erasing those who transcended or transgressed multiple identity categories simultaneously. That said, using a comparative frame enables us to understand similarities— and differences—across a wide geographic area. Comparing colonial strategies under the tutelage of the British, French, and Dutch empires, hopefully, will *decenter* these empires and focus more on questions of Indigeneity, anti-colonial resistance, and forms of living and being within and outside of colonialism.

While geography provides inherent opportunities and limitations, the category of sexuality does as well. Indrani Chatterjee has issued a bold reminder for scholars to acknowledge "the diverse ways in which our selves have been shrunk to fit puny bodies, and how a discourse of 'sexuality' has disciplined scholars and activists alike."[3] For Chatterjee, "the process of naming something as 'sexual'—was fundamentally the process of European colonialism." This happened as networks of devotion, education, and exchange became supplanted by European "parliamentary institutions, codes, and constitutionalism" that relied on hereditary inheritance and natal legitimacy to establish property rights and grow plantation-style economies.[4] This, for Chatterjee, meant that "certain practices had to be defined as 'sexual' before they could become 'homo,' 'hetero,' or 'any-other-kind of sex.'"[5] Colonialism and sexuality were mutually constituted and co-dependent, ushering in ways of thinking about sex and bodies that remain overburdened by the colonial past. This is especially true in South and Southeast Asia, where the material inequity of colonialism radically altered pre-existing understandings of sex.

Colonial archives, for Anjali Arondekar, are another impediment to studying colonial sexuality. Arondekar shares with Chatterjee the concern that many well-intentioned queer and feminist scholars have inadvertently reified colonial categories and epistemologies by searching for behavior and patterns that could be construed as homosexual in the past—without examining the material and cultural patterns that predated these concepts. These scholars want to make visible or legitimize contemporary identities by searching for sex acts in the archives. What they often find is that this search privileges the archives and their silences, reaffirming the power of these institutions to define and limit our understanding of sex. For example, colonial officials often portrayed sex through the lens of sin or conquest. This emphasis on sexual violence inherently privileged narratives of heterosexuality, obscuring other colonial threats to sexuality.[6] By contrast, it remains difficult to track down court cases and courts martial dealing with sodomy, or reports of male prostitution in the army, illustrating what was unspeakable among colonial officials.[7] To be documented was to be caught-out, unsuccessful, or prevented from existing. In other contexts, sexual acts were less about private desires than enacting power over space, communities, or political relationships. For example, those regulating legal, military, and religious codes might use sexual acts to humiliate, shame, or punish those who transgressed accepted norms of morality and belonging.[8] Sexual impulses could also be fluid according to situational circumstances, such as intimate barracks, living in a rigorous climate, or exposure to specific communities (often rationalized through theories of racial difference).[9] In order for historians to study sexuality it first must be recoverable and made legible from the colonial archive.[10]

Despite these challenges, studies of the early colonial period prove especially instructive for historians wanting to understand the multiple embodied and material traumas of colonization.[11] Barbara Watson Andaya and Michael Peletz have argued that sex helped to build kinship networks between traders and visitors in Southeast Asia during the sixteenth and seventeenth centuries.[12] Women often acted as sexual partners with traveling men to solidify the familial connection.[13] This practice of enlisting "temporary wives" facilitated trade across the region, rooting sex in a transactional network long before European presence.[14] Such networks afforded women some protections, as their families could ensure that visiting men respected women's marital rights. Men who transgressed acceptable behavior risked social and economic ostracism or even death.[15] In places like Batavia, Dutch men emulated local elites by gaining large "harems" full of women—which denoted status.[16] Due to the expense, however, Dutch officials increasingly forced slave women to complete domestic, income-producing, and sex work to increase their household income. European companies saved money by recruiting single men to serve overseas and outsourcing their care to local women.[17] As demands for women at colonial ports increased, colonial officials commodified women's sexual labor. The wealth that they produced was transferred to Europeans, dismantling existing systems of sex, kinship, and trade. This resulted in an almost full-scale breakdown of women's economic and sexual independence under colonialism.

Indrani Chatterjee suggests a similar loss of pre-existing sexual networks and autonomy in early colonial India. English East India Company officials glorified the heterosexual nuclear "family" due to the need to differentiate "legitimate" and "illegitimate" children.[18] This was rooted, in part, in British experiences with plantation slavery in the Atlantic. Economic imperatives meant assigning specific and unequal values to the simultaneous labors of childbirth performed by slave and wife.[19] The Company initially encouraged relationships between white men and Indian women to literally reproduce a labor force of mixed-race civil servants, plantation workers, domestic servants, and soldiers in the eighteenth century.[20] The categories of "legitimacy" and "orphan," in a British imperial context, increasingly commodified sex and delegitimized Indian women's rights as mothers.[21] Their categorization as "temporary wives," prostitutes, or concubines erased their claims to their children and their children's rights to the status of their father. For Michael Peletz, the encounters between Protestant Western missionaries and colonial officials proved just as influential. This contributed to the standardization of previously heterogenous systems of belief such as Sunni Islam, Theravada Buddhism, neo-Confucianism, and Iberian-style Catholicism, which hardened ideas of monogamy, legality, and male control of sexuality.[22] This delegitimized the previously prominent place of women and gender-fluid or transgender ritual practitioners across South and Southeast Asia. In the Philippines, Spaniards went so far as to regard women shamans as Satanists to circumscribe their agency.[23]

Early modern colonial officials were often just as concerned about regulating men's sexual acts as women's. In India, centuries-old intellectual and cultural lineages between students and teachers became "sodomy" performed by "eunuchs," according to the British colonial elite.[24] For Lee Wallace, the presumed opposition between homosexuality and heterosexuality emerged as a result of colonial encounters in the Pacific.[25] Captain James Cook became an emblematic icon of a paternalistic, stern, sober, and self-sacrificing military officer. Cook's colleague, Joseph Banks, meanwhile, inspired subsequent generations of elite European men to "go native." This meant traveling the world and participating in imperial knowledge-gathering, including the ethnographic study of, and participation in, taboo sex practices, such as sex between men.[26] Albeit in divergent ways, Cook's and Banks' performances of gender and desire served the imperial project. The ideal of British masculinity inspired by Cook emphasized sober sexual asceticism, which bolstered theories of racial difference hinging on notions of self-control. When "sober" men publicized sex practices in colonial spaces it produced moral outrage that justified British Christian interference.[27] At the same time, men like Banks exoticized such practices, promoting the titillating and erotic promise of travel to and study of colonial cultures. Though seeming to promote contradictory views of white, masculine sexuality, in Wallace's view, men like Banks could enjoy and gather information that men like Cook suppressed. This furthered the reach of the colonial state by allowing European men to envision many roles and purposes for themselves in colonial spaces.

As Wallace reminds us, sexual encounters were not simply British actors imposing imperial and sexual cultures across Asia and the Pacific. Instead, Indigenous concepts and expressions of desire, the erotic, and sex shaped European imperial codes of masculinity and desirability. Practices, acts, and ceremonies that could not fit into existing European categories, such as "sodomy," produced ambivalence about categorizing, condemning, or allowing alternative behaviors.[28] Richard Francis Burton's notorious investigation of boy brothels in Karachi in the 1840s, for example, led him to argue that prostitution, so common in Europe and the colonized world, was more damaging than practices such as polygamy.[29] He traveled in disguise to claim for himself the sexual freedom that he associated with traveling "East."[30] Later European officials, intellectuals, and sexologists—including John Addington Symonds, Richard Francis Burton, Havelock Ellis, and Edward Carpenter—carried this tendency into the nineteenth and twentieth centuries by participating in sexual experimentation and tourism under the pretense of imperial knowledge-gathering. Their readings and translations of texts such as *A Thousand and One Nights* and *The Kama Sutra* influenced European theories of sexology at the turn of the twentieth century, underscoring the constitutive role of overseas colonialism in the making of so-called "European" knowledge.[31] These voyages and travels reveal anxiety about the desirability—and penetrability—of the male body.

Some scholars have suggested that focusing on particular acts, rather than identity categories, demonstrates fluidity between Indigenous and colonial understandings of sex. Deborah Elliston, for example, argues that examining "semen practices" reveals how the Sambia of Papua New Guinea understood the exchange of semen from an older man to a younger man as part of a rite of passage and cultivation of appropriate masculinity, rather than a specific homosexual identity.[32] Similarly, scholars such as David Gordon White have examined how ancient and early modern Indian views of semen were key to understanding discussions of virility and immortality.[33] This was often linked to yoga, even though colonial cultures adopted, modified, and desexualized the practice. By the nineteenth and twentieth centuries, sexualized yoga became notorious and discredited due to the scandalous reputations of European occultists such as Aleister Crowley and Charles Leadbeater.[34] Nonetheless, poet, author, and Irish nationalist W.B. Yeats had a Steinach operation, similar to a vasectomy, to prevent the loss of semen. This was inspired by his selective understandings of yoga, tantra, and the Upanishads during his collaborations with Shri Purohit Swami.[35] Indian army Captain Francis Yeats-Brown, meanwhile, shared Yeats' enthusiasm for sexual yoga and the retention of sexual energy. For him it influenced a racialized understanding of the body that supported fascist beliefs.[36] Contemporary Indian jori club swingers and wrestlers, meanwhile, emphasize milk-based diets to evoke semen in a way that promotes celibacy and fertility. Physical culture, they argue, encourages discipline over both the body and desire which produces and contains semen and masculinity.[37] The focus on "semen practices," therefore, opens up many opportunities for thinking about the multiple meanings of acts frequently defined as sexual.

Non-binary and fluid identities have also gained their rightful space at the center of historical inquiry, revealing how sex and sexual identities and categories change over time. Evelyn Blackwood has examined the categorization of *banci* and *waria* (Indonesia) and *paway* (Malaysia) as they perform varied gender identities in rituals.[38] Peletz has identified these cross-regional identities as "gender and sexual pluralism."[39] Some have used the term "transgender," or assumed underlying homosexuality, even though these practices predate the categorization of "homosexual." The imposition of European categories in colonial archives has burdened historical actors with labels such as "men" or "women," and condemned their performances as "hermaphroditic" or "transvestic," despite the willful fluidity of gender categories.[40] Blackwood prefers to think instead in terms of "gender-transgressive ritual practitioner" to denote the performance of gender in a ritual duty, which did not necessarily lead to a transgression of gender or sexuality in daily life.[41] In fact, *banci* and *waria* were often members of a priestly class who took gender-ambiguous positions or "switched" genders during rituals. This entrusted them with the well-being of the community—a position of power. They did not exist peripherally, in secret, or at the margins of society, unlike in European contexts. The Dutch arrival in Indonesia complicated precolonial power and performance by imposing rigid categories of gender, emphasizing women's child-bearing capacities, and condemning same-sex intimacy and "cross-dressing."[42] As the Dutch consolidated their power over the East Indies in the nineteenth century, and a reformist strand of Wahabist Islam emerged, public and non-ritual performances of gender transgression increased rather than decreased. This indicates that these identities evolved to encompass grassroots resistance to colonial sexual regimes.[43]

As with *banci* and *waria* in Southeast Asia, Arondekar warns against "finding" groups such as *Hijra* in India as examples of gender non-conformity within liberation narratives because they often performed important and powerful roles as tax collectors under the Mughals.[44] These identities must be understood in relation to, rather than simply against, political power structures. British colonial officials, however, often discussed them only in regard to their sexuality, and, as a result, some scholars and non-scholars cannot help but do the same.[45] Adnan Hossain and Jessica Hinchy have done admirable work exploring how *Hijra* are enmeshed in other dynamics of power, including religious and political patronage.[46] For Hossain, *Hijra* in Bangladesh interpret Islamic knowledge and challenge authority while also blending more dominant Hindu and Muslim symbols, rituals, and myths.[47] For Hinchy, meanwhile, it is impossible to ignore the impact of the British government's "anti-Hijra campaign." She explains how "gender expression, sexual behaviours, domestic arrangements and intimate relationships were central to colonial governance" and helped to justify British campaigns of *Hijra* "extermination."[48] This has created a lasting difficulty of analyzing and understanding the community on its own terms. While *Hijra* may have held power in India under the Mughals, British leaders targeted these communities relentlessly, further circumscribing global understandings of gender and sexual difference.

The relationship between sex and colonialism is perhaps most transactional and entangled for historians of prostitution.[49] Philippa Levine argues that the prevalence of venereal disease determined the "centrality of sexual politics in the maintenance of empire." Without soldiers and colonial officials having guaranteed access to women's bodies, so the belief went, they would turn to rape or sex with one another.[50] Many European medical officials shared the perception that sexual diseases were conditions specific to the "East."[51] This resulted in the commodification and brutalization of the sex trade. Women were often subject to painful and humiliating medical inspections to search for venereal disease.[52] Yet the category of "prostitute" remained ambiguous. Chatterjee emphasizes how "nikka wives" were bought and exchanged between soldiers in cantonments in India, blurring the lines between slave and concubine.[53] The chakla system in India under the East India Company enabled the purchase of women through Indigenous agents, whose lack of freedom facilitated the invasive system of medical inspection first carried about by dhais, or midwives, but that became increasingly associated with colonial "lock hospitals."[54] Even those women who became wives rather than concubines or prostitutes lacked rights to citizenship or protection under English law.[55] This contrasted with the Dutch East India Company, which eventually allowed Asian women to obtain citizenship rights for marrying European men. At the same time, this created an "underclass" of Asian women who did not enjoy the privileged status of marriage and the claims to European citizenship that it enabled. These women's sexual labors helped European officials to assimilate, access knowledge networks, and have children to consolidate wealth and power.[56] Meanwhile, as Durba Ghosh has explored, these dynamics became even more complicated for categorizing individuals as "British" or "Indian" when they had mixed parentage.[57]

Scholars such as Arondekar, Ann Laura Stoler, Laurie Shrage, and Lenore Manderson have convincingly argued that prostitution made sexuality "raced" under colonialism.[58] In colonial Malaya, brothels maintained racial segregation. Tamil men visited Tamil brothels and Chinese men visited Chinese brothels. Europeans had free and unquestioned access to all ethnicities according to their personal preference—a sexual agency denied to Asian men. Women entered into the conversation only through racialized hierarchies of their sexual desirability. Japanese prostitutes were considered the most "clean," while European women, who were often Jewish migrants, were considered the most diseased.[59]

In the British-controlled Straits Settlements, more than 80 per cent of the Chinese population and roughly 75 per cent of the Indian population were men. Where men comprised more than 90 per cent of a group, homosexual acts and anally transmitted diseases were more widely reported. Prior to the encouragement of greater migration of women, prostitution flourished in areas near sugar and rubber plantations and mines.[60] Sexuality, therefore, is inseparable from the material context of labor and migration.

For Manderson, prostitution became one of many "institutions of sexuality." This naturalized "male sexuality" by arguing that access to women was necessary to maintain workers' morale and productivity.[61] Men's sexual desires were both discursively constructed as necessary for their productivity as workers but also fluid due to the male-dominated environments in which they lived and worked. The "ideal" male migrant worker had sex with women but could, out of perceived necessity, have sex with men as well. Efforts to regulate prostitution were rarely about protecting women and did not often lead to better employment or living conditions. Tan Beng Hui's study of Chinese prostitutes in Malaya, for example, suggests that demands for regulating Chinese prostitutes were raised most frequently by Chinese men, rather than women. Brothels tended to maintain control over women by insisting on filial piety common in women's Chinese households.[62] Women rarely went voluntarily to lock hospitals following the passage of the Contagious Disease Ordinance in 1870. This did not reduce abuses from traffickers and brothel keepers, inspiring passage of the Women's and Girl's Protection Ordinance in 1887.[63] When brothels were outlawed in the 1930s, elite brothels remained open while working-class and migrant brothels were closed. Entertainment venues such as cabarets and dance halls proliferated, often operating as fronts for unregulated prostitution.[64] Meanwhile, British colonial officials increasingly encouraged women to become laborers' wives rather than their prostitutes. Women's sexual and economic needs and desires, as a result, became largely irrelevant to the colonial state.[65]

For Arunima Datta there were instances when women could navigate the unequal, gendered, raced, and classed terrains of sex under colonialism. Indian Tamil migrants who worked as "coolie" laborers in Malaya, for example, had considerable sexual power despite colonial efforts to portray them as passive victims. Datta suggests that prevalent twentieth-century court cases involving "coolie" women reveal the tensions between Indian nationalists, the Malayan government, and the class structures of colonial labor and migration. These left an unexpected space for women to refuse marriage or switch sexual partners with greater ease due to the relative scarcity of women in and near coolie estates. Colonial intervention brought attention to women's relative sexual and economic agency. As a result it often increased, rather than decreased, their likelihood of facing domestic violence, particularly after cases of infidelity.[66] Nonetheless, both colonial leaders and Indian nationalists emphasized the passivity of coolie women to establish themselves as women's protectors, which rarely resulted in genuine concerns or actions to ensure their welfare.[67]

Many spaces in the colonial period confounded colonial control and undermined imperial understandings of sexuality. Satyasikha Chakroborty suggests that European women working as governesses and nurses in Indian princely households experienced European–South Asian same-sex intimacies that upended the raced and classed dynamics of migration and colonial rule.[68] European women were influenced by Europeans' eroticized understanding of the harem as a place of patriarchal control and sexual pleasure, which hinged on the eroticization and commodification of the "other." For Tamara Loos, places like Siam's Inner City of the Royal Palace were similarly condemned as an immoral "harem" by many European observers due to the existence of women's same-sex sexuality.[69] Yet life in India proved less sexually repressive and confining compared to work as a governess in Europe. White women enjoyed opportunities for status, travel, a better salary, and pleasure. Colonial elites nonetheless strictly monitored white women's labor in India and increasingly insisted that European women working in zenanas be "post-sexual" women of mature ages to avoid the possibility of their having sex with Indian men.[70]

Encouraging the employment of "aged" women for their presumed lack of sexuality relates to Rachel Leow's suggestion that age is an important category of gender analysis.[71] Age of consent debates, for example, were major and recurring issues for both British rulers in India and Dutch colonizers in Indonesia. British officials portrayed Indian men as "effeminate Bengalis" whose lack of "manly self-control" required the colonial state to intervene in the issue of child marriage in 1891.[72] For Ishita Pande, this reflected a change in colonial narratives from "woman-rescue" to "child protection" which defined sexual legal status through age.[73] Similar issues materialized in the interwar period, as Mrinalini Sinha explores, with the Child Marriage Restraint Act 1929, which made the state a mediator between women and their communities.[74] Leow, meanwhile, focuses on the youthfulness of the *muí tsai*, who were "young female bondservants" most common in diasporic Chinese households across Southeast Asia. Many *muí tsai* were formally adopted into families to work as domestic laborers, blurring the lines between categories such as wife, concubine, and prostitute, similar to Chatterjee's study of slavery in India.[75] *Muí tsai* could receive an elevated social position in Chinese households by "seducing the master of the house." This destabilized European categories of family by enabling girls and women to change status from adopted daughter to sexual intimate.[76] "Modern Girls" became a global phenomenon in this period, evoking similar sexual anxieties and fascination due to their youthfulness and association with consumerism and sexuality.[77] In many cases they transgressed the appropriate boundaries of family—forcing fathers to confront daughters as sexualized beings.[78]

Colonial preoccupations with the age of colonial subjects often obscure the license that Europeans had to abuse children due to their privileged status within colonial courts, as Jonathan Saha has argued. This was the case with a British rubber planter named Captain McCormick who raped, kidnapped, and held hostage a Malay child named Ainah, according to her own testimony, in early twentieth-century colonial Burma.[79] McCormick's account asserted that he captured Ainah to help her after she contracted gonorrhea from being prostituted by her parents. The courts privileged McCormick's account over both Ainah's testimony and a medical inspection indicating that she had been a victim of sexual assault. His perceived legitimacy and trustworthiness as a white male planter meant that he was never prosecuted for the crime, despite inconsistencies in his testimony and subsequent revelations about miscarriages of justice. Ainah's immediate and extended family filed petitions but courts did not consider their accounts credible due to inconsistencies (for which McCormick had been forgiven), even though they had to record them in McCormick's presence while he cleaned his gun.[80]

European men who participated in illicit and condemned sexual acts often enjoyed exemption from prosecution in colonial spaces due to the perceived need to maintain colonial racial hierarchies. This helps to explain why authors and artists such as J.R. Ackerley, Somerset Maugham, Paul Gaugin, and E.M. Forster romanticized the sexual release of travel in the empire.[81] Lieutenant Reginald Abel Lewis Moysey provides another striking example. He threatened to kidnap a general's daughter after the imprisonment of his companion—and likely lover—Nur Hussein Shah in 1920s colonial India. British officials associated Muslim men, like Nur, from northwestern India as likely "sodomites," but they hesitated to categorize British men as the same.[82] One British official nonetheless ascribed this label to Moysey, inspiring someone to scratch the word out of some copies of the official correspondence.[83] While the colonial state regarded colonized subjects as "habitual sodomites" naturally inclined toward "pederasty," Europeans had their so-called "tendencies" monitored, hidden, silenced, and obscured.[84] Men accused of sodomy could face military discharges and mental health assessments, but these usually occurred behind closed doors.[85] In the Dutch East Indies, Europeans accused of participating in "sodomy" faced severe hostility by the twentieth century, including prominent artists and intellectuals. Nonetheless, many British colonial elites saw gaining a position in South and Southeast Asia as an opportunity to participate in sexual acts shunned in Europe.[86] The threat of "outing" still remained for those who were detected—indicating the relative privilege in colonial spaces hinged on European homophobia. In 1930s British Malaya the diary of a Chinese professional fell into the hands of police. This resulted in an official inquiry and the disgrace of several prominent British leaders, including two suicides, due to implications of homosexuality.[87] Nonetheless, in 1930s India, Signalman H.H. Somerfield enjoyed sexual relationships with men living in and around military cantonments, including fellow signalman Sultan Mohammad and café owner Brij Lal. He made casual references to buying the companionship of various men, even though he was from a working-class background and therefore at the bottom of the British social hierarchy.[88]

Due to the imbrication of colonialism with sexuality, discussions about sex are also inseparable from struggles against colonialism. As Mrinalini Sinha and Charu Gupta have shown, many Indian nationalist leaders rejected or adopted colonial categories of sexual difference to critique colonial rule. Some resented and challenged the colonial state's right to intervene in social and cultural matters, such as the age of consent debates, because it limited their own ability to control women.[89] This did not stop colonial leaders from stifling and censoring sexual publications in the nineteenth and twentieth centuries by passing and encouraging numerous obscenity laws.[90] Some reformers chafed against these restrictions on the grounds that knowledge of sex and the erotic was important for married life.[91] However, as Ruth Vanita has argued, Pandey Becan Sharma, or "Ugra," wrote *Chaklet*, published in 1927, which became a source of concern for colonial and nationalist leaders alike. It dealt with sex between men and boys and became a commercial success.[92] Indian nationalists resented its critiques of heterosexual marriage and the depiction of apparently feminized men who had been dominated by colonialism.[93] Many nationalists responded by condemning homosocial spaces such as gymnasiums, military barracks, and boarding schools for encouraging same-sex activities.[94] Katherine Mayo's notorious 1929 tome *Mother India* did not help. It became a flashpoint of debate for portraying Hindu culture as oversexed and Hindu men as effeminate, making them inadequate for self-government. She condemned women, too, by castigating trained midwives and depicting Indian women as abused child wives.[95] This inspired a defensive response among many Hindu nationalists, who increasingly depicted their own strength and masculinity through sexual potency.

Interwar Hindu masculinist nationalism targeted anyone or any sexual identity or practice that could be considered an impediment to an imagined Hindu-nationalist state. For example, influential BBC broadcaster Zulfaqar Bokhari faced a severe backlash for both his Muslim cosmopolitanism and his perceived "queerness," including intimate relations with British BBC broadcaster Lionel Fielden.[96] The Hindu revivalist and reformist movement known as *Arya Samaj*, meanwhile, emphasized the notion of *brahmacharya* (celibacy), which was linked to the warrior god Krishna. Gita Thadani suggests that Hindu nationalists praised "Aryan heritage" as a key to heroic warrior manhood. In many cases the glorification of the Aryan hero erased women's sexuality entirely.[97] This depiction became important for constructing a nationalist masculinity that could fight for independence.[98] The "enemy," according to this worldview, was supposedly over-sexed Muslim men. Hindu nationalists accused them of targeting innocent—implicitly asexual—Hindu "sisters" for rape and abductions to increase the Muslim population.[99] Women like Sarala Debi Ghosal, niece of Rabindranath Tagore, urged the study of martial arts so that men could defend Indian women.[100] By 1926 Pandey Becan Sharma, or "Ugra," offered a counter-narrative in *Chand Hasinon ki Khutut*, which sensationalized a romance between a Hindu boy and a Muslim girl, re-centering the sexual vitality and attractiveness of Hindu men compared to Muslims.[101] These sexualized understandings of masculinity, nationality, and community difference contributed to the sexual violence of World War II, the struggle for independence, and the partition of India.[102]

The use of sexual violence to demoralize civilian populations featured in World War II as well as in wars over decolonization. Such practices built on the long history of colonialism and colonial rhetoric, which justified the dehumanization and commodification of colonial subjects. The colonial habit of using camps to confine, humiliate, or facilitate violence against so-called "enemy" populations was most notorious in the German Holocaust. Yet this strategy not only borrowed from longer European colonial methods but also linked the wartime efforts of many empires—from Britain and Japan to the United States.[103] Japanese forces conscripted *ianfu*, or "Comfort Women," who were *de facto* sexual slaves during their invasion and occupation of Southeast Asia during World War II.[104] The fear of wartime sexual violence inspired many families of the Indian diaspora to refuse their daughters permission to serve in all-women's regiments such as the Rani of Jhansi Regiment of the anti-colonial Indian National Army. However, promises of creating familial bonds through the leadership of women such as Lakshmi Sahgal gave families confidence about their daughters' safety.[105]

A similar familial appeal, and the admiration for women like Shamsiah Fakeh and Zainab Mahmud, inspired some women to join the Malayan Communist Party, which fought against Japanese occupation and against British forces in the "Malayan Emergency" in the 1940s and 1950s. Communist leaders, like colonial elites, saw the regulation of sexuality as integral to maintaining fighters' productivity. For example, married couples were kept separate so as to not cause problems of unwanted pregnancies out in the field, while polygamy was strictly prohibited in certain regiments.[106] However, British forces did report picking up babies from guerrilla camps after parents had been killed, captured, or forced to retreat. Many babies were also handed over to local villagers for safe-keeping.[107] Some Chinese-language British propaganda warned women of the dangers of getting pregnant in the jungle to persuade women against fighting as communist insurgents.[108] Accusations of women being "used" as sexual outlets for male fighters were common, betraying the promises of egalitarian gender relations.[109] Colonial officials, meanwhile, emphasized how military spaces could offer family-friendly accommodation to soldiers, mobilizing colonial and capitalist promises of heteronormative monogamy.[110] Yet wars against communism and decolonization often continued the colonial pattern of viewing subject populations as transactional objects useful for maintaining the morale of soldiers or demoralizing civilians. Sexual violence, according to this view, was a natural and inevitable by-product of war.[111]

Whether facing British, French, Dutch, Japanese, or American conquest, colonial subjects lived within and beyond the narrow parameters of colonial rule. Challenging the assumed binaries of men vs. women, homosexual vs. heterosexual, or colonial vs. Indigenous has proven an important starting point—although it remains inadequate—to express the fluidity and diversity of human experience. The colonial process of making land into concrete and quantifiable regions of conquest was inseparable from the desire to mark, define, and control sexed bodies across multiple, competing empires. By thinking about the historiography of sexuality and colonialism through the lens of "transactions," this essay suggests that discourses of identity and liberation cannot fully encompass the sacrifices, bargains, and concessions that people endured or forged to make sense of sex under colonialism. Recent scholarship makes it essential to understand sex within and beyond other material considerations. Forced migration, confinement, demographically skewed working conditions, homosocial environments, hierarchical courtrooms, and other institutions of confinement or opportunity influenced how and why people used, turned to, enjoyed, or anguished over sex.

Further research can and is being done to correct the scholarly tendency to emphasize both imperialism and nationalism in defining and excluding sexual "others." This, at times, runs the risk of overlooking alternative concepts born from debates about Indigeneity and human ties to specific lands, places, and ancestral understandings of sexed bodies across generations. Scholars such as T.J. Tallie remind us of how studies of sex and sexuality can and should be transnational and comparative in their analysis. By engaging with questions of Indigeneity in North American colonial contexts, for example, we can gain fresh insight about British colonial rule and settler colonialism more broadly.[112] Transnational archival projects are actively being constructed—especially using oral history—to document histories of sexuality and colonialism beyond national borders. This is part of a wider scholarly project to "decolonize" history by decentering colonial goals, desires, and restrictions. In some cases these projects emphasize the experiences of present-day communities owing to the on-the-ground vulnerability and urgency of marginalized peoples in various places. Yet they provide a roadmap for how to creatively and innovatively write histories of the colonial period despite the limitations of historical sources and the dominance of colonial epistemologies in many archives.[113] Further, eugenicist and other colonial models of restricting the growth of the human population might be counterbalanced by alternative understandings of the relationship between humans and non-human life.[114] This might reveal greater linkages between the systemic violence of colonialism and the continued emphasis on sexual violence in forging and defining militaristic postcolonial states. Yet more work can, will, and must be done. Only by dismantling the militarized tools of colonial power can we imagine alternative sexual futures and wrest ourselves from the bargains and transactions that humanity has made with the past.

Notes

1 Stoler, *Race and the Education of Desire*; Said, *Orientalism*.
2 Loos, "Transnational Histories of Sexualities in Asia," 1311.
3 Chatterjee, "When 'Sexuality' Floated Free of Histories," 957.
4 Ibid., 951.
5 Ibid., 952.
6 Arondekar, *For the Record*, ch. 1.
7 Arondekar, *For the Record*; conversations with Erica Wald.

8 Arondekar, *For the Record*, ch. 1.
9 Ibid.
10 See also Stoler, *Along the Archival Grain*.
11 For examples of scholarship examining modern gender identities, see Ong and Peletz, *Bewitching Women, Pious Men*; Blackwood and Wieringa, eds., *Female Desires*; Misra and Chandiramani, *Sexuality, Gender and Rights*; Luther and Ung Loh, "*Queer*" *Asia*.
12 Andaya, *The Flaming Womb*.
13 Andaya, "From Temporary Wife to Prostitute," 12.
14 Peletz, *Gender Pluralism*, 87, 91.
15 Andaya, "From Temporary Wife to Prostitute," 15.
16 Peletz, *Gender Pluralism*, 85, 96–97.
17 Andaya, "From Temporary Wife to Prostitute," 17; see also Stoler, "Making Empire Respectable."
18 Chatterjee, "Colouring Subalternity," 50–51.
19 Ibid., 51.
20 Ibid., 62–63.
21 Sinha, *Specters of Mother India*, 45. For more on the regulation of the family in India, see Sen, "The Savage Family."
22 Peletz, *Gender Pluralism*, 84.
23 Ibid., 84.
24 Chatterjee, "When 'Sexuality' Floated Free," 947; Hinchy, *Governing Gender and Sexuality in Colonial India*, 2.
25 Tracol-Huynh, "Between Stigmatisation and Regulation."
26 Wallace, *Sexual Encounters*, 10.
27 Ibid., 29–30.
28 Wallace, *Sexual Encounters*.
29 Kennedy, *The Highly Civilized Man*, 77–78, 214.
30 Ibid., 85.
31 Kennedy, "'Captain Burton's Oriental Muck Heap,'" 320; Dixon, "Out of your clinging kisses….I create a new world."
32 Elliston, "Erotic Anthropology"; Wallace, *Sexual Encounters*, 33.
33 White, *The Alchemical Body*; Wujastyk, "The Path to Liberation," 34.
34 Singleton, *Yoga Body*, 64; Dixon, "Out of your clinging kisses"; Owen, *The Place of Enchantment*.
35 Myers, "W. B. Yeats's Steinach Operation," 111.
36 Imy, "Fascist Yogis."
37 Alter, "Indian Clubs and Colonialism," 508; Gupta, *Sexuality, Obscenity, Community*, ch. 1.
38 For contemporary discussions of these identities and their meanings, see also Boellstorff, *The Gay Archipelago*; Blackwood, "Gender Transgression in Colonial and Postcolonial Indonesia," 849.
39 Peletz, *Gender Pluralism*.
40 Blackwood, "Gender Transgression in Colonial and Postcolonial Indonesia," 851.
41 Ibid., 852.
42 Ibid., 864.
43 Ibid., 865.
44 Arondekar, *For the Record*, ch. 2.
45 Ibid.
46 Ibid.
47 Hossein, "De-Indianizing Hijra"; Blackwood and Johnson, "Queer Asian Subjects," 444.
48 Hinchy, *Governing Gender and Sexuality*, 3.
49 Andaya, "From Temporary Wife to Prostitute," 11–34; Tambe, *Codes of Misconduct*; Whitehead, "Bodies Clean and Unclean"; Mitra, *Indian Sex Life*.
50 Levine, *Prostitution, Race, and Politics*.
51 Proschan, "'Syphilis, Opiomania, and Pederasty.'"
52 Legg, "Stimulation, Segregation and Scandal"; Wald, "Defining Prostitution and Redefining Women's Roles"; Wald, *Vice in the Barracks*.
53 Chatterjee, "Colouring Subalternity," 59.
54 Ibid., 66–67.
55 Ibid., 92–93.
56 Jones, *Wives, Slaves, and Concubines*.

57 Ghosh, *Sex and the Family in Colonial India.*
58 Stoler, *Race and the Education of Desire*; Manderson, "Colonial Desires," 377; Shah, "Race-ing Sex."
59 Manderson, "Colonial Desires," 379.
60 Ibid., 374.
61 Ibid., 372–388.
62 Hui, "'Protecting Women,'" 7.
63 Ibid., 1.
64 Ibid., 1–30.
65 Manderson, "Colonial Desires," 387.
66 Datta, "'Immorality,' Nationalism and the Colonial State in British Malaya," 584–601, 585.
67 Ibid., 598. Spivak famously described a foundational mentality of colonial governance as "white men saving brown women from brown men." Spivak, "Can the Subaltern Speak?" 271–313; see also Mani, *Contentious Traditions.*
68 Chakraborty "European Nurses and Governesses."
69 Andaya, "From Temporary Wife to Prostitute," 17; see also Peletz, *Gender Pluralism*, 85.
70 Chakraborty, "European Nurses and Governesses."
71 Leow, "Age as a Category of Gender Analysis," 977; age is also considered in Stoler, *Race and the Education of Desire*, 137.
72 Sinha, *Colonial Masculinity*, 18.
73 Pande, "Coming of Age"; Leow, "Age as a Category," 978.
74 Sinha, *Specters of Mother India,* 8.
75 Leow, "Age as a Category of Gender Analysis," 979.
76 Ibid.
77 Ibid., 977, 980; see also Weinbaum et al., *The Modern Girl Around the World.*
78 Leow, "Age as a Category of Gender Analysis," 983.
79 Saha, "Whiteness, Masculinity."
80 Ibid., 4.
81 Said, *Orientalism*; Chaudhury, "Controlling the Ganymedes," 48.
82 Sinha, *Colonial Masculinity*, 19.
83 Imy, "Kidnapping and a 'Confirmed Sodomite'"; Imy, *Faithful Fighters.*
84 Arondekar, *For the Record*, ch. 2; Proschan, "Syphilis, Opiomania, and Pederasty," 610–636.
85 Arondekar, *For the Record*, ch. 2.
86 Peletz, Gender Pluralism, 116.
87 Ibid., 117.
88 Imy, "Queering the Martial Races."
89 See also Mani, *Contentious Traditions.*
90 Gupta, *Sexuality, Obscenity, Community*, ch. 2.
91 Ibid.
92 Ibid.; Vanita, "The New Homophobia."
93 Gupta, *Sexuality, Obscenity, Community*, ch. 2.
94 Vanita, "The New Homophobia," 247.
95 Sinha, *Specters of Mother India*, 79.
96 Zivin, "'Bent,'" 204, 210.
97 Thadani, "The Politics of Identities and Languages," 67.
98 Gupta, "Anxious Hindu Masculinity in Colonial North India," 441–442.
99 Ibid., 449.
100 Singleton, *Yoga Body*, 99.
101 Gupta, "Anxious Hindu Masculinity," 452.
102 Khan, *India at War*; Khan, *The Great Partition.*
103 For Britain's long history of camps, see Forth, *Barbed-Wire Imperialism*; see also Hinchy, "Gender, Family, and the Policing of the 'Criminal Tribes.'"
104 Yoshiaki, *Comfort Women*; Kazue, "The 'Comfort women.'"
105 Lebra, *Women Against the Raj*, 63–66.
106 Musa, "Women in the Malayan Communist Party," 245.
107 Ibid., 247.
108 Imy, "Pregnant in the Jungle."
109 Musa, "Women in the Malayan Communist Party," 246.

110 Imy, "Pregnant in the Jungle."
111 Rydström, "Politics of colonial violence"; Maxwell, "Moving Beyond Rape as a 'Weapon of War.'"
112 Tallie, *Queering Colonial Natal.*
113 See for example, Luther and Loh, eds., *Queer Asia.* The National Archives of Singapore has an extensive oral history collection which has recorded a range of actors' perspectives of empire, https://www.nas.gov.sg/archivesonline/oral_history_interviews/. For an example of how oral history is enabling greater variety in historical inquiry, see Biswas and Tripathi, "History and/through Oral Narratives." Finally, the Visibility Project foregrounds contemporary histories of "the national queer Asian Pacific American women and transgender community," http://www.visibilityproject.org/
114 Tallbear, "An Indigenous Reflection"; Livingston and Puar, "Interspecies"; Haraway, *When Species Meet.*

Bibliography

Alter, Joseph. "Indian Clubs and Colonialism: Hindu Masculinity and Muscular Christianity." *Comparative Studies in Society and History* 46, no. 3 (July 2004): 497–534. doi:10.1017/S0010417504000258.

Andaya, Barbara Watson. "From Temporary Wife to Prostitute: Sexuality and Economic Change in Early Modern Southeast Asia." *Journal of Women's History* 9, no. 4 (Winter 1998): 11–34. doi:10.1353/jowh.2010.0225.

Andaya, Barbara Watson. *The Flaming Womb: Repositioning Women in Early Modern Southeast Asia.* Honolulu: University of Hawaii Press, 2006.

Arondekar, Anjali. *For the Record: On Sexuality and the Colonial Archive in India.* Durham, NC: Duke University Press, 2009.

Blackwood, Evelyn. "Gender Transgression in Colonial and Postcolonial Indonesia." *The Journal of Asian Studies* 64, no. 4 (November 2005): 849–879.

Blackwood, Evelyn and Mark Johnson. "Queer Asian Subjects: Transgressive Sexualities and Heteronormative Meanings." *Asian Studies Review* 36 (December 2012): 441–451. doi:10.1080/10357823.2012.741037.

Blackwood, Evelyn and Saskia E. Wieringa, eds. *Female Desires: Same-Sex Relations and Transgender Practices Across Cultures.* New York: Columbia University Press, 1999.

Boellstorff, Tom. *The Gay Archipelago: Sexuality and Nation in Indonesia.* Princeton, NJ: Princeton University Press, 2005.

Chakraborty, Satyasikha. "European Nurses and Governesses in Indian Princely Households: 'Uplifting that impenetrable veil'?" *Journal of Colonialism and Colonial History* 19, no. 1 (Spring 2018): 1532–5768. doi:10.1353/cch.2018.0001.

Chapman Lebra, Joyce. *Women Against the Raj: The Rani of Jhansi Regiment.* Singapore: Institute of Southeast Asian Studies, 2008.

Chatterjee, Indrani. "Colouring Subalternity: Slaves, Concubines and Social Orphans in Early Colonial India." *Subaltern Studies* X (1999): 49–97.

Chatterjee, Indrani. "When 'Sexuality' Floated Free of Histories in South Asia." *Journal of Asian Studies* 71, no. 4 (November 2012): 945–962. doi:10.1017/S0021911812001246.

Chaudhury, Zahid. "Controlling the Ganymedes: The Colonial Gaze in J.R. Ackerley's Hindoo Holiday." *Journal of South Asian Studies* 24, no. 1 (2001): 47–57. doi:10.1080/00856400108723435.

Datta, Arunima. "'Immorality,' Nationalism and the Colonial State in British Malaya: Indian 'Coolie' Women's Intimate Lives as Ideological Battleground." *Women's History Review* 25, no. 4 (2016): 584–601. doi:10.1080/09612025.2015.1114326.

Dixon, Joy. "'Out of your clinging kisses….I create a new world': Sexuality and Spirituality in the Work of Edward Carpenter." In *The Ashgate Research Companion to Nineteenth-Century Spiritualism and the Occult*, edited by Tatiana Kontou and Sarah Willburn, 143–164. Farnham, UK, and Burlington, VT: Ashgate, 2012.

Elliston, Deborah. "Erotic Anthropology: 'Ritualized Homosexuality' in Melanesia and Beyond." *American Ethnologist* 22, no. 4 (November 1995): 848–867.

Ghosh, Durba. *Sex and the Family in Colonial India: The Making of Empire.* Cambridge, UK: Cambridge University Press, 2008. doi:10.1017/CBO9781139878418.

Gupta, Charu. *Sexuality, Obscenity, Community: Women, Muslims, and the Hindu Public in Colonial India.* New York: Palgrave and Permanent Black, 2001. doi:10.1057/9780230108196.

Gupta, Charu. "Anxious Hindu Masculinity in Colonial North India: Shuddhi and Sangathan Movements." *Cross Currents* 61, no. 4 (December 2011): 441–442. doi:10.1111/j.1939-3881.2011.00194.x.

Hinchy, Jessica. *Governing Gender and Sexuality in Colonial India: The Hijra, c.1850–1900.* Cambridge, UK: Cambridge University Press, 2019. doi:10.1017/9781108592208.

Hinchy, Jessica. "Gender, Family, and the Policing of the 'Criminal Tribes' in Nineteenth-Century North India." *Modern Asian Studies* (2020). doi:10.1017/S0026749X19000295.

Hossein, Adnan. "De-Indianizing Hijra: Intraregional Effacements and Inequalities in South Asian Queer Space." *Transgender Studies Quarterly* 5, no. 3 (August 2018): 321–331. doi:10.1215/23289252-6900710.

Imy, Kate. "Queering the Martial Races: Masculinity, Sex and Circumcision in the Twentieth-Century British Indian Army." *Gender & History* 27, no. 2 (August 2015): 374–396. doi:10.1111/1468-0424.12130.

Imy, Kate. "Fascist Yogis: Martial Bodies and Imperial Impotence." *Journal of British Studies* 55, no. 2 (April 2016): 320–343. doi:10.1017/jbr.2016.1.

Imy, Kate. "Kidnapping and a 'Confirmed Sodomite': An Intimate Enemy on the Northwest Frontier of India, 1915–1925." *Twentieth Century British History* 28, no. 1 (March 2017): 29–56. doi:10.1093/tcbh/hww058.

Imy, Kate. *Faithful Fighters: Identity and Power in the British Indian Army.* Stanford, CA: Stanford University Press, 2019.

Luther, Daniel and Jennifer Ung Loh, eds. *Queer Asia: Decolonising and Reimagining Sexuality and Gender.* London: Zeb Books, 2019.

Jones, Eric. *Wives, Slaves, and Concubines: A History of the Female Underclass in Dutch Asia.* DeKalb, IL: Northern Illinois Press, 2010.

Kazue, Muta. "The 'Comfort women' Issue and the Embedded Culture of Sexual Violence in Contemporary Japan." *Current Sociology* 64, no. 4 (July 2016): 620–636. doi:10.1177/0011392116640475.

Kennedy, Dane. "'Captain Burton's Oriental Muck Heap': The Book of the Thousand Nights and the Uses of Orientalism." *Journal of British Studies* 39, no. 3 (July 2000): 317–339. doi:10.1086/386222.

Kennedy, Dane. *The Highly Civilized Man: Richard Burton and the Victorian World.* Cambridge, MA: Harvard University Press, 2005.

Khan, Yasmin. *The Great Partition: The Making of India and Pakistan.* New Haven, CT: Yale University Press, 2008.

Khan, Yasmin. *India at War: The Subcontinent and the Second World War.* Oxford, UK: Oxford University Press, 2015.

Legg, Stephen. "Stimulation, Segregation and Scandal: Geographies of Prostitution Regulation in British India, between Registration (1888) and Suppression (1923)." *Modern Asian Studies* 46, no. 6 (November 2012): 1459–1505. doi:10.1017/S0026749X11000503.

Leow, Rachel. "Age as a Category of Gender Analysis: Servant Girls, Modern Girls, and Gender in Southeast Asia." *The Journal of Asian Studies* 71, no. 4 (November 2012): 975–990. doi:10.1017/S0021911812001258.

Levine, Philippa. *Prostitution, Race, and Politics: Policing Venereal Disease in the British Empire.* New York: Routledge, 2003.

Loos, Tamara. "Transnational Histories of Sexualities in Asia." *The American Historical Review* 114, no. 5 (December 2009): 1309–1324. doi:10.1086/ahr.114.5.1309.

Luther, J. Daniel and Jennifer Ung Loh, eds. *'Queer' Asia: Decolonising and Reimagining Sexuality and Gender.* London: Zed Books, 2019.

Manderson, Lenore. "Colonial Desires: Sexuality, Race, and Gender in British Malaya." *Journal of the History of Sexuality* 7, no. 3 (January 1997): 372–388.

Mani, Lata. *Contentious Traditions: The Debate on Sati in Colonial India.* Berkeley, CA: University of California Press, 1998.

McClintock, Anne. *Imperial Leather: Race, Gender, and Sexuality in the Colonial Contest.* New York: Routledge, 1995.

Misra, Geetanjali and Radhika Chandiramani, eds. *Sexuality, Gender and Rights: Exploring Theory and Practice in South and Southeast Asia.* New Delhi: Sage Publications, 2005.

Mitra, Durba. *Indian Sex Life: Sexuality and the Colonial Origins of Modern Social Thought.* Princeton, NJ: Princeton University Press, 2020.

Musa, Mahani. "Women in the Malayan Communist Party, 1942–89." *Journal of Southeast Asian Studies* 44, no. 2 (June 2013): 226–249. doi:10.1017/S0022463413000052.

Myers, Kimberly R. "W.B. Yeats's Steinach Operation, Hinduism, and the Severed-Head Plays of 1934–1935." *Literature and Medicine* 28, no. 1 (Spring 2009): 102–137. doi:10.1353/lm.0.0038.

Ong, Aihwa and Michael G. Peletz. *Bewitching Women, Pious Men: Gender and Body Politics in Southeast Asia.* Berkeley, CA: University of California Press, 1995.

Owen, Alex. *The Place of Enchantment: British Occultism and the Culture of the Modern.* Chicago and London: University of Chicago Press, 2004.

Pande, Ishita. "Coming of Age: Law, Sex and Childhood in Late Colonial India." *Gender & History* 24, no. 1 (2012): 205–230. doi:10.1111/j.1468-0424.2011.01676.x.

Peletz, Michael G. *Gender Pluralism: Southeast Asia Since Early Modern Times.* New York and London: Routledge, 2009.

Proschan, Frank. "'Syphilis, Opiomania, and Pederasty': Colonial Constructions of Vietnamese (and French) Social Diseases." *Journal of the History of Sexuality* 11, no. 4 (2002): 610–636. doi:10.1353/sex.2003.0043.

Rydström, Helle. "Politics of colonial violence: Gendered atrocities in French occupied Vietnam." *European Journal of Women's Studies* 22, no. 2 (2014): 191–207. doi:10.1177/1350506814538860.

Saha, Jonathan. "Whiteness, Masculinity and the Ambivalent Embodiment of 'British Justice' in Colonial Burma." *Cultural and Social History* 14, no. 4 (2017): 527–542. doi:10.1080/14780038.2017.1329125.

Said, Edward. *Orientalism.* New York: Vintage, 1979.

Sen, Satadru. "The Savage Family: Colonialism and Female Infanticide in Nineteenth Century India." *Journal of Women's History* 14, no. 3 (2002): 53–79. doi:10.1353/jowh.2002.0075.

Shah, Nayan. "Race-ing Sex." *Frontiers* 35, no. 1 (2014): 26–36. doi:10.5250/fronjwomestud.35.1.0026.

Singleton, Mark. *Yoga Body: The Origins of Modern Posture Practice.* Oxford, UK: Oxford University Press, 2010.

Sinha, Mrinalini. *Colonial Masculinity: The 'Manly Englishman' and the 'Effeminate Bengali' in the Late Nineteenth Century.* Manchester, UK: Manchester University Press, 1995.

Sinha, Mrinalini. *Specters of Mother India: The Global Restructuring of an Empire.* Durham, NC: Duke University Press, 2006.

Stoler, Ann L. "Making Empire Respectable: The Politics of Race and Sexual Morality in 20th-Century Colonial Cultures." *American Ethnologist* 16, no. 4 (November 1989): 634–660. doi:10.1525/ae.1989.16.4.02a00030.

Stoler, Ann Laura. "'In Cold Blood': Hierarchies of Credibility and the Politics of Colonial Narratives." *Representations* 37 (Winter 1992): 151–189. doi:10.2307/2928658.

Stoler, Ann Laura. *Race and the Education of Desire: Foucault's History of Sexuality and the Colonial Order of Things.* Durham, NC: Duke University Press, 1995.

Stoler, Ann Laura. *Along the Archival Grain: Epistemic Anxieties and Colonial Common Sense.* Princeton, NJ: Princeton University Press, 2009.

Tallbear, Kim. "An Indigenous Reflection on Working Beyond the Human/Not Human." *GLQ: A Journal of Lesbian and Gay Studies* 21, no. 2/3 (2015): 230–235.

Tallie, T.J. *Queering Colonial Natal: Indigeneity and the Violence of Belonging in Southern Africa.* Minneapolis, MN: University of Minnesota Press, 2019.

Tambe, Ashwini. *Codes of Misconduct: Regulating Prostitution in Late Colonial Bombay.* New Delhi: Zubaan, 2009.

Tan Beng Hui. "'Protecting Women': Legislation and Regulation of Women's Sexuality in Colonial Malaya." *Gender, Technology and Development* 7, no. 1 (2003): 1–30. doi:10.1177/097185240300700101.

Thadani, Gita. "The Politics of Identities and Languages: Lesbian Desire in Ancient and Modern India." In *Female Desires*, edited by Evelyn Blackwood and Saskia E. Wieringa, 67–90. New York: Columbia University Press, 1999.

Tracol-Huynh, Isabelle. "Between Stigmatisation and Regulation: Prostitution in Colonial Northern Vietnam." *Culture, Health & Sexuality* 12 (August 2010): S73–S87. doi:10.1080/13691051003706561.

Vanita, Ruth. "The New Homophobia: Ugra's Chocolate." In *Same-Sex Love in India: Readings from Literature and History*, edited by Ruth Vanita and Saleem Kidwai, 246–252. New York: St. Martin's Press, 2000.

Wald, Erica. "Defining Prostitution and Redefining Women's Roles: The Colonial State and Society in Early 19th Century India." *History Compass* 7, no. 6 (November 2009): 1470–1483. doi:10.1111/j.1478-0542.2009.00647.x.

Wald, Erica. *Vice in the Barracks: Medicine, the Military and the Making of Colonial India, 1780–1868.* New York: Palgrave, 2014.

Wallace, Lee. *Sexual Encounters: Pacific Texts, Modern Sexualities.* Ithaca, NY: Cornell University Press, 2003.

Weinbaum, Alys Eve et al. *The Modern Girl Around the World: Consumption, Modernity, and Globalization.* Durham, NC: Duke University Press, 2008.

White, David Gordon. *The Alchemical Body: Siddha Traditions in Medieval India*. Chicago, IL: University of Chicago Press, 1998.

Whitehead, Judy. "Bodies Clean and Unclean: Prostitution, Sanitary Legislation, and Respectable Femininity in Colonial North India." *Gender and History* 7, no. 1 (April 1995): 41–63. doi:10.1111/j.1468-0424.1995.tb00013.x.

Wujastyk, Dominik. "The Path to Liberation through Yogic Mindfulness in Early Ayurveda," in *Yoga in Practice*, edited by David Gordon White, 31–42. Princeton, NJ: Princeton University Press, 2011.

Yoshiaki, Yoshimi. *Comfort Women: Sexual Slavery in the Japanese Military During World War II*. New York: Columbia University Press, 2000.

Zivin, Joselyn. "'Bent': A Colonial Subversive and Indian Broadcasting." *Past and Present* 162 (February 1999): 1995–1220. doi:10.1093/past/162.1.195.

7

SETTLER SEXUALITIES

Reproducing nations in the United States, Canada, Australia, and New Zealand

Gregory D. Smithers

"The art of putting men in their place is perhaps foremost in the science of government," Charles Maurice de Talleyrand declared in 1840.[1] Talleyrand, Napoleon I's foreign minister, understood the importance of controlling people and the geographical spaces they inhabited. He believed that if regions of "conquest" were to become permanently "settled" and "civilized," a socially compliant and culturally harmonious population was essential. Talleyrand's thinking, inflected as it was with an undemocratic spirit, echoed the sentiments of settler colonial officials throughout the nineteenth-century world. In the United States, Canada, Australia, and New Zealand—the focus of this chapter—government officials became alchemists of social order as they strove to conjure an idealized body politic; something the French philosopher Michel Foucault referred to as the "biopolitics" of population. Importantly, and as Foucault observed, such alchemy relied on the entrenchment of heterosexuality as normative and an insistence on the patriarchal family as essential to the reproduction of the settler body politic.[2]

In nineteenth-century settler societies, colonial officials, physicians, the clergy, and ethnologists used sex and sexuality to draw attention to myriad sociocultural anxieties. Controlling human bodies—what people did with them, and with whom they did it—revealed not only the historically specific ways in which corporeal meaning changed and was managed over time, but highlighted the constant unease that the architects of settler societies felt about their (in)ability to shape and reshape settler populations.[3] That seemingly constant sense of anxiety led to cycles of legal, political, and cultural prescriptions that entered colonial discourses and structured settler power dynamics. These discourses, and the structures they informed, did not go unchallenged by Indigenous people. That said, when settler colonial officials and their allies prescribed "normal" sexual behavior they laid claim to an understanding of, and power over, human bodies and the types of society those bodies inhabited.[4]

This chapter focuses on two interrelated aspects of sexuality in settler colonies. The first builds on what became popularly accepted Western understandings of sexuality at the end of the eighteenth century. These ideals informed cultural and policy prescriptions about "normal" forms of sexual behavior. The second, and related issue, emphasizes the struggle of settler states to control and contain Indigenous sexualities as a means of colonial conquest and territorial dispossession. Here my analysis ventures into the terrain of feelings, assumptions, and attitudes that historians have cataloged over the past half century—a field of inquiry that includes efforts to decolonize the history of sexuality in settler societies. While I'm cognizant of the racial, religious, and ethnic diversity of the settler societies covered in this chapter, space only allows for an engagement with the dynamics created by Indigenous–colonizer histories. This chapter therefore provides a historiographical overview of the above two issues to reveal not only the "eliminationist" tendencies of settler societies, but to highlight the complex ways in which settler sexualities intersected with, and were informed by, cultural and political constructions of race and gender and attempted to remake Native space into "white" space during the nineteenth century.[5]

The historian Jeffrey Weeks has argued that "the sexual and moral diversity of the past [can] lead us to be a little more accepting of the diversity of the present."[6] Acceptance, however, wasn't what the architects of nineteenth-century settler nations wanted to encourage. Anxieties about the meaning of national belonging fueled concerns about the policing of borders—both real and imagined—and led to calls for the engineering of demographically stable, homogenous populations.[7]

Defining settler sexualities in these contexts proved vital to the work of creating settler states in which white supremacy and racial exclusivity were characteristic features. First, however, I want to pause and offer a working definition of what I mean by the phrase "settler sexualities." In a broad sense, settler sexualities defined a panoply of sex acts and sexual identities during the nineteenth century. But as I argue below, narrow legal and cultural prescriptions of "normal" or "deviant" sexuality emerged as nineteenth-century doctors, politicians, and law enforcement officials defined sexuality in increasingly rigid and narrow terms. In other words, these agents of the settler state contrived a definition of "normal" sexual activity to privilege reproductive sexual behavior among settlers within marriage. These discourses nurtured fictions about monogamous marriages and patriarchal families being vital to the future wellbeing of settler societies.[8] Indeed, they built on sixteenth- and seventeenth-century efforts to undermine Indigenous traditions of marriage and kinship, and attacked, often violently, Native communities in which two-spirit people occupied important social and political positions of authority.[9]

Marriages recognized by the law and sanctified by religious officials became a way for nineteenth-century settler societies to organize society and build nations.[10] However, historian Nancy Cott reminds us that the denial of legal marriages to enslaved African Americans in the nineteenth-century United States is an example of how politically and legally defined notions of marriage preserved and protected white privilege.[11] Alternatively, settler stereotypes about Indigenous polygamy in Canada, Australian Aboriginal women engaging in prostitution, and European perceptions of Maori sexual libertines reveal how sex and gender constructs intersected with racial caricatures of Indigenous "otherness" to justify territorial invasion and dispossession, and to ultimately draw the parameters of settler citizenship for white people.[12]

Heterosexual monogamy was therefore an important racial and sexual tool for the settler state in clarifying social belonging and citizenship after the 1780s. Colonial officials used heterosexual monogamy to define normative sexual behavior, clarify categories of deviance, and exclude Indigenous people from "civilized" society—thereby providing a neat rationale for territorial dispossession.[13] Indeed, cultural and legal constructs of sexual deviance—and its increasingly explicit links with a medicalized vocabulary of "contagion" and "confinement" and eugenic concepts of "public health" throughout the nineteenth century—provided a flexible language that embedded settler patriarchy into the fabric of social and political life in the United States, Canada, Australia, and New Zealand.[14]

When George Washington became the United States' first president in 1789, sexual monogamy was far from the norm it became a century later. Christian monogamists constituted a minority of the world's population, but in the new United States the future of the settler state quickly became associated with personal mastery of one's sexual feelings and actions—a factor that helps to explain outrage about Mormon polygamists during the nineteenth century.[15] In a republic that proclaimed itself home to a virtuous citizenry, men and women ideally entered a marriage voluntarily, with mutual consent, and to reproduce the settler republic's white population.[16]

During the late eighteenth and early nineteenth centuries, couples of European descent married for a variety of reasons. This proved as true in Canada as it did in the nascent United States. Community connections, a shared religious belief, a common socioeconomic background, or access to property could precipitate a marriage. Marriage could also elevate the social standing of a couple in most parts of settler colonial Canada, although there were exceptions. In Montreal, for example, an increase in the immigrant population led to a decrease in the number of marriage licenses by the 1820s. This trend revealed the class dimensions associated with settler marriages, with the number of marriage licenses issued to bourgeois couples far outnumbering those of immigrant and working-class Canadians.[17]

The settler state's use of marriage as a tool to define normal sexual behavior, shape the categories of class and culture, and control labor became integral to the structures of settler colonial life in Canada and the United States during the nineteenth century—an important point that can also reveal fractures in "whiteness" during that century. Such frameworks built on English common law traditions that tied land and inheritance to patriarchal family formations.[18] As such, "love" wasn't just "a political event," as Elizabeth Povinelli observes, but a source of economic advancement and a statement about cultural belonging and stability.[19]

In North America, nineteenth-century white settlers viewed Indigenous and African American people as outside emerging bourgeois ideals of family and sexual propriety. White views of Native and African American sexuality both varied and overlapped. For example, when the Cherokee leader Elias Boudinot married Harriet Gold, a white woman, Gold's family accused the couple of indulging in "animal feeling" and warned Harriet that marriage to Elias would result in her loss of racial status—her "Gold shall shortly dim," Gold's brother warned. Not satisfied with these cruel barbs, Harriet Gold's brother-in-law warned that any children conceived in the marriage would result in "black young ones and a train of evil."[20] Such language, usually reserved for scandalized whites in describing "amalgamation" between white and African American couples, underscores how sexual and marital choices were connected to social, economic, and political concepts of power and privilege. As such, Indigenous communities had their land expropriated and African Americans were excluded from the means of production and their labor exploited.[21]

In Australia, focusing on the alterity of Aboriginal people began as soon as the First Fleet made anchor in Sydney Harbor. Australia was founded as a penal colony in January 1788. Over the past three decades, popular writers have portrayed the antipodean penal colonies as rough and violent places where "orgies" were commonplace and convicts routinely partook in the "great Sydney bacchanal."[22] These descriptions lack nuance, but they do remind us that for white women—be they convict or free—early colonial Australia wasn't a safe place. Women lived in a colony in which phrases like "have a grinding mill, to grind the fine corn" were used as euphemism for gang rape. Indeed, the historian Graham Willett argues that the term "pack-rape" was coined in colonial Australia.[23]

Colonial officials applied enlightenment principles in a bid to bring "civilization" to New South Wales by stamping out rape, sodomy, and sex with animals.[24] As in North America, sexual acts such as masturbation, rape, same-sex relationships, women who were sexually aggressive toward men, and bestiality (which occurred most commonly with dogs, sows, and horses) earned the ire of colonial officials. For example, in 1796 a laborer by the name of George Hyson was charged with having "carnal knowledge" with a dog, a crime that carried a potential sentence of death. Hyson avoided the gallows, however, after being convicted on the lesser charge of intent to have carnal knowledge with a dog.[25]

Early colonial efforts to police sexuality in Australia were riven with hypocrisies. If the United States' "founding fathers" engaged in sexual hypocrisy—most notably by keeping enslaved women to service their sexual desires—British officials in colonial Australia were no less unethical. Judge-advocate David Collins, who railed against Aboriginal sexual behavior and insisted that rape within colonial society "could not be passed with impunity," engaged in sexual behaviors that bankrupted his moral authority in the eyes of his contemporaries. In the initial years of the colony, Collins, who left his wife behind in England, took a convict mistress only to replace her with another—a 15-year-old girl.[26]

Reform, however, did eventually come to the Australian colonies with the arrival of the autocratic governor Lachlan Macquarie in 1810. Macquarie's reforms built on schemes initiated in the 1790s that sought to incentivize good behavior and marriage with offers of government employment or land. Colonial officials emphasized the importance of marriage to the maintenance of good moral character among colonial landholders. For example, an emancipated convict could receive 30 acres of land and an additional ten acres for each child produced in marriage. In this way colonial officials established incentives for emancipated convicts to contribute to the territorial dispossession of Aboriginal Australians by linking marriage and human reproduction to landholding and the accumulation of household wealth.[27]

Calls for reforms to colonial society grew louder in London following Commissioner John Bigge's report in the early 1820s. Among Bigge's recommendations were closer monitoring of convict sexuality and clearer class distinctions among convicts and free settlers, recommendations that undercut Governor Macquarie's rewarding of convicts for good conduct by giving them government posts. Additionally, arguments favoring protections for emigrating women grew louder—no small matter in a colony where men far outnumbered women.[28]

Despite all this, racial stereotypes about black, or Aboriginal, sexuality not only persisted but grew stronger.[29] Along the southeastern seaboard of Australia and Van Diemen's Land (Tasmania) a "sex industry" developed in the decades prior to New Zealand's founding as a British settler colony in 1840. This "industry" involved British and American men employed in the sealing trade and Aboriginal women (and, in some instances, Indigenous girls as young as eight).[30] Colonial discourse constructed the women and girls involved in this "sex industry" as prostitutes, a simplification that belied a far more complex set of relationship that ranged from the physically violent to something that the historian Lynette Russell calls "domestic arrangements."[31]

Sexual relationships between European men and Aboriginal women revealed the limits of the settler state's power to control intimate personal relationships. That said, it's important to remember that British invaders conceptualized colonial Australia as a masculinist space. Violent, often authoritarian, forms of masculinity persisted as the colonies prepared for self-government in the mid-nineteenth century. On the frontiers of settlement this meant that some settler men and local officials conspired to silence reports of interracial sexual violence—behavior that contradicted prescribed standards of sexual conduct for settlers.[32]

Masculinity in the southwest Pacific, as in North America, was never monolithic. However, by the mid-nineteenth century a form of masculinity that celebrated physical prowess and strength became part of settler colonial mythology in both Australia and New Zealand.

In Australia, this type of masculinity was viewed as essential for colonies. To settle the tropical north and conquer the vastness of Australia's interior and west coast, men of courage and strength were deemed essential. At the same time, colonial officials in Sydney and Melbourne and Christian missionaries broke the silence surrounding sexual violence against Aboriginal women and sometimes pointed to these men as contributing to a breakdown in racial order. Colonial officials identified these breakdowns in sexual self-control among white men at the end of the century as a contributing factor in the "half-caste problem," a shorthand for the growing population of mixed-race Aboriginal children born from illicit sexual encounters (including rape) involving white men and Indigenous women.[33]

Across the Tasman Sea in New Zealand, myths about individualistic forms of masculinity became linked to the founding of the colony in 1840. Narratives about an idealized type of settler male included commentary about the importance of comradeship among physically strong and tough men. Such qualities defined "real men" and ultimately became integral to the articulation of New Zealand nationalism. However, these qualities, which one scholar labels "hard" masculinities and typically associated with rural men, conceal an important point of comparison between British colonial New Zealand and Australia.[34]

When the New Zealand Company oversaw the transportation of 1,012 passengers to New Zealand between 1840 and 1842, more than 90 per cent traveled with kin. Traveling with family support networks, a factor that aligned with English working-class ideals, characterized this original settler population. Unlike the convict origins of neighboring Australia, family networks traveled to New Zealand. Edward Gibbon Wakefield wrote about the importance of this demographic reality to the future of settler society in New Zealand. Wakefield, whose ideas about systematic colonization were first tried with the founding of South Australia in the 1830s, insisted that the new settler colony of New Zealand "is a bad place for a young *single* man. To be single is contrary to the nature of a new colony, where the laws of society are labour, peace, domestic life, increase and multiply."[35]

Thousands of miles across the Pacific, the racially diverse western frontiers of the United States bore witness to both myths and more complex realities pertaining to gendered identities. In the American West, for instance, settlers and soldiers invaded, killed, and raped their way through Indigenous communities and stole their lands.[36] To the United States' north, a similar narrative unfolded in Canada.[37]

In New Zealand, anxieties about sexual violence were on full display by the 1850s and 1860s. Historians of New Zealand have demonstrated how court records reveal a steady stream of Pākehā (white) men being charged with rape, or assault with intent to rape Māori women. Recognizing this trend, nineteenth-century courts worked to give Māori people the impression that the colonial justice system operated to protect them as much as it operated to maintain law and order for settler communities. However, racial and gendered stereotypes tended to inform rulings. For example, courts routinely downgraded judgements against white men while undermining the "moral character" of Māori women in rape and attempted-rape cases.

Such was the case for Michael Caffrey. Caffrey stood before the Wellington Supreme Court in 1866 charged with assault with intent to rape. Although two Māori women observed Caffrey's assault and testified to the court about what they saw, Caffrey insisted that the Māori woman who brought the charge against him had plied him with liquor and taken advantage of him. Caffrey claimed that while intoxicated he discovered that "his trousers had been torn off." The court bought Caffrey's story. Satisfied, the court downgraded his charge and sentenced Caffrey to eighteenth months in prison for indecent assault.[38]

The historian Steven Maynard has argued that "nations depend on sex."[39] True enough. But just as immigration policy in the United States, Canada, Australia, and New Zealand revolved around "the right kind of bodies, those suited to building a white settler colony," so these settler states strove to manage sex and human sexuality in increasingly intrusive ways during the latter third of the nineteenth century.[40] During these final decades of the nineteenth century, European immigrants flocked to North America and the settler colonies of the southwest Pacific in record numbers. Internally, mixed-race populations attracted media headlines. During an era in which eugenics and xenophobic ideologies circulated (and often intersected) throughout the Anglo-colonial world, there were nativist demands for Anglo-Saxon "blood" to be protected from the immigrant hordes and subaltern lasciviousness lest the "blood" be replaced by "colored" races.[41] Within the settler states, managing bodies took on renewed urgency.[42]

All four settler states remained committed to white supremacy. In the United States and Canada, boarding schools and segregation laws operated to manage Indigenous bodies, keeping them separate from the increasingly variegated white masses.[43] In Australia and New Zealand, assertions that mixed-race Indigenous populations were on the rise produced some alarming claims about illicit sex on the frontiers of settlement. In some corners of the colonial bureaucracy, advocates for programs that would manage interracial marriage insisted that state oversight was the only way to stamp out illicit race mixing and "breed out the colour."[44]

By the late nineteenth century, cacophonous immigration debates had broken out in the United States, Canada, Australia, and New Zealand. The loudest and most sensational voices in these debates demanded stronger borders to protect the settler state from foreign threats. However, threats already existed within these four settler states. These threats required different types of borders—legal walls, physical separation, and moral vigilance to prevent racialized bodies mixing with white bodies.[45]

What emerges from more than two generations of sustained historical inquiry is a compelling case for how sexuality was used to create white settler states. If historians are to continue adding to our understanding of the kinds of histories that sex and sexuality had in settler colonial spaces, then we need to build on this scholarship by continuing to add new voices.[46] The histories we write in the future will undoubtedly reflect new archival discoveries as much as they will involve asking new questions about old sources. At the same time, historians of settler sexuality must continue being interdisciplinary in how we approach evidence and how we present historical analyses of the past. This will enable us to better represent the panoply of sexual expressions that existed in settler colonies but which the settler state tried to stifle and crush.

Notes

1 Crooks and Parsons, "Empires, Bureaucracy and the Paradox of Power," 18.
2 Foucault, *"Society Must Be Defended,"* 244. See also Katz, *The Invention of Heterosexuality*, 177.
3 Butler, "Performative Acts and Gender Constitution"; D'Emilio and Freedman, *Intimate Matters*, xii–xiii; Grosz, *Volatile Bodies*, xi; Comaroff and Comaroff, *Of Revelation and Revolution*, 324–325; Povinelli, *The Empire of Love*, 7. On persistent attempts and difficulties to shape settler and Indigenous sexualities, see Smithers, *Science, Sexuality, and Race,* 337; Ellinghaus, "Strategies of Elimination"; Morgan, "Creating Interracial Intimacies."
4 Collingham, *Imperial Bodies*, 6; Hawkes, *Sex and Pleasure in Western Culture*, 110–111; Sweet, *Bodies Politic*; Angier, *Sexing the Body*, 7–8; Lambert and Lester, "Imperial Spaces, Imperial Subjects"; Stoler, *Carnal Knowledge and Imperial Power*; Henderson, *Settler Feminism and Race Making in Canada*; Godbeer, *Sexual Revolution in Early America*; Levine, *Prostitution, Race & Politics*; Aldridge, *Colonialism and Homosexuality*; Burton and Ballantyne, "Introduction," 4; Laqueur, *Solitary Sex*; Edmonds and Nettelbeck,

eds. *Intimacies of Violence in the Settler Colony*; Aderinto, *When Sex Threatened the State*; Smithers, *Science, Sexuality, and Race*, 203; Morgan, "Creating Interracial Intimacies."

5 Weeks, *Making Sexual History*, 133–137; Harris, "How did Colonialism Dispossess?" see espec. 169; Forsyth, "After the Fur Trade"; Wolfe, "Settler Colonialism and the Elimination of the Native"; Veracini, *Settler Colonialism*. For a recent historical critique of settler colonial ideologies, see Greer, *Property and Dispossession*.

6 Weeks, *Making Sexual History*, 139.

7 Huttenback, "The British Empire as a 'White Man's Country'"; Ward, *White Canada Forever*; Kelley and Trebilock, *The Making of the Mosiac*, ch. 2; Jacobson, *Whiteness of a Different Color*; Bashford, "Immigration Restriction."

8 Lake and Reynolds, *Drawing the Global Colour Line*; Saler, *The Settlers' Empire*, 2.

9 Williams, *The Spirit and the Flesh*; Roscoe, *Changing Ones*; Morgensen, *Spaces Between Us*; Driskill, Justice, Miranda, Tatonetti, *Sovereign Erotics*; Rifkin, *When Did the Indians Become Straight?*; Rifkin, *The Erotics of Sovereignty*; Rifkin, *Settler Common Sense*; Driskill, *Asegi Stories*. See also my forthcoming *Reclaiming Two-Spirits*.

10 For example, see Sangster, *Regulating Girls and Women*, 168–193; Carter, *The Importance of Being Monogamous*; Wanhalla, *Matters of the Heart*; Seuffert, *Jurisprudence of National Identity*.

11 Cott, *Public Vows*, 32–33.

12 On this point, see Catlin, *Letters and Notes on the Manners*, 334; Yee, *Exotic Subversions in Nineteenth-Century French Fiction*; Waymouth, "Parliamentary Representation for the Maori."

13 Barman, "Taming Aboriginal Sexuality."

14 Anderson, *Imagined Communities*; Dauvergne, *The New Politics of Immigration and the End of Settler Societies*, 14; Harris, "Sex on the Margins," 1089.

15 Cannon, "The Awesome Power of Sex"; White, Jr., and White, "Polygamy and Mormon Identity."

16 Cott, *Public Vows*, 9–11, 19; Wood, *The Radicalism of the American Revolution*, 104.

17 Noël, *Family Life and Sociability in Upper and Lower Canada*, 62–63.

18 Ward, *Courtship, Love, and Marriage in Nineteenth-Century English Canada*, 15, 19, 42; Chambers, "Married Women's Property Law," espec. 429; Saler, *The Settlers' Empire*, 24.

19 Povinelli, *The Empire of Love*, 175.

20 Smithers, *The Cherokee Diaspora*, 89–90; McGrath, *Illicit Love*, ch. 1.

21 See for example, Catlin, *Letters and Notes*, 334.

22 For "orgies," see Hughes, *The Fatal Shore*, 563. For the "great Sydney bacchanal," see Kenneally, *Australians*, 12. For an insightful critique of these sensational accounts of early colonial Australia, see Bongiorno, *The Sex Lives of Australians*.

23 "Pack, local term," Letters to the Editor, *Australia*, July 18, 2002, 10. For fuller accounts of the experiences of convict women, see Damousi, *Depraved and Disorderly*; Rees, *The Floating Brothel*.

24 Gascoigne, *The Enlightenment and the Origins of European Australia*, 3.

25 Byrne, *Criminal Law and Colonial Subject*, 106–107; Bongiorno, *The Sex Lives of Australians*, ch.1.

26 Bongiorno, *The Sex Lives of Australians*, ch.1.

27 Smithers, *Science, Sexuality, and Race*, 51. See also Molony, *The Native-Born*.

28 Damousi, *Depraved and Disorderly*, 100; Benton and Ford, *Rage for Order*, 62.

29 For late-eighteenth- and early-nineteenth-century British perceptions of Aboriginal Australians as "black" and a branch of the "African race," see Smithers, *Science, Sexuality, and Race*.

30 Bongiorno, *The Sex Lives of Australians*, ch. 1.

31 Russell, "'Dirty Domestics and Worse Cooks,'" 19. See also Ryan, "The Struggle for Recognition"; McGrath, "Sex, Violence and Theft," 135; Taylor, "Savages and Saviours."

32 Berg and Kearns, "Naming as Norming," espec. 100.

33 McGregor, *Imagined Destinies*; Smithers, *Science, Sexuality, and Race*, 247, 251–272.

34 Woodward, "It's a Man's Life!"

35 Garnett, *Edward Gibbon Wakefield*, 320. For further analysis, see Tosh, *Manliness and Masculinities*.

36 Hurtado, *Intimate Frontiers*, 3; Spear, *Race, Sex, and Social Order*, 179, 181–182; Pascoe, *What Comes Naturally*, 94, 117; Deer, *The Beginning and End of Rape*; Ostler, *Surviving Genocide*.

37 Carter, *The Importance of Being Monogamous*, 29.

38 Paterson and Wanhalla, *He Reo Wahine*, ch. 6.

39 Maynard, "The Maple Leaf (Gardens) Forever," 71.

40 Perry, "Hardy Backwoodsmen," 343–360, 345. See also Smithers, "The 'Right Kind of White People.'"

41 Such anxieties peaked in the early twentieth century and typically came back to issues of "colored" races out-reproducing white races. See for example, Hart, "The Outcome of the Southern Race Question"; Stoddard, *The Rising Tide of Color Against White World Supremacy*.

42 Ward and Lin, "Immigration, Acculturation and National Identity in New Zealand," 156; Wang, "*His Dominion" and the "Yellow Peril*," 89; Daniels, *Coming to America*, 10–14; Moloney, *National Insecurities*, 23–25.

43 Pascoe, "Miscegenation Law"; Stoler, *Carnal Knowledge*; Grimshaw, "Interracial Marriages and Colonial Regimes"; Ellinghaus, *Taking Assimilation to Heart*; Haskins and Maynard, "Sex, Race, and Power"; McGrath, "Consent, Marriage, and Colonialism"; Hodes, *The Sea Captain's Wife*; Carter, *The Importance of Being Monogamous*; McGrath, *Illicit Love*.

44 Belich, *Making Peoples*, 251; McGregor, *Imagined Destinies*; Luker, "Zenith," 307–338; Garton, "Eugenics in Australia and New Zealand"; Smithers, *Science, Sexuality, and Race*.

45 Stasiulis and Yuval-Davis, "Introduction," 18–19.

46 Halperin, *How to Do the History of Homosexuality*, 105.

Bibliography

Aderinto, Saheed. *When Sex Threatened the State: Illicit Sexuality, Nationalism, and Politics in Colonial Nigeria, 1900–1958*. Urbana, IL: University of Illinois Press, 2015.

Aldridge, Robert. *Colonialism and Homosexuality*. London: Routledge, 2003.

Anderson, Benedict. *Imagined Communities: Reflections on the Origins and Spread of Nationalism*. London and New York: Verso, 1983.

Angier, Natalie. *Sexing the Body: Gender Politics and the Construction of Sexuality*. New York: Basic Books, 2000.

Barman, Jean. "Taming Aboriginal Sexuality: Gender, Power, and Race in British Columbia, 1850–1950." *BC Studies* 115/116 (Autumn/Winter 1997/98): 237–266. doi:10.14288/bcs.v0i115/6.1735.

Bashford, Alison. "Immigration Restriction: Rethinking Period and Place from Settler Colonies to Post-colonial Nations." *Journal of Global History* 9, no. 1 (March 2014): 26–48. doi:10.1017/S174002281300048X.

Belich, James. *Making Peoples: A History of the New Zealanders, from Polynesian Settlement to the End of the Nineteenth Century*. Honolulu: University of Hawaii Press, 1996.

Benton, Lauren and Lisa Ford. *Rage for Order: The British Empire and the Origins of International Law, 1800–1850*. Cambridge, MA: Harvard University Press, 2016.

Berg, Lawrence D. and Robin A. Kearns. "Naming as Norming: 'Race,' Gender, and the Identity Politics of Naming Places in Aotearora/New Zealand." *Environment and Planning D: Society and Space* 14 (1996): 99–122. doi:10.1068/d140099.

Bongiorno, Frank. *The Sex Lives of Australians: A History*. Collingwood, Australia: Black Inc., 2015.

Burton, Antoinette and Tony Ballantyne. "Introduction: the Politics of Intimacy in an Age of Empire." In *Moving Subjects: Gender, Mobility, and Intimacy in an Age of Global Empire*, edited by Antoinette Burton and Tony Ballantyne, 1–30. Urbana, IL: University of Illinois Press, 2009.

Butler, Judith. "Performative Acts and Gender Constitution: An Essay in Phenomenology and Feminist Theory." *Theatre Journal* 40, no. 4 (December 1988): 519–530.

Byrne, Paula J. *Criminal Law and Colonial Subject*. Cambridge, UK: Cambridge University Press, 1993. doi:10.1017/CBO9780511586101.

Cannon, Charles A. "The Awesome Power of Sex: The Polemical Campaign against Mormon Polygamy." *Pacific Historical Review* 43, no. 1 (February 1974): 61–82. doi:10.2307/3637591.

Carter, Sarah. *The Importance of Being Monogamous: Marriage and Nation Building in Western Canada to 1915*. Edmonton: University of Alberta Press, 2008.

Carter, Sarah. "'Daughters of British Blood' or 'Hordes of Men of Alien Race': The Homesteads-For-Women Campaign in Western Canada." *Great Plains Quarterly* 29 (Fall 2009): 267–286.

Catlin, George. *Letters and Notes on the Manners, Customs, and Condition of the North American Indians*. Philadelphia, PA: J.W. Bradley, 1859.

Chambers, Lori. "Married Women's Property Law, Reform, Couples, and Fraud in Canada West/Ontario, 1859–1900." In *Essays in the History of Canadian Law: Quebec and the Canadas*, edited by George Blaine Baker and Donald Fyson, 427–459. Toronto: University of Toronto Press, 2013.

Collingham, E.M. *Imperial Bodies: The Physical Experience of the Raj, c. 1800–1947*. Cambridge, UK: Polity Press, 2001.

Comaroff, John L. and Jean Comaroff, *Of Revelation and Revolution: The Dialectics of Modernity on a South African Frontier.* Vol. 2. Chicago, IL: University of Chicago Press, 1997.

Cott, Nancy F. *Public Vows: A History of Marriage and the Nation.* Cambridge, MA: Harvard University Press, 2000.

Crooks, Peter and Timothy H. Parsons. "Empires, Bureaucracy and the Paradox of Power." In *Empires and Bureaucracy in World History: From Late Antiquity to the Twentieth Century,* edited by Peter Crooks and Timothy H. Parsons, 3–28. Cambridge, UK: Cambridge University Press, 2016.

Damousi, Joy. *Depraved and Disorderly: Female Convicts, Sexuality and Gender in Colonial Australia.* Cambridge, UK: Cambridge University Press, 1997.

Daniels, Roger. *Coming to America: A History of Immigration and Ethnicity in American Life.* 2nd edition. New York: Perennial, 2002.

Dauvergne, Catherine. *The New Politics of Immigration and the End of Settler Societies.* Cambridge, UK: Cambridge University Press, 2016. doi:10.1017/CBO9781107284357.

Deer, Sarah. *The Beginning and End of Rape: Confronting Sexual Violence in Native America.* Minneapolis, MN: University of Minnesota Press, 2015.

D'Emilio, John and Estelle B. Freedman. *Intimate Matters: A History of Sexuality in America.* 2nd edition. Chicago, IL: University of Chicago Press, 1997.

Driskill, Qwo-Li, Daniel Heath Justice, Deborah A. Miranda, Lisa Tatonetti. *Sovereign Erotics: A Collection of Two-Spirit Literature.* Tuscon, AZ: University of Arizona Press, 2011.

Driskill, Qwo-Li. *Asegi Stories: Cherokee Queer and Two-Spirit Memory.* Tuscon, AZ: University of Arizona Press, 2016.

Edmonds, Penelope and Amanda Nettelbeck, eds. *Intimacies of Violence in the Settler Colony: Economies of Dispossession around the Pacific Rim.* Basingstoke, UK: Palgrave Macmillan, 2018.

Ellinghaus, Katherine. "Strategies of Elimination: 'Exempted' Aborigines, 'Competent' Indians and Twentieth Century Assimilation Policies in Australia and the United States." *Journal of the Canadian Historical Association* 18, no. 2 (2007): 202–225. doi:10.7202/018229ar.

Forsyth, Janice. "After the Fur Trade: First Nations Women in Canadian History, 1850–1950." *Atlantis* 29, no. 2 (Spring/Summer, 2005): 69–78.

Foucault, Michel. *"Society Must Be Defended": Lectures at the Collège de France, 1975–1976.* New York: Picador, 2003.

Garnett, Richard. *Edward Gibbon Wakefield, The Colonization of South Australia and New Zealand.* London: T. Fisher Unwin, 1897.

Garton, Stephen. "Eugenics in Australia and New Zealand: Laboratories of Racial Science." In *The Oxford Handbook of the History of Eugenics,* edited by Alison Bashford and Philippa Levine. 243–257. New York: Oxford University Press, 2010. doi:10.1093/oxfordhb/9780195373141.013.0014.

Gascoigne, John. *The Enlightenment and the Origins of European Australia.* Cambridge, UK: Cambridge University Press, 2002.

Godbeer, Richard. *Sexual Revolution in Early America.* Baltimore, MD: Johns Hopkins University Press, 2002.

Greer, Allan. *Property and Dispossession: Natives, Empires and Land in Early Modern North America.* Cambridge, UK: Cambridge University Press, 2018. doi:10.1017/9781316675908.

Grimshaw, Patricia. "Interracial Marriages and Colonial Regimes in Victoria and Aotearoa/New Zealand." *Frontiers: A Journal of Women's Studies* 23, no. 3 (2002): 12–28. doi:10.1353/fro.2003.0008.

Grosz, Elizabeth. *Volatile Bodies: Toward a Corporeal Feminism.* Urbana, IL: Indiana University Press, 1994.

Halperin, David. *How to Do the History of Homosexuality.* Chicago, IL: University of Chicago Press, 2002.

Harris, Cole. "How did Colonialism Dispossess? Comments from an Edge of Empire." *Annals of the Association of American Geographers* 94, no. 1 (2004): 165–182. doi:10.1111/j.1467-8306.2004.09401009.x.

Harris, Victoria. "Sex on the Margins: New Directions in the Historiography of Sexuality and Gender." *The Historical Journal* 53, no. 4 (2010): 1085–1104. doi:10.1017/S0018246X10000300.

Hart, Albert B. "The Outcome of the Southern Race Question." *The North American Review* 188, no. 632 (July 1908): 50–61.

Haskins, Victoria and John Maynard. "Sex, Race, and Power: Aboriginal Men and White Women in Australian History." *Australian Historical Studies* 126 (2003): 191–216. doi:10.1080/10314610508682920.

Hawkes, Gail. *Sex and Pleasure in Western Culture.* Cambridge, UK: Polity Press, 2004.

Henderson, Jennifer. *Settler Feminism and Race Making in Canada.* Toronto: University of Toronto Press, 2003.

Hodes, Martha. *The Sea Captain's Wife: A True Story of Love, Race, and War in the Nineteenth Century.* New York: W.W. Norton and Co., 2006.

Hughes, Robert. *The Fatal Shore: The Epic of Australia's Founding*. New York: Vintage Books, 1988.

Hurtado, Albert L. *Intimate Frontiers: Sex, Gender, and Culture in Old California*. Albuquerque, NM: University of New Mexico Press, 1999.

Huttenback, R.A. "The British Empire as a 'White Man's Country' – Racial Attitudes and Immigration Legislation in the Colonies of White Settlement." *Journal of British Studies* 13, no. 1 (November 1973): 108–137. doi:10.1086/385652.

Jacobson, Matthew Frye. *Whiteness of a Different Color: European Immigrants and the Alchemy of Race*. Cambridge, MA: Harvard University Press, 1998.

Katz, Jonathon Ned. *The Invention of Heterosexuality*. Chicago, IL: University of Chicago Press, 2007.

Kelley, Ninette and Michael Trebilock. *The Making of the Mosiac: A History of Canadian Immigration Policy*. Toronto: University of Toronto Press, 2000.

Kenneally, Thomas. *Australians: A Short History*. Sydney: Allen & Unwin, 2018.

Lake, Marilyn and Henry Reynolds. *Drawing the Global Colour Line: White Men's Countries and the Question of Racial Equality*. Carlton: Melbourne University Press, 2008.

Lambert, David and Alan Lester, "Imperial Spaces, Imperial Subjects." In *Colonial Lives Across the British Empire: Imperial Careering in the Long Nineteenth Century*, edited by David Lambert and Alan Lester, 1–31. Cambridge, UK: Cambridge University Press, 2006.

Laqueur, Thomas W. *Solitary Sex: A Cultural History of Masturbation*. New York: Zone Books, 2004.

Levine, Phillipa. *Prostitution, Race & Politics: Policing Venereal Disease in the British Empire*. New York and London: Routledge, 2003.

Luker, Vicki. "Zenith: Colonial Contradictions and the Chimera of Racial Purity, 1920–1940." In *Foreign Bodies: Oceania and the Science of Race, 1750–1940*, edited by Bronwen Douglas and Chris Ballard, 307–338. Canberra: ANU E-Press, 2008.

Maynard, Steven. "The Maple Leaf (Gardens) Forever: Sex, Canadian History and National History." *Journal of Canadian Studies* 36, no. 2 (Summer 2001): 70–105. doi:10.3138/jcs.36.2.70.

McGrath, Ann. "Sex, Violence and Theft." In *Creating a Nation*, edited by Patricia Grimshaw, Marilyn Lake, Ann McGrath and Marian Quartly, 131–150. Melbourne: McPhee Gribble, 1994.

McGrath, Ann. "Consent, Marriage, and Colonialism: Indigenous Australian Women and Colonizer Marriages." *Journal of Colonialism and Colonial History* 6, no. 3 (2005): 1–24. doi:10.1353/cch.2006.0016.

McGrath, Ann. *Illicit Love: Interracial Sex and Marriage in the United States and Australia*. Lincoln, NE, and London: University of Nebraska Press, 2015.

McGregor, Russell. *Imagined Destinies: Aboriginal Australian and the Doomed Race Theory, 1880–1939*. Carlton South: Melbourne University Press, 1997.

Moloney, Deirdre M. *National Insecurities: Immigrants and U.S. Deportation Policy since 1882*. Chapel Hill, NC: University of North Carolina Press, 2012.

Molony, John. *The Native-Born: The First White Australians*. Carlton South: Melbourne University Press, 2000.

Morgan, Cecilia. "Creating Interracial Intimacies: British North America, Canada, and the Transatlantic World, 1830–1914." *Journal of the Canadian Historical Association* 19, no. 2 (2008): 76–105. doi:10.7202/037749ar.

Morgensen, Scott L. *Spaces Between Us: Queer Settler Colonialism and Indigenous Decolonization*. Minneapolis, MN: University of Minnesota Press, 2011.

Noël, Françoise. *Family Life and Sociability in Upper and Lower Canada, 1780–1870*. Montreal: McGill-Queen's University Press, 2003.

Ostler, Jeffrey. *Surviving Genocide: Native Nations and the United States from the American Revolution to Bleeding Kansas*. New Haven, CT: Yale University Press, 2019.

Pascoe, Peggy. "Miscegenation Law, Court Cases, and Ideologies of 'Race' in Twentieth-Century America." *The Journal of American History* 83, no. 1 (June 1996): 44–69. doi:10.2307/2945474.

Pascoe, Peggy. *What Comes Naturally: Miscegenation Law and the Making of Race in America*. New York: Oxford University Press, 2009.

Paterson, Lachy and Angela Wanhalla. *He Reo Wahine: Maori Women's Voices from the Nineteenth Century*. Auckland: Auckland University Press, 2017.

Perry, Adele. "Hardy Backwoodsmen, Wholesome Women, and Steady Families: Immigration and the Construction of a White Society in Colonial British Columbia." *Histoire Sociale/Social History* 33 no. 66 (2000): 343–360.

Povinelli, Elizabeth A. *The Empire of Love: Toward a Theory of Intimacy, Genealogy, and Carnality*. Durham, NC: Duke University Press, 2006.

Rees, Siân. *The Floating Brothel: The Extraordinary True Story of an 18th-Century Ship and its Cargo of Female Convicts*. Sydney: Hodder, 2002.

Rifkin, Mark. *When Did the Indians Become Straight? Kinship, the History of Sexuality, and Native Sovereignty*. New York: Oxford University Press, 2011.

Rifkin, Mark. *The Erotics of Sovereignty: Queer Native Writing in the Era of Self-Determination*. Minneapolis, MN: University of Minnesota Press, 2012.

Rifkin, Mark. *Settler Common Sense: Queerness and Everyday Colonialism in the American Renaissance*. Minneapolis, MN: University of Minnesota Press, 2014.

Roscoe, Will. *Changing Ones: Third and Fourth Genders in Native North America*. New York: St. Martin's Press, 2005.

Russell, Lynette. "'Dirty Domestics and Worse Cooks': Aboriginal Women's Agency and Domestic Frontiers, Southern Australia, 1800–1850." *Frontiers: A Journal of Women Studies* 28, no. 1 (2007): 18–46. doi:10.1353/fro.2007.0035.

Ryan, Lyndall. "The Struggle for Recognition: Part Aborigines in Bass Strait in the Nineteenth Century." *Aboriginal History* 1/2 (1977): 27–51.

Saler, Bethel. *The Settlers' Empire: Colonialism and State Formation in America's Old Northwest*. Philadelphia, PA: University of Pennsylvania Press, 2015.

Sangster, Joan. *Regulating Girls and Women: Sexuality, Family, and the Law in Ontario, 1920–1960*. Toronto: University of Toronto Press 2001.

Seuffert, Nan. *Jurisprudence of National Identity: Kaleidoscopes of Imperialism and Globalization from Aotearoa New Zealand*. London and New York: Routledge, 2018.

Smithers, Gregory D. "The 'Right Kind of White People': Reproducing Whiteness in the United States and Australia, 1780s–1930s." In *Racism in the Modern World: Historical Perspectives on Cultural Transfer and Adaptation*, edited by Manfred Berg and Simon Wendt, 303–328. New York: Berghahn Books, 2011.

Smithers, Gregory D. *Science, Sexuality, and Race in the United States and Australia, 1780–1940*. Revised 2nd edition. Lincoln, NE, and London: University of Nebraska Press, 2017.

Spear, Jennifer M. *Race, Sex, and Social Order in Early New Orleans*. Baltimore, MD: Johns Hopkins University Press, 2009.

Stasiulis, Daiva and Nira Yuval-Davis. "Introduction: Beyond Dichotomies – Gender, Race, Ethnicity and Class in Settler Societies." In *Unsettling Settler Societies: Articulations of Gender, Race, Ethnicity and Class*, edited by Yuval-Davis Stasiulis, 1–38. New York: Sage, 1995.

Stoddard, Lothrop. *The Rising Tide of Color Against White World Supremacy*. New York: Charles Scribner and Sons, 1920.

Stoler, Ann Laura. *Carnal Knowledge and Imperial Power: Race and the Intimate in Colonial Rule*. Berkeley, CA: University of California Press, 2002.

Sweet, John Wood. *Bodies Politic: Negotiating Race in the American North, 1730–1830*. Philadelphia, PA: University of Pennsylvania Press, 2003.

Taylor, Rebe. "Savages and Saviours: The Australian Sealers and Aboriginal Survivors." *Journal of Australian Studies* 66 (2000): 73–84. doi:10.1080/14443050009387613.

Tosh, John. *Manliness and Masculinities in Nineteenth-Century Britain*. London and New York: Routledge, 2017.

Veracini, Lorenzo. *Settler Colonialism: A Theoretical Overview*. London: Palgrave Macmillan, 2010.

Wang, Jiwu. *"His Dominion" and the "Yellow Peril": Protestant Missions to Chinese Immigrants in Canada, 1859–1967*. Waterloo, Ontario: Wilfrid Laurier University Press, 2006.

Wanhalla, Angela. *Matters of the Heart: A History of Interracial Marriage in New Zealand*. Auckland: University of Auckland Press, 2014.

Ward, Colleen and En-Yi Lin. "Immigration, Acculturation and National Identity in New Zealand." In *New Zealand Identities: Departures and Destinations*, edited by James H. Liu, Tim McCreanor, Tracey McIntosh and Teresia Teaiwa, 155–173. Wellington: Victoria University Press, 2005.

Ward, Peter. *White Canada Forever: Popular Attitudes and Public Policy Toward Orientals in British Columbia*. Montreal: McGill-Queen's University Press, 1978.

Ward, Peter. *Courtship, Love, and Marriage in Nineteenth-Century English Canada*. Montreal: McGill-Queen's University Press, 1990.

Waymouth, Lyn. "Parliamentary Representation for the Maori: Debate and Ideology." In *Rere AtuTaku Manu! Discovering History, Language & Politics in the Maori-Language Newspapers*, edited by Jenifer Curnow, Ngapare Hopa and Jane McRae, 153–173. Auckland: Auckland University Press, 2002.

Weeks, Jeffrey. *Making Sexual History*. Cambridge, UK: Polity Press, 2000.

White, Jr., O. Kendall and Daryl White. "Polygamy and Mormon Identity." *Journal of American Culture* 28, no. 2 (June 2005): 165–176. doi:10.1111/j.1542-734X.2005.00161.x.

Williams, Walter L. *The Spirit and the Flesh: Sexual Diversity in American Indian Culture*. Boston, MA: Beacon Press, 1992.

Wolfe, Patrick. "Settler Colonialism and the Elimination of the Native." *Journal of Genocide Research* 8 (2006): 387–409. doi:10.1080/14623520601056240.

Wood, Gordon S. *The Radicalism of the American Revolution*. New York: Vintage Books, 1991.

Woodward, Rachel. "It's a Man's Life! Soldiers, Masculinity and the Countryside." *Gender, Place and Culture* 5 (1988): 277–300. doi:10.1080/09663699825214.

Yee, Jennifer. *Exotic Subversions in Nineteenth-Century French Fiction*. New York and London: Routledge, 2008.

PART II

Constructing race, controlling reproduction

8

SEXUAL INTERMIXTURE, BLOOD LINEAGE, AND LEGAL DISABILITIES IN EIGHTEENTH-CENTURY JAMAICA AND THE BRITISH ATLANTIC

Brooke N. Newman

In the past quarter century, scholars focused on gender, race, and power in the early modern British Atlantic have demonstrated that colonial legal innovations gave rise to the institution of slavery as a permanent, heritable condition perpetuated in the wombs of enslaved women.[1] More recent attention to the influence of Christian ideologies of enslavement derived from Iberian precedents has underscored the extent to which English colonial authorities yoked African birth and ancestry to lifetime bondage well before the enactment of provincial slave laws.[2] In British North America, doubts about the inheritance and continuation of slave status emerged when the presumed boundaries separating English colonizers from enslaved Africans blurred as a result of sustained sexual contact and social relations between free subjects and bound laborers. Beginning in the mid-seventeenth century, colonial legislatures grappled with the growing uncertainties surrounding the legal status of both the offspring of sexual unions between enslaved individuals and free colonists and enslaved converts to Christianity. To clarify who qualified for hereditary enslavement, the Virginia Burgesses pronounced in 1662 that all children would be enslaved or free depending on their mother's condition, and, in 1667, that Christian baptism did not confer freedom.[3] With the early exception of Maryland, assigning hereditary slave status on the basis of maternal descent became accepted practice across the Anglo-Atlantic world, enacted in the majority of cases by custom and judicial decision rather than by statute.[4]

During the first century of English colonization in mainland North America and the Caribbean, most colonial and British authorities assumed that enslaved mothers of African, Indian, and multiple ancestry transmitted permanent slave status to their offspring, unless a private act of manumission or positive law declared otherwise. By the mid-eighteenth century, with African slavery firmly entrenched throughout the Americas, both groups increasingly rejected the hereditary enslavement of Native peoples as illegitimate and detrimental to British imperial goals.[5] At the same time, as individuals of Native, African, and multiple heritage joined the ranks of the free, colonial authorities enacted local legislation according differing rights and responsibilities with regard to voting, office holding, property ownership, labor, and freedom of movement to categories of free people. The eighteenth century represented a pivotal period for the emergence of legal disabilities imposed on free communities of color, supplemented by social practices and gender and racial ideologies that created and reproduced inequalities.[6] To preserve and reinforce existing structures of wealth and power, authorities in colonial North America and the Caribbean defined English liberty as an exclusive inheritance, reserved solely for white European Protestants and their unmixed descendants— except in extraordinary cases.

Focusing on eighteenth-century Jamaica, but also drawing on other British Atlantic contexts, this essay explores how ideas about sexual mixture and inheritable blood informed the legislative strategies adopted by colonial officials to keep power and property in the hands of "white" subjects. It demonstrates that official racial classifications served colonial administrative needs by facilitating the division of the free population into categories of people ascribed varying rights and privileges on the basis of hereditary status. Notions of blood lineage empowered English officials in Jamaica and elsewhere to tighten control over free individuals of African, Native, and multiple heritage, whom they classified as racially inferior and "tainted" and thus unfit to claim the liberties of freeborn British subjects. Across the Anglo-Atlantic world, colonial legislatures subjected free communities of color to numerous legal restrictions that limited paths to economic and social mobility, blocked political participation, and stigmatized individuals descended from enslaved or Native ancestors. Justifying their actions on the basis of Europeans' supposed innate moral and intellectual superiority, colonial legislators used legal exclusions not only to shore up the institution of slavery but also to undercut the masculinity of free men of color by linking the full privileges of British inheritance directly to legal whiteness.

***

By the time the English established colonial settlements on the southern American mainland and the Caribbean islands in the early seventeenth century, the Spanish and Portuguese had long enslaved Native and African peoples in the Americas. Before the mid-1640s, indentured laborers recruited from the British Isles formed the bulk of the English colonial workforce. Over the following decades the rapid expansion of labor-intensive agricultural production, coupled with growing market demand in Europe and England's official entry into the transatlantic slave trade, dramatically increased the numbers of enslaved Africans imported to English North America and the Caribbean. Yet, due to the patchwork nature of imperial governance in the British Atlantic empire, the legal rules governing enslavement remained ill-defined, haphazard, and dependent on the agendas of local legislatures.[7] Prior to and alongside the emergence of English colonial slave laws, customary practices that developed in response to particular circumstances on the ground, as well as long-established Iberian traditions, shaped the conceptualization and treatment of enslaved people. Only after individuals of multiple heritage—such as Elizabeth Key in Virginia—challenged their enslavement on the basis of English paternal ancestry and Christian faith did colonial officials codify hereditary maternal slavery and decouple baptism from freedom.[8]

By favoring matrilineal descent instead of common law patrilineality to assign slave status, English colonial authorities adopted a civil law maxim widespread among European colonizers in the Americas and customarily associated with illegitimate birth and domestic animals. Roman law, which held that one became a slave by capture, self-sale, purchase, or birth to an enslaved mother, exerted significant influence on the development of rules regulating slavery in the overseas territories of Spain, Portugal, France, and Holland. The principle of *partus sequitur ventrem* (offspring follows the womb) enabled European colonizers to profit from enslaved women's sexual exploitation and reproductive labor. Emphasis on maternal bloodlines to determine eligibility for slavery also encouraged the ruling elites who dominated colonial assemblies to view the derogatory mental, physical, and moral traits associated with enslaved people as intractable and heritable, unless diluted through sexual mixture with white men over multiple generations. Gendered power dynamics and assumptions about African and Native women's bodies and sexualities played a significant role in shaping slave laws and practices throughout the Americas.[9] As clarified by the *Siete Partidas*, a medieval Spanish legal code that provided guidelines for Iberian colonial legislation, enslaved women, like other commercial items belonging to the head of a household, reproduced human commodities solely for their master's economic gain.[10] In Iberian colonial societies the rule of *partus sequitur ventrem* monetized enslaved women's wombs, leading to the enhanced surveillance of their sexual conduct, maternal practices, and bloodlines.[11] Similarly, French slave legislation, systematized in the *Code Noir* of 1685 for France's Caribbean colonies and later revised in 1724 for Louisiana, specified that the condition of the mother at the moment of birth determined her children's status.[12]

Although hereditary maternal slavery and restrictions on manumission curtailed paths to freedom for the vast majority of enslaved people in the British Atlantic, by the early eighteenth century a small population of individuals of African origin and descent had become free. Notions of heritable status that attended the rise and consolidation of slavery played a foundational role in shaping understandings of racial inheritance broadly, even in cases where people were not enslaved. Freedom from bondage did not erase the supposed negative inherited characteristics associated with servile African lineage that colonial and British imperial officials and enslavers had long used to justify chattel slavery. In the Chesapeake and Caribbean colonies, the presence of free people of African and multiple heritage prompted authorities to grapple with pressing questions related to gender, racial inheritance, and political participation. Would suffrage extend to all adult male freeholders, regardless of racial ancestry? Beginning in South Carolina, Barbados, and Virginia, colonial assemblies passed formal acts disfranchising men of African or Native origin and descent who under imprecise phrasing in earlier suffrage legislation might have claimed a voice in local elections. In 1716, South Carolina limited suffrage to "every white man, and no other, professing the Christian religion."[13] In 1721, Barbados officials, claiming that "sham Free-holders" had attempted to vote, denied the title of freeholder to any man "whose original extraction shall be proved to have been from a Negro," barring African-descended men from political participation.[14] Two years later Virginia prohibited all men of African, Native, and multiple heritage from voting. By 1732 the Virginia legislature had passed additional restrictions to prevent "Negroes, mulattoes, and Indians who professed themselves to be Christians" from serving as witnesses in trials against white colonists "forasmuch as they are People of such base and corrupt natures, that the Credit of their Testimony cannot be certainly depended upon," except in slave trials.[15]

The metropolitan councils and committees charged with overseeing English colonial affairs during the seventeenth century struggled to exercise systematic control. After 1696, with the establishment of the Board of Trade, a governmental advisory body composed of eight salaried commissioners and eight ex-officio unpaid members selected from the Privy Council, the legislative review process assumed greater importance in imperial administration. In an attempt to ensure the greatest possible uniformity in colonial policy, the board scrutinized colonial legislation and submitted recommendations to the King in Council to disallow acts declared repugnant to English law. At the same time, the Crown and the Privy Council continued to sanction legal diversity in the colonies in order to account for local circumstances.[16] As the Crown and its advisors recognized, the Atlantic slave colonies were nothing like England. Assessing Virginia's 1723 voting act, for example, Richard West, the royal attorney, reported "that it cannot be just by a general Law without any allegation of Crime or other demerit whatsoever to strip all free persons of a black complexion (some of whom may perhaps be of considerable substance) from those Rights which are so justly valuable to every Freeman."[17] Nonetheless, the King in Council permitted colonial laws enacted to prevent free blacks from exercising equal rights with white subjects in Virginia—and throughout the British Atlantic—to remain in force.

Restricting free men's liberties on the basis of racial lineage contradicted English legal precedents, but the board typically recommended that the Crown either confirm such controversial acts or let them "lye bye," neither confirming nor disallowing them.[18] When asked to justify Virginia's decision "to fix a perpetual brand upon free negroes and mulattos by excluding them from that great privilege of a Freeman [e.g., voting]," Governor William Gooch argued that conferring upon former enslaved men and their descendants the full privileges and responsibilities of manhood was a grave mistake. In the interest of public security, he explained, free men of servile African heritage needed to recognize "that a distinction ought to be made between their offspring and the descendants of an Englishman, with whom they never were to be accounted equal." Indeed, unless confined to a subordinate position, Gooch stressed, free men of African blood would necessarily imperil the development of an anglicized colonial society unburdened by racial intermixture and sexual contact between whites and blacks.[19]

***

In Jamaica, Britain's largest and most valuable Caribbean colony, laws restricting political participation by free men of African, Native, and non-Christian ancestry developed gradually and kept modifying in response to local developments. Beginning in 1711, in the wake of petitions from free blacks seeking English liberties and reports of attempts by Jewish men to vote, the Jamaica assembly barred free "Negroes," "mulattoes," Jews, and Indians from holding public office.[20] For the next two decades, custom alone sufficed to restrict voting rights to white, Protestant, propertied adult men. That is until members of the Jamaican legislature received a complaint on March 30, 1733, that John Golding of Vere and one of his sons, "both being mulattoes," had voted at an assembly election and "insisted on their right of voting."[21] A prosperous planter of mixed European and African descent, and the father of seven children whom he had raised Protestant, Golding had previously received permission from the legislature for his family members and servants to "pass as deficiencies," or count as white, in compliance with Jamaica's deficiency bill stipulating the minimum number of white residents per plantation.[22] Yet Golding had never claimed suffrage as his constitutional right as a British subject. As the assembly saw it, his public declaration of voting rights would reassure other free "mulattoes" that they could demand political rights if they met the property qualifications. In response, colonial legislators in Jamaica proposed a bill restricting the franchise to adult, Protestant men descended from white ancestors.

By the 1730s, discriminating against former enslaved men and their free descendants in suffrage laws had become unexceptional in Britain's Atlantic slave colonies. Still, the Board of Trade's tolerance of colonial statutes that diverged from English legal principles varied. Two years earlier, on the advice of the royal attorney, the Crown had ordered the repeal of a 1730 act passed in Jamaica to attach legal disabilities to "free negroes and mulattoes." Introduced during the First Maroon War, which pitted the British colonial government in Jamaica against bands of escaped slaves, the act was intended to monitor and suppress all free people in the colony descended from enslaved ancestors. Requiring free men and women to register with their local parish, the act also curtailed their ability to give evidence against whites in court, to sell goods freely, to purchase indentures for white servants, to carry arms (except on militia duty), or to live in or within five miles of Jamaica's three main urban centers: Port Royal, Kingston, or Spanish Town.[23] In response to the new restrictions, Francis Williams, an educated and affluent free Afro-Jamaican, petitioned the Crown directly. Williams argued that the law unfairly targeted his family and stripped free blacks of their rights as naturalized English subjects. Francis Fane, the royal attorney, sided with Williams, noting that the Jamaican legislature should have included exemptions for free blacks of substance, and the Crown declared the act null and void.[24]

In the spring of 1733, with Jamaica embroiled in turmoil as a result of the ongoing conflict with the Maroons, the assembly returned to the matter of the uncertain place of free men of African and multiple descent in a slave society. To protect the birthright of Englishmen as an exclusive inheritance, members of the Jamaica assembly resolved to restrict the franchise to "his Majesty's white Subjects." Yet a crucial matter of definition remained: how to delineate the precise legal division between whiteness and intermediate racial statuses. Like colonial officials throughout British North America and the Caribbean since the mid-seventeenth century, legislators in Jamaica had generally referred to all persons of mixed European and African or Native ancestry as "mulattoes," borrowing loosely from the Spanish.[25] In 1705, Virginia provided a statutory definition of "mulatto" for the first time in an act prohibiting any "negro, mulatto, or Indian" from holding public office. Those "accounted a mulatto" included "the child of an Indian, and the child, grandchild, and great-grandchild of a Negro." This definition persisted until 1785, when the legislature classified as mulatto "every person who shall have one-fourth or more Negro blood."[26] In Antigua the legislature pronounced free blacks ineligible for freeholder status as early as 1702, prohibiting them from owning more than eight acres of land. However, in an unusual move, Antigua permitted freeholders of multiple heritage to vote, a stance confirmed by an assembly committee in 1728.[27]

In Jamaica the legal demarcation between white and "mulatto" remained imprecise so long as free people of multiple ancestries lacked the requisite financial resources to attempt to claim the full rights of freeborn British subjects. As a result of the Goldings' action, colonial legislators moved to prevent free people descended from enslaved mothers from encroaching upon the exclusive birthright of Englishmen without official authorization. Preferring to maintain ongoing control over racial designations and the rights and obligations associated with them, the assembly devised a discretionary approach that preserved whiteness as the most privileged status by linking it to the ancient liberties of Englishmen. In exceptional cases, individuals and families with blood ties to prominent white men could apply for a private act declaring them "white" in the eyes of the law, ensuring that only white or legally whitened freeholders who met the property and religious qualifications for suffrage could vote. On April 19, 1733, the Jamaican legislature conferred the "Rights & priviledges of English men born of White Ancestors" on John Golding and his seven children, including suffrage. According to the act passed in his favor, Golding had acquired a fortune by his own industry and proved himself "a good and Loyall Subject and a Good Protestant." His legal whitening served as an initial test case intended to clarify whether "others of the Like Extraction would be Induc'd to Imitate or follow his Example."[28]

That same session, as the Jamaica assembly drew up a bill to restrict suffrage to white men, authorities realized that the legal parameters of whiteness remained indistinct. Passing a motion "that it should be ascertained who shall be deemed mulattoes and how far their corruption of blood should extend," members appear to have borrowed from the three-generation standard used by the Spanish to erase servile, non-Christian, and African/Native origins.[29] The 1733 voting act clarified that "no person who is not above three degrees removed in a Lineal Descent from the Negro Ancestor Exclusive shall be allowed to Vote or Poll in Elections and no one shall be deemed a Mulatto after the third generation as aforesaid but that they shall have all the Priviledges and Immunities of his Majesty's white Subjects of this Island provided they are brought up in the Christian Religion."[30] Reviewing Jamaica's new suffrage law the following year on behalf of the Crown, Fane noted that he had "no objections in Point of Law."[31] The imperial administration in Britain had accepted that divergent legal practices curtailing the rights of free people of African descent better fit the reality of life in Britain's Atlantic slave colonies. After 1733 the only recourse for free individuals in Jamaica less than three generations removed from an African forebear was to petition the assembly for a private act bestowing upon them some of the rights enjoyed by colonists of European Protestant ancestry.[32] Attaining legal whiteness in Jamaica without special dispensation became increasingly difficult for free men and women of multiple heritage.

By categorizing free persons and assigning them rights and privileges based on blood inheritance, Jamaican officials redefined British subject status in explicitly genealogical terms. Exclusive definitions of birthright citizenship at the local level concentrated legislative authority over exemptions granted to multiple-heritage individuals. Between 1733 and 1802, elite, well-connected men and women with blood ties to prominent white men petitioned the Jamaica assembly for private acts granting them white legal status, as if they "were free and Natural Born Subjects of the Crown of Great Britain and were Descended from White Ancestors." Official grants of limited white privileges to persons of mixed lineage nonetheless remained incredibly rare, accorded only to those with wealth and personal connections. Overall, the assembly approved 128 private bills granting white status to roughly 600 men, women, and children of multiple ancestry, only four of which granted the recipient all of the liberties of white male freeholders, including the right to vote and hold office. In response to the island's expanding enslaved African majority and pressing demand for more white settlers, the Jamaican legislature strategically whitened a select group of individuals with European and African blood while retaining the full privileges of British subject status for white colonists.[33] As Edward Long, a Jamaican planter who published a history of the island in 1774, observed, nearly all of the cases of legal whitening involved the enslaved or free sexual partners of white Creole men and their illegitimate mixed-race children.[34]

Following Tacky's Revolt in 1760, the largest uprising in the eighteenth-century Caribbean prior to the Haitian Revolution, the Jamaican legislature redefined white racial status as four degrees distant from an African ancestor. After 1760, Jamaican officials viewed the free community of color, including individuals whitened by their own discretionary policy, with mounting suspicion.[35] According to the assembly, men and women with known ties to African ancestors were naturally sympathetic to their enslaved brethren, despite having amassed substantial real and personal property in land and slaves. In time, people of color could potentially threaten white hegemony in an island colony where enslaved Africans outnumbered whites ten to one. Colonial authorities feared that a growing community of propertied, multiple-heritage individuals would demand political power and equal treatment with white colonists, driving away potential settlers from Britain, Europe, and North America and imperiling the slave system. The result was the 1761 Devises Act, which prohibited white colonists from leaving real or personal property worth more than £1,200 to persons of African descent. The law ensured that free blacks and people of color would remain economically subordinate to whites and granted the legislature full control over individual exemptions.[36]

Curtailing the ability of freeholders and free men and women to dispose of their property as they saw fit was controversial, even in colonial Jamaica. After several members of the Jamaica council complained that the Devises Act undermined their fundamental rights as British subjects, Lovell Stanhope, Jamaica's London agent, wrote to the Board of Trade in defense of the assembly. The act was necessary, he claimed, "to prevent the illegitimate Issue of Slaves [from] attaining a Superiority in Rank, Riches, and, in the Consequence, Power, over free men and their unmixed Descendants." Without strict measures in place to guarantee white supremacy, he argued, Jamaica would inevitably degenerate into "a Colony of Negroes and mulattoes" of no benefit whatsoever to the British empire.[37] Reliance on colonial slave labor left no room for free people descended from enslaved ancestors—especially free men of color, who could potentially acquire sufficient property to exercise the franchise—to participate as equals to white subjects in the British imperial polity.

***

The emergence and spread of notions of hereditary blood and racial inheritance in the eighteenth-century British Atlantic world facilitated the development of a range of local customary practices and legislation impacting the lives of enslaved and free people of African and Native origin and heritage. Colonial laws and customs that deviated from English common law perpetuated the institution of hereditary slavery while further encouraging racial and gender exclusion and inequality after freedom. Relying on the power of blood metaphors to shape both legal discourse and legal reasoning, Anglo-American and British Caribbean authorities made it impossible for free people of African, Native, or multiple heritage to participate as equals in English settler communities. Only a special legislative grant or the perceived dilution of non-European blood through sexual intermixture, and gradual erasure of the stigma of servile origins over many generations, enabled a fraction of multiple-heritage individuals to obtain the full benefits of British subject status.

In colonial Jamaica the conferral of white privileges on select persons of multiple ancestry stemmed from unsanctioned ties to elite white men, a Protestant upbringing, and wealth in land and slaves, all of which were supposed to dilute the negative and inferior traits ascribed to African blood. Yet assigning racial classifications and determining eligibility for English liberties on the basis of notions of hereditary blood foreclosed the possibility of economic and social mobility and political participation for the vast majority of free people of African and multiple parentage. As anticipated, few free people possessed the requisite lineage, property, and education to warrant legislative intervention and legal whitening. Colonists in eighteenth-century Jamaica and throughout the British Atlantic claimed the constitutional liberties and privileges of English men and women as their inherited and exclusive birthright, as "His Majesty's white subjects." By attaching legal disabilities to the free descendants of enslaved Africans and Native peoples, who were stigmatized and denied full membership in British settler communities, colonial officials defended long-held English liberties as the exclusive birthright privilege of white colonists and their heirs alone.

Notes

1 See esp. Brown, *Good Wives, Nasty Wenches, and Anxious Patriarchs;* Fischer, *Suspect Relations;* Morgan, *Laboring Women;* Gordon-Reed, *The Hemingses of Monticello.*

2 Goetz, *The Baptism of Early Virginia;* Guasco, *Slaves and Englishmen;* Handler, "Custom and Law"; Newman, *A Dark Inheritance.*

3 Banks, "Dangerous Woman"; Goetz, *The Baptism of Early Virginia;* Morgan, *"Partus sequitur ventrem."*

4 In 1664, Maryland instituted the common-law rule of patrilineal descent to assign slave status; New York and South Carolina later followed Virginia. See *Archives of Maryland*, 533–534; *Acts of Assembly Passed in the Province of New-York*, 65; *The Statutes at Large of South Carolina*, 397. Other English colonies adopted *partus sequitur ventrem* implicitly. See Handler, "Custom and Law"; Newman, "Blood Fictions, Maternal Inheritance, and the Legacies of Colonial Slavery."

5 Newton, "'Returns to a Native Land'," 115–116; Chaplin, "Enslavement of Indians in Early America," 46–47.

6 For a comparative perspective, see De la Fuente and Gross, *Becoming Free, Becoming Black*, 1–131.

7 Guasco, *Slaves and Englishmen*, 156–157; Newman, *A New World of Labor*, 54–55; Brown, *Good Wives, Nasty Wenches, and Anxious Patriarchs*, 3.

8 Hening, *The Statutes at Large*, 2: 170, 260. On the influence of Key's 1655 freedom suit in Virginia, see Banks, "Dangerous Woman: Elizabeth Key's Freedom Suit."

9 See esp. Higginbotham Jr. and Kopytoff, "Racial Purity and Interracial Sex in the Law of Colonial and Antebellum Virginia."

10 *Las Siete Partidas*, 977.

11 Dorsey, "Women Without History," 168–69; Cowling, *Conceiving Freedom*, 53–55.

12 Garraway, *The Libertine Colony*, 202–203; Spear, *Race, Sex, and Social Order in Early New Orleans*, 61–67.

13 An Act to Keep Inviolate and Preserve the Freedom of Elections, December 15, 1716, Cooper, ed., *The Statutes at Large of South Carolina*, 688.

14 Hall, *Acts, Passed in the Island of Barbados*, 252–253, 256.

15 Hening, *The Statutes at Large*, 3: 298, 4: 133, 327.

16 On the repugnancy and divergence principles underlying English understanding of colonial laws, see esp. Bilder, *The Transatlantic Constitution*, 1–11.

17 West to the Lords Commissioners of Trade and Plantations, January 10, 1724, CO 5/1323, f. 177.

18 *A Collection of All the Acts of Assembly, Now in Force, in the Colony of Virginia*, 474.

19 Newman, *A Dark Inheritance*, 92–93.

20 An act for regulating fees, May 19, 1711, *The Laws of Jamaica: 1681–1759*, 1: 111–112.

21 March 30, 1733, *Journals of the Assembly of Jamaica*, 3: 328.

22 June 24, 1730, and November 12, 1730, *Journals of the Assembly of Jamaica*, 2: 712, 714.

23 "An act for the better regulating slaves and rendering free negroes and mulattoes more useful," March 28, 1730, CO 139/12, ff. 76–79.

24 A Short Case of Francis Williams of Jamaica, rec'd June 30, 1731, CO 137/19, ff. 29–30; Francis Fane's Report on Six Acts Passed there in 1730, March 22, 1731; Delafaye to Popple, July 17, 1731, CO 137/19/part 1, ff. 31, 73–74.

25 Jordan, "American Chiaroscuro," 183–200.

26 Forbes, *Africans and Native Americans*, 195.

27 Gaspar, *Bondmen and Rebels*, 166.

28 An Act to Intitle John Golding Senior of the Parish of Vere planter & his family to the Rights & priviledges of English men born of White Ancestors, April 19, 1733, CO 139/13, f. 126.

29 March 30, 1733, and April 4, 1733, *Journals of the Assembly of Jamaica*, 3: 122, 130. On the significance of three generations to Spanish legal whitening, see Twinam, *Purchasing Whiteness*, 53, 202; Martínez, *Genealogical Fictions*, 49, 233.

30 6 Geo. II, c. 2, April 25, 1733, CO 139/13, ff. 139–142.

31 Fane to the Lords Commissioners, March 28, 1734, CO 137/21, ff. 79–80.

32 Hurwitz and Hurwitz, "A Token of Freedom," 423–431.

33 See Newman, *A Dark Inheritance*, ch. 3.

34 Long, *The History of Jamaica*, 3: 320.

35 2 George III c. 7, December 19, 1761, *Laws of Jamaica*, 23–26.

36 On the Devises Act, see Livesay, *Children of Uncertain Fortune*, 66–89; Newman, *A Dark Inheritance*, 111–120.

37 Stanhope, Reasons in support of the Bill to restrain exorbitant Grants to Negroes, June 13, 1763, CO 137/33, ff. 34–43.

Bibliography

Acts of Assembly Passed in the Province of New-York: From 1691 to 1725. London, 1726.

Archives of Maryland. Volume 1. Baltimore: Maryland Historical Society, 1883.

Banks, Taunya Lovell. "Dangerous Woman: Elizabeth Key's Freedom Suit—Subjecthood and Racialized Identity in Seventeenth Century Colonial Virginia." *Akron Law Review* 41, no. 3 (2008): 799–837. doi:10.2139/ssrn.672121.

Bilder, Mary Sarah. *The Transatlantic Constitution: Colonial Legal Culture and the Empire.* Cambridge, MA: Harvard University Press, 2008.

British National Archives, Kew. CO 5/1323, Board of Trade and Secretaries of State: Virginia, Original Correspondence, 1732–1736.

British National Archives, Kew. CO 5/1376, Board of Trade and Secretaries of State: Virginia, Acts, 1660–1682.

British National Archives, Kew. CO 137/19, Colonial Office and Predecessors: Jamaica, Original Correspondence, 1730–1732.

British National Archives, Kew. CO 137/21, Colonial Office and Predecessors: Jamaica, Original Correspondence, 1733–1735.

British National Archives, Kew. CO 137/33, Colonial Office and Predecessors: Jamaica, Original Correspondence, 1762–1765.

British National Archives, Kew. CO 139/12, Colonial Office and Predecessors: Jamaica, Acts, 1728–1730.

British National Archives, Kew. CO 139/13, Colonial Office and Predecessors: Jamaica, Acts, 1731–1733.

Brown, Kathleen. *Good Wives, Nasty Wenches, and Anxious Patriarchs: Gender, Race, and Power in Colonial Virginia.* Chapel Hill, NC: University of North Carolina Press, 1996.

Burns, Robert I., ed. *Las Siete Partidas*, trans. Samuel Parsons Scott, volume 4. Philadelphia, PA: University of Pennsylvania Press, 2001.

Chaplin, Joyce E. "Enslavement of Indians in Early America: Captivity without the Narrative." In *The Creation of the British Atlantic World*, edited by Elizabeth Mancke and Carole Shammas, 45–70. Baltimore, MD: Johns Hopkins University Press, 2005.

Collection of All the Acts of Assembly, Now in Force, in the Colony of Virginia. Williamsburg, VA, 1733.

Cooper, Thomas, ed. *The Statutes at Large of South Carolina: Acts, 1685–1716.* Volume 2. Columbia, SC: South Carolina, 1837.

Cowling, Camillia. *Conceiving Freedom: Women of Color, Gender, and the Abolition of Slavery in Havana and Rio de Janeiro.* Chapel Hill, NC: University of North Carolina Press, 2013.

De la Fuente, Alejandro and Ariela J. Gross. *Becoming Free, Becoming Black: Race, Freedom, and Law in Cuba, Virginia, and Louisiana.* Cambridge, UK: Cambridge University Press, 2020. doi:10.1017/9781108612951.002.

Dorsey, Joseph C. "Women Without History: Slavery, Jurisprudence, and the International Politics of Partus Sequitur Ventrem in the Spanish Caribbean." *Journal of Caribbean History* 28, no. 2 (1994): 165–207.

Fischer, Kirsten. *Suspect Relations: Sex, Race, and Resistance in Colonial North Carolina.* Ithaca, NY: Cornell University Press, 2002.

Forbes, Jack D. *Africans and Native Americans: The Language of Race and the Evolution of Red-Black Peoples.* Urbana, IL: University of Illinois Press, 1993.

Garraway, Doris L. *The Libertine Colony: Creolization in the Early French Caribbean.* Durham, NC: Duke University Press, 2005. doi:10.1215/9780822386513.

Gaspar, David Barry. *Bondmen and Rebels: A Study of Master-Slave Relations in Antigua.* (1985; reprinted.) Durham, NC: Duke University Press, 1993. doi:10.1215/9780822381778.

Goetz, Rebecca Anne. *The Baptism of Early Virginia.* Baltimore, MD: Johns Hopkins University Press, 2012. doi:10.1353/book.17321.

Gordon-Reed, Annette. *The Hemingses of Monticello: An American Family.* New York: W.W. Norton, 2009.

Guasco, Michael. *Slaves and Englishmen: Human Bondage in the Early Modern Atlantic World.* Philadelphia, PA: University of Pennsylvania Press, 2014.

Hall, Richard. *Acts, Passed in the Island of Barbados.* London, 1764.

Handler, Jerome S. "Custom and Law: The Status of Enslaved Africans in Seventeenth-Century Barbados." *Slavery & Abolition* 37, no. 2 (2016): 233–255. doi:10.1080/0144039X.2015.1123436.

Hening, W.W. *The Statutes at Large; Being a Collection of all the Laws of Virginia, from the First Session of the Legislature, in the Year 1619*, Volumes 1/2. New York, 1823.

Higginbotham Jr., A. Leon and Barbara K. Kopytoff, "Racial Purity and Interracial Sex in the Law of Colonial and Antebellum Virginia." *Georgetown Law Journal* 77 (1989): 1967–2029.

Jordan, Winthrop D. "American Chiaroscuro: The Status and Definition of Mulattoes in the British Colonies." *William and Mary Quarterly* 19, no. 2 (1962): 183–200.

Journals of the Assembly of Jamaica. Volume 2/3. Kingston, Jamaica, 1797.

Laws of Jamaica: 1681–1759. Volume 1. St. Jago de la Vega, Jamaica, 1802.

Livesay, Daniel. *Children of Uncertain Fortune: Mixed-Race Jamaicans and the Atlantic Family, 1733–1833*. Chapel Hill, NC: University of North Carolina Press, 2018.

Long, Edward. *The History of Jamaica*. Volume 3. London, 1774.

Martínez, María-Elena. *Genealogical Fictions: Limpieza de Sangre, Religion, and Gender in Colonial Mexico*. Stanford, CA: Stanford University Press, 2008.

Morgan, Jennifer L. *Laboring Women: Reproduction and Gender in New World Slavery*. Philadelphia, PA: University of Pennsylvania Press, 2004.

Morgan, Jennifer L. "*Partus sequitur ventrem*: Law, Race, and Reproduction in Colonial Slavery." *Small Axe* 22, no. 1 (2018): 1–17. doi:10.1215/07990537-4378888.

Newman, Brooke N. *A Dark Inheritance: Blood, Race, and Sex in Colonial Jamaica*. New Haven, CT: Yale University Press, 2018.

Newman, Brooke N. "Blood Fictions, Maternal Inheritance, and the Legacies of Colonial Slavery." *Women Studies Quarterly* 48, no. 1/2 (2020): 27–44. doi:10.1353/wsq.2020.0025.

Newton, Melanie J. "Returns to a Native Land: Indigeneity and Decolonization in the Anglophone Caribbean." *Small Axe* 17, no. 2 (2013): 108–122. doi:10.1215/07990537-2323346.

Spear, Jennifer. *Race, Sex, and Social Order in Early New Orleans*. Baltimore, MD: Johns Hopkins University Press, 2009.

Twinam, Ann. *Purchasing Whiteness: Pardos, Mulattos, and the Quest for Social Mobility in the Spanish Indies*. Stanford, CA: Stanford University Press, 2015.

9

CONCEIVING COLONIALISM

Contraceptive practices in colonial and postcolonial Mexico

Nora E. Jaffary

In the small town of Chiautla, Puebla, in 1829, parish priest *don* José Calletano received an anonymous letter requesting that community member Francisca de la Torres be punished for sacrilege and for consenting to the murder of her newly born baby. The writer, later revealed to be female, said she knew who had killed the child and declared that Torres had "tricked your honor by denying her pregnancy," claiming only to be ill when she had taken communion the previous Sunday.[1] Calletano turned the note over to a local judge who initiated a legal investigation into Torres' crimes that stretched out over the next four years. The court's investigation into Torres' guilt focused on whether she (or someone else) had smothered her baby at birth, and whether she had provoked the baby's miscarriage, as Calletano later alleged, by ingesting "certain medicines appropriate to another illness," administered by midwife *doña* Rosalia de Alarcoa, which "naturally caused a miscarriage."[2]

When she appeared before the investigating judge, Torres herself confessed that she had recently taken the medicinal herb *epazote*, but claimed she had been operating on the assumption that her ailment was the "detention of the menses, not that she was pregnant."[3] In her appearance, midwife Rosalia de Alarcoa declared that she had supplied Torres with a variety of medicines, including one mixture containing *escorzonera* ("viper grass") and the boiled flower *capitaneja* and another containing *alfolba* (fenugreek) and *manzanilla* (chamomile). Mexican women had long used all of these ingredients both to provoke miscarriages and to induce menstruation if it were "delayed" or "suppressed."[4] However, both de Alarcoa and several other witnesses declared that the medicines had been intended only for the latter objective.[5] They, like all the other historical actors treated here—judges, legal defenders, and community members—referred to these as two distinctive acts; inducing irregular menstruation was lawful and routine, whereas provoking a miscarriage was both criminal and immoral.[6] Despite their testimony to the contrary, my supposition is that in many of the colonial and nineteenth-century criminal trials I have studied, midwives and occasionally physicians (whether knowingly or unknowingly) supplied Mexican women with the abortifacients they sought to end unwanted pregnancies.

Fernanda Núñez has characterized late colonial and nineteenth-century Mexican women as possessing no "contraceptive mentality." In her view, contemporary medical literature's imperative that reproduction should accompany (exclusively marital) intercourse, along with

119

the contradictory evidence of high illegitimacy and low marriage rates in large sectors of the population and the "rampant fertility" of Mexican women, all indicate that, unlike in contemporary Europe, in Mexico a "contraceptive mentality did not yet exist."[7] On the contrary, however, the evidence I have gathered from abortion and infanticide criminal trials in several judicial archives suggests that Mexican women routinely employed a variety of pre-Columbian and newly introduced medicines to control reproduction through the colonial period and into the century following Mexican independence.

Crime and punishment in the colonial era

The comparison of judicial inquiries into the crimes of infanticide and abortion initiated in Mexico in the viceregal period (1521–1821) and the era beginning 50 years after Mexico's break from Spain reveals a striking discrepancy. Community members initiated criminal investigations into only a handful of women for these crimes during the 300-year period of colonial rule. My examination of various archival collections in Mexico has uncovered only 22 criminal investigations for both crimes during the entire colonial period.[8] Although evidence from criminal trials and medical texts suggest that women often used the same methods for controlling reproduction in both the colonial and postcolonial periods, denunciations and investigations for abortion and infanticide escalated dramatically after the mid-nineteenth century. For post-independence Mexico I have located a total of 111 investigations for abortion and 357 for infanticide in the 80-year period from 1829 to 1910.[9] As well as increasing in frequency, nineteenth-century abortion and infanticide trials also increased in severity. While colonial justices rarely convicted for these crimes, by the end of the nineteenth century justices convicted roughly half of those accused.

In the colonial era the paucity of denunciations for the crimes of abortion and infanticide, and the leniency with which colonial justices ruled over such cases, is striking. Numerous factors explain the low rates of denunciation and conviction in the colonial era: the secrecy of the crimes; the high rates of neo-natal mortality from natural causes; state disinterest in the involved offspring who were consistently illegitimate, poor, and often indigenous or of mixed race; and a community sense that women's reproductive practices were private, not public, business. Colonial-era inquiries are notable for the leniency or disinterest with which courts treated allegations of abortion. In several seventeenth- and eighteenth-century inquisitorial cases defendants under investigation for other crimes confessed in the course of their trials to having ingested abortifacients. Even though the papacy had ruled abortion punishable by excommunication in 1588,[10] New Spain's court of the Holy Office tended to ignore or sideline witnesses' descriptions of abortion or attempted abortion in such trials. Several witnesses, for instance, described María Marta de la Encarnación, a lay religious woman tried in 1717 for being a false mystic, practitioner of superstitions, and blasphemer, as having aborted a fetus. In an appearance before the court, de la Encarnación's father declared that, a year earlier, his daughter had experienced "the detention of her menses," while also displaying a "very elevated belly." He had discussed these symptoms with his wife, who arranged to have their daughter "bled from the ankle," an act both parents understood as provoking the "disappearance" of her belly.[11] A second witness in the trial described how de la Encarnación had once told him that she had realized she was pregnant and that she would "take something with which to abort and expel the fetus she carried (*tomaría algo con que abortase y hechase la criatura*)."[12] Nevertheless, neither the theological qualifiers who evaluated her deeds nor the inquisition's sentence against her even mentioned the allegations that María de la Encarnación had aborted a fetus; the court's condemnation of her focused on her falsifying sanctity.[13]

In a 1786 trial investigated by an ecclesiastical court, Juana Trinidad, a Spanish resident of the town of San Antonio Xacala in the current state of Hidalgo, initiated a suit against her second cousin, Antonio Márquez, for breach of the promise to marry, incest, and induction to commit abortion. Trinidad claimed that, under the pretext of promising to marry her, Márquez had seduced her and then, upon discovering her pregnancy, had encouraged her to "drink some herbs" in order to induce a miscarriage.[14] Márquez denied her claim and asserted it was Trinidad's mother who had counseled her to take such herbs, as she had done with her older sister months earlier, "since when she was already several months along, she gave her herbs so she would miscarry."[15] Trinidad eventually revealed she had provoked her miscarriage when she had "drunk a little *altamisa* (mugwort)."[16] The investigating judge found the couple guilty of committing incest and having procured an abortion, and ordered Márquez to pay Trinidad one hundred pesos for taking her virginity and to serve a one-year exile during which he was to perform set spiritual penances. However, neither the judge nor the various witnesses who appeared in the case devoted any attention to the question of how Trinidad had procured *altamisa,* nor did they dwell on the morality or criminality of the alleged abortion. Church doctrine called for excommunication for the crime, and several of the Iberian codes that lay at the foundation of the colonial legal system recommended the death penalty as the appropriate sentence for the commission of abortion.[17] Nevertheless, Trinidad's judge sentenced her with far greater leniency: she was to serve six months' supervised reclusion in a respectable household and perform the same spiritual penance as Márquez. Light as it was, Trinidad's was actually the strictest sentence issued from among the extant eighteenth-century abortion trials. Trinidad was no doubt convicted because, unlike most defendants, she confessed to her crime. Her sentence also indicates the court's interest in recuperating Trinidad—who was both Spanish and of a more elevated social class than the vast majority of women charged with these crimes—to conformity with the ideals of chaste femininity suitable to her station. However, the leniency of her sentence indicates the judicial and communal disinterest in reproductive crimes typical of the colonial era.

Intentional infanticide and medicinal abortion in New Spain

Notwithstanding the small number of criminal cases pursued against practitioners of abortion or infanticide in the colonial era, various types of evidence suggest that such practices were much more common than historians have hitherto acknowledged. For one, despite the widespread attribution of the "soaring fertility" of both colonial and nineteenth-century Mexican women, particular moments within this broad portrait imply a different reality. Historian Silvia Arrom, who drew her findings from a sample of 141 Mexico City wills dating from 1802 to 1855, found that more than 14 per cent of her sample had given birth to no children at all by the age of 45; a further 17 per cent had borne only one child; while another 15 per cent had only had two children.[18] Arrom observed that in the wills she studied women often commented that "during our marriage we had no children whatsoever despite the many years we were married."[19] Despite such suggestive evidence, Arrom commented that in this era "there is no evidence in the Mexican literature that contraception was used."[20]

Medical, religious, and legal texts also indicate that both abortion and infanticide were more widespread in colonial Mexico than the small number of criminal trials for either crime would suggest. Midwifery tracts circulating in the late eighteenth century, including Ignacio Segura's *Avisos saludables a las parteras* (1775) and Antonio Medina's *Cartilla nueva util y necesaria para instruirse las Matronas* (1750, 1806), explicitly admonished midwives for providing contraception or provoking abortion in their clients. Colonial confessional guides, such as

Bartolomé Alva's 1634 *Confessionario mayor, y menor*, required priests to interrogate women as to whether "when pregnant, they had taken some potion to expel the baby."[21] Judicial administrators and governors also lamented what they described as women's widespread practices of inducing miscarriage or murdering their newborns. In 1794 the Bourbon monarch Charles IV issued a *real cédula* (royal decree) which discussed the plight of foundlings in the Spanish possessions. The *cédula* sought to legitimize all foundlings, christening them "sons of the king." It also contained several specific measures designed to protect those apprehended in the act of transporting such children to foundling homes "in the interest of avoiding the many infanticides that occur" when those transporting babies killed them to avoid discovery and the resulting dishonor and prosecution.[22] Colonial officials expressed the same anxieties 25 years later when the public discovery in the streets of Popotla, a Mexico City suburb, of a group of four or five newborn corpses prompted a state investigation into the frequency of infanticide and the accessibility of *casas de expósitos* (foundling homes) to women across the viceroyalty.[23]

Defendants in colonial trials also occasionally hinted at the frequency of such practices. In an 1819 trial, María Dolores was accused of ordering one of her nieces to wring the neck of her newborn grandchild in order to protect the honor of her household (the baby had been conceived in an extra-marital and incestuous union with Dolores's son). In her defense statement, Dolores acknowledged that she had ordered the baby's death "out of anger in seeing that my niece had lacked respect for my household and exposed me to disquietude in my marriage ... and would cause my dishonor before the entire estate."[24] She also casually commented, however, that the murder of a newborn could be understood as commonplace: "It is so commonly said, when a baby cries, that it should be throttled or murdered, that there are really no parents who have not said this."[25] In the early postcolonial period, a Oaxacan midwife made a similar observation. Felipa Romero, charged with infanticide in 1837, defended herself by asserting that investigating judges should focus their attention in infanticide cases on post-partum mothers rather than the midwives who delivered their babies. Labor and childbirth were such physically devastating experiences that these alone often provoked women to destroy the babies they had just birthed. "How many times," she asserted, "has it happened that mothers murder their own children?"[26]

In the case of María Dolores's grandchild, the newborn died from strangulation. This, along with suffocation, was the second-most common cause of death in this body of infanticide cases, while exposure, which Mexican legal texts described as "infanticide by omission," was the most common.[27] In a substantial minority of the infanticide and abortion cases studied here, however, investigations turned on the question of whether defendants had taken abortifacients to provoke miscarriages. Such substances had a long history in New Spain.

When New Spain's Holy Office of the Inquisition seized the belongings of midwife Isabel Hernández, investigated for witchcraft in the central Mexican town of Tlaxcala in 1652, it discovered several known abortifacients among them. These included *cihuapatli* (the aster flower), the plant most often referenced in colonial and nineteenth-century medical texts as an effective abortifacient, and the dried tail of the *tlacuache* (a species of opossum).[28] Franciscan Bernardino de Sahagún's sixteenth-century indigenous informants had explained that pre-Columbian healers and midwives used both *cihuapatli* and *tlacuache* to stimulate menstruation, induce labor, or, administered in higher doses earlier in pregnancy, to provoke miscarriages; the latter because "the tail of this animal has the great virtue of provoking expulsion and of making the baby come out."[29] Hernández apparently made a practice of using such medicines as abortifacients. She recounted to the court how an "honorable family" in Tlaxcala had called her to aid a young woman, whom Hernández suggested to community members had suffered only from the "detention" of her menses. In fact, however, Hernández confessed to the court that she had attended the woman during her labor and misbirth. As was typical in such cases, the court asked for no further details about the cause of the infant's death or the disposition of its body.

Many women in the colonial era acquired medicines to induce miscarriages from midwives; others likely purchased them from *boticos* (pharmacies) or grew them in their own gardens. Paul Ramírez has recently commented on the genre of writing he terms medical self-care manuals, which circulated widely in New Spain throughout the colonial period.[30] Such texts, which included the friar Agustín Farfán's *Tractado breve de medicina y de todas las enfermedades* (1570, 1592), Jesuit Juan de Esteyneffer's important *Florilegio medicinal de todas las enfermedades* (1712), and physician Juan Manuel Venegas's *Compendio de la medicina* (1788), all discussed the routine medical complaint of women's "detention of the menses" and offered various medicinal remedies to treat the malady, many of which would have likely grown in household gardens. Venegas observed that various treatments could restore a woman's menses, including infusions of the plants chamomile, pennyroyal, and *altamisa.* [31] The prolific eighteenth-century scientific writer Antonio de León y Gama commented in his unpublished manuscript, "*Medicina mexicana,*" that *cihuapatli* could be used to treat "all the uterine illnesses from which women suffer," and also wrote that *pulque,* a popular beverage made from fermented maguey cactus, could be used to provoke detained menses in women.[32] The *Ensayo para la materia médica Mexicana* published in Puebla in 1832 recommended that the ubiquitous herb *epazote* be used to provoke menstruation "when it was detained by the atony of the uterus."[33]

One late-eighteenth-century text, an anonymous compilation of remedies and cures, included a recipe for an *altamisa* brew: "a tested, true, and infallible remedy to induce menstruation in women."[34] The *Gazeta de México,* one of New Spain's earliest news publications (and one published under state regulation and encouragement), also published a remedy for suspension of the menses. The September 18, 1795, edition announced that a daily dosage of a mixture formed by the reduction of the herb *viperina,* mixed with wine, cream of tartar, *aguardiente,* and *quina* leaves would successfully treat various chronic illnesses including menstrual detention, hysteria, hypochondria, and pulmonary disorders.[35] Another contemporary tract, a hand-written catalogue of Mexican medicines compiled by Jesuit missionary Lucas Vásquez, described several medicines that could be taken "to provoke childbirth and release the afterbirth." The main ingredient of one of these was *altamisa.* [36] Contemporaries believed there were many factors that might explain the "detention" of women's menses, including humoral imbalances, fright, weakness, hysteria, and age.[37] Nevertheless, then as now, the most common reason for the cessation of menstruation—although unspoken in these texts— would have been pregnancy, and many women no doubt knowingly ingested these medicines to address this state.

Post-independence change and continuity

In the postcolonial era, as the following cases demonstrate, Mexican women continued to use the same remedies to control reproduction as they had done in the colonial era. While defendants often claimed to have ingested medicines only to regularize menstruation, in some nineteenth-century criminal trials defendants confessed to having taken them to provoke abortions. Bernarda Sulú, for one, was tried and convicted in Chocholá, Yucatán, in 1854 for providing abortions to several women, provoked by an unspecified drink.[38] In Juana Aguirre's 1865 infanticide trial from Carmen, Yucatán, witnesses described how a woman administered castor oil *(aceite de higuerilla),* understood in the era to induce labor, to Aguirre.[39]

In Fernanda Canché's 1884 trial from Mérida, midwife Norberta Canché confessed to supplying a young woman who subsequently miscarried with a drink made from the leaves of *verbena,* but claimed this remedy was not intended to induce a miscarriage; rather it was meant to treat the subject's complaint of *pasmo,* a colloquial term for menstrual detention.[40] In Escálistica Alcozer's 1903 infanticide trial from Mérida, Yucatán, several witnesses testified that Alcozer and her mother had requested that a pharmacist supply her with medicines to induce an abortion.[41]

In the majority of such cases the suppliers of abortifacients were midwives. Occasionally, however, a doctor or male pharmacist (*boticario*) was involved. In the city of Puebla in 1836 a second anonymous note writer from Puebla denounced a young woman, Petra Sevilla, for having disposed of her newborn child in *los communes,* outdoor communal toilets. In her testimony Sevilla declared that the owners of the estate where she worked had called a doctor, *don* José Mariano Rivadenegra, to examine her on the night she had given birth because she had been complaining loudly of strong pains in her abdomen. The doctor had supplied her with a certain drink that she had taken and that "afterward she expelled that which she had in her womb" (later revealed to be a seven-month-old fetus).[42] When Rivadenegra gave his evidence he stated that he had visited Sevilla twice on the day she had given birth. For pains in the abdomen and intensive vomiting he had prescribed an "appropriate" remedy (*cosa analoga*) to "reduce the irritation." When he examined her a second time, alerted by household members who told him she was in heightened distress, he discovered her surrounded by a large quantity of coagulated blood, noting that those present were uncertain whether this had been caused by a "birth, miscarriage (*aborto*) or from the breaking of a detained menstruation."[43] Rivadenegra also declared that, since he had not been called to determine if Sevilla had recently given birth, he performed no internal examination of her cervix and limited himself to the observation of her abdomen's exterior, which he said appeared healthy. He prescribed a remedy for the "flow of blood" from which she was still suffering.[44] Whatever his official testimony, it seems highly improbable that a physician could have twice examined a woman during her third trimester, both while she was in active labor and moments after she gave birth, and not conclude that she had been pregnant. Either he was an incredibly incompetent physician or, as I suspect instead, he had deduced that Sevilla was pregnant and in labor and had supplied her with some sort of medicine to precipitate the process.

In nineteenth-century judicial proceedings, defendants and court officials often implied that the practice of abortion was common. Investigating officers in these trials frequently assumed and accepted the prevalence of abortion. When judges investigated alleged crimes of infanticide or abortion they routinely questioned defendants about whether or not they had consumed some medicine to induce the misbirth of their babies. In María Ambrosio's 1825 trial, for example, the *alcalde* (local judge) in the town of Tehuacán initiated an investigation after several community members reported the discovery of a newborn's corpse in an aqueduct. While Ambrosio's own testimony included no discussion of having taken an abortifacient to induce labor, in his summary of her crimes the *alcalde* included this characterization of such cases: "This crime is one of the most horrific possible and occupies, perhaps, the most pre-eminent place in its defiance of nature itself [he began]. It is indispensable, as such, to verify if María Ambrosio, propelled by the fear that her moral frailty [would be discovered], took some filthy drink [*bebistrajo*] that facilitated her miscarriage."[45]

Rather than suggesting the absence of a "contraceptive culture" in colonial and nineteenth-century Mexico, medical and legal documents show that women in both these periods actively sought to control reproduction through their ingestion of a variety of medicines that provoked abortions. In extant records for the colonial period, reproductive practices are most often discussed in medical and botanical texts, where medicines that acted as abortifacients are often described as innocent "menstrual regulators." As this chapter has demonstrated, evidence suggests that the authors of these texts were aware of the multiple purposes for which such substances might be used, including the induction of abortion. In Mexico's post-independence era, documentation of women's abortion practices is increasingly represented in criminal trials rather than in prosaic medical texts. The change in the means of documenting abortion's history indicates the intensification across time in Mexico of both the public scrutiny of female sexuality and the legal regulation of reproductive control.

The rise in criminal investigations for reproductive crimes in post-colonial Mexico, I have argued here, indicates a change in the formal and informal regulation of abortion and infanticide rather than an increase in women's actual practices. In the developing republic, regular Mexicans demonstrated a new penchant for scrutinizing and denouncing the sexual morality of the plebian women who constituted almost all of those accused of these crimes. State officers who tried these cases and members of the public who often initiated them seemed intent on ensuring the performance in lower-class communities of the gendered ideals of pre-marital virginity and marital chastity previously imperative particularly to elite families in the Mexican viceroyalty.

Notes

1 INAH, Archivo Histórico Judicial de Puebla (AHJP), caja 434, exp. 12745, fol. 1. I am grateful for the assistance of Hugo Rueda Ramírez in locating and photographing materials from the AHJP for me. I also acknowledge support for this research from the Social Sciences and Humanities Research Council of Canada.

2 Ibid., fol. 3. Calletano used the term *aborto*. In this era, court officials, physicians, and witnesses all used the term *aborto* to refer to both intentional abortions and those we now refer to as miscarriages.

3 AHJP, caja 434, exp. 12745, fol. 13v.

4 *Escorzonera* was used by indigenous groups in the colonial period to induce abortion, but also as emmenagogues to stimulate "delayed" menstruation. Kay, *Healing with Plants*, 66. *Capitaneja* was used to deal with problems in childbirth, including stimulation of the placenta's expulsion. Riddle, *Eve's Herbs*, 250, notes that women had long ingested fenugreek in Europe and eventually in the Americas to induce miscarriage. Quezada, "Métodos anticonceptivos y abortivos tradicionales," 235–238, observes that Mexican women in the colonial period and long after it also ingested *manzanilla* to provoke miscarriage.

5 AHJP, caja 434, exp. 12745, fol. 18–19.

6 Defendants repeatedly affirmed that they had understood themselves to be suffering from "detention of the menses" rather than pregnancy. See for example, María de la Luz López's 1851 case AHJP caja 942, exp. 33204 and María Rosa del Carmen's 1842 trial, AHJP, caja 721, exp. 22524, fol. 3v.

7 Becerra, "Imaginario médico," 152.

8 This body includes six inquisitorial rather than secular cases. The archives I have consulted for the viceregal era include Mexico's Archivo General de la Nación (AGNM), the Archivo Histórico Judicial del Estado de Oaxaca (AHJO), the Archivo General del Estado de Yucatán (AGEY), the municipal archives of both Mexico City and Oaxaca City, the Archivo Histórico del Estado de Tlaxcala, and the Archivo Histórico Judicial de Puebla. These cases include the few instances of the crimes that Sonya Lipsett-Rivera and Zeb Tortorici were able to locate in their own research. Rivera, "A Slap in the Face of Honor," 179–200; Tortorici, "Women at the Margins of the Unnatural." Dolores Encisco Rojas also comments on the paucity of such cases in the colonial period in "'Mal parir,'" 91–123.

9 I discuss about half of these, originating in archives from central Mexico and the state of Oaxaca in Jaffary, *Reproduction and Its Discontents in Mexico*. Subsequent to those treated in that volume I have collected further cases from judicial archives in the Mexican states of Yucatán, Puebla, Tlaxcala, and Oaxaca.

10 Noonan, *Contraception,* 344.

11 AGNM, Inquisición, vol. 788 exp. 24, fol. 406.

12 Ibid., fol. 503v.

13 Ibid., fols. 266, 453.

14 AGNM, Indiferente Virreinal, caja 6271, exp. 26, sn.

15 Ibid.

16 Ibid., fol. 4

17 The most important of these was King Alfonso X's thirteenth-century code, *Las Siete Partidas*, which in *Ley* 8, *título* 8, 7ª *Partida* called for capital punishment as the appropriate penalty for committing abortion. *Las Siete Partidas Del Sabio Rey Don Alonso el Nono, nuevamente Glosadas por Gregorio Lopez,* Vol. 7 (Diego Fernández de Cordóva, 1587).

18 Arrom, *The Women of Mexico City*, 125.

19 Ibid., 126. Historians have also unearthed instances earlier in the colonial period in other urban contexts, including seventeenth-century Guadalajara, of surprisingly low birth rates. Calvo, "The Warmth of the Hearth," 291.

20 Arrom, *The Women of Mexico City*, 318, fn 49.

21 Bartolomé Alva, *Confessionario mayor, y menor en lengua mexicana* (México: Por Francisco Salbago, impresor del Secreto del Santo Oficio. Por Pedro de Quiñones, 1634), 22.

22 AGNM, Bandos, vol. 19, exp. 78–79, fol. 1797.

23 AGNM, Indiferente Virreinal, caja 3503, exp. 1.

24 AGNM, Criminal, vol. 68, exp. 7, fol. 234v.

25 Ibid., fol. 235.

26 AHMO, Justicia, caja 15, Juzgado de la 1ª instancia 1836–1837, fol. 17.

27 Rafael Roa Bárcena, *Manual razonado de práctica criminal y médico-legal* (Mexico: Imp. De Andrade y Escalante, 1860), 609.

28 AGNM, Inquisición,vol. 561, exp. 6 fol. 557v; alternative spelling: *tlaquatzin*.

29 de Sahagún, *Historia general*, 609.

30 Ramírez, *Enlightened Immunity*, 62.

31 Juan Manuel Venegas, *Compendio de la medicina* (México: D. Felipe de Zúñiga y Ontiveros, 1788), 242, 341.

32 Huntington Library, Antonio de León y Gama, "Medicina Mexicana," HM 4297, 56, 70. Francisco Guerra identified the author of this unsigned manuscript as León y Gama.

33 Ensayo para la materia medica Mexicana:arreglado por una comisión nombrada por la Academia Médico-Quirúrgica de esta capital, quien ha dispuesto se imprima por considerarlo útil (Puebla: Oficina del hospital de S. Pedro, à cargo del C. Manuel Buen-Abad, 1832), 15.

34 Wellcome Library, "Mexico 18th century: Compendium of remedies," WMS Amer 58, fol. 26.

35 *Supplemento á la Gazeta de México del viernes 18 de septiembre de 1795*, 418, 422, 423.

36 Wellcome Library, Lucas Vasquez, "Florilegio medicinal para los misioneros entre las naciones bárbaras de México," WMS Amer 26, fol. 20v.

37 Juan Manuel Venegas, *Compendio de la medicina; ó Medicina practica* (México: Felipe de Zúñiga y Ontiveros, 1788), 241–243.

38 Archivo General del Estado de Yucatán (AGEY), Justicia, Penal, vol. 70, exp. 34, fols. 1–3.

39 AGEY, Justicia, Penal, caja 130, vol. 130, exp. 10, fol. 3.

40 AGEY, Justicia, Penal, vol. 132 exp. 34, fols. 3, 6.

41 AGEY, Justicia, Penal, Caja 533, vol. 29, exp. 10, fol. 10. Another case involving a defendant's confession to having taken an abortifacient is AGEY, Justicia, Penal, vol. 69, exp. 48.

42 AHJP, caja 595, exp. 18168, fol. 21.

43 Ibid., fol. 25v-26.

44 Ibid.

45 AHJP, caja 357, exp. 10659, fol. 10. The judge in Francisca de la Torres' case draws the same implication. AHJP, caja 434, exp. 12745, fol. 54v.

Bibliography

Alva, Bartolomé. *Confessionario mayor, y menor en lengua mexicana*. México: Por Francisco Salbago, impresor del Secreto del Santo Oficio. Por Pedro de Quiñones, 1634.

Arrom, Silvia Marina. *The Women of Mexico City, 1790–1857*. Stanford, CA: Stanford University Press, 1985.

Calvo, Thomas. "The Warmth of the Hearth: Seventeenth-Century Guadalajara Families." In *Sexuality and Marriage in Colonial Latin America*, edited by Asunción Lavrin, 287–312. Lincoln, NE: University of Nebraska Press, 1990.

Castilla, Alfonso X. (Rey). *Las Siete Partidas del Sabio Rey Don Alonso el Nono, nuevamente Glosadas por Gregorio López*, Vol. 7. Diego Fernández de Cordóva, 1587.

Encisco Rojas, Dolores. "'Mal parir', 'parir fuera de tiempo' o 'aborto procurado y efectuado'. Su penalización en Nueva España y el México independiente." *Dimensión Antropológica* 49 (May–August 2010): 91–123.

Jaffary, Nora E. *Reproduction and Its Discontents in Mexico: Childbirth and Contraception, 1750 to 1905*. Chapel Hill, NC: University of North Carolina Press, 2016.

Kay, Margarita Artschwager. *Healing with Plants in the American and Mexican West*. Tucson, TX: University of Arizona Press, 1996.

Lipsett-Rivera, Sonya. "A Slap in the Face of Honor: Social Transgression and Women in Late Colonial Mexico." In *The Faces of Honor: Sex, Shame, and Violence in Colonial Latin America*, edited by Lyman L. Johnson and Sonya Lipsett-Rivera, 179–201. Albuquerque, NM: University of New Mexico Press, 1998.

Noonan, Jr., John T. *Contraception: A History of Its Treatment by Catholic Theologians and Canonists, Enlarged Edition*. Cambridge, MA: The Belknap Press of Harvard University Press, 1986.

Núñez Becerra, Fernanda. "Imaginario médico y práctica jurídica en torno al aborto durante el ultimo tercio del siglo xix." In *Curar, sanar y educar: Enfermedad y sociedad en México, siglos xix y xx*, edited by Claudia Agoostoni, 127–161. México: UNAM, 2008.

Ramírez, Paul. *Enlightened Immunity: Mexico's Experiments with Disease Prevention in the Age of Reason*. Stanford, CA: Stanford University Press, 2018.

Riddle, John. *Eve's Herbs: A History of Contraception and Abortion in the West*. Cambridge, MA: Harvard University Press, 1997.

Roa Bárcena, Rafael. *Manual razonado de práctica criminal y médico-legal*. México: Imp. De Andrade y Escalante, 1860.

Sahagún, Bernardino de. *Historia general de las cosas de Nueva España*. México: CONACULTA, 1989.

Tortorici, Zeb. "Women at the Margins of the Unnatural: Abortion and Infanticide in New Spain," paper presented at the Latin American Studies Association Meeting, Rio de Janeiro, June 11–14, 2009.

Venegas, Juan Manuel. *Compendio de la medicina*. México: D. Felipe de Zúñiga y Ontiveros, 1788.

10

DEMOGRAPHIC ANXIETIES, PRO-NATALISM, AND GOVERNING DIFFERENCE IN THE LATE OTTOMAN EMPIRE

Gülhan Balsoy

The Ottoman state came into being circa 1300 in northwest Anatolia (Asia Minor).[1] At this time it was one of the many Turcoman tribal groups of Central Asian origin in Anatolia. Through a process of steady expansion that had accelerated with the conquest of Constantinople, the small principality had turned itself into a world empire by the sixteenth century. In global history, the Ottoman empire is perhaps the only political entity that has survived from the late-medieval era through to the modern period, enduring for almost 600 years until it finally disintegrated into numerous nation-states during World War I. At its height the Ottoman empire spread over three continents, with lands covering most of the Middle East, North Africa, and southeast Europe. Not only was it gigantic territorially but diverse in terms of its population. More than anything else, a great range of ethnic, religious, cultural, and geographical differences characterized the Ottoman society. As the nineteenth century approached, however, the main strength of the Ottomans turned into one of their main weaknesses. Imperialism and global expansionism, on the one hand, and nationalism, on the other, forced Ottomans to fight on two fronts simultaneously. As a result, organizing as well as consolidating difference became a major dilemma the Ottomans had to face.[2] While European powers were taking under their own control the Ottoman territories in North Africa and the Middle East, with the rise of nationalist sentiments, various groups under Ottoman rule started to fight nationalist wars aiming for independence and freedom. For the Ottoman power, this two-sided threat ripping apart its territories presented a difficult challenge. The Ottoman center had to formulate a common identity that would convince its subjects to support an Ottomanist project as a reaction to the nationalist independence movements. But at the same time it faced the need to turn itself into a colonial power and model colonialist behaviors or risk facing colonization itself.[3] Yet becoming a colonial power and fighting against separatist nationalisms were two clashing projects almost impossible to fulfill at one and the same time.

At the heart of colonialism was a rule of colonial difference that created a binary split into colonizers and colonized, which assumed the essential inferiority and inequality of the latter.[4] For Ottomans, drawing such boundaries was particularly difficult since the Ottoman Turkish rulers of Istanbul shared the same religion with the majority of subjects. In order to maintain group dominance, rulers had to gain the loyalty of their subjects and to stress similarity rather than difference for that purpose. Like other colonial powers, the Ottomans tried to base their rule on dual structures for governing the center and the peripheral colonies. More still, the Ottoman center legitimized its rule, especially in Arab provinces, as a mission to civilize and to uplift a "backward" population.[5] However, what distinguished the Ottoman case from European colonial rulers was an unwillingness to stress difference and to remake the local society,[6] since emphasizing difference would contradict the project of constructing a common identity to glue the empire together. The experiments initiated with the establishment of the Imperial School for Tribes (*Aşiret Mektebi*),[7] the formation and function of the Hamidian troops,[8] policies of conversion,[9] and changing practices of conscription[10] were all expressions of the intricate relation between the new politics of citizenship and methods of governing difference. Although extant scholarship has discussed the tension between similarity and difference mainly with reference to the male citizens and subjects, I argue that gender, sexuality, and reproduction were significant sites for the workings of the colonialist policy. Hence examination of the pro-natalist discourse and practices through the prism of colonialism will demonstrate some of the ways non-Turkish Muslims were included or excluded in the management of sameness and difference.

Ottoman politics of reproduction

The idea that having a healthy and large population as a precondition for creating a strong economy and military gained new importance in public discussion in the Ottoman empire from the mid-nineteenth century. For the Ottomans, the magnitude of population was particularly important since they were already losing territory due to wars, nationalist rebellions, and the emergence of new nation-states.[11] When incapable of reversing these major processes, the Ottoman elites turned their attention to the fecundity of women and sought ways to reduce high infant mortality rates and to increase birth rates. As I have argued in previous work, Ottoman pro-natalism was formulated through three registers: the medicalization of childbirth and the professionalization of midwifery; bans on abortion; and the medicalization of pregnancy and the discipline of the female body.[12]

The anxieties about the fate of the population were not universal, however. Ottoman pro-natalism was predicated on ethno-religious and class lines. For the Ottoman government authorities it was the "Muslim" population that was under threat of decline, while the non-Muslims enjoyed higher birth rates. According to officials, non-Muslim women did not induce abortions, as opposed to the Muslim women who made it a habit to terminate their pregnancies. Moreover, as bureaucratic and medical elites claimed, since non-Muslim men were not conscripted into compulsory military service, the portion of non-Muslims in the overall population continuously increased.[13] However, despite its popularity, this assumption was fundamentally flawed. Although Muslim and non-Muslim women could have had different attitudes toward terminating unwanted pregnancies, it is almost impossible to make conclusive assumptions due to the intimate nature of this choice. Women, regardless of their faiths, either kept their reproductive choices to themselves or shared them with only a few reliable friends or family members. Moreover, besides faith, poverty, or wellbeing, family size and the availability of family or community support were also among vital factors shaping women's reproductive decisions.

There was also a second and more concrete reason that countered the assumptions of the pro-natalist elites. Throughout the nineteenth century, and especially after the Berlin Treaty following the 1877–1878 Russo–Ottoman War, the share of Muslims in the overall population increased significantly due to the loss of territories that were marked by a higher proportion of non-Muslims as well as the migration of Muslim peoples from the lost territories to Anatolia. While at the start of the century the non-Muslims comprised almost 40 per cent of the Ottoman population, this share dropped to around 25 per cent after the 1877–1878 war.[14] Thus the position of intellectuals and bureaucrats worrying about the fate of the Muslim population was not sustained by the contemporary demographic figures; it was, instead, purely political and ideological.

Besides favoring the Muslims, Ottoman pro-natalism became increasingly class based from the late nineteenth century onwards. Especially in the early twentieth century, the debate about who should reproduce and who should avoid it was formulated along class lines more than ever. Particularly in the advice literature, a popular genre at that time,[15] the pro-natalist intellectuals lamented that the ignorant lower-class peoples, who were mostly of rural origins, kept on reproducing and having children. They assumed that the so-called degenerate characteristics such as ignorance, poverty, and unhealthiness were innate and heritable rather than the result of social and economic conditions, and hence passed on to succeeding generations. Thus the pro-natalists believed such ignorant and poor people were a burden for the economy and society. They believed that the educated, urban, middle-class professionals should be the ones to reproduce and have more children. It was their progeny that would elevate society and the economy.[16]

However, the pro-natalist anxieties were mostly referring to the Istanbul-based audience. Did different institutional, medical, and discursive principles apply to Istanbul, the center of the empire, as opposed to the periphery? How did Ottoman pro-natalism concern the peripheral populations? How, if at all, did reproductive policies approach the sexuality of these peripheral populations?

Midwifery, practices of childbirth, and cultural difference

The nineteenth century had been a time when midwifery practices came under increasing surveillance of pro-natalist Ottoman authorities. The education, training, and practice of midwives became subject to the scrutiny of pro-natalist bureaucrats and doctors. In that period the Ottoman state vigorously licensed, regulated, and controlled midwifery. The boundaries of midwifery practice were redrawn, with a sharp demarcation of midwives' tasks from those of doctors. For example, regulations barred midwives from using forceps and other novel obstetrical tools, reserving their use for male doctors. Midwives were also banned from turning the fetus inside the uterus—a task that they had probably been doing for centuries in the case of breech deliveries—and neither were they allowed to administer medicine.[17]

The expectations that ordinary people held of midwives and doctors were also changing. Numerous petitions from provincial towns and cities were sent directly to the School of Medicine or to the Ministry of the Interior asking for the appointment of licensed and trained midwives. Medine and Mekke, the two holy cities of Islam, were among those making requests.[18] As elsewhere, midwifery in the Ottoman empire was a skill that was passed on to succeeding generations without formal instruction; it could only be learned through experience. It had deep local and traditional roots and was one of the oldest female professions. Why then were the local people demanding medically trained midwives? Were they really embracing transformations in medicine, and why might they want to face a language barrier during the process of childbirth? Or was somebody else speaking for them? In order to address these questions, I trace the activities of four midwives who functioned in Medine from the late 1880s to the late 1890s.

In this ten-year period four midwives served in the city: Hâcce Hafize, Nefise Şadiye, Fatma Zehra, and a midwife recorded only as Şakire. Hâcce Hafize is the first midwife I was able to locate in the city. Her name is heavily loaded with notions of Islamic piety. *Hâcce* is a woman who has fulfilled her pilgrimage duty and *Hafize* is a woman who can recite the Quran by heart. It is unfortunately not possible to know whether she became a *hâcce* after she arrived in the city for midwifery or if she has another story, but she must have been appointed to the city early in 1888. From a petition submitted by her son in October 1889 we learn she had already been working as a midwife in the city for a year and a half, but in this time she did not receive a salary or stipend. Her son, who was a government official in Istanbul, wrote the petition on behalf of his mother and asked for the due payments.[19] We do not know the outcome of the petition, but from another document we know that she passed away in 1892.[20] After her death it took almost two years and frequent correspondence before a new midwife, Nefise Şadiye, was appointed to the city. She resigned and left after a few years due to health issues.[21] After her came Fatma Zehra, but the only evidence of her time in the city concerns her sudden death.[22] Finally, Şakire was appointed from Istanbul to Medine.[23] I was not able to trace how long she worked in the city, but apparently she was quite successful as she was awarded a medal for her services.

Among the four midwives, the story of Nefise Şadiye has some details that cast light on our questions. After Hâcce Hafize passed away, the governorate of Medine wrote to the Ministry of the Interior to report the death and to ask for the appointment of another midwife.[24] Nefise Şadiye seemed to be the best match, but there was a problem: she did not have a license issued officially by the School of Medicine.[25] Thus the local officials were informed that she was the only candidate but she could not be appointed. Disappointed by this information, the local officials wrote a memorandum to the Ministry of the Interior and complained that, since Hâcce Hafize's death, the broader region lacked a capable midwife. According to them, Turkish women in Yemen did not want Arab midwives to deliver their children and hence they were in urgent need of a midwife. In the meantime, another midwife, Ayşe, was found. However, Ayşe asked for a salary of 1,000 *gurus*, twice the amount that Nefise Şadiye would accept. The financial urgencies shaped the outcome in this case and Nefise Şadiye, who was first said to lack a proper license, was appointed to the city.[26] Unfortunately she fell ill not long after her arrival and, after two years, traveled back to Istanbul. There she decided she was too old and sick to continue midwifery and requested her retirement,[27] which she was able to secure.[28]

This information may be too scant and thin to reach conclusions about colonialist motivations and practices, but still there are several interesting hints in this story. The correspondence on the appointment of Nefise Şadiye is the clearest in terms of the function of the centrally appointed midwives. The documents insisting on her appointment to the city despite her lack of a license explicitly say that the "Turkish" women in the city did not want to have local midwives attending childbirths, creating a difficult situations due to the lack of centrally appointed midwives. Thus this request seems to be limited to the Turkish women and does not represent the demands or needs of local women. Given the demography of the city, we can also conclude that the Turkish women referred to in the petition were presumably the wives and sometimes sisters or daughters of the government officials appointed from the capital. As discussed, in the nineteenth century the practices of childbirth and midwifery were still strongly based in folk traditions of medicine. Moreover, language barriers could have made communication difficult. Thus local and Turkish women would have had reason to prefer a midwife sharing the same culture and language during this intimate experience. In any case, when the city administrators sent the request to Istanbul they were probably expressing a half-private need. They were speaking for themselves or for their close relations while pretending to express a public need.

A second issue concerns the opposite situation: the appointment of Arab midwives to Istanbul. Although midwives of all different backgrounds were licensed and served in the Ottoman medical sphere, when it came to official appointments the midwives from the peripheries were never moved to the center. In other words, the direction of appointment of the midwives was always from Istanbul to the peripheries. The midwives appointed from Istanbul to the peripheral regions were seen as the representatives of the newly emerging medical institution and its priorities.

Can we then call these midwives sent from Istanbul to Medine colonial midwives or agents of colonial medicine? In the nineteenth-century Ottoman context, medicine was a predominantly male field and women were excluded from the medical practice except for midwifery. Women were not admitted to medical schools or able to receive formal medical education. Even in midwifery the main focus of the state was to license and regulate rather than to train. Still, midwives were able to have access to the lives of women and female networks, and they were able to mediate between the state and local communities in many instances.[29] They also were entitled to many benefits, including pensions in return for negotiation with the state once they were licensed. Thus their appointment and practice in the provinces, in regions distant and different from the Ottoman center, was more than simply government service. It was a small but crucial step through which the state penetrated into female intimacy. Although there is still need of more exploration to reveal the role that medicine, and especially midwifery, played in the administration of the Ottoman "colonial" project, Ottoman pro-natalist policy extended to parts distant from the center through midwives.

A pamphlet on the harms of abortion

Prior to the nineteenth century, reproductive decisions were predominantly driven by religion. In a society like the Ottoman one, where different faith systems prevailed, women's reproductive decisions were shaped by a diversity of understandings and practices. In the early nineteenth century the Ottoman state started to intervene in the reproductive field in more overt ways. Although sporadic documents banning abortion had been issued previously, in 1838 the first document announcing a more coherent policy to fight abortion was released.[30] This document declared that abortion was a grave sin and women should avoid it in all cases. It was also sent to provincial authorities, telling them to take the necessary precautions to fight abortion.

Ottoman anti-abortion policies and measures were reshaped from the 1850s. Despite the official documents strictly banning abortion, the Imperial Penal Codes of 1840 and 1850 did not have articles defining punishments for this crime. The single measure to ban abortion was to ask doctors, pharmacists, and midwives to pledge oaths to their religious leaders against assisting in the termination of a pregnancy. The 1858 Penal Code was the first to cover abortion under its purview and define sanctions against it. The late 1850s also witnessed a greater transformation of the policies against abortion. Besides penalties for those inducing abortions, material incentives began to emerge to encourage women to have more births. For example, monthly stipends were offered to those having twins, having more than seven and later more than four children, and to those adopting babies. A state-run orphanage was also opened[31] and abortion was impacted by other public health measures. In other words, the wellbeing of the population was as important as its size.

Besides official documents, anti-abortion messages were also reiterated in printed media. To popularize the anti-abortion stance, a pamphlet on the harms of abortion was prepared.[32]

We do not know how and to whom this pamphlet was distributed, but we are lucky to have one copy available.[33] The pamphlet is 20 pages long and the ideas expressed are typical of contemporary views on abortion. The pamphlet cites verses from the Quran and also prophetic sayings (*hadith*).

The first verse cited in the pamphlet is the 31st verse of the al-Isrā' Surah, which says: "Kill not your children for fear or want: We shall provide sustenance for them as well as for you. Verily the killing of them is a great sin."[34] A few pages later this is followed by the 140th verse of Al-An'ām: "Lost are those who slay their children, from folly, without knowledge, forbid food which Allah hath provided for them, inventing [lies] against Allah. They have indeed gone astray and heeded no guidance."[35] Only the first part is taken, rather than the full verse. Finally, the 33rd verse of al-Isrā' is cited, which says: "Nor take life—which Allah has made sacred—except for just cause. And if anyone is slain wrongfully, we have given his heir authority: but let him not exceed bounds in the matter of taking life; for he is helped."[36]

In Islamic legal tradition there is a highly developed commentary literature that interprets the Quranic verses. Different schools of jurisprudence have different interpretations of abortion,[37] each interpreting these verses in different ways. Still, these verses are more broadly concerned with homicide than abortion specifically. Some commentators insist that the verses refer to the habit of infanticide. Prophetic stories were also cited in the pamphlet, which relate mostly to homicide rather than specifically abortion. Besides the Turkish version, 500–600 copies of an Arabic version were printed and sent for distribution in Jerusalem. As with the Turkish version, it was for religious or community leaders and not for women themselves.

Islam and the law of Islam, Sharia, did not have a fixed interpretation of abortion. Different legal schools (*mezhep*) of Islam displayed different opinions toward abortion with regard to the status of the fetus, its ensoulment, the conditions under which abortion is permissible, the start of pregnancy, and of abortion and contraception. While in Istanbul and Anatolia the Hanafi school, the most liberal school of Islam, was predominant, from Aleppo to Egypt and Yemen the Shafi'i school was most often followed. In the debate about abortion we see that although the ruling elites at the center and the subject populations at the periphery had shared the same religion, their interpretation of the requirements of their faith varied significantly in this matter. When Ottoman power intervened in the intimate lives of its subjects, it rationalized these measures at the center of Ottoman authority by citing concerns of public health. However, once these policies reached the peripheries neither concern for public health nor public welfare surfaced; rather, religion was the single tool to enable and legitimize state intervention in reproduction. In other words, the empire used different moral and political arguments to assert its authority over women's reproductive decisions. The pro-natalists did not make any effort to address interpretations and legal traditions of Islam in the religion. They did not establish welfare measures such as ones provided to the women in Istanbul either, and left the women in Middle Eastern peripheries to shoulder the consequences of their reproductive decisions on their own. While at the center the welfare and survival of children was a core component of pro-natalism, on the peripheries pro-natalism was more a matter of numbers, and the Ottoman state did nothing or little to ensure the wellbeing of its youth.

Pro-natalism was the main tool through which the empire penetrated into the intimate lives and practices of its peoples. Promoting an increase in its Muslim population was at the core of Ottoman pro-natalism. However, the Ottoman empire used different arguments and political tools when it was extending its reach into intimate experiences at the center and on the peripheries.

Despite increasingly sophisticated scholarship, there is still further need to investigate Ottoman methods of governing difference. Examining reproductive policies and Ottoman pro-natalism would help us to focus on bodies that serve as sites of regulation, discipline, surveillance, and social hierarchy. Topics such as medicine, sexuality, and arrangements of domestic space bear important potential for unfolding the nature of late Ottoman rule. Exploring intimacy might also give us a chance to go beyond the strict binary of colonizer and colonized, which does not work well in the Ottoman case and which would help us reconsider both the unequal importance of *and* the porosity between the Ottoman center and its periphery.

Notes

1　Imber, *The Ottoman Empire*, 4–17; Quataert, *The Ottoman Empire*; Inalcık and Quataert, *An Economic and Social History of the Ottoman Empire.*
2　For a meticulous discussion of the inner dynamics and background of the changing relations between the Ottoman communities as well as the transformation of the markers of difference, see Tezcan, *The Second Ottoman Empire.*
3　Deringil, "'They Live in a State of Nomadism and Savagery.'"
4　Chatterjee, *The Nation and Its Fragments*, 16–26.
5　Makdisi, "Ottoman Orientalism."
6　Kuehn, *Empire, Islam, and Politics of Difference.*
7　Rogan, "Asiret Mektebi."
8　Klein, *Power in the Periphery*, 256–340.
9　Deringil, "'There Is No Compulsion in Religion.'"
10　Gölbaşı, "Turning the 'Heretics' into Loyal Muslim Subjects"; Gölbaşı "'Devil Worshippers,'" 133–155.
11　Karpat, *Ottoman Population.*
12　Balsoy, *The Politics of Reproduction in Ottoman Society.*
13　Ibid., 51–75.
14　Quataert, "The Age of Reforms."
15　Although we do not have specific information as to the number of copies printed and sold, the existence of later editions and the multiple numbers of reprints for many of the advice books suggest that this genre received wide attention from middle-class men and women and also became a profitable business. See also Schick, "Print Capitalism."
16　Balsoy, *Politics of Reproduction*, 77–98. See also Demirci, *Body, Disease and Late Ottoman Literature.*
17　Balsoy, *Politics of Reproduction*, 27–49.
18　DH.MKT 1707/95 (1307.Z.14/1 September 1890), Ayniyat1024/181 (1286/1869–70), and NGG 772/18 (1285.Ca.18/6 September 1868) for Medina; İ.DH 601/41904 (1286.Ş.2/7 November 1869), Ayniyat1028/209 (1286/1869–70), and Ayniyat1024/202 (1286/1869–70) for Mecca. In references to the documents from the Ottoman Archives, I use the official acronym of the collection under which the document is classified, the document number, and finally the lunar and solar dates of the document.
19　DH.MKT 1621/124 (1306.09.7); DH.MKT 1666/19 (1307.02.12/13.10.1889); DH.MKT 1687/74 (14.05.1307).
20　DH.MKT 1976/38 (27.12.1309/23.07.1892).
21　DH.MKT 339/27 (1312.Ş.5/1.2.1895).
22　DH.MKT 2073/31 (1313.07.22).
23　İ.TAL 107/2 (01.07.1314); DH.MKT 2405/33 (25.05.1318).
24　DH.MKT 1976/38 (1309.Z.27/23.7.1892).
25　DH.MKT 1989/89 (1310.M.25/19.8.1892); DH.MKT 2004/99 (1310.S.29/22.9.1892). DH.MKT 59/30 (1311.B.27/3.2.1894).
26　DH.MKT 59/30 (1311.B.27/3.2.1894).
27　DH.MKT 236/34 (1311.Za.10/15.5.1894).
28　DH.MKT 295/77 (1312.R.15/16.10.1895); ŞD 934/62 (04.08.1312).
29　Demirci and Somel, "Women's Bodies, Demography, and Public Health."
30　"Meclis-i Umur-u Nafıanın Layihası," *Takvim-i Vekayi*, 1254.Ş.28/16.11.1838. See also Balsoy, *Politics of Reproduction*, 51–75.

31 Balsoy, *Politics of Reproduction*, 51–75; Maksudyan, *Orphans and Destitute Children.*
32 DH.MKT 1501/34 (1305.Ş.5/17 April 1888); DH.MKT 1481/55 (1305.Ca.16/30 January 1888).
33 Y.A.RES 61/15 (1310.Ra.14/6 October 1892).
34 The Holy Quran, trans. Abdullah Yusuf Ali (Wordsworth Classics of World Literature, 2000): 226.
35 Ibid., 111.
36 Ibid., 227.
37 Katz, "The Problem of Abortion in Classical Sunni *Fikh.*"

Bibliography

Baki, Tezcan. *The Second Ottoman Empire: Politics and Social Transformation in the Early Modern World.* Cambridge, UK, and New York: Cambridge University Press, 2010.

Balsoy, Gülhan. *The Politics of Reproduction in Ottoman Society, 1838–1900.* London: Routledge, 2013.

Cemil, Schick Irvin. "Print Capitalism and Women's Sexual Agency in the Late Ottoman Empire." *Comparative Studies of South Asia, Africa and the Middle East* 31, no. 1 (2011): 196–216. doi:10.1215/1089201X-2010-067.

Chatterjee, Partha. *The Nation and Its Fragments: Colonial and Postcolonial Histories.* Princeton, NJ: Princeton University Press, 1993.

Demirci, Tuba. "Body, Disease and Late Ottoman Literature: Debates on Ottoman Muslim Family in the Tanzimat Period (1839–1908)." Ph.D. diss., Bilkent University, 2008.

Demirci, Tuba and Selçuk Akşin Somel. "Women's Bodies, Demography, and Public Health: Abortion Policy and Perspectives in the Ottoman Empire of the Nineteenth Century." *Journal of the History of Sexuality* 17, no. 3 (2008): 377–420. doi:10.1353/sex.0.0025.

Deringil, Selim. "There Is No Compulsion in Religion': On Conversion and Apostasy in the Late Ottoman Empire: 1839–1856." *Comparative Studies in Society and History* 42 no. 3 (2000): 547–575. doi:10.1017/S0010417500002930.

Deringil, Selim. "'They Live in a State of Nomadism and Savagery': The Late Ottoman Empire and the Post-Colonial Debate." *Comparative Studies in Society and History* 45, no. 2 (2003): 311–342. doi:10.1017/S001041750300015X.

Gölbaşı, Edip. "Devil Worshippers' Encounter the State: 'Heterodox' Identities, State Building, and the Politics of Imperial Integration in the Late Ottoman Empire." In *The Ottoman East in the Nineteenth Century: Societies, Identities and Politics*, edited by Yaşar Tolga Cora, Dzovinar Derderian and Ali Sipahi, 133–155. London: I.B. Tauris, 2006.

Gölbaşı, Edip. "Turning the 'Heretics' into Loyal Muslim Subjects: Imperial Anxieties, the Politics of Religious Conversion, and the Yezidis in the Hamidian Era." *The Muslim World* 103, no. 1 (2013): 3–23. doi:10.1111/j.1478-1913.2012.01422.x.

Imber, Colin. *The Ottoman Empire, 1300–1650. The Structure of Power.* New York: Palgrave Macmillan, 2002.

Inalcık, Halil and Donald Quataert. *An Economic and Social History of the Ottoman Empire, 1300–1914.* Cambridge, UK, and New York: Cambridge University Press, 1995.

Karpat, Kemal. *Ottoman Population, 1830–1914.* Madison, WI: University of Wisconsin Press, 1985.

Katz, Marion Holmes. *The Problem of Abortion in Classical Sunni Islamic Ethics of Life: Abortion, War, and Euthanasia*, edited by Jonathan E. Brockopp, 25–50. Columbia, SC: University of South Carolina Press, 2003.

Klein, Janet. "Power in the Periphery: The Hamidiye Light Cavalry and the Struggle Over Ottoman Kurdistan, 1880–1914." Ph.D. diss., Princeton University, 2002.

Kuehn, Thomas. *Empire, Islam, and Politics of Difference: Ottoman Rule in Yemen, 1849–1919.* Leiden: Brill, 2011.

Makdisi, Ussama. "Ottoman Orientalism." *The American Historical Review* 107, no. 3 (2002): 768–796. doi:10.1086/ahr/107.3.768.

Maksudyan, Nazan. *Orphans and Destitute Children in the Late Ottoman Empire.* Syracuse, NY: Syracuse University Press, 2014.

Quataert, Donald. *The Ottoman Empire, 1700–1922.* Cambridge, UK, and New York: Cambridge University Press, 2000.

Rogan, Eugene L. "Asiret Mektebi: Abdulhamid II's School for Tribes (1892–1907)." *International Journal of Middle East Studies* 28, no. 1 (1996): 83–107. doi:10.1017/S0020743800062796.

11

SETTLER COLONIALISM AND THE CANADIAN CHILD WELFARE SYSTEM

Laura C.L. Landertinger

In the Canadian settler colony, few things are as permanent as Indigenous child theft. From its inception, Canada's "Indian policy" focused on severing Indigenous children from their communities; each new era in Indigenous–colonial relations brought new justifications and corresponding mechanisms to remove Indigenous children from their parents, communities, and land.[1] This was first accomplished through the rapid expansion of Indian Residential Schools after 1876 and later through the state-run child welfare system, which became an important conduit of child removal in the mid-twentieth century.

This chapter explores the themes of Indigenous child welfare and settler colonialism in Canada, focusing on the colonial relationship that is reproduced through the Canadian child welfare system in relation to the Indigenous peoples the state has formed around. It considers how, under the guise of child welfare, Indigenous child removal practices of the mid-nineteenth century—with, to be sure, lineaments in the earliest eras of settler colonization—persisted into the modern child welfare system. It puts forth the argument that Canada's child welfare system enacts and reproduces deeply colonial relations by disavowing Indigenous peoples' sovereign right to care for their own children and dissolving claims to kinship, culture, and land. Indeed, it suggests that the management of Indigenous children constitutes a central modality in colonial governance; taking the children of the dispossessed has been an enduring feature of Canadian nation-building.

The Canadian child welfare system is a decentralized system in which child welfare services fall under the jurisdiction of provincial and territorial authorities. While there are some differences in how child services are carried out across these jurisdictions, their commonality is the large-scale removal of Indigenous children. Several studies have shown that the Canadian child welfare system removes and institutionalizes Indigenous children at disproportionately high rates.[2] In 2016, while constituting seven per cent of the overall child population, Indigenous children constituted nearly half of all foster children across Canada.[3] In some provinces Indigenous children constitute the majority of children in child welfare custody. In Manitoba, Indigenous children make up almost 90 per cent of children in the system;[4] in Ontario, Indigenous children are 168 per cent more likely to be taken than white children.[5]

Jane Philpott, minister for Indigenous services, referred to this present-day situation as a "humanitarian crisis."[6] I suggest placing this crisis in its historical context to stress the continuity of colonial practice. What we may perceive as a crisis in the present is a continuation of practice that began in its "modern," institutionalized form in the late 1800s. Indigenous child removal/theft has thus been a crisis for almost two centuries.

Settler colonial governance

In a white settler colony such as Canada, governmental power is directed at particular goals. A settler colony comes into being via settler occupation of Indigenous territories and the attempted displacement of Indigenous nations. The emplacement and proliferation of a settler society is fueled by the large-scale acquisition and retention of land and the attempted annihilation of Indigenous peoples of that land.[7] Intent on "making a new home on the land," the settler society "insists on settler sovereignty over all things in their new domain."[8] Normalizing settler sovereignty involves the "systematic transformation and redefinition of the colonial terrain"[9] as rightfully belonging to the colonizer, and the continuous recasting of Indigenous peoples as a population to be managed by Canadian authorities. Violence is written into the very fabric of such a national formation.[10] "[T]he disruption of Indigenous relationships to land represents a profound epistemic, ontological, cosmological violence"[11]—a violence at once reaffirmed and disavowed by the settler colony's assertion of sovereignty as natural and normal, a violence that is endemic, structural, and enacted in the everyday: "This violence is not temporally contained in the arrival of the settler but is reasserted each day of occupation."[12] In sum, settler colonialism is a racial project of annihilation and accumulation.

I suggest that Indigenous child removal constitutes a central plank in colonial governance and the settler society's regime of the normal. The taking of the offspring of the Other represents a modality of colonial power directly aimed at interfering with and managing the reproduction, growth, and resurgence of Indigenous nations. "Everything within a settler society strains to destroy or assimilate the Native in order to disappear them from the land,"[13] Tuck and Yang remind us. The settler colony's sustained efforts to remove Indigenous children indicate a colonial modality intent on severing the bonds between Indigenous children and their communities, histories, cultures, and, most importantly, land. As Leanne Simpson states, "children are the glue that holds our families together."[14] Nishnaabeg resurgence and flourishment, Simpson explains, live and reverberate through the relations and interactions with families, children and communities.[15] Indigenous child removal seeks to interrupt this bond. Taking Indigenous children and hence interfering with the ability to pass on ways of being to future generations is an attempted form of erasure. As Patricia Monture writes, "Removing First Nations children from their culture and placing them in a foreign culture is an act of genocide."[16]

The emergence of child welfare

Child welfare emerged in the late nineteenth century, when a recently unified Canada sought to establish itself politically, economically, and culturally—as its own nation and as part of an empire.[17] This was a time characterized by heightened imperial anxieties over the future of the British empire, the national character of Canada, and overarching white fears over racial degeneration. British immigration propaganda began to promote Canada as a space for imperial renewal, one in which the white race could regenerate and flourish.[18] Indeed, in the words of Ernest Seton, some imagined Canada as the "White Man's Last Opportunity."[19]

Child welfare in Canada emerged as a project of white child-saving. Its aim was the proliferation of the white race and the building of a useful citizenry, whereby utility was defined according to Anglo-Saxon heteropatriarchal notions of bourgeois respectability.[20] It was a project directly opposed to the well-being of Indigenous nations, built instead on Indigenous dispossession.

At the first conference on child welfare in Canada on October 18–19, 1895, Rev. J. Edward Starr advised, "[t]ake care of the children and the nation will take care of itself."[21] This statement is at once a command for action as well as an observation of a causal-type relationship between nation-building and the well-being of children. It is also perhaps one of the more concise statements that sums up the impetus and core sentiment of the child welfare movement as it emerged at the turn of the twentieth century. Taking care of the children meant, by extension, taking care of the nation. Or, expressed differently, in order to build and mold the nation, one had to turn toward its children.

In this context the figure of the child became very important.[22] As future citizens,[23] and indeed the "future of the nation," the constitution, health, and virility of the white settler nation was believed to depend on its children. The children, it was believed, held the future of the empire in their hands (for better or for worse). As Dr Helen MacMurchy, chief investigator of infant mortality, explained: "We are only now discovering that Empires and States are built of babies. Cities are dependent for their continuance on babies. Armies are recruited only if and when we have cared for our babies."[24] Thus efficient nation-building efforts had to start with them. If raised "properly," the white child was said to embody the promise of a glorious future for the settler colony. If "neglected," the white child symbolized racial anxieties over the degeneration of the white race and fears over imperial decline. As an Anglican clergyman put it in 1912, "if Canada is to rear an imperial race it will not be by children raised in slums."[25]

Institutionalizing child theft

Having learned that a people's future was dependent on their offspring, the settler nation also turned to the children of the colonized. Excluded from the concerns of child-savers, yet of no less concern to the colonial state, this child population was to be managed differently. At the time child-savers were "saving" white children from racial degeneration, the colonizers' management of Indigenous children was a more complete and deadly undertaking, effected through the Indian Residential Schools system.

Indian Residential Schools have a long history in Canada. The first failed attempts, created by Catholic missionaries, date back to the early to mid-1600s in New France. In the 1820s Indian boarding schools began to reappear (first by an Anglican missionary) and by the 1860s the Anglicans, Protestants, Catholics, and Methodists all operated several schools. Upon confederation in 1867 and increasing waves of westward settler expansion, more schools were built in the prairies and western Canada. In 1876, Indian Residential Schools were consolidated by the passing of the Indian Act, officially establishing the schools as a church-operated, government-funded undertaking—a joint-management strategy that remained in place until 1969, after which the federal government assumed control. From 1876 on, the number of Indian Residential Schools expanded considerably, with 80 such schools in operation by 1931. The last school closed its doors in the late 1990s.[26]

Through Indian Residential Schools settler colonization was to be effected by capturing those children whose very presence on the land signified an obstacle to settler colonial success. As the schools' proverbial maxim "to kill the Indian in the child" proclaimed, the attempted erasure of Indianness was the system's defining feature. Its prime objective was breaking the ties between Indigenous children and their parents, families, communities, cultures, and their land. In 1920 an amendment to the Indian Act made school attendance compulsory for "[e]very Indian child between the ages of seven and fifteen years."[27] The Act gave the Superintendent General the authority to "appoint any officer or person to be a truant officer to enforce the attendance of Indian children at school, and for such purpose a truant officer shall be vested with the powers of a peace officer, and shall have authority to enter any place where he has reason to believe there are Indian children."[28] While Indian Agents would comb the country rounding up Indigenous children, the Act made it illegal for Indigenous caregivers to resist the capture of their children. If they resisted, the "parent, guardian or person with whom an Indian child is residing" was "liable on summary conviction … to a fine … or imprisonment" and the children could be "arrested without a warrant and conveyed to school."[29]

Prevented from and punished for speaking their languages, practicing their cultures, and adhering to their spiritual beliefs, these institutions sought to break the children's epistemic and ontological understandings of the world. Children were taught that who they were, where they came from, and what they thought and believed in was inherently wrong, evil, and inferior.[30] Through these institutions, white colonizers systematically abused generations of Indigenous peoples. Alongside epistemic and psychological violence, many sadistic stories of torture, rape, and unfathomable physical violence have also been documented.[31] More than 150,000 First Nations, *métis*, and Inuit children had to attend an Indian Residential School, and, according to the Truth and Reconciliation Commission of Canada (2015), at least 6,000 children did not make it out alive.

Institutional adjustments

After World War II the discursive and legislative landscapes began to change. Newly appalled by racial discrimination and state-sanctioned persecution in the wake of the Holocaust, Canada began to promote the principles of liberal equality. Though no less annihilative in effect, the nation transitioned from using explicit annihilative language to colonial gestures of inclusion. Canada began to focus on Indian integration.[32] Indigenous peoples were presented as damaged, deprived, and mistreated—framed not as a result of colonialism but of racial exclusion from Canadian society. To address this, integration was presented as a just and equitable solution. In child welfare the argument went as follows: having thus far been *excluded* from child protection services that were available to white children, now deemed a form of racial discrimination, Indigenous children were to be *included* in this system. Importantly, when we witness a shift to liberal gestures of inclusion, dispossession and the bedrock of violence on which it rests continue apace.

The management of Indigenous children thus became the purview of the child welfare system while Indian Residential Schools were slowly phased out. Put differently, the child welfare system replaced the residential school system as the settler society's primary mechanism of Indigenous child removal. The number of residential schools dropped from 72 in 1948 (holding 9,368 students) to 52 schools in 1969 (holding 7,704 students) and 12 schools in 1979 (holding 1,899 students).[33] Simultaneously, about 15,500 Indigenous children had been taken into the child welfare system.[34]

To enable this transition, Canada's legislative framework had to adapt. In 1951, changes to the Indian Act allowed for the extension of provincial child welfare legislation on to reserves.[35] Previously, reserves fell under federal jurisdiction, limiting the power of the provinces. Child theft was now effected through provincial social workers who would enter reserves and remove children "by the busloads."[36] Consequently their number in the child welfare system grew exponentially. In 1959 only one per cent of children in the child welfare system were Indigenous. By the end of the 1960s, 30–40 per cent of children in the system were "status Indians."[37] Patrick Johnston termed this large-scale removal effort the "Sixties Scoop," drawing from the statements of a social worker who recounted "that provincial social workers would, quite literally, scoop children from reserves on the slightest pretext,"[38] sometimes removing entire generations of newborns.[39] As a result, virtually every extended Indigenous family across Canada lost someone to the child welfare system.[40]

Once taken, Indigenous children "typically vanished with scarcely a trace,"[41] their Indigenous identities purposefully obscured. Most Indigenous children were transferred to white, middle-class families.[42] More than 10,000 "status Indian" children who were adopted between 1960 and 1990[43] and 75 per cent of Indigenous children adopted between 1971 and 1981 ended up in white homes.[44] In addition, many children were sent to faraway places. Indigenous children were transferred to households across Canada and even outside the country—in particular to the United States and, to a smaller extent, to Europe.[45] Maggie Blacksmith, whose son was stolen by the Manitoban government, recounts it as follows:

> Big, shiny American cars would come onto the reserve, followed by the social worker's car. ... When they left, there'd be a little Indian child sitting in the back of the American car, bawling their eyes out. The social worker always had a piece of paper saying it was legal. ... If parents tried to keep their kids, the social worker called the Mountie.[46]

The centrality of land needs to be kept in mind. The purpose of Indian Residential Schools was to remove children from their families, communities, cultures, histories, and land—seeking to sever the children from their "Indianness"—and, in doing so, to free up the land for the colonizers. Attempting to strip Indigenous children of their roots by, for example, obscuring or keeping the children's ancestry a secret, keeping shoddy or no records of where they would be sent or where they came from, and having children adopted into white settler homes was directed toward the same end. For without "Indians," there would be no contestation over land. These were attempts to erase or "disappear" Indigenous peoples from the landscape, for "if 'Indians' are disappearing, the settler can legitimately become the original owner of the land."[47]

Curating a crisis

Indigenous child theft is authorized by Canadian law. Indigenous nations never consented to have their children taken. On the contrary, Indigenous nations fought to keep their own offspring. Yet it was never deemed illegal by settler law for the state to remove Indigenous children and to place them in Indian Residential Schools. Nor was it deemed illegal to transfer them to Euro-Canadian settler families or to sell them[48] to the United States. It was, however, illegal for Indigenous peoples to raise their own offspring, to hide their children from the social worker, the Indian Agent, or the Royal Canadian Mounted Police.

Marlee Kline and Patricia Monture remind us that race and coloniality are inherent to the operation of child welfare. Colonialism, as they point out, gave rise to its laws, policies, and protocols and, as such, their applications extend and perpetuate relations of coloniality in the present.[49] The colonizer's discursive and legal mechanisms continue to reaffirm a relationship in which power, control, and the exercise of sovereignty firmly rest with

Canada, asserting that it is right and just for the colony to remove the children of other nations. This self-authorized position of the colonizer violates and undermines the sovereignty of dozens of independent nations.

Canada holds more Indigenous children in child welfare custody today than it institutionalized during the height of the Indian Residential School era.[50] This permanency of practice highlights that the high number of institutionalized Indigenous children in Canada's child welfare system is neither surprising nor an anomaly, but the predictable outcome of an annihilative tactic the settler state has pursued for centuries. The practice of Indigenous child removal was implemented to enact Indigenous dispossession and erasure, deliberately and intentionally used to further the settler colonial project. By continuing the practice of Indigenous child removal, the child welfare system sustains the settler society's annihilative and accumulative impulses in the present, continuing to dispossess Indigenous peoples of their lands and sovereignty.

Notes

1 Fournier and Frey, *Stolen from our Embrace*, 17.
2 Ontario Human Rights Commission, "Interrupted Childhoods"; Pon, Gosine, and Phillips, "Immediate Response"; Sinha et al., *Kiskisik Awasisak*; de Finney et al., "All Children are Equal"; MacDonald and MacDonald, "Reflections of a Mi'kmaq Social Worker"; Gough et al., "Pathways to the Overrepresentation of Aboriginal Children"; Blackstock et al., "Wen:de – We Are Coming to the Light of Day"; Walmsley, *Protecting Aboriginal Children*; Bennett, "First Nations Fact Sheet."
3 Turner, "Insights on Canadian Society."
4 Palmater, "From Foster Care to Missing or Murdered."
5 Ibid.
6 Kassam, "Canada welfare system is 'humanitarian crisis.'"
7 Snelgrove, Dhamoon and Corntassel, "Unsettling Settler Colonialism"; Razack, "When Place Becomes Race."
8 Tuck and Yang, "Decolonization is not a Metaphor," 5.
9 Scott, "Colonial Governmentality," 36.
10 Slotkin, *Gunfighter Nation*; Bruyneel, "The American Liberal Colonial Tradition"; Fanon, *The Wretched of the Earth*; Razack, *Dying from Improvement*.
11 Tuck and Yang, "Decolonization," 5.
12 Ibid.
13 Ibid., 9.
14 Simpson, *Dancing on Our Turtle's Back*, 135.
15 Ibid., 145.
16 Ibid.
17 In 1867 the British North American colonies of Nova Scotia, New Brunswick, and the Province of Canada (Ontario and Quebec) united into the Dominion of Canada, officially establishing Canada as its own nation within the British Commonwealth.
18 Devereux, "New Woman, New World," 175.
19 Seton, "The White Man," 525.
20 Landertinger, "Child Welfare and the Imperial Management of Childhood in Settler Colonial Canada."
21 City of Toronto Archives. Children's Aid Society of Toronto. Fonds 1001, Series 533. Fonds Title: Children's Aid Society of Toronto, reports of the Superintendent of Neglected and Dependent Children of Ontario. Dates of Creation: 1894–1914, 1939. In "Report of the Superintendent: Dependent and Neglected Children of Ontario." Appendix. Proceedings of the First Ontario Conference on Child-Saving, Toronto, Oct. 18–19, 1895. File 1. Date 1894. Box 146483, Folio 1.
22 Davin, "Imperialism and Motherhood"; Comacchio, *Nations are Built of Babies*; Chen, *Tending the Gardens of Citizenship*.
23 From 1763 until the Canadian Citizenship Act in 1947, people born in Canada were British subjects. Since British immigrants were already British subjects, they did not have to obtain citizenship or become naturalized in Canada.

24 Quoted in Finkel, *Social Policy and Practice in Canada*, 72.
25 Ibid., 138.
26 Royal Commission on Aboriginal Peoples (RCAP), "Residential Schools"; Truth and Reconciliation Commission of Canada (TRC), *Canada's Residential Schools*, Pts. 1 and 2.
27 Indian Act, 1920 s.10(1).
28 Indian Act, 1920 s.10(3).
29 Ibid.
30 Milloy, *A National Crime*; Miller, *Shingwauk's Vision*; Chrisjohn, Young, and Maraun, *The Circle Game*.
31 See for example, TRC, *The Survivors Speak*.
32 Stevenson, "Intimate Integration"; Shewell. *'Enough to Keep Them Alive.'*
33 RCAP, "Residential Schools," 351.
34 McKenzie and Hudson, "Native Children"; Monture, *Thunder in my Soul*, 192.
35 Indian Act, 1985, s.88.
36 Fournier and Crey, *Stolen*; Palmater, "From Foster Care to Missing or Murdered."
37 Fournier and Crey, *Stolen*, 83.
38 Quoted in MacDonald and MacDonald, "Reflections," 39.
39 Sinclair, "Identity Lost and Found," 66.
40 Fournier and Crey, *Stolen*, 86.
41 Ibid., 81.
42 Fournier and Crey, *Stolen*; MacDonald and MacDonald, "Reflections"; Sinclair, "Identity."
43 Gough et al., "Pathways."
44 Walmsley, *Protecting*, 14; Fournier and Crey, *Stolen*.
45 Ibid.; Sinclair, "Identity."
46 Fournier and Crey, *Stolen*, 89.
47 Razack, *Dying from Improvement*, 10, 293.
48 Many Indigenous children were bought by American families. The Children's Bureau of New Orleans, for example, charged $4,000 per child. Marlene Orgeron's Louisiana parents bought her for $30,000. Diane Fast's brother was bought for $10,000. "His mother used to say she owned him," Fast recounts in Carreiro "Indigenous children for sale."
49 Kline, "Child Welfare Law"; Monture, "Vicious Circle."
50 Blackstock, "First Nations Child and Family Services"; Kassam, "Ratio," *The Guardian*.

Bibliography

Bennett, Marlyn. *First Nations Fact Sheet: A General Profile on First Nations Child Welfare in Canada*. Ottawa: First Nations Child and Family Caring Society of Canada (FNCFCS), 2004.
Blackstock, Cindy. "First Nations Child and Family Services: Restoring Peace and Harmony in First Nations Communities." In *Child Welfare: Connecting Research Policy and Practice*, edited by Kathleen Kufeldt and Brad McKenzie, 331–343. Waterloo, Ontario: Wilfrid Laurier University Press, 2003.
Blackstock, Cindy, Tara Prakash, John Loxley and Fred Wien. *Wen:de – We Are Coming to the Light of Day*. Ottawa: First Nations Child and Family Caring Society of Canada (FNCFCS), 2005.
Bruyneel, Kevin. "The American Liberal Colonial Tradition." In *The Settler Complex: Recuperating Binarism in Colonial Studies*, edited by Patrick Wolfe, 193–206. Los Angeles, CA: UCLA American Indian Studies Center, 2016.
Carreiro, Donna. "Indigenous children for sale: The money behind the Sixties Scoop." *CBC News*, September 28, 2017.
Chen, Xiaobei. *Tending the Gardens of Citizenship. Child Saving in Toronto. 1880s-1920s*. Toronto: University of Toronto Press, 2005.
Chrisjohn, Roland and Sherri L. Young (with Michael Maraun). *The Circle Game: Shadows and Substance in the Indian Residential School Experience in Canada*. Penticton, British Columbia: Theytus Books, 2006.
Comacchio, Cynthia R. *Nations are Built of Babies: Saving Ontario's Mothers and Children, 1900–1940*. Montreal: McGill-Queen's University Press, 1993.
Davin, Anna. "Imperialism and Motherhood." *History Workshop Journal* 5 (1978): 9–65. doi:10.1093/hwj/5.1.9.
de Finney, Sandrina, Mackenzie Dean, Elicia Loiselle and Johanne Saraceno. "All Children are Equal, but Some are More Equal than Others: Minoritization, Structural Inequities, and Social Justice Praxis in Residential Care." *International Journal of Child, Youth and Family Studies* 3/4 (2011): 361–384.

Devereux, Cecily. 1999. "New Woman, New World: Maternal Feminism and the New Imperialism in the White Settler Colonies." *Women's Studies International Forum* 22, no. 2 (1999): 175–184.

Fanon, Frantz. *The Wretched of the Earth*. Translated by Constance Farrington. New York: Grove Press, 1963.

Faulkner, William. *Requiem for a Nun*. London: Chatto & Windus, 1919.

Finkel, Alvin. *Social Policy and Practice in Canada: A History*. Waterloo, Ontario: Wilfrid Laurier University Press, 2006.

Fournier, Suzanne and Ernie Crey. *Stolen from Our Embrace*. Toronto: Douglas & McIntyre, 1997.

Gough, Pamela, Nico Trocmé, Ivan Brown, Della Knoke and Cindy Blackstock. "Pathways to the Overrepresentation of Aboriginal Children in Care. CECW Information Sheet #23E," *CECW Information23E* (2005): 1–3.

Kassam, Ashifa. "Ratio of Indigenous children in Canada welfare system is 'humanitarian crisis.'" *The Guardian*. November 4, 2017. www.theguardian.com/world/2017/nov/04/Indigenous-children-canada-welfare-system-humanitarian-crisis

Kline, Marlee. "Child Welfare Law, 'Best Interest of the Child' Ideology, and First Nations." *Osgoode Hall Law Journal* 30, no. 2 (1992): 375–425.

Landertinger, Laura. "Child Welfare and the Imperial Management of Childhood in Settler Colonial Canada, 1880s–2000s." Ph.D. diss., University of Toronto, 2017.

MacDonald, Nancy and Judy MacDonald. "Reflections of a Mi'kmaq Social Worker on a Quarter of a Century Work in First Nations Child Welfare." *First Peoples Child and Family Review: A Journal on Innovation and Best Practices in Aboriginal Child Welfare Administration, Research, Policy & Practice* 3, no. 1 (2007): 34–45. doi:10.7202/1069525ar.

McKenzie, Brad and Pete Hudson. "Native Children, Child Welfare, and the Colonization of Native People." In *The Challenge of Child Welfare*, edited by K.L. Levitt and B. Wharf, 125–141. Vancouver: UBC Press, 1985.

Miller, J. R. *Shingwauk's Vision*. Toronto: University of Toronto Press, 1996.

Milloy, John. *A National Crime: The Canadian Government and the Residential School System, 1878–1986*. Winnipeg: University of Manitoba Press, 2006.

Monture, Patricia. "A Vicious Circle: Child Welfare and the First Nations." *Canadian Journal of Women and the Law* 3, no. 1 (1989): 1–17.

Monture, Patricia. *Thunder in my Soul: A Mohawk Woman Speaks*. Nova Scotia: Fernwood Publishing, 1995.

Ontario Human Rights Commission (OHRC). "Interrupted Childhoods: Over-representation of Indigenous and Black Children in Ontario Child Welfare." Last modified February, 2018. http://www.ohrc.on.ca/en/interrupted-childhoods

Palmater, Pamela. "From Foster Care to Missing or Murdered: Canada's Other Tragic Pipeline." *Maclean's Magazine*. April 12, 2017.

Pon, Gordon, Kevin Gosine and Doret Phillips. "Immediate Response: Addressing Anti-Native and Anti-Black Racism in Child Welfare." *International Journal of Child, Youth and Family Studies* 3, no. 4 (2011): 385–409.

Razack, Sherene, ed. "When Place Becomes Race." In *Race, Space, and the Law: Unmapping a White Settler Society*, 1–20. Toronto: Between the Lines, 2002.

Razack, Sherene. *Dying from Improvement: Inquests and Inquiries into Indigenous Deaths in Custody*. Toronto: University of Toronto Press, 2015.

Royal Commission on Aboriginal Peoples (RCAP). "Chapter 10: Residential Schools." In *Looking Forward, Looking Back. Vol. 1, Report of the Royal Commission on Aboriginal Peoples*. Ottawa: Canada Communication Group, 1996.

Seton, Ernest Thompson. "The White Man's Last Opportunity." *Canada-West* 3, no. 6 (April 1908): 525–532.

Shewell, Hugh. *'Enough to Keep Them Alive', Indian Welfare in Canada, 1873–1965*. Toronto: University of Toronto Press, 2004.

Simpson, Leanne. *Dancing on Our Turtle's Back: Stories of Nishnaabeg Re-Creation, Resurgence, and a New Emergence*. Winnipeg: Arbeiter Ring Publishing, 2011.

Sinclair, Raven. "Identity Lost and Found: Lessons from the Sixties Scoop." *First Peoples Child and Family Review: A Journal on Innovation and Best Practices in Aboriginal Child Welfare Administration, Research, Policy & Practice* 3, no. 1 (2007): 65–82.

Sinha, Vandna, Nico Trocmé, Barbara Fallon, Bruce MacLaurin, Elizabeth Fast and Shelley Thomas Prokop. *Kiskisik Awasisak: Remember the Children. Understanding the Overrepresentation of First Nations Children in the Child Welfare System*. Ontario: Assembly of First Nations, 2011.

Slotkin, Richard. *Gunfighter Nation: The Myth of the Frontier in Twentieth-Century America.* Norman, OK: University of Oklahoma Press, 1998.

Snelgrove, Corey, Rita Kaur Dhamoon and Jeff Corntassel. "Unsettling Settler Colonialism: The Discourse and Politics of Settlers, and Solidarity with Indigenous Nations." *Decolonization: Indigeneity, Education & Society* 3, no. 2 (2014):1–32.

Stevenson, Allyson. "Intimate Integration: A Study of Aboriginal Transracial Adoption in Saskatchewan, 1944–1984." Ph.D. diss., University of Saskatchewan, 2015.

Truth and Reconciliation Commission of Canada (TRC). *Canada's Residential Schools: The History, Part 1, Origins to 1939. The Final Report of the Truth and Reconciliation Commission of Canada*, Volume 1. Montreal: McGill-Queen's University Press, 2015.

Truth and Reconciliation Commission of Canada (TRC). *Canada's Residential Schools: The History, Part 2, 1939 to 2000. The Final Report of the Truth and Reconciliation Commission of Canada*, Volume 1. Montreal: McGill-Queen's University Press, 2015.

Truth and Reconciliation Commission of Canada (TRC). *The Survivors Speak: A Report of the Truth and Reconciliation Commission of Canada.* Montreal: McGill-Queen's University Press, 2015.

Tuck, Eve and K. Wayne Yang. "Decolonization is not a Metaphor." *Decolonization: Indigeneity, Education & Society* 1, no. 1 (2012): 1–40.

Turner, Annie. "Insights on Canadian Society: Living arrangements of Aboriginal children aged 14 and under." *Statistics Canada.* Last modified April 13, 2016. www150.statcan.gc.ca/n1/en/pub/75-006-x/2016001/article/14547-eng.pdf?st=sa4AyAwv

Walmsley, Christopher. *Protecting Aboriginal Children.* Vancouver: UBC Press, 2005.

12

IMPERIAL WET-NURSING IN ITALIAN EAST AFRICA

Diana Garvin

Italian imperialism in East Africa began as an economic venture, a late entrée into the European Scramble for Africa. Missionary Giuseppe Sapeto, based in Abyssinia, gained the ear of King Vittorio Emanuelle II. Italian presence in the area, he argued, would promote trade. At the same time, Raffaele Rubattino planned to establish a steamship line through the newly opened Suez Canal and the Red Sea to India. The King, the monk, and the magnate agreed: Rubattino's company would purchase the Bay of Assab (in the future Eritrea) in its own name and with its own funds, but would use the port to further Italy's national interests. By March 1870 an Italian shipping company had thus become claimant to territory at the northern end of Eritrea, with its beaches and outlying islands. Two years later Italy formally took possession of the nascent colony from its commercial owners. Eritrea became Italy's *colonia primogenita*, the first-born colony, soon to be followed by Somalia and Ethiopia in the formation of Italy's East African empire, known by the Italian acronym AOI.

Military action bolstered financial outlay, pushing Italian imperial rule southward across the Horn of Africa. In 1887, roughly 500 men comprising the Italian forces were defeated at Dogali, the famous *cinquecento* for whom the Roma Termini's Piazza Cinquecento is named.[1] The Battle of Adwa, another disaster for the Italians, took place in 1896. Feeling that these two military defeats were insults to be avenged, the Italians strove to establish other forms of control. Further south, in Somalia, Italians worked to establish indirect rule, again through economic means. First, they placed the Filonardi Company in charge of the Somali Benadir Concession. New oil refineries and banana plantations further increased trade between Mogadiscio and Rome. Next, commercial treaties with Sultan Said of Zanzibar established Italian access to ports up and down the Somali coastline. Somalia was declared an Italian colony three years later, in 1908.

Ethiopia was not a colony but rather an occupied territory in Benito Mussolini's East African empire. Italian forces invaded in 1935, taking Addis Ababa and deposing Emperor Haile Selassi. Occupation turned on brutality. Geneva Convention violations included the use of dum dum bullets and poison gas.[2] Marshal Graziani's troops bombed military outposts and Red Cross hospitals alike. In 1938 the Race Laws underwrote and further developed a policy of segregation into the colonial urban sphere. Different city quarters in Addis, Asmara, and Mogadiscio separated Italians, East Africans, "mixed races," and industrial zones along regularized grids, incorporating rivers and trees as buffers between the homogenized neighborhoods. It is in this milieu that interracial wet-nursing emerged.

On April 5, 1939, the racialist periodical *The Defense of Race* (*La difesa della razza*) published recommendations for the proper nutrition for Italian infants born in the colonies. The guidelines condemned one feeding practice in particular: *il baliatico mercenario indigeno* (Figure 12.1). Interracial wet-nursing, or "mercenary breastfeeding" in the regime's parlance, was a

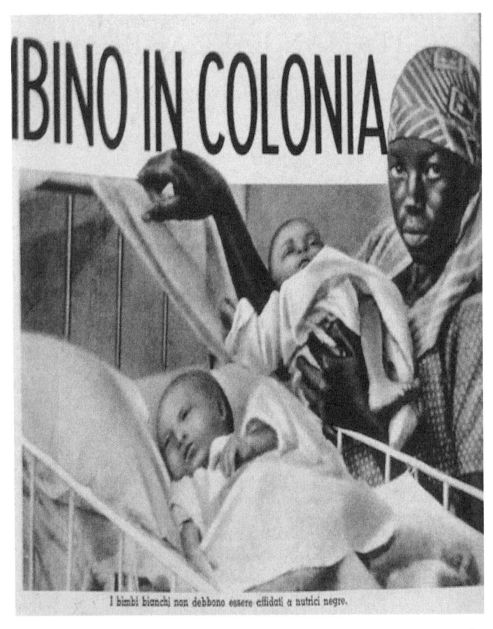

I bimbi bianchi non debbono essere effidati a nutrici negre.

Figure 12.1 An illustration for an article on interracial wet-nursing, "Feeding children in the colonies," in *The Defense of the Race* (*La difesa della razza*). The text reads, "White infants should not be trusted to black wet-nurses." Article by Giuseppe Lucidi, Rome, Italy, April 1939. (Archivio Centrale dello Stato, Rome, Italy)

common form of domestic labor in the colonies, a fact decried by Giuseppe Lucidi, the article's author.[3] He cited dubious studies claiming to have analyzed African women's milk in comparison with that of European mothers, and found it too high in fat and too rich for consumption by colonists' children. Lucidi went so far as to say that native pathogens would render Ethiopian wet-nurses' milk undigestible for Italian infants. Fascist women's groups unleashed fleets of prophylactic pamphlets decrying interracial wet-nursing by equating light color with superior nutrition. How could white milk come from black bodies? Fake science and Fascist government intertwined (Figure 12.2) and leapt toward literature. The opening car crash of F.T. Marinetti's famous Futurist Manifesto sends the protagonist flying from metallic vehicle to muddy earth, and from European adulthood to colonial infancy: "Oh maternal ditch, brimming with muddy water! Fair factory drain! I gulped down your bracing slime (*melma*), which reminded me of the sacred black breast of my Sudanese wet-nurse."[4] The *melma* he speaks of refers to a factory run-off.

Why devote so much panting press to interracial wet-nursing? In a historical period when the Fascist Italian press actively worked to construct racial difference, this particular form of domestic labor challenged the binary of dark and light at a cellular level. Scholars of the colonial intimate such as Ann Stoler and Anne McClintock have focused on the bodily

ı controsenso e
pericolo: balie
gre per bambini
bianchi.
16

Figure 12.2 An illustration for an article on interracial wet-nursing, "Feeding children in the colonies" in *The Defense of the Race* (*La difesa della razza*). The text reads, "A contradiction and a danger: black wet-nurses for white children." Article by Giuseppe Lucidi, Rome, Italy, April 1939. (Archivio Centrale dello Stato, Rome, Italy)

contact of interracial sexuality. This analysis builds on Stoler's account of wet-nursing in the colonies and expands the scope of intimacy to include childrearing practices. I argue that the physical intimacy and exchange of fluids involved in wet-nursing and breastfeeding are critical to our understanding of race, gender, and sexuality in the colonial world. Feeding and eating transcended the gap between self and other, blurring the line between subject and object as food turned into tissue, muscle, and nerve and provided the energy to fire them all.[5]

Interracial wet-nursing was a "reproductive regime." Through ingestion and digestion it held Fascist imperial power in place by consolidating hierarchies of bodily labor in colonial homesteads. At the same time, it also defied the 1938 Race Laws that segregated urban space and criminalized sexual contact across racial lines. This paradox points to divergent meanings of white lips on black breasts in Italian East Africa: the intimacy of interracial wet-nursing differs from the intimacy of interracial sex. Interracial sex eventually produced a generation of children who confused racial borders and boundaries. But the problems associated with interracial breastfeeding were more subtle and more immediate. Proximity and ingestion between wet-nurses and infants muddled an Italian understanding of motherhood in which breastfeeding implicated biological and cultural inheritance.

Broadly speaking, the Fascist regime objected to wet-nursing as the moral foe of breastfeeding. More and better breastmilk promised to minimize infant mortality while fortifying the national body, a key plank in the regime's platform for demographic control of the Italian populous. Recognizing how this food could promote their party's pro-natalist goals, the Fascist regime approached the promotion of breastfeeding and the denigration of wet-nursing with biopolitical considerations in mind. Key objections were two-fold. First, faulty knowledge of biological inheritance framed wet-nursing as a threat to the nascent racial hierarchy that the regime attempted to build in the Italian empire. In Medieval Rome, breastmilk was believed to transmit moral qualities as well as fats and vitamins.[6] Previously these concerns had been couched in terms of class. Accounts of wet-nursing in Renaissance Florence decried wealthy infants' absorption of base moral values via peasant wet-nurses.[7] During the 1930s the cooking magazine *La Cucina Italiana* provided recipes for nursing mothers that aimed to improve the flavor of their breastmilk (Figures 12.3 and 12.4). The tastes of the infant, not the mother, mattered: these recipes aimed to fortify the bodies of the nation's future soldiers. With the invasion of East Africa in 1935, interracial contact replaced interclass contact as the key threat. If white infants suckled from a black breast, they were believed to inherit the crude characteristics of their wet-nurse rather than the civilized traits of their biological mother. The industrialization of women's health care during the interwar period aimed to bring reproductive care under state control in continental Italy. Italian wet-nurses lacked formal association with the Fascist government. Because of their status as independent practitioners dealing with women's reproductive health and labor, wet-nursing evoked privacy issues and created woman-to-woman relationships of financial interdependence and physical intimacy between adult and infant bodies across social classes. Transferring these concerns from Italy to Ethiopia, wet-nursing undermined regime efforts to uphold its tenuous grasp on white superiority by bringing non-white, colonized subjects into precisely the domain deemed most sanctified: the Italian homestead with its Catholic family.

Put more broadly, wet-nursing threatened to undermine Fascist hierarchies of race, gender, and class by placing local infant foodways in private homes, outside of regime control. By extension, wet-nurses—working-class women and, crucially, women of color—could have an outsize impact on the regime's national economic and demographic projects. Little surprise, then, that Fascist propaganda worked to ameliorate wet-nurses' moral hygiene through greater intensity of medical surveillance and regimentation of feeding.

Figure 12.3 Magazine cover for *La Cucina Italiana*. September 1938, Rome, Italy. (Biblioteca Gastronomica, Parma, Italy)

This antipathy is evinced by increasing use of the term *baliatrico mercenario* in the Fascist and far-right press.[8] While so-called mercenary wet-nurses (*sensale* or *mandarine*) provided the necessary nutrients of human milk, regime propaganda linked wet-nurses to mud: that of the Italian countryside and the muck of East Africa as an undistinguished whole. Dirt carried moral opprobrium. Concrete and abstract filth combined to form a lack of moral hygiene. Because some women were physically incapable of breastfeeding, Giovanni Fagioli, founder of the Wet-Nurse Institute "The Nourisher" (*Istituto di Baliatico "La nutrice"*), framed wet-nursing as a necessary evil. At best, the wet-nurse menaced the "material and moral health of the family" ("*la salute materiale e morale della famiglia*"). At worse, she threatened "a moral danger to its physical and moral integrity" ("*un pericolo mortale per la sua integrità fisica e morale*").[9]

A poll of Roman doctors and pediatricians conducted by the right-leaning newspaper *Giornale d'Italia* framed the perceived problem of the wet-nurse as one of hygienic and unhygienic built environments. The newspaper characterized their January 1929 poll as an "exercise in the surveillance of hygiene," regarding the "sanitary conditions," of the wet-nurses' surroundings.[10] But the poll was also an exercise in state surveillance: the regime's

149

Figure 12.4 Magazine cover for a themed issue of *La Cucina Italiana*, "Woman and Race" ("*La Donna e la razza*"). October 1938, Rome, Italy. (Biblioteca Gastronomica, Parma, Italy)

Office of Hygiene (*Ufficio d'Igiene del Governatorato*) examined, and edited, all interview results prior to publication.[11] Though these medics certainly condemn the wet-nurse for her chief interest in payment rather than infant health, they primarily decry the unhygienic built environments where wet-nursing occurs. Dimestore novel language colors the descriptions: wet-nurses supposedly worked in "lurid and fetid dens" and "altogether unhealthy environments."[12] This booklet highlights regime-affiliated centers for wet-nurses as a hygienic solution, a move that also increased medical surveillance and government oversight of this practice. The only photos in this book show the interior rooms of one such center. In every photo a male doctor surveys the scene, whether in-person at a desk, as in the photo "The Management" ("*La Direzione*") or from the height of a wall-hung portrait, as in "Room for the Selection of Wet-nurses" ("*Salottino per la scelta delle balie*") (Figure 12.5). Portraits of the King and Mussolini hang just to the right of the Director's, creating a space of classed and gendered hierarchy to bring wet-nursing under regime control. In a textual reflection of this visual argument, the article also applauds the regime's recent decision to criminalize wet-nursing without government documentation. Wet-nurses endangered Fascist motherhood.

Figure 12.5 Photograph of *Istituto Baliatrico "La Nutrice,"* 1940, front office. (*Il bimbo al seno: Le grave conseguenze del baliatico mercenario*, 103 [1940])

But why? Collapsing breastfeeding with motherhood allowed the Fascist government to monitor women as well as children. Wet-nursing limited the regime's reach by giving middle- and upper-class women control over their time, and by giving poor and working-class women control over their finances. To the regime, the problem with wet-nursing lay not in its nutritional deficits but its social ones.

To parse the imperial intimacies of feeding and eating, let us examine two photos taken mere moments apart in a marketplace in Harar, Ethiopia, on May 8, 1936. The first of the two images (Figure 12.6) shows an Ethiopian fruit vendor as she breastfeeds her child. The camera work tells us how the photographer framed Ethiopian breastfeeding as anthropological, thus estranging what should have been a common, global feature of motherhood. The mother's head and the background are both blurry, suggesting that the photo was taken in haste, without the subject's consent. It purports to "capture" breastfeeding as through it were an anthropological moment exhibiting characteristic or stereotypical Ethiopian culture. But the furtive nature of the photographer's approach also suggests a latent, secondary motive: the erotics of breastfeeding. And, indeed, the second version of this market scene changes the tenor of the photo (Figure 12.7). Between shutter clicks one and two, the photographer must have interacted with the photo's subjects. He seems to have made two requests: one to the mother alone, asking her to look up

Figure 12.6 Photograph of woman breastfeeding at the Harar market, "Breastfeeding Woman" ("*Donna che allata*"). Photographed for LUCE by unknown photographer, May 8, 1936, Harar, Ethiopia. (Archivio LUCE Photo Code AO00008522, Series S.O. Various 5, Rome, Italy)

from her infant's face to face his camera's lens, and one to the crowd and the mother, asking them all to smile. This smile is key, because it places this second photo within the Italian tradition of Black Venus photography.

How did the regime use these images? Whose hands would have held them, and how would they have understood their content? The Fascist regime's *Milizia Volontaria di Sicurezza Nationale* established and diffused the concept of the "*Venere nera*" by turning these photos into postcards which they distributed to young Italian males, potential soldiers, at barber shops in Italy during the first months of the Ethiopian Campaign in 1936 and later to enlisted soldiers in Italian East Africa. This fact is already a matter of historical record. But perhaps more significant is what happened next: Italian soldiers wrote on these erotic postcards and mailed them home to their wives, mothers, and daughters in mainland Italy. In their texts they often call the loved one's attention to the postcard's illustration, noting that the woman shown is a "characteristic" one. In other words, the soldiers who used these postcards often framed these women in anthropological terms rather than erotic ones.[13] They used the pretext of strangeness to excuse and obfuscate the potential for arousal.

Figure 12.7 Photograph of woman breastfeeding at the Harar market, "An Indigenous Woman Breast-feeding her Son in the Harar Market" ("*Una donna indigena che allata il figlio al mercato di Harar*"). Photographed for LUCE by unknown photographer, May 8, 1936, Harar, Ethiopia. (Archivio LUCE Photo Code AO00008548, Series S.O. Various 6, Rome, Italy)

Anthropological pretexts for looking at erotically posed East African women frame race and ethnicity as unassailable differences, walls that separate the gazer and the object of the gaze. Tautological reasoning ruled soldiers' decisions to send a postcard depicting a topless woman to a female relative in Italy: if they sent the postcard, they declared it to be anthropological in the postcard text, because they would not send pornography to a female family member. If they kept it for themselves then it was pornographic, because they would use it as such. As a result of these two factors, the definition of pornography rested, oddly, on the use of ephemera rather than its content. Read in isolation, the second photo of the smiling Ethiopian fruit vendor does not appear to be particularly sexualized. But when read in relation with the vast iconography of calendars, postcards, and advertisements that sexualized East African women, the photographer's request to smile changes the tenor of the woman's slightly bare breast from maternal to erotic.

More broadly, this photo exemplifies an early twentieth-century variant of a long tradition of the European eroticization of African breastfeeding. For comparison, in Sander L. Gilman's much-quoted essay "Black Bodies, White Bodies: Toward an Iconography of Female Sexuality in Late Nineteenth-Century Art, Medicine, and Literature," he details the history of "the wet-nurse of Negus" (*"la balia del negus"*) or, simply, "the wet-nurse" (*"la nutrice"*).[14] In the first images of a series of 21.5cm by 16.5cm photographs,[15] she appears as a late middle-aged woman with huge fallen breasts, leaning on rock while holding a tambourine.[16] Later images in the same set show her holding one breast, then both, pinching the nipples. Instead of smiling to beckon the viewer, she grimaces instead, her eyes glazed over with a vague look suggesting mental impairment. The wet-nurse, rendered archetypal by her appellation alone, bridges the erotic and the grotesque via her breastfeeding work. The eroticization of East African breastfeeding also appears in Cesare Lombroso and Guillaume Ferrero's work, where she pops up in a criminal anthropology table as "Dancer and Abyssinian prostitute" (*"Ballerina e prostituta Abissina"*). During the Fascist period her images also appeared on Libyan colonial postcards advertising the Hotel de l'Europe and Oriental and General Stores. This progression from wet-nurse to dancer/prostitute supports Gilman's point that "The perception of the prostitute in the late nineteenth century merged with the perception of the black."[17] It also extends it, and not just temporally into the twentieth century. These images blended nourishment and titillation under the general aegis of the black breast, suggesting not so much a dichotomy as an utter conflation: the *Madonna lattante* and the whore.

While the British army brought an end to the Italian Fascist regime's colonial projects in Italian East Africa in 1941, imperial constructions of race continue to reverberate to the present day. The anthropological and erotic framing of Ethiopian women diffused into a more generalized racism that saturates visual culture in Italy. Companies continue to use race as an advertising gimmick (Figure 12.8), conflating sexualized, dark-skinned women with luxurious, dark-colored food products such as coffee and chocolate. One might argue that, in Italian mass media, all women are sexualized. While this essay readily concedes the point, it nonetheless maintains that contemporary Italian mass media sexualize black and white women in different ways, largely due to the legacy of colonialism in East Africa. Today, Italian advertisements featuring black women overwhelmingly use the color of their skin as a visual pun to connote their similarity to former colonial products, such as chocolate or coffee. Further, the erotic portrayal of black women continues to be tinged with the anthropological. Along those lines, Italian fascination with interracial wet-nursing resurfaces in an image photographed by Oliviero Toscani for the United Colors of Benetton. The Black Venus of this photograph is not only topless but headless. We are meant to notice two iconic elements: her bare, black breast and the white infant she feeds. Even in the modern era, interracial wet-nursing exerts an outsize pull on the Italian imagination. This advertisement for the United Colors of Benetton has won more awards than any other ad in the company's history. I do not include it among the images contained in this chapter. While both the Vergani chocolate advertisement and the United Colors of Benetton spot raise racist tropes anchored in the Italian colonies, only the Benetton ad makes active use of the ongoing wounds of this history, relying on interracial breastfeeding as a visual shockwave to sell its colorful cotton tee-shirts.

This arresting image brings up a broader debate. How should we read the visual archive of empire? Two broad camps have emerged and are aptly illustrated by the conversation surrounding Tamara Lanier's 2019 lawsuit against Harvard University. The Swiss-born Harvard professor and zoologist Louis Agassiz posed "Papa Renty," the Lanier family patriarch, for a photo as part of a pseudo-scientific study of race. He and his daughter, Delia, were enslaved. They were ordered to strip naked for the demeaning photographs. Now this image illustrates

Figure 12.8 Chocolate box, "WhiteBlack" ("*Bianconero*"). Produced by Vergani Chocolate Company. (https://eng.winestyle.ru/products/Vergani-Praline-Bianco-Nero.html)

the cover of a Harvard anthropology publication that sells in bookstores for forty dollars. Lanier argues that Harvard is "perpetuating the systematic subversion of black property rights that began during slavery and continued for a century thereafter."[18]

For Lanier, these images are personal and they are painful. Because they depict family members, and were taken by force, they do not belong to the public. For historians, they are a critical and damning account: a vital visual testimony to the intimate horrors of slavery. Herein lies the problem: the wrenching moment when Agassiz's shutter clicked matters deeply to both the family and to the historical record of racial violence. Privatizing the photos or, at the extreme, destroying them erases irreplaceable knowledge that could be used to avoid similar horrors in the future. Publicizing the photos or, at the extreme, replicating them in large, glossy books risks replicating racist power. In a parallel debate focused on museum objects rather than archival images, curators and communities ask what to do with the sacred artefacts on display. They too were originally taken by colonial force. Such debates leave us with the question: what concrete steps can we take to study the history of gender and race in a more thoughtful way?

Feminist pedagogy might guide these discussions through models for diffused authority and inclusive debate. The primary goal must always be to promote better relationships between people. Feminist pedagogy decenters the scholar and focuses on the scholarship. It changes monologues to dialogues and creates the space to apologize and to learn new approaches. As Ijeoma Oluo has phrased it in her oft-quoted guide, *How to Talk about Race*, "It is not about feeling better. It is about doing better."[19] To apply these ideas to the visual archive of empire, we need to think about how style signals values. There is more than one way to reproduce a colonial image, and some choices replicate imperial power structures overtly. Consider the controversy surrounding the publication of *Sexe, Race, & Colonies.* [20] This compendium, co-edited by 97 historians, included more than 1,200 paintings, drawings, and prints of colonized women and men from across the French, Spanish, American, and Japanese imperial regimes. Typography centered the word "Sexe" on the book cover, in a font three times larger than the words "Race" and "Colonies." Set against a darkened backdrop, the glowing white title evoked strip-bar lighting. Critics noted that the book's large, glossy images evoked a coffee table book, a genre that provokes voyeurism and its lurid pleasures. By contrast, a book focused on text, with small images on matte paper, might communicate similar messages but to a lesser degree. Museums such as the Luigi Pigorini National Museum of Prehistory and Ethnography in Rome have started to address the politics of presentation by restructuring their display boxes. Objects are now presented according to their creator's intended meaning and cultural context: art, not anthropology. As per contemporary gallery conventions, Pigorini now presents these objects alone, where they had previously been massed into rough groups. Glass cases provide a black background lit by multiple beams to accentuate each art piece. Problems remain: the provenance and authorship are still unstated. None of these solutions is perfect. But having these conversations, however uncomfortable, is the first step toward learning from and representing the history of empire through the voices of those most affected by its brutality.

Strikingly, Italian portrayals of interracial wet-nursing continue to speak to larger issues of how race and racism are constructed and consumed. Eroticism and anthropology constitute two planks in the platform. But a less obvious element of these images accounts for their resonance: they are, ultimately, about how people figure in foodways. Although we rarely characterize breastmilk as a food, or breastfeeding as a foodway, both bear consideration as public, political activities. Because the food producer—the mother—and the consumer—the infant—physically connect in a mutual act of feeding and eating, breastfeeding provides a key to understanding all other foodways by clarifying their most basic essence: a one-to-one exchange of nutrients, fats, and vitamins between two human bodies. In the context of imperialism, the Fascist focus on East African wet-nursing and breastfeeding points to the desire to eat the other, to both erase and appropriate through aggressive consumption. Eating the Other, as theorized by bell hooks, revolves around edible power play. One person assumes the power of another by consuming their heart.[21] This theory untangles the cultural significance of breastfeeding photography in the rural marketplace in Harar. Desire intermingles with aggression, which is incarnated through hunger. Mouths sink into flesh. hook's theory underscores a Fascist fear as well. Eating the other was step one. But what happened next? Digestion did not mean disappearance—it meant incorporation. Every meal presented a racial risk: if food remade the body from the inside out, then an Italian infant that consumed East African milk could no longer be considered wholly Italian—local food began to reshape the foreign body that consumed it. This is the second, logical, step of eating the other. With apologies to Salman Rushdie, the empire bites back.[22]

Notes

1 Igiaba Scego and Rino Bianchi reckon with the colonial monuments of the Italian metropole in their textual and photographic exploration, *Roma Negata*.
2 Sbacchi, *Legacy of Bitterness* and *Italian Colonialism in Ethiopia*.
3 Giuseppe Lucidi, "L'Alimentazione del bambino in colonia," in *La difesa della razza* (Rome: La difesa, 1939).
4 Marinetti, "The Futurist Manifesto."
5 For a comparative study of race and ingestion in the American context, see Tompkins, *Racial Indigestion*. Also see Parasecoli, *Bite Me*, ch. 5.

6 Bynum, *Jesus as Mother*.
7 Manes, "The Power of Mother's Milk."
8 Both prior to and after the Fascist period the unmodified term *fare la balia* was more commonly applied to wet-nursing. It could also indicate more general forms of paid infant care provided by a non-relative.
9 Fagioli, *Il bimbo al seno*, 185.
10 *Giornale d'Italia* January 1929 poll cited in Fagioli, *Il bimbo al seno*, 182.
11 Ibid.
12 *Giornale d'Italia* January 1929 poll cited in Fagioli, *Il bimbo al seno*, 186.
13 Sòrgoni, *Parole e corpi*. Also see Tilley and Gordon, *Ordering Africa*.
14 In contrast with the term *balia*, which evokes the wet-nurse in terms of a type of paid work, the word *nutrice* underscores the content and goal of this work in its evocation of nourishment. See Zanichelli, *l'Etimologico minore*.
15 Testifying to the long-lasting international interest in the *balia del negus,* multiples copies of this photographic series can be found in museums in France, Italy, and the United States. Ponzanesi and Gilman cite the locations of the photographs as the Musée Bourdelle in Paris, the Peabody Museum in Boston, and the Società Africana d'Italia in Naples. Image info: H. Arnoux, Port Said, nrs. 1304–1306, Nourrice du Negus d'Abyssinie. (S. Palma in Impero nel cassetto 89).
16 Also see Jennifer Morgan's examination of seventeenth-century travelogue illustrations depicting African women suckling children over their shoulders. Morgan argues that these images laid the foundation for racial slavery by suggesting that African women could simultaneously perform plantation and reproductive labor. Morgan, *Laboring Women*.
17 Gilman, "Black Bodies, White Bodies."
18 Hartocollis, "Who Should Own Photos of Slaves?"; Daley, "Why These Early Images of Slavery Have Led to a Lawsuit Against Harvard."
19 Oluo, *So You Want to Talk about Race*.
20 Blanchard et al., *Sexe, race, & colonies*. Also see Prinscille Lafitte, "Sex, Race, & Colonies book hits nerve in post-colonial France," *France 24*, October 22, 2018.
21 bell hooks, "Eating the Other."
22 Rushdie, "The Empire Writes Back with a Vengeance," 8.

Bibliography

Blanchard, Pascal et al. *Sexe, race, & colonies: La domination des corps du XVe siècle à nos jours*. Paris: La Decouvert, 2018.

Bynum, Caroline Walker. *Jesus as Mother: Studies in the Spirituality of the High Middle Ages*. Berkeley, CA: University of California Press, 1984.

Daley, Jason. "Why These Early Images of Slavery Have Led to a Lawsuit Against Harvard." *Smithsonian Magazine*, March 22, 2019.

Fagioli, Giovanni. *Il bimbo al seno: Le grave conseguenze del baliatico mercenario*. Rome: Istituto Baliatrico, 1937.

Gilman, Sander. "Black Bodies, White Bodies: Toward an Iconography of Female Sexuality in Late Nineteenth-Century Art, Medicine, and Literature." *Critical Inquiry*. 12, no. 1 (1985) 204–242.

Hartocollis, Anemona. "Who Should Own Photos of Slaves? The Descendants, not Harvard, a Lawsuit Says." *The New York Times*, March 20, 2019.

hooks, bell. "Eating the Other: Desire and Resistance." In *Black Looks: Race and Representation*. Cambridge, UK: South End, 1999.

Lafitte, Prinscille. "Sex, Race, & Colonies book hits nerve in post-colonial France." *France 24*, October 22, 2018.

Manes, Yael. "The Power of Mother's Milk." In *The Renaissance: Revised, Expanded, Unexpurgated*, edited by Medina Lasansky. 362–376. New York: Periscope Publishing, 2014.

Marinetti, Filippo Tommaso. "The Futurist Manifesto." In *Filippo Tommaso Marinetti: Critical Writings*, edited by Günther Berghaus. 11–17. New York: Macmillan, 2007.

McClintock, Anne. *Imperial Leather: Race, Gender, and Sexuality in the Colonial Context*. New York: Routledge, 1995.

Morgan, Jennifer. *Laboring Women*. Philadelphia, PA: University of Pennsylvania Press, 2011.

Oluo, Ijeoma. *So You Want to Talk about Race*. New York: Hachette, 2018.

Palma, Silvana. *L'impero nel cassetto: L'Italia coloniale tra album privati e archivi pubblici*. Edited by Paolo Bertella Farnetti, Adolfo Mignemi and Alessandro Triulzi. Milan: Mimesis, 2013.

Parasecoli, Fabio. "Jam, Juice, and Strange Fruits: Edible Black Bodies." In *Bite Me: Food in Popular Culture*, 103–126. New York: Berg, 2008.

Ponzanesi, Sandra. "Beyond the Black Venus: Colonial Sexual Politics and Contemporary Visual Practices." In *Italian Colonialism: Legacy and Memory*, edited by Jacqueline Andall and Derek Duncan, 165–190. London: Peter Lang, 2005.

Ponzanesi, Sandra. "The Color of Love: *Madamismo* and Interracial Relationships in the Italian Colonies." *Research in African Literatures*. 43, no. 2 (2012): 155–172.

Rushdie, Salman. "The Empire Writes Back with a Vengeance." *The Times* (UK), 3 July 1982.

Sbacchi, Alberto. "Italian Colonialism in Ethiopia, 1936–1940." Ph.D. diss., University of Illinois, 1979.

Sbacchi, Alberto. *Legacy of Bitterness: Ethiopia and Fascist Italy, 1935–1941*. Lawrenceville NJ: Red Sea Press, 1997.

Scego, Igiaba and Rino Bianchi. *Roma Negata: Percorsi coloniali nella città*. Rome: Ediesse, 2014.

Sòrgoni, Barbara. *Parole e corpi: antropologia, discorso giuridico e politiche sessuali interrazziali nella colonia Eritrea, 1890–1941*. Naples: Liguori, 1988.

Stoler, Ann Laura. *Carnal Knowledge and Imperial Power: Race and the Intimate in Colonial Rule*. Berkeley, CA: University of California Press, 2002.

Tilley, Helen and Robert J. Gordon. *Ordering Africa: Anthropology, European Imperialism and the Politics of Knowledge*. Manchester, UK: Manchester University Press, 2007.

Tompkins, Kyla Wazana. *Racial Indigestion: Eating Bodies In the 19th Century*. New York: New York University Press, 2012.

13

RACE, GENDER, COLONIALISM, RACIAL CAPITALISM, AND BLACK WOMEN'S WOMBS

Françoise Vergès

In June 1970 in a small city in Réunion Island, a French post-colony and an "overseas department" in the Indian Ocean, a general physician was called to check on a 17-year-old girl who was bleeding profusely. He understood that she was the victim of a botched abortion, still a crime under French law. The physician summoned the gendarmes whose investigation soon confirmed what the Catholic Church—which was against abortion—and the Communist party—which saw the abortions as a colonial racial practice—had denounced the preceding year: that French, white, male doctors had been performing thousands of abortions per year since the mid-1960s in a clinic that belonged to Doctor Moreau, a wealthy white *réunionnese* and a leader of local conservatives. *Témoignages*, the communist newspaper, reported daily on the inquiry, linking the forced abortions with the general political neo-colonial situation, sexism and racism, and raising questions about the misappropriation of public funds. The doctors had, after all, received reimbursements from social security in the order of millions of francs after declaring they were performing minor surgeries rather than abortions. Soon "The Island of Doctor Moreau," a title borrowing from H.G Wells' book,[1] was making the front pages of national media outlets. Thirty women who had been aborted and sterilized agreed to have their testimonies published in *Témoignages* and to come forward as plaintiffs. It was the first time in the history of Réunion that poor women of color constituted themselves as a collective of plaintiffs in the court against powerful white men. Trials and appeals followed. In the final trial, in February 1971, white French doctors went unpunished but the two other men who had been indicted—a surgeon of Moroccan origin and the first male head nurse of Indian descent on the island—were fined and forbidden to practice their jobs for a while. Race and republican coloniality protected white patriarchy. Réunion women never received reparation.[2]

In France, the state wanted women to bear children; in the *département d'outre-mer* (DOM) it launched aggressive birth control campaigns and systematically hampered the establishment of social legislation that would protect pregnant women. Indeed, one might argue that in both cases women's bodies were used as tools to serve the interests of the state. That said, it is no less true that the difference between the two is crucial. In the colonies-cum-overseas departments, reproduction was integrated into the logic of racial capitalism, a capitalism in which processes of racialization are central, as Cedric Robinson has shown.[3] Put another way, the politics of reproduction were adapted to the exigencies of the color line in the organization of labor: women's wombs were racialized.

Though some French feminist groups were aware of the forced abortions and sterilizations in Réunion Island, the latter never occupied a central role in their analysis of social reproduction, patriarchy, capitalism, and gender. On April 5, 1971, two months after the trial in Réunion, 343 French women published a manifesto in which they publicly declared that they had abortions, breaking the silence around the one million women who had abortions every year, performed under terrible and life-threatening conditions. French Planned Parenthood and feminist groups had already circumvented the anti-abortion law by either proposing trips to the Netherlands or England, where abortion was legal, or by performing abortions themselves. The thousands of abortions and sterilizations that had been performed without consent, and the wide state-supported public campaign that encouraged Réunion women to abort or to be sterilized and to accept contraception, were entirely ignored. This occurred despite the fact that the scandal had been largely covered by the very newspapers in which members of Women's Liberation published and which these French women surely also read. Their indifference and willful ignorance, however, was not surprising. The state had communicated that French colonialism ended with Algerian independence, definitively closing this historical chapter, and that it was now time to concentrate on France. French feminism accepted the state narrative and did not seriously consider that anti-colonialism was still alive in overseas departments or that patriarchy and conceptions of female sexuality and birth control continued to be racialized. During what has been called the "second wave" of feminism, race remained on the margins.

The reproductive policies of the 1960s–1970s hearken back to 1945, when the decision was made not to develop or diversify local industries on Réunion Island. As a consequence, there was no longer a need for local labor. Successive reports, speeches, and studies began to invoke the notion of overpopulation, and the idea that population growth would exceed available jobs and resources began to take root at all levels of policy-making. Fearing an uprising, given the global context of decolonization, experts proposed two policies: birth control and state-controlled emigration. Two measures put these policies into practice during the 1960s, and an ideological opinion thus gradually became cemented as truth: non-white women were having too many babies and were the cause of underdevelopment and poverty. Birth control policies in Réunion were then inscribed not only in state policy as the nation reconfigured its borders during the postwar moment, but also in the international politics of birth control launched throughout the Third World by the major world powers. It is, therefore, unsurprising that in Réunion (and the Antilles) doctors, social workers, and nurses felt encouraged, legitimated, and fully supported in their abortionist activities. Once the "overpopulation" of the French overseas departments had become a national concern, it attracted zealous advocates. This scandal, which remains marginal in the study of women's struggles in France, shows that there cannot be a study of women's rights and emancipation without a study of the ways in which race, gender, sexuality, patriarchy, colonialism, and capitalism intertwine.

Social reproduction, primitive accumulation, slavery, and colonialism

French efforts to control the fertility of women of color on Réunion Island were not unique to the twentieth century, nor to France, and indeed connect to a longer history of racial slavery, racial capitalism, and state control of black women's wombs. To guarantee a continuous connection to a bonded workforce, European powers faced two problems: one was to ensure unlimited access to captives to fill the holds of slave ships on the coasts of Africa; the second was to resolve the reproduction of the enslaved population in the colonies. If the second aspect has been studied,[4] the first one remains neglected. Yet the history of the racial control of black women's wombs is arguably anchored in the invisible but necessary work of reproduction performed by African women during the slave trade. Each deported African man and woman had a mother. For each captive, an African woman had carried a human being, had helped to make a child a speaking and thinking person before she or he was snatched by slave traders and sent to a plantation in North and South America, the Caribbean, or the Indian Ocean. African women's wombs were made into capital to feed—year after year and for four centuries—the holds of slave ships. The production of their wombs was transformed into merchandise, objects of commerce, money, or, in the terms used by the French Code Noir, into "pieces of furniture."[5] Access to African-born labor, which represented a consistent form of capital for the global capitalist system, relied on the essential but invisible fact of its reproduction in Africa. In Europe, as Cedric Robinson has noted, the vast reserves of the labor force had been lumped together in poor districts surrounding the big cities;[6] Africa had been forced to "spill" into the black Atlantic the human beings it had birthed.

This management of bodies was the object of negotiations among colonists, the state, and intermediary bodies (ship-owners, bankers, industrialists) who all had the same interests: to profit from the supply of an exploitable and limitless labor force. Early on, slave owners had to decide whether this supply would be ensured by organizing its reproduction locally or by guaranteeing the source of its capture and importation. Social reproduction of the enslaved labor force varied from one slave colony to the other. Two main policies were enforced. One (mostly in the United States) was to create a "slave-breeding industry,"[7] the other (in French and British colonies) was first based on a constant importation of captives, relying less on local reproduction. In French colonies, except during specific instances such as when slave trade routes were hindered by wars or blockaded by English forces, owners of large plantations rejected the creation of a local slave-breeding industry and instead continually chose to import enslaved Africans. Since male bonded labor was preferred over female labor, the number of men thrown into the global market for bonded labor largely exceeded that of women. This led to an increased imbalance between the sexes and a very low birth rate in French slave colonies. In both instances, enslaved women were systematically raped to produce a natally-bonded workforce. A pregnant slave was not considered a woman; she could be flogged, punished, and forced to work until the end of her pregnancy. Black women were said to have a depraved sexuality, to be able to easily support the physical suffering of giving birth and to have no maternal feelings.[8] The white woman, conceived of as fragile, modest, and sexually demure, was invented in contrast to the black woman. Capitalism was possible because a drain on African societies was organized, in an industrial fashion, over the course of several centuries. And the invisible source of this drain was nothing other than the wombs of African women, whose children were being captured for deportation. The reproduction of the labor force was thus assured by millions of African women whose work would not be recognized in the analysis of reproduction and the international division of labor. Reproduction, the international division of labor, the organization of the slave trade, and rape are all elements of wealth's accumulation.

After the abolition of the slave trade and slavery, the predation on the wombs of women of color continued. The millions of male indentured workers from Asia and in lesser number from Africa and Madagascar were also taken by force and sent to European colonies under restrictive contracts. They left countries devastated by wars, famines, and dispossession caused by European imperialist powers. Again, the ratio of women to men was deeply imbalanced.

Hence, for centuries, European colonialism and imperialism transformed black and brown women's wombs into capital to reproduce the workers needed for bondage or indenture. The colonial organization of a mobile, racialized, sexualized, and gendered workforce for the plantations, mines, railways, and other industries during slavery and after produced a heavily biased male racialized workforce whose reproduction rested on the invisible production of women of color's wombs, and to whom the feelings of maternity and normative female sexuality had been systematically denied.

Silvia Federici's analysis of social reproduction in *Caliban and the Witch* linked several important events: the privatization of land in Europe, the disappearance of the commons, colonial expansion, the African slave trade, and the subjugation of women. But to this analysis we must also add the racialization of non-white women and men, of their sexualities and capacity for parenting.[9] Though Federici notes the role of race in the history of social reproduction and capitalism, we must add the history of rape—the predation of indigenous, black and brown women's wombs—to her description of the "imbrication of a population crisis, an expansionist theory of population, and the introduction of policies promoting demographic growth"[10] and the correlation as of the sixteenth century between demographic growth, an increase in the nation's prosperity and power, and the "promotion of population" that went "hand in hand with a massive destruction of life."[11] As soon as we consider the rape of black women and the theft of their wombs as elements of capitalism, the analysis of patriarchy as a universal phenomenon that expresses itself everywhere in the same way no longer holds. Reproductive policies, wherein—either by capture or by rape—living beings carried by black women become merchandise, make clear that patriarchy is racialized.

Racial capitalism, imperialism, decolonization, and birth control

After World War II the new needs of imperialism and capitalism for a precarious, racialized, and vulnerable workforce transformed once again. Colonies were becoming independent, Western settlers were leaving the colonies, the United States was emerging as a hegemonic power, and the reconstruction of western Europe required a flexible workforce. Capitalism and imperialism were entering a new phase consolidating the North/South axis, instigating coups and wars in different parts of the world even as formal colonial control ostensibly ended. Imperialism no longer required the transport of large amounts of labor from one colony to another. Instead, migrant workers were now summoned to reconstruct Europe and to work in its factories or to labor in agro-business in the United States. The exploitation of the wombs of women of color for the colonial global labor market had to be revised. It was alleged that women from parts of the globe that would soon be called the "Third World" made too many babies and thus represented an obstacle to global development and the eradication of poverty, concerns that began to dominate international meetings and development programs without consideration of historical causality or responsibility. It is important to turn back to the ideology of global birth rate programs in the period following World War II in order to understand how the French state was inspired by this ideology and borrowed its premises, as well as how the reorganization of the racialized division of labor in France connected to its division on an international level.

At the end of the 1950s the control of the birth rate in the so-called Third World was at the heart of international politics; it became inseparable from development and structural adjustment policies. The birth rate in the Third World was the object of particular scrutiny, not only by the institutions charged with studying global demographics but also by those who managed labor, migration, and security: those subjects are, in effect, imbricated. Later, in the 1970s, the environment was added to the list of fields linked to demographics and security. The IMF (created in 1944) and the World Bank (created in 1945) were going to include the demographics of the Third World in their analyses of the progress of the global economy. The prevailing ideology was the following: demographics in the Third World are at once an obstacle to its development and a threat to global security; "development"—an idea and a policy forged in the Global North and aimed at the Third World—and demographics would henceforth be inextricable. The United States took control of the campaign that linked birth rates in the Third World to anxiety about the security of the "free world." During the second conference on population, held in Belgrade in 1965, representatives from the United States gave a speech on birth control that explicitly targeted the Third World: "A constant increase in population generates permanent problems, revolutions that call into question the established order and the security of the interests of the great industrial powers, the United States in particular, and constrain them to pacification missions."[12] Third World women's fertility was thus equated with a terrorist threat.[13] The United States recommended accelerating the deployment of contraceptive and family planning programs throughout the world. It garnered the support of the Indian government, which introduced compulsory male sterilization. Racialized policies that sought to limit the fertility of poor and non-white women, and which the government of the United States had imposed within its own borders, were subsequently expanded throughout the world. However, it is important to trace more carefully the politics of state, capitalist, and patriarchal control over non-white women's wombs—indigenous women, black women, Muslim women—and how they are affected on the one hand by ethno-nationalism or invented tradition and, on the other, by neoliberal feminism.

Support for these so-called "population policies" soon found its way into emerging progressive movements. Over-population in the Third World came to be seen as a threat to the environment. The publication in 1968 of *The Population Bomb* by Paul Ehrlich, which sold millions of copies, set the tone with its first sentence: "The battle to feed all of humanity is over." Ehrlich advocated for coercive measures to reduce global population, including compulsory sterilizations. "Advertisements for contraception and sterilization as birth control methods led to the conclusion that over-population was the principal cause of poverty in under-developed countries," Chandra Talpade Mohanty has written.[14] The impact of Ehrlich's book was tremendous, lending support to the nascent environmental movement and galvanizing the anti-population-growth crusade. Some Western feminists also cited over-population to support the case for reproductive rights. The ideology of birth control taken out of its racial history took over and the image of a free, emancipated woman that was based on Western representations of freedom and unfreedom became the norm. Third World feminists battled at once with pro-natalist nationalist patriarchies—which saw population growth as necessary to the formation of new nations—and restrictive Western birth control policies. Far from being opposed to the "individual right of people of color to control the birth rate," black, Chicana, and Indigenous feminists criticized "racist population control strategies."[15]

Neoliberalism, birth control, and race

In the late 1990s the dominant trend of neoliberalism, even among right-wing or conservative parties, came to embrace feminism. "Feminist" was no longer an insult; anyone could claim to be feminist and gender became a required topic in research. The limits of a formalistic approach to gender equality and of the representation of women in elected institutions was clear. By the 2000s, women's rights had become a trump card in the hands of capitalism and imperialism.

The politics of birth control were now framed within a universal ideology of rights that did not integrate its racial history. Societies of the Global South were said to be *by nature* hostile to women's rights. In this move, the politics of reproduction under slavery and imperialism were forgotten and states' policies in the North and the South were analyzed along the line of civilized/non-civilized.

In this context, white Western feminism turned to the vocabulary and politics of a *civilizing* feminism, borrowing from the ideology of a civilizing mission and of postcolonial development, which could in turn be adopted by states and bourgeois feminists in the Global South. The West, in other words, had a new civilizing mission—a good one because it led to women's empowerment, women's choice, and "women's agency." "Saving women of color from men of color"—once a feature of paternalistic colonial policies—now became the task of the mainstream women's movement. The postcolonial state policies of population control in the Global South of the 1970s—including forced sterilizations of women or men in India or Peru and the one-child policy in China—were decried by Western women's groups because they had not respected women's choice. Birth control campaigns that respected women and empowered them became, by the 2000s, the credo of Western foundations and institutions, which contrasted their true concern for women of the Global South against the conservative politics of evangelist churches or other ostensibly conservative religions. Against the latter, which defended the family and patriarchy, civilizing feminism offered women autonomy. The campaign for birth control led by the Bill and Melinda Gates Foundation strategically applied the vocabulary of the feminist struggle for women's rights: "Voluntary family planning is one of the great public health advances of the past century. Enabling women to make informed decisions about whether and when to have children reduces unintended pregnancies as well as maternal and newborn deaths. It also increases educational and economic opportunities for women and leads to healthier families and communities. Family planning is a smart, sensible, and vital component of global health and development."[16] The Foundation promised that access to birth control will be "without coercion or discrimination."

Girls and women in the Global South have thus become the targets of neoliberal capitalism and imperialism in the twenty-first century. They have given a new configuration to Frantz Fanon's famous summary of colonial policy toward women: "Let's win over the women and the rest will follow."[17] Birth control, girls' education, and women's economic empowerment are still regarded as vital for protecting world security and hindering migrations from the Global South to the Global North. Only, these objectives are now presented as progress for women. The accelerated integration of women in the global economic financial system through micro-credit, the private investment in girls' education, birth control, and women's entrepreneurship all show a strategic interest in winning over the women so the rest will follow. The "rest" is not only to separate women of the Global South from the anti-racist, anti-imperialist, and anti-capitalist struggle but to earn women's support for their integration in a global financial economy. Women of the Global South are presented as a good financial investment, on the same level as a material resource or a commodity. "The world's fastest growing emerging market is not a country or a region; it is the world's women," the US Government's development finance institution OPIC2X has declared. The economic calculation is clear: "The female economy represents a market more than twice the size of India and China combined. By 2028, female consumers will control around $15 trillion of global consumer spending" and "closing the gender labor gap could add $28 trillion to global GDP by 2025."[18]

Following a Group of Seven summit in August 2019, Emmanuel Macron, president of France, announced the creation of Affirmative Finance Action for Women in Africa (AFAWA), which takes "a comprehensive approach based on improving access to finance for women-owned and -controlled businesses; capacity building for women entrepreneurs and financial institutions; and the mobilization and even support of African governments in implementing the legal, policy and regulatory reforms needed to develop women's entrepreneurship."[19] Commenting on the AFAWA initiative at the press conference, President Macron said, "As the current G7 Chair, I am particularly proud that the program we support today—the AFAWA initiative, comes from an African organization, the African Development Bank, which works with the African Guarantee Fund and a network of African banks."[20] The same Macron had warned in 2017 against the birth rate in Africa:

> The challenge of Africa … is civilizational. What are the problems in Africa today? The failed states, the complex democratic transitions, the demographic transition, which is, as I recalled this morning, one of the essential challenges of Africa. When countries still have seven to eight children per woman today, you can decide to spend billions of euros there, you will not stabilize anything.[21]

A year later, though, he insisted on the fact that giving birth had to be a woman's choice:

> Ask yourself the question: wherever you have seven, eight, nine children per woman, each time, in each family, you are sure that it is the choice of this young woman? There are families in my country who have made this choice, there are in France families where there are seven, eight, nine children per woman, it is their choice, it is very good … I don't judge it, I never speak of it anyway. And I do not have to judge for a family and an African woman, but I want to be sure that everywhere in Africa, it is the choice of this girl or this woman.[22]

This investment in women in the Global South fulfills many goals that arguably serve Western self-interest: hindering migrations to the wealthy North, demonstrating the natural feminism of the West, and weakening the political struggle against neoliberalism, imperialism, and civilizing feminism. As Catherine Rottenberg has shown in *The Rise of Neoliberal Feminism*, feminism is now conscripted to "solve" these thorny issues.[23] Neoliberal feminism is expected to ease the tensions created by neoliberalism between women's work and women's duties. The right to work is framed within the ideology of gender equality which ignores divisions created by class and race, by the international division of labor, and by regulations imposed by the North on production, trade, and migration. The politics of birth control were never exclusively about "women giving birth." We must look at all the elements that produce them.

In Europe during the 1960s and 1970s, women of color from former colonies were drafted into the cleaning/caring industry, but the economic and cultural transformations in the 2000s led to what Sara Farris has termed "femonationalism"—the process by which right-wing nationalists, neoliberals, and some feminists and women's equality agencies invoke women's rights to stigmatize Muslim men and advance their own political objectives, thus creating a "convergence" across these groups despite their obvious differences.[24] The consequences of neoliberalism and of structural adjustment programs were felt more violently on a global scale in the 2000s. The creation of large institutions and offices built in cities around the world, the changing standard of living of employees—bankers, traders, insurers, experts—and the multiplication of meetings and congresses to manage the new order all required a vast workforce to clean, feed, and provide care. Caring—cleaning, feeding, doing sex work, taking care of the bodies and souls of women, men, elderly, and children of the neoliberal class—led to a greater industrialization of the field. White women aspired to "lean in" and talks, magazines, and books about positive reinforcement techniques for women in the workforce became a successful genre, providing practical advice on mentorship and building a satisfying career so white women could combine professional achievement with personal fulfillment. The cleaning/caring work of women of the Global South was expected to help white women to fulfill these goals while white women were simultaneously fashioned as role models for their cleaners and caretakers, showing the latter the benefits of having fewer children, managing a professional career and home life, and being a loving companion and mother. In Europe, civilizing feminism became an advocate of Islamophobia, turning to cultural racism to justify their attacks on Muslim women and men. The argument ran that Muslim men were naturally hostile to women's equality, that Muslim women who had to wear the veil and preserve their virginity until marriage were then forced into multiple pregnancies, and that Muslim communities were homophobic. The colonial tropes of non-Western sexualities were mobilized again.

The discourse of the "*grand remplacement*"—European populations being overwhelmed in number by Muslims—gained traction through incessant chatter about the irresponsible birth rate in Muslim countries and among Muslim communities in Europe. "The racialization of the world," Nikhil Pal Singh has written, "has helped to create and re-create 'caesuras' in human populations at both the national and global scales that have been crucial to the political management of populations." He adds: "We need to recognize the technology of race as something more than skin color or biophysical essence, but precisely as those historic repertoires and cultural, spatial, and signifying systems that stigmatize and depreciate one form of humanity for the purposes of another's health, development, safety, profit, and pleasure." Ruth Wilson Gilmore has called this "the state-sanctioned or extralegal production and exploitation of group-differentiated vulnerability to premature death."[25]

In their essay "Bio(necro)polis: Marx, Surplus Populations, and the Spatial Dialectics of Reproduction and 'Race,'" Michael McIntyre and Heidi J. Nast introduce the notions of "bio (necro)polis" and "necro(bio)polis" to emphasize the geographical fluidity of accumulation and racialized difference.[26] They study how surplus populations "are the effect of racially striated regimes of biological reproduction," arguing "that the workings of capitalism must be under-stood in terms of the linked contradictions of reproduction and race."[27] They go on to write that racial marking of lands and bodies continues to be a way of rendering certain bodies superfluous. Canalized, criminalized, ostracized, stigmatized, the necropolis—that spatiality through which the necropolitan is defined or constituted—becomes a reserve of multifarious material proportions: of negative symbolic potential and death's liminal pleasures; a reserve of labor; a nature reserve open for appropriation; a reserve of potentially fecund land for settlers; and a reserve of waste land for colonialism's human and environmental detritus.

Colonialism and racial capitalism constructed black, indigenous, and brown women's lives as both superfluous *and* necessary. Their lives were disposable but their reproduction and their work was necessary. Their rights were denied, they were said to be unable to under-stand freedom. Neoliberalism has understood how the Western discourse of women's rights could aid its objective of integrating women of the Global South into its financial banking system, of transforming them into a peaceful army spreading its ideology of women's empowerment, delinking women's liberation from social emancipation and decolonization. Yet the growing movement of Indigenous and non-white people worldwide against the economy of overproduction and overconsumption that continually produces more death and devastation of societies and their environments resists this post-industrial economy that condemns the majority of humanity to death. It is in these movements that a post-racist, post-capitalist, post-patriarchal approach to social reproduction is emerging.

Notes

1 Wells, *The Island of Doctor Moreau*. Doctor Moreau, the character imagined by Wells, created human-like hybrids from animals.
2 In *Le ventre des femmes*, published in English as *The Wombs of Women*, I told this story in detail and analyzed French feminists' silence and the long history of racial politics regarding black and brown women's wombs. This essay is largely based on the book.
3 Robinson, *Black Marxism*.
4 See Sublette and Sublette, *The American Slave Coast*; Stanley, "Slave Breeding and Free Love."
5 The title *Black code* was given to the royal decree or royal edict of March 1685. A second version was edited in 1724. Article 44 said that the enslaved were *meubles* (furniture) and as such were entered on the same level as tables or chairs into the slave owner's capital.
6 Robinson, *Black Marxism, 309.*
7 See Sublette and Sublette, *The American Slave Coast*.
8 See Dorlin, *La matrice de la race*.
9 Federici, *Caliban et la sorcière, 30.*
10 Ibid.
11 Ibid.
12 George and Rochefort, "L'ombre de Malthus à la Conférence mondiale," 554. See also the text of the declarations from the UNFPA global conferences on population. http://www.unfpa.org/
13 National Security Memorandum, *Implications of Worldwide Population Growth for US Security and Overseas Interests*, December 10, 1974.
14 Mohanty, "Cartographies of Struggle," 12.
15 Davis, *Femmes, race et classe, 271.*
16 Bill and Melinda Gates Foundation, "Family Planning."
17 Fanon, "Algeria Unveiled," 37.
18 2X Challenge, "Investing in Women."
19 "Le G7 augmente l'accès."
20 Ibid.
21 Ranc, "Macron pointe."
22 Gaboulad, "Sept ou huit enfants."
23 Rottenberg, *The Rise of Neoliberal Feminism*. See also Grewal, *Transnational America.*
24 Farris, *In the Name of Women's Rights*.
25 Gilmore, *Golden Gulag, 28.*
26 McIntyre and Nast, "Bio(necro)polis."
27 Ibid., 1471.

Bibliography

2X Challenge. "*Investing in Women.*" Accessed September 3, 2020. https://www.2xchallenge.org/
Agence Ecofin. "Le G7 augmente l'accès au financement des femmes grâce à l'initiave AFAWA, la BAD & AGF." *Agence Ecofin*. Accessed September 3, 2020. https://www.agenceecofin.com/investissement/0209-68842-le-g7-augmente-l-acce-s-au-financement-des-femmes-gra-ce-a-l-initiave-afawa-la-bad-agf
Bill and Melinda Gates Foundation. "Family Planning: Strategy Overview." Accessed September 3, 2020. https://www.gatesfoundation.org/what-we-do/global-development/family-planning
Davis, Angela. *Femmes, race et classe*. Paris: Éditions des femmes, 1983.
Dorlin, Elsa. *La matrice de la race. Généalogie sexuelle et coloniale de la nation*. Paris, La Découverte, 2009.
Fanon, Frantz. "Algeria Unveiled." In *A Dying Colonialism*, translated by Haakon Chevalier. New York, Grove Press, 1965.
Farris, Sara. *In the Name of Women's Rights. The Rise of Femonationalism*. Durham, NC: Duke University Press, 2017.

Federici, Silvia. *Caliban et la sorcière. Femmes, corps et accumulation primitive* (2004). Paris: Entremonde, 2014.

Gaboulad, Adrien. "'Sept ou huit enfants par femme': le refrain africain de Macron." *Paris Match.* Accessed September 3, 2020. https://www.parismatch.com/Actu/Politique/Sept-ou-huit-enfants-par-femme-le-re frain-africain-de-Macron-1554563

Gilmore, Ruth Wilson. *Golden Gulag: Prisons, Surplus, Crisis, and Opposition in Globalizing California.* Berkeley, CA: University of California Press, 2006.

Grewal, Inderpal. *Transnational America: Feminisms, Diasporas, Neoliberalisms.* Durham, NC: Duke University Press, 2018.

McIntyre, Michael and Heidi J. Nast. "Bio(necro)polis: Marx, Surplus Populations, and the Spatial Dialectics of Reproduction and 'Race.'" *Antipode* 43, no. 5 (2011): 1464–1488. doi:10.1111/j.1467-8330.2011.00906.x.

Mohanty, Chandra Talpade. "Cartographies of Struggle: Third World Women and the Politics of Feminism." In *Third World Women and the Politics of Feminism*, edited by Chandra Talpade Mohanty, Ann Russo and Lourdes Torres. Bloomington, IN: Indiana University Press, 1991.

Ranc, Agatha. "Macron pointe les '7 à 8 enfants par femme' en Afrique: un raccourci qui passe mal." Accessed September 3, 2020. https://www.nouvelobs.com/politique/20170711.OBS1954/macron-p ointe-les-7-a-8-enfants-par-femme-en-afrique-un-raccourci-qui-passe-mal.html

Robinson, Cedric J. *Black Marxism. The Making of the Black Radical Tradition*, 2nd edition. Chapel Hill, NC: University of North Carolina Press, 2000.

Rottenberg, Catherine. *The Rise of Neoliberal Feminism.* Oxford, UK: Oxford University Press, 2018. doi:10.1093/oso/9780190901226.001.0001.

Stanley, Amy Dru. "Slave Breeding and Free Love. An Antebellum Argument over Personhood." In *Capitalism Takes Command: The Social Transformation of Nineteenth Century America*, edited by Michael Zakim and Gary J. Kornblith, 119–144. Chicago, IL:University of Chicago Press, 2012.

Sublette, Ned and Constance Sublette. *The American Slave Coast. A History of the Slave-Breeding Industry.* Chicago, IL: Lawrence Hill Books, 2016.

Vergès, Françoise. *Le Ventre des femmes. Capitalisme, racialisation, féminisme.* Paris: Albin Michel, 2017.

Vergès, Françoise. *The Wombs of Women: Race, Capitalism, Feminism.* Translated by Kaiama L. Glover. Durham, NC: Duke University Press, 2020.

Wells, H.G. *The Island of Doctor Moreau.* London: Heinemann, 1896.

PART III

Sexuality in law

14

NEGOTIATING ADULTERY IN COLONIAL QUITO

Chad Thomas Black

The setting

The middle of the eighteenth century was a tumultuous time for the Audiencia of Quito.[1] A series of volcanic eruptions, earthquakes, droughts, and epidemics struck the region.[2] The misfortunes made a lasting impact on the city. In 1765, when imperial officials from Bogotá sought to increase taxation and monopolize the sale of alcohol, city leaders defensively recited the burdens of natural disasters as evidence that the reforms were unfeasible. This resistance led to the most important eruption in Quito of the eighteenth century, the Rebellion of the Barrios.[3] In May 1765 the city's neighborhoods erupted in protest and drove colonial officials, and particularly European Spaniards, out of town. The rebellion was a deep rupture of authority for Europeans in Quito. Fifteen months after it began, the Governor of Guayaquil entered the city at the head of a contingent of royal troops whose arrival sparked fear amongst Quiteños that reprisals by the empire would be swift and cruel. One Jesuit priest at the time remarked that, with the appearance of troops and the restoration of colonial authority, a fearful "Quito took up the yoke of the law, and subordinated itself to it."[4]

Indeed, in the decades following the Rebellion of the Barrios the yoke of law was used to transform unruly barrios into orderly neighborhoods and households, subordinated to colonial authority by a series of Audiencia Presidents who revolutionized policing and detention. Late-colonial authorities in Quito changed the city's policing practices, creating a neighborhood-level magistracy to monitor and correct the city's public sins.[5] Magistrates encouraged denunciations of sexual crimes and zealously prosecuted offenders.

The enhanced legal regime of the period 1765–1790 left us with a large set of concubinage and adultery cases that reveal how sex became a proxy for other conflicts in late colonial Quito. Reading the cases exposes, ironically, popular toleration of illicit relationships and flexible understandings of what constituted legitimate marriage. In this chapter I use a set of some 40 cases to show how historians can use criminal trials and procedures to reconstruct popular moral economy, an unintended consequence of an activist colonial judicial regime. With one particular case as an anchor, we walk through the three main phases of a prosecution, and find that, from a political and economic desire for orderly streets and orderly households, colonial officials built an infrastructure of policing and discipline that turned neighbors into accomplices in reshaping colonial authority. Let us begin, then, with the case of Francisca Naranjo.

171

Phase I: sumaria

On April 20, 1770, a hat maker named Alexo Merino denounced his wife before a city magistrate for her 15 years of abandonment. Merino accused Francisca Naranjo of long-term "notorious adultery and daring haughtiness," carrying on publicly with her lover, a soldier named Xavier Sandoya.[6] Merino complained that the two lovers frequented the city's *pulperias* (small grocery stores that could double as taverns in the evening), and had twice in the past been apprehended together by the city's *ronda*.[7] Merino noted that on these occasions he had sent Jesuit priests to visit Naranjo in the women's jail, the Recogimiento de Santa Marta, to implore her to return to married life. In the early 1760s, judicial authorities tried to separate the lovers by banishing Sandoya to Guayaquil. In secret, Naranjo funded her lover's return to Quito, providing him with the astonishing sum of 300 pesos for the trip.[8]

And now, in April 1770, Francisca Naranjo again sat in jail, arrested by a neighborhood magistrate on patrol for cavorting publicly with her lover. Faced with this provocation, Merino denounced her to the court and asked that she be incarcerated and her lover sentenced to labor in a royal textile factory. Within the week the magistrate collected testimony from three witnesses suggested by Merino, all of whom swore to the defendant's long-term relationship. Arrest warrants were issued, and by the end of April both were jailed to await trial for public, scandalous cohabitation.[9]

Alexo Merino's denunciation initiated a *sumaria*, the opening stage of a criminal prosecution of adultery and cohabitation in which an investigating magistrate gathered information about the allegations. Significantly, the tenor of a case was set in the *sumaria* by the terms of the denunciation because the Spanish legal system presumed guilt. On the merits of this presumption, the opening phase of a case saw the imposition of an interventionist and moralizing colonial order, often even peering right into people's bedrooms.

Merino's denunciation and the magistrate's investigation reveal a number of trends of the policing of illicit sex in the wake of Quito's crisis of Spanish colonial authority. First, many prosecuted relationships were long-term relationships. Naranjo and Sandoya maintained their affair for more than a decade. The phrase *muchos años* (many years) repeatedly described the age of suspect relationships, emphasizing the incorrigibility of the accused but also revealing long-term toleration of affairs in the barrios. For cases with more exact descriptions, the shortest were one-night stands or relationships of less than a month, but the longest exceeded 30 years. Don Martín Díaz de Cervantes, who was married in Spain, lived in Ibarra north of Quito for 20 years with a woman not his wife.[10] An investigation of Josef Garay in Cuenca, to the south, in 1779 alleged he maintained a relationship with María Acosta for more than 30 years.[11] The median length of relationships described with a specific time span was three years. Long years together were not the only evidence of neighborhood toleration of relationships. Enrique Alban and Antonia Pazmiño were arrested for illicit cohabitation in 1782, despite having an eight-year-old child together.[12]

What, then, changed to make these long-term relationships suddenly subject to judicial scrutiny? A second common feature was that some public event, often unrelated to the relationship in question, spurred a denunciation of sexual transgression. Frequently, witness testimonies inadvertently revealed what events triggered denunciations of long-term relationships. Adultery prosecutions formally required a jilted spouse to denounce their partner, or for a couple to be caught in the act of an illicit rendezvous. To circumvent the requirement, magistrates often used the ronda to try to surprise couples in bed at home or out together at one of the city's taverns or nightspots. The use of the ronda proved to be a third remarkable feature, with 24 (60 per cent) of the prosecutions including a visit by the patrols. Often, where officials got their information on suspected couples cannot be determined. It is likely, though, that someone in the barrio informally denounced them to the magistrate, who waited for night to surprise couples. At times we can guess from later information in a case (witness statements, admissions by magistrates) who might have made such a denunciation and why. Offended spouses, such as Alexo Merino, would very rarely make a denunciation without some public provocation, especially if they were already leading separate lives from their partners. Often, denunciations of illicit behavior were used to punish unrelated grievances.

In January 1777, Fernando Ortega was arrested for illicit cohabitation after he helped his lover, Doña María Josefa Gavilanes, leave the city of Cuenca. Ortega insisted that Doña María's husband knew about their relationship and tolerated it (*con ciencia y tolerancia*).[13] In July 1781, Mariano Ayala was arrested for a brutal assault on his lover, Antonia Hidalgo. The couple had quarreled one morning over a hat that she was supposed to sell for Mariano. That afternoon, when the two met for their usual rendezvous in one of Quito's ravines, Mariano viciously attacked Antonia, giving her 100 lashes, cutting her hair, and stuffing a package of ground chile peppers into her "secret parts."[14] Victimized by Mariano, Antonia sought help from a magistrate to whom she was forced to confess a six-year relationship with her abuser. Mariano was still a minor, and substantially younger than the 22-year-old Antonia, but had been raised as a servant in her household and confessed that for years the two of them went to the ravine under the pretext of bathing, but really for other activity. Such cases reveal that men were targeted for prosecution during the late eighteenth century as well as women.

In June 1783, a tavern owner named Brigida Alban was arrested on charges of illicit cohabitation with Antonio de la Cruz after his wife, Gregoria Rojas, turned him in.[15] The pretext of the complaint against Alban was a publicly humiliating scene in which Rojas was taunted by Flora Lara, a friend of Alban, for being a cuckquean. Antonio de la Cruz, though, maintained that he had provoked his wife into denouncing him by demanding that she give him money she made running her own shop (*tienda*), despite years of neglect and abandonment. Four years later Flora Lara turned in her own sister, Josefa Lara, for a same-sex relationship with Manuela Palis after their parish priest threatened to excommunicate Josefa for *not paying ecclesiastical taxes.*[16] In another case of same-sex allegations, in 1788 Custodio Legendres beat up Mariano Espinosa in a dispute over some property. A few days later he found himself accused of sodomy in a case that resulted in allegations against no less than ten other men.[17]

In other cases, defendants saw themselves as collateral damage of zealous judges, political fights, or other people's disputes. In the 1779 case of Josef Garay, he claimed he was targeted by the Lieutenant Governor, Mariano Coello, as retribution for a dispute that Coello had with Garay's boss, a public notary.[18] Garay was accused of carrying out 30 years of "illicit commerce" with María Acosta, and the two were picked up by the ronda. After 70 days in jail Garay managed to get a petition to the Audiencia court, which ordered his immediate release and accused Coello of abuse of authority.

In October 1760, Antonio Gálvez, a notary in the town of Zaruma, found himself arrested for drunkenness, bad living, abuse of power, causing scandal, and illicit cohabitation.[19] The charges were brought after one particularly robust evening of drinking that ended with Gálvez, sword in hand, in the middle of the town's plaza loudly insulting the credit and lineage of the local priest and other citizens. The magistrate who made the arrest was related to the priest.

In 1779, a native leader from the village of Pelileo snuck a petition accusing magistrate Antonio Villalobos of illicit cohabitation into a case file in which Villalobos was prosecuting an indigenous community member for assault and refusing to pay tribute.[20] Investigating further, the Audiencia discovered that this attempt to sabotage Villalobos was retaliation for yet another case in which two women were living with priests in sacrilege, and with the consent of their father and the community.[21] Thus one unwanted prosecution begat another.

Outside of direct denunciations by offended spouses, magistrates tried hard to catch couples in the act in order to avoid jurisdictional problems, and because the Audiencia often threw out cases where no *flagrante delicto* evidence could be provided. The ronda became increasingly central to this dynamic, and in the early 1780s the Audiencia explicitly ordered local magistrates to use the ronda to identify and correct public sins and scandals. It was an effective strategy to find and prosecute disorderly households, but could also backfire when defendants had substantial social and financial status. For example, in September 1783 a neighborhood magistrate on patrol in the parish of San Blas came across loud music and a scandalous party.[22] He banged on the door repeatedly until he was let in by one of the many prostitutes (*mujeres de trato*) present, only to realize that the party was being held for one of the city's leading caballeros. The men and their women companions laughed the magistrate and his patrol out of the house while the musicians mockingly followed them into the street. Despite the magistrate reporting the party to the Audiencia, the case went nowhere.

Phase II: prueba

Long-standing relationships, targeted by the ronda and zealous magistrates, produced an ever increasing number of adultery and cohabitation cases into the 1780s. But the allegations did not go uncontested. In the second phase of trial, the *prueba*, defendants questioned the most basic assumptions of magistrates pursuing orderly households, including the nature of marriage. In confessions and written petitions, defendants negotiated intrusive colonial power and sought to turn the state's moralizing language against itself.

Returning to the case of Alexo Merino, Francisca Naranjo, and Xavier Sandoya, the magistrate took the confessions of the two defendants from the respective jail cells with questions taken directly on Merino's framing. The couple denied wrongdoing. Following established procedure, the confessions were forwarded to Merino, who asked that Sandoya again be banished from Quito and his wife held in the Santa Marta jail to "learn her reformation."[23] In response, Sandoya filed a petition that questioned the *a priori* assumption that he and Naranjo were even committing adultery. He first demurred, claiming that any actual sexual congress had occurred years before, outside the customary limitations for accusations. Further, he reasoned, for adultery to exist there had to be a functioning marriage, "It is equally certain that legally there is no Adultery if there has been no violation of a Conjugal Bed." This had not existed, he explained, because Merino had long lived "a scandalous life," cheating on his wife, beating her to the point of causing a miscarriage, and voluntarily abandoning her. "It was in these circumstances that I met [her], the marital bed of his wife abandoned for years. One could not call [their marriage] conjugal, as the word insinuates the cohabitation of consorts." The greater sin was Merino's, not his wife's. Her transgression was rooted in weakness, in the search for the companionship and care of a substitute relationship when faced with an abusive, duplicitous husband.[24]

Francisca Naranjo's petition echoed the arguments of her lover. She asked the magistrate to investigate her husband's infidelities before passing judgment on her unfortunate lot, reasoning,

> it is well known through municipal, canon, and civil law that in order for a male
> spouse to have the right and ability to accuse his wife of the crime of adultery, it is

necessary to have complied exactly with the obligations of an honorable husband; that is, to provide her with food and clothing … as well as to be well ordered in his habits and morals ….

Merino's habits and morals were, according to his wife, anything but orderly. Naranjo's appeal to the law was inexact, referring only to a vague body of law upholding a certain form of honorable marital obligation. The phrase "it is well known" inverted the innuendo of gossip and accusation in order to question the legitimacy of her marriage. The couple then provided their own list of witnesses and questions for investigating Merino's behavior, which the magistrate followed up on.

These strategies fit with an array of common arguments and actions defendants used to shift rhetoric after the *sumaria*. Often paramours claimed they were not living as married couples. After a surprise visit by the ronda, male defendants often alleged that their lovers were actually just providing domestic service, usually cooking or tending to their laundry. In one case in 1779 the ronda tried to surprise Ignacio Hiraeta and his married lover at 8:30 p.m., but she was not at his home. So the patrol came back for a second visit and arrested the couple together at 11:00 p.m. In his defense, Hiraeta complained that the tactic was an abuse of power by a zealous magistrate, and claimed that his alleged lover tended to his laundry because he had no family contacts in town.[25] In November 1775, Joaquín de Zerri and Paula Villarroel were arrested after a surprise visit by the ronda and accused of scandalously living together for years. The magistrate claimed they were caught in the act, but later testimony revealed they were caught sitting together in Zerri's kitchen. The defendant claimed that Villarroel was not his lover but rather his cook. She operated and lived in a shop at the street-level entrance to his home and thus her presence was fully understandable. Zerri mitigated his confession, claiming that if any adulterous relationship had happened between the two it had happened years prior, was no longer going on, and was the result of his own fragility as a man.[26]

For those with incontrovertible evidence of past dalliances, such as children, their confessions and petitions during the *prueba* tried to diminish their relationships by claiming that any sexual "commerce" or "correspondence" was long over. For example, Matías Casimiro Benavides, described as an old man at age 65, was accused of maintaining a two-year relationship with Teresa Villagran after they were picked up by the ronda.[27] Benavides admitted that they lived together but claimed their sexual relationship had ended after the first year and that they were cohabitating only out of poverty. Admissions of sexual impropriety were often explained by both men and women as examples of their own personal failing, of weakness and fragility. Even couples surprised in bed by the ronda presented creative explanations for their misdeeds. Manuela Palis and Josefa Lara, accused of sodomy, claimed they were sharing a bed because the night they were found together was cold, Palis was too drunk to walk home alone late at night, and that the apartment only had one bed.[28] Petrona Ayala made a similar argument after she was discovered sleeping in bed with her brother-in-law, Miguel Lagos, while her husband, Fernando, was passed out drunk on the floor. At confession, the three insisted they were not engaged in a love triangle but rather that they were simply poor and could only afford one bed shared by everyone in the house.[29]

Defendants also regularly complained of magistrate abuse and blamed enemies seeking revenge for their legal woes. In 1764, Antonio Solano, a royal official, was surprised by the ronda and found in bed with a married woman.[30] Solano and Doña Teresa de Encalada reportedly had had a scandalous relationship for years. But it was only after Solano became embroiled in a dispute with magistrate Juan Chica's uncle that the ronda showed up. Chica's decision to arrest the couple was not uniformly hailed in the neighborhood. After their arrest, a group of local musicians followed the patrol to the jail, making up songs on the spot that lampooned the magistrate and defended the couple. Solano complained to the Audiencia that Chica abused his power and used the ronda for harassment. After the couple denied their relationship during the *prueba*, the Audiencia ordered them released. Antonio Solano was a well-connected individual, but his complaint about abuse at the hands of magistrates was a common refrain.[31]

These rounds of confession and petition created a counternarrative crafted by defendants and their legal representatives. At the end of the *prueba*, cases were forwarded to the Crown attorney (*fiscal*) for an opinion before sentencing. The fiscal might take into account expressions of contrition, mitigations, and diminishments from the *prueba*, but most often simply explained to the court what the recommended punishment was for substantiated allegations. Based on all the accumulated information and the fiscal's recommendations, magistrates then handed down sentences in the final phase of the trial.

Phase III: autos

As a result of their arguments, Francisca Naranjo and Xavier Sandoya were eventually released from jail by order of Audiencia judge Sebastián Salzedo y Oñate. Officially he was unwilling to accept the force of the couple's deconstruction of the meaning of marriage and adultery, but justified his decision to release them by citing Alexo Merino's complicity in the same transgression. New witnesses introduced during the *prueba* provided evidence of his infidelities; the adultery of one party cancelled the other's out. Naranjo and Sandoya's freedom came with an admonition to abandon their illicit relationship under pain of future severe punishment. While the accused couple were ultimately released, they did spend five months in jail. For his part, Merino was scathed only by an order to pay one third of the court costs. By all rights Francisca Naranjo could have denounced her husband, leading to his incarceration years earlier. She did not, it seems, because she had long ago accepted that her marriage was a farce. It was the invasive presence of royal authority in the form of the ronda and a vigilant magistrate that brought this into "public" light and forced a long-term relationship into the category of scandal and notoriety. Neighborhood surveillance and magistrate discretion made the adultery fit the requirements for prosecution.

City magistrates and Audiencia judges alike were not required to justify the *autos* (sentences) they handed down. This final phase of the case offered an opportunity for judges to resolve confrontations through leniency and punishment. Still, defendants who ultimately were cleared of wrongdoing suffered greatly under the system. Such was the potency of making allegations of illicit sexual behavior, with tragic consequences for falsely or problematically accused individuals. For example, in 1804 a 15-year-old boy named Geronimo Berveran was accused of bestiality by a *mulato* slave, Juan Campoverde.[32] He was quickly tried and convicted of having a sexual encounter with a mare by officials who, it turns out, were allies with Campoverde. Beveran was sentenced to ten years' service on the Rio Chagras in Panama, while the mare was lanced to death.[33] On appeal, Beveran's mother was able to secure her son's freedom with two arguments: casting doubt on the mechanics of the allegations by proving the horse in question had never been broken, and demonstrating that Campoverde was a family enemy in league with local officials. The court recognized the disqualifying allegiance between Beveran's accuser and local judicial authorities, but not before Beveran had endured more than two years in jail. Sexual allegations were extremely powerful because accusers and defendants understood that royal officials had identified sexual sin as a threat to the orderly and docile colonial power they were trying to maintain.

35 See for example, the case of María Anguieta and Matías Tapia. Anguieta's husband denounced her for their adulterous affair in September 1782. Anguieta was ordered back to married life, and Tapia received six months in the tobacco factory. ANE CR 97, exp. 7, 2-ix-1782.

36 On tobacco, see ANE Fondo Especial (FE) 1778, Volume 1, Documento 3858. On the administration of tribute, see ANE FE 1778, Vol. 1, Doc. 3859. On the alcohol monopoly, see ANE FE 1778 Vol. 1, Doc. 3860. On playing cards and gunpowder, see Archivo General de Indias (AGI) Quito, 239, N.115 "Estanco de naipes y pólvora."

37 ANE CR 102, exp. 1, 6-vi-1783.

38 ANE, Juicios de Primer Notaría, 75 12-i-1782, "Visita de Cárcel."

39 García de León made the claim in an Inquisition case, where the defendant was moved from the Audiencia court's own jail to a tobacco factory in spite of the danger he posed to orthodoxy. ANE CR 98, exp. 3, 22-x-1782.

40 See for example the case against Doña Theresa Veintemilla who was banished for her relationship with Father Gabriel Endana. ANE CR 122, 15-vi-1787.

41 ANE CR 111, 18-v-1785.

Bibliography

Andrien, Kenneth J. "Economic Crisis, Taxes and the Insurrection of 1765." *Past & Present* 129 (1990): 104–131. doi:10.1093/past/129.1.104.

Andrien, Kenneth J. *The Kingdom of Quito, 1690–1830: The State and Regional Development.* Cambridge, UK: Cambridge University Press, 1995. doi:10.1017/CBO9780511529054.

Andrien, Kenneth J. "The Politics of Reform in Spain's Atlantic Empire during the Late Bourbon Period: The Visita of José García de León y Pizarro in Quito." *Journal of Latin American Studies* 41, no. 4 (2009): 637–662. doi:10.1017/S0022216X0999054X.

Black, Chad Thomas. *The Limits of Gender Domination: Women, the Law, and Political Crisis in Quito, 1765–1830.* Albuquerque, NM: University of New Mexico Press, 2010.

Black, Chad Thomas. "Prosecuting Female-Female Sex in Bourbon Quito." In *Sexuality and the Unnatural in Colonial Latin America*, edited by Zeb Tortorici, 120–140. Berkeley, CA: University of California Press, 2016.

Cutter, Charles. *Libro de los principales rudimentos tocante a todos juicios.* Mexico City: UNAM, 1994 [1764].

Germeten, Nicole von. *Profit and Passion: Transactional Sex in Colonial Mexico.* Berkeley, CA: University of California Press, 2018.

González Suárez, Federico. *Historia general de la república del Ecuador.* Vol. 2. Quito: Casa de la Cultura, 1970.

Komisaruk, Catherine. *Love and Labor in Guatemala: The Eve of Independence.* Stanford, CA: Stanford University Press, 2013.

Kuethe, Allan J. and Kenneth J. Andrien. *The Spanish Atlantic World in the Eighteenth Century: War and the Bourbon Reforms, 1713–1796.* Cambridge, UK: Cambridge University Press, 2014. doi:10.1017/CBO9781107338661.

McFarlane, Anthony. "The Rebellion of the Barrios: Urban Insurrection in Bourbon Quito." In *Reform and Insurrection in New Granada and Peru*, edited by Allan J. Keuthe, John R. Fisher and Anthony McFarlane. Baton Rouge, LA: Louisiana State University, 1990.

Minchom, Martin. *The People of Quito, 1690–1810: Change and Unrest in the Underclass.* Boulder, CO: Westview Press, 1994.

Recio, S.J.P. Bernardo. *Compendiosa relación de la cristianidad de Quito*, Vol. 2, Biblioteca misionera. Edited by P. Carlos Garcia Goldaraz. Madrid: Consejo superior de Investigaciones Científicas, 1957 [1773].

"Relación sumaria de las dos sublevaciones de la pleve de Quito." *Boletín de la academica nacional de historia* XV, no. 42 (1937).

Robins, Nicholas. *Of Love and Loathing: Marital Life, Strife, and Intimacy in the Colonial Andes.* Lincoln, NE: University of Nebraska Press, 2015. doi:10.2307/j.ctt1d9nhx8.

Tortorici, Zeb, ed. *Sexuality and the Unnatural in Colonial Latin America.* Berkeley, CA: University of California Press, 2016.

Tortorici, Zeb. *Sins Against Nature: Sex and Archives in Colonial New Spain.* Durham, NC: Duke University Press, 2018.

Voekel, Pamela. "Peeing on the Palace: Bodily Resistance to Bourbon Reforms in Mexico City." *Journal of Historical Sociology* 5 no. 2 (1992): 183–208. doi:10.1111/j.1467-6443.1992.tb00161.x.

Walker, Charles F. "Shaking the Unstable Empire': The Lima, Quito, and Arequipa Earthquakes, 1746, 1783, and 1797." In *Dreadful Visitations: Confronting Natural Catastrophe in the Age of Enlightenment*, edited by Alessa Johns, 113–144. New York: Routledge, 1999.

15

REGULATED PROSTITUTION IN FRENCH-COLONIZED NORTHERN VIETNAM AND ITS FAILURES, 1920–1945

Christina Firpo

During World War I the French colonial government faced a growing threat of venereal disease in Tonkin, the northeastern-most protectorate in Indochina and currently part of modern-day Vietnam. Sexually transmitted infections were a matter of major concern to the colonial government, as they could potentially weaken whole military units or result in serious birth defects for children of infected mothers. Authorities identified sex workers as the main source of contagion and implemented measures to stymie the spread of venereal disease. The colonial state instituted a strict regulation system, imported from the metropole, that required sex workers to register with police, pay steep taxes, submit to invasive venereal exams, and, if results were positive, be quarantined. Yet the strict rules of the regulation system, which limited sex workers' profits, mobility, and freedom, drove many women to work in Tonkin's black market for unregistered prostitution, which thrived during the late colonial period.

This article investigates the colonial regulation system in Tonkin, its founding and its failures. In exploring two of the most popular and openly practiced forms of clandestine prostitution—*à đào* singing houses and Western-style dance halls—this study explores the limits of colonial policing power and sex workers' ability to exploit those limits.

The colonial regulation system and the black market

Tonkin's strict regulatory regime for prostitution was based on metropolitan trends in bureaucratic systems and the science of regulation that had emerged during the nineteenth century. Though prostitution had been legal in France since the Middle Ages, the state did not begin to regulate sex work until the early 1800s.[1] By the mid-nineteenth century, France faced a growing threat of venereal disease, and authorities identified sex workers as the primary source of transmission.[2] Across Europe, governments enacted regulation codes, known in the anglophone world as the Contagious Diseases Acts, to prevent the spread of venereal disease.[3] These anti-venereal disease regulations evolved in the context of mid-nineteenth century trends in policing, as demonstrated by scholars such as Michel Foucault, Jann Matlock, and Judith Walkowitz.[4] Concurrently the emergence of the nation-state and its associated bureaucratic policies to "make populations legible" shaped the system for the registration and regulation of sex work.[5] Over the course of the nineteenth century a regulation system developed in France that required sex workers to submit to venereal exams and that dictated the age of sex workers, where the work was performed, and the taxes owed.[6]

In the 1880s, as France was colonizing Tonkin, the colonial government established municipal-level ordinances, loosely based on metropolitan statutes, to regulate sex work in the French-controlled cities of Hai Phòng (1886) and Hanoi (1888).[7] Yet, like their equivalents in the metropole, these municipal ordinances proved largely ineffective in preventing the spread of venereal disease. By World War I the French colonial government faced rocketing rates of venereal disease, which was considered one of the colony's top health threats, particularly to the military. In 1915 the General Commander Superior of the Indochina troops reported that venereal disease was the main infection afflicting the French troops stationed in Annam and Tonkin.[8]

Of greatest concern to French healthcare professionals in the colony was the potential for a venereal disease outbreak that would infect entire military units. The concern was multifaceted. Officials feared not just that venereal disease would render soldiers unable to fight but also that the disease could potentially spread to France when infected troops returned home.[9] Moreover, French and Vietnamese doctors—as well as Vietnamese intellectuals—feared that the birth defects caused by venereal disease could lead to racial degeneracy among both the French and Vietnamese populations.[10] As in the metropole, colonial doctors identified sex workers as the source of contagion,[11] and the state aimed to maintain control over the sex trade by regulating, taxing, and policing prostitution.

In 1921, to slow the spread of venereal disease, the colonial state adopted a stronger, more uniform legal code that regulated prostitution throughout the French concessions in Tonkin. The 1921 law, which was based on the metropolitan regulation system, required sex workers to register with the state. The law taxed the sale of sex and required sex workers to submit to regular gynecological examinations; those who tested positive were sequestered in venereal disease clinics until the infection passed. This system proved financially devastating for some women, who could not earn a living while interned at a clinic. Moreover, once sex workers had registered with the state it was difficult for them to deregister. Women who wished to be removed from the police list had to prove they had an "honorable" profession or were married to a man who had the means to support them, both of which were nearly impossible to prove.[12]

Colonial Tonkin's regulatory system, notwithstanding its underpinning of bureaucratic science, proved to be a failure. With such stringent regulations, many sex workers avoided registering with the state and submitting to its regulations, choosing instead to operate in the black market. Ironically, the 1921 law, designed to prevent the spread of venereal disease, would only drive more sex workers into a clandestine market void of the very regulations that colonial authorities believed would thwart the proliferation of infection.

The black-market sex industry succeeded because sex workers found ways to flout the 1921 law. Devised for the metropole, the regulation system did not account for Tonkin's unique situation. For one thing, the particularities of Tonkin's political landscape provided legal sites of refuge for clandestine sex work. As a protectorate, Tonkin was an indirect colony and hence subject to the indigenous legal code. The main cities of Hanoi and Hai Phòng, as well as provincial capitals and military bases, by contrast, were French concessions where French law prevailed. In this patchwork of Vietnamese territory and French-ruled concessions,[13] French agents looking to police Tonkin's sex industry enjoyed only limited powers in the countryside. Sex workers aiming to escape the regulatory system set up shop just outside city limits or on military bases to profit from the urban and military customer base while evading colonial laws. Located just beyond the reach of French colonial jurisdiction, suburbs became a site of debauchery. The result was, as one French health official put it, a "belt of Venus that crowns the suburbs of Hanoi and the other urban zones of Tonkin."[14] By 1938 there were more than 1,400 clandestine sex workers residing in *ả đào* singing houses in the suburbs of Hanoi alone.[15]

Clandestine sex workers also capitalized on the way that the 1921 law characterized prostitution. Instead of stipulating which acts could be considered prostitution or what kinds of transactions constituted payment, the law defined it as "the deed of using one's body for business with any and all takers indiscriminately, in exchange for monetary remuneration."[16] This definition complicated police efforts to force clandestine sex workers to register with the state and follow the rules of the regulation system. For one thing, the 1921 definition appears to have applied only to those whose main profession was prostitution, not necessarily those who only occasionally sold sex. The clause "with any and all takers indiscriminately" allowed those in question to make the case that they enjoyed the free will to turn down whatever clients they wished. Finally, the definition of prostitution as an exchange of sex for monetary compensation excluded those who were paid in-kind with gifts or room and board. By limiting the range of activities that could be considered sex work, the law hindered police efforts to force clandestine prostitutes to register with the state and follow the regulatory system. Moreover, because the law was crafted to protect the personal liberties of metropolitan French men and women, it implicitly restricted the ability of police to enter the kinds of private businesses that served as covert venues for sex work, such as *ả đào* singing clubs and dance halls, both of which were ubiquitous in the colony and neither of which were registered as brothels. In short, the 1921 law had the unintended effect of restraining, rather than reinforcing, state authority over clandestine prostitution. The result was a booming black market for prostitution that often operated in very public ways.

Sex work in *ả đào* singing houses

During the late colonial period (1920–1945) sex workers looking to dodge regulations used Tonkin's *ả đào* singing houses as a front for clandestine prostitution. *Ả đào* music, variations of which date back to the fourteenth century, had historically found an audience with the scholarly gentry. The musical genre was held in high esteem throughout the centuries and associated with the Vietnamese literary revival of the late nineteenth century. In the colonial period, however, the reputation of *ả đào* entertainment suffered as the social standing of the mandarin class declined with French rule.[17] During this time, *ả đào* singing houses became associated with clandestine prostitution.

From its early iterations, *ả đào* singing had been associated with sensuality. Pretty young singers—always women—carried the tune, backed up by a long-neck lute player. The manner of vocal control and the breathy nature of their singing was known to stir the passions. The lyrics were typically famous works of Chinese poetry, or occasionally a poem that a customer had written himself and slipped to the singer only moments before she went on stage. The music was spontaneous and enhanced by audience participation, creating the feel of a personal relationship between the performer and the crowd.

During the colonial period many of the *ả đào* houses capitalized on the sensual nature of the singing. Exclusively male audiences gathered to listen to pretty women sing, flirt with servers, gamble, and smoke opium.[18] Along with the music, customers at *ả đào* houses enjoyed "intimate discussions and some passion," as one journalist wrote in the *Việt Báo* newspaper in 1939.[19] Owners encouraged workers to flirt with customers, many of whom patronized their favorite singers and showed up with gifts of clothing or fine jewelry to win their affections. Some men even fell in love and grew jealous when *ả đào* singers paid too much attention to other customers.[20]

Ả đào singing houses became a refuge from Tonkin's strict regulation laws. Located in suburbs just outside city limits, the singing houses drew from the large urban customer base but remained beyond the jurisdiction of colonial police. As *ả đào* singing houses were private establishments, police lacked the legal authority to enter without due cause. Moreover, *ả đào* singing served as an effective front for prostitution. Singers managed to avoid the penalties associated with the 1921 law, which defined prostitutes as those who sold sex as their main profession, simply by claiming singing as their full-time profession.

Clandestine prostitution in *ả đào* singing houses was a public secret. As evidenced by government documents, colonial officials were well aware that clandestine prostitution was taking place in *ả đào* houses. In 1939, officials complained that brothels were mis-identifying women who engaged in sex work as "singers" in order to avoid registering them as prostitutes and, in turn, paying the requisite taxes and submitting them to the regulatory prescriptions of the 1921 law.[21] As for Vietnamese officials, some were known to frequent singing houses even while publicly condemning them for clandestine prostitution.[22] And Vietnamese newspapers regularly featured stories exposing the link between prostitution and *ả đào* venues. A poignant 1938 article in the *Đông Pháp* newspaper addressed the prevalence of venereal disease among singers, suggesting their role as sex workers. Referring to *ả đào* houses as brothels [*nhà lầu xanh*], the reporter estimated that 90 per cent of the singers at the *ả đào* houses had venereal disease, which was assumed to be contracted through sex work.[23]

As the 1921 law increasingly proved ineffective for regulating sex work in *ả đào* venues, colonial officials sought alternative ways to limit clandestine prostitution in singing houses. In the 1930s French officials shifted policing powers to Vietnamese officials in the provinces to implement city planning codes that limited business opportunities. To further restrict sex work in *ả đào* houses, French officials also drew upon public health measures that provided reason for policing private establishments. Vietnamese authorities attempted to force singers to register as prostitutes in Nam Định in 1932 and in Hanoi in 1938, but singers refused.[24] In Hà Đông in July 1938, officials banned street solicitation and briefly closed offending *ả đào* singing houses.[25] That August, the *Thời Vụ Báo* newspaper ran a story about singers caught violating city codes in Nam Định. The singers were fined and forced to "get familiar with the duck's beak" (*làm quen với cái mỏ vịt*)—Vietnamese slang for the speculum used by gynecologists in venereal exams. Those who refused to submit to, or had otherwise managed to avoid, venereal exams were slapped with fines ten times greater than those imposed on singers in Hanoi.[26]

Women who worked in *ả đào* singing houses made every effort to present their profession as an art form, however sexualized it may have been. Indeed, while prostitution was prevalent in *ả đào* signing houses, not all singers were sex workers and some sold sex only occasionally. Throughout the late colonial period there was a constant back and forth between the colonial administrators who were trying to police the sex work in *ả đào* venues and the professional *ả đào* singers themselves, who were doing their best to defend the reputation of their craft. As one owner of a singing house in Nam Định insisted, singers "do not make a living [by prostitution] because all we sell is singing … for men of fine character and noble men of letters."[27]

Sex workers found clever ways to defy ordinances and regulations. Take, for example, a case that occurred in Nam Định in 1938, when clandestine sex workers escaped forced venereal check-ups either by fleeing the province or, more humorously, by posting "For Rent" signs outside their *à đào* houses to trick police into thinking they were vacant while continuing to accommodate customers on the sly.[28] Other singers, also in Nam Định, went on strike when authorities tried to force them to submit to venereal disease testing and pay prostitution taxes. Still others continued to see clients in secret.[29] Later that year, when authorities in Ninh Bình directed *à đào* singers to submit to weekly venereal exams, singers bribed officials to look the other way.[30]

Sex work in dance halls

A second means of evading the colonial regulation system was the surreptitious selling of sex in Tonkin's dance halls. Initially popular in Europe and other parts of Asia, a Western-style dance trend took Tonkin by storm in the mid-1930s.[31] Youths lined up nightly outside dance halls; inside, patrons danced with their friends or bought tickets to tango, waltz, and foxtrot with professional dancers. Dance halls hired young women as professional dancers to keep the party going, elevate the level of dance, and encourage young men to spend money on drinks.

Dance halls attracted a diverse clientele and were sites of interracial mingling. Vietnamese and Chinese youth joined European and Foreign Legion soldiers on the dance floor, laughing, chatting, and holding their bodies close as they danced to the beat of the music. With their European music, decor, cocktails, and cigarettes, dance halls provided a familiar cultural environment for homesick soldiers from France and other European countries. As such they became one of the main venues for European–Vietnamese social and romantic inter-actions. While most patrons came to dance halls for entertainment and coquetry, the atmosphere was ripe for black-market prostitution, and professional dancers quickly earned a reputation as clandestine prostitutes.[32]

Like *à đào* singing houses, sex work in dance halls was hardly a secret. Pimps and madams sent unregistered sex workers into dance halls to find customers, and young men arrived at the halls looking for a night of love.[33] French authorities more or less assumed that professional dancers were clandestine prostitutes,[34] calling professional dancing "a new pseudo-artistic means of selling oneself expensively."[35] As Vietnamese journalist Trọng Lang, who was himself pro-positioned by dancers while researching his articles, wrote, "In the dance clubs, girls go from timidly dancing the foxtrot to dancing the debauched dance."[36] Similarly, journalist Vũ Trọng Phụng famously wrote that "the Bạch My spirit," the patron saint of sex workers, "has acquired a new type of prostitution."[37]

Authorities identified dancers as the main source of venereal disease transmission among soldiers. In 1938, Hanoi Mayor Virgitti and the colony's top venereal disease expert, Dr Bernard Joyeux, went so far as to deem dance halls the "new halls of contamination for Europeans, particularly European troops."[38] That same year military doctor Marcel Piere considered dancers to be the "most dangerous" threat to European troops.[39] A 1943 hygiene inspection report on Hai Phòng noted an increase in the number of reported cases of venereal disease in the city due to raids on dance halls, "which are considered to be establishments like brothels."[40]

As in the case of *à đào* singing houses, the colonial government searched for alternative ways to limit sex work in the dance halls. Like *à đào* singers, dancers were not considered sex workers according to the 1921 law that defined prostitution, and authorities thus had little policing powers over them. In 1934 the Hanoi government imposed heavy taxes on the halls. As taxes limited profits, dance hall owners moved their businesses to the suburbs, co-locating with *à đào* singing houses to benefit from their customer base and evade colonial policing and taxes.[41] Initially, local governments in the suburbs attempted to exert control through city ordinances that imposed limits on the hours that dance halls could operate. For example, those found open after midnight (except on Saturday) were slapped with fines.[42] Those that stayed open to 1 a.m. paid 0.80 piasters; those that remained open past that time had to pay five piasters.[43] Given that dance halls reaped enormous profits by staying open late, such fines were negligible in their impact.

Interestingly, colonial authorities refrained from policing dance halls with the zeal that they applied to *à đào* singing houses. Acutely aware of the popularity of dance halls among French and Foreign Legion troops, authorities kept policing efforts to a minimum so as to keep the troops happy and strengthen their virility, which military leaders assumed would carry over onto the battlefield. Authorities also found the dance halls, which were culturally familiar, less threatening than the *à đào* singing houses and were hence less inclined to restrict them. As a result, sex work continued largely unfettered in Tonkin's dance halls.

Conclusion

Tonkin's colonial regulation system for prostitution ultimately failed. Originally intended for the metropolitan environment and based on bureaucratic strategies to prevent the spread of venereal disease, the regulatory system was unsuccessful in the colony because it did not account for the intricacies of colonial rule. For one thing, the law did not take into account the complicated political geography of the protectorate, which was a patchwork of Vietnamese and French rule. Sex workers thus managed to exploit the protectorate system by locating their work just outside the jurisdiction of the French colonial state. Moreover, given that the 1921 law defined prostitution narrowly, sex workers were able to conceal their illicit activities in venues showcasing legitimate popular female performance arts: *à đào* singing houses and dance halls. While local governments attempted to thwart their operations by passing ordinances that limited the profitability and hours of operation of these establishments, sex workers still managed to practice more or less freely and easily sidestepped policing efforts. As a result, the black market for unregistered prostitution in Tonkin flourished as an entertainment-based industry until the beginning of World War II.

Notes

1 The spread of venereal disease led the city of Paris to establish venereal clinics to treat sex workers; the city then required sex workers to register with the state as a means of tracking prostitutes and ensuring they submitted to venereal exams and treatment. Miller, "'The Romance of Regulation,'" 1–7.
2 For an excellent discussion of gendered discourse on venereal disease, see Spongberg, *Feminizing Venereal Disease.*
3 Decree of February 3, 1921, printed in Joyeux, *Le Péril Vénérien et la prostitution à Hanoi,* 184–189; Charbonnier, "Contribution à l'étude de la prophylaxie antivénérienne à Hanoi," 37–38.
4 See Foucault, *Discipline and Punish*; Foucault, *The History of Sexuality,* vol. 1; Matlock, *Scenes of Seduction*; Walkowitz, *Prostitution and Victorian Society.*
5 On the use of bureaucratic systems to control populations, see Scott, *Seeing Like a State.*
6 The regulation codes were initially developed ad-hoc. Miller, "'The Romance of Regulation,'" 17.
7 Decree of April 28, 1886 (Hải Phòng) and decree of December 21, 1888 (Hanoi), printed in Annex of Bernard Joyeux, *Le Péril vénérien et la prostitution à Hanoi.* On the Contagious Diseases Acts, see Levine, *Prostitution, Race, and Politics.*

8 General of Division Lombard to GGI, February 8, 1916. Centre des Archives d'Outre Mer (CAOM), files of the Résidence Supérieure de Tonkin Nouveau Fonds (RSTNF) 3856.

9 General of Division Lombard to GGI, February 8, 1916. CAOM, RSTNF 3856.

10 The Director of the Bureau of Hygiene in Hanoi told Vietnamese journalist Vũ Trọng Phụng that in one study of 4,000 infant deaths, 1,000 were found to have resulted from syphilis. Vũ Trọng Phụng, *Lục Xì: Phóng Sự* (1937), 31; a French public health report from 1928 deemed syphilis the primary cause of newborn mortality (through miscarriage, stillbirth, or infantile death), as well as child mortality generally. "Rapport sur le fonctionnement du service de l'assistance médicale au Tonkin pendant l'année 1928." Vietnam National Archives, Center 1 (VNNA 1), Résidence Supérieure de Tonkin (RST) 32032.

11 "Comité local d'hygiène du Tonkin séance du mardi 2 mars 1920." VNNA 1, RST 32024.

12 Decree of February 3, 1921, printed in B. Joyeux, *Le Péril Vénérien et la prostitution à Hanoi*, 184–189; Charbonnier, "Contribution à l'étude de la prophylaxie antivénérienne à Hanoi," 37–38.

13 As per the 1884 Patenòtre treaty (Treaty of Hue) that established French protectorate status over Annam and Tonkin, Tonkin was officially under the jurisdiction of the Vietnamese king in Huế, who maintained sovereignty over most domestic affairs while remaining subordinate to the French colonial government. Yet, while Tonkin was only indirectly under colonial rule, an 1888 royal ordinance had conceded the cities of Hanoi and Hải Phòng, as well as provincial capitals and military bases, to the French government. Phúc, *Lịch Sử Thăng Long Hà Nội*, 265–267.

14 L'Inspecteur général de l'hygiène et de la sante publique to Directeur des finances de l'Indochine, November 4, 1936. VNNA 1, Maire de Hanoi (MH) 2593.

15 Nguyễn Đình Lạp, "Than niên trụy lạc," 204.

16 Joyeux, *Le Péril Vénérien*, 184–189.

17 Ethnomusicologists Stephen Addiss and Barley Norton date the genesis of modern *á đào* music style to the early years of the Lê Dynasty-era (1428–1777) musical forms called Hát Cửa Đình and Hát Cửa Quyền. Addiss, "Hat a dao," 19–20 and Norton, "Singing the Past," 27–56.

18 "Rapport sur le fonctionnement du service des moeurs du 1er janvier au 31 decembre 1926." VNNA 1, RST 78667.

19 "Bốn quan viên cố ngủ lấy một đêm cuối cùng nữa ở nhà *á đào* để sáng ngày ra gây thành một tấn náo kịch," *Việt Báo*, November 24, 1939, 4.

20 Virgitti and Joyeux, "Les maisons de chanteuses à Hanoi," 81–86. "Lấy đồng-hồ chi chầu hát, một quan viên mới ra thoát nhà cô đầu," Đông Pháp, July 23, 1936.

21 Pettelat to RF Bắc Giang, February 25, 1939. CAOM, RSTNF 746.

22 "Thái Bình: Chị em xóm Vũ Tiên gửi bức thư ngỏ cho ông hội Thiều," *Việt Báo*, August 30, 1939, 3.

23 "Nay mai cô đầu ở Ninh Bình sẻ phải đi khám bệnh," Đông Pháp, October 5, 1938, 1, 5.

24 "Note pout M. le Chef de Bureau," October 25, 1938. CAOM, RSTNF 746.

25 "Mấy nhà hát cô đầu bị phạt 8 hôm không được mở cửa," Đông Pháp, July 19, 1938.

26 "Vậy còn cô đào Hà Nội thì sao?" *Thời Vụ Báo*, August 12, 1938.

27 Nguyễn Thị Loan to RST, September 1, 1938. CAOM, RSTNF 746. For more on the defense of singers, see Firpo, *Black Market Business* and "Sex and Song."

28 "Chị em dưới xóm hồng-lâu đã dọn nhà đi gần hết," Đông Pháp, August 17, 1938.

29 "Muốn tránh nạn đi khám bệnh và theo chị em phố Rợp, chị em Ngã Sáu quyết định đình nghiệp," Đông Pháp, August 13, 1938, 1, 5.

30 "Nay mai cô đầu ở Ninh Bình sẻ phải đi khám bệnh," Đông Pháp, October 5, 1938, 1, 5.

31 Tuy-Tinh, "Tôi ngày, chị nhảy, chúng ta nhảy…," *Hà Thành Ngọ Báo*, September 30, 1933, 1.

32 For example, see Lê Kym Vân, "Hai con dường," *Thời vụ báo*, July 18, 1939, 5; Trần Văn Lý, "Cái Hại Khiêu-Vũ," *Trung Hoà Báo*, June 19, 1937, 1–2; Bạch Đinh, "Những tiệm nhảy ở trước cửa Bồ Đề"; J. Leiba, "Một thiếu nữ ở Hà Thành (Đời thực của một cô gái sống một mình giữa cảnh phồn hoa gió bụi)."

33 Dance halls offered both male and female sex workers, though the sources provide scant information about male sex workers. Marcel Piere and Bernard Joyeux, "Contribution à l'étude des maladies vénériennes au Camp de Tong (Tonkin) et plus spécialement dans l'effectif Furopéen," 1938. VNNA 1, MH 2593.

34 Vũ Trọng Phụng. *Lục xì*, 109–110, 122–128.

35 Virgitti and Joyeux, *Le Péril Vénérien*, 16.

36 Trọng Lang, *Hà Nội lầm than*, 40, 46.

37 Bạch My was the spirit associated with sex workers. Phụng, *Lục xì*, 122.
38 Virgitti and Joyeux, *Le Péril Vénérien*, 16–17.
39 Marcel Piere and Bernard Joyeux, "Contribution à l'étude des maladies vénériennes au Camp de Tong (Tonkin) et plus spécialement dans l'effectif Européen," 1938. VNNA 1, MH 2593.
40 "Rapport d'inspection du 28 avril au 1 mai et du 4 au 6 mai 1943, Municipalité de Haiphong." CAOM, RSTNF 1387.
41 Xuân Chào, "Gập Dâu Nói Dấy: Giêm thuế 'nhầy' tăng giá diện," *Thời Vụ Báo*, February 22, 1938, 7.
42 Trọng Lang, *Hà Nội lầm than*, 28.
43 "Hanoi: Giảm thuế cho các tiệm khiêu vũ," *Trung Hoà Báo*, March 3, 1938, 2.

Bibliography

Addiss, Stephen. "Hat A Dao, The Sung Poetry of North Vietnam." *Journal of the American Oriental Society* 93 (1973): 18–31. doi:10.2307/600514.

Bạch Đinh. "Những tiệm nhảy ở trước cửa Bồ Đề." In *Phóng Sự Việt Nam, 1932–1945, tập 2*, edited by Phan Trọng Thưởng, Nguyễn Cừ, Nguyễn Hữu Sơn, 1239–1243. Hanoi: NXB Văn học, 2000.

Charbonnier, Roger. "Contribution à l'étude de la prophylaxie antivénérienne à Hanoi." Ph.D. diss., Faculté de médecine de Paris, 1938.

Firpo, Christina. "Sex and Song: Clandestine Prostitution in Tonkin's Ả Đào Music Houses, 1920–1940." *Journal of Vietnamese Studies* 11, no. 2 (2016): 1–36. doi:10.1525/jvs.2016.11.2.1.

Firpo, Chirstina. *Black Market Business: Selling Sex in Northern Vietnam*. Ithaca, NY: Cornell University Press, 2020.

Foucault, Michel. *Discipline and Punish: The Birth of the Prison*. Translated by Alan Sheridan. New York: Vintage Press, 1979.

Foucault, Michel. *The History of Sexuality*. Vol. 1. Translated by Robert Hurley. New York: Vintage Press, 1980.

Joyeux, B. *Le Péril Vénérien et la prostitution à Hanoi: État actuel—bibliographie réglementation*. Hanoi: Imprimerie d'Extrême-Orient, 1930.

Leiba, J. "Một thiếu nữ ở Hà Thành (Đời thực của một cô gái sống một mình giữa cảnh phồn hoa gió bụi)." In *Phóng Sự Việt Nam, 1932–1945, tập 2*, edited by Phan Trọng Thưởng, Nguyễn Cừ, Nguyễn Hữu Sơn, 1223–1231. Hanoi: NXB Văn học, 2000.

Levine, Philippa. *Prostitution, Race, and Politics Policing Venereal Disease in the British Empire*. New York: Routledge, 2003.

Matlock, Jann. *Scenes of Seduction: Prostitution, Hysteria, and Reading Difference in 19ᵗʰ Century France*. New York: Columbia University Press, 1994.

Miller, Julia Christine Scriven. "'The Romance of Regulation': The Movement Against State-Regulated Prostitution in France, 1871–1946." Ph.D. diss., New York University, 2000.

Nguyễn Đình Lạp. "Than niên trụy lạc." In *Phóng Sự Việt Nam, 1932–1945, tập 1*, edited by Phan Trọng Thưởng, Nguyễn Cừ, Nguyễn Hữu Sơn, 204. Hanoi: NXB Văn học, 2000.

Nguyễn Vinh Phúc, ed. *Lịch Sử Thăng Long Hà Nội*. Hanoi: Nhà Xuất Bản Thời Đại, 2010.

Norton, Barley. "Singing the Past: Vietnamese Ca Trù, Memory and Mode." *Asian Music* 6 (2005): 27–56. doi:10.1353/amu.2005.0023.

Scott, James. *Seeing Like a State: How Certain Schemes to Improve the Human Condition Have Failed*. New Haven, CT: Yale University Press, 1998.

Spongberg, Mary. *Feminizing Venereal Disease: The Body of the Prostitute in Nineteenth-Century Medical Discourse*. New York: NYU Press, 1997.

Trọng Lang. *Hà Nội lầm than*. Hanoi: NXB Hội Nhà Văn, 2015.

Virgitti, M.H. and B. Joyeux. *Le Péril Vénérien dans la Zone Suburbaine de Hanoi*. Hanoi: Imprimerie d'Extrême-Orient, 1938.

Virgitti, M.H. and B. Joyeux. "Les maisons de chanteuses à Hanoi." *Revue du Paludisme et de Médecine Tropicale* 5 (1947): 81–86.

Vũ Trọng Phụng. *Lục Xì: Phóng Sự (1937)*. Hanoi: Nhà Xuất Bản Văn Học, 2004.

Walkowitz, Judith R. *Prostitution and Victorian Society: Women, Class, and the State*. London: Cambridge University Press, 1980.

16

THE LEAGUE OF NATIONS AND COLONIAL PROSTITUTION

Liat Kozma

The League of Nations, founded in 1920, aspired to bring together former enemies and pre-empt, through international arbitration, armed conflicts. The assumption was that the trauma of World War I was powerful enough to enlist international goodwill and prevent the recurrence of a global war. Alongside these political aspirations, the League had a key role in the emergence of international humanitarian norms. It coordinated international efforts to alleviate disease; nurture intellectual, technological, scientific, and economic collaboration; and suppress traffic in humans and in drugs. The League's involvement in social questions was motivated, at least in part, by a belief that social ills could be eliminated through international collaboration.[1] The role of the League in sanctioning interwar colonialism, but also as a stage for anti-colonial criticism, has been the topic of some scholarly debates in the last 15 years.[2]

One issue that the League took upon itself was traffic in women and children for prostitution. Members of the League signed the 1921 International Convention for the Suppression of the Traffic in Women and Children, and an Advisory Committee on Traffic in Women (henceforth CTW) was founded to monitor compliance. Its members included 11 representatives of the Convention's signatory countries (such as Spain, France, the United States, Britain, Japan, and Uruguay) and five representatives of international organizations against traffic in women.[3] The impact of the CTW's efforts was, first, in restricting the international migration of women traveling alone and, second, by arguing for a connection between regulated prostitution and traffic in women it affected regulation policies worldwide. Philippa Levine, for example, ascribes the abolition of regulation policies in Britain's Asian colonies in the 1920s and 1930s in part to the League's interest in traffic in women and children.[4] Similarly, Leonore Manderson argues that regulated prostitution in British Malaya was suppressed in the 1920s due to political pressure from and commitment to the League of Nations and to British abolitionist organizations.[5]

My purpose here is to explore the connections between the League and interwar colonialism by focusing on the CTW and colonial prostitution in the Middle East and South Asia. I argue here, first, that, instead of mapping coerced traffic in women, the CTW focused on women's migration for prostitution. This focus served the dual purpose of supporting migratory restrictions on undesirable women and the global abolition of licensed brothels. Second, I argue that debates on traffic in women in "the East"—as the CTW's protocols referred to Asia in general, and sometimes to South and Southeast Asia more specifically—reflected colonial

and children from traffic. The declared purpose of these reports was to map the international traffic in women, trace sources of supply and demand, and monitor compliance with the Convention.

In practice the data included information about a variety of topics, such as sexual offenses, immigration policies, and deportation figures. Annual reports on mandatory Iraq, for example, included cases of abduction, rape, and solicitation of minors. These reports also regularly included cases of pederasty—procuring or rape of boys—which was not included in any of the other country reports I reviewed. The reason for the inclusion of such cases is not clear, especially since most of them involved Iraqi men and boys (and, rarely, Persian ones). As for deportation and repatriation, the reports listed mainly the deportation of Syrian and Persian women for prostitution or "immoral character."[19]

Importantly, many of the measures taken to protect women from traffic had the effect in practice of blocking the entry of prostitutes and restricting the migration of unaccompanied women. Country reports for Syria and Lebanon, for example, noted the deportation of French, Greek, Turkish, and Iraqi women, mostly for clandestine prostitution. The report also listed cases in which visas were denied to artists, prostitutes, and women whose request was "considered suspect." In addition, travel documents were issued to women and children only after a thorough enquiry into the reasons for a journey.[20]

In the 1937 Bandung Conference of Central Authorities in Eastern Countries (further discussed below), French representative Prof. A.P.R. Labrouquère of the University of Hanoi listed Chinese and Annamese singing girls in Saigon and Hanoi, "whose position was often difficult to distinguish from that of prostitutes." As for prevention measures, he provided details of enquiries made as to the morals of applicants—not a measure to detect victims but rather a means to detect morally suspicious immigrants. The Japanese delegate, Chikayuki Akaghi, the secretary of the Department of Overseas Affairs, similarly listed Japanese prostitutes in Hong Kong and Singapore, while the Dutch Mr Meyer mentioned measures taken against the migration of prostitutes to the Netherland Indies.[21] Mrs Mukerjee, the Indian representative, noted that the purpose of the measures taken against traffic was "to make it difficult for foreign prostitutes and souteneurs to enter India."[22]

Measures aimed at protecting women from traffic, then, in practice amounted to an international coordinated effort to restrict the mobility of unaccompanied women in an increasingly mobile age. These discussions said nothing about traffic victims or protective measures, but focused instead on the migration of prostitution and measures to contain it. Non-European women's mobility across international borders, moreover, was seen as a threat to their port of destination but not to themselves. In addition, these deliberations reflected colonial biases regarding the sexuality of colonized populations: be it pederasty in the Iraqi case or, as we will see below, Islamic oppression of women or Indian promiscuity. These reports, moreover, absolved colonial authorities of any responsibility for prostitution in the colonies.

Besides these annual reports, the CTW conducted on-the-ground investigations, designed to detect those aspects of traffic in women that governments were trying to conceal. The first traveling commission (1924–1925) was composed of three American investigators who visited more than 100 cities in the Americas, Europe and around the Mediterranean. They interviewed state officials and conducted undercover investigations that brought them into contact with the underworld of migratory prostitution. Their visits to the Middle East and North Africa were marked by little interest in local prostitution or in French or British regulation policies. The mandate of the commission was to investigate international traffic in women, so local women were of little interest. Moreover, since they spoke only European languages, they had no means of interviewing, for example, Syrian prostitutes in Palestine,

Lebanon, or Egypt. Importantly (and controversially), the ensuing report concluded that licensed brothels had an adverse effect on efforts to stem international traffic in women. This conclusion, which had little basis in the report's own data, paved the way for adoption of the abolition of licensed brothels as the CTW's main policy goal in the following years.[23]

The "Travelling Commission to the East" (1932) concentrated on traffic in women in Asia and was intended to fill the lacuna created by the first traveling commission. It visited regions that the first one had not, namely most of Asia, as well as some territories that the first had already visited, namely Palestine and Lebanon. Due to criticism of the first commission's clandestine methods, the second one now conducted its investigations in collaboration with state authorities and interviewed only state officials.[24] The initial mission of the Travelling Commission to the East relied on the assumption of a "profound difference of mentality between East and West and even between different Eastern countries." The CTW instructed the commission to "bear these differences carefully in mind in determining the nature and extent of the enquiries to be made and the methods to be followed in conducting the investigation."[25]

The products of the annual reports and both traveling commissions echoed colonial biases on Asian and Middle Eastern sexuality. These reports understood prostitution in Islamic societies, for example, in terms of women's seclusion and the threat of "honor killing." Country reports on the Middle East maintained that integration into regulated brothels virtually saved women from being murdered by their kin, as "fallen women" had no chance of reintegration into society.[26] For Transjordan, the British report explained that precautions against traffic in women were "unnecessary in a country composed of small villages or nomads where everybody knows what the others do and where children and women are very jealously guarded."[27]

The traveling commission's report on the East similarly concluded that Islam provided enough protection against prostitution as to obviate measures on the part of colonial authorities: "The custom of the Muslims tends strongly to prevent prostitution and traffic. Women are kept in seclusion and have few opportunities of meeting men. In certain districts, infidelity on the part of women is visited with death and generally speaking, the tenets of their religion enforces strongly the protection of the chastity of women."[28] In Lebanon the commission similarly concluded, "there is the restraining effect that women with Moslems mostly keep to the house and are rigorously watched when they go out."[29] For Iraq, the police told the commission that inquiries about prostitution were necessarily incomplete, since "many women thought to be prostitutes would have risked death had their families even suspected that enquiries were being made about them in this connection."[30] For Islamic societies, then, prostitution did not require any intervention. If native prostitution did exist, it was only because local societies left women with little choice; or because women themselves went to great lengths to circumvent protection. Seclusion and the threat of murder presumably protected Muslim women from prostitution.

In other societies, reports to the League highlighted indigenous promiscuity. British and Portuguese authorities in India blamed the ban on widows' remarriage for the prevalence of prostitution in India, and claimed that as many as 30 per cent of Indian prostitutes were young widows.[31] Special attention was paid to the devadasis, women dedicated to Hindu temples. Trained in dancing and poetry, these women also formed sexual unions with high-class men. Colonial authorities saw them as prostitutes and designed policies that, in practice, criminalized and impoverished the women, eventually driving them into actual prostitution.[32] British and Portuguese oral and written reports to the League reflected similar biases. In the Bandung Conference, the delegate from Portuguese India explained that "Devadasism" was virtually "compelling women of a certain caste to become prostitutes."[33]

As for European women, the second traveling commission concluded that their migration for prostitution to the East (here, Asia in general) was in decline, and that "prostitutes who go to the Middle or Far East seek their clients among their own race."[34] The implication of this observation was that, as long as migrant European prostitutes did not fraternize with colonized men, their limited presence in the East could be tolerated. The reason for the decline in demand was that European officials now settled in the colonies with their wives, since "conditions in the East are more suitable to family life of Occidentals." "Prostitutes from the Occident," moreover, "are replaced by Russians in the Far East, as well as by women of mixed blood."[35]

Concerns about miscegenation were shared by the Japanese government, which made significant efforts to repatriate Japanese prostitutes abroad by pressuring or convincing them to leave. The presence of these women in foreign countries "reflected on the prestige of Japan and adversely affected the sound development of Japanese interest abroad." The objection of the Japanese government and Japanese communities abroad was to "Japanese prostitutes catering for men of other races." Like European women, the presence of Japanese prostitutes was tolerated if their number was limited to a level "required to meet an almost exclusive demand by Japanese men in the cities concerned."[36]

Since numbers of European prostitutes in Asia were dropping, the CTW's attention shifted to Russian women in the East; in this case China, and particularly Shanghai. Following the Russian Revolution and subsequent civil war, White Russians found refuge in Manchuria, where large clusters of Russian settlements had already existed around the Russian-owned China Eastern Railroad. Several processes—including the Soviet takeover of the railroad company, economic hardship, and later Japanese occupation—pushed White Russians to other parts of China, including Shanghai, in search of livelihoods. Poverty and male unemployment drove some women to the entertainment industry and to prostitution to supplement household income. Foreign commentaries subsequently raised concerns about the threat these women posed to white prestige.[37] Reporter John Pal, who lived in Shanghai in the 1930s, ascribed the League's interest in the fate of White Russians to European colonial anxieties: "The appearance of white women in such disgraceful capacity as that of prostitutes among the natives of the lower class affects very deeply the prestige of the Western Nations in the Orient."[38]

In 1934 the League's assembly asked the CTW to examine the problem of those Russian women who had fallen into prostitution. The ensuing report found that the women constituted "a source of supply for almost the entire occidental prostitution in the great international commercial centers of China." The CTW concluded that the most effective way to address the problem would be "to increase considerably the social measures available to women of Russian origin in Harbin and other places in Manchuria," and thus prevent them from drifting into prostitution.[39] Indeed, unlike Chinese prostitutes, whose rehabilitation was never discussed, the future employment of these women was crucial. The 1934 report recommended "to direct women and girls into the following professions: shorthand and typewriting, bookkeeping, accountancy, correspondences, etc.," namely "fields in which Chinese labor cannot compete."[40]

In conclusion, then, the discussion of traffic in women was in line with colonial interests and priorities. Central to these debates were concerns about miscegenation, white prestige, and the ability to contain the migration of undesirable women. The policy implications of these debates targeted both migration policies and the abolition of licensed houses. Both brought to the fore, most powerfully, colonial modes of control.

The Bandung Conference and the abolition of licensed houses in South and Southeast Asia

In 1934, following the report of both traveling commissions, the League's assembly passed a resolution urging governments to abolish the system of licensed brothels.[41] This report helped to convince governments to move toward abolition.[42] The same year, a report of the CTW on abolition of licensed houses sought to assess the outcome of the abolition of licensed brothels on traffic in women, venereal diseases, sex offences, public order, and former prostitutes themselves. The report was based, partially, on data received from Britain, France, and the Netherlands regarding their experiences with abolition in their South and Southeast Asian colonies.[43] The suitability of various cultures to abolition was at the heart of the discussion.

Three years later a Conference of Central Authorities in Eastern Countries was held in Bandung. Its purpose was to coordinate regional efforts to contain traffic in women and to follow up on the CTW's report on traffic in women in Asia.[44] The conference was composed of representatives of British, French, Dutch, and Portuguese authorities in South and Southeast Asia, alongside Japanese and Siamese authorities and representatives of international voluntary organizations.[45]

In the conference's opening speech, K.L.J. Enthoven, Director of the Department of Justice, the Netherland Indies, declared that "The initiative for convening it did not arise in the Far East. This event comes rather as a surprise to the East. A great proportion of public opinion in the Far East is still very little acquainted with the problems to be dealt with."[46] Joseph Avenol, the Secretary General of the League, dispatched a similar message that was read at the conference opening: "The subject with which this Conference is called upon to deal, the part of the world with which it is concerned, and the place in which it is being held should confound all those who have alleged that the League of Nations is chiefly a European organization, and that it is almost exclusively interested in political questions.[47]"

Both statements reflected the conference's aspirations as well as its blind spots. Both reflect an attempt to situate the League's work as truly global, rather than European. The list of colonial officers and the absence of indigenous ones, however, reflects the limitation of this aspiration. Both quotes, moreover, present regulated prostitution and traffic in women as social problems that the East had not yet come to recognize. As we will see below, delegates debated why local societies were not yet ready for abolition and immigration control but ignored the colonial authorities' role in regulated prostitution and in creating preconditions for migratory prostitution. It was noted with satisfaction that the conference's stand on abolition was a "milestone in the progress towards abolition … it was the first occasion on which not a single delegation had tried to justify regulation outright."[48] For many of the delegates, however, this aspiration was no more than lip service.

Both the 1934 report on abolition and the 1937 Bandung Conference reflected ambiguity regarding the suitability of South and Southeast Asian societies for abolition. In 1934 the British maintained that the closing of licensed brothels would not eliminate prostitution in India, "so long as an abnormal [i.e., local] demand for promiscuous intercourse on a commercial basis remains." Reducing demand would have to include "increase in recreational facilities for adults and young people," women's literacy, "popular enlightenment on the harmful personal and social effects of commercialized prostitution," and sex education that would raise a generation "favorable to the increased sense of personal responsibility for personal, social and racial health." According to the British authorities, then, Indian society needed to be re-educated for abolition to be effective.[49]

Such cultural shifts were arguably happening elsewhere in the empire. For the Straits Settlements, Federated Malay States, Johore, and Kedah the British noted a decrease in prostitution and traffic in women alongside an increase in clandestine prostitution. A decline in prostitution was attributed to leisure activities: "steadily increasing appreciation of games and outdoor sports ... dancing is becoming more popular with Asians, and dance-halls, respectable in character, are increasing in number. ... The custom of 'walking out' openly with friends of the opposite sex appears to be rapidly taking hold of the Chinese. Asiatic adults are taking an increasing interest in outdoor games."[50] This report concluded, moreover, that the shutting of licensed houses "closed the market provided by the brothels, and to that extent reduced the commercial value of the business." In addition, after the abolition of compulsory examinations, voluntary venereal disease clinics now attracted men and women, both married women and clandestine prostitutes. Finally, where propaganda campaigns prepared the ground for abolition, women were reabsorbed into the general social structure.[51]

Similarly the British authorities highlighted changing migration patterns, which had led to a more balanced gender ratio among the Chinese in Malaya. The outcome was that more locally born Chinese women took to prostitution, "leaving less demand for prostitutes from China." More Chinese men were getting married, which further decreased the demand for prostitution. More stringent immigration regulation, moreover, made the examination of passengers easier and more effective, thus making traffic in women more difficult.[52]

The Dutch representative to the Bandung Conference, J.A. Meyer, Inspector of Discipline, Education, Reclassification and Public Assistance in the Netherland Indies, claimed that the native society in the Netherland Indies might be more receptive to abolition than European societies because prostitution was not stigmatized as in Europe. Local society was "not yet so individualist," and thus "had proved more capable than Europe of absorbing and taking care of the victims of prostitution. The causes leading to prostitution were less active and less incurable than in Europe, and could therefore be more easily removed."[53]

Other colonial representatives, on the other hand, explained at length why abolition was not yet feasible in their respective colonies. In French Indochina, for example, Prof. Labrouquère explained that illiteracy and the absence of birth registration made the protection of women from traffic impossible without state-regulated brothels. In addition, the sex trade suffered from an influx of women of mixed ancestry, marginalized by both European and indigenous society. These women "desire to live like Europeans," but cannot make European salaries and thus become "easy victims to prostitution."[54] The Portuguese delegate, from Macao, stated that prostitution was indeed an "evil which should be eliminated from society," but it was first necessary to reform economic and social conditions "of a district, of a country, and of the world in general." Abolition of regulated prostitution would lead to increased clandestine prostitution and the spread of venereal disease and increase the display of vice in the street and brothels accessible to inexperienced youth.[55]

The conference concluded that "public opinion would not yet condemn brothels on such grounds as, for instance, that to be kept in a brothel was against human dignity of a woman ... in some countries, public opinion has only just begun to count in this question."[56] It was therefore advisable not to rush "the East" and instead wait for favorable public opinion to develop. After that point, abolition would be accompanied by administrative, medical, and social measures.[57] "Abolitionism, which was a very fine aspiration of the human soul," claimed Prof. Alberto Correia, Sub-Director of the Health Service in Portuguese India, "could not be put into practice everywhere with the same facility as in certain countries which had long been prepared for it."[58]

Conclusion

Deliberations on traffic in women in Asia ascribed the phenomenon to Chinese families who sold their daughters, to Indian temple dedication, or to Muslims' reluctance to accept women's premarital sexuality. The creation of regional ports such as Hong Kong and Singapore and the ensuing formation of male worker communities was not discussed. It was therefore only white women who could be trafficked to begin with, and whose forced prostitution deserved international intervention. In addition, Chinese and Indians were supposedly not ready for abolition of regulated prostitution; but it was colonial authorities that imposed regulation to begin with, and the CTW did not bother to ask local societies what their actual aspirations were.

Elsewhere I have analyzed what Egyptian feminists were saying about abolition. They employed the League's reports to press the British colonial authorities to abolish licensed houses in their country. To complement the present article, more research is needed to trace Indian, Chinese, and Vietnamese voices and examine what impact, if any, the CTW's policies had on local debates on prostitution, migration, and regulation.[59]

Notes

1 See for example, García, Rodogno and Kozma, *The League of Nations*; Pedersen, "Back to the League of Nations"; Borowy, *Coming to Terms With World Health*; Watenpaugh, "The League of Nations' Rescue of Armenian Genocide Survivors."
2 See for example, Pedersen, *The Guardians*; Anghie, *Imperialism*, 115–195.
3 Limoncelli, *The Politics of Trafficking*; Kozma, *Global Women*; Chaumont, *Le Mythe de la Traité des Blanches*.
4 Levine, *Prostitution, Race, and Politics*, 126.
5 Manderson, "Colonial Desires," 386.
6 Warren, *Ah Ku and Karayuki-san*; Manderson, "Colonial Desires," 374; Sinn, "Women at Work."
7 Levine, *Prostitution, Race, and Politics*; Manderson, "Colonial Desires," 386.
8 Levine, *Prostitution, Race, and Politics*.
9 Ibid.; Warren, "*Ah Ku and Karayuki-san*," 362.
10 Levine, *Prostitution, Race, and Politics*, 134.
11 "International Conference on Traffic in Women and Children: Final Act," *League of Nations – Official Journal* (July-August 1921), 598–599.
12 LNA, Traffic in Women and Children, resolutions adopted by the Assembly, the Council and the Traffic in Women and Children Committee, CTFE 359 (1), 20.11.1929.
13 Chaumont, *Le Mythe de la Traité des Blanches*; Limoncelli, *The Politics of Trafficking*.
14 LNA, Box 669, Dossier 25965, document no. 26004, Traffic in women and children in mandated territories: Various Correspondences with Associations for Moral and Social Hygiene & other Associations.
15 League of Nations, Permanent Mandate Commission (PMC), *Minutes of the Sixth Session, Held at Geneva from June 26th to July 10th 1925*, C.648.M.237.1925.VI. (Geneva: The League of Nations, 1925), 100–1, 116–117, 169–170.
16 Ibid., 134.
17 League of Nations, PMC, *Minutes of the Seventh Session, Held at Geneva from October 19th to October 30th 1925*, C.648.M.237.1925.VI. (Geneva: The League of Nations, 1925), 79.
18 LNA, Traffic in women and children: extension of the enquiry on traffic in women and children in the East: information concerning French mandate territories, C.T.F.E Orient/10, 21.8.1930; LNA, Traffic in women and children: extension of the enquiry on traffic in women and children in the East: A report concerning Palestine, CTFE Orient/29, 25.7.1932.
19 League of Nations, *Traffic in Women and Children, Summary of Annual Reports for 1926, prepared by the Secretariat, Geneva, January 31st, 1928*, C.28. M. 14. 1928 IV, p. 3, 10; League of Nations, *Traffic in Women and Children, Summary of Annual Reports for 1928, prepared by the Secretariat, Geneva, January 15th, 1930*, C.85. M. 12. 1930 IV, p. 5.

20 League of Nations, *Traffic in Women and Children, Summary of Annual Reports for 1933–34, prepared by the Secretariat, Geneva, March 19th*, 1935, C.127. M. 65. 1935 IV, p. 20.
21 *Conference of Central Authorities in Eastern Countries (Bandoeng, Java, February 2nd to 13th, 1937): Minutes of Meetings* (Geneva: League of Nations, 1937), 12–13.
22 Ibid., 30.
23 Chaumont, *Le Mythe de la Traité des Blanches*.
24 Kozma, *Global Women*, 37.
25 LNA, "Traffic in women and children: Preliminary information for the enquiry of the traffic in women in the East," C.T.F.E Orient/1, 14.8.1930, p. 6.
26 *Report by His Britannic Majesty's Government to the Council of the League of Nations on the administration of Iraq for the Year 1925* (London: Colonial Office, 1926), 6.
27 LNA, Advisory Committee on Social Questions, Summary of Annual Reports for 1937–38, prepared by the Secretariat, Obscene Publications, Geneva, 1.1.1939. C.69.M.31. 1939. IV, p. 4.
28 *Commission of Enquiry into Traffic in Women and Children in the East: Report to the Council* (Geneva: The League of Nations, 1932), 15–16.
29 Ibid., 426.
30 Ibid., 407.
31 *Conference of Central Authorities*, 40.
32 Sreenivas, "Creating Conjugal Subjects."
33 League of Nations, *Traffic in Women and Children: Work of the Bandoeng Conference*, C.516.M.357.1937. IV. (Geneva: The League of Nations, 1937), 9.
34 *Commission of Enquiry*, 16.
35 Ibid., 22–24, 145.
36 Ibid., 69–70.
37 Newham, "The White Russians of Shanghai."
38 Pal, *Shanghai Saga*, 20–21; quoted in Hershatter, *Dangerous Pleasures*, 429n145.
39 *Position of Women of Russian Origin in the Far East* (Geneva: League of Nations, 1935), 1.
40 Ibid., 5, 15.
41 *Conference of the Central Authorities*, 36.
42 Ibid., 43.
43 *Abolition of Licensed Houses* (Geneva: League of Nations, 1934).
44 *Work of the Bandoeng Conference*, 27.
45 Ibid., 25.
46 *Conference of Central Authorities*, 6.
47 Ibid., 8.
48 Ibid., 42.
49 *Abolition of Licensed Houses*, 62.
50 Ibid., 82–83.
51 Ibid., 62–63.
52 *Conference of Central Authorities*, 83.
53 Ibid., 62.
54 Ibid., 36.
55 Ibid., 38.
56 *Work of the Bandoeng Conference*, 48.
57 Ibid., 53.
58 *Conference of Central Authorities*, 53.
59 Kozma, *Global Women*, 135–136.

Bibliography

Anghie, Antony. *Imperialism, Sovereignty, and the Making of International Law*. Cambridge, UK: Cambridge University Press, 2004. doi:10.1017/CBO9780511614262.
Borowy, Iris. *Coming to Terms With World Health: The League of Nation's Health Organisation 1921–1946*. Frankfurt: Peter Lang, 2009.
Chaumont, Jean-Michel. *Le Mythe de la Traité des Blanches: Enquête sur la Fabrication d'un Fléau*. Paris: Decouverte, 2009.

García, Magaly Rodríguez, Davide Rodogno and Liat Kozma. *The League of Nations' Work On Social Issues: Visions, Endeavours and Experiments*. Geneva: United Nations, 2016.

Hershatter, Gail. *Dangerous Pleasures: Prostitution and Modernity in Twentieth-Century Shanghai*. Berkeley, CA: University of California Press, 1997.

Kozma, Liat. *Global Women, Colonial Ports: Prostitution in the Interwar Middle East*. Albany, NY: SUNY Press, 2017.

Levine, Philippa. *Prostitution, Race, and Politics: Policing Venereal Disease in the British Empire*. New York: Routledge, 2003.

Limoncelli, Stephanie. *The Politics of Trafficking: The First International Movement to Combat the Sexual Exploitation of Women*. Stanford, CA: Stanford University Press, 2010.

Manderson, Lenore. "Colonial Desires: Sexuality, Race, and Gender in British Malaya." *Journal of the History of Sexuality* 7 no. 3 (1997): 372–388.

Newham, Fraser. "The White Russians of Shanghai." *History Today* 55, no. 12 (December 2005): 20–27.

Pedersen, Susan. "Back to the League of Nations: Review Essay." *American Historical Review* 112 (2007): 1091–1117. doi:10.1086/ahr.112.4.1091.

Pedersen, Susan. *The Guardians: The League of Nations and the Crisis of Empire*. Oxford, UK: Oxford University Press, 2015.

Sinn, Elizabeth. "Women at Work: Chinese Brothel Keepers in Nineteenth-Century Hong Kong." *Journal of Women's History* 19, no. 3 (2007): 87–111.

Sreenivas, Mytheli. "Creating Conjugal Subjects: Devadasis and the Politics of Marriage in Colonial Madras Presidency." *Feminist Studies* 37 (2011): 63–92.

Warren, James Francis. *Ah Ku and Karayuki-san: Prostitution in Singapore, 1870–1940*. Singapore: Singapore University Press, 2003.

Watenpaugh, Keith David. "The League of Nations' Rescue of Armenian Genocide Survivors and the Making of Modern Humanitarianism, 1920–1927." *American Historical Review* 115 (2010): 1315–1339. doi:10.1086/ahr.115.5.1315.

17

"IN CONSONANCE WITH THEIR SACRED LAWS"

The colonial remaking of religious courts in Iraq

Sara Pursley

In most modern Middle Eastern states, laws related to marriage and divorce are based on the religion or sect to which particular citizens belong rather than on a unified civil code applicable to all citizens.[1] This system of "legal dualism"—whereby family laws are adjudicated differently from other laws—is often contrasted with legal systems in modern European states, where "marriage came to seen as contractual and regulated by secular civil codes that applied uniformly to all European subjects."[2] Until the past two decades, scholars typically explained legal dualism as a "traditional" remnant. It was imagined either as a failure of Muslim-majority societies to secularize within the "sacred" arena of family law or, more specifically, as a legacy of the late nineteenth-century Ottoman millet system, in which recognized non-dominant religious communities (millets), in particular Christians and Jews, maintained some jurisdiction over personal status laws, or codes related to marriage, divorce, child custody, and inheritance.

Recent scholarship has challenged these explanations, positing systems of legal dualism instead (or also) as a legacy of the global colonial order and the emergence of the secular nation-state. In an influential intervention, Talal Asad argued that the concept of "family law"—and indeed of "family" itself—was unknown in Islamic legal discourse prior to the nineteenth century, and linked its emergence to that of the liberal secular nation-state and its public–private distinction. As religion, morality, and the family were all relegated to the modern private sphere, they became linked to one another in unprecedented ways.[3] Saba Mahmood, extending Asad's argument, linked this process to new religious conflicts and struggles over "minority rights" in modern Egypt, as family law came "to bear an inordinate weight in the reproduction and preservation of religious identity" under secular logics of governance.[4]

In this article I build on these interventions in several ways. I focus mainly on a historical context that has not received much attention in this scholarship, that of Iraq during the British wartime occupation (1914–1920) and mandate (1920–1932) periods. I first trace a colonial genealogy of modern legal dualism in Iraq, showing how the British radically overhauled the Ottoman system of family-law courts and jurisdictions even while (sometimes) claiming to have simply maintained it. The emerging colonial notion of "development along native lines" provided justification for maintaining separate religious laws for personal status issues, which on the face of it resembled the Ottoman millet system. Thus Noga Efrati, a rare historian who has discussed family law in Iraq during this period, asserts that British policy was to "maintain the Ottoman court system and laws to the greatest extent possible."[5]

In contrast to this assertion, I argue that "development along native lines" did not translate into a simple continuation of Ottoman legal institutions. Rather, it involved active state intervention to define and contain different types of natives through the regulated application of their existing laws in new ways. The concept applied not only to the Iraqi population as a whole but also to specific populations defined along sectarian or racial lines. In the case of the former, each sect was imagined to exist partly through the particularity of its family law. Rather than attempt to reform the content of religious family laws, British policy was concerned with confining "religion" to the private sphere of family and morality and with reducing the porosity of boundaries between religious and sectarian communities. Starting during the occupation of Ottoman Iraq in World War I, and continuing under British mandate rule in the 1920s, reforms of family-law jurisdiction aimed to produce a religious identity between court, judge, litigants, and the law—thus ending Ottoman forms of porosity between religious communities, such as through the practice of "forum shopping"—and to bring religious courts under state supervision. This contributed to the hardening of communal boundaries and curtailed the independence of non-Sunni systems of religious law in comparison to Ottoman times.

Finally, I identify a second genealogy of Iraq's dual legal system, that of international law, whose constitutive role in shaping Iraq's legal system was intimately related but not entirely reducible to that of British colonial law. Ultimately, colonial law worked together with international law, building on the existing system of Ottoman law, to fortify communal boundaries through the regulation of family-law courts.

"Sacred laws and racial ideals": development along native lines

Upon the British army's occupation of Baghdad in March 1917, military commander Stanley Maude issued a proclamation to the city's residents:

> But you people of Baghdad, whose commercial prosperity and whose safety from oppression and invasion must ever be a matter of the closest concern to the British Government, are not to understand that it is the wish of the British Government to impose upon you alien institutions … [O]nce again the people of Baghdad shall flourish, enjoying their wealth and substance under institutions which are in consonance with their sacred laws and their racial ideals.[6]

The promise that Britain would not impose "alien institutions" upon the people, but would instead respect their "sacred laws" and "racial ideals," was drawn from existing colonial practices of rule. But the form of British governance that emerged in Iraq also differed from earlier colonial experiences. It was shaped by the emerging colonial notion of "development along native lines," which in Iraq involved particular forms of regulating religious and racial affiliations.

As I have argued elsewhere, British policy in Iraq was oriented toward producing a stable and ultimately independent state whose territory would be open to projects of "economic development," which in this period referred to the creation of infrastructure to enable the extraction of resources (in Iraq's case taxes, agricultural products, and oil). Disciplining the population in the interest of this stability was to be attained in two main ways: the direct application of violence, especially through the new technology of airpower; and the creation of a pluralistic legal system based on principles of separation and containment rather than the application of uniform disciplinary mechanisms. In other words, British policy in Iraq was not oriented toward the kinds of biopolitical interventions into the population and its everyday forms of life that have been the focus of much scholarship on colonial policy in Egypt, India, and elsewhere. Iraq was Britain's (and the world's) first large-scale imperial experiment in "rule from the air," or what British officials called "control without occupation." This had significant effects on the application of the theory of development along native lines.[7]

The "sacred laws" invoked in Maude's proclamation almost surely referred to religious family laws. And, indeed, a few months later the British implemented a radical alteration to the Ottoman system of family-law courts, despite the fact that occupying forces, under international law, were responsible for maintaining existing legal systems in territories occupied during wartime. In December 1917—remarkably, given that the war was still raging and the occupation expanding northward—the British military issued an ordinance limiting the jurisdiction of the existing Ottoman shari'a courts, which ruled on personal status cases in accordance with Sunni Hanafi law, to "suits concerning Sunni Mohammedans." Personal status suits involving Shi'i Muslims, Jews, or Christians would be transferred to British-run civil courts and decided in accordance with the religious law of the litigants. "Suits concerning Shi'ahs will be decided in accordance with Shi'ah law; those concerning Christians in accordance with the customs of the sect to which they belong and those concerning Jews in accordance with Jewish law." The ordinance directed that civil court judges, who were unlikely to be trained in the relevant religious law, refer to a "Shi'ah religious jurist or to the Christian or Jewish religious authorities as the case may require."[8]

British officials justified this reform on the grounds that non-Sunnis should not be subject to Sunni family laws, thus heralding it as a "measure of justice to the Shi'ah, Christian and Jewish communities."[9] What such explanations failed to mention was that, under Ottoman rule, members of these communities had not been *required* to use the official Hanafi shari'a courts, though they were free to avail themselves of those courts if they wished. Alternatively, they could and did appeal to the rulings of their own religious authorities.[10] Christians and Jews did this through the officially recognized "millet" courts. The Ottoman state did not officially recognize Shi'ism as a religious community nor the Ja'fari (Shi'i) madhhab as a legitimate Islamic legal school, but, in practice, Shi'i laypeople often simply took disputes to their own religious authorities. The ordinance thus did not extend new rights to non-Sunni communities. Rather, it had two different effects. First, it removed the option of "forum shopping" for non-Sunni subjects, who would now be required, as Sunni Muslims already were, to follow *only* the family laws of their own religious authorities. Second, court hearings and rulings on personal status cases for all recognized religious communities would now be regulated by the fledgling state of the British military occupation rather than, or at least in addition to, autonomously within those communities.

Both effects were strengthened by other reforms over the next few years. As it turned out, the use of civil courts for personal status cases for non-Sunni litigants was only a temporary measure. In the second phase of the process, separate religious personal status courts for each recognized non-Sunni community were either created (in the case of the Shi'a) or brought under direct state supervision (in the case of Christians and Jews), and litigants were instructed to stop using civil courts for family-law disputes. The establishment of a Shi'i shari'a court system, in which Shi'i judges were appointed and paid by the state, was a particularly radical innovation in comparison to both the Ottoman system of Hanafi shari'a courts and the existing system of Shi'i jurisprudence that functioned outside of state supervision.

Sexual decadence, religious morality, and the law

British justifications both for maintaining the Ottoman Sunni courts and for breaking with the Ottoman system by establishing official Shiʻi personal status laws and courts stood in some tension with a prevalent British colonial discourse on the sexual decadence and historical backwardness of Islamic family law in general and Shiʻi family law in particular. This discourse condemned all schools of Islamic law for allowing male unilateral divorce and polygamy, while Shiʻi law was singled out for permitting *mutʻa*, or temporary, marriage—i.e., marriage contracted for a specified period of time, which might be one hour or 99 years. Thomas Lyell, a criminal court judge in the British military administration, wrote that *mutʻa* marriage provides Shiʻa with "a life of uncontrolled libertinism" and that the Sunnis "rightly regard this system with extreme disgust."[11] He invoked the horror of *mutʻa* marriage as a reason for continuing the British occupation of Iraq: "To have relieved them from the tyranny of the Turk would be a small matter, if we leave them under the tyranny of their own 'Holy Men,' with full opportunity to promulgate their revolting doctrines of temporary marriage, and concubinage, resulting in an ever-increasing degeneracy and ineptitude."[12]

Indeed, British claims of the backwardness of sexual and gender norms in Iraq were typically invoked, not to argue for modern disciplinary interventions into everyday life but rather to establish the need for British governance.[13] Noting "a most distressing prevalence of homosexuality, and even bestiality" in the Shiʻi shrine cities, Lyell asserts that "one is literally aghast at the thought of such people having any say in the matter of their government."[14] Yet, even in a commentator as biased against Islam and Shiʻism as Lyell, there are hints of the reasoning that shaped British support for parallel Sunni and Shiʻi shariʻa personal status courts. He distinguished between the corruption of modern-day jurists and the essential morality of religion. "I do not, of course, refer to the actual teaching of the Quran. Were the standard of morality therein laid down strictly observed, there would be little ground for complaint. But as the vast majority of Muslims are utterly ignorant of their Holy Book, we cannot judge them by it."[15] As an example, he pointed to "promiscuous divorce," which had "grown up through a misunderstanding of Quranic teaching."[16]

British justifications for maintaining the Ottoman shariʻa courts in the first place centered on the desirability of keeping family law within the domain of the "sacred," a discourse that aligned religion, family, and morality and located all of them within the private sphere, beyond the reach of universal or public civil law, the type of law that British jurists might provide. Edgar Bonham-Carter, Senior Judicial Officer of the British military occupation, wrote a report in December 1917 on the administration of law in the occupied territories. He justified maintaining the Hanafi shariʻa courts for personal status cases for Sunnis, rather than transferring such cases to British civil magistrates, on the grounds that such courts were "interpreters of the sacred law," even when the law in question was at odds with British norms.

> [A] judge should be in accord with the law which he is administering, and this is especially the case as regards a religious law … [W]hen as head of the Sudan Legal Department, which comprised a large number of Mohammedan Courts, I received a petition from a litigant dissatisfied with the application to his or her case of a principle of Mohammedan Law, which is not in accord with Western ideas, such as the law of divorce or the right to the custody of children, I always felt that my position and that of the Government was a much stronger one, than, if as a British judge I had given the decision myself.[17]

This notion of a desired religious identity between court, judge, litigants, and the law was very different from the logic shaping the Ottoman system within which the Hanafi courts had previously functioned. These courts had been available to all Ottoman subjects as the "official" shari'a courts of the realm, though not as the only option for non-Sunnis. They reflected the primacy of Sunni Islam as the foundation of universal law in the empire as well as the policy of granting limited autonomy to other religious communities within a hierarchical but semi-porous order. The British system, while building on the existing Ottoman legal infrastructure, was guided by a very different form of reasoning, based on the notion of equal but discrete religious identities whose jurisdictional boundaries would be policed by the state and whose recognition by the state would bestow legal rights and constraints.[18] Family law was key to this system.

The new legal dualism

The new system was established in two phases. For several years after the 1917 ordinance banning Shi'a, Christians, and Jews from using the Ottoman Hanafi courts, a majority of cases heard in the civil courts involved personal status disputes between litigants from those communities. In Baghdad in 1919, of 3,280 cases initiated in the civil courts of first instance there were 1,966 Shi'i and 505 Christian or Jewish personal status cases.[19] During the same year, 1,203 personal status cases were heard in the Sunni shari'a court in Baghdad.[20] Meanwhile, non-Sunnis continued to also take disputes directly to their own religious authorities, the Shi'a informally and Christians and Jews through the millet courts that had been recognized by the Ottoman state.

The second phase, of establishing specific religious courts under state supervision, started early for the Shi'a. The idea was to create a system of shari'a courts applying Ja'fari (Shi'i) law that was fully parallel to the Hanafi shari'a court system. The first courts were created at the end of 1919; i.e., before the League of Nations had recognized the British mandate over Iraq.[21]

The 1923 Organic Law, or Iraqi constitution, divided the judicial system into three types of courts: civil, religious, and special. The religious courts were further subdivided into two types: shari'a courts for Muslims and "spiritual councils of the communities" for Christians and Jews. The shari'a courts had exclusive jurisdiction over "actions relating to the personal status of Muslims and actions relating [to] the administration of their waqf foundations." In other words, Shi'a were no longer allowed to use the civil courts for personal status cases. Judgments were to be administered in accordance with "the particular shari'a rulings of each of the Islamic sects," and each qadi, or judge, of a religious court "shall be a member of the sect [*madhhab* in the Arabic version] to which the majority of the inhabitants of the place to which he is appointed belong"; Baghdad and Basra were to have both Sunni and Shi'i qadis.[22]

Also in 1923, in line with the constitution, a law was passed mandating that judges appointed to all official shari'a courts be either Shi'i or Sunni according to "the prevailing sect in the locality."[23] While the judge of each district's shari'a court was henceforth to be a member of the majority sect in the district, he was always to apply the family law of the sect to which the litigants belonged, consulting with authorities from that sect as needed. This system was a significant break both from the Ottoman system, whereby judges of the official shari'a courts ruled in accordance with Hanafi law regardless of the sect or *madhhab* (legal school) of the litigants, but also from existing Shi'i systems of jurisprudence. In contrast to the latter, judges in the new courts were appointed and paid by the state and assigned to particular geographical districts rather than being chosen by the litigants themselves from among the qualified jurists.

For some time into the 1920s and possibly 1930s, Christians and Jews continued to have the option of taking their cases either to the civil courts or to their own communal courts, officially recognized but not directly overseen by the state. This lack of government oversight of the communal courts was a cause of increasing discomfort to British authorities, and they were slowly brought under closer supervision. In 1924 a British report noted that the existing Christian and Jewish courts were still not "included in the judicial system, and legislation is required in the near future to provide for their proper establishment, in accordance with the Organic Law."[24] Laws establishing the parameters for Armenian Orthodox and Jewish personal status courts were only passed in 1931, the year before formal Iraqi independence.[25]

Development along Shi'i lines

The effects of the reforms on Shi'i personal status disputes and on those for Christians and Jews were thus similar in the sense that they resulted in separate religious courts, regulated by the state but applying the law of the sectarian community in question. But there were also important differences, both because Shi'i law was not treated the same as Christian and Jewish law in Ottoman times and because the British had different kinds of interests in each community. Shi'i Muslims constituted a significant majority in Basra and Baghdad provinces, both occupied by Britain during World War I, and a slight majority in the territory that became Iraq. They were also seen by the British as a political problem: the Shi'i shrine cities were centers of resistance to the occupation throughout the war and the early 1920s. One official wrote in 1927:

> There is fundamental difference between the Shia and the ordinary minority position. The Shia, aware that they are both more numerous and better armed than the Sunni Arabs, know that they could destroy the present Government if British forces were not behind it, though they could not replace it without British help.[26]

This quote betrays some ambiguity about the position of the Shi'a, who were not dominant in government but were not a minority at all, let alone an "ordinary" one. It also reveals British anxiety about Shi'i capacities for political mobilization.

Examining the creation of a separate system of Shi'i shari'a courts challenges a number of common narratives of this period. Yitzhak Nakash, one of the foremost historians of the Shi'a in modern Iraq, writes that, in contrast to the lack of "separation between religion and state" in neighboring Shi'i-majority Iran, "successive Sunni governments in Iraq strove to isolate the Shi'i mujtahids and established clearer boundaries between religion and politics in Iraq."[27] This argument resonates with familiar claims that the British dismantled the cross-sectarian coalition of forces behind the 1920 revolt and contributed to the production of Iraq as a "Sunni state" by co-opting the revolt's Sunni leaders into the government while isolating and in some cases deporting its Shi'i clerical leadership in the shrine cities. By ignoring institutional reforms in the adjudication of family-law disputes, the narrative has missed a key mechanism used by the British to bring members of the Shi'i clerical class into the Iraqi state apparatus. It also fails to elucidate how the state did not simply engage in the separation of religion from politics but, rather, redefined "religion" as properly belonging to the private sphere of morality and the family. In doing so it reconfigured sectarian communities as discrete entities whose development was driven internally (according to forms of reasoning endemic to each community's "sacred laws") but regulated externally (through institutional appointment and oversight by the emerging state apparatus).

British officials often justified the reforms by referring to the oppression of Shiʻa in Otto-man Iraq, especially how they were purportedly required to follow Sunni family laws: "the law which was administered was Sunni law, and the Shiahs had to make the best of it."[28] They also asserted that bringing the politically oppositional Shiʻa closer to government was an explicit aim of the reforms, the importance of which

> rests not only on the fact that it is a measure of justice to Shiʻah litigants that such cases should be tried and settled by judges of their own faith and in accordance with their own law; but also on the fact that it opens the Government service to Shiʻah ʻAlims, a class who have hitherto always kept aloof from the Government and in general have tended to adopt an attitude of opposition to the Government.[29]

Judicial Secretary Bonham-Carter similarly stated that the goal was to foster "the asso-ciation of Shiʻah jurists with the Government by the establishment of Shiʻah Courts."[30] Dissident Shiʻi religious figures involved in the 1920 revolt and other uprisings were frequently appointed as judges in the new courts, sometimes after being returned from British-imposed exile or released from imprisonment.[31] By 1918, officials were already proclaiming the reforms as a major accomplishment, invoking the language of develop-ment along native lines. "In the four years of British occupation great changes have been effected ... Sunni and Shiʻah Courts have been separated, and a judicial system has been established, based on the existing law of the land, and permitting the fullest use possible of native personnel."[32]

In the early years, officials noted some tension between state-appointed Shiʻi jurists in the new courts and the mujtahids at the highest level of the Shiʻi clerical establishment, who tended to stay clear of official appointments. One British authority remarked on "some jealousy on the part of the Shiʻah religious chiefs at the jurisdiction exercised by the Courts in Shiʻah personal cases," and further explained that "[o]wing to the privileged position of the Shiʻah religious chiefs at Najaf and Karbala, the appointment of Shiʻah Judges at those places presents special difficulties."[33] For my purposes here, these claims point to what British officials chose to ignore when claiming to have expanded the "rights" of Shiʻa in Iraq: that Shiʻi litigants in Ottoman times had not been compelled to use the official Sunni courts for personal status rulings but could and did take their disputes to their own religious authorities: hence the "jealousy" when state-sanctioned Shiʻi courts were established.

International law and the making of minorities

Parallel to the colonial ordinances issued during the occupation, and to the British-influenced national laws passed after Iraq's formation as a state in the early 1920s, a series of international laws and treaties helped to enshrine modern legal dualism in Iraq. In these interventions, dualism came to be understood as the protection of "minority rights," based on the emerging concept that in a global postcolonial order of sovereign nation-states each newly created state would consist of a "majority" population and remainder "minority" populations, the latter requiring legal protection backed by international oversight. While the mandate-era recon-struction of religious personal status courts in Iraq appeared in some ways to treat each reli-gious identity as an equal but discrete entity, in other ways it constructed "Muslim" as the dominant national religious identity of Iraq (a construction that paralleled that of "Arab" as the dominant national ethnic identity). The other, minority, identities were subject to international oversight, largely through the protection of their family laws.

For Iraq and the other post-Ottoman mandate states, the principle of legal dualism was enshrined in the League of Nations mandate agreements.[34] The original agreement for Iraq constrained Britain to respect existing law regarding "questions arising out of the religious beliefs of certain communities (such as the laws of Wakf and personal status)."[35] This agreement was never ratified and was instead replaced with the Anglo-Iraqi Treaty of 1922, which did not mention personal status questions. But in 1932 the principle as laid out in the original League of Nations mandate texts was codified—now phrased specifically in relation to "non-Muslim minorities"—in Iraq's agreement to join the League of Nations as an independent state.

> The Iraqi Government undertakes to take, as regards non-Moslem minorities, in so far as concerns their family law and personal status, measures permitting the settlement of these questions in accordance with the customs and usage of the communities to which those minorities belong. The Iraqi Government will communicate to the Council of the League of Nations information regarding the manner in which these measures have been executed.[36]

Despite the significance of these provisions, the role of international law is absent from most histories of legal dualism in the modern Middle East. Scholars of Muslim-majority states tend to write in dialogue with one another, rather than engaging with relevant scholarship on, for instance, the emergence of "minority rights regimes" in Europe or with the broader history of international law in relation to family law from the nineteenth through the twentieth centuries. Comparative histories even of post-Ottoman states, especially those with non-Muslim majorities, are lacking. For example, in current scholarship Egypt might be compared to Syria but not to Greece or Israel, though all of these post-Ottoman states emerged with systems of legal dualism in which religious minorities maintained their own personal status laws and courts. International law played a key role here. In Greece, for example, the Muslim minority was granted the right to maintain shari'a courts and personal status laws through a series of international treaties starting in the late nineteenth century. In Greek Thrace, where Muslims were exempted from the 1923 forced population exchange with Turkey, the Muslim minority continues to maintain its own religious laws and courts for family-related disputes.[37]

Conclusion

Ironically, by the end of the mandate period in 1932, when Iraq became formally independent, it was less common for British officials to assert that they had implemented a radical break from the Ottoman system of family-law courts, as some had asserted during the war and 1920s. Instead they now often claimed that they had simply maintained that system. "The right of separate religious communities in Iraq to have their own courts competent to give valid decisions on matters of personal status has been inherited from the regime of the old Ottoman Empire and has been confirmed in the Constitution of Iraq."[38] But the system established under British governance was neither a continuation of the Ottoman millet system nor an expansion of rights to marginalized groups. It was a project of fixing communal boundaries and a radical reconfiguration of the relation between family law, religion, and the state.

Meanwhile, the disavowal of this reconfiguration allowed the Ottoman state to be blamed for what was now often perceived as the backwardness of a system in which family law was adjudicated in separate religious courts by religious laws rather than in civil courts by a unified civil code. British officials sometimes acknowledged that the system was against "public opinion generally," which "appears to incline to the modern Turkish judicial system, which has placed all personal status cases within the jurisdiction of the Civil Courts," and that the maintenance of separate religious courts "may be somewhat of an anachronism." Nevertheless, a unified civil code in Iraq was "not now constitutionally possible."[39]

Despite the crucial role played by both colonial and international intervention in establishing modern legal dualism in Iraq (and elsewhere), many accounts of Muslim-majority post-Ottoman states continue to explain these systems through reference to "tradition." For example, legal scholar Dan Stigall asserts that the "paradigm of legal dualism" in modern Iraqi and Egyptian law is a "remnant" of the role of "religious traditionalists" in those states, who opposed the efforts of reformers to draft a unified family-law code for Muslims and Christians. He claims that it was because of this conservative religious opposition that family law remained separate "from the modernity of [the] civil code," which applied equally to all citizens.[40] As this article has shown, however, Iraq's legal system was constrained to dualism by British colonial policy and the emerging state's obligations under modern international law.

This article is a preliminary investigation into the remaking of Iraqi family-law courts and jurisdictions in the early twentieth century. Its focus on colonial and international interventions points to the need for further research in several directions. First, the role of religious authorities and jurists—Shi'i, Sunni, Jewish, and the various Christian sects—in the creation or reconstruction of separate religious courts under state regulation needs to be better understood. A second related but not identical question is how the content of specific religious family laws, and their availability to members of different communities, may have changed during this process. As just one example of the availability question, the research in this article suggests that the drive to fix boundaries around each religious community and its family law—creating obstacles to earlier forms of religious promiscuity such as conversion, intermarriage, and forum shopping—may not have been entirely disconnected from the drive to contain the imagined sexual promiscuity of Islamic law, even while no direct effort was made to change that law itself. For example, the closing down of forum shopping with the 1917 British ordinance would certainly have narrowed divorce options for Christians, who had long availed themselves of Ottoman Hanafi shari'a courts when seeking divorce.[41] The hardening of boundaries around sectarian communities likely also meant a hardening of boundaries around certain aspects of marital and sexual life in Iraq.

Notes

1 This is the case even in many states that have a so-called national or civil family law, such as Iraq; it is often not understood that Iraq's "civil" family law, originally promulgated in 1959 and amended several times, applies only to Muslim citizens. The system in Lebanon is often seen as exceptional for having no national family law, but the main difference between Lebanon and states such as Iraq and Egypt may simply be that there is no clear religious majority in the former and thus no religious law that could have been designated the "national" law.

2 Mahmood, *Religious Difference in a Secular Age*, 123.

3 Asad, *Formations of the Secular*, ch. 7. See also Agrama, *Questioning Secularism*; Scott, *Sex and Secularism*.

4 Mahmood, *Religious Difference*, 9.

5 Efrati, *Women in Iraq*, 52.

6 Ireland, *Iraq*, 458.

7 See Pursley, *Familiar Futures*, ch. 1.

8 "Review of the Civil Administration of the Occupied Territories of Al 'Iraq, 1914–1918" [L/P&S/10/752], in *Iraq Administration Reports 1914–1932* (Melksham: Archive Editions, 1992) [hereafter *IAR*], 1:64.

9 Ibid.

10 This is acknowledged, albeit in a contorted and misleading way, in Ibid., 1:62.

11 Lyell, *Ins and Outs of Mesopotamia*, 145.

12 Ibid., 158.

13 See Pursley, *Familiar Futures*, ch. 1.

14 Lyell, *Ins and Outs*, 157–158.

15 Ibid., 175.

16 Ibid., 178.

17 "Review of the Civil Administration of the Occupied Territories of Al 'Iraq, 1914–1918" [L/P&S/10/752], *IAR*, 1:63.

18 On how personal status law reforms in French mandate Syria in 1938 "reconfigured the Ottoman practice of granting privileges and immunities to communities of Christians and Jews with the secular sovereign power of recognition," see Abillama, "Contesting Secularism," 151.

19 "Report on the Administration of Justice for the Year 1919" [L/P&S/11/175], *IAR*, 3:386.

20 Ibid., 3:390.

21 "Administration Report of the 'Amarah Division for the Year 1919" [CO 696/2], *IAR*, 4:20.

22 For the English constitution, see *Records of Iraq* 4:5–21; for the Arabic version, see 'Abd al-Razzaq al-Hasani, *al-'Iraq fi Dawray al-Ihtilal wa-l-Intidab* (Beirut: Dar al-Rafidayn, 2013), 92–114.

23 "Report by His Brittanic Majesty's Government on the Administration of Iraq for the Period April 1923-December 1924," *IAR*, 7:658–9. On the establishment of a system of Ja'fari shari'a courts in French mandate Lebanon, see Weiss, *In the Shadow of Sectarianism*, 124.

24 "Report by His Brittanic Majesty's Government on the Administration of Iraq for the Period April 1923-December 1924," 7:659.

25 "Report by His Majesty's Government in the United Kingdom of Great Britain and Northern Ireland to the Council of the League of Nations on the Administration of Iraq for the year 1931," *IAR*, 10:416, 10:419.

26 Quoted in Sluglett, *Britain in Iraq*, 219.

27 Nakash, *The Shi'is of Iraq*, 87.

28 "Indian Desiderata for Peace Settlement," December 1918, in *Papers on British Policy and the Arab Movement*, Mss Eur F112/277, Qatar Digital Library, http://www.qdl.qa/en/archive/81055/vdc_100000001491.0x00028b, p. 290.

29 "Report on the Administration of Justice for the Year 1920" [C/O 696/3], *IAR*, 6:445.

30 "Review on the Administration of Civil Administration for the Year 1918" [L/P&S/11/165], *IAR*, 2:579.

31 al-Bahadili, *al-Sayyid Hibat al-Din al-Shahrastani*, 49–51.

32 "Indian Desiderata for Peace Settlement," 290.

33 "Report on the Administration of Justice for the Year 1919" [L/P&S/11/175], *IAR*, 3:376, 3:379.

34 See White, *Emergence of Minorities*, 50.

35 "Final Draft of the Mandate for Mesopotamia," in *Records of Iraq 1914–1966*, ed. Alan de L. Rush (Chippenham: Archive Editions, 2001), 2:734.

36 "Declaration of the Kingdom of Iraq, made at Baghdad on May 30th, 1932, on the occasion of the termination of the Mandatory Regime in Iraq, and containing the guarantees given to the council by the Iraqi Government," League of Nations, Distr. Assembly, Council, Members A.17.1932.VII (VII. Political. 1932. VII. 9), 16 August 1932.

37 Tsoukala, "Marrying Family Law to the Nation"; Tsitselikis, "The Legal Status of Islam in Greece."

38 "Report by His Majesty's Government in the United Kingdom of Great Britain and Northern Ireland to the Council of the League of Nations on the Progress of Iraq during the period 1920–1931," *IAR*, 10:281.

39 Ibid., 10:78–79. "Public opinion" referred to a prominent nationalist discourse that criticized legal dualism as both anti-modern and a "divide and rule" colonial technique. See al-'Umari, *Hikayat Siyasiyya*, 122.

40 Stigall, "Iraqi Civil Law," 47.

41 This was increasingly true over the empire's last two centuries, as Eastern Christian sects slowly adopted the Roman Catholic ban on divorce. Farha, "Stumbling Blocks," 35n10. For use of Hanafi courts for divorce, and by women for alimony, among Greek Orthodox Ottoman subjects, see Tsoukala, "Marrying Family Law to the Nation."

Bibliography

Abillama, Raja. "Contesting Secularism: Civil Marriage and Those Who Do Not Belong to a Religious Community in Lebanon." *PoLAR: Political and Legal Anthropology Review* 41, no. S1 (2018): 148–162. doi:10.1111/plar.12259.

Agrama, Hussein Ali. *Questioning Secularism: Islam, Sovereignty, and the Rule of Law in Modern Egypt.* Chicago, IL: Chicago University Press, 2012.

Asad, Talal. *Formations of the Secular: Christianity, Islam, Modernity.* Stanford, CA: Stanford University Press, 2003.

al-Bahadili, Muhammad Baqir Ahmad. *al-Sayyid Hibat al-Din al-Shahrastani: Atharuhu al-Fikriyya wa-Muwaqifuhu al-Siyasiyya.* Beirut: Mu'assasat al-Fikr al-Islami, 2002.

Efrati, Noga. *Women in Iraq: Past Meets Present.* New York: Columbia University Press, 2012.

Farha, Mark. "Stumbling Blocks to the Secularization of Personal Status Laws in the Lebanese Republic." *Arab Law Quarterly* 29, no. 1 (2015): 31–55. doi:10.1163/15730255-12341290.

al-Hasani, 'Abd al-Razzaq. *al-'Iraq fi Dawray al-Ihtilal wa-l-Intidab.* Beirut: Dar al-Rafidayn, 2013.

Ireland, Philip. *Iraq: A Study in Political Development.* London: Alden Press, 1937.

Lyell, Thomas. *Ins and Outs of Mesopotamia.* London: A.M. Philpot, 1923.

Mahmood, Saba. *Religious Difference in a Secular Age: A Minority Report.* Princeton, NJ: Princeton University Press, 2015.

Nakash, Yitzhak. *The Shi'is of Iraq.* Princeton, NJ: Princeton University Press, 1994.

Pursley, Sara. *Familiar Futures: Time, Selfhood, and Sovereignty.* Stanford, CA: Stanford University Press, 2019.

Scott, Joan. *Sex and Secularism.* Princeton, NJ: Princeton University Press, 2018.

Sluglett, Peter. *Britain in Iraq: Contriving King and Country*, rev. ed. New York: Columbia University Press, 2007.

Stigall, Dan. "Iraqi Civil Law: Its Sources, Substance, and Sundering." *Journal of Transnational Law & Policy* 16, no. 1 (2006): 1–72.

Tsitselikis, Konstantinos. "The Legal Status of Islam in Greece." *Die Welt des Islams* 44, no. 3 (2004): 402–431. doi:10.1163/1570060042562507.

Tsoukala, Philomila. "Marrying Family Law to the Nation." *American Journal of Comparative Law* 58, no. 4 (2010): 873–910. doi:10.5131/ajcl.2010.0005.

al-'Umari, Khayri. *Hikayat Siyasiyya.* Baghdad: Dar al-Qadisiyya, 1980.

Weiss, Max. *In the Shadow of Sectarianism: Law, Shi'ism, and the Making of Modern Lebanon.* Cambridge, MA: Harvard University Press, 2010.

White, Benjamin Thomas. *Emergence of Minorities in the Middle East: The Politics of Community in French Mandate Syria.* Edinburgh: Edinburgh University Press, 2011.

18

"THE RIGHT TO MY DAUGHTER"

African women, French men, and custody of *métis* children in twentieth-century French colonial Africa

Rachel Jean-Baptiste

While scholarly publications have increasingly centered sexuality in our understanding of colonialism, indigenous societies' and indigenous women's experiences and perceptions of interracial sexuality—becoming pregnant from and parenting children born from such relationships in contexts of colonial rule—have largely been ignored. In part, this lacuna derives from limited source materials; indigenous women's direct voices rarely enter into colonial state and religious archives. Yet the gap also results from a failure of historical imagination, scholarly focus on colonial states' and societies' representations of interracial sex and multiracial persons. In consolidating colonialism in twentieth-century Africa and Asia, European states and societies emphasized "the creation of racial boundaries as a means of consolidating the colonial rule" and thus worried greatly about "sex across the color line."[1] Nevertheless, interracial sexual and domestic relationships occurred, mainly between indigenous women and European men in the form of concubinage, prostitution, marriages according to local customary laws, other arrangements, as well as rape.[2]

Interracial sex resulted in the biological reproduction of multiracial persons, liminal figures whose very existence both undergirded and called into question the asymmetrical racialized relations of power that were foundational to colonial rule. Following the pioneering work of Ann Stoler, a now substantial colonial studies literature has analyzed how European colonial states and societies—the Dutch, British, and French in Africa and Asia—were anxious about and articulated the small numbers of multiracial persons as a "problem."[3] With these anxieties, European colonial states in some regions in Southeast Asia and Africa intervened in the upbringing of scores of multiracial children, carrying out forced or coerced removals from their mothers to European metropoles or into orphanages and mission stations in the colonies that were segregated from indigenous societies.[4] However, more multiracial African-Europeans stayed in Africa than left. African societies, pluralistic and diverse, absorbed multiracial children into maternal kinship networks, with some multiracial persons conceptualizing themselves according to multiple African identities and some calling themselves *métis*, colored, or Anglo-European.[5]

This essay considers how our understanding of the intersectional histories of sexuality and colonialism deepens with analyses that center African women, their relationships with their children, and interactions with colonial states and individual Europeans in navigating parenting and parental rights. This essay focuses on a single case study that took place in the 1930s in colonial French Africa—a vast region spanning the Atlantic Ocean, inland into the Sahel, and southwest along the Congo River—and in France. It is the story of an African woman from the Ivory Coast; her *métis* daughter who went on to live in the Congo and France; a French man and his wife who claimed parental rights over the girl; and French colonial civil and court personnel who adjudicated competing custody claims over the girl. The central struggle, between the African woman and the French man, unfolds over the course of an epistolary exchange and legal battle. Their letters open a window into little-explored themes of emotion, motherhood, and family life in the histories of colonialism and sexuality. The story that unfolds is marked by intense expressions of intimacy, bitterness, love, and loss, and it reveals the porousness of seemingly rigid hierarchies in colonial contexts.

In February 1938 an African woman named Adama Diallo living in Abidjan, Ivory Coast, petitioned the French colonial Attorney General of the Ivory Coast.[6] Her letter protested that a Pierre Dauriat, who resided in Brazzaville, Congo, had "detained illegally and against my will my daughter Germaine Diallo." Colonized by the French since the early twentieth century, the Ivory Coast and the Congo respectively were divided into the governing units of French Occidental Africa (FOA) and French Equatorial Africa (FEA) and separated by a 3,000 kilometer journey by boat. The letter continued:

> I do not understand and have never understood the goal that M. Dauriat is pursuing. For two months, he has tried with all his relations to intimidate me into abandoning my daughter brought up at the price of ten years of sacrifices. The copies of acts and correspondence included with this letter will prove to you the whole extent of our accord. This is why I take recourse with your highest justice so that my daughter is given back to me as soon as possible.[7]

Written in French, the letter contained spelling and grammar mistakes. Adama had likely engaged a professional male African letter-writer to compose it. Few African women in Ivory Coast had formal French education and thus literacy. The letter relayed that she had written repeatedly to Pierre, since March of 1937, for the return of her daughter. She claimed that, after several written demands, Pierre had at last responded and promised to return her daughter in August of 1937.

This particular letter, and others attributed to Adama, survived in French colonial archives, in the records of the highest French colonial appeals court in FOA, because that court took up the question of parental rights over her daughter. In June 1938 the Governor General of FEA sent a letter stamped "Confidential" to the FOA Governor General informing him that he was forwarding yet another petition by Adama. Adama, he outlined, had written to him that she had "entrusted" her daughter, Germaine, to Lieutenant Pierre Dauriat—whom the Governor General identified as a French man. From Brazzaville, where he resided with Germaine, Pierre had placed a petition before the highest French colonial court in Dakar to have the girl declared a French citizen and him her legal guardian. Adama contested Pierre's rights to file the naturalization petition and demanded her daughter's return.

Adama also forwarded letters and telegrams between her and Pierre, and a copy of the French colonial legal document recording the supposed accord between them granting Pierre's guardianship of Germaine. This agreement was recorded in a report authored by a regional colonial official in Ivory Coast in July 1934.[8] The document relayed a gathering of Pierre, who was second in command of a colonial infantry troop of African soldiers, Tié-moko Diara, identified as a clerk employed at a wharf, Adama, identified as "the wife of Diara and without profession," and two French colonial civil servants who were listed as witnesses. The report summarized Adama as declaring under oath "that they [presumably her and her husband] consented entirely to confide the *métisse* daughter of Adama Diallo, named Marguerite Germaine born in 1925 in Bobo-Dioulasso of an unknown father" to Pierre and that, "It remains agreed that Mr. Dauriat takes on as his cost and entire responsibility the care and education of the young Germaine until she reaches the age of majority."[9] The gathering, and the French court document that summarized it, silenced Adama. It was her husband Tiémoko who spoke on her behalf, with the document con-ferring to him the legal right to speak for her and to confer guardianship of her daughter to Pierre. It racialized Germaine as *métisse*, a shifting French term and social identifier denot-ing a person with one European parent and one "other" parent.

How were the parties—Adama, her husband, and Pierre—connected? Pierre and Adama likely had a sexual relationship during Pierre's time in Ivory Coast and he was Germaine's biological father. Yet it was rare for a French man to legally recognize a child with an African mother. Pierre likely wanted to raise his daughter, and perhaps Pierre's French wife agreed to this arrangement on condition that he not sully his reputation and white manhood by legally claiming biological fatherhood. Adama may have reluctantly but willingly entrusted care of her daughter to Pierre, seeking the best material circumstances for her daughter. Or Adama could have been coerced or convinced by Pierre and/or Tiémoko, potentially with promises of financial compensation for relinquishing guardianship. Perhaps during 1934 legal proceedings Adama did not fully comprehend that she was ceding parental rights or perhaps such a legal hearing never took place. Indeed, Adama later accused Pierre of fraudulently using his con-nections to colonial administrators to draw up legal proceedings. The parties may have privately agreed that Adama would occasionally see Germaine. Regardless, Adama consistently requested her daughter's return, beginning in 1936, and insisted that she, not Pierre, had full legal rights over Germaine.

After the 1934 hearing, Pierre left with Germaine, then nine or ten years old, for France and Adama, Tiémoko, and Pierre remained in contact about Germaine. Correspondence initially suggested cordial collaboration and mutual respect and agreement about Germaine's living situation, and even warmth and familiarity. In letters addressed to Tiémoko from Paris, Pierre wrote about Germaine's acclimation to French education, describing her as a "little European" and that his family in France had come to "adore" her.[10] Pierre alluded to future travel to Ivory Coast with Germaine at which time Tiémoko and Adama would be able to see her. Yet by October 1936, in a series of telegrams and letters between Adama, Tiémoko, and Pierre, the tenor of these discussions changed drastically.

By then Germaine, Pierre, and a person identified in Pierre's letters as "my wife" were in Brazzaville, Congo. Germaine was 11 or 12 years old and had been away from Africa and her mother Adama for two years. Adama wished to see her daughter and had Tiémoko cable Pierre, notifying him of her plans to travel to Brazzaville for this purpose. Pierre's response, addressed to Tiémoko, was "No," retorting tersely that he "categorically refuses to receive Adama."[11] In a more extensive letter addressed to Tiémoko, Pierre insisted that Adama's presence would be "harmful to Germaine and that the authorities would not allow Adama to debark in Pointe-Noire," the closest port to Brazzaville.[12] He insisted that, "I am doing my duty for Germaine to give her a European upbringing and education that will allow her to become naturalized as French as soon as she is 16 years old."

Centering the interpretation of events from Adama's perspective presents the following tale. Two years after trusting her daughter to Pierre, she was experiencing regret. She missed her daughter and wished to see her. She refused to disappear from Germaine's life and, moreover, selected the European tools of pen, paper, and telegram to convey to Pierre her continued rights as a mother. Adama continued to voice her emotional attachment to her daughter and her legal parental rights, given that she was the biological mother. Adama generated a paper trail of "written agency"[13] that threatened Pierre's surety in his position as a French man.

Despite Pierre's refusals, Adama demanded to see her daughter. In November 1936 Adama sent a letter by registered mail to Pierre in Brazzaville. In it Adama complained that it was the third letter she had sent to him without acknowledgment of receipt. Written in the first person, she continued that she did not understand Pierre's response in the cable that he "categorically refuses to receive" her in Brazzaville. Adama reiterated that she had already informed Pierre that she and Tiémoko were now divorced. She relayed that she had since remarried and was still "waiting for her daughter." She complained that Pierre and Germaine had stopped by the port of Port-Bouet near her home. However, because Pierre communicated only with Tiémoko, she only learned of their visit afterward and had missed the chance to see her daughter. Expressing her anguish, she continued:

> I assume that you love Germaine as much as me. I do not see the reason why you are opposed to my departure [to Brazzaville]. I neither gave nor sold my child … we are in the Republic and however much a poor mother I am I think that human laws give me the right to my daughter. I don't know myself well enough your kindness towards Germaine but I find your opposition to me seeing her uncalled for.[14]

Adama questioned whether the cable saying that Pierre refused to see her if she came to Brazzaville had really come from him. She reminded Pierre that they shared emotions of love for Germaine, both wanted what was best for the girl, and that she, as the biological mother, was naturally suited to care for her.

Adama shifted from expressing the right to visit her daughter in Brazzaville to demanding that Pierre return Germaine. She cited French law, human rights, and moral and ethical behavior. She also emphasized her love for her daughter and hoped that Pierre's own affection for Germaine would compel him to empathize.

Finally, directly responding to Adama instead of her now ex-husband Tiémoko, Pierre sent her a certified letter in December 1936 dismissing her previous letter as "insulting!" Pierre wrote that he assumed it was not Adama who was "the instigator of this dishonest 'machination' mounted against him and his wife. Thank goodness, I recognized that it was 'a writer' by the way the letter was written and its stupidities. I hope that the person who translates [reads] this letter to you will explain its terms." Dismissing Adama's initiative, he alleged that a "dishonest" individual had fooled Adama into believing he had "bought" Germaine. He apologized that their ship's short one-hour docking at Abidjan prevented Germaine and him from seeing her, and he denied knowing about Adama's divorce or ever receiving her three earlier letters. He added that, "Germaine and my wife are doing well and greet you and wish you good health." But, in an abrupt change of tone, he again dissuaded Adama from coming to Brazzaville and continued: "Let me give you some advice: follow-through with your promises as I do myself vis-à-vis Germaine."[15]

Pierre's reply dismissed Adama's insistence that the best place for her daughter was with her biological mother. Pierre also dismissed any agency that Adama expressed about her legal parental rights, in the process elevating his French wife as a more suitable mother for Germaine. He alluded to the project of making Germaine "a little European" as one that he and Adama had originally agreed to, and insisted it was still the best path for Germaine. He beseeched Adama to relinquish any thought or mention of seeing her daughter or living with her again. Pierre and his wife knew that public respectability of their marriage and their nuclear French family with their "adopted" daughter depended on erasing links with her African mother and African cultures.

The photo referenced in the letter, with an inscription on the back that said "Something to Remember Germaine By For Adama," has not survived in the archives, but the type-written letter bearing Germaine's purported signature has. The document began, "I say hello to you and wish you happy new year. Right now, I will be very happy if you leave my mother and father alone. I am doing well in their home and I wish to stay with them."[16] How heartbreaking for Adama it must have been to hear—as someone is likely to have read the letter aloud to her—Germaine refer to Pierre and his wife as her "mother and father" and that she wished to stay with them.

Adama's January 1937 response was distraught and unrelenting in her demands for her daughter's return. She replied that the "words in the last letter came well from me, however insulting you found them to be. I will not allow you to accuse of stupidity an honest man who was willing to write my thoughts." With this sentence, Adama disclosed that she did not write the letters. Yet she insisted that the letters' content was her own. She accused Pierre, however, of his own act of epistolary ventriloquism, claiming "What is really stupid is the letter written by Germaine under your dictation." Referring to how the letter addressed Adama by the first name, she rejoined that the letter should have at least referred to her as "Mommy (*Maman*)," as this would reflect how Germaine truly felt about Adama in spite of Pierre's efforts to wipe away Germaine's memory of Adama over the course of the three years she had lived with him.

Adama questioned the very legitimacy of the 1934 court document agreement between her, her ex-husband, and Pierre. As she asserted, "I want the pure and simple return of my daughter. The so-called educational contract that was drawn up due to your relations with highly-ranked people in Bingerville does not bind me." In fact she accused Pierre of fabricating her agreement and the legitimacy of his guardianship through well-placed contacts with colonial administrators.[17] She threatened to lodge a complaint with colonial administrators in Ivory Coast.

Rather than honor this direct request, Pierre sought to solidify and legalize his custody under French law. At some point in 1937 he petitioned Brazzaville's colonial administrators to have Germaine declared a French citizen. French nationality law was dictated by the principle of *jus sanguinis*, blood and affiliation. For the most part, only those born of persons who were already "French," as defined in the Civil Code, were legally "French."[18] Africans born in French colonies in FEA and FOA held the legal status of "native," not French nationality. French colonial law subjected Africans to separate codes through which they could obtain French nationality under widely shifting criteria over the course of the twentieth century—including having won a Legion of Honor for military service, marrying a French woman, and fluency in French.[19] Yet Pierre applied for Germaine to receive French nationality based on a specific set of laws promulgated for *métis* in Indochina and French Africa in the 1920s and 1930s.

These laws opened a door for French citizenship by way of "racial filiation."[20] They allowed people born in Africa of a legally unknown parent of French or European origin to petition for French citizenship. African adults, men or women over the age of 21, as well as children if an adult petitioner applied on their behalf could apply for French nationality with proof of being *métis*. Qualifying as *métis* involved an ambiguous set of criteria based on skin color, culture, language, lifestyle, moral character, socio-economic status, and that one of the parents was French or European.[21]

The legal conundrum over whether or not Germaine could receive French nationality as a *métis* hinged not on her racial status before French law but on who had parental rights over her: Adama as her biological African mother, or Pierre as a French man who claimed no biological ties yet asserted that Adama had conferred guardianship to him? Pierre's petition in Brazzaville for Germaine to be declared a French citizen hit a legal hiccup owing to this question of parental rights. Adama's communication with colonial officials in Ivory Coast, contesting that he was unlawfully detaining Germaine, intersected with Pierre's petition.[22] Before Pierre's case could proceed further, colonial officials in January and February of 1938 had to settle the question of parental rights. Referring to Germaine's case and the 1930 law for *métis* and French citizenship, the Attorney General relayed in an April 1938 letter that "the person qualified to institute the legal proceedings" would have to file the request.[23]

At first, colonial administrators conceded that they could not proceed with the citizenship question without Adama's consent and that she, as the biological mother, was "the person qualified."[24] However, the Attorney General in Ivory Coast judged Pierre as having rights over Germaine and looked for justifications to deny Adama hers. He wrote to the Attorney General of FOA that he would have a police officer in Abidjan conduct "a confidential investigation on the morals and lifestyle" of Adama and would transmit the results when ready.[25] With this addition of an investigation into Adama's "morals and lifestyle," colonial officials inserted that they could have grounds to strip her of her parental rights. That police report has not survived the archives, yet Pierre ultimately prevailed.

Colonial court officials ruled that Pierre was Germaine's legal guardian and could petition for her to be declared a French citizen. In July 1938 court documents of the Court of Appeals of FOA, the highest French colonial court, decreed that Germaine Marguerite *dite* (otherwise known as) Dauriat was recognized as a French citizen.[26] How did colonial personnel justify that Pierre had the legal right to submit the petition despite Adama's objections?[27] The court utilized the very 1934 document conferring Germaine to Pierre, the one that Adama protested had been brokered coercively by Pierre's friends in the colonial administration, to strip her of her rights. The decree that declared Germaine a French citizen permanently nullified Adama's legal rights over her daughter, citing that she had "confided" Germaine to Pierre to be raised and cared for until she reached the age of majority.

Furthermore, the court cited the emotional attachment of "Mr. and Mrs. Dauriat" to Germaine as justifying their legal guardianship. The decree elaborated that Germaine had "always lived with Mr. and Mrs. Dauriat, who brought her with them to France, gave her a European education, treating her like their own child and showing her deep affection, that she gives back to them completely." The decree did formally acknowledge "the opposition of her mother Adama Diallo" but justified the abrogation of her parental rights owing to her "morals and lifestyle," which demonstrated that "it is in the well-understood interest of the minor *métisse* girl to remain confided in the care of the Dauriat spouses who will assure her an education and living conditions that her mother would certainly be unable to provide for her." Thus officers of the court admitted that they were denying Adama her parental rights, but maintained the nullification was in the best interest of Germaine.[28]

Adama's clamoring had reached the heights of the French legal system, yet her claims proved futile. The decree that declared Germaine a French citizen not only conferred to her French nationality but also conferred parentage to Dauriat and his wife. The document listed the biological father as "unknown" and the biological mother as Adama, yet otherwise erased any genealogical, social, or legal ties between mother and child. Yet in codifying Germaine's surname as "otherwise known as Dauriat," the court document also signaled that she could carry that name due to legal decree and not because Dauriat was her biological father. Though I haven't found further archival traces of Germaine, she likely moved to France with the Dauriat couple and had no subsequent contact with or perhaps even memory of her mother, Adama.

At first glance this case study drawn from personal letters preserved in French colonial archives represents the triumph of racialized power and colonial masculinity. In her TED Talk, "The Danger of a Single Story," Nigerian author and intellectual Chimamanda Ngozi Adichie criticizes how "Africa" is often represented in Western literature and imaginaries as a single story of catastrophe, and Africans as "incomprehensible people … unable to speak for themselves." The archival documents analyzed in this article represent a seemingly singular story of the loss of Adama's dignity and the erasure of Adama and any ties to Africa for Germaine's sense of self and legal status. Adama lost her struggle to retain custody of her daughter and likely never saw her again. However, Adichie counteracts, "Many stories matter. Stories have been used to dispossess and to malign, but stories can also be used to empower and to humanize. Stories can break the dignity of a people, but stories can also repair that broken dignity."[29] In this vein, the paper trail that Adama generated reveals multiple stories of how an African woman's persistent efforts to assert her personhood and parental rights compelled European private citizens and the colonial state and society to continually reconfigure laws, systems of thought, and moral landscapes in order to maintain power and dispossess her of her child.

Thus Adama did not disappear and nor was she incomprehensible. Rather, the clarity and tenacity with which she maintained her claims in communications with Pierre and colonial employees exposed the tenuousness of colonial racial and gendered relationships of power. As a French man, Pierre represented the historically constructed category of "colonial masculinity"[30] on which European states and societies built the scaffolding of colonial power. However, the sexual relationship he may have had with Adama, the emotional sentiments of warmth toward Tiémoko and bitterness and anxiety in reaction to Adama, and the attachment he exhibited toward Germaine also laid bare his vulnerability. Pierre is atypical in that a small number of European men claimed paternity and sought to care for the children they had with African women.[31] Yet this tale suggests that this may have had as much to do with the tenaciousness with which African women sought to keep their multiracial children as it had to do with the feelings of European men toward the children. Though Adama was not able to directly write for herself, she did find ways to speak for herself as a mother and to speak of her love for her daughter in terms that were intelligible, thereby leaving in the archives a singular story of the persistent belief and practice of human dignity even in the starkest of colonial contexts.

Notes

1 Ray, *Crossing the Color Line*, 9–10.
2 Gosh, *Sex and the Family in Colonial India;* Jean-Baptiste, "A Black Girl Should not Be with a White Man."
3 European fathers largely didn't acknowledge paternity nor did they provide material resources for their children's upbringing. *Métis*, French colonial government officials from Southeast Asia to French Africa worried, were *déracinés* (uprooted), *déclassés* (removed from one's social class), dangerous, and could rebel against colonial states and societies, as had occurred in Haiti centuries earlier. Stoler, *Carnal Knowledge and Imperial Power*.
4 European missionaries, civil servants, private citizens, and some *métis* adults who managed these projects endeavored to acculturate *métis* children into cooperative partners of colonial rule, or, if in the metropole, integrated and adopted by Europeans. White, *Children of the French Empire*; Firpo, *The Uprooted*; Budagwa, *Noirs, blancs, métis*.

5 Milner-Thornton, *The Long Shadow of the British Empire;* Lee, *Unreasonable Histories;* Ray, *Crossing the Color Line.*

6 National Archives of Senegal (ANS), 3M52 (184), Letter from Adama, chez Samba Diallo, demeurant à Treichville to the Attorney General of the Republic in Grand-Bassam, Letter Arrived # 3399/AN stamped February 5, 1938, Dated February 4, 1938.

7 ANS, 3M52 (184), Letter from Adama, February 4, 1938.

8 ANS, 3M52 (184), Letter from the Governor-General of AEF to the Governor-General of AOF, Letter #397c A/P, June 23, 1938.

9 ANS, 3M52 (184), Procès-Verbal, Colony of Ivory Coast, Lagunes Circle, Summary, no document #, July.

10 ANS, 3M52 (184), Letter from M.P. Dauriat, Ministry of War, Office of the Secretary General to My Dear Tiémoko, No document #, October 10, 1935.

11 ANS, 3M52 (184), Cable # 496 W 9, October 29, 1936.

12 ANS, 3M52 (184), Letter from Dauriat, Commander of the transition of troops of AEF to My Dear Tiémoko, October 10, 1936.

13 Lee, *Unreasonable Histories.*

14 ANS, 3M52 (184), Letter from Adama Diallo, Living at the residence of Samba Diallo, Treichville, Abidjan to My Dear Mr. Dauriat, Certified mail Letter # 023 A.R, November 30, 1936, delivered to the addressee on December 11, 1936.

15 ANS, 3M52 (184), Letter from Dauriat to Adama, Certified mail Letter # 085, December 11, 1936.

16 ANS 3M52 (184), Letter from Germaine to Adama, December 12, 1936.

17 ANS 3M52 (184), Letter from Adama, chez Pierre Beraud, Railway, Abidjan to M. Dauriat, Certified letter # 448 A.R., January 16, 1937.

18 Weil, *How to Be French,* 12–13.

19 Semly, *To Be Free and French.*

20 Saada, *Empire's Children.*

21 Jean-Baptiste, *Multiracial Identities.*

22 ANS, 3M52 (184), Letter from Adama, residing with Samba Diallo in Treichville to the Attorney General of the Republic in Grand-Bassam, Letter Arrived # 3399/AN stamped February 5, 1938, Dated February 4, 1938.

23 ANS 3M52(184): Letter from the Head of the Justice Department, Court of Appeals of FEA to the Attorney General, Letter # 992 P.G; March 25, 1938; Letter from The Attorney-General of the Court of the First Instance of Brazzaville to the Chief Police Commissioner, Letter # 457, April 12, 1938; Note from the Chief Police Commissioner, French Congo to the Attorney General of the Republique, Letter #316 D.68, April 13 1938.

24 ANS 3M52(184): Letter from the Attorney General of Ivory Coast, Court of the First Instance, Grand-Bassam to the Attorney General of AOF, Letter #397 H P.G., December 15, 1937.

25 ANS 3M52(184): Letter from the Attorney General of Ivory Coast, Court of the First Instance, Grand-Bassam to the Attorney General of AOF, Letter #25 P.G., January 14, 1938.

26 ANS 3M52(184): Letter from the Attorney General of AOF to the Attorney General, Head of Judiciary Service of the Court of Appeals of AEF, Letter #9923, March 25, 1938.

27 ANS, 3M52: Letter from the Governor General of FOA to the Governor General of FEA, Letter # 104 A.J, August 16, 1938; Letter from the Attorney General to the Minister of Colonies, Letter # 3442 P.G., September 27, 1938.

28 ANS 3M52(184): Letter from the Attorney General of AOF to the Ministry of Colonies, Office of Archives, Letter #3443 P.G., September 27, 1938.

29 Adichie, "The Danger of a Single Story."

30 Sinha, *Colonial Masculinity.*

31 Jean-Baptiste, "'Miss Eurafrica.'"

Bibliography

Adichie, Chimamanda Ngozi. "The Danger of a Single Story." Filmed July 2009 at TEDGlobal. Video. https://www.ted.com/talks/chimamanda_ngozi_adichie_the_danger_of_a_single_story/transcript?language=en

Budagwa, Assumani. *Noirs, blancs, métis: La Belgique et la segregation du Congo Belge et du Ruanda-Urundi (1908–1960).* Self-published, 2019.

Firpo, Christina. *The Uprooted: Race, Children and Imperialism in French Indochina, 1890–1980*. Honolulu: University of Hawai'i Press, 2006.

Gosh, Durba. *Sex and the Family in Colonial India: The Making of Empire*. Cambridge, UK: Cambridge University Press, 2008. doi:10.1017/CBO9781139878418.

Jean-Baptiste, Rachel. "'A Black Girl Should not Be with a White Man': Sex, Race, and African Women's Social and Legal Status in Colonial Gabon, c. 1900–1946." *Journal of Women's History* 22, no. 2 (2010): 56–82. doi:10.1353/jowh.0.0140.

Jean-Baptiste, Rachel. "'Miss Eurafrica': Men, Women's Sexuality, and Métis Identity in Late Colonial French Africa, 1945–1960." *Journal of the History of Sexuality* 20, no. 3 (2011): 568–593. doi:10.1353/sex.2011.0053.

Jean-Baptiste, Rachel. *Conjugal Rights: Marriage, Sexuality, and Urban Life in Colonial Libreville, Gabon*. Athens, OH: Ohio University Press, 2014.

Jean-Baptiste, Rachel. *Multiracial Identities in Twentieth Century French Colonial Africa: Childhood and Citizenship*. Cambridge, UK: Cambridge University Press, Forthcoming.

Lee, Christopher. *Unreasonable Histories: Nativism, Multiracial Lives, and the Genealogical Imagination in British Africa*. Durham, NC: Duke University Press, 2014.

Milner-Thornton, Juliette. *The Long Shadow of the British Empire: The Ongoing Legacies of Race and Class in Zambia*. New York: Palgrave Macmillan, 2012. doi:10.1057/9781137013088.

Ray, Carina. *Crossing the Color Line: Race, Sex, and the Contested Politics of Colonialism in Ghana*. Athens, OH: Ohio University Press, 2015.

Saada, Emmanuelle. *Empire's Children: Race, Filiation, and Citizenship in the French Colonies*. Chicago, IL: University of Chicago Press, 2012.

Semly, Lorelle. *To Be Free and French: Citizenship in France's Atlantic Empire*. Cambridge, UK: Cambridge University Press, 2017. doi:10.1017/9781316181669.

Sinha, Mrinalini. *Colonial Masculinity: "The Manly Englishman" and the "Effeminate Bengali" in the Late Nineteenth Century*. Manchester, UK: Manchester University Press, 1995.

Stoler, Ann L. *Carnal Knowledge and Imperial Power: Race and the Intimate in Colonial Rule*. Berkeley, CA: University of California Press, 2002.

Weil, Patrick. *How to Be French: Nationality in the Making since 1789*. Durham, NC: Duke University Press, 2008.

White, Owen. *Children of the French Empire: Miscegenation and Colonial Society in French West Africa, 1895–1960*. Oxford, UK: Clarendon Press, 1999. doi:10.1093/acprof:oso/9780198208198.001.0001.

19

PINING FOR PURITY

Interracial sex, the South African Immorality (Amendment) Act (1950), and "petty" apartheid

Susanne M. Klausen

On January 17, 1962, a white man named John Hibbert Ferreira and Sarah Titus, a Coloured woman, were arrested for sitting on a blanket together, fully clothed, near the city of Port Elizabeth. The police had seen Ferreira's car "parked half in the bush" and, upon investigation, found the couple together about 75 yards away from the road.[1] They were arrested on suspicion of intending to have sex in contravention of the Immorality Act that prohibited heterosexual white South Africans from having, or even intending to have, extra-marital sex with people of color.[2] Titus was taken away in the patrol van. Her fate is unknown; however, there is a history of women of color being raped by police officers that makes it troubling to consider what may have happened to her.[3] Simultaneously, a sergeant drove with Ferreira in the latter's car to the police station and on the way, according to the officer, he "pleaded with me to drop the case." Once they arrived the sergeant got out of the car and waited for Ferreira to park his vehicle as directed. Instead Ferreira suddenly accelerated and took off for the nearby harbor where, according to a witness, he sped along a quay "and landed in the sea." By the time the police retrieved him he was dead. At the subsequent inquest his death by drowning was pronounced a suicide, an act committed, it was assumed, because he was "fearful of being charged under the Immorality Act."[4] The verdict had been expected by contemporary observers because suicide by white men caught contravening the Immorality Act was not unusual, as critics were repeatedly pointing out.[5] That the fear of being publicly exposed for desiring a women of color literally drove Ferreira, and other white men, to suicide is testimony to how intensely stigmatized interracial sex had become in white South Africa by the 1960s.

Criminalizing interracial sex between heterosexual whites and people of other "races" had been a matter of urgency for the Afrikaner National Party (NP) upon attaining power. Elected in 1948, the NP implemented apartheid (1948–1994), the racist national policy of "separate development" for the four official race categories of "white," "native" (Africans), "Coloured" (mixed race), and "Indian."[6] For the new regime a fundamental objective of apartheid was to protect white racial purity; therefore ending whites' involvement in interracial sexual relationships was of paramount importance.

The NP's absolute intolerance of interracial sex was an abrupt change in the official approach to an issue that has a complex history dating back to the mid-seventeenth century, when the Dutch East India Company established a slave-based colony in the Cape. Initially authorities permitted European men to marry free women of color and to engage in extra-marital interracial sex with women of color, free and enslaved. Starting in the eighteenth century, when significant numbers of European women began settling in the colony, mixed marriage became stigmatized among people of European descent but was never prohibited before NP rule; widespread disapprobation made criminalization superfluous. With regards to extra-marital sex, though perceived by the respectable settler population as disreputable to white prestige, white men rarely faced significant social consequences for having illicit sex, whether coercive or consensual, across the color line.[7] The first laws criminalizing interracial sex outside of marriage, passed at the turn of the twentieth century, targeted white prostitutes selling sexual services to African men.[8] After Union in 1910, the government extended the prohibition to include white men with the Immorality Act (1927) that criminalized extra-marital sex between whites and Africans. However, the 1927 law was not aimed at eliminating interracial sex; instead it was intended to educate whites—especially poor, white men—in whiteness by associating membership in the white race with respectable, "civilized" behavior, which was explicitly stated to preclude sex with the "primitive" races.[9] In contrast, the NP government genuinely sought to prevent white heterosexual South Africans from having any further extra-marital sexual contact with people of color.

Afrikaner nationalism and white racial purity, 1914–1948

The NP was the political embodiment of the Afrikaner nationalist movement that was forged in the aftermath of the Boers' crushing defeat by British imperialism in the South African War (1899–1902). Middle-class Boers, who were deeply resentful toward the British and fearful of losing their distinct cultural identity, succeeded, with the vigorous support of the Afrikaner churches, in forming an Afrikaner ethnic identity and a nationalist movement that proclaimed Afrikaans-speaking whites a *volk* (nation/people) with a God-given duty to ensure the survival of Christian *blanke beskawing* (white civilization) in South Africa by maintaining white rule.[10] From the outset the NP (est. 1914) opposed interracial sexual relationships, preaching that the *volk* should preserve their racial and cultural purity by maintaining social distance from other races. The claim to be racially "pure" was in fact wishful thinking because, as was widely known (and Afrikaners strenuously denied), Boers had a history of interracial marriage, concubinage, and extra-marital sex dating back to the earliest days of Dutch settlement in the Cape.[11]

Though consistently hostile to "race mixing," Afrikaner nationalist elites perceived the concept of race in inchoate, overlapping religious, historical, and biological terms. During the 1930s they increasingly conceptualized race as a biologically marked concept, a consequence of the movement's embrace of far-right ideas being promulgated in Europe.[12] Proclaiming that God had created races as biologically as well as culturally distinct groups and desired the races to remain distinct, the NP began vehemently demanding a law banning mixed marriages. Intense opposition to mixed marriage was consistent with the NP's increasingly virulent racist ideology. At the same time, attacking the ruling United Party (UP) government for not doing enough to prevent "racial admixture" was a cynical bid to win poor and working-class white supporters away from its competitors, the UP and Labour Party, by whipping up anger at the widespread white poverty that resulted in poor whites and people of color cohabitating in urban slums. Particularly alarming to patriarchal nationalists were "mixed" marriages between white women and men of color.[13] Some of the most effective speeches given in the late 1930s by D.F. Malan, leader of the NP, stressed the vulnerability of Afrikaner culture and white racial purity; in 1938, for example, he declared "social mixing [of the races] readily leads to sexual intercourse which then causes the disappearance of the pure white colour ..."[14]

During the 1938 national election the NP made the criminalizing of mixed marriage the focus of its campaign and, though it lost to the UP, exhortations about the danger of race mixing clearly resonated with whites, especially Afrikaans-speakers who were undergoing a process of ethnic mobilization that emphasized the duty of the *volk* to remain "pure."[15] Months later the party held a national conference where the "race problem" was a central issue. Malan told delegates, "We have gathered here with one great aim in mind, and it is to safeguard South Africa for the white race and to preserve the white race, pure and conscious of its calling, for South Africa."[16] The conference organized a petition demanding miscegenation between whites and so-called non-whites be made a criminal offence, as well as calling for residential, economic, and political segregation. The petition, submitted to Parliament in 1939, was signed by 230,619 white men and women, more than 25 per cent of the total number of white votes cast in the election the previous year.[17]

While victorious at the polls, the UP government was so rattled by the accusation of being "soft" on miscegenation that it immediately formed a commission of inquiry to investigate the desirability of criminalizing mixed marriages. The Report of the Commission on Mixed Marriages in South Africa (1939) affirmed miscegenation was a threat to white supremacy, and the majority of commissioners recommended criminalizing interracial marriage. Unbidden, they also went a step further and asserted that miscegenation via "immorality"—sex outside of marriage between white men and women of color—was a far greater danger, given how few mixed marriages were by then taking place.[18] Four out of five commissioners recommended criminalizing *both* types of sexual contact to assist "the white race to keep its head above water in a sea of color" and pursue "the ideal of a 'White South Africa,' by which is meant the hegemony of the white."[19] When World War II erupted, the report was shelved but, for the NP, not forgotten.

During and immediately after the war, opposition to miscegenation became fundamental to the party's *raison d'être*: God, the NP repeatedly declared in these years, had bestowed racial boundaries as part of His divine plan.[20] In the aftermath of the war the NP's popularity surged as Afrikaans-speaking unskilled and working-class whites, facing food shortages and a rising cost of living, became resentful toward the UP government. Whites were also extremely anxious at the prospect of competing for jobs with the tens of thousands of Africans who had migrated to the cities during the war to find employment in the rapidly expanding manufacturing sector.[21] In addition, the visibility and close proximity of so many "native" bodies fanned whites' longstanding fear of "swamping," meaning demographic displacement by the far larger population of so-called non-whites: by 1946, whites comprised only 20.8 per cent of the total population, roughly half English-speaking and half Afrikaans-speaking.[22] The combination of job competition, urbanization among the African population, the spread of mixed-race slums, and rising black labor militancy had a deeply unsettling effect on whites already feeling economically insecure.

By the 1948 election the NP, the Broederbond (a secretive and powerful "brotherhood" of elite Afrikaner nationalists), and Afrikaner churches had succeeded in their joint task of Afrikaner ethnic mobilization and the NP was the undisputed political voice and home of Afrikaner nationalists. The party was also perceived by many as the true champion of white supremacy. The UP had begun to acknowledge, pragmatically, that racial integration in South Africa was inevitable but, still wholly committed to white supremacy, envisaged gradual political reform occurring at an unspecified time in the future.[23] In contrast to such equivocation, the NP excelled at exploiting whites' frustrations and fears provoked by the social and economic changes unleashed by the war. As a panacea, the NP promised a hard-right policy called *apartheid* (Afrikaans for apartness) to safeguard white supremacy and racial capitalism by separating the races as far as possible spatially, politically, economically, and socially. The proposed policy was ambiguous and contradictory regarding a number of fraught features of South African society, especially the economy's total dependence on cheap African labor.[24] But the NP at that time was led by men who were genuinely passionate and unequivocal on the emotional matter of *bloedvermenging* (blood mixing): it was evil in the eyes of God and, if elected, they would finally stamp it out. Surprisingly to everyone, including its own members, the NP won the election.

Under apartheid the issue of race became the main "faultline" and "organizing principle" of society.[25] The NP enacted a battery of laws to ensure that a person's racial identity would, in profoundly gendered ways, largely determine the course of her or his life trajectory; consequently, demarcating and policing racial boundaries was essential to the success of apartheid. In 1950, for example, the regime passed the Population Registration Act requiring all South Africans, including whites, to be racially categorized by registering with the Office for Race Classification. That same year it also criminalized extra-marital interracial sex to help preserve whites' (fictional) blood purity, inculcate whiteness, and prevent increasing the size of the already large Coloured population.

Passage of the Immorality (Amendment) Act, 1949–1950

The NP's first major piece of legislation was a miscegenation law: the Prohibition of Mixed Marriages Bill (PMM Bill) that made it illegal for "Europeans" to marry "non-Europeans." T.E. Dönges, Minister of the Interior, introduced the PMM Bill in Parliament on May 19, 1949, with this blunt declaration: "The object of this Bill is as far as possible to check blood mixture, and as far as possible to promote racial purity."[26] As historians have shown, the UP, long divided over the issue of miscegenation, mounted a weak attack on the proposed legislation, on the one hand agreeing with the regime that "race mixing" was a social evil while on the other hand opposing the prohibition of mixed marriage on the grounds, mainly, that it was "unchristian" to prevent marriage between people who love one another, regardless of race.[27] Despite the UP's objections, the Bill passed and the Prohibition of Mixed Marriages Act received royal assent on July 1, 1949.

Ending mixed marriage was the first half of a carefully planned two-pronged legislative attack on miscegenation to protect white racial purity. When introducing the PMM Bill in Parliament, Dönges was clear that, in keeping with the recommendations of the Report of the Commission on Mixed Marriages in South Africa (1939) (discussed above), the NP intended also to prohibit *extra-marital* interracial sex. With rhetoric revealing how deeply the NP was still enamored of far-right ideas about the evils of "blood mixing," he declared:

> This is naturally only the first step and it must be followed up by the prohibition of extra-marital blood mixture. Here we have only to deal with it within the marriage tie, but it is inadequate and incomplete and hon. Members can therefore well understand that the Government … will have to follow it up by also prohibiting extra-marital blood mixture.[28]

Just weeks after introducing the PMM Bill the NP tabled the Immorality (Amendment) Bill (I(A)A Bill) that extended the 1927 law to prohibit extra-marital sex between whites and all other races (the original law had prohibited sex with Africans only). During the second reading the Minister of Justice reiterated that criminalizing extra-marital interracial sex was a "necessary and logical sequel to the Mixed Marriages Act," otherwise, he said, "we would be placing a premium on immorality; if such persons are prevented from marrying they would be encouraged to live immorally."[29]

During debate about the I(A)A Bill in the House of Assembly, Members of Parliament across party lines concurred that protecting white blood from "contamination" was imperative; indeed, the need to maintain white racial purity was invoked at least 20 times, with some members of the NP also defiantly rejecting the emergent human rights discourse rapidly gaining recognition globally.[30] The (relatively) liberal members of the UP opposed the proposed law, but the party was divided and stymied in an attempt to mount an effective challenge. The UP mainly criticized the authoritarian solution of policing sex, arguing it was impossible to legislate morality. In the words of one UP parliamentarian, the government should instead try to teach whiteness to recalcitrant white men: "It is not force that we should use on this type of individual. Force will not bring us anywhere. It is education that we must concentrate upon."[31]

The UP also tried to manipulate (and thereby affirmed) white racism by repeatedly calling the suggestion that whites would engage in interracial sex "insulting" to the race. The UP had, during the 1938 national election, successfully used the "insult" argument in an earlier political confrontation with the NP over miscegenation. During the campaign the NP had distributed a poster intended to foment anger at the UP's refusal to criminalize mixed marriages by depicting a white woman with an African husband and mixed-race children. The UP had responded by condemning it as an insult to white womanhood: by suggesting that white women would want to marry black men, the NP had "slandered" white women.[32] The UP's racist counter-attack was a turning point in the election in their favor. However, just over a decade later, in 1950, the tactic failed to rouse white outrage and the party's inability to gain traction was telling: white fear and loathing of miscegenation had hardened in the intervening years, something the UP was unable to come to grips with politically. The Immorality (Amendment) Act (hereafter the Act) was assented to on May 1, 1950.

"Petty" apartheid? Impact of the Immorality (Amendment) Act

Few contemporary observers foresaw how destructive the Act would be to many South Africans' lives, including members of the race that apartheid was designed to benefit: whites. One astute politician who had an inkling of what was to come was Sam Kahn, the sole MP for the Communist Party who, when the I(A)A Bill was introduced in Parliament, made this prediction:

> We are told a Bill is to be introduced against immorality. I say life in South Africa is going to become a very dangerous thing for hundreds of thousands of Europeans, apart from the strangers who will visit our shores, on account of the fantastic laws in force in South Africa. ... We are told that there is going to be a Bill dealing with immorality, but the most wonderful thing is the exploitative extra-marital sexual relations which go on between European and non-European in every walk of life. ... One day this Government will begin to see that those who are going to suffer most under measures of this kind are not merely Coloured people but many "White" people who are at present supporters of this Government.[33]

Kahn's warning was prophetic. From 1950, prosecutions for contravening the Act became commonplace—so frequent, in fact, that they drew international attention as both a source of salacious fascination and fodder to critics highlighting the hypocrisy of Afrikaners' supposedly Christian apartheid project.[34] Between 1950 and 1985, the year the Act was repealed, at least 20,000 South Africans were arrested for having, or attempting to have, "illicit" sex across the color line, with the overwhelming majority of couples comprised of white men (often Afrikaner) and women of color.[35] The risk of arrest grew after 1957, the year the NP expanded the Immorality Act (as it was renamed) to make it illegal to "attempt, solicit, importune or incite" extra-marital sexual intercourse across the white–black color divide.[36] However, what constituted such acts was not defined in law, which meant that a bewildering variety of behaviors could be interpreted as an indication of forbidden desire, such as sitting on a blanket together as Titus and Ferreira had done in 1962. The nature of sexual encounters for which couples were arrested included actual or attempted rape, casual sex, and prostitution, although a significant number of couples were in loving relationships. The police enforced the law using an infamous assortment of methods, ranging from using women to entrap white men to perching in trees in order to peer into people's bedrooms.[37]

The personal and social costs of enforcing the Act were severe and have yet to be assessed by historians. Clearly the experience of arrest was gendered and raced, in ways repeatedly highlighted by contemporary critics. For example, women of color would be imprisoned while the white men with whom they were arrested were acquitted or given suspended sentences, for the simple reason that men often had sufficient financial resources to hire lawyers.[38] The consequences of imprisonment for women's employment and family life have not been examined. Also, an alarming number of white men, overcome with feelings of either shame or pain resulting from severe stigmatization, committed suicide after being arrested. Already by 1962, the year Ferreira drove his car into the sea, so many white men had killed themselves that critics, Afrikaner as well as English, were demanding the "devastating" law be repealed or amended.[39]

The NP's rush to pass the Act after winning power and its rigorous enforcement by the state made it clear that sex regulation was to be a cornerstone of apartheid. Nevertheless, the fundamental importance of sexuality has yet to be sufficiently integrated into the prevailing dominant historical understanding of this political era. For decades the foundational role of sexuality in the construction and maintenance of apartheid was marginalized by a radical research agenda focused primarily on the operation of apartheid machinery in the public sphere—the application of measures attacking the land, labor, and political rights of oppressed people of color. The impact of apartheid in the private sphere, including the damage and degradations wrought on people's sex and love lives, seems to have appeared less "political" and therefore not as urgently in need of investigation. A sign that the meaning and impact of the Act on South African society has been underestimated by historians is the tendency to allocate it to the "petty" half of apartheid's dizzying array of oppressive laws. Here I am referring to the longstanding convention dating back to the 1960s of dividing apartheid laws into two types: there was "grand" apartheid, comprising racist laws related to land, labor, and political representation; and "petty" apartheid, made up of laws that regulated everyday life by dictating segregation in myriad spaces from benches to beaches.[40]

The two laws imposing a color bar on sexual relationships, the Prohibition of Mixed Marriages Act and the Immorality Act, started being called examples of "petty" apartheid in the 1980s when debate was raging over their repeal. When P.W. Botha became prime minister in 1978 he told white South Africans that if they wished to maintain the existing social order they must "adapt or die," meaning inaugurate a number of reforms to undercut the increasingly militant domestic anti-apartheid movement and appease international detractors of apartheid. While a hardcore faction of Afrikaner nationalists wished to retain miscegenation legislation to continue "protecting" white racial purity, the most powerful members of the regime decided it would gain credibility and goodwill by repealing the two laws. The laws were intensely hated by people of color, especially the Immorality Act which, by 1980, was considered "the ultimate symbol of racism."[41] Leading Afrikaners asserted the sex laws were no longer essential to white survival. As the Minister of National Education, Gerrit Viljoen, stated in 1983, "I do not believe that the White people of this country need either of these Acts to maintain their identity. I don't think the White people will collapse ... without these Acts."[42] Botha rocked Afrikanerdom by making similar comments.[43] At the same time, the NP fully intended to maintain fundamental apartheid measures that enabled "individual communities" (meaning the "races") to maintain their "way of life," leading to accusations that the offer to repeal the miscegenation laws was "purely cosmetic."[44]

When the regime finally abolished the two sex laws in 1985 it did so without simultaneously doing away with legislation dictating where, depending on their race, South Africans could live and work, thus fueling opponents' anger even further.[45] Anti-apartheid activists agreed the two laws were "cornerstones" of apartheid but insisted they were not "as basic to structural racial discrimination" as legislation such as the Group Areas Act or influx control (controlling the movement of Africans from rural to urban areas).[46] For example, Bishop Desmond Tutu, general secretary of the South African Council of Churches, said he was "not particularly impressed" by the regime's intention to address only "peripheral" issues (interracial marriage and sex) and not "the total problem of apartheid."[47] The altered perception by the 1980s that the Act was merely "peripheral" was undoubtedly because, in the 1970s, the regime had stopped enforcing it as aggressively as in previous decades; not because of newfound approval of "race mixing" but because it wanted to end the onslaught of negative publicity accompanying the constant arrests.[48] In the 1980s, in other words, the Act started being viewed more as a hateful symbol of apartheid and no longer as a profoundly harmful weapon. As a result, some contemporary observers and researchers labelled the Act as an aspect of "petty," never "grand," apartheid, and the privileging of the latter over the former is explicit in the very terminology.[49] In subsequent decades historians looking back have done the same, although mainly the Act has simply been overlooked.[50] The gap in the historiography is all the more striking given the rich body of work on many of the political and social meanings of miscegenation in southern Africa prior to 1948, particularly in relation to the myth of the Black Peril (rape of white women by African men).[51] In contrast, scholars from other disciplines such as sociology and legal studies, as well as cultural producers outside the academy, began in the 1950s to explore many of the Acts' extremely detrimental aspects because, one surmises, they witnessed for themselves the harsh enforcement and saw at first hand the degrading, even tragic, consequences.[52]

Unfortunately, the lack of serious scholarly historical attention has meant the Immorality Act's very purpose is frequently misunderstood as a law that banned sex between "the races," as though it was aimed in a general way at containing all South Africans' sexual activities within their allocated race.[53] Instead, it was aimed solely at preventing sex between whites and racial "others" (and not between, for example, Indians and Coloureds or Africans and Indians). That is because, as this essay has shown, the Act was intended to buttress white supremacy by maintaining white racial purity and preventing transgressive members of the white race from further increasing the size of the already far larger "non-white" population. Since the inauguration of liberal democracy in 1994, the new political context has certainly spurred and fostered historical interest in the deployment and meanings of sexuality during apartheid.[54] Nevertheless, much remains to be documented and understood, not least about the damage inflicted by the NP's merciless attempt to end "race mixing" and the ways South Africans evaded detection when acting on their forbidden desire for interracial sexual contact.

Notes

1 The research for this essay was supported by the generous financial assistance of the Social Sciences and Humanities Research Council of Canada (SSHRC), the Gerda Henkel Institute, and the Netherlands Institute for Advanced Study in the Humanities and Social Sciences (NIAS-KNAW). *Cape Argus*, "Immorality Act Fear."

2 Government of South Africa, "Immorality (Amendment) Act (Act No. 21 of 1950)"; Government of South Africa, "Immorality Act (Act No. 23 of 1957)."

3 For example, in 1967 two constables were charged with raping an African woman at Emmarentia Dam; one committed suicide before trial. *Cape Argus*, "Constable On A Charge."

4 This and previous quotes from *Cape Argus*, "Immorality Act Fear."

5 See for example, the debate spurred by the attempt of Helen Suzman of the Progressive Party (PP) to decriminalize interracial sex in 1962. South Africa House of Assembly Debates (hereafter *Hansard*), February 23, 1962, columns 1531–1562.

6 Racial terminology is inescapably problematic when writing about South Africa, past or present. The Population Registration Act (1950) decreed there were three official race categories: white, native (African) and Coloured (descendants of interracial sexual encounters between whites, indigenous peoples, and imported slaves from Africa and Indonesia). See South African History Online, "The Population Registration Act." In 1961 the government recognized Indians as permanent residents and added "Indian" as an official category.

7 MacCrone, *Race Attitudes in South Africa*; Fredrickson, *White Supremacy*, 108–123; Van Den Berghe, "Miscegenation in South Africa"; Giliomee, "Eighteenth Century Cape Society"; Scully, "Rape, Race, and Colonial Culture."

8 Van den Berghe, "Miscegenation in South Africa," 71.

9 Martens, "Citizenship, 'Civilisation.'"

10 Moodie, *The Rise of Afrikanerdom*; Furlong, "The Mixed Marriages Act (1949)."

11 Fredrickson, *White Supremacy*.

12 Dubow, "Afrikaner Nationalism."

13 Hyslop, "White Working-Class Women."

14 Cited in Fourie and Inwood, "Interracial Marriages in Twentieth-Century Cape Town," 632.

15 Hyslop, "White Working-Class Women," 74.

16 Cited in Koorts, "'The Black Peril,'" 572.

17 Ibid., 574; *South Africa 1982 Official Yearbook*, 129.

18 An analysis of statistics available prior to passage of the Prohibition of Mixed Marriages Act (1949) reveals that only 1.38 per cent of all people entering registered marriages did so outside their racial group, with whites being "by far the most endogamous." Van Den Berghe, "Miscegenation in South Africa," 72.

19 Government of South Africa, *Report of the Commission on Mixed Marriages*, 9.

20 Cited in Furlong, "The Mixed Marriages Act," 72.

21 Between 1939 and 1945 the manufacturing workforce grew 7.7 per cent annually. Nattrass, "Economic Growth and Transformation in the 1940s," 24–25.

22 Beinart, *Twentieth-Century South Africa*, Table 1.

23 Dubow, "Introduction: South Africa's 1940s."

24 On the ambiguous meaning of apartheid, see Posel, *The Making of Apartheid*.

25 Posel, "What's In A Name?" 52.

26 *Hansard*, May 19, 1949, column 6164 (T.E. Dönges, Minister of the Interior).

27 See Chapter 3 of Furlong's assessment of the parliamentary debate in "The Mixed Marriages Act."

28 *Hansard*, May 19, 1949, column 6164 (T.E. Dönges, Minister of the Interior).

29 *Hansard*, March 1, 1950 column 2164 (C.R. Swart, Minister of Justice).

30 See for example, *Hansard*, March 1, 1950, columns 2208 (J.E. Potgieter, NP).

31 *Hansard*, March 2, 1950, column 2268 (L.C. Gay, UP).

32 Hyslop, "White Working-Class Women," 76.

33 *Hansard*, May 24, 1949, columns 6419, 6422 (Sam Kahn, CP).
34 One of many international newspapers to cover South African "immorality" cases was *The Times* of London. See as an example, "S. African Couple."
35 Klausen, "Sex, Shame, and Suicide."
36 Government of South Africa, "Immorality Act (Act No. 23 of 1957)."
37 For one example, see *Sunday Times*, "Man and Woman Watched."
38 *Cape Argus*, "Two Women to Appeal."
39 Quote in *Hansard*, Feb. 23, 1962, column 1531 (Helen Suzman, PP); "Morals Act."
40 As a representative example of this longstanding analytical bifurcation by historians, see Beck, *The History of South Africa*, 125–126.
41 *Rand Daily Mail*, "Sex Laws."
42 *Natal Witness*, "Viljoen."
43 *Citizen*, "Sex Act Repeal."
44 *Sunday Times*, "Repeal of Laws."
45 *Star*, "It's Official."
46 *Cape Argus*, "Mixed Marriage."
47 *Star*, "Committee to Probe."
48 Klausen, "Sex, Shame, and Suicide"; "Fewer Prosecutions"; "Soft Pedal on Race Sex Laws."
49 See Giffard and Hachten, *The Press and Apartheid*, 8.
50 For example: "… 'petty apartheid' [is] the name given to apartheid laws concerned with the regulation of day-to-day life, most notably the Immorality Act, Mixed Marriages Act, and the Separate Amenities Act." South African History Online, "South Africa Repeals Separate Amenities Act 1953."
51 Exemplary studies include: van Onselen, "The Witches of Suburbia"; Etherington, "Natal's Black Rape Scare of the 1870s"; Pape, "Black and White"; Lubbe, "The Myth of 'Black Peril'"; McCulloch, *Black Peril, White Virtue*; Martens, "Settler Homes, Manhood and 'Houseboys.'"
52 See Van Den Berghe, "Miscegenation in South Africa"; Lewin, "Sex, Colour and the Law," 9–12; McClure's novel *The Steam Pig*; Brink's novel, *Looking on Darkness*; Fugard's play, "Statements After an Arrest Under the Immorality Act."
53 Two representative examples: "The Immorality Amendment Act 21 of 1950 criminalized sexual relations between members of different races…" in Heyns, *Human Rights Law in Africa*, 247; and Miller, *An African Volk*, 38.
54 Significant studies include Achmat, "'Apostles of Civilised Vice'"; Gevisser and Cameron, eds., *Defiant Desire*; Walker and Reid, "Sex Then and Now"; Erlank, "Sexuality in South Africa and South African Academic Writing"; Klausen, *Abortion Under Apartheid*.

Bibliography

Achmat, Zackie. "'Apostles of Civilised Vice': 'Immoral Practices' and 'Unnatural Vice' in South African Prisons and Compounds, 1890–1920." *Social Dynamics* 19, no. 2 (1993): 92–110. doi:10.1080/0253395930458553.
Beck, Roger B. *The History of South Africa*. Westport, CT: Greenwood Press, 2000.
Beinart, William. *Twentieth-Century South Africa*. Oxford, UK: Oxford University Press, 2001.
Brink, André Brink. *Looking on Darkness*. London: W.H. Allen, 1974.
Cape Argus, The. "Two Women to Appeal." May 31, 1958.
Cape Argus, The. "Immorality Act Fear: Suicide." February 23, 1962.
Cape Argus, The. "Constable On A Charge Shoots Himself." May 31, 1967.
Cape Times, The. "Mixed Marriage Law Offer by Botha." April 22, 1983.
Citizen, The. "Sex Act Repeal Likely to be Recommended." April 14, 1985.
Dubow, Saul. "Afrikaner Nationalism, Apartheid and the Conceptualization of 'Race.'" *The Journal of African History* 33, No. 2 (1992): 209–237. doi:10.1017/S0021853700032217.
Dubow, Saul. "Introduction: South Africa's 1940s." In *South Africa's 1940s: Worlds of Possibilities*, edited by Saul Dubow and Alan Jeeves, 1–19. Cape Town: Double Storey Books, 2005.
Erlank, Natasha. "Sexuality in South Africa and South African Academic Writing." *South African Review of Sociology* 39, no. 1 (2008): 156–174. doi:10.1080/21528586.2008.10425083.
Etherington, Norman. "Natal's Black Rape Scare of the 1870s." *Journal of Southern Africa Studies* 15, no. 1 (October 1988): 36–53. doi:10.1080/03057078808708190.

Fourie, Johan Fourie and Kris Inwood. "Interracial Marriages in Twentieth-Century Cape Town: Evidence from Anglican Marriage Records." *The History of the Family* 24, no. 3 (2019): 629–652.

Fredrickson, George. *White Supremacy: A Comparative Study of American and South African History*. New York: Oxford University Press, 1981.

Fugard, Athol. "Statements After an Arrest Under the Immorality Act." In *Statements: Three Plays* (Athol Fugard, John Kani and Winston Ntshona). London and Oxford: Oxford University Press, 1974.

Furlong, Patrick. "The Mixed Marriages Act (1949): A Theological Critique Based on the Investigation of Legislative Action and Church Responses to This Legislation." MA thesis, University of Cape Town, 1984.

Gevisser, Mark and Edwin Cameron, eds. *Defiant Desire: Gay and Lesbian Lives in South Africa*. New York and London: Routledge, 1995.

Giffard, Anthony C. and William Hachten, *The Press and Apartheid: Repression and Propaganda in South Africa*. Madison, WI: University of Wisconsin Press, 1984.

Giliomee, Hermann. "Eighteenth Century Cape Society and Its Historiography: Culture, Race, and Class." *Social Dynamics* 9, no. 1 (1978): 18–29.

Government of South Africa. *Report of the Commission on Mixed Marriages in South Africa*. Pretoria, 1939.

Government of South Africa. "Immorality (Amendment) Act (Act No. 21 of 1950)." Accessed September 19, 2020. https://disa.ukzn.ac.za/sites/default/files/pdf_files/leg19500512.028.020.021.pdf

Government of South Africa. "Immorality Act (Act No. 23 of 1957)." Accessed September 19, 2020. https://disa.ukzn.ac.za/sites/default/files/pdf_files/leg19570412.028.020.023.pdf

Heyns, Christof, ed. *Human Rights Law in Africa*. Vol. 2. The Hague: Kluwer Law International, 1997.

Hyslop, Jonathan. "White Working-Class Women and the Invention of Apartheid: 'Purified' Afrikaner Nationalist Agitation for Legislation against 'Mixed' Marriages, 1934–9." *Journal of African History* 36, no. 1 (1995): 57–81. doi:10.1017/S0021853700026979.

Klausen, Susanne M. *Abortion Under Apartheid: Nationalism, Sexuality, and Women's Reproductive Rights in Apartheid South Africa*. Oxford, UK, and New York: Oxford University Press, 2015.

Klausen, Susanne M. "Sex, Shame, and Suicide: Policing White Male Heterosexuality in South Africa During Apartheid." Department of History Seminar Series, University of Johannesburg, February 28, 2017.

Koorts, Lindie. "'The Black Peril Would Not Exist If It Were Not For A White Peril That Is A Hundred Times Greater': D.F. Malan's Fluidity on Poor Whiteism and Race in the Pre-Apartheid Era, 1912–1939." *South African Historical Journal* 65, no. 4 (2013): 555–576. doi:10.1080/02582473.2013.858764.

Lubbe, Henriette. "The Myth of 'Black Peril': Die Burger and the 1929 Election." *South African Historical Journal* 37, no. 1 (November 1997): 107–132. doi:10.1080/02582479708671294.

MacCrone, D. *Race Attitudes in South Africa: Historical, Experimental and Psychological Studies*, repr. ed., Johannesburg, 1937.

Martens, Jeremy. "Settler Homes, Manhood and 'Houseboys': An Analysis of Natal's Rape Scare of 1886." *Journal of Southern African Studies* 28, no. 2 (June 2002): 379–400. doi:10.1080/03057070220140766.

Martens, Jeremy. "Citizenship, 'Civilisation,' and the Creation of South Africa's Immorality Act, 1927." *South African Historical Journal* 59 (2007): 223–241. doi:10.1080/02582470709464779.

McClure, James. *The Steam Pig*. Letchworth, UK: Garden City Press, 1971.

McCulloch, Jock. *Black Peril, White Virtue: Sexual Crime in Southern Rhodesia, 1902–1935*. Bloomington, IN: Indiana University Press, 2000.

Miller, Jamie. *An African Volk: The Apartheid Regime and Its Search for Survival*. Oxford, UK: Oxford University Press, 2016.

Moodie, T. Dunbar. *The Rise of Afrikanerdom: Power, Apartheid, and the Afrikaner Civil Religion*. Berkeley and Los Angeles, CA: University of California Press, 1975.

Morsink, Johannes. "World War Two and the Universal Declaration." *Human Rights Quarterly* 15, no. 2 (May 1993): 357–405. doi:10.2307/762543.

Naicker, Linda. "The Role of Selected Churches and Communities in the Development and Maintenance of Inter-Racial Relationships in Natal in the Context of Apartheid (1970–1994)." MA thesis, University of Kwa-Zulu Natal, 2012.

Natal Witness, The. "Viljoen: Whites Can Do Without Immorality Act." February 2, 1983.

Nattrass, Nicoli. "Economic Growth and Transformation in the 1940s." In *South Africa's 1940s: Worlds of Possibilities*, edited by Saul Dubow and Alan Jeeves. Cape Town: Double Storey Books, 2005.

Pape, John. "Black and White: The 'Perils of Sex' in Colonial Zimbabwe." *Journal of Southern African Studies* 16, no. 4 (1990): 699–720. doi:10.1080/03057079008708257.

Posel, Deborah. *The Making of Apartheid, 1948–1961: Conflict and Compromise*. Oxford, UK: Oxford University Press, 1991.

Posel, Deborah. "What's In A Name? Racial Categorisations Under Apartheid and Their Afterlife." *Transformation* 47 (2001): 50–74.

Rand Daily Mail, The. "Morals Act: Nats Becoming Concerned." February 1, 1971.

Rand Daily Mail, The. "Sex Laws: 'Deleting Them Is the Only Way'." September 4, 1980.

Scully, Pamela. "Rape, Race, and Colonial Culture: The Sexual Politics of Identity in the Nineteenth-Century Cape Colony, South Africa." *American Historical Review* 100, no. 2 (1995): 335–359. doi:10.1086/ahr/100.2.335.

South African History Online. "South Africa Repeals Separate Amenities Act 1953." Accessed September 19, 2020. www.sahistory.org.za/dated-event/south-african-parliament-repeals-separate-amenities-act-1953

South African History Online. "The Population Registration Act." Accessed September 19, 2020. www.sahistory.org.za/sites/default/files/DC/leg19500707.028.020.030/leg19500707.028.020.030.pdf

Star, The. "Committee to Probe Sex Colour Bar Acts." June 30, 1983.

Star, The. "It's Official: There's No Special Dispensation for Mixed Race Couples." July 7, 1985.

Sunday Times, The. "Man and Woman Watched with Binoculars." November 1, 1971.

Sunday Times, The. "Repeal of Laws 'Not Just Cosmetic'." April 30, 1985.

Sunday Tribune, The. "Soft Pedal on Race Sex Laws." June 21, 1981.

Thakur, Vineet. *Jan Smuts and the Indian Question*. Pietermaritzburg: University of KwaZulu-Natal Press, 2017.

Times, The [London]. "S. African Couple Given Suspended Sentences." April 10, 1969.

Times, The [London]. "Fewer Prosecutions Under Apartheid Sex Law." February 18, 1974.

Van Den Berghe, Pierre L. "Miscegenation in South Africa." *Cahiers d'Études africaines* 4 (1960): 68–84. doi:10.3406/cea.1960.3680.

van Onselen, Charles. "The Witches of Suburbia: Domestic Service on the Witwatersrand, 1890–1914." In *Studies in the Social and Economic History of the Witwatersrand 1886–1914: New Nineveh*, edited by Charles van Onselen, 45–60. Johannesburg: Longman, 1982.

Walker, Liz and Graeme Reid. "Sex Then and Now: Exploring South Africa's Sexual Histories." *South African Historical Journal* 50 (2004): 77–83. doi:10.1080/02582470409464796.

PART IV

Subjects, souls, and selfhood

20

SINGLE WOMEN AND SPIRITUAL CAPITAL

Sexuality and devotion in colonial Guatemala

Brianna Leavitt-Alcántara

Feminist and postcolonial studies of sexuality and colonialism have tended to focus on nineteenth- and twentieth-century British, French, and Dutch empires. Given that sexuality is a modern construct, its application to early modern Latin American empires is more methodologically fraught. As Zeb Tortorici recently put it, "how might we speak of sexuality ... in an epoch before the advent of 'sexuality'—a term, concept, and organizing principle of the self that emerged only in the nineteenth century?"[1] Spaniards and Portuguese colonizers certainly relied upon sexual mores and ideologies tied to legitimacy, religiosity, honor, and "clean" Christian (then European) blood to sustain a caste hierarchy and legitimize colonial rule. But Iberian colonialism emerged out of a late medieval and early modern context which lacked the rigid biological conceptions of race and sex that undergirded modern empire building. There were other significant disconnects between early modern Spanish and Portuguese empires and modern European colonial projects. Spain and Portugal developed inclusive colonial societies which contrasted with the exclusive settler colonialism of modern European empires. Indeed, by the late colonial period, racial mixture was a defining feature of Latin American societies. As Kimberly Gauderman puts it, the Spanish "colonization of the intimate" was at best incomplete, at worst a failure.[2]

The distinctive context of sexuality and empire in colonial Latin America has led several scholars to move away from a Foucauldian emphasis on power and domination and toward an exploration of sexual desires and lived experiences, including significant gaps between ideals and realities and widespread engagement in "alternative" or "diverse" sexualities.[3] Studies have shown, for example, how informal unions, prostitution, sexual witchcraft, erotic religiosity, and same-sex sexual practices were remarkably common and often tolerated in the daily life of colonial Spanish America.[4] Nor were alternative sexualities firm markers of non–European "otherness," given Spanish and *criollo* (Spanish American) engagement in these sexual practices as well. And yet other studies complicate this picture. Tolerance did not always mean acceptance. Within the complex internal hierarchies of non–elite communities, sexual practices and reputation, legitimacy, and formal marriage mattered and shaped social standing, including vulnerability to verbal or physical violence and vital access to credit, mutual aid, and favorable outcomes in court.[5]

This study considers how some laboring and mixed-race single women in the colonial Guatemalan capital navigated these tensions in their daily lives and in the documentary record. While many studies have productively mined the meaty testimonies of court records, criminal cases, and Inquisition trials, I approach this topic from the distinct vantage point of wills, an admittedly unlikely source for accessing sexuality. But a surprising number of laboring single women left wills in Guatemala's colonial capital, and these documents uniquely highlight how non-elite, unmarried women engaged Catholic notions of morality even as they reworked official discourses of gender, sexual mores, and religiosity and constructed pious personas for themselves.[6] Much as scholars recognize that race in colonial Latin America was a flexible category and individuals might claim multiple racial identities simultaneously, this study considers how gender and sexual ideals were malleable and multifaceted and poor, single women could sometimes claim more than one moral status.

Wills, sexuality, and spiritual networks

In 1705, María Nicolasa de Aparicio, a former slave and single mother, found herself sick in bed and called a local notary so that she could make out her will.[7] María Nicolasa's words and wishes were undeniably mediated that day by the notary and the formulaic will-making script. So, like all other sources and the archive itself, María Nicolasa's will was "constructed" and she was just one player in that construction. But examining her will alongside hundreds of others illuminates patterns and ways in which non-elite and mixed-race single women developed and invoked alternative sexual, gender, and religious ideals in their lives and in the archival record. It's unclear where María Nicolasa was born, but she appears to have been a longtime resident of Santiago de Guatemala, the colonial capital of the Kingdom of Guatemala (a province of New Spain corresponding roughly to modern Central America). She notably declined to identify her birth legitimacy and marital status, but did opt, rather unusually, to declare her racial or caste status. She described herself as a "*mulata libre*," a free woman of mixed African descent. While many mulatto Guatemalans were born into freedom by this time, María Nicolasa was not. An oblique reference later in her will indicates that she was an adult before she gained her freedom. Given these circumstances, María Nicolasa likely opted to identify herself as a free mulatta woman as a point of honor and pride or as a way of distancing herself from her former enslaved status. Circumventing the standard testamentary formula, María Nicolasa waited until the very last lines of her will to discuss matters of family and inheritance. Only then did she acknowledge that she was a single mother of three children, one of whom was still enslaved and whose inheritance was meant to purchase his freedom. In a Spanish American system that recognized gradations of illegitimacy, María Nicolasa described her children as "*hijos naturales*" (natural children). This was an intermediate status of illegitimacy for children born to parents who could legally marry, as opposed to an adulterous or other scandalous union. But her claim was tenuous, given that she did not identify the father or fathers of her children.

Although Spanish and Catholic officials and prescriptive sources heavily emphasized feminine ideals of chastity and enclosure, María Nicolasa's situation as a laboring single woman, and even as a single mother of illegitimate children, was not unusual in colonial Spanish American cities. Labor and migration patterns often produced urban female majorities and high numbers of unmarried women and female-headed households.[8] Indeed, the provincial capital of Santiago de Guatemala was very much a mixed-race "city of women" by the eighteenth century. At the time María Nicolasa made out her will, well over half of the city's population of 40,000 was mixed-race, and by the mid-eighteenth century mulattoes like her constituted the single largest demographic group.[9] A 1740 census taker pointedly remarked that among the "common poor ... the feminine sex abounds in total profusion."[10] And illegitimacy rates hovered around 45 per cent among the non-elite population, down from a high of 77 per cent in the mid-seventeenth century. Even among the elite Spanish population, illegitimacy rates were almost 30 per cent.[11]

Viewed in this context, María Nicolasa's experience reflects widespread complacency among Spanish American officials toward "illicit" sexuality. Of course, complacency toward non-elite and mixed-race sexuality was also strategic. Elite Spanish and *criollo* men guarded their own gendered sexual privileges to engage in "concubinage" or extramarital unions with women of color. And lacking a fully-formed racial ideology, the Spanish colonial system relied upon assumptions about the sexual immorality of indigenous and African peoples, the illegitimacy of mixed-race births, and the neophyte religious status of all but pure-blooded Europeans to sustain the caste hierarchy and justify European colonial control. Many historical sources—including Inquisition and criminal cases, prescriptive literature, and early modern Catholic decrees—would suggest that single, laboring women like María Nicolasa made their way under a hostile official gaze.

But María Nicolasa's will also powerfully countered that narrative, highlighting her economic achievements and successful development of devotional networks and a pious persona in her community. It's unclear how María Nicolasa made a living, but she owned her own house and some basic furnishings in a poor and swampy neighborhood of the city. She was a member of the Brotherhood of Charity, a racially integrated lay confraternity in the Cathedral Church, and counted on them to ensure a proper funeral and burial. She was also a longtime member and *capitana* (captain) of a black confraternity, the Black Brotherhood of Our Lady of the Rosary, which cared for one of the Dominican convent church's most visited chapels.[12] In Guatemala, *capitanas* and other female leaders were elected annually by confraternity members and were usually responsible for tending images and altars, collecting alms, and/or serving as patrons for celebrations.[13] It seems her devotional activity and reputation made it possible for María Nicolasa to profess in the prestigious Franciscan Third Order on her deathbed and gain authorization to wear the tertiary habit in her final days and when she was laid to rest. She also planned to be buried under the floors of the Dominican chapel she had tended, a prime burial location that communicated prestige in this life and access to spiritual rewards in the next. Finally, she positioned herself as a pious, albeit humble, benefactor, leaving one donation to support the Black Brotherhood's feast of Our Lady of the Rosary and another for the construction of the Church of Our Lady of Carmen. In the last lines of her will, María Nicolasa invoked the support of one priest who served as witness and another priest along with a local notary who served as executors to her will.

By allying with priests, positioning herself as a pious benefactor and leader, and developing active devotional networks, María Nicolasa challenged sexual and racial ideologies and laid claim to a moral status within her community. And she was not alone. An analysis of more than 500 wills from Guatemala's capital illustrates how many mixed-race and laboring single women employed similar strategies. Elsewhere I have explored each of these strategies in detail, as well as why many priests allied with these women. But in the interests of space I will focus my attention here on single women's participation in confraternities and Third Orders. Religious brotherhoods were powerful lay organizations and central players in Spanish America's vibrant ritual life. They provided mutual aid for members, including care in sickness, a decent funeral and burial, and suffrages for the soul; they also supported collective devotions to a particular saint, caring for the image and sponsoring feast-day celebrations. In Santiago de Guatemala, confraternities further provided key economic support to parishes and their priests, contributing liturgical necessities such as wax and wine as well as funding church construction and repair.[14] There were more than 70 confraternities in Santiago by the eighteenth century, with each chapel, parish, or convent church hosting multiple brotherhoods. Entry fees were modest and often reflected a sliding scale based on social status. While some of Santiago's confraternities were organized along racial or caste lines, many were racially integrated by the eighteenth century.

Scholars have explored how non-elite men, particularly black and mulatto men in colonial Spanish America, utilized confraternities as well as black militias to cultivate a positive black identity, gain social mobility, and access corporate privileges and vassal status.[15] Less attention has been paid to non-elite women's participation in confraternities and how that participation shaped women's personal status within their communities as well as broader sexual and racial ideologies. And yet it appears that, by the eighteenth century, women, and particularly non-elite women, made up the majority of confraternity members in Guatemala and beyond. Surviving confraternity records in eighteenth-century Santiago de Guatemala and Mexico indicate that women accounted for approximately 60 per cent of confraternity memberships.[16]

Evidence indicates that many of those female confraternity members were laboring single and widowed women. Consistently, from 1700 to 1770, approximately 65 per cent of non-elite unmarried female will-makers in Guatemala's capital affirmed membership in a confraternity, compared to 35 per cent or less of elite women and laymen of all social statuses. Indeed, it was not uncommon for non-elite single women to belong to multiple confraternities affiliated with different churches and religious orders across the city. For example, Isabel de Pinzón, a non-elite woman and single mother of six children, noted in her 1705 will that she belonged to two confraternities, one in her parish church and one in the Mercedarian convent church.[17] Antonia de Leiva, a mulatta woman, freed slave, and single mother of two sons still enslaved, belonged to four different confraternities in as many churches across the city.[18] Although surviving confraternity records for Guatemala do not reveal the social status of members, evidence from wills reflects trends documented in colonial Mexico. Nicole von Germeten found that poor and laboring women of mixed-race descent "dominated the membership lists, of almost every one of the hundreds of confraternity record books available in parish and diocesan archives."[19] She further notes that baptism records confirm that some of these women were single mothers laboring in urban environments.[20]

For poor, single women navigating the tensions between gender and sexual ideals and the realities of their daily lives, participation in confraternities offered opportunities to build and buttress a pious persona through membership in spiritual communities. Entry into most confraternities required a "spiritual contract," which demanded virtuous habits as well as attendance at religious functions and sermons.[21] Confraternities, which encompassed men and women, often from different socio-racial backgrounds, also nurtured new kinds of relationships and identities based on communal religious practices rather than distinctions of social, racial, marital, or sexual status.[22] This could be especially important for poor or mixed-race women, who were more vulnerable to accusations of criminal behavior, particularly sexual or religious deviance. For example, one study points to a Mexican Inquisition case in which a free mulatta woman and confraternity member successfully challenged allegations that she had made a pact with the devil. Although her accuser was a Spanish man and social superior, the local Inquisition official rejected the allegations based on his own personal knowledge of the woman's leadership position in a confraternity and her regular engagement in confession and communion.[23]

As seen in the case of María Nicolasa, some of Santiago's confraternities provided enhanced opportunities for poor, single women to establish their spiritual status and authority through leadership positions. For urban plebeian communities, militia and confraternity leadership posts offered the most powerful public roles available within colonial society. These positions played an important role in establishing internal non-elite hierarchies and social status within the broader community. In Spain, confraternity leadership was restricted to male members, but African and indigenous influence led to the creation of female leadership positions in Spanish America. Indeed, evidence suggests that, in Santiago de Guatemala, African and indigenous traditions broadly reshaped the local religious landscape as female leadership positions extended beyond ethnically segregated native and black brotherhoods and also survived well into the nineteenth century.[24] The Black Brotherhood of the Rosary's repeated election of single-mother María Nicolasa into a key religious leadership post certainly could be taken as evidence of how the black and mulatto community's sexual mores diverged from or directly challenged Spanish elite sexual ideals of female chastity. But María Nicolasa's pious persona was also clearly recognized beyond Santiago's black community. Her ability to profess in the prestigious Franciscan Third Order and don the tertiary habit in her final days indicates that Franciscan friars and elite leaders of the Franciscan Third Order recognized her piety and honorable reputation alongside her status as a freed slave and single mother. Her story highlights a broader acceptance of more flexible gender ideals and a weakening of Spanish colonial "strategies of exclusion" based on sexual and racial ideologies.[25] This tangible breakdown in colonial Spanish America's gender and racial hierarchy reflects a variety of complex local, regional, and global factors, including internal conflicts within Spain's colonial model which sought to create an inclusive Catholic colonial society while also maintaining a rigid caste hierarchy. María Nicolasa's case also reflects encounters of local and global Catholicism, as Guatemalan church leaders in the modest provincial capital adapted official regulations according to local needs and circumstances at the same time that the eighteenth-century renewal of Catholic missionary movements promoted more diverse models of piety and clerical alliances with laypeople of color in the interests of evangelization and spiritual renewal.[26]

Refashioning identities: clothing, sexuality, and the Franciscan Third Order

Nearly one third of female will-makers in early eighteenth-century Santiago de Guatemala identified as members of the Franciscan Third Order, that is as Franciscan tertiaries. The Franciscan Third Order represented a "middle state between the cloister and the world."[27] Tertiaries went through year-long novitiates, made revocable vows, and followed a common "Rule" that involved strict moral standards, private and public devotions, and charitable activities. Some gained authorization to mark their status by publicly wearing modified habits. The Rule of the Franciscan Third Order in Guatemala and other parts of Spanish America also technically required novitiates to demonstrate wealth, legitimacy, pure Spanish descent, and impeccable virtue. Indeed, the few existing studies of the Franciscan Third Order in colonial Latin America emphasize that its membership was elite and mostly male and that the women who joined were wealthy and either wives or laywomen enclosed in religious houses.[28] And yet most female will-makers who identified as Franciscan tertiaries in early eighteenth-century Santiago de Guatemala were non-elite and living outside marriage. Among them were poor widows, abandoned wives, single mothers (including María Nicolasa, a mulatta freed slave), and women born illegitimate, of potentially mixed-race backgrounds. As I have argued elsewhere, the diverse make-up of Santiago de Guatemala's Franciscan Third

Order in part reflected Franciscan missionary zeal and tactics, particularly as they were adapted to Guatemala's local context.[29] But it also resulted from non-elite women's own devotional enthusiasm and persistent efforts to join this prestigious religious organization.

Evidence from wills suggests that women who gained authorization to wear the Franciscan tertiary habit were especially well positioned to highlight their virtue and piety. Single-mother Antonia de Aguilar, who had raised two illegitimate daughters, somewhat unusually pointed to her status as a Franciscan tertiary of the *habito descubierto* (habit worn in public) in the opening lines of her will. She identified herself as "Antonia de Aguilar, a *soltera* (single woman) dressed in the habit of the Third Order of Penitence of Saint Francis."[30] Antonia's juxtaposition of terms is striking. The term *soltera* referred to a single woman who could not claim virginity, as opposed to the morally elevated status of *doncella*, or maiden. Many female will-makers simply left their status blank rather than identify themselves with this term. And yet Antonia acknowledged her position as a *soltera* and in the same breath identified herself as a Franciscan tertiary who had gained the honorable authorization to wear a habit in public. The emphasis Antonia placed on her tertiary status was replicated by the notary, who identified her in the sidebar as "Antonia de Aguilar, Spanish, Tertiary." Although notaries sometimes included women's marital status in the sidebar notes, Antonia's notary opted to emphasize her ethnic status of Spanish descent and her tertiary identity rather than her position as a *soltera*. Abandoned-wife Juana de la Fé y Velasco also pointed to her identity as a Franciscan tertiary in the opening lines of her will, immediately before acknowledging her morally ambiguous status as an abandoned wife.[31] She presented herself as "Juana de la Fé y Velasco, *vecina* (citizen) of this city of Santiago de Guatemala, sister of the Third Order of Penitence of Saint Francis, legitimate wife of Don Juan de Salazar, who has been absent from this city for more than twenty years." She was also sure to emphasize later in her will that she was authorized to publicly wear the tertiary habit and had been an upstanding member paying her dues for many years.

As numerous scholars point out, clothing played a powerful role in the construction of identities in colonial Spanish America. Most studies examine the ways in which non-elite and mixed-race individuals regularly adopted elegant attire as a means of altering their social or ethnic status.[32] Tamara Walker's recent study further points out that stylish clothing allowed enslaved peoples to "lay claim to their bodies as sites of pride and pleasure" and to "nurture relationships and fashion dynamic social identities."[33] The coarse and humble Franciscan tertiary habit was purposefully the opposite of sumptuous elegance, but adopting the habit similarly allowed poor, single women and single mothers to make claims about their bodies, develop devotional networks, and construct pious personas in their communities. Perhaps the tertiary habit effaced the moral ambiguities of poor, unmarried women's status and allowed them to pass as moral exemplars, much as poor or mixed-race people passed as wealthier or whiter individuals through lavish displays of silk, lace, and jewels. Or perhaps the penitential nature of the tertiary habits did not conceal women's poverty or ambiguous moral status so much as transform their meaning into the sacred categories of humility and repentance.[34]

Social and racial status could, of course, extend or limit women's abilities to construct or manipulate their public personas. Antonia de Aguilar's ability to identify herself as a *soltera* and single mother, and to have professed in the Franciscan Third Order with permission to wear the tertiary habit in public, highlights the privileges she enjoyed as a woman of Spanish descent. As a mulatta and freed slave, María Nicolasa de Aparicio notably declined to identify herself with the term "*soltera*" and only admitted to having illegitimate children in the last lines of her will. It also appears she was only allowed to profess in the Third Order on her deathbed. Still, María Nicolasa's profession directly undermined the Franciscan Third Order's exclusionary Rule, which restricted access to elite and "pure-blooded" Spaniards with honorable reputations. In so doing, she participated in a broader challenge to religious, sexual, and racial ideologies underpinning caste restrictions, with wide-reaching implications over time. Decades after María Nicolasa's death, a wealthy donor in Santiago de Guatemala left a sizeable grant, 30,000 pesos, to fund a religious house for mulatta members of the Franciscan Third Order. The foundation was ultimately unsuccessful, most likely due to the fallout associated with the massive earthquakes of 1773 and protracted relocation of the capital. But the attempt suggests the existence of a thriving local community of mulatta women in the Franciscan Third Order. Elsewhere I have speculated that this community may have played a leading role as teachers and administrators in Guatemala's first free primary school for girls, founded in the 1770s and open to girls of all racial backgrounds.[35]

Conclusion

A century after María Nicolasa de Aparicio left her will, the provincial Franciscan head in Guatemala passionately lobbied the king to remove most caste restrictions on people of African descent so that they might enter universities, religious orders, and elite professions. He argued that discriminatory policies were irrational, given that among the mulatto population "there are many of both sexes endowed with admirable qualities and virtuous customs, sustained by the frequency of prayer and the sacraments."[36] Within a decade his rather radical proposition was superseded by independence movements that abolished the colonial caste system and declared legal equality for all American-born males. Recent studies have illuminated how mixed-race men actively and gradually eroded caste restrictions over centuries through militia service and lawsuits, laying the foundation for equal citizen status after independence from Spain. African, indigenous, and mixed-race women have typically figured in this story as the sexual partners of white or lighter-skinned men and as mothers of mixed-race offspring who further blurred racial lines. Evidence from wills reveals another side to this story. Laboring single women who developed devotional networks and pious personas reworked official discourses of sexuality, morality, and religiosity in their own daily lives, as well as in local institutions and the archival record. In so doing they participated in the slow weakening of "racialized forms of rule" in colonial Spanish America.[37]

Notes

1 Tortorici, *Sins Against Nature,* 5.
2 Gauderman, "It Happened on the Way to the *Temascal* and Other Stories," 177.
3 See Pizzigoni, "Alternative Sex and Gender in Early Latin America"; Germeten, *Violent Delights, Violent Ends,* 10–11. On loopholes accessed by elite women, see Twinam, *Public Lives, Private Secrets.*
4 See for example, Tortorici, ed., *Sexuality and the Unnatural*; Germeten, *Profit and Passion.*
5 See for example, Boyer, "Honor Among Plebeians," 152–178; Lipsett-Rivera, *Gender and the Negotiation of Daily Life.*
6 This study emerges from a broader analysis of close to 550 wills in Guatemala's capital between 1700 and 1870. In order to ensure the most representative sample possible, I examined every will, both male and female, in 13 selected years. During the eighteenth century, 45–50 per cent of will makers in any given year were women, with over 80 per cent of those women living outside of marriage. Non-elite laboring women made up a sizeable percentage (ranging from 40–70 per cent) of female will makers in the eighteenth century. For more discussion of sources and method, see Leavitt-Alcántara, *Alone at the Altar,* 9–14.
7 Will of María Nicolasa de Aparicio, 1705, Sig. A1, Leg. 1006, Exp. 9499, Escribano Francisco Herrera Samayoa, Fols. 196v-198f, Archivo General de Centroamérica (AGCA).

8 Kinsbruner, *The Colonial Spanish-American City*, 113.
9 Lutz, *Santiago de Guatemala*, 92–93.
10 Cited in Komisaruk, *Labor and Love in Guatemala*, 115.
11 Lutz, *Santiago de Guatemala*, 234.
12 Girón, Menéndez, and Axpuac, "Las capillas de morenos y naturales del templo de Santo Domingo en Santiago de Guatemala," 1515.
13 See for example, Libros de Cofradías de San Sebastián, Fondo Parroquial, San Sebastián, Sección Sacramental, Archivo Histórico Arquidiocesano de Guatemala (AHAG).
14 Añoveros, *Población y estado sociorreligioso de la Diócesis de Guatemala*, 67, 72.
15 See Twinam, *Purchasing Whiteness*; Vinson III, *Bearing Arms for His Majesty*; Germeten, *Black Blood Brothers*.
16 See Libros de Cofradías de San Sebastián, Fondo Parroquial, San Sebastián, Sección Sacramental, AHAG; Libros de Cofradías de Remedios, Fondo Parroquial, Nuestra Señora de los Remedios, Sección Sacramental, AHAG. For Mexico, see Chowning, "La feminización de la piedad en México," 481, 483.
17 Will of Isabel de Pinzón, 1705, Sig. A1, Leg. 740, Exp. 9233, Escribano José de León, Fols. 75f-77f, AGCA.
18 Will of Antonia de Leiva, 1705, Sig. A1, Leg. 1006, Exp. 9499, Escribano Francisco Herrera Samayoa, Fols. 173f–175v, AGCA.
19 Germeten, *Black Blood Brothers*, 46.
20 Ibid., 41. Margaret Chowning similarly found that many single women joined confraternities alongside sisters and other female relatives. Chowning, "La feminización de la piedad en México," 481, 483.
21 Lavrin, "Cofradías Novohispanos," 50.
22 This analysis builds upon Matthew O'Hara's application of Vered Amit's notion of "relational identities" to religious brotherhoods in colonial Mexico. O'Hara, "The Orthodox Underworld of Colonial Mexico," 243.
23 Germeten, *Black Blood Brothers*, 42.
24 Libros de Cofradías de San Sebastián, Fondo Parroquial, San Sebastián, Seccion Sacramental, AHAG.
25 Stoler, "Tense and Tender Ties," 832.
26 Leavitt-Alcántara, *Alone at the Altar*, 42–53.
27 Belanger, "Between the Cloister and the World," 157.
28 See Voekel, *Alone Before God*, 118–120; See de Gentile, "Familias de la Orden Tercera de San Francisco en Buenos Aires," 59–70.
29 Leavitt-Alcántara, *Alone at the Altar*, 42–53.
30 Will of Antonia de Aguilar, 1717, Sig. A1, Leg. 1410, Exp. 9901, Escribano Diego Leonardo Valenzuela, Fols. 55v–57v, AGCA.
31 Will of Juana de la Fé y Velasco, 1717, Sig. A1, Leg. 1375, Exp. 98661, Escribano Juan de Ulloa y Moscoso, Fols. 141f–144v, AGCA. On the morally ambiguous status of women living apart from their husbands, see van Deusen, *Between the Sacred and the Worldly*, 58, 84.
32 See for example, Earle, "'Two Pairs of Pink Satin Shoes!' and Germeten, *Violent Delights, Violent Ends*, 145–147.
33 Walker, *Exquisite Slaves*, 44.
34 I am grateful to Gretchen Starr-Lebeau for alerting me to this possibility. Personal communication, April 2015.
35 Leavitt-Alcántara, *Alone at the Altar*, 106.
36 Cited in Matthew, "'Por que el color decide aquí en la mayor parte la nobleza,'" 162.
37 Stoler, "Tense and Tender Ties," 840.

Bibliography

Belanger, Brian. "Between the Cloister and the World: The Franciscan Third Order of Colonial Querétaro." *The Americas* 49, no. 2 (October 1992): 157–177. doi:10.2307/1006989.

Boyer, Richard. "Honor Among Plebeians: Mala Sangre and Social Reputation." In *The Faces of Honor: Sex, Shame, and Violence in Colonial Latin America*, edited by Lyman Johnson and Sonya Lipsett-Rivera, 152–178. Albuquerque, NM: University of New Mexico Press, 1998.

Castañeda García, Rafael. "Piedad y participación femenina en la cofradía de negros y mulatos de San Benito de Palermo en el Bajío novohispano, siglo XVIII." *Nuevo Mundo, Mundos Nuevos Débats* (2012). doi:64478.

Chowning, Margaret. "La feminización de la piedad en México: Género y piedad en las cofradías de españoles. Tendencias coloniales y pos-coloniales en los arzobispados de Michoacán y Guadalajara." In *Religión, política, e identidad en la independencia de México*, edited by Brian Connaughton, 475–514. México City: Universidad Autónoma Metropolitana, 2010.

Earle, Rebecca. "'Two Pairs of Pink Satin Shoes!!' Race, Clothing, and Identity in the Americas (17th–19th Centuries)." *History Workshop Journal*, no. 52 (2001): 175–195.

Gauderman, Kimberly. "It Happened on the Way to the *Temascal* and Other Stories: Desiring the Illicit in Colonial Spanish America." *Ethnohistory* 54, no. 1 (Winter 2007): 177–186. doi:10.1215/00141801-2006-043.

Germeten, Nicole von. *Black Blood Brothers: Confraternities and Social Mobility for Afro-Mexicans*. Gainesville, FL: University Press of Florida, 2006.

Germeten, Nicole von. *Violent Delights, Violent Ends: Sex, Race, and Honor in Colonial Cartagena de Indias*. Albuquerque, NM: University of New Mexico Press, 2013.

Germeten, Nicole von. *Profit and Passion: Transactional Sex in Colonial Mexico*. Berkeley, CA: University of California Press, 2018.

Lavrin, Asunción. "Cofradías novohispanos: Economías material y espiritual." In *Cofradías, capellanías, y obras pías en la América colonial*, edited by María del Pilar Martínez López-Cano, Gisela von Wobeser and Juan Guillermo Muñoz Correa, 49–64. México City: Universidad Nacional Autónoma de México, 1998.

Leavitt-Alcántara, Brianna. *Alone at the Altar: Single Women and Devotion in Guatemala, 1670–1870*. Stanford, CA: Stanford University Press, 2018.

Lipsett-Rivera, Sonya. *Gender and the Negotiation of Daily Life in Mexico, 1750–1850*. Lincoln, NE: University of Nebraska Press, 2012.

Lutz, Christopher. *Santiago de Guatemala, 1541–1773: City, Caste, and the Colonial Experience*. Norman, OK: University of Oklahoma Press, 1994.

Kinsbruner, Jay. *The Colonial Spanish-American City: Urban Life in the Age of Atlantic Capitalism*. Austin, TX: University of Texas Press, 2005.

Komisaruk, Catherine. *Labor and Love in Guatemala: The Eve of Independence*. Stanford, CA: Stanford University Press, 2013.

Mannarelli, María Emma. *Private Passions and Public Sins: Men and Women in Seventeenth-Century Lima*. Translated by Sidney Evans and Meredith Dodge. Albuquerque, NM: University of New Mexico Press, 2007.

Matthew, Laura E. "'Por que el color decide aquí en la mayor parte la nobleza': Una carta de Fr. José Antonio Goicoechea, Guatemala, siglo XIX." *Mesoamérica* 55 (enero-diciembre 2013): 153–167.

O'Hara, Matthew. "The Orthodox Underworld of Colonial Mexico." *Colonial Latin American Review* 17, no. 2 (2008): 233–250. doi:10.1080/10609160802393831.

Rodríguez Girón, Zoila, Dámaris Menéndez and Octavio Axpuac. "Las capillas de morenos y naturales del templo de Santo Domingo en Santiago de Guatemala." In *XX Simposio de Investigaciones Arqueológicas en Guatemala, 2006: Museo Nacional de Arqueología y Etnología*, edited by Simposio de Investigaciones Arqueológicas en Guatemeala, Juan Pedro Laporte, Bárbara Arroyo and Héctor E. Mejía, 1512–1528. Guatemala: Ministerio de Cultura y Deportes, Instituto de Antropología e Historia, 2007.

Siegrist de Gentile, Nora. "Familias de la Orden Tercera de San Francisco en Buenos Aires. Identidad de sus miembros y relaciones con España en los siglos XVIII Y XIX." In *Familias iberoamericanas: Historia, identidad, y conflictos*, edited by Pilar Gonzalbo Aizpuru, 59–79. México City: Colegio de México, 2001.

Stoler, Ann. "Tense and Tender Ties: The Politics of Comparison in North American History and (Post) Colonial Studies." *The Journal of American History* 88, no. 3 (2001): 829–865. doi:10.2307/2700385.

Tortorici, Zeb, ed. *Sexuality and the Unnatural in Colonial Latin America*. Berkeley, CA: University of California Press, 2016.

Tortorici, Zeb. *Sins Against Nature: Sex and Archives in Colonial New Spain*. Durham, NC: Duke University Press, 2018.

Twinam, Ann. *Public Lives, Private Secrets: Gender, Honor, Sexuality, and Illegitimacy in Colonial Spanish America*. Stanford, CA: Stanford University Press, 1999.

Twinam, Ann. *Purchasing Whiteness: Pardos, Mulattos, and the Quest for Social Mobility in the Spanish Indies*. Stanford, CA: Stanford University Press, 2015.

van Deusen, Nancy E. *Between the Sacred and the Worldly: The Institutional and Cultural Practice of Recogimiento in Colonial Lima*. Stanford, CA: Stanford University Press, 2001.

Vinson, Ben. *Bearing Arms for His Majesty: The Free-Colored Militia in Colonial Mexico.* Stanford, CA: Stanford University Press, 2001.

Voekel, Pamela. *Alone Before God: The Religious Origins of Modernity in Mexico.* Durham, NC: Duke University Press, 2002.

Walker, Tamara. *Exquisite Slaves: Race, Clothing, and Status in Colonial Lima.* Cambridge, UK: Cambridge University Press, 2017.

21

MIXED MARRIAGE AND THE EMBODIMENT OF LAW IN FRENCH ALGERIA

Judith Surkis

According to the French demographer and politician René Ricoux, the failure of population mixing or "fusion" between "*indigènes*" and "Europeans" in colonial Algeria was not merely the result of religious and legal difference. Their sexual incompatibility had, he claimed, a physiological basis: "Two causes that are more powerful than the difference of religions can explain the small amount of interbreeding with *indigènes*, and allow us to predict that they will not become more frequent: they are *syphilis* and *sodomy*." For Ricoux, a doctor at the civil hospital in Philippeville, these "endemo-constitutional vices" explained past resistance to fusion and rendered any future reconciliation between the populations "an unrealizable utopia." For Ricoux, "the French people has no interest in compromising its native qualities, its moral superiority, in mixing with these corrupt races whose blood is polluted [*vicié*]."[1] This corporealized conception of Algerian sexual perversity made "Franco–Muslim" mixing unfeasible as a strategy of colonization. By contrast, he and other demographers sought to show that "European" mixed marriages, optimally between French men and "Southern" or Latin women, would physically and politically solidify French domination.[2] Published in the wake of the 1870 advent of civilian rule in the colony, Ricoux's study lent scientific ground to arguments for "European" fusion and settlement.[3]

Official reports underscored that mixed marriages with Muslims were exceedingly rare. Based exclusively on the civil registry, the *Annuaire statistique de France* for 1876 recorded, for example, 11 marriages between European men and Muslim women and four between Muslim men and European women. In 1880 there were five and six total marriages, respectively.[4] While apparently uncommon, officials nonetheless continued to worry about the legal questions these marriages posed. Their arguments contributed to an increasingly corporealized conception of the difference between "Europeans" and Algerians. A colonial legal construction of Muslim civil or "personal status" and its difference from a secular French Civil Code elaborated a corporealized conception of Islam. The legal status of French citizens, "European" nationals, and Algerian colonial subjects, or *indigènes*, thus took on bodily attributes and qualities. In their doctrine and jurisprudence, colonial jurists and administrators linked claims made by racist demographers about Algerians' perverse physicality to law.

For Algerian colonial jurists, Muslim men remained stubbornly attached to their personal status because it granted them patriarchal sexual privileges such as polygamy, repudiation, and forced marriage. An 1873 property reform (the Warnier law) had territorialized French civil law, while setting aside "personal status" as a distinct jurisdiction of family law.[5] Land transactions in selected areas were made subject to French civil law, while marriage, divorce, and inheritance "as matters of the freedom of conscience, of religion, of the intimate life of families" were regulated by Muslim and customary law.[6] This new legal category of "Muslim personal status" condensed and confused religious attachment and patriarchal sexual rights.

Polygamy, child marriage, and repudiation became metonyms for Muslims' conflation of religious and civil law. They explained why Algerians refused to become citizens by adopting the Civil Code, as had been outlined in an 1865 *sénatus-consulte*. Charles Roussel, who had been a magistrate in Algeria in the 1860s, thus claimed in 1875: "Because their religious status is confounded with their civil status, naturalization [i.e., becoming a citizen] touches their faith in modifying their civil status. Polygamy, divorce, and repudiation, which it eliminates, are fundamental institutions in Islam, the abandonment of which implies a certain heresy."[7] The prominent specialist of international private law, André Weiss, similarly presented naturalization as a loss of men's sexual rights: "for him no more divorce by mutual consent or simple repudiation, no more polygamy."[8] For Albert Hugues, "polygamy, repudiation, wife purchase, paternal constraint" were all "rights that are cherished in the heart of every believer."[9] In the eyes of colonial jurists, Algerian men's embodied investment in Muslim law made legal assimilation impossible. Their studies of mixed marriage imagined and explored this (im)possibility. The juridical conflicts associated with mixed marriage demonstrate how, while nominally based on a religious rather than racial difference, colonial jurists increasingly represented Muslim law and legal difference as intimately linked to bodies.[10]

Mixed-marriage jurisprudence sheds light on the colonial history of secularism and the legal production of a secular European as well as Muslim body. In pondering these cases, French colonial administrators and jurists elaborated fantasies of Muslim law as bound to men's sexual rights and women's sexual degradation. They projected those fantasies onto the bodies of Muslim persons while casting French civil law as integral and dignified, especially in its treatment of women. In the process, Muslim personal status and French civil status each assumed an embodied meaning, combining and confusing racial, religious, and sexual difference. This chapter illuminates an apparent paradox: how the legal rhetoric of secularism and religious freedom shaped a corporealized—and particularized—conception of Muslim personal law and sex.[11]

Corporealizing codes

As a religious jurisdiction *internal* to the French state's system of secular law, Muslim personal status set aside marriage, divorce, and inheritance as matters to be adjudicated by state-appointed Muslim jurists.[12] The religious basis of Muslim personal status was nonetheless ambiguous. It could not be acquired and it could only be abandoned according to the procedures outlined in the 1865 *sénatus-consulte*. Persons were born into Muslim personal status by virtue of the fact that they had "indigenous" ancestors. While religious sensibility served as its purported ground, the status was, in fact, based on and limited by "blood ties" of filiation to former inhabitants of the Regency of Algiers. In this sense it was a *jus sanguinis* with a religious name. Religious conversion alone (i.e., without recourse to official "naturalization") did not alter Muslim legal status. Inversely, converts to Islam did not acquire it. Conversion remained a matter of private personal faith and not public law. Secular legal status was distinct from individual religious belief.[13]

Because neither individuals nor clerical authorities could alter personal status, converts to Christianity remained legally Muslim. (Some jurists would hence argue that a more accurate description in this case was "*indigène catholique.*"[14]) Christian converts to Islam likewise kept their French or other European nation's civil status. Muslim personal status was at once "ethno-political" *and* implicitly religious, in part because secular public law claimed independence from what it designated as religious matters.[15] The *de facto* ethnicization of Muslim status was thus a partial effect of French civil law's claim to secularity.[16] The ambiguity of Muslim personal status—as at once religious and not—actually made it an effective node of Algerian colonial governmentality.[17] As I show in this chapter, legal accounts of Islamic faith as implacably bound to a gendered juridical organization of sex and kinship consolidated this ethnicized understanding of personal status. Because it lacked a national territorial referent, the status was anchored in Muslim bodies and affects instead.

In contrast to conversion, marriage profoundly affected personal status, especially for women. A French woman's marriage to a foreigner altered her nationality. Article 12 of the 1804 Civil Code established that a foreign woman who married a French man became French, while article 19 determined that "a French woman who marries a foreigner follows the condition of her husband."[18] Up until a 1927 reform, the Civil Code privileged "legal unity" within the conjugal family.[19] This legal construction of conjugality (as distinct from extended kinship) subordinated married women to their husbands' law.

By the end of the nineteenth century, new divorce laws, rising rates of immigration and emigration, concerns about demography, and the development of organized feminism put new pressures on the principle of conjugal legal unity. Jurists and feminists debated married women's relationship to nationality at international private law conferences, feminist congresses, and in proposals for new civil codes and nationality laws. Some small reforms in 1889 helped widows and divorcées regain French nationality and protected women who did not gain nationality by marriage. The principle of marital unity based on patriarchal prerogative nonetheless remained in place. In one of the many dissertations devoted to the topic at the end of the nineteenth-century, Albert Cauwès explained how legal uniformity in marriage was wedded to national sovereignty: "Marital power is an essential factor in the principle of nationalities: the state must, in itself, assure unity everywhere." In his view, "the power that it attributes to the husband to modify the original nationality of his wife by marriage" was a "translation" of the state's power.[20] Sovereign and marital authority coincided in the conjugal family.

Colonial mixed marriages raised pointed questions about this patriarchal principle by testing the unity of law within both the family and the state. Such marriages made the lacunae and contradictions of colonial legal pluralism visible. Jurists, politicians, and administrators continually grappled with how to assign legal status to the husbands, wives, and children whose kinship and property relations were governed by conflicting codes. At the beginning of colonization, administrators and jurists improvised answers to these questions, often in ways that preserved patriarchal prerogatives. By the end of the nineteenth century, however, they devised fixed rules with which to manage them. Unlike in the early nineteenth century, these legal "fixes" stopped prioritizing the principle of patriarchy—or the subordination of a married woman to the husband's law—and instead upheld the superiority of the French Civil Code, placing principles of French legal sovereignty and superiority above that of patriarchy, at least for Muslim men. By juxtaposing conflicts over the course of the nineteenth century and into the twentieth, we grasp the import and extent of this shift.

Preserving patriarchy

An 1836 trial before the Tribunal of First Instance of Algiers prompted an initial response to this legal quandary.[21] It involved Si Hamdan ben Abderaman Bourkaïeb, an Algierian notable who had worked with the French after the capitulation in 1830 but who soon fell into disgrace with French authorities. Twice exiled to Paris, he married the daughter of a French consul, Josephine Zabel, before a French official, even though he already had two wives. Ailing, he returned with Josephine to his residence in Algiers, after which he soon died and left behind a considerable fortune.[22] Before his death, Bourkaïeb had, in a document drawn up before a qadi, named his nephew Mustapha, not Josephine, as administrator of his son Ismaïl's inheritance. Josephine, meanwhile, claimed that French law should govern their marital regime and its effects on the person and fortune of her son.[23]

Following international legal principles of *jus gentium*, the Tribunal of First Instance found in the nephew's favor. It decided that Bourkaïeb could contract marriage before French authorities while maintaining his own civil law status. As an inhabitant of the former Ottoman Regency of Algiers he contracted under "Moorish law," which permitted a Muslim man to marry Christian women. The court also decided that because "a woman follows the condition of her husband," his widow was also subject to that law. She remained Catholic, but the marriage and its effects would be regulated by her husband's law. The initial decision explained that, "according to French law [i.e., article 19 of the Civil Code], because she became the wife of a Muslim, she must be governed by 'Moorish law,' at least relative to the effects of her marriage." The court had little patience for Josephine's attempt to reclaim French legal status. In its view, "she engaged in advance to submit" to that law, "in uniting her destiny to that of a man who she knew benefited from civil rights different from her own."[24] The court granted Josephine custody over Ismaïl's young person, but upheld Mustapha's authority as administrator of his possessions.

Josephine appealed but made no further headway. The court did, however, use the occasion to clarify her legal status: "One cannot conclude from this marriage that it had the effect of rendering the dame Zabel indigenous to the territory of Alger ... since the quality of *indigène* can only belong to a person who was born in this territory." The court thus placed a legal limit on local status: one had to be born an *indigène*; one could never become one. The Superior Tribunal of Algiers nonetheless affirmed the patriarchal principle according to which "women follow the condition of their husbands." Zabel's marriage to Hamdan Bourkaïeb and its effects were "Muslim."[25]

This early decision is remarkable from the perspective of subsequent jurisprudence. By the last third of the nineteenth century, jurists and politicians actively worked to protect the French legal status embodied by "European" women and occasionally by Algerian women who had been "naturalized." They upheld the primacy of French civil law over a subordinate and exceptional Muslim law and castigated the Tribunal of Algiers' early finding.[26] Later mixed-marriage cases instead appealed to "European" women's status in order to affirm a sexualized hierarchy between "French" and "Muslim" law.

Containing conflicts

Mixed-marriage cases assumed heightened significance for jurists and legislators in later decades. These concerns emerged in tandem with the legal delineation of "Muslim personal status." According to the civil registry, mixed marriage increased moderately in the 1860s and 1870s. An estimation based on the names and family histories included in the marriage acts suggests that there were at least 25 in the 1860s, 59 in the 1870s, and 71 in the 1880s, up from eight between 1839 and 1849 and 15 in the 1850s.[27] While these numbers remained low, jurists' concern about the unions increased, especially after the advent of civilian settler rule in 1870. The presumptive rarity of the romances spurred both legal and novelistic imaginations, as jurists worked to distinguish French and European from "Muslim" law. The imagined fate of French and European women in mixed marriages came to embody what jurists saw as grave conflicts of law. Intervening in the name of women's protection, they asserted the sexual and civilizational superiority of French civil law.[28]

Coinciding with the advent of civilian rule, the case of Aurélie Tijani, née Picard, attracted considerable official attention. Its singular circumstances were worthy of a novel. In 1870, Aurélie, the daughter of a gendarme who had served in Algeria, met Ahmed al-Tijani, the powerful and wealthy head of the Tijaniya Islamic confraternity that was close to colonial authorities.[29] The couple met in Bordeaux, where Ahmed was in exile. Aurélie accepted his marriage proposal and returned with him to the Algerian south. After the move, she developed a measure of political influence in the Tijaniya, while working with her husband to expand the French presence in the Sahara. When Ahmed died in 1897 she married his brother. By the end of her life she had become a colonial heroine of sorts, garnering public recognition and praise.[30] By influencing the subsequent juridical treatment of mixed marriage, her union with al-Tijani left a legal as well as political legacy.

Picard and al-Tijani's marital project provoked official resistance. They could not wed under French civil law because al-Tijani already had two other wives, while qadis had no jurisdiction over French and European subjects. Unwilling to displease French authorities, the qadi of Algiers refused to contract their union. Al-Tijani and Picard's appeal before the Cour d'Alger ended in failure.[31] Their "marriage," eventually overseen by an *imam* and blessed by Cardinal Lavigerie, went unrecognized by French authorities.[32] Other "mixed" unions officiated at the *mairie* and recorded in the civil registry that same year did not produce similar legal wrangling.[33] The non-recognition of Picard's marriage, meanwhile, provided a unique occasion to outline the hierarchal relation between civil and "Muslim law" at the moment of Algeria's transfer to civilian rule.

Named governor general in March 1871, Admiral Louis Henri de Gueydon implemented civilian rule by eliminating many of the administrative structures of the Second Empire's ongoing military government and "Arab Kingdom."[34] Fusionist fantasies of Franco–Muslim marriage were another facet of the previous regime that settler advocates had long sought to dismantle.[35] Mobilizing this politico–legal critique of hybridity, Gueydon firmly opposed the prospect of Picard's "Muslim" union and issued a November 1871 circular on "mixed marriage" to Algeria's new prefects, mayors, and qadis in response. His text denounced the "anomalies caused by undefined legal relations between two populations, European and *indigène*, each having, one and the other, their own personal status and real property status." He targeted both the "impossibility of property transactions" and the purportedly "more serious inconveniences" in matters of personal status. More specifically, he underscored that "the existing state of legislation already poses, notably regarding mixed marriages, certain obstacles to what I will call the abuse of Muslim law." As Gueydon's circular explained: "In no case can a mixed marriage be celebrated according to Muslim law, without the production of a marriage act certifying that a civil marriage has taken place before a French official."[36] Because Picard was a French citizen (albeit a second-class one), she could only marry under French civil law.

According to this rule, Picard's French law status trumped that of her prospective husband, even though the reverse rule applied in international private law—and in the 1836 Bourkaïeb case. When French legal sovereignty was still uncertain at the outset of colonization, Zabel's French statute did not prevail, her husband's "Moorish law" did. By the 1870s, jurists asserted the Civil Code's ascendency over a subordinate and exceptional Muslim law. In an ironic reversal and denegation of the Code's own patriarchal principles of marital unity, colonial jurists argued that "European" women needed to be protected from the patriarchal excesses of Muslim law.[37] This gendered inversion came to distinguish colonial law from international conflicts of law. The sexual integrity and dignity of European women thus embodied the sovereignty and secularity of the Civil Code.

The presumptive rarity of Muslim–European marriages shored up arguments about the superiority of French civil law. Starting in 1878, yearly listings on Algeria in the *Statistique générale de France* publicized these small numbers.[38] Listed in the single digits, unions between "*Européen et musulmane*" and "*Musulman et Européenne*" paled in significance beside the hundreds listed between French and foreigners, and the thousands contracted between French nationals or foreigners among themselves. These small numbers supposedly proved European women's dignity. How the census arrived at these numbers is unclear. As Kamel Kateb has demonstrated, even those demographers who played a crucial role in the development of the Algerian statistics bureau, such as Ricoux, questioned their reliability.[39] The so-called "European" *état-civil* does contain traces of French civil marriages contracted between Muslims and Europeans that were not necessarily recorded as such in the published statistics. Official counting was no doubt uneven and inconsistent, especially since civil marriage made religious affiliation irrelevant. The registries do sometimes signal the partners' legal status. In the registry of Mustapha from 1872, the marriage between Jeanne Nadal and a daily laborer named Ali ben Saïd has the word "*indigène*" scribbled in the margin.[40] How the marriages were categorized on the census, if at all, is unclear.[41]

Labeling in the marriage registry was occasional and far from uniform. It reflected an unstable relationship between religion, ethnicity, and nationality in the minds and actions of officials who worked to form "Muslim" and "European" into statistical and legal realities. The annual production of demographic tables as well as the scientific studies and public policy that were based on them called attention to these marriages, in part because of, rather than despite, their small number. In contrast to Aurélie Picard's exotic and romantic union with Ahmed al-Tijani, these marriages occurred between modest characters. Despite this banality, statistical and legal accounts presented them as exotic exceptions to the normative endogamy of European settlement, marriage, and law.

Invalid acts

Despite the 1871 Gueydon circular, cases involving conflicting laws continued to come before French courts. Among them was the trial of a 26-year-old Corsican woman, Emilie Danési, who married an Algerian Muslim in 1878. Acting in the name of the public order of French law, the state itself put Danési on trial. At issue was the legitimacy of her "Muslim law" marriage to Ismaël ben Boursali following her sworn "abjuration" of Christianity and embrace of Islam before the Hanefi qadi of Algiers. Using her newly adopted name, Mimi bent Abdallah registered her Muslim marriage contract with Boursali on August 25, 1878. Calling Danési before the Muslim Chamber of the Appeals Court of Algiers, the public prosecutor, Jean Baptiste Fourcade, sought to annul both acts because her conversion and marriage were "contrary to public order" and "illegal assaults on the personal status of citizens."[42] Stepping in to protect the French personal status that she embodied, the state overruled her own wishes to the contrary.[43]

As in the Picard marriage, the Muslim Chamber threw the case out on the basis of jurisdiction. Despite Danési's religious conversion, her French nationality and citizenship required her to appear before a French civil court, rather than the tribunal set aside to hear Muslim law cases and litigants. When the case passed to the Court of First Instance it denied its competency to judge Danési's conversion, "which only had the effect of changing her religion and not her nationality." It had no jurisdiction over a purely "religious" act: "from no point of view can courts interfere with or recognize an act of this nature, which depends solely on the conscience of those who submit to it."[44] The marriage act was, however, fully in the domain of secular French law and hence subject to public concern and policing. Danési's marriage act was found to be "radically null and void" because "the personal status reserved for Muslim *indigènes* of Algeria can never apply to a person who does not have the quality of *indigène*."[45] Extending beyond the inner life of conscience, marriage altered legal personality, especially for women. Matters of spirit were to one side, personal law on the other.

The court's decision affirmed a principle that soon became axiomatic: that French and "European" women could never assume Muslim law status, even by marriage. As the adamantly secular colonial jurist Émile Larcher explained in the case of foreign women, "A European woman, in marrying a Muslim *indigène*, becomes, not an *indigène*, but a French citizen: her personal status is governed by French law, not Muslim law."[46] Up until 1927 the Civil Code subordinated married women to their husbands' "foreign" law. In Algeria, by contrast, a foreign European woman's civil law status took precedence over that of her husband, even as she acquired "his" French nationality in the marriage. "European" women, both French and foreign, personified the French Civil Code's superiority. This apparently "protective" legal gesture was always also disciplinary. In the Danési case it set the terms according to which a Corsican migrant could marry a Muslim man.

The question of how to manage conflicts of law in mixed marriage remained a persistent spur to jurists' legal imaginations. In numerous tracts and dissertations they criticized the effects of mixed marriage on "French" or "European" women and considered how a husband's "naturalization" might impact his Muslim wife.[47] In subsequent decades the dangers posed by "mixed marriage" would be used to argue against extending political rights to Algerian men who maintained their Muslim status.[48] Both during and after World War I, colonial and military officials increasingly worried that relations between North Africans and French women would become much less exceptional. At once citing and reproducing pervasive concerns about polygamy, they underscored the sovereign precedence of French civil, over exceptional "Muslim," law.[49]

The unions and their legal effects remained a persistent object of official concern over the course of the next two decades. In response, the Ministries of Justice and the Interior drew up a law regularizing how apparent conflicts between "French" and "indigenous" legal statutes—particularly in the case of French women and Algerian men—were to be resolved. The reports drafted in favor of the law demonstrate how the arguments and conclusions elaborated in earlier court decisions came to operate as common sense. The presentation before the Chamber of Deputies in 1925 affirmed the "logical preeminence of the colonial power over the indigenous," and hence of "a certain moral abandonment of personal status, which makes possible the presumption of a certain assimilation of European moeurs, while it is impossible to conceive of a renunciation of European moeurs by the French spouse."[50] Adopted by the Chamber in 1928, the legislation remained stalled in the Senate. Its underlying principles were nonetheless reconfirmed in subsequent doctrine and judicial decisions. As one law professor in Algiers remarked in reference to the proposed legislation, "In the domain of the conflicts of law the inequality of civilization and the mission of the more evolved country translates into the predominance of the more civilized legislation."[51] The prospect of mixed marriages nonetheless continued to haunt the imaginations of French officials as an unfair "privilege" of Muslim men. Octave Depont, a colonial administrator and migration expert, opposed extending citizenship to Algerians on this basis. He complained, "Muslims take the right to marry European women, but it is not reciprocal, because under no pretext can their girls be given over to Christians." Comparing this attitude to that of "prehistoric" men, he decried how the "tribe jealously guards the excess of its feminine element, wanting to keep it exclusively for itself."[52] Depont depicted Muslim Algerians as a primitive horde who kept a surplus of women and sexual pleasures for themselves, hence denying equal enjoyment to French men.

The abuse of this sexual "privilege" was penalized. A case in 1929 criminalized the perceived "exploitation" of personal status by a Muslim Algerian man who was eventually sent to prison for contracting two marriages: one under French civil law and the other under customary law, the latter of which was subsequently rendered void.[53] A treatise on the Algerian civil registry from 1937 reiterated the principle, underscoring that it was "repugnant" to assign a French woman—or her children—Muslim status, thus making them subject to "forced marriage," repudiation, or polygamy.[54] Muslim status, in other words, continued to evoke fears of a sexual violation of French women—and civil law.

Conclusion

Despite their apparent statistical insignificance, cases of mixed marriage incited considerable colonial juridical inquiry as synedoches of the conflict between a secular Civil Code and Algerian Muslim law. Present from the outset of colonization, these questions became more pointed once the "intimate" domain of Muslim personal status emerged as a legal shorthand for family, sex, and confessional sentiment. Cleaved from a universal and universalizable French law of property transaction, Muslim personal status (including Kabyle customary law) signified the particularized "quality" of the *indigène* and his patriarchal sexual rights. Matrimony was its ground (i.e., "marriage, divorce, and inheritance" defined its jurisdiction) and its limit, since indigenous status was not transferable by marriage. In court decisions, legislative reports, and legal treatises French jurists and politicians construed Muslim religiosity, legality, and kinship as intertwined and intimately bound to the embodied Muslim person.

This story resonates with other accounts of deep social ambivalence about ethno–religious mixing in colonial societies. In focusing on juridical developments we see how the secular status and sovereignty of French civil law gave form to a corporealized religio–legal personhood for Muslims, and implicitly for French and European subjects as well. From the outset of colonization, mixed marriages remained legally protected by principles of religious freedom. Conversion, as a pure matter of private conscience, was beyond the domain of secular law. But the legal effects of mixed marriage were a subject of public concern. At a crucial moment of political and legal transition in the 1870s, the cases of Aurélie Picard and Emilie Danési reveal how this secular logic, dividing private conscience from public law, outlined the contours not only of Muslim legal persons but also of "French" and "European" persons. Indeed, protecting the integrity of *French* personal status from the implicitly sexual incursions of Muslim law such as repudiation and polygamy became a crucial question of "public order" and hence of the sovereignty of French civil law. Inverting the conjugal logic of legal unity that governed international law, French women's civil status took precedence over their husbands' "Muslim" status. French women became bearers of abstract claims about French law's sovereign dignity, while Muslim men's legal status was particularized. In a revealing twist on the paradoxes of post-revolutionary French citizenship, women thus embodied the universality of French personal status.[55]

Notes

1 Ricoux and Bertillon, *La démographie figurée de l'Algérie*, 262.
2 Dessoliers, *De la fusion des races européennes*; Demontès, *Le peuple algérien*; Peyerimhoff de Fontenelle, *Enquête sur les résultats de la colonisation officielle*. On demography and European settlement, see Andersen, *Regeneration through Empire*.
3 Ricoux and Bertillon, *La démographie figurée de l'Algérie*, 258–259. On "Arab syphilis," see Amster, "The Syphilitic Arab?"
4 Ministère du Commerce, *Annuaire statistique de la France*, 653.
5 On "family law" as a novel legal domain, Halley and Rittich, "Critical Directions in Comparative Family Law"; Halley, "What is Family Law?"
6 Warnier, "Loi relative à l'établissement," 400.
7 Roussel, "La naturalisation des étrangers en Algérie," 914.
8 Weiss, *Traité théorique et pratique de droit international privé*, 399.
9 Hugues, *La nationalité française chez les musulmans de l'Algérie*, 194.
10 On Algerian concerns with mixed marriage, despite its seeming rarity, see Saada, *Empire's Children*, 25–30.
11 Scott, *Sex and Secularism* and *The Politics of the Veil*; Mahmood, *Religious Difference in a Secular Age*; Fernando, "Intimacy Surveilled."
12 Christelow, *Muslim Law Courts*.
13 Larcher, "Des effets juridiques du changement de religion"; Bonnichon, *La conversion au christianisme l'indigène musulman algérien*.
14 Larcher, "Des effets juridiques du changement de religion en Algérie."
15 Weil, *Qu'est-ce qu'un Français?* 235.
16 For parallel discussions of Jewish racialization, Brown, *Regulating Aversion*; Markell, *Bound by Recognition*.
17 On ambiguity as a mechanism of secular power, Agrama, *Questioning Secularism*.
18 Heuer, *The Family and the Nation*, 131–132.
19 Camiscioli, *Reproducing the French Race*.
20 Cauwès, *Des rapports du mariage avec la nationalité*, 3. See also, Gruffy, *De l'unité de nationalité dans la famille*; Garcin, *Du changement de nationalité entre époux*.
21 Droit-Tribunaux, *Revue africaine*, 113; Dame Hamdan Bourkaïeb v. Mustapha ben Ahmed ben el Adji Sehid, Tribunal Superier d'Alger, June 20, 1836, in Estoublon, *Jurisprudence algérienne*, Vol. 1 (1836), 15–17.
22 Reynaud, *Annales algériennes*, 381–382.
23 Droit-Tribunaux, *Revue africaine*, 108. Dame Hamdan Bourkaïeb v. Mustapha ben Ahmed ben el Adgi Sehid, Estoublon, *Jurisprudence algérienne*, Vol. 1, 15–17.
24 Droit-Tribunaux, *Revue africaine*, 113.
25 Dame Hamdan Bourkaïeb v. Mustapha ben Ahmed ben el Adgi Sehid, Estoublon, *Jurisprudence Algérienne*, Vol. 1 (1836), 15–17.
26 Clavel, "Mariage contracté devant l'officer de l'état civil français," 1003; Larcher, "Des effets du mariage," 214. See also, Norès, "Essai de codification," 46.
27 This was no doubt an effect of increased migration of "European" women. Statistics compiled from ANOM État Civil, Algérie.
28 On judicial "chivalry," Sharafi, "The Semi-autonomous Judge in Colonial India."
29 For a colonial account, Coppolani and Depont, *Les confréries religieuses musulmanes*, 496–531.
30 Bertrand, "Madame Aurélie," 196. See also, Trumbull, *An Empire of Facts*, 116–125.
31 Tedjani v. Demoiselle Picard, Cour d'Alger, October 24, 1871, in Estoublon, *JA*, Vol. 4 (1871), 25.
32 Liauzu, *Passeurs de rives*, 22.
33 ANOM État Civil, Algérie.
34 Mussard, "Réinventer la commune?"
35 See the attack on Ismaël Urbain's marriage, Warnier, *L'Algérie devant l'Empereur*, 156.
36 Circular, November 3, 1871, *BOGGA*, Vol. 11 (1871), 558–559.
37 See also, Renucci, "Confrontation entre droit français et droits indigènes."
38 See, Ministère du Commerce. *Annuaire statistique de la France*. Vol. 1–13, Paris: Imprimerie nationale, 1878–1890. The earlier serial publication, *Tableau de la situation des établissements français dans l'Algérie (1838–1866)*, did not have an equivalent statistic. It listed marriages between "French" and between "French and foreigners." *Indigènes* were treated separately. On the organization of the new statistical service in Algeria, see Kateb, *Européens, "indigènes" et juifs en Algérie (1830–1962)*, 103.

39 Ibid., 107.
40 Mustapha, Marriage, Ali ben Saïd and Jeanne Nadal, Marriage, Mustapha, 1872. See also, Antoine Dubois and Josephine Marie Aïcha bent Mohammed, Marriage, Mustapha, 1875; Kaddour ben Allouah and Marie Josephine Raibaldi, Marriage, Mustapha, 1876. ANOM État Civil, Algérie.
41 See, "Algérie-Tableau 2," 569.
42 Proc. Gen. v. Boursali et Emilie Danési, Cour d'appel d'Alger (Ch. des appels musul.), October 28, 1878, *Bulletin Judiciaire d'Algérie*, January 16, 1879, Vol. 3, n. 50, 24–29.
43 On "public order" as a mechanism of state sovereignty and governmentality, see Agrama *Questioning Secularism*; Mahmood, *Religious Difference in a Secular Age*.
44 Min. Pub. v. Emilie Danési et Ismael ben Mohamed Boursali, *BJA*, January 16, 1879, Vol. 3, n. 50, 31.
45 Min. Pub. v. Emilie Danési, idem., 32. The public prosecutor who pleaded the case, M. Valette, would subsequently argue in favor of the abolition of Muslim personal status *tout court*, Valette, *Un projet de loi*.
46 Larcher, "Des effets du mariage d'une femme indigène," 212, n. 1. For a strong statement of Larcher's commitment to the "secularization" of Algerian law, "Des effets juridiques du changement de religion." Reprinted in *RA*, 1910.
47 Dunoyer, *Étude sur le conflit des lois*; Hamel, "De la naturalisation des indigènes musulmans"; Besson, *La législation civile de l'Algérie*; Hugues, *La nationalité française chez les musulmans de l'Algérie*.
48 "La naturalisation des musulmans dans leur statut," 427.
49 Lapradelle and Morand, "Du mariage en France des marocains."
50 Projet de loi réglant les conflits entra la loi française et le statut indigène algérien en matière d'état des personnes, J.O. Chambre., Doc. Parl., annexe 1365, March 10, 1925: 383–384.
51 Chauveau, "Le conflit des lois dans l'Afrique du Nord," 50. See also Maunier, *Loi française et coutume indigène en Algérie*. Meylan, *Les mariages mixtes en Afrique du Nord*.
52 Depont, *L'Algérie du centenaire*, 117–118.
53 Min. Pub. c. Mezdad Amar, Cour de Cassation, February 14, 1929, *Revue Algérienne, tunisienne, et marocaine de jurisprudence*, Part 2, 1929: 99.
54 Benet, *L'état civil en Algérie*, 397–398. Cited in Saada, *Empire's Children*, 30.
55 Scott, *Only Paradoxes to Offer*.

Bibliography

Agrama, Hussein Ali. *Questioning Secularism: Islam, Sovereignty, and the Rule of Law in Modern Egypt*. Chicago, IL: University of Chicago Press, 2012.

Amster, Ellen. "The Syphilitic Arab? A Search for Civilization in Disease Etiology, Native Prostitution, and French Colonial Medicine." In *French Mediterraneans: Transnational and Imperial Histories*, edited by Patricia Lorcin and Todd Shepard, 320–346. Lincoln, NE: University of Nebraska Press, 2016.

Andersen, Margaret Cook. *Regeneration through Empire: French Pronatalists and Colonial Settlement in the Third Republic*. Lincoln, NE: University of Nebraska Press, 2015.

Bellon, Laurence. "Logiques judiciaires et couples mixtes." *Le Genre humain* 1, no. 2 (1997): 63–74.

Benet, Henri. *L'état civil en Algérie: traité théorique et pratique de la constitution de l'Etat civil des indigènes algériens*. Alger: Imprimerie Minerva, 1937.

Bertrand, Augustin, "Madame Aurélie," *Annales Africaines* 43, no. 13 (July 1, 1931): 196.

Besson, Emmanuel. *La législation civile de l'Algérie: étude sur la condition des personnes et le régime des biens en Algérie*. Paris: Marescq, 1894.

Bonnichon, André. *La conversion au christianisme de l'indigène musulman algérien et ses effets juridiques (Un cas de conflit colonial)*. Paris: Recueil Sirey, 1931.

Brown, Wendy. *Regulating Aversion: Tolerance in the Age of Identity and Empire*. Princeton, NJ: Princeton University Press, 2006.

Camiscioli, Elisa. *Reproducing the French Race: Immigration, Intimacy, and Embodiment in the Early Twentieth Century*. Durham, NC: Duke University Press, 2009.

Cauwès, Albert. *Des rapports du mariage avec la nationalité*. Paris: L. Larose, 1901.

Chauveau, Paul. "Le conflit des lois dans l'Afrique du Nord." *Revue algérienne de jurisprudence*, no. 2 (1928): 45–52.

Christelow, Allan. *Muslim Law Courts and the French Colonial State in Algeria*. Princeton, NJ: Princeton University Press, 1985.

Clavel, Eugène. "Mariage contracté devant l'officer de l'état civil français, entre un musulman algérien français et une chrétienne française." *Journal international de droit privé* (1897): 997–1009.

Coppolani, Xavier and Octave Depont. *Les confréries religieuses musulmanes.* Alger: A. Jordan, 1898.

Déjeux, Jean. *Image de l'étrangère: unions mixtes franco-maghrébines.* Paris: Boîte à documents, 1989.

Demontès, Victor. *Le peuple algérien: essais de démographie algérienne.* Alger: Impr. algérienne, 1906.

Depont, Octave. *L'Algérie du centenaire– L'Oeuvre française de libération, de conquête morale et d'évolution sociale des indigènes - Les Berbères en France - La Représentation parlementaire des indigènes.* Paris: Recueil Sirey, 1928.

Dessoliers, Félix. "Le peuple algérien." *Revue politique et parlémentaire* 52, no. 154 (1907): 34–47.

Droit-Tribunaux, *Revue africaine*, no. 6 (October 1837): 108–113.

Dunoyer, Léon. *Étude sur le conflit des lois special à l'Algérie.* Paris: Pedone-Lauriel, 1888.

Estoublon, Robert. *Jurisprudence algérienne de 1830 à 1876.* Vol. 1/4Alger: A. Jourdan, 1890.

Estoublon, Robert and Adolphe Lefébure. *Code de l'Algérie, Vol. 1 (1830–1895).* Alger: A. Jourdan, 1896.

Fernando, Mayanthi L. "Intimacy Surveilled: Religion, Sex, and Secular Cunning." *Signs: Journal of Women in Culture and Society* 39, no. 3 (2014): 685–708.

Garcin, René. *Du changement de nationalité entre époux.* Paris: L. Boyer, 1902.

Gruffy, Georges. *De l'unité de nationalité dans la famille, étude sur la naturalisation des femmes mariées et des mineurs.* Paris: E. Duchemin, 1893.

Halley, Janet. "What is Family Law? A Genealogy." *Yale Journal of Law and Humanities* 23, no. 1 (2011): 1–109.

Halley, Janet and Kerry Rittich. "Critical Directions in Comparative Family Law: Genealogies and Contemporary Studies of Family Law Exceptionalism." *American Journal of Comparative Law* 58, no. 4 (2010): 753–776.

Hamel, Louis. "De la naturalisation des indigènes musulmans de l'Algérie." *Revue algérienne de jurisprudence*, no. 1 (1890): 19–32.

Heuer, Jennifer. *The Family and the Nation: Gender and Citizenship in Revolutionary France, 1789–1830.* Ithaca, NY: Cornell University Press, 2005.

Hugues, Albert. *La nationalité française chez les musulmans de l'Algérie.* Paris: A. Chevalier-Maresq, 1899.

Kateb, Kamel. *Européens, "indigènes" et juifs en Algérie (1830–1962): représentations et réalités des populations.* Paris: Institut national d'études démographiques, 2001.

La Revue Indigène. "La naturalisation des musulmans dans leur statut: Opinion de M. Arthur Giraud [sic]," Vol. 6, (July–August, 1911): 427.

Lapradelle, Albert and Marcel Morand. "Du mariage en France des marocains et des indigènes musulmans d'Algérie." *Revue de droit international privé* (1919): 223–233.

Larcher, Émile. "Des effets du mariage d'une femme indigène musulmane avec un indigène admis à la jouissance des droits de citoyen après la dissolution du mariage." *RA*, no. 2 (1908): 209–221.

Liauzu, Claude. *Passeurs de rives: changements d'identité dans le Maghreb colonial.* Paris: l'Harmattan, 2000.

MacMaster, Neil. "The Role of European Women and the Question of Mixed Couples in the Algerian Nationalist Movement in France, circa 1918–1962." *French Historical Studies* 34, no. 2 (2011): 357–386. doi:10.1215/00161071-1157376.

Mahmood, Saba. *Religious Difference in a Secular Age: A Minority Report.* Princeton, NJ: Princeton University Press, 2015.

Marchand, Henri. *Les mariages mixtes franco-musulmans.* Alger: Vollot-Debacq, 1954.

Markell, Patchen. *Bound by Recognition.* Princeton, NJ: Princeton University Press, 2003.

Maunier, René. *Loi française et coutume indigène en Algérie.* Paris: Editions Domat-Montchrestien F. Loviton et Cie, 1932.

Meylan, Philippe. *Les mariages mixtes en Afrique du Nord.* Paris: Sirey, 1934.

Ministère du Commerce. *Annuaire statistique de la France.* Vol. 1–13. Paris: Imprimerie nationale, 1878–1890.

Mussard, Christine. "Réinventer la commune? Genèse de la commune mixte, une structure administrative inédite dans l'Algérie coloniale." *Histoire@ Politique*, no. 3 (2015): 93–108.

Norès, E. "Essai de codification," *Revue algérienne et tunisienne de jurisprudence*, 1905, Part 1, 39–65.

Pellissier de Reynaud, Henri-Edmond. *Annales algériennes*, vol. 2. Paris: Anselin et Gaultier, 1836.

Peyerimhoff de Fontenelle, Henri de. *Enquête sur les résultats de la colonisation officielle de1871 à 1895.* Alger: Torrent, 1906.

Renucci, Florence. "Confrontation entre droit français et droits indigènes: le cas desmariages mixtes en Afrique du Nord (1870–1919)." *Cahiers Aixois d'Histoire des Droits de l'Outre mer Français* (2002): 147–191.

Ricoux, René and Louis-Adolphe Bertillon. *La démographie figurée de l'Algérie: étude statistique des populations européennes qui habitent l'Algérie.* Paris: G. Masson, 1880.

Roussel, Charles. "La naturalisation des étrangers en Algérie." *Revue des deux mondes* 45 (1875): 682–695.

Saada, Emmanuelle. *Empire's Children: Race, Filiation, and Citizenship in the French Colonies*. Translated by Arthur Goldhammer. Chicago, IL: University of Chicago Press, 2012.

Scott, Joan Wallach. *Only Paradoxes to Offer: Feminism and the 'Rights of Man' in France, 1789–1940*. Cambridge, MA: Harvard University Press, 1996.

Scott, Joan Wallach. *The Politics of the Veil*. Princeton, NJ: Princeton University Press, 2007.

Scott, Joan Wallach. *Sex and Secularism*. Princeton, NJ: Princeton University Press, 2017.

Sharafi, Mitra. "The Semi-autonomous Judge in Colonial India: Chivalric Imperialism meets Anglo-Islamic Dower and Divorce law." *Indian Economic & Social History Review* 46, no. 1 (2009): 57–81. doi:10.2139/ssrn.1661197.

Shepard, Todd. *The Invention of Decolonization: The Algerian War and the Remaking of France*. Ithaca, NY: Cornell University Press, 2006.

Trumbull, George R. *An Empire of Facts: Colonial Power, Cultural Knowledge, and Islam in Algeria, 1870–1914*. Cambridge, UK: Cambridge University Press, 2009.

Valette, Victor. *Un projet de loi sur la réorganisation de l'Algérie*. Alger: Cheniaux-Franville, 1881.

Warnier, Auguste. *L'Algérie devant l'Empereur*. Paris: Challamel, 1865.

Weil, Patrick. *Qu'est-ce qu'un Français? Histoire de la nationalité française depuis la Révolution*. Paris: Grasset, 2002.

Weiss, André. *Traité théorique et pratique de droit international privé*, vol. 1. Paris: L. Larose & L. Tenin, 1892.

22

WHITE FRENCH WOMEN, COLONIAL MIGRATION, AND SEXUAL LABOR BETWEEN METROPOLE AND COLONY

Caroline Séquin

In her memoirs, *Vie d'une prostituée,* the former French sex worker Marie-Thérèse recalled that following the promulgation of the Law of 13 April 1946 in metropolitan France, which put an end to more than a century of *maisons de tolérance* (tolerated brothels), some French women resettled in the French empire, where they could continue selling sex in colonial brothels.[1] It was easier, she opined, to move overseas to ply their trade than to find a different job locally.[2] Another sex worker who left France for Dakar at that time marveled at the opportunity the colonial sex industry offered: "We had just arrived on one of the 'Pasteur' … We were making big bucks … The industry was marvelous … We used to have a prime clientele … men who were high in the hierarchy and who would secretly give us 1,000 bills [francs]."[3] Like many of their contemporaries, women involved in the sex trade equated colonial migration with financial reward.

In these two examples, a key legal reform in the metropole—the official closing of the *maisons de tolérance*—prompted white French prostitutes to leave for the French empire. Their migration for sexual labor between metropole and colony, however, long predated the mid-twentieth century. Historians of empire have stressed how colonial governments condemned the presence of white women whose sexual behavior deviated from bourgeois norms, because white women were perceived as "the bearers of a redefined colonial morality"[4] in the twentieth century. Yet, as this essay shows, in the interwar period the migration of white French prostitutes had become a common occurrence, especially to Dakar, the capital of French West Africa on the westernmost tip of the continent. Lured by a desire to increase their earnings, these women yearned to improve their lives through colonial migration for sexual labor. The reality, however, often sharply contrasted with their expectations. Caught in a liminal position, white French sex workers present in colonial Dakar found themselves free to engage in trans-imperial mobility yet rigidly constrained in their movements once in the colony. Their presence at once bolstered the colonial project by serving the purported sexual needs of white colonists yet, at the same time, threatened the colonial logic by undermining French claims of white respectability.

I have identified 55 cases of French women who were suspected of moving to Dakar to work as registered prostitutes between 1915, when the first brothel opened, and 1947, when the Law of 13 April 1946 was finally extended to French West Africa. Unfortunately there are few first-hand testimonies of sex workers that have survived, let alone of women who sold sex across the French empire. However, other documents can provide a valuable insight into white French women's experiences of migration for sex work. In the opening decades of the twentieth century a growing number of countries, including France, sought to repress what they called "white slavery"—the sexual trafficking of women and children. The institutions created to combat this phenomenon have left a thick paper trail for historians interested in examining the migration of women across national borders for sexual labor, whether consensual or coerced.[5] These included the *police des moeurs,* which was the local police force in charge of controlling prostitution at a city level; the special commissioners (*commissaires spéciaux*) who were posted in harbors and train stations across the metropole from the turn of the century to detect women travelling alone or in suspicious company; and the *Contrôle Général du service des recherches judiciaires,* a branch of the police in charge of investigating criminal law offenses, including the traffic in women. Additionally, from the 1920s to 1939, colonial governors compiled annual reports detailing prostitution and sex trafficking in the territories they administered, which they sent to the League of Nations' Advisory Committee on the Traffic in Women and Children. Together these reports offer mediated accounts of migration for sex work between metropole and colony and make legible women's aspirations, experiences, and, more often than not, their disillusionment with imperial mobility.

Historians have noted the presence of white French prostitutes in the French empire as early as the second half of the seventeenth century. In November 1680 the hospital Saint-Louis in Paris sent to Martinique 128 women, initially swept from the streets for presumably engaging in prostitution; King Louis XIV would have partially covered the cost of their expatriation. In September 1682 another 50 Parisian women, some of whom were accused of being "of ill repute," similarly reached Martinique. Once on the island the women, whose ages ranged from 15 to 22, were expected to serve as wives for the white colonists—a remarkable shift in status that would become unthinkable in twentieth-century colonial discourses.[6] Such arrangements were not limited to Martinique; they also took place in other parts of the French empire, such as Louisiana and Saint-Domingue in the seventeenth and eighteenth centuries.[7] For French authorities these initiatives presented two benefits. On the one hand, it rid the metropole of its "undesirable" subjects who, through their behaviors and supposed predispositions, upset the social and moral order; on the other, the influx of white women could help offset the imbalanced ratio of white men to white women in the colony. Although further research would need to be undertaken to fully understand the motives behind what seems like the forced migration of women deemed prostitutes, this scheme can be interpreted as an early attempt to limit the occurrence of intimacy across the racial line well before the mid-eighteenth century "proliferation of social penalties against whites who committed the misdeed of *mésalliance* (marrying a non-white person)."[8]

Denunciations of the presence of white prostitutes recurred throughout the colonial period. Yet these accusations should be treated with caution, as they often tell us more about existing gender and sexual norms than actual acts of commercial sex.[9] Take, for example, the case of a white woman in Martinique who, in 1757, was labelled a prostitute. Initially arrested on the charge of having killed her child, she was later found innocent. And yet she was still banished for "having prostituted herself *with a negro* and [for] the uproar that this affair created among the public."[10] Such an accusation, however, left unclear whether she had actually sold sex, or whether the mere act of engaging in sexual intercourse with a black man was enough to relegate her to the rank of prostitute, given how interracial sex transgressed social mores in eighteenth-century Martinique—especially when involving a white woman. As historian Emily Landau explains, "Prostitution was, and is, a powerful metaphor, and because interracial and commercial sex both fell beyond the limits of respectable sexuality, they were easily conflated."[11] Thus it is possible that authorities could only fathom white women's desire for black men as transactional. Whether or not this sexual exchange was commercial, what transpires from this example is that white colonists expressed concerns about interracial intimacy and, more specifically, about the political and social implications of white women's sexual activity on the colonial order.

The proliferation of licensed brothels across the empire in the opening decades of the twentieth century, especially in urban centers where the French colonial presence was expansive, illuminates new configurations of the management of sex in French colonial settings. The infamous *quartier réservé* (red-light district) of Bousbir in Casablanca, Morocco, opened in 1912, while others were created in Saigon and Hanoi in 1934 and 1936 respectively.[12] These establishments provided a "sexscape"[13] where the growing population of white European men—whether colonial administrators, sailors, soldiers, or other colonists—could indulge their erotic desires. While white Europeans could patronize both European and indigenous prostitutes, brothel keepers typically denied indigenous men sexual access to brothels staffed with white prostitutes.[14] Though enforced informally, racial segregation within these spaces of sexual regulation reinforced colonial hierarchies by dictating who could have sex with whom.

Dakar did not have a red-light district *per* se, but the French district, known as the Plateau, nonetheless counted up to five houses of prostitution in the interwar years. The first licensed brothel had been established in the mid-1910s, shortly after the colonial administration designated the port city as the capital of French West Africa in 1902. One particularity of Dakar's brothels was that all of the women registered were white and the majority of them were French. In 1923 the Governor General in Dakar noted in his annual form sent to the League of Nations that "there were 47 registered prostitutes, among whom 39 French, 2 Portuguese, 1 Italian, 1 Romanian, and 4 Spanish"[15] split between three brothels. Crucially, their services were reserved for "Europeans," or white colonists, only.[16] White-only licensed brothels played a key role in the empire-building project, as they fulfilled the purported sexual needs of white male colonists at a time when interracial sexual–conjugal relations were becoming increasingly controversial.[17] Once accepted as a feature of colonial life, concubinage between French men and indigenous women, also known as *mariages à la mode du pays*, were at the turn of the twentieth century construed as a threat to the colonial order. These relationships, moral observers claimed, blurred the boundaries between colonizer and colonized, as well as between black and white. To be sure, white brothel prostitution did not garner unanimous support among colonial authorities and moral observers. French women's sexual transgressions, including their engagement in transactional sex, could tarnish notions of French superiority in the eyes of the colonized populations. But, if discreet, white brothel prostitution could provide an alternative sexual outlet to interracial sex and thus help to maintain the racial boundaries upon which the French colonial project rested.[18]

Supplying brothels with white prostitutes, however, was no easy task considering the limited number of French women living in Dakar. In 1907 the colonial city counted about 400 French women for 2,000 French men, among an overall population of 25,000. By the early 1940s there were 17,500 French people living in Dakar, of whom only 2,000 were women.[19] As a result, brothel keepers relied heavily on the migration of women from the metropole to respond to the sexual demand among white male colonists. Significantly, most of these women did not fit the typical portrayal of white slave victim that filled the pages of newspapers at the time—the young, innocent, and virgin woman who was lured into prostitution abroad. Out of the 55 women suspected of moving to Dakar to sell sex between 1915 and 1947, more than half (31) claimed to have been registered as prostitutes in the metropole prior to their departure. Another seven, when questioned by a special commissioner, insisted they were artists—a milieu which, according to French authorities, was filled with prostitutes in disguise. Only three asserted they were moving to marry a man living in the colony. The status and motivations of the remaining 14 are unclear.

Often an intermediary like Henri Lagrezas facilitated their journey. Born around the turn of the century in Périgueux, in the 1920s Lagrezas managed a hotel in Vancouver until a conviction for trafficking in women led to his expulsion from Canada.[20] Following his eviction he resettled in France where, in 1930, he opened a brothel with his wife in Angoulême, a medium-sized French city located about 70 miles from the Atlantic coast. Sometime in the 1930s he also acquired two other brothels, "Ginette" and "Georgette," located on 19 and 24 Raffenel Street in Dakar's Plateau.[21] In 1935 a police officer working for the *Service des moeurs* in Angoulême described the well-established system Lagrezas had devised:

> The prostituted women who come to work in the brothels [in Angoulême] are generally here [for a short period of time], some only stay for a couple of days, others for a few weeks, very few spend several months, by the time they leave they take their ID back and let us know where they are going. *None of them ever told us she was going to Dakar. Most claim they are going to Bordeaux.* It is only a while after that we receive a request for additional information from the Chief Administrator of the Colonies in Dakar, regarding a prostitute who had claimed she was coming from Angoulême.[22]

Lagrezas sought to recruit women who already worked in his metropolitan business. Those interested in pursuing sex work in Dakar first headed to Bordeaux, a major Atlantic port city with regular maritime routes to French West Africa and South America. After a short stay in the city, where some found temporary employment in a local brothel, the women embarked on a steamship to Dakar. As the police report above suggests, few divulged their plan until they were about to leave French shores.

How women framed their motivations for migrating for sex work determined the authorities' responses and, consequently, whether they would be able to undergo their travel. Legally speaking, French officials could not stop women who were *willingly* migrating to sell sex abroad, given that the 1921 international anti-trafficking accord, which France had signed in 1926, only targeted the trafficking of underaged girls and non-consenting adult women. The cases of 25-year-old Marguerite M. and 22-year-old Gabrielle M. are particularly instructive.[23] On January 9, 1932, a port commissioner stopped the two French women in Bordeaux's harbor. He suspected they were planning to join one of Lagrezas's brothels in Dakar but could not intervene. Marguerite, he claimed, "was over the age of majority and her desire to go and prostitute herself was evident." And even though Gabrielle had just become of age (which at the time was 21), she had already worked in a brothel. The commissioner interpreted Gabrielle's prior involvement in sex work as evidence of her willingness to migrate for commercial sex. Similarly, when Mireille R.—another woman who left Bordeaux for Dakar in May 1938—reported to an agent that she had been deceived into moving to Dakar to sell sex in horrendous conditions, the police did not view her as a victim of sex trafficking because she had previously been engaged in the metropolitan sex industry.[24] As Stephanie Limoncelli notes, French authorities displayed "no desire to stop trafficking, only to control it."[25]

What motivated white French women to settle in colonial Dakar to sell sex? Prostitutes in the twentieth century were generally speaking highly mobile. They frequently moved from one brothel to another, and from brothel prostitution to street prostitution.[26] They associated physical mobility with better financial prospects, and their decision to move to Dakar fit this pattern, as police interrogations of these women reveal. Most of them came from modest backgrounds and had little family support; at least 20 per cent of them had lost one or both parents by the time they were on their way to Dakar.[27] Rumor had it that brothel prostitutes were to find wealth in colonial houses of prostitution. Between 1932 and 1935 alone, 11 women stopped on their way to Dakar expressed their hope to make more money overseas. Take, for example, Marguerite R., 26, and Octavie Louise C., 27. They had already worked in Lagrezas's brothel in Angoulême as well as other institutions in Bordeaux when they decided to make the move to Dakar in November 1932. Convinced that they would make more money selling sex in Dakar than in the metropole, they headed to Lagrezas's brothels in Dakar.[28] It is unclear whether it was Lagrezas himself who spread hope among prospective worker migrants, but it would not be surprising if he did, given that his colonial businesses' success hinged upon the migration of white sex workers. Some women also reported receiving letters from friends already practicing sex work in the colony, stating that they would make more money there. More rarely, a woman relied on her own previous experience selling sex in Dakar to give her confidence that she would increase her income in the colony—a scenario suggesting that some women moved back and forth between metropole and colony.[29] In hoping for economic advancement in the colony, the women who migrated for sexual labor shared the same aspirations as the 60 million European men and women who, between 1870 and 1940, left their native lands to find economic prosperity in the United States, South America, and in European colonies, sometimes never to return.[30]

Wealth accumulation, however, was at best an uncertain—and, at worst, an unrealistic—outcome for most prostitutes on the move. Several reasons made it challenging for women to boost their earnings in a colonial brothel. There were the typical hurdles that brothel prostitutes could expect anywhere, such as reimbursement to the brothel keeper of living expenses—which included personal products, food, and clothing—usually with interest.[31] There was, too, the economic crisis of the 1930s that equally plagued the colony and the metropole and affected the demand for transactional sex.[32] And then there were the constraints that were specific to selling sex in a colonial brothel: the costs of a ticket on a steamship sailing from Bordeaux to Dakar which, although increasingly affordable to the average person by the late nineteenth century, remained expensive.[33] Additionally, each passenger paid 2,500 francs in a security deposit to the shipping companies to cover repatriation costs should their stay in the colony go wrong. Sex procurers like Lagrezas usually assumed these initial costs, but they expected to be paid back and often with interest. The high cost and meticulous planning that bringing white women from the metropole entailed for brothel keepers made them reluctant to let women leave after a short time. A Dakar brothel owner was reported to have yelled at one of his employees after she expressed her desire to return to the metropole: "For ten years I have spent money on people like you and you can do nothing against me. [...] You owe me money, you won't leave."[34] Full awareness of these financial hurdles could have deterred some women from pursuing sex work in the colony in the first place.

It was not just that life in a colonial brothel did not yield the expected financial gain; it also presented specific constraints tied to the racial and social dynamics in a colonial setting. The presence of single white women—a category that indubitably included prostitutes in the eyes of the colonial administration—deeply worried colonial observers. As Stoler explains, "[single women] presented the dangerous possibility that straitened circumstances would lead them to prostitution and thus to degrade white prestige at large."[35] In Dakar a 1926 colonial ordinance required brothel keepers to prevent their employees from leaving the brothel out of fear that they would offer their sexual services in public—an activity that threatened the image of the respectable white French woman in the colony.[36] One exception to this policy specified brothel prostitutes could exit the brothel if a client requested to spend the night in their company in another location—perhaps because such a scenario dissimulated her status as a prostitute.[37] Abolitionists denounced the pervasive corruption among brothel keepers, Dakar police, and doctors who wrongly diagnosed rebellious brothel prostitutes with venereal disease so as to lock them in a nearby hospital and deter them from escaping.[38] In sum, the liminal position in which white prostitutes found themselves in the colony limited their mobility; their racial identity upheld them to standards of white respectability while their occupation compelled authorities and brothel keepers to render them invisible beyond the confines of the whites-only brothels.

The demise of state-tolerated brothel prostitution in the colony on the eve of 1947 did not put an end to the presence of white prostitutes in Dakar. Colonial authorities feared that former brothel prostitutes would turn to clandestine prostitution to survive, making white prostitution more visible than ever in the colony.[39] To some extent they were right. Although colonial officials advocated for the repatriation of former brothel prostitutes to the metropole, some women were reluctant to leave. A few weeks after the closing of brothels, a journalist estimated that 20 out of the 60 former brothel prostitutes remained in the colonial capital.[40] Reporting the presence of a former brothel prostitute sitting at the table of a fancy restaurant along with three other women and a Lebanese man, he noted, "Not all of these 'Ladies' had returned to France; after the closing of brothels they slept here and there, waiting for a boat that they hoped they did not have to take."[41] Those who wished to stay developed strategies to curtail colonial authorities' attempts to expel them from the colony, hiding from the police or missing their boat "on purpose."[42] Years later, some women had devised new ways to identify potential customers from the safety of their home. "My name is Rose of Naples," a small ad from 1949 posted in the local newspaper *Les Échos Africaines* read: "Tired of Lebanese men who pay well but do not know how to 'make love à la française,' would like to find a disinterested colonist, 50 to 60 years old, likely to buy me a car. Ask the *Échos Africaines*."[43] Whether or not this woman had been a brothel prostitute in the recent past, she sought to capitalize on the sexual needs of French men to make a life for herself in the colony while also playing into Orientalist stereotypes about effete Middle Eastern men and flattering the putative sexual superiority of the white French colonist. Despite the closing of licensed brothels in postwar Dakar, white women selling sex adapted to the new legislative landscape and continued to find ways to provide their sexual services to white colonists, thus showing, once again, the limits of colonial state control over sexuality.

French women involved in the sex industry shared the aspirations of their time. Like millions of European men and women, they equated geographic and social mobility. They viewed the French empire as a desirable destination to increase their wealth through their placement in a colonial brothel. Yet analyzing the experiences of the 50 or so white French women who engaged in labor migration for sex work between the metropole and colonial Dakar in the first half of the twentieth century provides a bleaker picture. Most women willingly settled in the colony to sell sex, but the outcome once there rarely matched their expectations. Colonial mobility did not always bring more freedom and financial autonomy; in fact, it could limit their range of options, as colonial incentives to limit the occurrence of interracial intimacy and maintain fragile notions of white respectability made the presence of white prostitutes at once problematic and necessary. If sex work offered an entryway to the French empire, it was far from a golden ticket.

Notes

1 The "regulationist" regime of licensed brothels gradually emerged across French cities in the early nineteenth century and, later, in parts of the French empire. According to the system known across the world as the "French model," women working in prostitution were required to register with the police, undergo mandatory medical examinations, and to be enclosed in lock hospitals if they were symptomatic of venereal diseases or evaded police surveillance. See Corbin, *Women for Hire*; Harsin, *Policing Prostitution in Nineteenth-Century Paris*. The Law of 13 April 1946 was initially applied to the metropole only, before being selectively extended to some French colonies in the following months. See Séquin, "Prostitution and the Policing of Race in the French Atlantic," especially ch. 6.
2 Cointre, *Vie d'une Prostituée*, 95.
3 "La crise du logement sévit à Dakar," *Les Échos africaines*, February 4–7, 1947. The "Pasteur" was a steamship that connected Bordeaux to Dakar.
4 Stoler, "Making Empire Respectable," 640.
5 The coercive or consensual nature of the so-called white slave trade has been heavily debated among historians. Key works include Guy, *Sex and Danger in Buenos Aires*; Limoncelli, *The Politics of Trafficking*; Pliley, *Policing Sexuality*; Stauter-Halsted, *The Devil's Chain*, 117–195; Kozma, *Global Women, Colonial Ports*; Camiscioli, "Coercion and Choice."
6 Debien, *Les Engagés pour les Antilles*, 181.
7 Schafer observes a similar phenomenon taking place in eighteenth-century Louisiana in *Brothels, Depravity, and Abandoned Women*, 1.
8 Garraway, *The Libertine Colony*, 30.
9 Tabet, *La Grande Arnaque*.
10 Peytraud, *L'Esclavage aux Antilles françaises avant 1789*, cited by Gautier, *Les Soeurs de Solitude*, 135. Emphasis added.
11 Although her observation pertains to the United States at the turn of the twentieth century, it is pertinent to other societies where race structured power relations. Landau, *Spectacular Wickedness*, 37.
12 Taraud, *La Prostitution coloniale*; Limoncelli, *The Politics of Trafficking*, 126.
13 Staszak, "Planning Prostitution in Colonial Morocco."
14 Letter from the Governor General of AOF to the Directeur du Cabinet, Affaires réservées, Dakar, June 27, 1938, 14MIOM 3071, Archives Nationales d'Outre-Mer (ANOM).
15 General Government in AOF, Answers to the form given by the League of Nations on the Traffic in Women and Children, year 1923. 2K1, National Archives of Senegal (ANS).
16 Gouverneur Général de l'AOF to Directeur du Cabinet, Dakar, June 27, 1938, 14MIOM3071, ANOM.
17 Stoler, "Making Empire Respectable"; Osborn, *Our New Husbands are Here*; White, *Children of the French Empire*.
18 Séquin, "Prostitution and the Policing of Race."
19 1941 Annual Medical Report, 2G41/7, ANS, and 14 MIOM/1835, ANOM.
20 Letter from Commissaire Spécial de Police to Procureur de la République in Angoulême, October 8, 1932, Angoulême, F/7/14862, Archives Nationales de France (AN).
21 Report from inspecteur de Police mobile Dejean to Commissaire Divisionnaire in Bordeaux, February 22, 1935, Bordeaux, 4M88, Archives Départementales de Charente (ADC).
22 Report from the inspector of *service des moeurs* to the Central Commissioner, March 22, 1935, 4M88, ADC. The sentence in italics is my emphasis.
23 In order to not participate in the process of labelling and stigmatizing the women deemed prostitutes that I discuss in this essay, I have chosen to not divulge their last names.
24 I discuss more extensively the case of Mireille R. in Séquin, "Marie Piquemal, the 'Colonial Madam,'" forthcoming. It is important to note that the 1933 International Convention for the Repression of the Traffic in Women of the Full Age condemned the traffic in all adult women, even with their consent, but France did not sign it until 1947, and even then it included a colonial clause that precluded its colonial territories from the purview of the treaty.

25 Limoncelli, *The Politics of Trafficking*, 132.
26 The few memoirs written by French former sex workers support this claim. Cointre, *Vie d'une Prostituée*; Watts, *The Men in my Life*.
27 Among the 55 cases I have identified, 12 women claimed to have lost one or both parents, and 23 provided the identity of their parents with no further information. The remaining cases make no mention of their filiation.
28 Report from Commissaire divisionnaire de Police Spéciale to Préfet de la Gironde, November 5, 1932, Bordeaux, 4M340, ADG.
29 Ibid.
30 Nugent, *Crossings*; McKeown, "Global Migration."
31 Report from inspecteur de Police mobile Dejean to Commissaire Divisionnaire in Bordeaux, February 22, 1935, Bordeaux, 4M88, ADC.
32 *Comité pour la lutte contre la prostitution réglementée* to Chef Adjoint du Cabinet de la Préfecture au Commissaire Spécial, October 27, 1932, Bordeaux, 4M340, ADG.
33 Ibid.
34 Renseignements, Dakar, undated, 14MIOM3071, ANOM.
35 Stoler, *Carnal Knowledge and Imperial Power*, 61.
36 Arrêté relatif à la surveillance de la prostitution, January 3, 1926, n°14 bis, *Journal Officiel du Sénégal*.
37 Untitled, undated document, 14 MIOM 3050, ANOM.
38 *Comité pour la lutte contre la prostitution réglementée* to Chef Adjoint du Cabinet de la Préfecture au Commissaire Spécial, October 27, 1932, Bordeaux, 4M340, ADG.
39 Note from Médecin Principal Audibert, chef du Service de Santé, to Capitaine de frégate Chef d'Etat Major, Dakar, January 27, 1947, 14 MIOM 3050, ANOM.
40 Ibid.
41 "La Crise du logement sévit à Dakar," *Les Échos Africaines*, February 4–11, 1947.
42 "Les propos d'un célibataire," *Les Échos Africaines*, March 15–22, 1947.
43 *Les Échos Africaines*, January 14–20, 1949.

Bibliography

Betts, Raymond. "Dakar: Ville Impériale (1857–1960)." In *Colonial Cities: Essays on Urbanism in a Colonial Context*, edited by Robert Ross and Gerard J. Telkamp, 2 :193–206. Dordrecht: Martinus Nijhoff Publishers, 1985.

Camiscioli, Elisa. "Coercion and Choice: The 'Traffic in Women' between France and Argentina in the Early Twentieth Century." *French Historical Studies* 42, no. 3 (Summer 2019): 483–507. doi:10.1215/00161071-7558357.

Cointre, Marie-Thérèse. *Vie d'une Prostituée*. Genève: Gonthier, 1964.

Corbin, Alain. *Women for Hire: Prostitution and Sexuality in France after 1850*. Cambridge, MA: Harvard University Press, 1996.

Debien, Gabriel. *Les Engagés pour les Antilles (1634–1715)*. Paris: Société de l'histoire des colonies françaises, 1952.

Garraway, Doris Lorraine. *The Libertine Colony: Creolization in the Early French Caribbean*. Durham, NC: Duke University Press, 2005.

Gautier, Arlette. *Les Soeurs de Solitude: Femmes et esclavage aux Antilles du XVIIe au XIXe siècle*. Rennes: Presses Universitaires de Rennes, 2010 [1985].

Guy, Donna. *Sex and Danger in Buenos Aires: Prostitution, Family, and Nation in Argentina*. Lincoln, NE: University of Nebraska Press, 1991.

Harsin, Jill. *Policing Prostitution in Nineteenth-Century Paris*. Princeton, NJ: Princeton University Press, 1985.

Kozma, Liat. *Global Women, Colonial Ports: Prostitution in the Interwar Middle East*. Albany, NY: SUNY Press, 2016.

Landau, Emily Epstein. *Spectacular Wickedness: Sex, Race, and Memory in Storyville, New Orleans*. Baton Rouge, LA: Louisiana State University Press, 2013.

Limoncelli, Stephanie. *The Politics of Trafficking: The First International Movement to Combat the Sexual Exploitation of Women*. Stanford, CA: Stanford University Press, 2010.

Nugent, Walter T.K. *Crossings: Transatlantic Migrations, 1870–1914*. Bloomington, IN: Indiana University Press, 1992.

Osborn, Emily Lynn. *Our New Husbands are Here: Households, Gender, and Politics in a West African State from the Slave Trade to Colonial Rule*. Athens, OH: Ohio University Press, 2011.

Pliley, Jessica R. *Policing Sexuality: The Mann Act and the Making of the FBI*. Cambridge, MA: Harvard University Press, 2014.

Schafer, Judith Kelleher. *Brothels, Depravity, and Abandoned Women: Illegal Sex in Antebellum New Orleans*. Baton Rouge, LA: Louisiana State University Press, 2009.

Séquin, Caroline. "Prostitution and the Policing of Race in the French Atlantic, 1848–1947." Ph.D. diss., University of Chicago, 2019.

Séquin, Caroline, "Marie Piquemal, the 'Colonial Madam': Brothel Keeping, Migratory Prostitution, and Racial Politics in the French Empire." *Journal of Women's History* (forthcoming).

Staszak, Jean-François. "Planning Prostitution in Colonial Morocco: Bousbir, Casablanca's Quartier Réservé." In *(Sub)Urban Sexscapes: Geographies and Regulation of the Sex Industry*, edited by Paul J. Maginn and Christine Steinmetz, 175–196. London: Routledge, 2014.

Stauter-Halsted, Keely. *The Devil's Chain: Prostitution and Social Control in Partitioned Poland*. Ithaca, NY: Cornell University Press, 2015.

Stoler, Ann Laura. "Making Empire Respectable: The Politics of Race and Sexual Morality in 20th-Century Colonial Cultures." *American Ethnologist* 639, no. 4 (November 1989): 634–660. doi:10.1525/ ae.1989.16.4.02a00030.

Stoler, Ann Laura. *Carnal Knowledge and Imperial Power: Race and the Intimate in Colonial Rule*. Berkeley, CA: University of California Press, 2002.

Tabet, Paola. *La Grande Arnaque: Sexualité des femmes et échange économico-sexuel*. Paris: L'Harmattan, 2004.

Taraud, Christelle. *La Prostitution coloniale: Algérie, Tunisie, Maroc (1830–1962)*. Paris: Payot, 2003.

Watts, Marthe Hucbourg. *The Men in my Life*. New York: Lyle Stuart, 1960.

White, Owen. *Children of the French Empire: Miscegenation and Colonial Society in French West Africa, 1895–1960*. Oxford, UK: Clarendon Press, 1999.

23

TRANSGENDER HISTORY IN SINOPHONE TAIWAN

Howard Chiang

In the summer of 1953 the Taiwanese press initiated an era of extensive coverage of Xie Jianshun. The media construed Xie as the "first" Chinese transsexual and labeled her the "Chinese Christine." Xie's widely circulated nickname was an allusion to the American ex-G.I. transsexual star Christine Jorgensen, who had received her sex reassignment surgery in Denmark two years prior and then became a worldwide household name due to her personality and glamorous looks.[1] In fact, the short span of two years between 1952 and 1953 captured a global moment of the Christine narrative. Around the same time, a Japanese Christine, Nagai Akiko, underwent a sex change operation at the Nippon Medical University hospital in Tokyo, and Marta Olmos, the Mexican Christine, was treated with a similar procedure in Mexico City. Soon after, both Tokyo and Mexico City became an early surgical destination.[2]

In the case of Taiwan, the Christine analogy reflected the growing influence of American culture on the Republic of China at the initial peak of the Cold War. Within a week the characterization of Xie in Taiwanese media changed from an average citizen whose ambiguous sex provoked uncertainty and national anxiety to a transsexual icon whose fate contributed to the global staging of Taiwan on a par with the United States. Saturated with national and trans-Pacific significance, Xie's experience made "*bianxingren*" (transsexual) a household term in the 1950s. Centering on the making of Xie's celebrity, this chapter argues that the publicity surrounding her transition worked as a pivotal fulcrum in shifting common understandings of transsexuality, the role of medical science, and their evolving relation to the popular press in mid-twentieth-century Sinophone culture.

As the press coverage escalated, new names and startling medical conditions grabbed the attention of journalists and their readers. The examples aside from Xie's life history tell stories of gender transgression, defects of the reproductive system, uncommon problems related to pregnancy, the marriages of individuals with cross-gender identification, transsexual childbirth, human intersexuality, and sex metamorphosis itself, emanating from both domestic contexts and abroad. Although these stories came to light within an overall narrative of Xie's transition, they provide crucial evidence for the growing frequency of sex-change-related discussions in Chinese-speaking communities in the era immediately after World War II.

The excavation of a series of trans formations in postwar Taiwan maps gender and sexual marginality onto the region's global (in)significance in and beyond the 1950s.[3] After weaving together Xie's narrative with other stories of gendered corporeal variance, this chapter concludes with a historiographical framework in which these diverse examples of "transing" could be adequately appreciated.[4] Within the field of Sinophone postcolonial studies, these stories have broader historical import, bringing new analytic angles, new chronologies, and new conceptual vocabularies. The Sinophone world, in this context, refers to Sinitic-language communities and cultures situated outside of China or on the margins of China and Chineseness.[5] By contesting the epistemic status of the West as the ultimate arbiter in queer historiography, the history of trans formations in Sinophone Taiwan offers an axial approach to provincializing China, Asia, and "the rest." The queerness of the trans archive delineated in this chapter is underpinned not only by the very examples of trans subjectivities retrieved and documented but also by the enabling effect of their Sinophonicity to de-universalize existing historiographical hegemonies, whether defined in the conventions of writing the twentieth-century "Chinese" or "Taiwanese" past.[6]

Trans in the spotlight

Born in Chaozhou, Guangdong, on January 24, 1918, Xie joined the army when she was 16 and lost both her parents by the age of 18. She came to Taiwan with the Nationalist army in 1949. On August 6, 1953, the 36-year-old Xie visited the Tainan 518 Hospital for a physical examination due to regular abdominal cramps. The chair of the external medicine division, Dr Lin Chengyi, immediately discovered Xie's intersexed condition and initiated a series of sex change operations. Some news reports suggested that Xie had in fact been fully aware of her feminine traits since childhood but had kept them a secret until their recent "revelation" under the close attention of doctors in Tainan. Xie's story soon triggered an avalanche of media sensationalism in postwar Taiwan.

Two weeks after Xie's initial visit, Dr Lin performed the first "sex change" operation. In fact, as the public would soon realize, this was simply an exploratory laparotomy. Confirming the presence of ovarian tissues in Xie's reproductive anatomy, Dr Lin asserted that "Xie Jianshun should be converted into a woman in light of his physiology" and that this procedure would have "a 90 percent success rate."[7] Detailed coverage of this preliminary surgery appeared in the *United Daily News* (*Lianhebao*) the following day, August 21, with the headline claiming "Soldier Destined to Become a Lady."[8] This echoed the headline of the *New York Daily News* front-page article that announced Jorgenson's sex reassignment in December 1952, "Ex-GI Becomes Blonde Beauty." The *Shin Sheng Daily* headline read "Yin-Yang Person's Yin Stronger than Yang," while *China Daily News* concluded that Xie's bodily biology was "thoroughly female."[9] From this point on, Xie was frequently dubbed the "Chinese Christine." Whereas in the first week of publicity reporters had used either the masculine pronoun "he" or both the masculine and the feminine pronouns, they thoroughly changed to the feminine pronoun "she" in referring to Xie in all subsequent writings.

As doctors, the authorities, and Xie became more self-conscious about what they said in public, the press met increasing obstacles in sensationalizing new narratives about the alleged "first" Chinese transsexual. After the exploratory laparotomy, reporters lacked direct access to information about Xie's medical care so they began to look for other tantalizing stories of gender transgressive behavior or bodily ailment. Between late 1953 and late 1954 the popularity of Xie's transsexual narrative instigated the appearance of other similar accounts of unusual body morphology—though sometimes deviating from the actual transformation of sex—in the Taiwanese press. During the pivotal moments when the media attention on Xie took a back seat, these stories of physical trans anomaly came to light in the shadow of

Christine's glamor and thereby played an important role in sustaining popular interest in sex change in Cold War Taiwan.

The media coverage of the Xie story enabled some readers to consider the possibility of experimenting with their own gender appearance. For instance, toward the end of September 1953 the 19-year-old crossdresser Lü Jinde, who used to work as a hairdresser, was identified by one of her former clients living in the Wanhua district. This client followed Lü around briefly before turning to the police, explaining that Lü "walked in a funny way that was neither masculine nor feminine." After being arrested on the ground of indecency, Lü told the police, "Because I enjoy posing as a lady, starting roughly two months ago, I have been wandering around the street in female attire after sunset on a daily basis." Lü confessed that cross-dressing enabled him to "align with his psychological interest" and that, sexually, he was "attracted to women." "Although Lü emulated a modern lady quite successfully," a *United Daily News* article insisted, "his feminine attire still fails to conceal his masculine characteristics, which are easily recognizable in the eye of any beholder."[10] One exceptional observer considered Lü's cross-dressing behavior unproblematic, pointing out the counter-example of the increasing number of women who had begun imitating the roles of men in society.[11] Most commentators reacted conservatively, though, claiming to have witnessed "an immoral, confusing, and gender ambiguous persona that provokes disgust."[12]

Apart from explicit gender transgressive behaviors, the press reported on other astonishing accounts of bodily irregularity. In writing about these stories, the reporters always began by referring to Xie Jianshun's experience as a departing point for framing these rare disorders of the reproductive system. For example, a gynecologist came across a young woman with two uteruses in Tainan.[13] The woman was pregnant and near the end of her third trimester when she showed up at the Provincial Tainan Hospital for treatment. Upon discovering two uteruses inside her womb, Dr Huang Jiede decided that, for this woman's delivery, he would first perform a cesarean section, followed by a tubectomy (tubal ligation). The purpose of the tubectomy, according to Dr Huang, was to prevent "gestation in both uteruses, which may lead to undesirable side effects in the future." Interestingly, in contrast to the tremendous degree of publicity accorded to Xie Jianshun, journalists complied with the medical team's instruction to withhold the personal information, including the full name, of this particular patient. What is certain, though, is that the media exposure of this bi-uteral condition hinged on its potential for forthright comparison to the Xie story, given that both shared a certain feature of "rareness [to be investigated by] the medical community."[14]

In November 1953 the press discovered another individual with uncommon pregnancy problems. Only this time the patient was a man. Born in 1934, the farmer Liao had experienced persistent cramps and abdominal discomfort over the past two decades. The pain had become more pronounced over time, especially in recent years, reaching an intolerable state that forced Liao to seek medical assistance with the company of his family. Although this was not the first time that Liao consulted doctors about his condition, it was the first instance that he received surgical (and possibly terminal) treatment for it. Dr Yang Kunyan, the president of the Jichangtang Hospital, situated on Zhongzheng Road in the Luodong district of Yilan County, operated on Liao on November 7. News of this male pregnancy was circulated on two levels: the local district level and the county level. In Dr Yang's view, Liao was indisputably male. The county-level coverage disclosed Dr Yang's confirmation that Liao "was neither a woman nor a hermaphrodite."[15] The venturing into Liao's sexual identity led to greater clarification of his physical ailment. "The growth," Dr Yang speculated, "may have been the result of twin conception during his mother's pregnancy and that one of the fetuses formed prematurely and remained in his body."[16] Although neither the woman with two uteruses nor the pregnant man expressed medical symptoms related to sex change per se, the Xie story provided an immediate optic for coming to terms with these problems. The news accounts claimed that, like Xie's transsexuality, these were extraordinary biological phenomena with the potential to contribute to the advancement of biomedical research. On their end, in both cases, the doctors justified surgical intervention for these "unnatural" bodily defects.

In the midst of Xie Jianshun's relocation to Taipei in December 1953, the press recounted the story of another transsexual: Gonggu Bao, a foreign criminal who at times disguised herself as a man but, more often, appeared as a woman, and who had lived in various parts of Asia at different points of her life. Born in Siberia in 1902, Gonggu entered the world as Gonggu Baozi. Her father was Chinese and her mother was half Koryak and half Japanese. After her mother died due to malnutrition during the Russo–Japanese War (1904–1905), her father married another Japanese woman and moved to Tokyo. At the age of seven, Gonggu Baozi discovered that her facial and other physical appearances began to exhibit "masculine traits." Doctors performed plastic surgery on her (how intrusive this surgery was in terms of direct genital alteration is unclear from the newspaper account) but she still appeared "neither womanly nor manlike." Given the situation, her father and stepmother decided to change her name to Gonggu Bao, believing that by adopting this new, more masculine, name she was destined to pass as a normal man.[17]

At the age of 13, however, Gonggu Bao began to menstruate. This horrified her, as someone who had been assigned a male identity for half of her life up to that point. She began to alienate herself. She never played with other kids at school. Her parents, hugely disappointed with the situation, decided to send her away to live with her grandmother. Since the age of 15, so the newspapers claimed, Gonggu had committed at least 38 crimes across the world, including in Shanghai, Hong Kong, Singapore, Japan, and even Alaska and Canada. But more importantly, what Gonggu Bao's story confirmed was that Xie Jianshun's sex change was neither exceptional nor the first in Asia. Although their life trajectories proceeded in vastly different social, cultural, political, and historical contexts, Gonggu and Xie followed the same legacy of bodily transformation through medical intervention.[18] Moreover, the renewed interest in Gonggu Bao implied that it would be too simplistic to consider her, like Christine Jorgensen, merely as a historical precedent to Xie's popularity; rather, it was precisely the ways in which the popular press served as a central vehicle for disseminating the possible idea of sex change that enabled the stories of Gonggu, Jorgensen, and Xie to command public interest as interwoven and interrelated in Cold War Sinophone culture.

By the end of 1954, reporters had lost almost all contact with Xie Jianshun and her medical team. Xie's case gradually moved from current events to yesterday's news, but, as other stories of unusual bodily problems arose and resurfaced, the media reminded the public that manhood, womanhood, and their boundaries were neither as obvious nor as impermeable as they once had seemed. From Lü Jinde's transvestism to the lady with two uteruses, and from Liao's male pregnancy to Gonggu Bao's sex transformation, the earlier publicity on Xie provided cogent leverage for both the journalists and health care professionals to relate other nominal stories of bodily irregularity to the idea of "transsexuality." Although not all of them were directly or necessarily about sex change per se, these stories enabled some readers to take seriously the possibility of sex/gender transgression. With an elevated awareness of the malleability of gender, they began to learn what the label "*bianxingren*" meant and appreciate the immediate role of medical intervention in the reversing of one's sex. Through the press coverage, stories of intersexuality and sex transition cast questions about human identity in a new light. The alleged authority of doctors to unlock the secret of sexual identity, in particular, became more firmly planted in the popular imagination.

On October 28, 1955, the No. 1 Army Hospital in Taipei finally released a full-length report on Xie, entitled "The Completion and Success of Xie Jianshun's Sex-Change Operation."[19] The official report revealed numerous aspects of the Xie story that overthrew earlier speculations. Of these revelations, the most surprising was probably the fact that Xie's most recent operation was actually her fourth and not her third. By June 1954, from reading the scattered newspaper accounts, interested readers could gain a vague impression that doctors in Taipei had performed a second surgery on her, but its date, nature, and purpose lacked transparency. According to this official report, however, Xie's second operation, which was also an exploratory laparotomy but with the additional step of removing parts of her male gonadal tissues, had taken place on April 10, 1954. Based on the samples extracted from her body during this operation, the doctors confirmed Xie's status as a true hermaphrodite, meaning that she had both ovarian and testicular tissues in her gonads. The doctors also clarified that, by that point, her "testicular tissues were already deteriorating and unable to generate sperm" but her "ovarian tissues were still functional and able to produce eggs." In light of a stronger presence of female sexual characteristics, the medical team performed a third operation on August 26, 1954. After the surgery, Xie's penis was replaced by an artificial vaginal opening. All this happened more than a year prior. Xie's most recent and fourth genital surgery, which took place on August 30, 1955, was simply a vaginoplasty. Now with "a normal woman's vaginal interior," Xie Jianshun's "transformation from a soldier into a lady is now indisputable."[20] Brought to light by the report, Xie's personal triumph encapsulated the postwar fears and hopes about the possibilities of medical science.

The final media blitz surrounding the Xie story occurred in the late 1950s, during which it was reported that Soong Mei-ling, Chiang Kai-shek's wife, and a number of celebrities had visited Xie in Taipei and that Xie had begun working at the Ta Tung Relief Institute for Women and Children under the new name Xie Shun after *nine*, not four, surgeries.[21] Ever since the birth of "the Chinese Christine," the comparison of Xie to Jorgensen had intrigued, satisfied, and resonated with observers time and again, but never without limits.

Sinophone postcoloniality

The saga of Xie Jianshun, and that of other trans stories that followed in her wake, attests to the emergence of transsexuality as a form of modern sexual embodiment in Chinese-speaking society. As one *United Daily News* front-page article asserted, "to reconstruct a thirty-something year-old man into female is unprecedented in the history of clinical medicine [in Taiwan]."[22] Xie's story, in particular, became a lightning rod for many post-World War II anxieties about gender and sexuality, and it called dramatic attention to issues that would later drive the feminist and gay and lesbian movements in the decades ahead. In a different way, these stories of trans formation bring to light a genealogy that exceeds, even subverts, familiar historicizations of Taiwan's postcoloniality. They illustrate the ways in which the Chinese community in Taiwan inherited a Western biomedical epistemology of sex from not only the Japanese colonial regime (a conventional reading of Taiwan's colonial past) but also, more importantly, the sophisticated scientific globalism that characterized the Republican period on the mainland.[23] This genealogy from Republican-era scientific modernity to postwar Taiwanese transsexuality, connected via the Sinitic language but also made possible culturally by the migration of more than one million people from the mainland in the late 1940s, underscores the ways in which the Nationalist government regained sovereignty in Taiwan beyond a monolithic framing of Japanese postcolonialism. Parallel to British colonial Hong Kong, Taiwan experienced the highly institutionalized establishment of Western biomedical infrastructure under Japanese occupation.[24] In the 1950s, when Mao "nationalized" Chinese medicine in continental China, both Taiwan and Hong Kong represented the most advanced regions in modern Western medicine situated on the geo-margins of the Sinosphere.[25] Adding to its catalytic role in the transmission of Western biomedical knowledge and practice, British colonialism was instrumental in establishing Hong Kong as a more permissive cultural space when other parts of mainland China were strictly governed by a socialist state.[26] These historical factors thus allowed for the immense media publicity showered on Xie Jianshun and on sex change more broadly. Together, the rapid technology transfer of Western biomedicine and the availability of a fairly open social and cultural milieu enabled the Sinophone articulation of transsexuality to emerge first and foremost across the postcolonial East Asian Pacific Rim.

The examples of gender transformation unearthed here must be identified with the broader horizon of Sinophone production, by which I mean a broadening of queer Sinophonicity to refer to a mode of cultural engendering coalescing around the multiple peripheries of dominant geopolitical and social formations. The queer historicity of the transvestites, the bi-uteral woman, the pregnant man, intersexed persons, and other trans characters who came to light in the shadow of Xie rested on epistemological–historical pillars that came from outside the geopolitical China proper, including the legacies of Japanese postcolonialism, American neo-imperialism, the recontextualization of the Republican state's scientific globalism, and Taiwan's cultural and economic affiliations with other sub-regions of Cold War East Asia, such as Hong Kong and Japan. None of the queer subjects and embodiments that emerged in 1950s Taiwan can be sufficiently appreciated according to the historical logic of Republican China, Communist China, imperial Japan, or the modern United States alone, but their significance must be squarely situated at their discrepant and diffused intersections.

Considering Xie's celebrity and influence as a Sinophone (re)production of transsexuality is instructive in four other regards. First, the Sinophone approach pushes postcolonial studies beyond its overwhelming preoccupation with "the West." Postcolonial critics have problematized the West either by deconstructing any variant of its essentialist invocation or by provincializing the centripetal forces of its greatest imperial regimes, such as Europe and the United States.[27] On the contrary, viewing trans formations in postwar Taiwan as historical *events* of Sinophone production repositions our compass—and redraws our map—by recentering the non-West, Asia, and China more specifically. While the dispersed circuits of knowledge that saturated the "Chinese Christine's" glamor may question any straightforward conclusion about the Chineseness or Americanness of Xie's transsexuality, the other contemporaneous stories of trans corporeality represent a highly contingent and conditional response to the nascent genealogy of sex change emerging out of regional currents and global tensions. This chapter in 1950s Taiwanese history refocuses our attention from the "influence" of Western concepts and ideas to the inter- and intra-Asian regional conditions of subjectivity formation—from denaturalizing the West to provincializing China, Asia, and the rest.

Second, by provincializing China, the Sinophone framework enables us to see and think beyond the conventions of China studies. In the spirit of marking out "a space in which unspoken stories and histories may be told, and to recognize and map the historically constituted cultural and political effects of the cold war," I have aimed in this chapter to raise a series of interrelated questions that challenge the various categorical assumptions still haunting a "China-centered perspective."[28] Was Xie Jianshun's transsexuality "Chinese" or "American" in nature? And "transsexuality" in whose sense of the term? Was it a foreign import, an expression (and thus internalization) of Western imperialism, or a long-standing indigenous practice in a new light? How can we take the Republican state's administrative relocation in the late 1940s seriously? Is it possible to speak of a "Republican Chinese modernity" that problematizes the familiar socialist narrative of twentieth-century Chinese history? Which China was alluded to by the Chineseness of the label "Chinese Christine"? In the yet-to-appear discourse of Taiwanese nativism, did the Republican regime exemplify settler colonialism, migration, immigration, or diaspora? Evidently, the complexity of the history far exceeds the common terms used to describe the historical characteristics of postwar Taiwan. To call the GMD a regime from the outside or a colonial government only partially accounts for its proto-Chineseness or extra-Chineseness, and, precisely because of the lack of a precedent and analogous situations, it is all the more difficult to historicize, with neat categorical imperatives or ways of periodization, the social backdrop against which and the epistemic conditions under which the first Chinese transsexual became a comprehensible concept. The queerness of Sinophone Taiwan, as evinced through trans-archiving, calls into question not only the conventions of China studies; it invariably casts light on a symmetrically nested agenda to decenter the normative orientation of Taiwan studies as well. Like China, Taiwan has never been a *straight*-forward geobody, a political container of sorts, carrying evolving historical cultures that merely reflect a series of colonial governmentality displacements.

Third, understood as "a way of looking at the world," the epistemological rendition of the Sinophone not only breaks down the China-versus-the-West binary; it also specifies the most powerful type, nature, and feature of transnationalism whose interest-articulation must lie beyond the hegemonic constructions of the nation-state. In particular, the kind of *minor* transnationalism proposed by François Lionnet and Shu-mei Shih contextualizes the global significance of Taiwan without being routed through a center, whether it is China or the West.[29] The peripheral ontologies of Sinophone queerness demand carefully executed place-based analyses while never losing sight of the ever shifting parameters of the norms and centers of any given regional space. The transnationalism and interregionalism of the trajectory from Republican China to postwar Taiwan make it evident that any hegemonic understanding of "China" and "Taiwan" as sovereign nation-states will always fall short in capturing the genealogical grounding of those queer livelihoods, maneuvers, and experiences encapsulated in the two categories' politically contested relationality.

Although I have used mid-twentieth-century Taiwan as the exemplary context of queer Sinophone (re)production, its implications obviously extend beyond Taiwan and the early Cold War period. By bringing the theoretical category of the Sinophone to bear on the non-identitarian history of trans formations narrated here, my aim is to bring together, historically, the reciprocal rigor of queer and Sinophone theoretical critiques, thematizing the coproduction of gender heteronormativity and the hegemonic (Chinese) nation-state as they are articulated through one another. Together, the queerness of Sinophone perspectives and the anti-Sinocentric logic of queering settle on unsettling the overlapping recognitions of Xie Jianshun's transsexuality as a Chinese copy of a Western original, a Sinophone production of a Chinese original, a straight mimesis of a male-to-female transgendered body, a queer reproduction of an American blonde beauty, and so forth. A social history of trans formations in Sinophone Taiwan that exceeds a conventional Japanese postcolonial paradigm comprises the broad spectrum of these potential straightforward convergences and postnormative divergences. The resulting historiographical task challenges a homogenous postcolonial interpretation of twentieth-century Taiwan that figures in either Chinese imperial hegemony or Japanese colonialism (or American neo-colonialism for that matter) as its exclusive preoccupation. The history of contemporary Taiwan therefore invites multiple interpretative strategies and approaches to account for its "colonial" (read global) past—a historicism that decenters rather than recenters the hegemony of formal imperial giants such as China, Japan, the United States, and so forth.

This brings us to the last, yet perhaps the most important, contribution of the Sinophone methodology: to appreciate the formation of Sinophone modernity that began to distinguish itself from and gradually replaced an older apparatus of colonial modernity in the course of twentieth-century Chinese history.[30] The queer Sinophone framework underscores the ways in which the particular polities mediating the transmission of foreign/Western knowledge to China (such as Japan in the early Republican period as often viewed through the lens of colonial modernity), at least in the areas of gender and sexuality, have been gradually replaced by Sinophone communities by the end of the twentieth century.[31] Taken together, what the cases of gender transgression recollected in this chapter reveal is a much earlier moment of historical displacement, in the immediate postwar era, when the sociocultural articulation of non-normative genders and sexualities was rerouted through—and thus re-rooted in—Sinitic-language communities and cultures on the periphery of Chineseness.

Notes

1 This chapter is adapted from *After Eunuchs: Science, Medicine, and the Transformation of Sex in Modern China*, by Howard Chiang. Copyright © 2018 Columbia University Press. Reprinted with permission of Columbia University Press. On Christine Jorgensen, see Serlin, "Christine Jorgensen and the Cold War Closet"; Meyerowitz, *How Sex Changed*; Skidmore, "Constructing the 'Good Transsexual.'"

2 On Nagai Akiko, see McLelland, *Queer Japan from the Pacific War to the Internet Age*, 113. On Marta Olmos, see Jones, "Mexican Sexology and Male Homosexuality."

3 This chapter's focus on the 1950s hinges on two particular chronological frameworks: the (immediate) post-WWII and the Cold War. Whereas the former calls attention to the global trends of gender normativization following the six-year global war, the latter emphasizes a new international configuration in which most nations are divided into either US- or USSR-led spheres of influence. Taiwan, in this sense, epitomizes both characterizations: a highly virile state under the dictatorship of the Nationalist Party (led by Chiang Kai-shek) and a "Chinese" US-protectorate in opposite to the USSR-backed Maoist regime. In light of the unique historical situation, I use "postwar" and "Cold War" interchangeably throughout the essay. On placing Taiwan on the map of gender and sexual marginality in the 1950s, see Chiang, "Archiving Peripheral Taiwan."

4 On "transing," see Stryker, Currah and Moore, "Introduction: Trans-, Trans, or Transgender?"

5 In this sense, Sinophone studies are distinct from Chinese studies by disrupting the chain of equivalence typically assumed between nation, culture, language, ethnicity, and politics that obfuscates what the label "Chinese" holds. Sinophone communities bear a historically embedded and political contested relationship to China, akin to the relationship between the Francophone world and France and the Anglophone world and Britain. The monograph that has inaugurated the field of Sinophone studies is Shih, *Visuality and Identity*. See also Shih, Tsai and Bernards, eds., *Sinophone Studies*.

6 On queer Sinophonicity, see Chiang and Heinrich, eds., *Queer Sinophone Cultures*.

7 *Lianhebao*, "Burang Kelisiding."

8 Ibid.; "Shoushu shunli."

9 *Taiwan xinshengbao*, "Yinyangren yinsheng yangshuai"; *Zhonghua ribao*, "Nanshi yinyangren."

10 *Lianhebao*, "Dianyingjie."

11 *Lianhebao*, "Yidu dianying."

12 *Lianhebao*, "Renyao zhanzhuan."

13 *Lianhebao*, "Ji yinyangren hou."

14 *Lianhebao*, "Ji yinyangren hou."

15 *Lianhebao*, "Qingnian nanzi."

16 Ibid.

17 *Lianhebao*, "Yinyangren liulangji."

18 Ibid.

19 *Lianhebao*, "Lujun diyi zongyiyuan."

20 *Lianhebao*, "Sici shoushu."

21 *Lianhebao*, "Xiaoyangnü."

22 *Lianhebao*, "Woguo yixue shishang."

23 For a succinct execution of this thesis, see Dikötter, *The Age of Openness*.

24 Lo, *Doctors within Borders*; Liu, *Prescribing Colonization*.

25 Taylor, *Chinese Medicine in Early Communist China, 1945–1963*.

26 Carroll, *A Concise History of Hong Kong*, 140–166.

27 Sakai, "Modernity and Its Critique"; Chakrabarty, "Provincializing Europe."

28 Chen, *Asia as Method*, 120. See also Chun, *Forget Chineseness*. On the "China-centered perspective," see Cohen, *Discovering History in China*.

29 Lionnet and Shih, eds., *Minor Transnationalism*.

30 On colonial modernity, see Barlow, ed., *Formations of Colonial Modernity in East Asia*.

31 On Japan's role in mediating linguistic and cultural change in early twentieth-century China, see Liu, *Translingual Practice*.

Bibliography

Barlow, Tani, ed. *Formations of Colonial Modernity in East Asia*. Durham, NC: Duke University Press, 1997. doi:10.1215/9780822399117.

Carroll, John M. *A Concise History of Hong Kong*. Lanham, MD: Rowman & Littlefield, 2007.

Chakrabarty, Dipesh. "Provincializing Europe: Postcoloniality and the Critique of History." *Cultural Studies* 6, no. 3 (1992): 337–357. doi:10.1080/09502389200490221.

Chen, Kuan-Hsing. *Asia as Method: Toward Deimperialization*. Durham, NC: Duke University Press, 2010. doi:10.1215/9780822391692.

Chiang, Howard. "Archiving Peripheral Taiwan: The Prodigy of the Human and Historical Narration." *Radical History Review*, no. 120 (2014): 204–225. doi:10.1215/01636545-2704110.

Chiang, Howard and Ari Larissa Heinrich, eds. *Queer Sinophone Cultures*. New York: Routledge, 2013.

Chun, Allen. *Forget Chineseness: On the Geopolitics of Cultural Identification*. Albany, NY: State University of New York Press, 2017.

Cohen, Paul A. *Discovering History in China: American Historical Writing on the Recent Chinese Past*. New York: Columbia University Press, 1984.

Dikötter, Frank. *The Age of Openness: China before Mao*. Berkeley, CA: University of California Press, 2008.

Jones, Ryan. "Mexican Sexology and Male Homosexuality: Genealogies and Global Contexts, 1860–1957." In *A Global History of Sexual Science, 1880–1960*, edited by Veronika Fuechtner, Douglas E.Haynes and Ryan M. Jones, 232–257. Oakland, CA: University of California Press, 2018. doi:10.1525/9780520966673.

Lianhebao "Burang Kelisiding zhuanmei yuqian dabing jiang bianchen xiaojie" (Christine will not be America's exclusive: Soldier destined to become a lady). August 21, 1953.

Lianhebao "Dianyingjie zuowan chuxian renyao shaonian qiaozhuang modengnü zikui shengwei nan'ersheng" (Human prodigy appeared on movie street last night: A man dressing up like a modern woman, loathing a natural male body). September 25, 1953.

Lianhebao "Ji yinyangren hou you yi yiwen poufu qutai fang nanchan chuyun shaofu liang zigong" (Another strange news after the hermaphrodite: C-section performed on a woman with two uteruses). September 28, 1953.

Lianhebao "Lujun diyi zongyiyuan xuanbu Xie Jianshun shoushu chenggong" (No. 1 Hospital announces the completion and success of Xie Jianshun's sex change operation). October 28, 1955.

Lianhebao "Qingnian nanzi sheng youyun yishi pouchu renxingliu" (Doctor excised a human-form growth from a pregnant man). November 13, 1953.

Lianhebao "Renyao zhanzhuan qijie nongde mianwu qunxie shangfeng baisu juliu santian" (The human prodigy no longer appears fabulous: Detained for three days for offending public morals). September 26, 1953.

Lianhebao "Shoushu shunli wancheng gaizao juyou bawo" (Surgery successfully completed: Alteration is feasible). August 21, 1953.

Lianhebao "Sici shoushu yibian erchai Xie Jianshun bianxing jingguo" (Male to female transformation after four surgeries: The sex change experience of Xie Jianshun). October 28, 1955.

Lianhebao "Woguo yixue shishang de chuangju Xie Jianshun bianxing shoushu chenggong" (A new chapter in the nation's medical history: The success of Xie Jianshun's sex change surgery). August 31, 1955.

Lianhebao "Xiaoyangnü Fu Xiuxia zhu Tatong Jiaoyangyuan" (Little girl Fu Xiuxia boarding Tatong Relief Institute). June 7, 1959.

Lianhebao "Yidu dianying duanzuo youtian" (A trip to the movie: Fast becoming worries). September 26, 1953.

Lianhebao "Yinyangren liulangji" (The tale of a hermaphrodite). December 30, 1953.

Lionnet, Françoise and Shu-mei Shih, eds. *Minor Transnationalism*. Durham, NC: Duke University Press, 2005.

Liu, Lydia H. *Translingual Practice: Literature, National Culture, and Translated Modernity—China, 1900–1937*. Stanford, CA: Stanford University Press, 1995.

Liu, Shiyung. *Prescribing Colonization: The Role of Medical Practice and Policy in Japan-Ruled Taiwan*. Ann Arbor, MI: Association for Asian Studies, 2009.

Lo, Ming-Cheng. *Doctors within Borders: Profession, Ethnicity, and Modernity in Colonial Taiwan*. Berkeley, CA: University of California Press, 2002.

McLelland, Mark. *Queer Japan from the Pacific War to the Internet Age*. Lanham, MD: Rowman & Littlefield, 2005.

Meyerowitz, Joanne. *How Sex Changed: A History of Transsexuality in the United States*. Cambridge, MA: Harvard University Press, 2002.

Sakai, Naoki. "Modernity and Its Critique: The Problem of Universalism and Particularism." *South Atlantic Quarterly* 87, no. 3 (1988): 475–504.

Serlin, David. "Christine Jorgensen and the Cold War Closet." *Radical History Review*, no. 62 (1995): 136–165. doi:10.1215/01636545-1995-62-137.

Shih, Shu-mei. *Visuality and Identity: Sinophone Articulations Across the Pacific*. Berkeley, CA: University of California Press, 2007.

Shih, Shu-mei, Chien-hsin Tsai and Brian Bernards, eds. *Sinophone Studies: A Critical Reader*. New York: Columbia University Press, 2013.

Skidmore, Emily. "Constructing the 'Good Transsexual': Christine Jorgensen, Whiteness, and Heteronormativity in the Mid-Twentieth Century Press." *Feminist Studies* 37, no. 2 (2011): 270–300.

Stryker, Susan, Paisley Currah and Lisa Jean Moore. "Introduction: Trans-, Trans, or Transgender?" *Women's Studies Quarterly* 36, no. 3/4 (2008): 11–22.

Taiwan xinshengbao "Yinyangren yinsheng yangshuai" (Hermaphrodite's yin flourishes and yang depletes). August 21, 1953.

Taylor, Kim. *Chinese Medicine in Early Communist China, 1945–1963: A Medicine of Revolution*. New York: Routledge, 2005.

Zhonghua ribao "Nanshi yinyangren dongshoushu shengli jiego quanshu nüxing" (Tainan hermaphrodite's female biology revealed after surgery). August 21, 1953.

24

QUEER SOVEREIGNTIES

Re-imagining sexual citizenship from the Dutch Caribbean

Wigbertson Julian Isenia

This chapter is a theoretical re-imagination of sexual citizenship through an engagement with the cultural practices of the Curaçaoan-born theater-maker Fridi Martina. Traditionally the concept of sexual citizenship outlines the sexual rights and duties of individuals relating to the nation-state, encompassing legal disputes about same-sex marriage, among other things. Throughout this chapter I discuss how Martina's articulation of ideas about sexuality contribute to broader theoretical and collective political efforts to radically re-imagine sexual citizenship; that is, a critique of heteronormativity as well as an intersectional analysis that brings into focus axes of sexuality, class, gender, and race.[1] More importantly, I foreground a re-imagination of sexual citizenship from below, which prioritizes minoritarian perspectives and does so from the perspective of the fragmented sovereignty of the Dutch Caribbean. Currently the Dutch Caribbean consists of the constituent countries Aruba, Curaçao and Sint Maarten, and the special municipalities of Bonaire, Sint Eustatius, and Saba.[2] The Kingdom of the Netherlands includes the Dutch Caribbean and the European mainland Netherlands. Being a Dutch Caribbean might mean at once being a citizen of one of the special municipalities or constituent countries within the Kingdom (living on one of the Caribbean islands); a citizen of the European mainland Netherlands (born in the Caribbean and living in the Netherlands); a European citizen (having a Dutch European passport by legal membership in the Kingdom); and a Caribbean citizen (identify culturally with one of the islands). This chapter underlines the longstanding, complex, and fragmented sovereignty of the Dutch Caribbean islands, yet sees this political context as a unique entry point to devise social transformations outside the idea of the nation-state and Euro-American centered scholarship.

Sexual citizenship as more than legal and state membership

This chapter offers cultural practices of citizenship as a way to re-imagine a rights-based understanding of sexual citizenship. The notion of sexual citizenship emerged in the context of Euro-American legal discussions in the 1990s. The concept relates to the demands of sexual minorities and transgender persons as political subjects to institutional rights ensured by the nation-state, such as the right to marriage, the right to join the military, the right to choose a gender identity, the right to essential health care benefits, and protection against discrimination.

However, gender and queer scholars have been critical of state inclusion and protection. Lisa Duggan explains that the political and social recognition of gay individuals comes with the condition that heterosexual and monogamous relationships continue to be upheld as the societal norm. This, in turn, favors the already privileged and disregards subjects that fail to meet this norm.[3] Dean Spade, on the other hand, argues that a rights-based LGBT framework focused on legal recognition and equality claims is not a viable strategy to ensure the safety and livelihood of transgender people. Instead, there should be a focus on practices and processes in contrast to a symbolic endpoint.[4] Rather than expanding the literature on rights-based citizenship to the geopolitical setting of Curaçao, I turn to cultural practices aimed at achieving social transformation without prioritizing state inclusion and protection. This would bring about a kind of sexual citizenship that critiques not only the heterosexualization and masculinization of the state but also considers how colonialism and imperialism, and their effects, dictate the socioeconomic lives of queer people.[5]

Subjects deemed as queer in the Dutch Caribbean seek to claim belonging in the local cultural community of the non-independent Dutch Caribbean islands, while at the same time exploring the advantages of belonging to the sovereign nation-state of the Netherlands. Simultaneously, these actors also seek to mobilize themselves outside of the state or state-centered politics within public spaces or through cultural practices such as public appearances or theater. Such an approach to "citizenship from below" highlights practices that foster social change or reject dominant ideals of morality, respectability, and heteronormativity. As Mimi Sheller argues, to study "citizenship from below" is to engage with popular culture such as dance and performance, "which overflow beyond the political realm."[6] According to Sheller, these practices are related to forms of material struggle within hegemonic systems and direct us to more culturally shaped counter-hegemonic processes.[7]

To think citizenship from below, I situate Fridi Martina's cultural practices within the context of the fragmented sovereignty of the Dutch Caribbean. Neither independent nor officially a colony, the Dutch Caribbean—much like other non-sovereign formations in the British, French, and US Caribbean—represents a form of strategic and neo-colonial entanglement with the former metropolis. This particular political situation offers rich terrain from which to conceptualize what I term *queer sovereignties*. The Dutch Caribbean islands compel us to rethink questions of sovereignty and political imaginations within movements for social justice. I borrow Yarimar Bonilla's idea of strategic entanglement to construct an understanding of queer sovereignties. Focusing on labor activists in the French Caribbean, Bonilla argues that this particular form of national non-sovereignty produces what she calls *strategic entanglement*: "a way of crafting and enacting autonomy within a system from which one is unable to fully disentangle."[8] In this political praxis, the past, particularly the occupation of indigenous land, the history of colonialism, displacement, and enslavement, is wielded in the present. But also, how activists are "working *within and against* the constraints of postcolonial sovereignty … as an effort to break free from the epistemic binds of political modernity, even while still being compelled to think through its normative categories."[9] Hence this chapter asks what kind of queer politics this fragmented sovereignty might produce.

Through the concept of *queer sovereignties* I complicate the varied and complex ways in which social, political, and economic structures shape queer Dutch Antillean intimacies. Thus *queer sovereignty* in the context of the Dutch Caribbean implies subjects working *within and against* the epistemology of sexual identity or working *within and against* the (neo)-colonial construction of the Dutch Caribbean. It is taking a closer look at the different Dutch Caribbean islands' histories, needs, and demands and the need to consider the complexity of our political world and to adopt various pragmatic strategies depending on the specific context.[10]

For instance, *queer*, as is the case with *queer of color critique*, by no means only focuses on sexuality, but is also attentive to the intersections of class, gender, race, and citizenship that determine one's position within political economy.[11] At the same time, there is a realization that race and sexuality operate in distinctive ways, which necessarily have implications for how we address these intersections in our political and intellectual projects. The chapter interweaves two different materials. First, a critical analysis of interviews with Martina about the difference between same-sex relationships and desires in Curaçao and the Netherlands. Second, a close reading of Martina's performance *Siegu pa Kolo* (Papiamentu, the creole language of Aruba, Curaçao, and Bonaire, for *Colorblind*, 1978). Through this material I join cultural practices with broader social movements.

"I live and work with a woman, but don't call that lesbianism"

Fridi Martina is known for her performances in the national theater of Curaçao and her plays in neighborhood centers and on television and radio. When Martina was 22 years old she migrated to the Netherlands from Curaçao and was admitted to the Academy of Dramatic Arts in Amsterdam. Martina gained fame with the play *Colorblind* (1978), a performance about colorism and racism that, depending on where she staged it, was performed in either English, Dutch, or Papiamentu. In 1986, together with her then-partner Margareth Adama (Madama), she opened Villa Baranka, an art salon for and by artists with a migrant background in the Netherlands. She was appointed as a drama teacher and later as executive officer to promote intercultural studies of performing arts at the Utrecht School of the Arts. After 25 years in the Netherlands, Martina moved back to Curaçao and lived there for 20 years. During this period she recorded four albums, co-produced a film, and directed a drama series for the local television station. In 2014 she died of the effects of ALS/Lou Gehrig's disease.

In 1986 Martina spoke during the Lesbian Festival that was part of a broader commemoration of the fortieth anniversary of the Dutch national LGBT+ organization COC. An audience member asked how it was to be a person who identified as a lesbian in the Dutch theater landscape and how she dealt with the theme of lesbianism in her theater practice. Martina replied: "Well, I would like to ask other questions. So far, [the term] lesbian is not clear to me. That is one. How it works in practice [makes a questioning gesture. You hear laughter from the audience] … Furthermore, I think if you only approach being a lesbian from [either] a social or a romantic perspective, it's incredibly limited. … I live and work with a woman, but don't call that lesbianism."[12]

A few months earlier there had been a public conversation between the writers Astrid Roemer and Audre Lorde in Amsterdam. Roemer, who was born in Suriname, asked: "Why is [it] necessary to declare oneself a lesbian[?] There are, after all, things which aren't to be given names—giving them names kills them … [W]e do have age-old rituals originating from Africa by which women can make quite clear that special relations exist between them."[13] The American-Barbadian Audre Lorde, who calls herself "a Black lesbian," in contrast asserted: "If you speak your name, you represent a threat to the powers that be," and, besides, other women "may see that it is possible to speak your name and to go on living."[14] Instead of classifying one position as purely "political," and the other as strictly "personal" and a way of surviving,[15] I argue that the views espoused by Roemer, Martina, and Lorde set the foundation for a political and intellectual project that attends to a particular Black female sexual liberation merged with racial justice and class. Roemer and Martina extend this political and intellectual project by adopting a theorization from the margins; in this case, from the cultural practices of the former Dutch Caribbean colonies. Simultaneously, this theorization from the Dutch Caribbean must be analyzed hand in hand with how the European mainland Netherlands was and is defined over and against subjects from the former colonies, despite having the same Dutch citizenship. This means that an analysis of sexuality should, at the same time, question the very idea of state membership and colonialism. Such consideration does not dismiss the radical political potential of Black lesbianism. Instead, it seeks to theorize an underexplored position, which I term *queer sovereignties*.

First, in a surprising and witty manner, Martina questions the self-evident and universal meaning of the term "lesbian." Like many other Caribbean thinkers, she questions this term in the local context of the Dutch Caribbean. Martina even does so within the context of the diaspora in the Netherlands. These terms, mainly originating in a Euro-American context, are devoid of any cultural and historical specificity to the Caribbean and contribute to the erasure of local words and culture relating to gender and sexuality.[16] However, Martina is not propelling a homogenous and monolithic idea of the sexual cultures that exist in the Dutch Caribbean. Actually, Martina repeatedly acknowledges the existence of Dutch Caribbean lesbians with whom she partied at Villa Baranka.[17] Indeed, as Madama, Martina's ex-partner recounts in an oral history interview I did with her in 2018, Martina met her in an LGBT bar in Amsterdam.[18] This shows that although Martina rejected such sexual markers, she occasionally frequented so-called LGBT spaces. Nevertheless, Martina's rejection of the category "lesbian" can be interpreted as a rejection of a global (read Euro-American) LGBT identity-based politics and instead opens a possible way to de-center the focus on the Global North in theoretical understandings of sexual citizenship.[19]

Other interviews show that Martina was fairly consistent in shunning identitarian markers or categories of sexuality. Martina describes herself in another interview in a LGBT radio program by stating: "It's not that I feel the need [to have a relationship] right now. So, the moment I do that, it is also with someone I feel something for. And then it makes no difference for me whether it is a man or a woman. However, indeed, I often choose women [over men] because I cannot muster the patience to be with men."[20] Martina describes her sexuality and the motivations she has for entering into a relationship with a person. She continues in the interview about an acquaintance:

> I find it incredibly difficult the way of thinking here in the west where everything should be put in a box ... I have a friend who lives with another woman ... Only that it is [not visible] to the community. Because I did not know it myself for a long time, I suspected it. However, officially, they shared a house. That was possible too. Do you understand? ... For the outside world, they are just two friends. They have also adopted three children. So, they are also two parents.[21]

Second, Martina's non-identitarian sexual praxis extends other erotic traditions in the Dutch and broader Caribbean, suggesting the possibility of their survival and mobility. To be more precise, we might situate Martina's sexual practices within an old Afro-Curaçaoan social and sexual institution called *kambrada*. *Kambrada*, as is the case with Suriname's *mati* and English-Creole's *zami,* is a non-identitarian practice of female same-sex relations and can imply an erotic relationship, a platonic relationship, or an erotic desire.[22] Despite the colonial male- and Western-centered early descriptions of women in *kambrada* relationships at the end of the nineteenth century and the beginning of the twentieth, these accounts give a multi-dimensional perspective to the relationships these women have in which issues of race, gender, sexuality, and colonialism collide.[23] Martina's answer documents that parts of this practice of *kambrada* may still have existed in the 1990s and might have even traveled from the former (post)colony to the old metropolis. Martina points out what she considers to be a limited way of looking at intimate female same-sex relationships, and also brings a material component by emphasizing labor and co-dependence as necessary to her relationships: I live and *work* with a woman.

Martina's repeated refusal of the term "lesbian," while also participating in a lesbian festival or a LGBT radio program, is indicative of politics within *queer sovereignty*. It reverberates with what Yarimar Bonilla terms *strategic entanglement*. In the case of Martina, one might participate within and at the same time against the hegemonic seduction of traditional LGBT, perhaps for material compensation or recognition, and also be questioning its very core. *Queer sovereignty* in this case is not a kind of gay nationalism or a territorial claim.[24] It moves away from big narratives of freedom and national sovereignty and seeks instead odd, unusual, or *straño* (queer/odd in Papiamentu) sovereignties. For example, *queer sovereignty* is constituted by queer people engaging in cultural practices and struggles for political subjectivity to improve their collective lives. Sometimes these practices are not always visible to the law or the state; and notions of "politics" may not relate solely to the nation-state or the government. *Queer sovereignty* questions the legitimacy of Western models and incorporates analyses of race, class, and gender in its consideration of cultural practices of sexuality, while at the same time being vigilant not to seek a pure and uncontaminated "indigenous" sexuality. More importantly, it re-imagines ways of being in the world without adding *kambrada* into the LGBTQIA+ mix and stir; it does not, in other words, seek institutional legibility, but collective betterment. Instead, queer sovereignties encourage us to think about how the cultural practices of Martina can orient our political and intellectual project elsewhere.

Cathy Cohen directs us toward a political and intellectual project that shifts attention from queer theory's primary focus on sexuality to "the multiple and intersecting systems of power that largely dictate our life chances."[25] Cohen critiques queer theory's narrow focus on sexuality that reinforces the binary logic between queerness and heterosexuality, instead of strategically challenging heteronormativity. According to Cohen, this might mean investing politically in the lives of Black women who may belong to the category of heterosexual women but who are not considered by the society as "normal, moral or worthy of state support."[26] In our case, this might mean to ask whether the women who engaged in *kambrada* relationships (sometimes unmarried, simultaneously or successively in relationships with men and raising children together or of other families) would qualify in what some criticize as an understandable, legible, and apparent LGBTQIA+, and thus deserving or able to claim various forms of state support. As the next section documents, through a close reading of the performance *Colorblind*, Martina's cultural practices show that not only sexuality but also the intersections of race and citizenship play a role in the re-imaging of sexual citizenship as *queer sovereignty*.

"You shouldn't be here, 'cause you're black"

Martina's work is characterized as "the emotional state of mind of pain, sorrow, impotence" of one individual in which the viewer experiences the performance as an "emotional roller coaster."[27] The performance of *Colorblind* following this characterization consists of four women's monologues in four different scenes or acts. Martina performs and sings the four monologues while being accompanied musically by a conga player and a male singer. The four monologues are about four women of different ages and from different economic upbringings. The first monologue chronicles a woman who wants to escape the small Caribbean-Dutch island of Curaçao for the social and economic benefits of the Netherlands.

Once she's migrated she is confronted with problems such as racism and colorism. The second monologue is about a woman who speaks about her ex-boyfriend, who was not accepted by her parents because he is a touch darker than herself. The third monologue is about the Black mother that puts her white child on a pedestal, to be scorned later by the same child due to her blackness, and, finally, the fourth monologue is about a social worker who got stuck in her color complexes.

Colorblind invites the viewer to reflect on the problem of colorism, which is inter-group racism, in a racist, patriarchal, capitalist, and postcolonial society. Like Zora Neale Hurston's *Color Struck* (1926) five decades earlier, the play *Colorblind* "dramatizes the fact that color prejudice takes many forms."[28] In both pieces by Martina and Hurston the protagonists discuss racism, colorism and the remnants of colonization and enslavement through the intimate, the personal, and the home. This features, for instance, in the second monologue in Martina's play on the disapproval of a romantic relationship due to colorism, or the third monologue on the rejection of a Black mother by her lighter-skinned daughter. In Hurston's play, the main character is overtly fixated on skin color and is only sexually attracted to lighter-skin people. Yet Martina's play also emphasizes the differentiation made by government officials from the 1960s on between Kingdom citizens originating in the European Netherlands and the Dutch Caribbean, which I argue is entrenched with racism and colorism. For example, in the fourth monologue a social worker who functions as an intermediary says: "If too many of us live in the same neighborhood, we are spread out all over [the Netherlands]. Whether you like it or not."[29] Here the character possibly refers to the settlement and distribution policy in the Netherlands in the 1970s and 1980s to hinder the housing of Surinamese, Dutch Caribbean, Moroccan, and Turkish people in the four big cities. They were forced to disperse throughout the Netherlands as much as possible in order to prevent any kind of "problems." Through the cultural practice of theatre, Martina expresses a social and political framework in which the postcolonial subjects with a Dutch passport were situated.

Colorblind shows that racism and colorism are interwoven with citizenship. Since people from the Dutch Caribbean and Suriname (until 1975) have a Dutch passport, they have free movement between the Netherlands and the Caribbean. Politicians have repeatedly tried to regulate these migration flows. These attempts led to further administrative and legal divisions in society between so-called *allochtoon* (emerging from another soil) and *autochtoon* (emerging from this soil) within the Kingdom. In 1972, for example, European Dutch parliamentary leaders suggested introducing a visa requirement for Surinamese and Antillean citizens.

A recent example is a bill from then minister Rita Verdonk in 2006 to send back so-called Antillean "problem youths." Both proposals were ultimately deemed unlawful because they made a distinction between European Dutch and Caribbean Dutch citizens. In addition to the legal dimensions, Martina's play shows that these migrations also had social consequences for people from the Dutch Caribbean in the Netherlands. After a year, the woman in the first monologue notices that her landlord is subjecting her to discriminatory treatment: "It's the way they look at you, … tells you … you shouldn't be *here*, 'cause you're black."[30] *Here,* in this instance, refers to the European Netherlands, which, as Gloria Wekker suggests, is imagined "as homogenously white."[31] This myth of racial purity functions to trivialize the Dutch colonial past and, in doing so, confuses national identity with race and ethnic identity.

Colorblind resists portraying Blackness as an ontology of victimization and precarity while still being attuned to the aftermaths of chattel slavery. Instead, the play creates a space of possibility. In this space Black people, in the words of Christina Sharpe, do "not simply or only live in subjection and as the subjected" but are "politically and socially astute,"[32] which is articulated most clearly at the end of the play: "that's why I protest with all the others who can see through [color]."[33] Furthermore, the play proves how cultural practices such as theater performances can act as an alternative archive of orality that counters the "discourse of shame" of race and color in Curaçaoan society.[34] Martina underscores this in an interview: "One must rebel against the injustices that one faces by forming a unity and fighting for your rights."[35] This form of camaraderie and radical coalition work through the discussion of colorism means that we should combat racism *and* colorism independently and synchronously.

The last part of *Colorblind* emphasizes that colorism, next to racism, remains a tenacious problem in our imaginations of freedom. Within these imaginations, people are often eager to eradicate differences in order to build stronger coalitions. This racelessness, as Angela Roe argues in the case of Curaçao, aids rather than dispels racial difference, because it remains anchored in the very fabric of the state, its bureaucratization, and social interactions.[36] Racelessness, following Roe, eliminates the vocabulary with which racial inequality can be examined and addressed, and it hinders the historical and structural roots of racial difference from being countered.[37] Somehow *Colorblind* offers to contribute to this vocabulary in the way that it articulates and showcases, in the words of Martina, how the colonial past is "engraved in the present, how refined [colonial prejudices] are reproduced and educated, how we [as Black people] are set up against each other … and white people against [Black people]."[38]

Conclusion

There has been a global effort in recent years to revisit the histories of the intersectional politics of the Black feminist movements, the radical queer movements, and the politics of queer of color collectives. These studies challenge the presumption that intersectional politics is a recent phenomenon and document that these multidimensional projects had different geopolitical origins and consequences. Others, such as Fatima El-Tayeb, examine queer of color collectives outside of the United States of America to look at how, in the case of the Netherlands, groups such as Strange Fruit from the 1990s refused to prioritize particular struggles over others. They rejected "the normativity of a white western model of homosexual identity."[39] Through this chapter I hope to contribute to this global project to investigate how the life and works of an individual—Fridi Martina, living and working both in the Netherlands and Curaçao—can help us reflect on the intersections of colonialism, sexuality, nationalism, and race within a left political project.

Notes

1 Cohen, "Punks, Bulldaggers, and Welfare Queens," 440.
2 Suriname is also often considered part of the Dutch Caribbean because of its official language and its colonial past. But for this chapter I will mainly focus on the islands that currently still belong to the Kingdom of the Netherlands.
3 Duggan, *The Twilight of Equality?*
4 Spade, *Normal Life.*
5 Alexander, "Not just (Any)Body can be a Citizen"; Kamugisha, "The Coloniality of Citizenship."
6 Sheller, *Citizenship from Below,* 38.
7 Ibid., 33.
8 Bonilla, *Non-Sovereign Futures,* 43.
9 Ibid., 15. My emphasis.
10 I borrow this insight from Groenewoud, "Les Mobiliations Féminines dans les Antilles Néerlandaises."
11 Ferguson, *Aberrations in Black.*

12 Registration on DVD of the Lesbian Festival (December 5 and 6, 1986) on the occasion of the 40th anniversary of the COC, 5316 and 5440, IHLIA LGBT Heritage archives.
13 Wekker, "Mati-ism and Black Lesbianism," 153–154.
14 Ibid., 153.
15 Ibid., 157.
16 Wekker, *The Politics of Passion*.
17 Registration of radio interview with Fridi Martina and Felix de Rooy (July 20, 1990), 657753, Beeld en Geluid archives.
18 Margareth Adama, interview with the author, July 19, 2018.
19 Richardson, "Rethinking Sexual Citizenship," 219.
20 Radio interview (my translation).
21 Ibid.
22 Wekker, *Politics and Passion*; Tinsley, *Thiefing Sugar*.
23 Isenia, "Looking for Kambrada."
24 Lattas, "Queer Sovereignty."
25 Cohen, "Punks, Bulldaggers and Welfare Queens," 203.
26 Ibid., 205.
27 Echteld and Severing, "Over een Meertalige Bloemlezing," 192–193.
28 Carpenter, "Addressing 'The Complex-ities of Skin Color,'" 22.
29 Theatrical script of *Colorblind* (1978) by Fridi Martina and translated by Maryke Veugelers, LMA/4463/C/09/05/004, Metropolitan Archives, 11.
30 Theatrical script, 2. My emphasis.
31 Wekker, *White Innocence*, 4.
32 Sharpe, *In the Wake*, 4.
33 Theatrical script, 56.
34 Roe, "The Sound of Silence," 174.
35 van Dijs, "Fridi Martina," 11.
36 Roe, "The Sound of Silence," 246.
37 Ibid.
38 *La Prensa*, "Fridi Marina Sensashonal den Ciegu pa Kolo," July 29, 1978. Mongui Maduro Library archives.
39 El-Tayeb, *European Others*, xlv.

Bibliography

Alexander, Jacqui. "Not just (Any)Body can be a Citizen: The Politics of Law, Sexuality and Postcoloniality in Trinidad and Tobago and the Bahamas." *Feminist Review* 48, (Autumn 1994): 5–23. doi:10.1057/fr.1994.39.

Bonilla, Yarimar. *Non-Sovereign Futures: French Caribbean Politics in the Wake of Disenchantment*. Chicago, IL: Chicago University Press, 2015.

Carpenter, Faedra Chatard. "Addressing 'The Complex'-ities of Skin Color: Intra-Racism and the Plays of Hurston, Kennedy, and Orlandersmith." *Theatre Topics* 19, no. 1 (2009): 15–27. doi:10.1353/tt.0.0048.

Cohen, Cathy. "Punks, Bulldaggers, and Welfare Queens: The Radical Potential of Queer Politics?" *GLQ: A Journal of Gay and Lesbian Studies* 3, no. 4 (1997): 437–465. doi:10.1215/10642684-3-4-437.

Duggan, Lisa. *The Twilight of Equality? Neoliberalism, Cultural Politics, and the Attack on Democracy*. Boston, MA: Beacon Press, 2003.

Echteld, Elisabeth and Ronald Severing. "Over Een Meertalige Bloemlezing Met Gedichten, Liedteksten En Monologen van Fridi Martina (1950–2014)." In *Creative Contradictions: Unsettling Resonances in the Study of the Languages, Literatures and Cultures of the Dutch Caribbean and Beyond*, edited by Nicholas Faraclas et al., 189–198. Curaçao and Puerto Rico: University of Curaçao and Puerto Rico, 2019.

El-Tayeb, Fatima. *European Others: Queering Ethnicity in Postnational Europe*. Minneapolis, MN: University of Minnesota Press, 2011.

Ferguson, Roderick. *Aberrations in Black: Toward a Queer of Color Critique*. Minneapolis, MN: University of Minnesota Press, 2004.

Groenewoud, Margo. "Les Mobiliations Féminines dans les Antilles Néerlandaises (Curaçao et Aruba, 1946–1993)." *Clio* 50 (2019): 63–85. doi:10.4000/clio.17001.

Isenia, Wigbertson Julian. "Looking for Kambrada: Sexuality and Social Anxieties in the Dutch Colonial Archive, 1882–1923." *Tijdschrift voor Genderstudies* 22, no. 2 (2019): 125–143. doi:10.5117/TVGN2019.2.002.ISEN.

Kamugisha, Aaron. "The Coloniality of Citizenship in the Contemporary Anglophone Caribbean." *Race & Class* 49, no. 2 (2007): 20–40. doi:10.1177/0306396807082856.

Lattas, Judy. "Queer Sovereignty: The Gay & Lesbian Kingdom of the Coral Sea Islands." *Cosmopolitan Civil Societies Journal* 1, no. 1 (2009): 128–139. doi:10.5130/ccs.v1i1.883.

Richardson, Dianne. "Rethinking Sexual Citizenship." *Sociology* 51, no. 2 (2017): 208–224. doi:10.1177/0038038515609024.

Roe, Angela. "The Sound of Silence: Ideology of National Identity and Racial Inequality in Contemporary Curaçao." Ph.D. diss., Florida International University, 2016.

Sharpe, Christina. *In the Wake: On Blackness and Being*. Durham, NC: Duke University Press, 2016.

Sheller, Mimi. *Citizenship from Below: Erotic Agency and Caribbean Freedom*. Durham, NC: Duke University Press, 2012.

Spade, Dean. *Normal Life: Administrative Violence, Critical Trans Politics, and the Limits of Law*. Durham, NC: Duke University Press, 2011.

Tinsley, Omise'eke Natasha. *Thiefing Sugar: Eroticism between Women in Caribbean Literature*. Durham, NC: Duke University Press, 2010.

Van Dijs, Mayra. "Fridi Martina: Via Toneel iets Overbrengen in de Maatschappij." *Amigoe*, August 5, (1978). Consulted on Delpher: https://resolver.kb.nl/resolve?urn=ddd:010639365:mpeg21:a0111.

Wekker, Gloria. "Mati-ism and Black Lesbianism: Two Idealtypical Expressions of Female Homosexuality in Black Communities of the Diaspora." *Journal of Homosexuality* 24, no. 3/4 (1993): 145–158. doi:10.1300/J082v24n03_11.

Wekker, Gloria. *The Politics of Passion: Women's Sexual Culture in the Afro-Suriname Diaspora*. New York: Columbia University Press, 2006.

Wekker, Gloria. *White Innocence: Paradoxes of Colonialism and Race*. Durham, NC: Duke University Press, 2016.

25

COLONIALIST INTIMACIES

Loving and leaving on lesbian land

Katherine Schweighofer

It is January of 1978 and a young Puerto Rican woman finds herself and her young child on a women's land in southern California recovering after fleeing an abusive husband: "There are no men and no rules and where we live, in our house in the desert, there is no power. The men and the power and the violence are all outside the gates. We have managed to keep them out of here, so far."[1] She is full of energy imagining the possibilities of this new life. Yet just a few years and multiple women's lands later, it would become clear to her that power and violence were not only outside the gates but, in fact, were part of these radical communities as well. Declaring her intention to pursue her love for another Native-identified woman, she focuses on a strategy for the ensuing power dynamics, "I choose the Indian from now this day forward. I choose the Indian womyn[2] and the indian [sic] way but I must be careful and play the role of womyn who succeeds in the world or they will all turn on me."[3]

Grounded in feminist and queer methodological practices, this project finds a rarely discussed history in the journal accounts of a Native woman named Juana Maria Paz, whose story demands consideration of the complex position of white lesbian women in relation to settler colonialism. How did a movement of predominantly white women invested in resisting patriarchal norms and institutionally enforced gender roles, and even undermining capitalistic systems of production and ownership, engage, resist, and rewrite colonialist legacies? In both politics and in daily practice, evidence of white landers' erasure, manipulation, and assimilation of Native women within the land movement suggests an example of how queer counterculture groups also struggle with a colonialist mindset. My use of "colonialist" to describe these practices emphasizes the ongoing nature of the process of gaining political control over others, rather than focus on the legacy of colonial systems in social organization that is central to Anibal Quijano's "coloniality of power" and other similar concepts.[4] This lesbian land history highlights the operation of settler colonial sexualities, not only on the macro level of culture and nation but on the individual level of interpersonal relationships. In fact, I argue that intimacy is central to the operation of many contemporary forms of colonialist violence and rhetoric.

In this analysis I examine the interpersonal, questioning the politics of intimacy and the dynamics between individuals and small groups. In the histories of lesbian lands, "intimacy" might refer to a range of interactions. Most clearly, women on these lands often found themselves in sexual relationships with one another, whether casually or for extended or committed relationships. Intimacy also accurately describes the non-sexual relationships formed between women living communally on lands. The day-in, day-out interactions meant women knew each other's habits, bodies, needs, quirks, insecurities, fears, and dreams. In living settings where food, personal space, division of labor, and even political positions were frequently negotiated collectively, these women were very intimate with each other's inner thoughts and habits. Lesbian lands were a practical extension of the powerful rallying cry of second-wave feminism, "the personal is political." That catchphrase's emphasis on political meaning is designed to be liberating, helping women bring meaning to the everyday and forge connections across difference. Yet, as examples from the archive suggest, lesbian lands produced situations where the personal became a site of nation-state politics and a place of maintaining settler colonial power.

A land of one's own

The history of lesbian lands has largely been excluded from LGBTQ histories, rural histories, and feminist histories, and as such may not be familiar even to those who lived or have studied counterculture movements of the second half of the twentieth century. This movement saw its heyday between 1970 and 1985, and incorporated lesbian–feminism, identity politics, anti-capitalism, nascent forms of environmentalism, and a back-to-the-land DIY ethos. Though its participants are often misrepresented as separatist, exclusionary, and disconnected, they were in fact frequently engaged in local communities, national mainstream issues, and creating networks of like-minded individuals through publications, workshops, and ideology.[5] Lesbian lands varied in membership, acreage, policies, geographic location, physical layout, and organization. Regardless of these differences, I refer to any individual property that was home to women with a strong commitment to living feminist and radical politics as a lesbian "land."[6] This category therefore stretches from pieces of property owned by one or two women, to sites with a handful of permanent members and hundreds of visitors, to communes where a group of women shared resources and lived collectively. Though there are no hard and fast numbers of lesbian lands, given the parameters described here, there were at least two or three thousand individual lands operational between 1970 and 1985, with likely upwards of 10,000 women living on them in various states of permanence and impermanence. This number is a combination of several pieces of information, including the 90 lands that author Joyce Cheney solicits for her collection *Lesbian Lands,* the lesbian women *not* participating in the music and community scene, and women who embraced feminism without connection to urban lesbian–feminist politics or communities.[7] Using magazine subscription data and reader surveys to ground estimates for the latter two groups, there were certainly 2,000 lands formed between 1970 and 1985, and possibly twice that number.[8] Using "land" and "landers" as shorthand for these communities and their members is intended to underscore the geographical specificity of this movement, emphasizing its rural character and separation from urban communes and other shared living experiences.

Despite their varied external appearances and operating structures, lesbian lands shared important identity and political connections. Women on lesbian lands were redefining their relationships to the earth, agriculture, mass consumption, their bodies, and each other. They often shifted their food production and consumption practices by growing much of their own food using organic and sustainable methods, purchasing only the necessities, and developing informal trade and exchange networks. Bodies were also a site of change: women explored sexual possibility with one another, got in touch with their own physiological systems and physical abilities, and experienced new phenomenological relationships between bodies and spaces through activities as simple as working outside topless. Examining the political implications of their food, housing, consumer, sexual, relationship, bodily, and spiritual activities meant a complete reworking of daily life.

One part of the process of applying "the personal is political" to everyday existence meant engaging with settler ideologies of land ownership. For many landers, escaping the landlord–tenant relationship was an important part of the independence they sought. Yet, as women within patriarchal systems of power, they often struggled to access the resources, information, and even confidence required to purchase property. Those who were able to navigate local bureaucracies and everyday sexism were often motivated to share their knowledge with others.[9] Beyond the practical challenges, many women in the land movement asked important political questions in a decolonialist spirit about ownership, Native removal, and land destruction. The work of Native American writers often served as inspiration for white women exploring different relationships to the earth. Indigenous-authored selections appeared in feminist and land movement magazines, reinforcing an image of Native people as earth-wise and non-Natives as earth-destroyers.[10] This idea became central in how landers envisioned themselves as caretakers of the land. One woman in 1973 wrote,

> In a place where men [… think] they can own land, I must own land too, to prevent their leaving scars on "my" land also, Indians [sic] felt their place and could be trusted to love and nurture the earth that supported them. White men cannot be trusted to nurture anything. And I, a white woman owning land, must use all the power of my possession to dispossess white men's destruction from this piece of land.[11]

Thus white women in the land movement envisioned themselves in a position separate from white men, one in which they might be responsible for protecting land in the (presumed) absence of Native caretakers.[12] The analyses of land ownership, privilege, and destruction by lesbian land members did not address either the histories of white women in early colonial settler systems or how contemporary white women might intentionally or inadvertently re-engage those systems of power. While this position embraced some traditional Native modes of relating to land, it did not incorporate solidarity with First Nation political movements or prompt support for contemporary Indigenous communities. For, like other forms of "playing Indian" or "going Native," these representations of Indigeneity required the absence of Native Americans.[13]

The sexual is political

> As a celibate womyn during most of my time on lesbian land, I had less power in terms of the overall group than womyn whose lovers could always be counted on for support. I believe a political white lover could have provided me with safe passage through situations I found no way out of.[14]

Lesbian land members' inattention to colonialist power dynamics played out vividly in the sexual politics of these communities, most notably in the ways white women engaged with Native-identified women emotionally, politically, and personally on lesbian lands. In his examination of homonationalism and settler colonialism, Scott Morgensen employs "settler sexuality" to denote the forms of white, national heteronormativity that regulate Indigenous sexuality and gender by supplanting them with the sexual modernity of settler subjects.[15] Elsewhere I argue that there are ways in which settler sexuality operates in relationship to

Indigenous individuals and cultures that also regulate Indigenous sexuality and gender by disciplining them via the sexual modernity of homosexual settler subjects, and not through the heteronormative mainstream. Queer cultures also produce systems of sexuality that oppress individuals and control spaces. Within the mostly lesbian context of women's lands, the normative (settler) sexuality demanded women engage sexually with other women. While celibacy was tolerated, women's lands directly or indirectly promoted lesbian relationships, whether monogamous or polyamorous. One woman writing about the sexual practices on a land called Dragon Wimmin Outpost mused, "Why do we say 'women's land' or even 'wimmin's land' when we mean 'lesbian land'? We talk that way to be open-minded and sisterly, I suppose, but if a womoon isn't a lesbian when she comes here, she probably is by the time she leaves. It's one of the Dragon's tricks."[16] Suggesting this "trick" originates in the land and not in the actions of the women involved removes responsibility and in fact naturalizes the lesbian sexuality practiced there. Trick or not, the normative sexuality on land was in fact homosexual, and operated in similarly oppressive ways as Morgensen's settler (hetero)sexuality for non-white and Indigenous landers. This settler homosexuality regulated bodies and desires as a tool for white settler advancement; white women able to wield these advantages had greater say over group political, economic, and relationship decisions, increasing the likelihood they would remain on and benefit from women's lands longer than their Native counterparts.

Juana Maria Paz, whose words open this piece, was a woman of Puerto Rican descent who identified with her Native roots. She initially went to women's land with her infant daughter to escape an abusive heterosexual marriage, but soon found a reborn identity through her experiences on women's land: "it seemed that the new self I had discovered was linked with the land and would leave if I came back [to the outside world]."[17] Part of this newfound self was exploring sexual attraction to women, including a love affair with another Native woman who would haunt her journals for many years. Her journals chronicle her daily life on several different lands across the US, and the turbulence in her love life that accompanied many years living on lesbian land. As fits the time, she did not often spend time parsing the terms of her sexual identity in her writing, nor did she focus on declaring a fixed lesbian or bisexual identity. Instead, Paz writes about "loving women" and ongoing sexual desires for men. Paz is clear about her multiple attractions and describes sexual choices as central to feminist politics: "I want the ability to love men and womyn equally, not label one the enemy and one the answer. Hating and rejecting have not been the answer."[18] This was not an uncommon perspective at this time and is similar to the sexual fluidity practiced by other women on lands.

And yet, despite the frequency of women engaged in sexual exploration after leaving heterosexual lives to live on lands, the sexual openness that appears at first glance characteristic of many land communities was much more complicated. In some cases, sexuality appears to have been used as a tool of political manipulation. As a single, often celibate, bisexual woman of color in communities dominated by white lesbian women, Paz's journals reveal the ongoing operation of settler sexualities in the communities she joined. She ruminates on how a "political white lover" would guarantee safety, revealing how the politics and leadership on lands were frequently interwoven with personal and sexual dynamics. Paz wonders if a white woman lover would have enabled her a smoother path through conflict in her community; a natural ally and protection from potential isolation. She also recalls other times when these power dynamics operated as forms of racialized exoticization and sexualization:

Every once in a while someone would plan an exquisite game of torture called, "Let's flirt with the little Puerto Rican," and then appear shocked when I seemed to expect that something would follow. I was too new and inexperienced to call this what it was, a game and a rip-off, and I was afraid of their labels and their put-downs … so I backed off.[19]

Here, even when Paz participates in the culture of lesbian sexuality in this community, she finds herself rebuffed. Paz appears to have restricted agency in these sexual and political interactions; when she attempts to withdraw from these hurtful intimate interactions, "the same womyn who felt oppressed by my needs followed me to the tipi for visits to continue the energy."[20] While sexual culture was not the same on all women's land communities, Paz's journals include other similar events, indicating she experienced regular sexual policing in many places. Paz is no wallflower, and time and time again speaks her mind, challenges her fellow landers, or finds herself engaged in conflict with another woman. Though her experience is her own, her struggles were echoed by other women of color in the land movement and in feminist organizations more broadly during this time. Lesbian sexual attraction, flirting, and sexual rejection were manipulated as tools for controlling individual women's behavior and establishing power hierarchies in many feminist and radical settings; so much so that even the most vocal of critics might still find herself subsumed by such forces.

The settler *homo*sexuality outlined here operated similarly to settler (hetero)sexuality in its oppression of non-white members using norms drawn from radical, feminist, and counter-culture values. In the case of lesbian lands, these queer norms included non-monogamy and sexual desire for other women. These intimate politics require reading on the level of colonialist violence, and not simply as interpersonal racism, because of the role of land in these women's lives. Land is at the root of these conflicts: the ability to stay, the ways the land would operate, and the identities individual women had embedded in a particular terrain were at the center of nearly every conflict on land. In the formation of the American nation-state, settler colonists used settler sexualities to tighten their hold on colonized territories and ground nascent forms of American identity. Ideologically, settler sexual ideology tied Puritanical heteronormative sexual practice to whiteness, citizenship, and morality, thereby marking a diverse array of Native sex/gender practices (same-sex sexuality, extra marital, non-binary genders) as deviant and dangerous. Practically, this settler sexual ideology meant Native women and third gender people were sexually assaulted and killed, and Native children were systematically removed from their homes and communities in centuries-long campaigns with the ultimate goal of elimination and removal.[21] Thus the enforcement of settler sexualities is interwoven with the land acquisition goals of the settler colonial project.

In the 1970s and 1980s, lesbian landers also used a form of settler sexuality to accomplish their liberatory and identity-based goals. These women sought respite from the continuous policing of gendered behavior, misogynistic violence and harassment, and the general struggle of everyday living in heteropatriarchal culture. Seeking freedom in land, however, led white women in this movement to utilize colonialist power structures—including an ideology of liberation emphasizing land acquisition and access to some financial and legal resources—to achieve their own freedoms, while compromising the access of women of color to the same forms of liberation. The operation of settler sexualities in these spaces was particularly damaging, as women of color and Indigenous women sought land communities specifically as an escape not just from patriarchal abuses but from race-based oppression as well.

Women of color who were tired of struggling against racism and settler sexuality in the predominantly white land movement sometimes sought out one another. Some garnered support from white communities or organizations, and others scraped together their own resources for a down payment or several month's rent. Paz's path included stays on multiple women of color lands; she wrote often of her desire to find a community filled with women of color and other Native women for prospective partners, friends, and allies. In 1978 she was involved in founding a land exclusively for women of color in California named La Luz de la Lucha (The Light of the Struggle). Sadly, La Luz folded 18 months later and Paz had to move on. She tried a land outside Fayetteville, Arkansas, founded when two Native women negotiated with white landers a division of their property to establish a women of color space. Unfortunately, none of these communities proved to be a long-term option for Paz. She describes her hurt and frustration:

> I don't want to put all my eggs in one basket again, don't want to be totally dependent on womyn of colour for all my support. ... Feel some questions from womyn of colour already about why I'm going back into the whyte wommyn's community. The answer is simple—because third world womyn's support is not organized enough to meet all my needs or accept all my energy and I am tired of waiting.[22]

Despite a longing to be in community with other Native women and non-Native women of color, Paz's experience brought her face to face with the realities confronted by nearly all lands—not enough money and too much disagreement almost always led to difficulties sustaining land communities. Here, her comments also suggest the racial politics of her choices among the women of color and the difficulty she faced moving between these different land communities. Sadly, one of the results of this ongoing personal struggle against intimate forms of settler sexuality and racialized violence was the toll it took on a passionate and fierce woman. "I feel destroyed by the lesbian of colour struggle and I need some time off," she wrote.[23] A few months later, Paz appears to have given up on her women's land dreams:

> The womyn's community. Womyn of colour land. A lesbian nation. They won. I can't take it any more [sic]. All my freedoms have to be personal. There is no group that can help me, save me, make my life real.[24]

On these lesbian lands, white, partnered homonormativities regulated Indigenous sexuality by establishing social and political structures in which non-settler sexualities had real consequences in daily life. Life on lesbian lands was always precarious: financially, women struggled to make rent or mortgage payments on little or no income, and, logistically, they faced challenges ranging from building structures for shelter to growing food to sharing resources. These pressures meant that when interpersonal inequities were added, women on the short end would very quickly find their residency on land untenable. Intimacy, the "personal" in the euphemistic feminist phrase "the personal is political," became the very tool with which individual women were discouraged from benefiting from the land movement.

Conclusions: moving on?

The lesbian land movement attempted to turn myriad and complex political beliefs into everyday reality. Upending patriarchal values and messages demanded examining everything, from power tools and beer to food stamps and sexual practices. Despite consideration of the colonialist implications of land ownership, the discourse within the land movement about land ownership set white women apart from legacies of colonialism and did not consider the possibility of these women perpetuating a colonialist mindset. White landers' interest in and embrace of Native writing that propagated traditional Native perspectives on caring for the earth produced a complicated set of images and stereotypes that left Native-identified women like Paz in a bind. Sometimes Native women were able to use these representations to their benefit. "Dressing in feathers" refers to instances where Indigenous people strategically perform a white settler representation of Indianness, according to Native Studies scholar S. Elizabeth Bird.[25] This strategic embracing of "The Indian" was part of how the Native women on a land in Arkansas successfully convinced their community members they needed a portion of land for just women of color. The founders of Arco Iris pointed to dream visions of Native "warriors on the cliffs" overlooking the land beckoning to them, messages from a spirit guide, and the influence of the Great Spirit as support for their case. Yet even these strategic uses of Indianness recall settler conflict; one of the women explained the difference between her and the white owner they negotiated with via the meaning of land, "To her, her heritage had taught her that land was money. To me, land is our survival, and our future."[26] At other times the political power of Native messages and ideas seemed only to hold up in the absence of Native women, as evident in instances when Paz felt she was explicitly excluded from having a voice in the politics of her community.

Landers policed many modes of sexual engagement, and, while these homonormative forces were not solely applied to Native and non-Native women of color, they stemmed from a white, middle-class normative coupling structure and were woven into power and decision making within these groups. The intimacy between landers combined with the settler ideology behind the meaning of land produced conflict that disenfranchised Native women. White lesbian landers simultaneously integrated Indigenous ideas on land, sexuality, and spirituality into their politics while also occluding Native-identified women from full participation in the versions of sexual modernity they were creating. Doing so relied upon settler ideologies to structure dynamics of sexuality and power, and upon intimacy as the vehicle for enacting this power. Whether masked as "the Dragon's tricks" or as white women's attempts to remedy white male settler destruction of land, uncovering the politics of intimacy reveals colonialism's ability to invade even the most personal of feminist spaces.

Notes

1 Juana Maria Gonzalez/Third World Women's Earth Collective, "La Luz de la Lucha," January 1978.
2 Writers in the land movement were invested in linguistic resistance and so used alternative spellings of "women" and "woman" that remove men/man. Spellings include "womyn," "wimmin," and "wommin" and even "womoon" or "wombyn" to suggest connections to nature. This paper uses the standard spelling but does not correct or indicate error for sources using spelling alternatives as a way of legitimizing those choices.
3 Juana Maria Paz, "One Mad Dreamer, 10/1/80–5/13/81," Dec 2, 1980.
4 Quijano, "Coloniality of Power." The work of María Lugones on the gender dynamics of coloniality also was an influence. See "Heterosexualism and the Colonial/Modern Gender System."
5 See my work in "Legacies of Lesbian Land."
6 Shewolf, a lesbian feminist who has compiled and updated a "Directory of Wimmin's Lands" regularly since 1990, defines her parameters for inclusion as "Places where some lesbians and other wimmin have escaped the patriarchy, to some degree, and created settlements of feminist and/or lesbian-friendly communities living in harmony with Mother Earth." Shewolf, *Shewolf's Directory of Wimmin's Land and Lesbian Communities*, 1.
7 Cheney, *Lesbian Land*.

8 *Country Women* publication data, including a peak circulation of 11,000 with over a third of those subscribers with lesbian or bisexual identities, is central to this number. See "Country Women is All of Us," *Country Women* 19, March 1976, 64.

9 For example, see Sherry Thomas's article, "Would You Like to Buy Rhode Island?" *Country Women* 7, June 1973, 4.

10 In particular, rural-living focused magazines like *Country Women* and *Maize* included this kind of material. For example, the back cover of *Country Women* #7 published in June 1973 declared, "The Indians [sic] never hurt anything, but the white people destroy all."

11 Thomas, "Would You Like to Buy Rhode Island?" 4.

12 See Schweighofer, "A Land of One's Own."

13 I use "going native" to refer to Huhndorf's *Going Native*. "Playing Indian" references Deloria's *Playing Indian*. Rayna Green's analysis also contributed to these ideas, see "The Tribe Called Wannabee."

14 Paz, "La Luz de la Lucha," 73.

15 Morgensen, "Settler Homonationalism," 106.

16 Teena Delphina Brown, "DW Outpost," 49.

17 Paz, "La Luz de la Lucha journal," n.d., approximately February 1, 1980.

18 Paz, "La Luz de la Lucha journal," December 28, 1980.

19 Paz, "La Luz de la Lucha," 68.

20 Ibid.

21 For a historical overview, see Smith's "Sexual Violence as Tool of Genocide." Her essay "Native American Feminism, Sovereignty, and Social Change" elucidates the ongoing operation of this settler ideology.

22 Juana Maria Paz, "Journal: Winter 1979–1980," March 1980.

23 Paz, "Journal: Winter 1979–1980," April 9, 1980.

24 Juana Maria Paz, "One Mad Dreamer, 10/1/80–5/13/81," November 10, 1980.

25 Bird, *Dressing in Feathers*.

26 Maria, "Arco Iris," 36.

Bibliography

Bird, S. Elizabeth. *Dressing in Feathers: The Construction of the Indian in American Popular Culture*. Boulder, CO: Westview Press, 1996.

Carrithers, Susie. "None of the above ranch." *Country Women* 7 (June 1973), 14–15.

Cohn, Fern. "Finding our place." *Country Women* 7 (June 1973), 17.

Deevy, Sue, Kaufer, Nelly, Wagner, Dian, Newhouse, Carol, Miracle, Billie. *Country Lesbians: The Story of the WomanShare Collective*. Grants Pass, OR: WomanShare Books, 1976.

Deloria, Philip. *Playing Indian*. New Haven, CT: Yale University Press, 1998.

Driskill, Qwo-Li, Chris Finley, Brian Gilley and Scott Morgensen, eds. *Queer Indigenous Studies: Critical Interventions in Theory, Politics, and Literature*. Tucson, TX: University of Arizona Press, 2011.

Goodyear, Carmen. "No trespassing." *Country Women* 7 (June 1973), 25.

Green, Rayna. "The Tribe Called Wannabee: Playing Indian in American and Europe." *Folklore* 99, no. 1 (1988): 30–55. doi:10.1080/0015587X.1988.9716423.

Huhndorf, Shari. *Going Native: Indians in American Cultural Imagination*. Ithaca, NY: Cornell University Press, 2001.

Justice, Daniel Heath (Cherokee Nation), Mark Rifkin and Bethany Schneider. "Introduction." *GLQ: A Journal of Lesbian and Gay Studies* 16, no. 1/2 (2010): 5–39. doi:10.1215/10642684-2009-011.

Lugones, María. "Heterosexualism and the Colonial/Modern Gender System." *Hypatia* 22, no. 1 (Winter 2007): 186–209. doi:10.1111/j.1527-2001.2007.tb01156.x.

Meyer, Carter Jones and Diana Royer, eds. *Selling the Indian: Commercializing and Appropriating American Indian Cultures*. Tucson, TX: University of Arizona Press, 2001.

Morgensen, Scott. "Settler Homonationalism." *GLQ: A Journal of Lesbian and Gay Studies* 16, no. 1/2 (2010): 105–131. doi:10.1215/10642684-2009-015.

Mujeres de Arco Iris. "Arco Iris." In *Lesbian Land*, edited by Joyce Cheney, 30–40. Minneapolis, MN: Word Weavers, 1985.

Mujeres de Arco Iris. "La Luz de la Lucha – Where do dreams go when they die?" In *Lesbian Land*, edited by Joyce Cheney, 66–75. Minneapolis, MN: Word Weavers, 1985.

Quijano, Anibal. "Coloniality of Power, Eurocentrism, and Latin America." *Nepantla: Views from the South* 1, no. 3 (2000): 533–580. doi:10.1177/0268580900015002005.

Schweighofer, Katherine. "Legacies of Lesbian Land: Rural Feminist Spaces and the Politics of Identity and Community." Ph.D. diss., Indiana University, 2015.

Schweighofer, Katherine. "A Land of One's Own: Whiteness and Indigeneity on Lesbian Land." *Settler Colonial Studies* 8, no. 4 (2018): 489–506. doi:10.1080/2201473X.2017.1365410.

Shewolf. *Shewolf's Directory of Wimmin's Land and Lesbian Communities 2013–2016*, 6th edition. Melrose, FL: Target Blue Enterprises, 2013.

Smith, Andrea. "Sexual Violence as Tool of Genocide." In *The Feminist Philosophy Reader*, edited by Alison Bailey and Chris Cuomo, 421–438. Boston, MA: McGraw-Hill, 2008.

Smith, Andrea. "Native American Feminism, Sovereignty, and Social Change." In *Feminist Theory Reader: Local and Global Perspectives*, edited by Carole McCann and Seung-kyung Kim, 3rd edition, 321–331. New York: Routledge, 2013.

Stoler, Ann L. "Making Empire Respectable: The Politics of Race and Sexual Morality in 20th-Century Colonial Cultures." *American Ethnologist* 16, no. 4 (1989): 634–660. doi:10.1525/ae.1989.16.4.02a00030.

Thomas, Sherry. "Would you like to buy Rhode Island?" *Country Women* 7 (June 1973), 4–5.

Warrior, Robert. *Tribal Secrets: Recovering American Indian Intellectual Traditions*. Minneapolis, MN: University of Minnesota Press, 1994.

PART V

Pleasure and violence

26

A SPANISH NOTARY IN A NAHUA TOWN IN POST-CONTACT MEXICO

A case of sexual and cultural liminality

Martin Nesvig

In the 1570s, in Tuxpan (in the current state of Jalisco, Mexico) in the farthest western reaches of New Spain, a peninsular Spanish man had, by all appearances, not only married a Nahua woman but had fully integrated himself into the ritual, cultural, and religious life of the indigenous pueblos of the region. Details of the man's biography are scattered throughout Colima's municipal and state archives and in one medium-length case file, housed in Mexico's national archive in its Inquisition section. The Inquisition case was the result of an investigation by the diocesan court into accusations that he had engaged in idolatry and pagan rites, worshipping the Mexica deity Xolotl. He had also slept with many indigenous women, including one who would become his wife. The case file consists of 25 sworn testimonies, a legal commission to the judge in the case, an arrest warrant, and an inventory of confiscated property. The file has remained, presumably, in the Inquisition archive since that time, yet no trial is extant. We cannot know the legal fate of the man, but we learn a great deal about the town's culture, its persistent pre-Hispanic cosmology and ritual practice, and the sexual and amorous lives of women and the Spanish man.

Using the Tuxpan Investigation[1] as its point of focus, this essay examines the boundaries of desire, consent, colonial rule, and inter-ethnic relationship. The setting is sixteenth-century Mexico, under formal Spanish rule. Most rural areas of New Spain remained largely indigenous in culture, language, and custom. In this nascent phase of colonization and at the margins of colonial rule, the Tuxpan Investigation brings to mind some central questions. What kind of (sexual) relationship did the notary have with his (many) indigenous mistresses? How can we take seriously inequities in power while also considering space for women's agency and motivations to enter such relationships? What was the man's relationship with his Nahua wife? We know that he formed a lasting marriage with her. What can we know about these marriages between Spanish men and indigenous women? Were all these relationships coercive, or how might we conceive of "consent" before this notion enjoyed popular currency? What do we make of acculturation of the Spanish man to indigenous custom? This essay explores these questions through a case study which reflects fluid indigenous–Spanish cultural and sexual dynamics.

While the idea of and word for a mestizo—someone of mixed indigenous and Spanish ancestry—was just forming in the sixteenth century, there were a good deal of sexual or marital relationships between Spanish men and indigenous women.[2] This essay does not discuss or analyze the later colonial period (seventeenth and eighteenth centuries), when widespread ethnic mixing and intermarriage were thorough and regular in Latin America.[3] Rather, this essay probes the boundaries of frontier marriages in which one person lived in *nepantla* (a Nahuatl word and concept for living in between cultures, lands, territories; for example, Spanish men in indigenous cultural worlds in rural areas) and how we might think about that dynamic.[4] The idea of liminality is also helpful; while Victor Turner originally conceived of liminality as an in-between life stage often surrounding rites of passage, it applies to cultural states of being in between.[5] Spanish colonial rule was initially limited in its reach over rural indigenous towns, concentrated as it was primarily in Mexico City, with its representatives in provincial cities. Encomenderos and indigenous elites (*pipiltin; caciques, gobernadores, principales*) were much more likely to exercise quotidian power over indigenous commoner (*macehual*) communities than royal or ecclesiastical agents in the sixteenth century, especially in rural areas. This was precisely the dynamic where the Tuxpan Investigation took place.

It is no secret that, from the earliest phases of Spanish presence in the Americas, Spanish men engaged in a wide range of sexual, amorous, and marital practices with indigenous women. These ran the spectrum from outright rape to arranged political marriages between conquistadors and *pipiltin* women. There are high-profile cases of the latter category, such as that between Moctezuma's daughter *doña* Isabel Tecuichpotzin and Alonso de Grado, but we know relatively little about middling Spanish men who married or cohabitated with indigenous women, primarily commoners (plural, *macehualtin*).[6] Men who migrated to the Americas from the Iberian peninsula outnumbered women on a massive scale in the sixteenth century. Indeed, from 1493 to 1540, women represented less than 10 per cent of all Europeans in the Americas. By the 1570s there were more European women migrants, but they still only accounted for a third of European immigrants.[7] The Black Legend propagates a ghoulish assumption that Spanish men would rape indigenous women—and, indeed, contemporaneous evidence shows that it did occur. But in rural areas, where indigenous customs and leaders prevailed, is it possible that indigenous women entered willfully into relationships with Spanish men? The question of consent is complicated, given the uneven power structures of colonial society. Nevertheless, close reading of microhistorical case studies can tell us a good deal about a specific community's value systems at a time when "consent" and "coercion" were not necessarily conceived as the binary terms under which one engaged in sexual acts or relationships.

Though facts are scattered, we know there was a wide range of relationships between Spanish men and indigenous women in the sixteenth century.[8] Such relationships were fraught, complex, and often defy accepted truisms about machismo and, the other side of its conceptual coin, female meekness and lack of autonomy.[9] Even studies of one of colonial Latin America's most famed female figures, Malintzin—Spanish conquistador Hernan Cortés's translator and later mother to his son, Martín—reflect that Malintzin was coerced into a union with Cortés but that she also used her intellect and linguistic aptitude to navigate a man's political world.[10] Critical scholars now accept that women were subject to very real forms of surveillance, control, and violence but that they were not passive victims in this "man's world." They were conscious and smart actors who operated within the anthropological rules of the world which regulated them.[11] Beneath the more obvious stories of conquest, women acted to carve out little spaces of comfort, engaged in businesses, or seemed unconcerned about the acknowledgment of casual sex.

Social standing and class powerfully inflected relationships between Spanish men and indigenous women. On the one hand, there were notable marriages between conquistador men and *pipiltin*-princess women. Spanish conquistadors hoped to become attached to the indigenous woman's land claims and hold rights to land and vassalage through *encomiendas* (labor drafts).[12] On the other hand, marriages and unions between non-elite indigenous women and non-conquistador and unlanded Spanish men are not well known or studied. Pedro Carrasco argues that Spanish men who adopted indigenous customs were viewed poorly.[13] Moreover, non-conquistador Spanish men who married indigenous women tended to marry *macehual* women in cities, but both *macehual* and *pipiltin* women in rural areas.

Lacking extensive demographic data, we can look to case studies, microcosms, possibly, of life in New Spain which reflect the dynamic of inter-ethnic unions. The Tuxpan Investigation offers a brief vista onto the inter-ethnic world of post-contact Mexico and details part of the life of an unlanded Spanish man and a Nahua woman who may or may not have been *pipiltin*. As with the Tuxpan Investigation, inquisitional and ecclesiastical court prosecutions into charges such as heresy, bigamy, or secret Judaizing frequently included other details about the lives of those who testified and the accused. Often richer in quotidian details are the ordinary denunciations, confessions, and depositions created in the local context, whether rural or small-town, when people were accused of sorcery or witchcraft. The Tuxpan Investigation, for example, tells us that the ceremonies were called *mitotes*, a Nahuatl word for ritual dance, and *areitos*, a Taino word for ritual festival/dance. How a Taino loanword made its way into a rural community much closer to the Pacific than the Caribbean is a mystery. But the point is that we can glean valuable cultural evidence—in this case, linguistic fluidity in a monolingual Nahuatl-speaking town—from these kinds of sources. These testimonies reveal the mentalities, or cultural assumptions, of the people who testified.

A Spanish notary and a Nahua local

The Tuxpan Investigation concerned a Spanish man, presumably from Seville. Related sources tell us that he had married a Nahua woman later in life who was from the area of Tuxpan-Zapotlan of southern Jalisco.[14] The man, Francisco López de Avecilla, was a notary—a position of some modest influence—in the provincial city of Colima possibly as early as 1560. While he had been married to a Spanish woman who lived in Mexico City, he apparently bedded dozens of indigenous women (some teenagers) in Tuxpan over the years. He later married one of these girls, Magdalena de los Reyes, and lived with her for some time through the 1580s. It is unclear if she appears specifically as a witness in the primary investigation, as the Nahua witnesses are not identified by surname. We know almost nothing about de los Reyes except that she was indigenous and presumably Nahua.[15] Witnesses identify one of López de Avecilla's most long-standing lovers as Magdalena, a daughter of a principal, though we cannot know if this is Magdalena de los Reyes.

The Tuxpan Investigation was not concerned with sex per se. Rather, the court heard rumors that López de Avecilla was a central promoter of a regional worship of Xolotl, the Mexica trickster deity. Accordingly, the principal reason the ecclesiastical court investigated López de Avecilla was that he had become an idolater and promoter of pre-contact religion. The diocesan and inquisitional courts were not generally interested in sex unless there was a case of bigamy. Inquisitors viewed polytheism or sorcery, especially if committed by a Spaniard, as much more serious than sexual peccadillos. But because the notary was also a potential bigamist there was added interest in the case, despite the distance from the capital of the polity in Pátzcuaro, a journey of about a week by horseback and more if by burro or foot.

Additionally, there were reports that López de Avecilla had claimed he possessed a papal bull that exempted him from the standard ban on adultery. The ecclesiastical investigation was not interested especially in the sex itself but was very concerned about the counterfeiting or fraudulent claims about papal bulls. That he used those bulls to procure sex only aggravated the offense. While the investigation began as a doctrinal one, it revealed incidentally a great deal about his sex life. The reason may be that the women found his sexual behavior to be something the authorities should know about, whereas they showed little interest in his religious deviations.

Francisco López de Avecilla was the kind of middling Spanish immigrant from Seville who sought a better life—perhaps even while fleeing the law—in the Americas. We do not know when he came to Mexico. He was variously the notary public of the villa and notary of the *alcalde* (mayor) of Colima from as early as 1566 until 1593.[16] He had no university degree, though he was obviously literate and trained as a notary. While his background in the 1550s and 1560s is uncertain, we know that in 1573 the diocese of Michoacán, which had jurisdiction over Colima and Tuxpan, investigated López de Avecilla for a series of offenses.

The main charges were the following: incest (for having engaged sexually with various pairs of sisters and for claiming that he had a papal bull which exempted him from ecclesiastical prohibitions on incest) and idolatry (for engaging in the worship of and leading a cult dedicated to the deity Xolotl). Ecclesiastical law defined incest broadly and one individual man having sex with two sisters was legally a form of incest. That we learn so much about his sexual behavior is incidental from a legal perspective. Again, while the church court viewed his religious behavior as graver than any sexual behavior, the indigenous women who testified clearly viewed his sexual behavior as fair game in the context of a formal deposition.

The diversity of the witnesses reflects the predominantly indigenous ethnicity of the town, which had a smattering of Spanish officials and residents.[17] Of the 25 witnesses, at least 17 were indigenous, monolingual Nahuatl speakers. Four Spanish men were summoned to testify, though as a town the population was probably more than 90 per cent Nahua. There were five witnesses whose ethnicity is unclear but may have included mestizos and mulattoes. Among the indigenous witnesses were five *principales*, one of whom, Don Juan de Guzmán, was the Spanish *alcalde*'s notary. He too lived in *nepantla*, acting for the non-Nahuatl-speaking magistrate as his conduit to the indigenous community over which he presided as representative of royal justice. Yet Don Juan did not speak or understand Spanish well enough to testify in that language and gave his deposition via *nahuatlato*, or interpreter.

The ecclesiastical court named two *nahuatlatos* for the case. Both were citizens of Tuxpan and both European, ethnically, but bilingual Spanish–Nahuatl speakers. One, Juan Marín Aragoces, was generically Spanish, possibly part Croatian. The second, Juan Gallegos, was a criollo born in Mexico City. Both presumably came to their command of Nahuatl through immersion in everyday life and also possibly from their wet-nurses or housekeepers. The other indigenous and Spanish witnesses appear to be monolingual, which means that bilingualism in the town probably acted as an entrée to the other ethnic world—Nahua or Spanish. Such bilingualism brought cultural prestige and thus possible economic benefits as well as risks; interpreters were often distrusted by both cultures as they knew too much about each and were viewed with suspicion for their privileged level of cultural information.

The range of witnesses told the same basic story. The pattern suggests a high level of general knowledge about López de Avecilla and his ceremonial and sexual eccentricities. Testimonies varied little in their portraits of his behavior, only in degree of moral commentary. Most agreed that the notary was a notorious lecher, womanizer, and possible rapist. He was married to a Spanish woman, Isabel de Vargas, who lived in Mexico City but, for all purposes, he lived as if he were unmarried. One witness, Gallegos, the criollo interpreter, accused López de Avecilla of having poisoned his Spanish wife in an attempted murder, though she survived—but for how long we do not know. Most agreed that he had had sex with far too many indigenous girls and women. But these affairs were enumerated somewhat prosaically. The accusations of affairs were a by-product of an ecclesiastical investigation into doctrinal errors and for idolatry. Such accusations functioned as an airing of grievances against the Spanish notary. But it is also clear from witness testimony that López de Avecilla had formed some kind of mutual bond with some of the witnesses, as well as with several *pipiltin* who did not testify.

The language used by the women witnesses, as well as the way the Spanish notary who rendered it, is notable. The main thing that female witnesses said about López de Avecilla was that he was well known to have been "hooked up with," living with, or partnered with several different women. The word the Spanish notary chose for this was *amancebado/ amancebamiento*, which was common also in the Spanish men's testimonies. The word refers to a state or a couple that has some kind of bond beyond sex and usually refers to people who live together. It also specifically refers to people not married to each other. In some statements, witnesses—both indigenous and Spanish, male and female—say this was evidence that López de Avecilla was a bad Christian. Others say nothing. Typical of the matter-of-fact tone was the testimony of María de Castilla, a Nahua girl whom the notary described as being "about 15 years old." She plainly stated that she had been hooked up with López de Avecilla for about a year but that she had left him. She expressed no opinion of López de Avecilla. She said that after she left him it was well known that he had slept with a Magdalena, a daughter of the indio principal of Tuxpan, as well as with her sister, Catalina. María de Castilla added in her testimony that her sister-in-law had asked her: "Well, aren't you ashamed that you slept with Francisco López?" to which she responded, "It has been a long time since I slept with him."[18] The notary's choice for the verb for the sexual act was *echarse*: to lie down with, sleep with, have sex with while lying down. It may strain our twenty-first century values, but she seemed to view her sexual relationship with López de Avecilla at age 14 as normative, adding an intriguing detail: she claimed López de Avecilla had raped a girl but she did not say who, nor did she claim that he had raped her.

Other witnesses described sexual as well as quasi-marital engagements. For example, it appears that he had indeed slept with a pair of sisters and a pair of cousins, one of whom may have been Magdalena de los Reyes. Her cousin, María Magdalena, testified that it was well known that she slept with him (*se ha echado*) but added that it was also well known that he provided for her as if she were his wife. Others made similar remarks. María Sánchez claimed that López de Avecilla had administered a type of herbal abortifacient to Magdalena, his quasi-wife. María Magdalena repeated the claim. The word was *pahtli* (various spellings exist in the case file), a Nahuatl word for remedy, potion, or drug. The notary or the interpreter did not translate this word. Here we see further the extent to which this world, while monolingually Nahuatl, had a high degree of linguistic variety, with loanwords from Nahuatl and Taino in the Spanish transcription—this a document intended for an exclusively Hispanolexic juridical audience.

The Tuxpan Investigation elucidates several points about colonial relationships. First, it is clear that López de Avecilla was fluent in Nahuatl and well integrated in the community. The witnesses who remarked on his whereabouts all said that the notary lived full-time in Tuxpan, even though he was a notary in Colima, a horse trip of two or three days away. While his profession as notary was a good civil-servant job, he was far from wealthy. He augmented this salary by buying and selling dry goods—chiles, cotton, dried fish and meat, cactus prickly pears, and such. The notary could not have been so thoroughly integrated into this society without a good command of Nahuatl language, which is the only language people in the town spoke.[19] That he was able to communicate so well even though he had not studied Nahuatl in a school or monastery also indicates that he learned by immersion and that this immersion had taken place over several years.

Second, witnesses all agreed that he was sexually promiscuous. Witnesses described a womanizer who had bedded as many as 40 individual Nahua girls and women, but they recounted this sexual history in language that varied from plain and pragmatic to intense moral indignation. A number of these statements were offered not by women but by men, including the Nahua principal, Don Juan de Guzmán. He may have exaggerated the numbers, possibly for political effect. And Don Juan's denunciations of López de Avecilla's sexual relationships may have been motivated by political distrust or rivalry. It is telling that, among the witnesses, the *pipiltin* men showed the greatest level of outrage. The *pipiltin* men tended to describe López de Avecilla in morally disapproving terms ("he was a bad Christian" was a common refrain). The *macehual* women, meanwhile, described their own or others' sexual affairs with the notary in practical terms. We do not have any women *pipiltin* witnesses in the case, so we lack their perspective.

Third, the several indigenous female witnesses who testified described unions both consensual and others forced on some level. For example, 20-year-old Nahua Luisa Caravajal admitted to having sex (twice) with López de Avecilla and attached no further significance to the acts. The 40-year-old Nahua woman Madalena López, the servant of the *alcalde*, disapproved of López de Avecilla, whom, given his many lovers, she considered a bad Christian. She considered these relationships consensual but immoral. Women like María de Castilla, María Magdalena, and María Sánchez expressed little outrage, but, rather, mild distaste. In some cases the young women defended him, noting that he provided for them economically. That same arrangement roused the moral ire of the *pipiltin* men. In some ways the sexual world was a kind of marketplace of status and socioeconomic power.

The women, all of them Nahua, offered little moral scorn for López de Avecilla. Telling, however, are the testimonies of the indigenous *pipiltin* men. Their complaint was that López de Avecilla plied these women with gifts, food, and coconut wine as a method of seduction. This type of testimony is the same as that provided by at least three young women: that López de Avecilla compensated them for their sexual favors with gifts and economic support. The women who related this form of exchange offered no moral observations about it. But the *pipiltin* men tried to leverage this general charge against López de Avecilla—one of lechery—into a broader charge against him as a bad Christian, defending themselves as fully Catholic. They do not state their motives but they may have viewed López de Avecilla as an economic or political rival in addition to being a sexual competitor. Theirs may have been a political strategy to drive López de Avecilla out of town. It did not appear to have worked, as he continued to spend time in Tuxpan after the investigation.

The charge that López de Avecilla was a ringleader of a Mesoamerican religious ritual reveals his deep cultural involvement with the pueblos of Tuxpan, Zapotlan, and Tamazula. Several *principales* and López de Avecilla led a local cult to the deity Xolotl, a trickster deity associated with Venus, the evening star, who was the twin of Quetzalcoatl. Xolotl was also viewed as a sort of monstrosity, sometimes depicted with canine features. Why the peoples of this area venerated Xolotl remains a mystery. Yet it was clear that the *indios principales* and López de Avecilla held positions of leadership in this underground religious group. They celebrated the deity with parties that resembled semi-sexual orgies, with ritualized alcohol consumption. Many witnesses claimed that López de Avecilla and one of the *indios principales* hosted the parties. Among the most fascinating details is that this group constructed statuettes, called *tzoalli*, of Xolotl, made with amaranth, which they ritually consumed. There were many false rumors among Spanish clergy that they used blood of human sacrifice victims. Rather, honey was likely used as a binding agent. The Mexica of central Mexico engaged in similar activities, though their statuettes were replicas of the war god Huitzilopochtli.[20] Again, we see Nahuatl loanword concepts entering the Spanish transcript, underscoring the linguistic–cultural fluidity of the region.

López de Avecilla was one of the principal leaders of the Xolotl cult and he was the one to go out into the countryside to collect amaranth. Not a single witness disputes this and all agreed that he was instrumental in reviving the ancient cult. This second point seems contrived as a way for the indigenous elites to ingratiate themselves with the diocesan inspector by claiming that they had, in fact, become devout Catholics. Regardless of whether their claims were honest or not, it is not possible that a Spanish man could simply stumble upon a carefully planned and recurrent religious event. Indeed, the opposite appears to be the case. López de Avecilla had spent years living in and around Tuxpan and had become a trusted cultural intermediary, an outsider who had become an insider. The *pipiltin* who were implicated in the inquiry by their participation in the Xolotl festivals did not testify in the Tuxpan Investigation. For all we know, they might have provided a more positive evaluation of López de Avecilla. That he remained, as far as we know, married to his second (Nahua) wife, Magdalena, offers further evidence that he was acculturated to an extent to the region. Two witnesses said that Magdalena was the daughter of a principal.

López de Avecilla was living in *nepantla* but had also in effect become a *compadre* (godfather) of some of the *pipiltin* families, making him a de facto member of the town's *pipiltin* class. If Pedro Carrasco is correct, he would have suffered distrust from his Spanish colleagues and friends, and contempt for having taken on the cultural ways of the Nahuas of western Mexico. He was even eventually formally married to his Nahua lover, de los Reyes. She, in turn, operated an illegal liquor store or bar from their house. It is not clear what exactly she sold in the locale.[21] It may have been the popular coconut liquor of the region or pulque, a fermented drink made from the milky liquid of the agave cactus.[22] Many witness in the Tuxpan Investigation claimed that the Xolotl orgies were rife with alcohol consumption, of *vino de la tierra*, probably pulque in this case since coconut liquor was not yet widespread in 1573.

López de Avecilla was deeply enmeshed in the cultural world of Tuxpan, populated almost exclusively by indigenous peoples. Encomenderos and magistrates were more easily empowered to abuse indigenous women sexually than were lower-status Spanish men. The women in those cases could appeal to royal justice, but it was difficult to exact guilty verdicts against such powerful men who could in many cases ignore the law. López de Avecilla was not as powerful. Though he wielded some influence as notary of Colima, in Tuxpan his status depended on his ability to ingratiate himself with the local custom and with the *pipiltin*. Witnesses felt free to air their grievances against what they largely perceived to be slightly scandalous behavior. But if he had been a serial rapist or consistent sexual predator, the local indigenous men and women probably would have expelled him. They had legal means to incriminate him but there are no criminal complaints against him from people in Tuxpan. There are, however, hints in the 1573 depositions that at least one of the *principales* asked the diocesan inspector to have him expelled from the town as a threat to good order. However, because he continued to be connected to Tuxpan for many years to come, it appears he had more supporters than enemies among the *pipiltin*.

I have used this opportunity to pose some questions about the history of intimacies that are difficult to excavate. My goal was not to cast moral judgment on the case but to highlight the ways witnesses framed López de Avecilla's behavior in ambiguous terms. While it is difficult to know whether these relationships were steadfastly amorous or perhaps hierarchical, they nevertheless appear distinct from the countless examples of outright sexual violence toward women during the contact period. Malintzin, for example, had simply no choice when she was given away to Cortés as war spoils, as if she were a set of dishes or an old table. Through her intellectual–linguistic brilliance and political cunning she managed to survive and even accumulate an *encomienda*. But unlike Cortés, López de Avecilla was a low to middling socioeconomic sort; as court records show, town residents—especially men—could and did criticize López de Avecilla without risk to their own status, prestige, or wellbeing. He was not a man who commanded great power or means; he could offer some modest stability but hardly wealth to a potential indigenous bride. There would have been plenty of indigenous suitors for Magdalena de los Reyes, if she were indeed the daughter of a principal, yet she chose to remain married to a middling Spaniard who died in poverty and brought her no great prestige in the Spanish world.

The Tuxpan Investigation offers perplexing portraits. The main charge against López de Avecilla, idolatry, was quite serious, but we have no record of the investigation ever advancing to trial or sentence. He was arrested at the end of the investigation, in the Pátzcuaro in November 1573, and then released to house arrest after his property was embargoed. No trial is extant. He continued to work as the notary of Colima uninterrupted from 1575 until 1593 and died around 1598.[23] The result of the Tuxpan Investigation is that we know more about the peccadillos of people in Tuxpan. It shows that Nahua women openly discussed non-monogamous forms of relationship and sex; that men and women willingly entered into non-monogamous relationships, a practice which missionaries continued to try to suppress five decades after putative Christianization. In the *nepantla* world, in between, which eventually just became Mexico in general, bilingual and bicultural peoples flitted in and out. The indigenous women who stayed in the world of their Nahua domus viewed Nahuatlized Spaniards with a measure of skepticism mixed with practicality.

Notes

1 For our purposes here I identify the collective contents of the forty-folio file as the Tuxpan Investigation. The investigation is found in Archivo General de la Nación, México (AGN), Inquisición (Inq.), volume (vol.) 116, expediente (exp.) 2.

2 Masters, "A Thousand Invisible Architects."

3 For some excellent recent treatments of the phenomenon and of the development of the "sistema de castas," see Schwaller, *Géneros de Gente* and Vinson III, *Before Mestizaje*.

4 For an excellent discussion of cultural intermediaries in the colonial period, see Yannakakis, *The Art of Being In-Between*.

5 Turner, "Betwixt and Between."

6 See Chipman, *Moctezuma's Children*.

7 Boyd-Bowman, *Patterns of Spanish Emigration*.

8 Ibid.; Socolow, *The Women of Colonial Latin America*, 39.

9 For representative works, see Lavrin, ed., *Sexuality and Marriage*; Johnson and Lipsett-Rivera, eds., *The Faces of Honor*; Calvo, "Concubinato y mestizaje en el medio urbano"; Gonzalbo Aizpuru, *Educación, familia y vida cotidiana*; Gonzalbo Aizpuru, "La familia novohispana"; Muriel, *Los recogimientos de mujeres*.

10 Townsend, *Malintzin's Choices*.

11 For this argument, see especially Sousa, *The Woman Who Turned into a Jaguar*; Germeten, *Profit and Passion*; Germeten, *Violent Delights, Violent Ends*.

12 Himmerich y Valencia, *The Encomenderos of New Spain*; Townsend, *Malintzin's Choices*.

13 Carrasco, "Indian-Spanish Marriages"; Carrasco, "Matrimonios hispano-indios."

14 Archivo Histórico del Municipio de Colima (AHMC), Reyes 161.

15 The region was home to an outpost of Nahuatl-speaking peoples, west of the Purépecha kingdom-federation. See Sauer, *Colima of New Spain*.

16 The earliest proof for his exercise of the office comes in 1566: Romero de Solís, *Andariegos y pobladores*, 280. He was still acting as notary when he was investigated in 1573: AGN, Inq., vol. 116, exp. 2. He continued as notary in 1577: Archivo Histórico del Estado de Colima (AHEC), fondo virreinal, caja 3, carptea 1, f. s/n [image 89]. He renounced the position in 1593: AGN, Indiferente, 527, L. 1, f. 163.

17 There is also extensive population data after 1540 that show it to be almost exclusively an indigenous town. See, e.g., "Relación de Tuxpan," in *Relaciones geográficas de la Diócesis de Michoacán*.

18 AGN, Inq., vol. 116, exp. 2, f. 216: "pues como no teneis vosotras vergüença que te eches tu con Francisco López … y respondió ya a mucho que yo no me echo con el."

19 AGN, Tierras, vol. 59, exp. 5; "Relación de Tuxpan."

20 Mazzetto, "¿Miel o sangre?"

21 AHMC, caja A-23, exp. 27.

22 For overviews of the Colima region's coconut liquor industry in the sixteenth and seventeenth centuries, see Machuca Chávez, *El vino de cocos en la Nueva España*.

23 Romero de Solís, *Andariegos y pobladores*, throughout and esp. 280–282.

Bibliography

Boyd-Bowman, Peter. *Patterns of Spanish Emigration to the New World (1493–1580)*. Buffalo, NY: SUNY, 1973.

Calvo, Thomas. "Concubinato y mestizaje en el medio urbano: El caso de Guadalajara en el siglo XVII." *Revista de Indias* 44 (1984): 203–212.

Carrasco, Pedro. "Matrimonios hispano-indios en el primer siglo de la colonia." *Cincuenta años de historia en México* 2 (1991): 103–118.

Carrasco, Pedro. "Indian-Spanish Marriages in the First Century of the Colony." In *Indian Women of Early Mexico*, edited by Susan Schroeder, Stephanie Wood and Robert Haskett, 87–104. Norman, OK: University of Oklahoma Press, 1997.

Chipman, Donald. *Moctezuma's Children: Aztec Royalty Under Spanish Rule, 1520–1700*. Austin, TX: University of Texas Press, 2005.

Germeten, Nicole von. *Violent Delights, Violent Ends: Sex, Race, and Honor in Colonial Cartagena de Indias*. Albuquerque, NM: University of New Mexico Press, 2013.

Germeten, Nicole von. *Profit and Passion: Transactional Sex in Colonial Mexico*. Oakland, CA: University of California Press, 2018.

Gonzalbo Aizpuru, Pilar. "La familia novohispana y la ruptura de los modelos." *Colonial Latin American Review* 9 (2000): 7–19. doi:10.1080/713657405.

Gonzalbo Aizpuru, Pilar. *Educación, familia y vida cotidiana en México virreinal*. Mexico: El Colegio de México, 2013.

Gruzinski, Serge. "Las cenizas del deseo: Homosexuales novohispanos a mediados del siglo XVII." In *De la santidad a la perversión: O de por qué no se cumplía la ley de Diós en la sociedad novohispana*, edited by Sergio Ortega, 255–281. Mexico: Grijalbo, 1986.

Himmerich y Valencia, Robert. *The Encomenderos of New Spain, 1521–1555*. Austin, TX: University of Texas Press, 1991.

Johnson, Lyman L. and Sonya Lipsett-Rivera, eds. *The Faces of Honor: Sex, Shame and Violence in Colonial Latin America*. Albuquerque, NM: University of New Mexico Press, 1998.

Lavrin, Asunción, ed. *Sexuality and Marriage in Colonial Latin America*. Lincoln, NE: University of Nebraska Press, 1989.

Machuca Chávez, Paulina. *El vino de cocos en la Nueva España. Historia de una transculturación en el siglo XVII*. Zamora: Colegio de Michoacán, 2018.

Masters, Adrian. "A Thousand Invisible Architects: Vassals, the Petition and Response System, and the Creation of Spanish Imperial Caste Legislation." *Hispanic American Historical Review* 98 (2018): 377–406. doi:10.1215/00182168-6933534.

Mazzetto, Elena. "¿Miel o sangre? Nuevas problemáticas acerca de la elaboración de las efigies de *tzoalli* de las divinidades nahuas." *Estudios de Cultura Náhuatl* 53 (2017): 73–118.

Mörner, Magnus. *Race Mixture in the History of Latin America*. Boston, MA: Little, Brown and Company, 1967.

Muriel, Josefina. *Los recogimientos de mujeres: Respuesta a una problemática social novohispana*. Mexico: UNAM, 1973.

Relaciones geográficas de la Diócesis de Michoacán, 1579–1580. Guadalajara: n.p., 1958.

Romero de Solís, José Miguel. *Andariegos y pobladores. Nueva España y Nueva Galicia (Siglo XVI).* Colima: Universidad de Colima, 2001.

Sauer, Carl. *Colima of New Spain in the Sixteenth Century.* Berkeley, CA: University of California Press, 1948.

Schwaller, Robert C. *Géneros de Gente in Early Colonial Mexico: Defining Racial Difference.* Norman, OK: University of Oklahoma Press, 2016.

Socolow, Susan. *The Women of Colonial Latin America.* New York: Cambridge University Press, 2015. doi:10.1017/CBO9781139031189.

Sousa, Lisa. *The Woman Who Turned into a Jaguar, and Other Narratives of Native Women in Archives of Colonial Mexico.* Stanford, CA: Stanford University Press, 2017.

Tortorici, Zeb, ed. *Sexuality and the Unnatural in Colonial Latin America.* Oakland, CA: University of California Press, 2016.

Tortorici, Zeb. *Sins Against Nature: Sex and Archives in Colonial New Spain.* Durham, NC: Duke University Press, 2018.

Townsend, Camilla. *Malintzin's Choices: An Indian Woman in the Conquest of Mexico.* Albuquerque, NM: University of New Mexico Press, 2006.

Turner, Victor. "Betwixt and Between: The Liminal Period in Rites of Passage." In *Betwixt and Between: Patterns of Masculine and Feminine Initiation*, edited by Louise Carus Mahdi, Steven Foster and Meredith Little, 3–22. La Salle, IL: Open Court, 1987.

Vinson, Ben. *Before Mestizaje: The Frontiers of Race and Caste in Colonial Mexico.* New York: Cambridge University Press, 2018. doi:10.1017/9781139207744.

Yannakakis, Yanna. *The Art of Being In-Between: Native Intermediaries, Indian Identity and Local Rule in Colonial Oaxaca.* Durham, NC: Duke University Press, 2008.

27

A TRACE OF LAW

State building and the criminalization of buggery in Jamaica

Tracy Robinson

Many durable laws criminalizing sex between men around the world today can be traced to colonial criminal codes and consolidated criminal legislation introduced in the second half of the nineteenth century in the British empire in Africa, Asia and the Caribbean.[1] In this essay I look at the history of criminalization of sex between males in Jamaica, a former British Caribbean colony, in two periods of state formation in the nineteenth and twentieth centuries; the half century after slavery ended in 1838 and the decolonizing years of the 1950s and 1960s leading to Jamaica's independence in 1962.

Jamaica's laws criminalizing anal sex or the "abominable crime of buggery" with mankind or animal, indecent assault upon a male, and gross indecency by a male with another male—a combination of serious and minor offenses—are all found in the 1864 Offences against the Persons Act (OAPA), modeled on the 1861 UK legislation of the same name (though gross indecency became an offense through an amendment some 40 years later, in 1906).[2] These laws have changed little since their enactment. Violence and intolerance as well as these locked-in criminal laws have contributed to Jamaica's global reputation as a site of exceptional homophobia. If there is a "ritualizing of a certain 'idea of homophobia' as a stable discursive formation," then histories of enduring buggery laws in the Global South of the common law world are a part of its logic.[3]

There is a risk that the backwards gaze on enduring criminal laws flattens the "lumpiness of imperial formations,"[4] and legislation is seen as a definitive and unobstructed archive of institutionalized anti-gay affect. Looking at decriminalization legal advocacy in India, Anjali Arondekar argues that "[e]ven as the discourse of law becomes the space of reform ... the very sign of law as evidence needs to examined."[5] She suggests that we think of the object of historical investigation "as a trace," a decentered subject that eludes "discovery," and as a "recalcitrant event [that] reads the notion of the object against a fiction of access, where the object eschews and solicits interpretative seduction."[6] In this essay I take up Arondekar's idea of reading colonial law as a trace rather than offering a self-evident univocal truth about colonialism and male homosexuality. In decentering the OAPA, buggery becomes more of a "metaphor ... a dense transfer point of multiple shifting significations,"[7] and one that shows up the "mechanisms through which state and nation are mediated."[8]

In the first section, this essay examines the modernizing post-slavery criminal and penal justice system that utilized corporal punishment to index the ungovernable black man—one prone to sex crimes like buggery and rape and a necessary site of physical punishment. The second section looks at the practices of legality to secure power in and govern a race-based political system evident in the aftermath of the Morant Bay uprising, including the failed attempt at criminal law codification in Jamaica. The buggery law is but one facet of that enduring post-emancipation foundation for law and order in contemporary Jamaica. The final section is set against the backdrop of the intimacies of the decolonizing realm—mass migration of West Indians to Britain, political negotiations and constitution making, and intense debates about law and morality—and it considers how colonial laws such as the OAPA 1864 gained new import as normative and fundamental law in Jamaica in the wake of independence.

Punishing sex

Jamaica became a British colony in 1655, when it was seized from Spain. In early British Jamaica there were a few reports of arrests and convictions of men, mostly sailors and soldiers, for buggery.[9] During this period it was assumed that the law related to sexual offenses like buggery and rape was English statute law received in Jamaica at the time of British colonization. English statutes of general application were deemed to be in force in West Indian colonies from the date of settlement, and Jamaica was treated as a settled colony. In England, buggery evolved from an ecclesiastical offence to a felony when committed with mankind or beasts. This felony was made perpetual law in 1562 (5 Eliz. c. 17) and was punishable by death.

The end of slavery in 1838 ushered in a new era of state formation and the expansion and modernization of penal and criminal justice in the British Caribbean. There was a flurry of new legislating across the region dealing with vagrancy, offenses against the person, master and servant, and immigration which heavily criminalized plantation laborers and the new peasantry and created forms of legal coercion to support the plantation labor system.[10] As slave courts became defunct, common law courts expanded with a more professionalized judiciary of trained lawyers administering them. Penal reform that began before abolition led to the construction of a large prison complex in 1845, at first aimed at rehabilitation, though this goal was soon abandoned. Criminal prosecutions became largely a matter for the state. By 1867 the Jamaica Constabulary Force, a more modern police force, was established. Another key dimension of social and legal regulation after slavery was the emphasis placed on constructing "a proper gender order" for black colonial subjects grounded in marriage, patriarchy, and female dependency.[11]

Jonathan Dalby's excellent research shows that there was a dramatic rise in prosecutions for sex crimes in the two decades after slavery ended in 1838, largely prosecutions of black men who were former slaves.[12] The abolition of the onerous death penalty for buggery and rape in 1842 made it easier to prosecute these crimes after slavery ended, as would have the more modernized system for prosecuting crimes.[13] Prosecutions for sexual offenses rose from one per cent of all cases before the assizes courts between 1750 and 1834 to 14 per cent of the total offenses prosecuted in the assizes courts in the two decades after slavery ended.[14] Dalby was able to distinguish cases of buggery with animals—bestiality—and with mankind.[15] Just 30 of the 183 sexual offenses cases in the 1840s and 1850s related to buggery with man-kind.[16] Twenty of these 30 prosecutions involved men who were convicts residing at the just-established General Penitentiary,[17] an indication that the post-slavery legal ordering and the modern prison complex produced heightened surveillance of sex between men. The revelation in 1849 of "crimes, revolting to human nature, which are admitted to be of constant occurrence within the walls of the Penitentiary"—cases of buggery—amplified the moral panic about emancipation and its subjects after slavery ended, and contributed to the reintroduction of flogging.[18]

Flogging, a mainstay of slave punishment, was abolished as a judicial punishment following the end of slavery. Yet, in 1850, flogging was reintroduced for all major sex crimes in Jamaica, permitting a maximum of 117 lashes for rape, buggery with mankind or animal, carnal abuse, and attempts to commit these offenses. Over the next 15 years the sentence of corporal punishment was extended multiple times, including to crimes related to property, but 75 per cent of the recorded sentences of flogging in the 1850s and 1860s handed down by the assize and circuit courts related to sex crimes.[19] Corporal punishment became an integral part of the modernized penal system in Jamaica.[20] Flogging "index[ed] social others" by race and gender.[21] Sex crimes subject to flogging, such as buggery, were offenses that, by definition, were committed by *men* and the subjects of this punishment were largely *black* men,[22] described by a Jamaican newspaper as "depraved beings, who are the slaves of unruly passions."[23]

Discovering the content of law related to offenses against the person in early British Jamaica was a difficult task as there was little relevant statute law made for Jamaica, and much of the law related to these offenses was presumed to have been received from England.[24] The enactment of the OAPA in 1864 marked a critical development in modern criminal law in Jamaica by making this law accessible in a single statute. It was Jamaica's most comprehensive legislation dealing with offenses against the person and was a close replica of the 1861 English legislation of the same name aimed at consolidating and amending the criminal law. The OAPA separated buggery from rape and fashioned the former into "an exceptional crime against carnal order."[25] Under the heading, "Unnatural Offences," the OAPA provided that "LII. Whosoever shall be convicted of the abominable crime of buggery, committed either with mankind or with any animal, shall be liable, at the discretion of the Court, to be kept in penal servitude for life, or for any term not less than ten years."[26] This offence could be committed between a male and a female, though throughout Jamaica's history this aspect of the law appears to have been subject to "an organized forgetting."[27] Two additional sections dealt with a lesser offence of an attempt to commit buggery or an indecent assault upon a male person, and provided that "carnal knowledge" for the purposes of this offence is deemed complete upon proof of anal penetration only.[28] The 1885 Labouchere Amendment in England, which made it a minor offence for a male person to commit an act of gross indecency with a male person in public or private, was not a priority for the Jamaican legislature. It became law in Jamaica in 1906, 18 years after the Colonial Office encouraged the governor of Jamaica to enact the provisions of the UK Criminal Law Amendment Act 1885 (48 & 49 Vic. c. 69.), which included the Labouchere Amendment.[29]

While 1864 marked an important moment in the development of sex offenses, the moral boundaries of "unnatural sex" offenses were most defined by the legal debates in Jamaica before and after 1864 related to their *punishment*. In 1893, Jamaica's governor forwarded to the Colonial Office an amendment to the OAPA made by the Legislative Council that sought to reduce the heavy sentence of imprisonment for buggery, which was thought to discourage convictions, and to add a mandatory sentence of corporal punishment and a requirement that the flogging be administered prior to the release of the convict. Three elected members of the Legislative Council made strong objections to the flogging provisions to the Colonial Office on the ground that flogging was not a punishment for the same offense in England and was associated with slavery. The Colonial Office was less concerned about the inclusion of corporal punishment, and more its nature—mandatory rather than discretionary, and administered prior to the release of the convict, after the term of imprisonment had been served. Facing a risk that the law would be disallowed, a new version of the law, without the provision of corporal punishment, was enacted in 1894.

In showing up the gap between the proposed colonial punishment and imperial punishment for buggery, the aim of the dissident Jamaican legislators in 1893 was to position post-slavery flogging as "an aberration of modernity."[30] The failure of the corporal punishment amendments was not a victory for their position and a disavowal of the use of corporal punishment to discipline the black male body. It reflected the pragmatism of colonial officials and legislators in ensuring that colonial legislation was allowed. That Jamaican legislators at the end of the nineteenth century were still deeply engaged in debates about flogging as a punishment for buggery, as they had been in the decade after slavery ended, highlights the racialization and gendering of corporal punishment to position black male others on the margins of civilization, and as those whose "bodies were not properly subject to control by their minds and therefore punishment should be addressed to the body rather than the mind."[31] The governance of race, gender, and sex in the post-emancipation period through criminal law and punishments named people, practices, and moments that embodied "nonnormativity, a break in the line of gender," shards of Caribbean queerness.[32]

A love of law

The repressive post-slavery colonial regime and the failure of the colonial government to respond to the demands of Afro-Jamaicans for economic, social, and political reforms led to the Morant Bay uprising in Jamaica in 1865, a year after the OAPA was enacted. Martial law was declared for a month and a "protracted and calculated reign of terror" was unleashed on the black peasantry in which more than 400 blacks were shot or executed and more than 600 flogged.[33] The intense political and intellectual debates after 1865 in England and Jamaica about martial law generated strong conservative opinions about imperial rule, racial differences between whites and blacks, and the inevitability of force and violence to secure law and order over unruly black subjects.[34] These debates, as well as the attempts to hold the governor and others accountable in England, were marked by a preoccupation on both sides of the Atlantic with law and legality.[35] The Jamaica controversy and debates were marked by an "unabashed chauvinism" that it was law that made England great.[36] Morant Bay confirmed that legal exceptions such as martial law were inside, not outside, the colonial rule of law.[37]

In the wake of Morant Bay, and amid the fear of the white minority of the Afro-Caribbean masses, Jamaica's elites voluntarily gave up its representative assembly and accepted Crown colony government, whereby the Crown assumed direct and full responsibility for the administration of the colonies through a governor who was subject to close metropolitan supervision. The new Legislative Council in Jamaica was made up of official and unofficial nominated members over whom the governor could exercise control, though by 1884 elected members were added. Crises like the Morant Bay uprising helped to precipitate codification exercises in the British empire.[38] With strengthened imperial control of the colony, R.S. Wright, an English barrister, was commissioned in 1870 to draft a criminal code and code of criminal procedure for Jamaica that would serve as a model in other colonies.

Wright's first draft of the Penal Code was completed in 1874. The Colonial Office asked James Fitzjames Stephen, a prominent criminal law drafter, to review the draft code and to pay close attention to the provisions "not conforming to the English criminal law, but designed to introduce improvements."[39] One of these related to unnatural offenses. Stephen disagreed strongly with Wright's proposal to distinguish buggery with consent from buggery without consent, placing the former in a section headed "Public Nuisances" and punishing it by a maximum two-year sentence of imprisonment.[40] After Stephen's strong objection, the Colonial Office raised the proposed penalty for buggery without consent in the Jamaica draft code from two years to ten years. Wright's Criminal Law and Criminal Procedures Codes were enacted in 1879 by Jamaica's Legislative Council at the request of the Colonial Office, with a clause suspending their entry into force. The Criminal Code included one provision for unnatural carnal knowledge with force and without consent, with a penalty of penal servitude for life and flogging; the other dealt with unnatural connections and carried a ten-year imprisonment term and the possibility of flogging or whipping.[41] Wright later said that the extension of corporal punishment to offenses such as these "was part of the instructions by which I was bound."[42] The Colonial Office had doubts about bringing the codes into operation while another criminal code was being considered for adoption in England, since it thought that the fate of the latter might have implications for Wright's codes and their "novelties."[43]

Within a few years the codes, which had been enacted without opposition in Jamaica, faced open criticism from the legal profession there. When contemporaneous attempts at codification in England failed, elites in Jamaica pushed back against imperial control and negotiated their power in the name of a love of and ownership of English law. A Supreme Court Memorandum from its judges, who were all trained in England, complained that the Jamaican legislature should not "be invited to give a lead to Imperial Legislation on vexed questions of such vital importance," given that efforts at codification in England had ended in failure.[44] The judges complained that "the decisions of the English courts would cease to be of assistance to us in deciding the numerous questions which are in the administration of Criminal Justice."[45] There was also suspicion that Jamaica, now a Crown colony and under the thumb of the Colonial Office, was the "victim of a great experiment" and at risk "of being immolated on the altar of legal reform," in a context where efforts at codification had failed in the metropole.[46] The governor ultimately asked the Colonial Office to permit the repeal of the codes, which took place in 1889, ten years after the law was initially enacted in Jamaica.

Jamaica's failed Criminal Code of 1879 invites and refuses "interpretative seduction." The possibilities hinted at in the code's initially more liberal provisions on offenses dealing with sex between males haunt the OAPA to an extent. While the Criminal Code's repeal had little to do with its provisions on sex crimes, the rejection of Wright's novel provisions on consensual sex between men indicates that, in the colonial context, codification was not just aimed at providing clear legal rules; it was also "a force for moral conquest" and a tool of colonial civilization.[47] The vigorous post-slavery legislating for crimes, the effort at codification, and the resistance to it in the name of the love of English law were all investments in the rule of law in a "racialized political system" premised on fear of, contempt for, and disenfranchisement of the non-white population, and in which "legality became the preeminent signifier of state legitimacy and of 'civilization.'"[48] Elizabeth Kolsky explains that "colonial rule pressed against its own limits of legality and produced new forms of law that sanctioned spectacular displays of power and violence."[49] The "modern" structures of legality that accompanied emancipation—criminal law, prisons, courts, the police—have been remarkably resilient in the Anglophone Caribbean.[50] Equally durable have been the "new forms of law" that made the legal regimes of exception, such as martial law, intrinsic to the maintenance of power and legality.

The intimacies of decolonization

By the twentieth century "the center of gravity" of the British empire had shifted away from Jamaica, which at one stage was its most important colony, and the rest of the Caribbean.[51] Poor economic and social conditions and an authoritarian crown colony system of government fueled nationalist uprisings in Jamaica and the rest of the British West Indies in the 1930s, where less than 10 per cent of the population had the right to vote before World War II.[52] In the wake of social and labor disturbances, there was a dismantling of the crown colony government, constitutional advances were made toward self-government, and universal adult suffrage was introduced across the British Caribbean, beginning with Jamaica in 1944. A short-lived West Indies Federation made up of ten territories, including Jamaica, was established in 1959 but fell apart three years later as Jamaica abandoned it and became independent in 1962 with a new constitution with a bill of rights.

The waning years of colonization in the 1950s and 1960s were marked by new entanglements between Caribbean colonies and Britain. There were intense political negotiations between nationalist politicians and colonial officials and copious constitution-making for the colonies. Wide-scale immigration from Jamaica and other Caribbean colonies to Britain started after the end of World War II and tourism expanded and opened Jamaica to an influx of white visitors. These close encounters sharpened racialized geographies of sexuality.[53] While the statutory framework for criminalization of sex between males and unnatural sex in the OAPA was virtually untouched in the first half of the twentieth century—but for the addition of the offence of gross indecency in 1906—by the 1950s homosexuality in Jamaica was described as a practice induced by white male tourists or other foreigners.[54] When Lady Foot, the governor's wife, in 1952 criticized a lack of shame about high rates of illegitimacy in the black population in Jamaica and described illegitimacy as the problem of a "smelly alley,"[55] Wills Isaacs, a black nationalist politician, responded that she "should remember that there are Alleys in England that smell much worse than ours," citing "homosexualism" as one of England's "great social evils."[56]

Jamaicans closely followed the law and morality debates that accompanied the work of the Departmental Committee on Homosexual Offences and Prostitution, chaired by Sir John Wolfenden, which was set up in 1954 as a response to a moral panic about sex work and the increase in arrests and prosecutions in England of homosexual men for buggery and gross indecency. The Committee's recommendation to decriminalize homosexual sex between consenting adults in private was rejected initially by the metropolitan government, and it took ten years for that recommendation to become law in England and Wales. The transatlantic Wolfenden debates about criminalization did more than associate male homosexuality with the buggery and indecency laws; through the debates, the law gave further shape to the notion of a male homosexual identity. When Sir John visited Jamaica in 1960, an interviewer told him, "Your name has run from one end of Jamaica to the other because of the Wolfenden Report, I think that everybody in Jamaica has heard or read about that."[57] The interviewer also advised him that, "The picture has been painted that London was the most wicked city in the world."[58]

In negotiations between local politicians and colonial officials over arrangements for decolonization, British authorities viewed the Caribbean as underdeveloped and often adopted a racist and condescending attitude toward the local leaders.[59] In an internal office discussion, a senior Colonial Office official said the motto of the failed West Indian Federation should be "Ten little nigger boys,"[60] betraying the metropolitan racial anxieties about both decolonization and West Indian immigration. As the West Indian Federation fell apart, the black nationalist politicians tasked with drafting the independence constitution claimed an emblem of Englishness, the common law tradition, as part of their own identity and as a signal of their maturity to lead.[61] The debates on the readiness of the West Indies for independence often turned on questions of whether black and brown West Indian men could "prove themselves to be the masculine equals of Englishmen."[62] Norman Manley, the most important drafter of the independence constitution, asserted, "We had a system which we understand [understood]; we have been operating it for many years with sense. It is a system which is consistent with the sort of ideals we have in this country. … Let us not make the mistake of describing as colonial, institutions which are part and parcel of this country."[63]

The 1962 independence constitution included a chapter devoted to the protection of fundamental rights and freedoms, with stark exceptions to the new rights regime for colonial laws and colonial punishments. One savings law clause ensured that colonial punishments, such as capital and corporal punishment, could not be challenged on the grounds that they were inhuman and degrading.[64] In the parliamentary debates on the draft constitution, Manley conceded that "flogging is inhuman and degrading punishment" and intentionally so.[65] Manley then explained, "Well, that is why you have to have [the savings law clause]. Otherwise you would have at once abolished the right to flog people whether for rape or for stealing coconuts or any other form of mischievous theft."[66] Manley ended there abruptly, making it clear that degrading physical punishments were necessary as modern tools of power and control in the new nation-state, distinguishing the ungovernable black male who disrupted the moral and economic order from the mature, governing black man, entitled to lead the independent nation-state.[67]

These savings law clauses sharpened a sphere of higher order law comprised of constitutions and colonial law in which the latter became sacrosanct and exalted "as part and parcel of this country." Another savings law clause in the 1962 constitution preserved and protected colonial laws, like the OAPA 1864, from challenge on the grounds that they violated any of the guaranteed rights.[68] The imperial court, the Judicial Committee of the Privy Council, based in London and which Jamaica retained as its final court of appeal after independence, gave early moral meaning to this clause. In 1967 the Privy Council explained that the exception for colonial laws from the new rights regime "proceeds on the presumption that the fundamental rights that [the Constitution] covers are already secured to the people of Jamaica by existing law."[69]

In 1967, five years after Jamaica's independence, the Sexual Offences Act decriminalized sex between men in England and Wales. It has been suggested that decriminalization "came too late for most of Britain's colonies," like Jamaica, which gained independence in the early sixties "with sodomy law still in place,"[70] conjuring up a gap between here and there in the wake of decolonization as the "civilizing" reach of empire waned. The regular media reports in Jamaica on the 1967 reforms, the intimate legal ties between postcolony and metropole sustained through retention of the Privy Council, and that court's decisive interpretation of Jamaica's constitution in 1967 belie this notion of distance. Still, the intimacies of decolonization deepened the differentiated jurisdictional and constitutional spaces of the similarly worded buggery law in Jamaica and the one in England prior to 1967. In the wake of the Wolfenden debates, the UK buggery law was *ordinary* criminal law made by and always open to legislative reform by a sovereign Parliament. By contrast, in 1962 in Jamaica, there was a new independence constitution that was supreme. The combined effect of savings law clauses in the Jamaican constitution and its interpretation by the Privy Council in 1967 repositioned Jamaica's colonial laws, including OAPA and its buggery provisions, as venerated law, *higher order* "saved" laws, and as legacies of colonialism's civilizing mission that should not be easily changed.

In the decade leading to decriminalization in England, discourses of deviance in Britain were deeply racialized. Nadia Ellis notices that the "black queer" was nowhere explicit in the Wolfenden Report and other documents on homosexuality in the 1950s, but that "he lurks and sidles" in such documents since discussions around immigration "were as voluble as those on the homosexual."[71] She concludes that "the sad, blunt truth about this period in British history is that sexual freedom, aligned with whiteness, trumped black freedom of movement and access to metropolitan citizenship."[72] Britain responded to the "deviance" of black Caribbean immigrants by enacting legislation limiting their access to British citizenship. The intimacies of decolonization produced different codes of freedom in Jamaica and Britain, in the Jamaican constitution and the UK sexual offenses and immigration reforms respectively. They governed different spaces and they also guaranteed differentiated and hierarchical freedoms.

Conclusion

The history of the buggery law in Jamaica is a history of the regulation of sex, race, and gender on both sides of the Atlantic. Through this law we can trace how legality buttresses state development in Jamaica and is reworked in different moments and jurisdictions. The imprecision of the saved colonial offence of buggery in "making sense and nonsense of the male genital body,"[73] sexual acts, and identities has only heightened its normativity. Buggery was amenable to shifting interpretations over time, which reinforced its capacity to "invent persons who yet remain in a negative relation to law."[74]

Notes

1 See Human Rights Watch, *This Alien Legacy*; Han and O'Mahoney, *British Colonialism and the Criminalization of Homosexuality*.
2 Jamaica Offences against the Person Act 1864, sections 76, 77, 79.
3 Amar Wahab, "Calling 'Homophobia' into Place," 911.
4 Benton, *A Search for Sovereignty*, 7–8.
5 Arondekar, "Without a Trace," 21.
6 Ibid., 22.
7 Moran, *The Homosexuality of Law*, 87.
8 Alexander, *Pedagogies of Crossing*, 192.
9 Edwards, *The Development of Criminal Law in Jamaica*, 423.
10 Paton, *No Bond but the Law*, 54.
11 Hall, *Civilizing Subjects*, 122.
12 Dalby, *Crime and Punishment in Jamaica*; Dalby, "Luxurious Resting Places for the Idle and Vicious," 193; Dalby, "Such a Mass of Disgusting and Revolting Cases," 136.
13 Dalby, *Crime and Punishment*, 43.
14 Dalby, "Such a Mass of Disgusting and Revolting Cases," 136–137.
15 Ibid., 142.
16 Dalby, "Luxurious Resting Places," 155.
17 Ibid.
18 *Falmouth Post*, "The General Penitentiary," May 8, 1849, cited in Dalby, "Luxurious Resting Places," 154–155.
19 Dalby, "Luxurious Resting Places," 157.
20 Paton, *No Bond but the Law*, 143.
21 Geltner, *Flogging Others*, 10.
22 Paton, *No Bond but the Law*, 143.
23 *Falmouth Post*, "Editorial," October 26, 1852, cited in Paton, *No Bond but the Law*, 141.
24 Edwards, *The Development of Criminal Law in Jamaica*, 419.

25 Moran, *The Homosexuality of Law*, 81.
26 Jamaica Offences Against the Person Act 1864, section LII.
27 Halley, "Reasoning about Sodomy," 1722.
28 Jamaica Offences Against the Persons Act 1864, sections LIII, LIV.
29 Jamaica Criminal Law Amendment Law, 1906, section 10.
30 Geltner, *Flogging Others*, 10.
31 Paton, *No Bond but the Law*, 142
32 Ellis, "Out and Bad," 12.
33 Kostal, *A Jurisprudence of Power*, 13.
34 Hall, *Civilizing Subjects*, 424.
35 Kostal, *A Jurisprudence of Power*, 461.
36 Ibid.
37 Hussain, *The Jurisprudence of Emergency*, 19–20.
38 Wright, "Criminal Law Codification and Imperial Projects," 26.
39 CO/137/478/395, J.F. Stephen to R.G.W. Herbert, January 19, 1876.
40 R.S. Wright's Jamaica Criminal Code, sections 65, 345, cited in Friedland, "R.S. Wright's Model Criminal Code," 307, 328.
41 Jamaica Criminal Code 1879, sections 65, 345.
42 Quoted in Friedland, "R.S. Wright's Model Criminal Code," 335.
43 CO 137/498/350, Memo from R.G.W. Herbert, the Permanent Under-Secretary, January 19, 1880, cited in Friedland, 334.
44 CO 137/536, Norman to Knutsford, November 1, 1888, enclosed Memo of Supreme Court.
45 Norman to Knutsford.
46 *Gall's Weekly News Letter*, "Editorial," September 29, 1888.
47 Farmer, *Making the Modern Criminal Law*, 157.
48 Hussain, "Towards a Jurisprudence of Emergency," 100.
49 Kolsky, "The Colonial Rule of Law and the Legal Regime of Exception," 1219.
50 Newton, "Freedom's Prisons," 165.
51 Knight, *The Caribbean*, 275.
52 Alomar, *Revisiting the Transatlantic Triangle*, 14.
53 Chin, "In the Shadows of Kinship," 8.
54 Ibid. By the 1950s the *Jamaica Gleaner* regularly published reports of court cases related to buggery and gross indecency, giving the most visibility to those involving Jamaican men working in the tourist industry and foreign men.
55 *Daily Gleaner*, "Lady Foot Hits at Illegitimacy."
56 Isaacs, "Letter."
57 Audio interview between Ivy Cunningham of Jamaica Broadcast Corporation and Professor Arthur Lewis, Sir Charles Morris, and Sir John Wolfenden, January 17, 1960, Mona Hotel, St. Andrew, to be kept at the Radio Education Unit (on file with the The UWI Archives). In 1960, Sir John Wolfenden, who was then vice chancellor at an English university, visited Jamaica as part of a special committee looking at the financial situation of the University College of the West Indies (UCWI). During that visit he met with students and discussed the Wolfenden Report (Gleaner University Correspondent, "Attend Local University, West Indians Advised," *Daily Gleaner* February 2, 1960, 19). He also participated in the BBC's programme, "Calling the Caribbean" in a question and answer session with Caribbean students at the West Indian Student Centre in London on March 9, 1960 ("Sir John Wolfenden for BBC Carib Programme," *Daily Gleaner*, March 7, 1960, 7).
58 Interview.
59 Alomar, *Revisiting the Transatlantic Triangle*, 69.
60 CO 1031/3376, Poynton Minute, October 22, 1962.
61 Robinson, "Gender, Nation and the Common Law Constitution," 740.
62 Edmondson, *Making Men*, 8.
63 Norman Manley, Proceedings of the House of Representatives Session 1961–62, January 23, 1962, 719.
64 Jamaica Constitution 1962, section 17(2), now repealed.
65 Norman Manley, Jamaica Proceedings of the House of Representatives, Session 1961–62, January 25, 1962, 765.
66 Manley, January 25, 1962.

67 Paton, *No Bond but the Law* 142. Just a year after independence, following reports about a phantom rapist, flogging was provided for as an additional punishment for rape in the Prevention of Crime (Special Provisions) Act 1963–42.

68 Jamaica Constitution 1962, section 26(8), now repealed.

69 *DPP v Nasralla* [1967] AC 238, 247–248 (Privy Council, Jamaica).

70 Human Rights Watch, *This Alien Legacy*.

71 Ellis, *Territories of the Soul*, 132–133.

72 Ibid., 132.

73 Moran, *The Homosexuality of Law,* 79.

74 Dayan, "Rituals of Belief," 197.

Bibliography

Alexander, M. Jacqui. *Pedagogies of Crossing: Meditations on Feminism, Sexual Politics, Memory, and the Sacred.* Durham, NC: Duke University Press, 2005.

Arondekar, Anjali. "Without a Trace: Sexuality and the Colonial Archive." *Journal of the History of Sexuality* 14 nos. 1/2 (January 2005/April 2005): 10–27. doi:10.1353/sex.2006.0001.

Benton, Lauren. *A Search for Sovereignty: Law and Geography in European Empires, 1400–1900.* Cambridge, UK: Cambridge University Press, 2010.

Chin, Matthew. "In the Shadows of Kinship: Revisiting Sexual Politics in the 1950s Jamaica." Paper presented at "The Jamaica 1950s" Symposium, University of Pennsylvania, April 2019.

Cox Alomar, Rafael. *Revisiting the Transatlantic Triangle: The Constitutional Decolonization of the Eastern Caribbean.* Kingston: Ian Randle Publishers, 2009.

Daily Gleaner. "Lady Foot Hits at Illegitimacy." January 11, 1952.

Dalby, Jonathan. *Crime and Punishment in Jamaica: A Quantitative Analysis of the Assize Court Records, 1756–1856.* The Social History Project, Department of History. Mona: University of the West Indies, 2000.

Dalby, Jonathan. "'Luxurious Resting Places for the Idle and Vicious'?: The Rise and Fall of Penal Reform in Jamaica in the 1840s." *Small Axe: A Caribbean Journal of Criticism* 15, no. 1 (34) (2011): 147–163. doi:10.1215/07990537-1189593.

Dalby, Jonathan. "'Such a Mass of Disgusting and Revolting Cases': Moral Panic and the 'Discovery' of Sexual Deviance in Post-Emancipation Jamaica (1835–1855)." *Slavery & Abolition* 36, no. 1 (2015): 136–159. doi:10.1080/0144039X.2014.929815.

Dayan, Colin. "Rituals of Belief, Practices of Law." *Small Axe: A Caribbean Journal of Criticism* 14, no. 1 (31) (2010): 193–199. doi:10.1215/07990537-2009-051.

Edmondson, Belinda. *Making Men: Gender, Literary Authority, and Women's Writing in Caribbean Narrative.* Durham, NC: Duke University Press, 1999.

Edwards, Adolph. "The Development of Criminal Law in Jamaica." Ph.D. diss., London School of Economic and Political Sciences, 1966.

Ellis, Nadia. "Out and Bad: Toward a Queer Performance Hermeneutic in Jamaican Dancehall." *Small Axe* 15, no. 2 (35) (2011): 7–23. doi:10.1215/07990537-1334212.

Ellis, Nadia. *Territories of the Soul: Queered Belonging in the Black Diaspora.* Durham, NC: Duke University Press, 2015.

Falmouth Post (Jamaica). "The General Penitentiary." May 8, 1849.

Falmouth Post (Jamaica). "Editorial." October 26, 1852

Farmer, Lindsay, *Making the Modern Criminal Law: Criminalization and Civil Order.* Oxford, UK: Oxford University Press, 2016. Friedland, Martin. "R.S. Wright's Model Criminal Code: A Forgotten Chapter in the History of the Criminal Law." *Oxford Journal of Legal Studies* 1 (1981): 307–346. doi:10.1093/ojls/1.3.307.

Farmer, Lindsay. "Reconstructing the English Codification Debate: The Criminal Law Commissioners, 1833–45." *Law and History Review* 18 (2000): 397–425. doi:10.2307/744300.

Gall's Weekly News Letter (Jamaica). "Editorial." September 29, 1888.

Geltner, G. *Flogging Others: Corporal Punishment and Cultural Identity from Antiquity to the Present.* Amsterdam: Amsterdam University Press, 2014.

Hall, Catherine. *Civilizing Subjects: Metropole and Colony in the English Imagination 1830–1867.* Chicago, IL: University of Chicago Press, 2002.

Halley, Janet. "Reasoning about Sodomy: Act and Identity in and after Bowers v Hardwick." *Virginia Law Review* 79, no. 7 (1993): 1721–1780.

Han, Enze and Joseph O'Mahoney. *British colonialism and the criminalization of homosexuality: Queens, crime and empire.* London: Routledge, 2018.

Human Rights Watch. *This Alien Legacy: The Origins of "Sodomy" Laws in British Colonialism.* New York: Human Rights Watch, 2008. Accessed October 10, 2019. https://www.hrw.org/report/2008/12/17/a lien-legacy/origins-sodomy-laws-british-colonialism

Hussain, Nasser. "Towards a Jurisprudence of Emergency: Colonialism and the Rule of Law." *Law and Critique* 10, no. 2 (1999) 93–115. doi:10.1023/A:1008993501958.

Hussain, Nasser. *The Jurisprudence of Emergency: Colonialism and the Rule of Law.* Ann Arbor, MI: University of Michigan Press, 2003.

Isaacs, Wills O.Letter. *Daily Gleaner*, January 21, 1952.

Knight, Franklin W. *The Caribbean Second Edition.* New York: Oxford University Press, 1990.

Kolsky, Elizabeth. "The Colonial Rule of Law and the Legal Regime of Exception: Frontier 'Fanaticism' and State Violence in British India." *American Historical Review* 120, no. 4 (2015): 1218–1246. doi:10.1093/ahr/120.4.1218.

Moran, Leslie. *The Homosexuality of Law.* London: Routledge, 1996.

Newton, Melanie J. "Freedom's Prisons: Incarceration, Emancipation, and Modernity in *No Bond but the Law.*" *Small Axe* 15, no. 1 (34) (March 2011): 164–175. doi:10.1215/07990537-1189602.

Paton, Diana. *No Bond but the Law: Punishment, Race, and Gender in Jamaican State Formation, 1780–1870.* Durham, NC: Duke University Press, 2004.

Robinson, Tracy. "Gender, Nation and the Common Law Constitution." *Oxford Journal of Legal Studies* 28, no. 4 (2008): 735–762. doi:10.1093/ojls/gqn024.

Wahab, Amar. "Calling 'Homophobia' into Place (Jamaica)." *Interventions* 18, no. 6 (2016): 908–928. doi:10.1080/1369801X.2015.1130641.

Wright, Barry. "Criminal Law Codification and Imperial Projects: The Self-governing Jurisdiction Codes of the 1890's." *Legal History* 12, no. 1 (2008): 19–49.

28

GENDER, SEXUAL VIOLENCE, AND THE HERERO GENOCIDE

Elisa von Joeden-Forgey

The genocide committed by the German empire against the Herero and Nama peoples in the colony of German South West Africa (present-day Namibia) from 1904 to 1908 was the first genocide of the twentieth century and took the lives of an estimated 80 per cent of the Herero and 50 per cent of the Nama peoples. Despite the comprehensive nature of the genocide, it is still a little-known event in human history, its memory eclipsed by what came after: the Armenian genocide in World War I and the Holocaust in World War II. In the past 20 years, both scholars and the wider public have begun to recognize the Herero genocide. There is a growing scholarly literature on the genocide, and the Herero people have maintained a steady pressure on Germany to both recognize the genocide and offer reparations. Still neglected, however, is the history of women and sexuality during the genocide. Herero women's experiences are rarely included in studies of gender, sexuality, and genocide, with the notable exception of the pathbreaking work of Gesine Krüger.[1]

As scholarship on colonialism has shown, European empires were as much constructed through gender and sexual categories as through race and class. The ways in which gendered experiences of colonialism intersect with their experiences of genocide thus help us to better understand both processes. In the Herero case, we see the colonial conflict between competing gendered politics of patriarchal power that resulted, on the German side, in a root-and-branch genocide pursued with the aim of shoring up German masculine authority. In this case, the leadership of both sides instrumentalized the treatment of women as part of their explicit communication with one another about their war aims. This chapter will examine the secondary literature on women and the Herero genocide, and argue that a gendered and sexualized concept of power, constructed through the process of colonization, greatly facilitated the choice among German authorities to turn to a policy of genocide.

Colonial relationships and the path to genocide

Despite its long-term historical silencing, the Herero genocide was very well known in Germany as it was occurring. Debates in the news, in the public sphere, and in parliament resulted in a full-fledged political crisis for the imperial German state.[2] During and after World War I, the Herero genocide was used by the entente powers as evidence of a particular German brutality that made the country unfit for overseas colonization. An important

British government Blue Book, originally published in 1918 and recently reissued and edited by Jeremy Silvester and Jan-Bart Gewald,[3] is still one of the few collections of survivor testimonials in existence. The genocide was, of course, also integrated into Herero oral tradition and became a core focus of collective memory among survivors and their descendants.[4]

The experiences of Herero and Nama women during the genocide were directly influenced by the gendered structures of power that had characterized German domination up to 1904. German South West Africa (*Deutsch-Südwest Afrika*, or DSWA) had the greatest number of German settlers in the German empire, making it Germany's largest settler colony when measured by German population.[5] Unlike Germany's tropical colonies, DSWA was free of the diseases that exacted a high toll on Europeans. It was rich in arable land and had a thriving cattle culture before Germans arrived. It is the only colony that the central state in Berlin ever identified as suitable for mass emigration and settlement by Germans. The state planned to use DSWA to solve the emigration crisis of the mid- to late nineteenth century, when Germans were leaving the country in large numbers. DSWA was thus viewed as an integral part of the future of the metropole, a place where Germans could return to the simpler life of the pre-industrial era. These plans set the stage for conflict and eventual genocide.

As in other settler colonies at the turn of the century, the early years of colonial domination were characterized by a German imperial patriarchy in which unequal power between the colonizer and the colonized coexisted with multilateral diplomatic relationships and the possibility of horizontal exchange. Herero leaders represented themselves as analogous to German aristocrats and conducted themselves accordingly.[6] The early German colonists, who were mostly administrators, officers, soldiers, and missionaries, relied on local culture to survive and were deeply embedded in local politics and commerce.[7] Their labor force was supplied to them by Herero leaders and, in the early years of the colony, these leaders saw it as a matter of pride to offer their daughters to work in German households. Of course, the presence of young Herero women in the homes of German male settlers frequently led to sexual relationships, both consensual and coerced. At this time, instances of sexual relations between German men and African women, as well as formalized marriages between the two, were not met with the same hostility as they later came to be; indeed, in these early years they were accepted as the norm. There was in fact a relatively high level of intermarriage, and the benefits of this practice for European men were well recognized.

Although no comprehensive study of women in Herero society exists for the period before the genocide, it appears that women enjoyed significant social power in patriarchal Herero society. The Herero practice a bilateral descent system, according to which children trace their heritage through both their father's and their mother's lineages. Inheritance of land and cattle is also traced bilaterally. As in other southern African societies, Herero families were often polygamous, with men heading the homestead and women comprising separate households within it. While the leadership position of the homestead was usually conferred to male family members, women could also inherit these powerful positions. Traditionally, cattle raising and trading were seen as men's work, while women were responsible for milking cattle, taking care of the households, and trading in other goods.[8] Before the genocide, German men commented on the "helpfulness and obedience" of African women in comparison with "spoiled and demanding" German women.[9] Europeans also commented on what they believed to be the relatively high status of Herero women in Herero society, basing this assessment on the fact that women were not involved in the backbreaking agricultural work seen elsewhere in Africa.[10]

Companionate marriage between German men and African women, including Hereros, was widespread in the early years of German imperial rule in DSWA. German men often married into prominent African families in order to gain status, land, cattle, and trading connections.[11] They spoke local trade languages, used local farming techniques and commercial norms, and founded families. However, once the colonial administration began to formalize its rule, and the settler population began to grow, these sorts of liaisons came under scrutiny. "Race mixing" became a central preoccupation among Germans in Germany's colonies as well as in pro-colonial circles in the metropole. So-called mixed marriages were believed to undermine the position of whites in the colonies and lead to politically destabilizing and racially inferior mixed-race children. DSWA was the first colony to ban mixed marriages (during the Herero genocide) and the citizenship status of the children of these marriages was constantly called into question.[12]

In German South West Africa, sexualized violence was widespread. This did not change in practice once the marriage ban was in place. Among the most widely publicized colonial scandals in Germany were those involving sexualized violence against colonized women. One case, which occurred in the German West African colony of Cameroon, involved the flogging and mass rape of the wives of the colony's African police force, ordered by the interim governor, Karl Theodor Heinrich Leist.[13] In another case, this one in German East Africa, the famous adventurer and colonial administrator Carl Peters, out of jealousy, had his sex slave and her lover hanged and their villages destroyed, an atrocity that, once it became known, ended his government career.[14] These scandals in Cameroon and German East Africa resulted in uprisings against the German colonizers.

So commonplace was the sexual assault of African women by German men that settlers developed special terms for it, such as *Verkafferung* (going native) and *Schmutzwirtschaft* (dirty trade).[15] As these terms indicate, no distinction was made in colonial discourse between consensual and forced sex. Indeed, sexual relations between European men and African women were described with reference to the race hierarchy that governed the German social order, such that violent criminal acts by white German men were normalized and excused with reference to native custom. The consent of African women was completely irrelevant to naming. To wit, in May 1904, Governor Leutwein, in a letter to the Colonial Department of the Foreign Office, conflates rape and sexual relations: "Throughout the years I have spent in the Protectorate, not a single case of rape has been brought to the notice of the authorities, although it cannot be denied that sexual relations between whites and natives are common."[16]

As was the case with the scandals in German East Africa and Cameroon, the Social Democratic Party publicized incidents of rape in DSWA. The Social Democratic paper *Berliner Tagwacht*, for example, published the description of the gang rape of an African woman by three German settlers as follows:

> The overseer of the kraal, a German, and two of his cronies had locked themselves in with the wife of a native, probably after having administered a heavy dose of schnapps to her. Her husband, who had got wind of the matter, rushed to their house, hammering at the door and demanding the release of his wife. Thereupon one of these heroes came out to give the black man a good hiding, a practice which, albeit forbidden, is fairly commonplace here. However, the black man offered resistance and, after having himself struck a blow, fled into his hut. The whites, blazing with anger, dragged him out and maltreated him, subsequently bundling him off to the police station where he was given fifty lashes into the bargain for having assaulted a white man.[17]

Subsequent reports on the incident by the District Office and the Imperial Railway Authority at Swakopmund confirmed the details of the case, but, independently of one another, remarked that such goings-on were so commonplace that they did not deem the case worthy of note.[18]

Rape and sexual violence played a role in creating the conditions for the outbreak of the Herero anticolonial rebellion in 1904. One case that was particularly offensive to the Herero was the attempted rape and murder of the wife of the son of Herero Chief Zacharias in 1903. A German trader traveling with the family had attempted to rape her at night when everyone was sleeping; when she protested, he shot her, killing her and injuring her newborn. The German was acquitted of charges of manslaughter and subsequently, on appeal, sentenced to three years' imprisonment. Such violent and disrespectful treatment of Herero of high standing is cited alongside loss of land and cattle as a contributor to the Herero decision to revolt.[19]

Herero survivors of the genocide were still speaking of these degradations, including the specific case of Chief Zacharias's daughter-in-law, when the British gathered testimony for their Blue Book during World War I. Samuel Kariko (son of Subchief Daniel Kariko) told the interviewers: "Our people were shot and murdered [before the outbreak of the revolt]; our women were ill-treated; and those who did this were not punished. Our chiefs consulted and we decided that a war could not be worse than what we were undergoing. … We all knew what risks we ran … yet we decided on war, as the chiefs said we would be better off even if we were all dead."[20]

During the genocide

As Gesine Krüger has pointed out, men, women, and children were intentionally killed during the Herero genocide. Neither sex nor age determined Herero chances of survival. Women and children were directly targeted by the German military, which aimed to destroy the social body of the Herero in its totality. The German military made no distinction between combatants and non-combatants.[21] Like men, women and children died from dehydration, starvation, disease; they were killed in battle, shot as prisoners, and worked to death in concentration camps.[22] According to eyewitnesses, women and children were also hanged, bayonetted, burned alive, and mutilated. Nevertheless, despite the gender-neutral outcome of the genocide in terms of lives lost, we do see gendered patterns within the genocidal process in DSWA that are similar to other cases of genocide, both in imperial and national contexts.

The genocide against the Herero occurred in the context of a German counterinsurgency campaign against what they believed had been a Herero revolt. Most scholars now view the outbreak of war to have been the result of a series of misunderstandings, driven by a national security paranoia on the part of German settlers and administrators, who were constantly afraid of a Herero rebellion.[23] The Germans mistook a meeting of Herero chiefs regarding inheritance issues as a sign of imminent attack. The panicked German response led the Herero to believe that the Germans planned to kill their paramount chief, Samuel Maherero. In response, on January 14, 1904, a small group of Hereros revolted, murdering 123 white Germans, including three women.[24]

> After this, the rest of the Herero were forced into war by the strong German military response. Samuel Maherero issued a letter to Herero chiefs in which he delineated legitimate and illegitimate targets, saying, "I have issued an order, a straight word, meant for all my people, that they should no longer lay their hands on the following:

namely Englishmen, Basters, Bergdamaras, Namas, Boers; we do not lay hands on these. Do not do this. I have sworn an oath to this, that this case does not become open, also not to the missionaries. Enough."[25]

In a similar fashion, Maherero also guaranteed the safety of German women and children.[26] Subchief Daniel Kariko reported that "[a]t our clandestine meetings our chiefs decided to spare the lives of all German women and children. ... Only German men were regarded as our enemies."[27] There are examples of Herero soldiers escorting German women and children to safety at great personal risk. In point of fact, no more than four women and one child were killed by Herero forces during the war. Many German women described their good treatment by Herero soldiers for the full period of the war, up to the German defeat of the Herero at Waterberg on August 11, 1904.

Despite this humane treatment of women and children by Herero soldiers, atrocity stories ran rampant among settlers and especially in pro-colonial circles in Germany. They contributed to the overall sense in Berlin of a national security emergency as well as the redefinition of what was a very limited colonial conflict as a "race war." Propaganda described rapes, eviscerations, breast mutilations, and murders of German women by Herero soldiers.[28] Equally destructive were propaganda images of Herero women as "castrating Amazons."[29] In fact, colonial authorities named Herero women as the most ferocious and cruel of all fighters, despite the lack of evidence that women participated as soldiers.[30] Instead, as was the case across Africa, Herero women followed behind their male family members in battle, singing songs of support and taking care of the logistics of feeding and caring for the troops.[31]

With few known exceptions, German women embraced the concept of the "race war." Lora Wildenthal describes the pervasive view among German women that "Africans had inexplicably turned on German men and women using duplicitous, unconventional methods and were never again to be trusted with any notable measure of liberty."[32] German women who arrived after the end of the genocide were even more racist, as they "took up the race war thesis and applied it to peacetime life."[33] Memoirs written by German women displayed inveterate support of General Lothar von Trotha's measures against the Herero (and later the Nama), which can be interpreted as the consequence of German women's reliance on a strict colonial race hierarchy for their position of relative power vis-à-vis African populations, and especially African women.

For the most part the atrocity stories circulating among German settlers must be seen as fabrications. Even at the time, missionaries sought to disabuse Germans in the metropole of their false—and radicalizing—impressions.[34] However, some instances of mutilation may have occurred. One missionary wrote in the Social Democratic paper *Der Reichsbote*: "Certain newspapers report that appalling atrocities have been perpetrated by the Herero, alleging that they have massacred the wives of settlers and also castrated a number of men. As far at the latter assertion is concerned, they have indeed done so in the case of whites who have raped their womenfolk in the most brutal manner."[35]

The German colonial military force (*Schutztruppe*), first under the command of Governor Leutwein and, after June 1904, under General von Trotha, responded to the initial Herero attack with typical colonial ferocity. Settlements were raided, the inhabitants murdered, and all structures burned. Because German soldiers would not distinguish between African groups, all African settlements were at risk, not just the Herero.[36] Though this approach was taken in other colonial rebellions—including in the Maji Maji rebellion in German East Africa—a distinctive feature of the Herero genocide was the comprehensive nature of orders given to soldiers. According to the memoirs of one marine who arrived in DSWA soon after the start of the war, for example, he and his fellow soldiers had been told that men, women, and children were all to be slaughtered—no one was to be left alive.[37] While there does not appear to have been an overall order to this effect from Governor Leutwein or metropolitan authorities, localized orders such as this resulted in gender-neutral massacres on the ground even before the arrival of von Trotha.[38]

Throughout the first eight months of the war the Herero sought a negotiated settlement and were encouraged in their efforts by Governor Leutwein, who believed "[i]n colonial issues there must always be a diplomat standing next to a leader. The rebels must know that their route back is still open, one that does not always lead to death."[39] However, neither General von Trotha nor the authorities in Berlin had plans to negotiate. Von Trotha wished to destroy the Herero to the fullest extent possible; in his words, "the nation as such should be annihilated."[40] He embraced a view of the war as a "race war" and conducted the conflict accordingly. When he took over the war effort in June 1904 he switched to a new policy of annihilation, one that involved defeating the Herero militarily and forcing the entire population into the Omaheke desert, where all points of exit as well as the watering holes were to be sealed off and the Herero nation starved to death.

Henrik Campbell, commander of the Rehoboth force that fought alongside the Germans at Waterberg, testified to Germany's gender-neutral policy of murder: "When the engagement was over, we discovered eight or nine sick Herero women who had been left behind. Some of them were blind. They had a supply of water and food. But the German soldiers burned them alive by setting fire to the hut in which they were lying."[41] A similar fate awaited a group of men, women, and children—all prisoners—who were confined in a small enclosure of thorn bushes. Kindling was heaped upon them and set on fire. In another instance, a group of 50 prisoners, again of mixed sex and age, were bayonetted to death.[42] Some young women were eviscerated by German troops. A baby was impaled on a bayonet as soldiers let out "roars of laughter."[43]

A Griqua African man who traveled with German troops reported that

> [t]he Germans took no prisoners. They killed thousands and thousands of women
> and children along the roadsides. They bayoneted them and hit them to death with
> the butt ends of their guns. Words cannot be found to relate what happened; it was
> too terrible. They were lying exhausted and harmless along the roads, and as the
> soldiers passed they simply slaughtered them in cold blood. Mothers holding babies
> at their breasts, little boys and little girls; old people too old to fight and old
> grandmothers, none received mercy; they were killed, all of them, and left to lie
> and rot on the veld for the vultures and wild animals to eat.[44]

During the war, women and girls were also subjected to rape in what appears to be very high numbers. One African observer testified that "[o]ften, and especially at Waterberg, the young Herero women and girls were violated by the German soldiers before being killed. Two of my Hottentots [the witness was a chief] … were invited by the German soldiers to join them in violating Herero girls. The two Hottentots refused to do so."[45]

The horror of the direct assault by German forces on defeated Herero soldiers and civilians was matched by the conditions they faced in the desert. Von Trotha made sure that the desert was sealed off and all means of escape barred. He then ordered the watering holes to be sealed and, in some instances, poisoned. Women constructed makeshift huts from branches and leaves to shelter their children. They attempted to endure the freezing nights with small fires in these shelters as well as using them to find shade from the harsh sun of daytime.

Families tried to stay together. In one instance, an emaciated married couple emerged from the desert together and approached German troops to surrender because they could no longer go on—the man's leg was badly wounded by a bullet and he was forced to lean on his wife's arm to walk. After having been given some provisions by a kindly transport driver, the couple was unceremoniously shot by German soldiers.[46] Even in the desert, Herero families were constantly threatened by German patrols, which would ambush and slaughter them down to the last child. German patrols often came upon lone children and infants, whom they murdered. Herero oral traditions tell of children who lost their mothers and of women who took care of orphans whom they found in the desert.[47] As in other cases of genocide, these stories of individual family tragedies carry the full weight of the sorrow of the crime of genocide committed against the larger group.

Eventually the imperial government in Berlin, concerned about the economic impact of von Trotha's policy as well as the reputation of Germany as a colonial power, recalled von Trotha and installed Friedrich von Lindequist as Governor. Lindequist's orders were to coax the remaining Herero to surrender. A survivor described their condition on surrender in the following stark terms: "We then had no cattle left, and more than three-quarters of our people had perished, far more. There were only a few thousands of us left, and we were walking skeletons, with no flesh, only skin and bones."[48]

Concentration camps

Surviving Herero were placed as forced laborers in concentration camps on and near the coast, and on white farms. In these camps thousands of Herero perished—they were murdered, worked to death, mistreated, and starved. Unaccustomed to the damp climate, they also died from disease at very high rates. It is in the camps that we begin to see gender differentiation in the treatment of victims. All Herero men of fighting age and Herero leaders were "systematically sought out, tried in 'courts-martial' and executed, usually by hanging."[49] Everyone else was subjected to hard labor. As had been the case throughout the war and genocide, women and girls were additionally raped in high numbers. Helmut Bley notes that rape in the camps reached "catastrophic proportions."[50] Women and girls as young as seven years old were raped, not only by the military personnel who guarded the camps but also by white civilians, who would come to the camps and take women and girls to be abused as sex slaves.[51] Starting in 1906, girls and women were also subject to humiliating internal exams, ostensibly to inhibit the further spread of sexually transmitted diseases, which had reached epidemic proportions. These examinations, which were conducted by male doctors, were so humiliating that Herero women eventually openly protested.[52]

David Olusoga and Casper Erichsen point out that not only was rape common in the camps, it was "actively celebrated." They describe a postcard that circulated at the time, one of many atrocity postcards that were popular among Germans, as depicting "a naked, adolescent Herero girl standing in a tiny shack, probably the interior of the guards' shelter … Squeezed between the girl's thighs, in an unconscious effort to retain some semblance of dignity, are the torn remains of her dress that had been ripped from her body."[53]

Missionaries in the camps were powerless to protect Herero women from sexual exploitation. In fact, when faced with evidence of rampant sexualized violence, rather than lay responsibility for it on German soldiers and civilians, the missions instead blamed the victims. One missionary wrote, "I was appalled by what you reported on the disgusting activities of the Herero women. Of course one cannot really expect anything different from these people. Even if they have become Christians, we cannot allow ourselves to forget the deep immoral dirt out of which they have come, and again and again with our love and patience we must attempt to show them the disgusting and shameful aspects of their activities."[54]

Herero women, because they were not summarily executed like battle-age men, were often left to do some of the most horrific of tasks related to genocide. For example, Olusoga and Erichsen cite evidence that women prisoners were forced to aid the research efforts of Eugen Fischer and other scientists. Among other things, they were put to work boiling the heads of dead inmates and scraping off remaining skin and eyes with shards of glass to prepare the heads for skull studies. As the authors note, these may have been the heads of the women's family and community members.[55]

The dream of one dying Herero woman, retold by Gewald, is indicative of the extent to which the struggles that women faced in the desert to keep family members alive and together followed them to the concentration camps. This prisoner told a missionary named Meier how she had seen in a dream two "spotlessly clean men" who asked her if she was ready to come with them to heaven. She told the men that she wanted to take her one-year-old child with her. Meier relates that, as the woman told him about her dream, he "saw how her sunken face glowed with inner joy." Shortly afterward, her daughter died; the woman followed within days.[56]

Conclusion

The evidence we have for the experiences of Herero and other African women during the genocide in DSWA conforms to patterns we know from the total genocides of the twentieth century, in which men and women were killed in fairly equal numbers by perpetrators who saw them as cosmic "internal enemies." The period during which von Trotha's extermination order was in effect mirrors in this respect much larger genocides of the twentieth century, such as the Armenian genocide, the Holocaust, the Cambodian genocide, and the 1994 genocide of Rwandan Tutsis. As with several of these larger scale genocides, the genocide of the Herero involved many different genocidal tactics; from direct killing, to starvation, to murder in concentration camps through hard labor and exposure.

Once the extermination order had been lifted, however, the genocidal pattern reverted to a more common and gender-selective type, in which men and boys of battle age are killed outright, and women and children subjected to sexualized violence and genocide by attrition. Like all genocides, mass rape and other forms of sexualized violence existed throughout the entire process.

The colonial nature of the genocide cannot be overlooked. This is especially true because of the sexual transgressions committed by German men, which contributed directly to the environment in which war would break out and all but ensured that what could have been a limited conflict would develop into catastrophe. A culture of impunity regarding rape of African women clearly links the genocide to the pregenocide era. German claims about Herero atrocities in 1904 were a mirror image of what they themselves had been committing and planned to commit. As is the case in many genocides, the genocidaires here—the people in the grip of a genocidal mentality—accused their victims of constituting sexual threats, as rapists and as castrators.[57] These rumors and stories helped create a sense of panic and national security crisis among Germans in DSWA and back in the metropole, reaffirming existing commitments to an all-out "race war."

The consequences of the genocide are felt up to this day in terms of continued dislocation from historical lands, long-term underdevelopment of affected communities, and memories of violence written deeply into family stories. Especially with cases of mass rape, the physical traces of genocide are present in daily reminders across many generations. Festus Muundjua, a descendant of Herero victims, for example, recently told the German newspaper *Deutsche Welle*, "I have to look at my great-grandmother every day, she looks like a German, she has green eyes." Muundjua added, "It always come [sic] to my mind, how many times was [her mother] raped, how did she feel, did anyone come to her help?"[58]

Notes

1 This chapter is adapted from Elisa von Joeden-Forgey, "Women and the Herero Genocide," in *Women and Genocide: Survivors, Victims, Perpetrators*, edited by Elissa Bemporad and Joyce W. Warren, 36–57. Copyright © 2018, Indiana University Press. Reprinted with permission of Indiana University Press. Krüger, *Kriegsbewältigung*.
2 Smith, "The Talk of Genocide."
3 Silvester and Gewald, *Words Cannot Be Found*.
4 Gewald, *Herero Heroes*, 5.
5 In 1896 there were 2,000 Europeans (including German military forces); in 1903 the population was 4,700; in 1907 it was 8,000 (excluding German military forces); and in 1914 it was 14,000. These Europeans, and especially German settlers, constituted a ruling class that controlled a population of 500,000 Africans. See Bley, *Namibia,* 73–74. The female European population is estimated to have been 306 women in 1899 and 670 in 1903. See: Kundrus, *Moderne Imperialistin*, 78n117.
6 Bley, *Namibia*, 88.
7 Ibid., 86–91.
8 Gibson, "Double Descent," 109–139.
9 Wildenthal, *German Women*, 82.
10 Silvester and Gewald, *Words Cannot Be Found*, 63.
11 Wildenthal, *German Women*, 80.
12 Ibid., 92.
13 Stoecker, *Drang nach Afrika*, 59–60; Gann and Duignan, *The Rulers of German Africa*, 145–146.
14 Reuss, "The Disgrace and Fall."
15 Sarkin, *Germany's Genocide*, 107.
16 Bundesarchiv-Berlin (BA), Reichskolonialamt (RKA) 1001 2115, Leutwein to the Colonial Department, May 17, 1904, cited in Drechsler, *Let Us Die Fighting*, 168n12.
17 *Berliner Tagwacht* 75, September 18, 1901, cited in Drechsler, *Let Us Die Fighting*, 133.
18 Drechsler, *Let Us Die Fighting*, 168.
19 Krüger, *Kriegsbewältigung*, 45; Madley, "Patterns of Frontier Genocide." See also Silvester and Gewald, *Words Cannot Be Found*, 96.
20 Silvester and Gewald, *Words Cannot Be Found*, 95–96.
21 Sarkin, *Germany's Genocide*, 110.
22 Krüger, "Bestien und Opfer," 144.
23 Gewald, *Herero Heroes*, 142–156; Schaller, "Herero and Nama," 89–114, 91.
24 Drechsler, *Let Us Die*, 150. The plaque at the foot of the Reiter statue in Namibia, which was erected in 1914 to memorialize the 1,633 Germans who died during the war, cites four German women and one child killed; Silvester and Gewald, *Words Cannot Be Found*, 101n104.
25 Gewald, *Herero Heroes*, 157.
26 Krüger, "Bestien," 148.
27 Drechsler, *Let Us Die*, 144.
28 Krüger, "Bestien," 148.
29 Krüger, *Kriegsbewältigung*, 149.
30 BA-Berlin, RKA 2089, Chief of the Army General Staff von Schlieffen to Chancellor von Bülow, December 16, 1904, cited in Drechsler, *Let Us Die*, 174n113.
31 Krüger, *Kriegsbewältigung*, 116–122.
32 Wildenthal, *German Women*, 152–153.
33 Ibid., 154.
34 Drechsler, *Let Us Die*, 146.
35 *Der Reichsbote* 69 (March 22, 1904), cited in Drechsler, *Let Us Die*, 146.
36 Drechsler, *Let Us Die*, 159.

37 G. Auer, In *Südwestafrika gegen die Hereros: Nach den Kriegs-Tagebüchern des Obermatrosen G. Auer,* bear-beitet von M. Unterbeck, 2nd ed. (Berlin 1911), 30, cited in Gewald, *Herero Heroes*, 164.
38 Dreschler, *Let Us Die*, 152; Zimmermann, "Rassenkrieg." For a discussion of the orders that German soldiers may have received at different moments in the war, see Hull, *Absolute Destruction*, 28.
39 Gewald, *Herero Heroes*, 168
40 Sarkin, *Germany's Genocide*, 112.
41 Dreschler, *Let Us Die*, 158.
42 Schaller, "Genocide of the Herero," 106.
43 Ibid., 107 and 104.
44 Silvester and Gewald, *Words Cannot Be Found*, 117.
45 Ibid.
46 Schaller, "Genocide of the Hereros," 105.
47 Krüger, "Bestien," 155.
48 Silvester and Gewald, *Words Cannot Be Found*, 177.
49 Gewald, *Herero Heroes*, 197.
50 Cited in Sarkin, *Germany's Genocide*, 122
51 Krüger, "Bestien," 154–155.
52 Wallace, "A Person," 77–94.
53 Olusoga and Erichsen, *Kaiser's Holocaust*, 213.
54 Gewald, *Herero Heroes*, 201.
55 Olusoga and Erichsen, *Kaiser's Holocaust*, 224.
56 Gewald, *Herero Heroes*, 197.
57 Cooper, "Reparations."
58 Rengurash, "Is Germany Moving."

Bibliography

Bley, Helmut. *Namibia Under German Rule*. Hamburg: LIT Verlag, 1996.
Cooper, Alan D. "Reparations for the Herero Genocide: Defining the Limits of International Litigation." *African Affairs* 106, no. 422 (January 2007): 113–126. doi:10.1093/afraf/adl005.
Drechsler, Horst. *Let Us Die Fighting: The Struggle of the Herero and Nama against German Imperialism 1884–1915*. London: Zed Press, 1980 [1966].
Gann, L.H. and Peter Duignan. *The Rulers of German Africa, 1884–1914*. Stanford, CA: Stanford University Press, 1977.
Gewald, Jan-Bart. *Herero Heroes: A Socio-Political History of the Herero of Namibia 1890–1923*. Oxford, UK: James Currey, 1999.
Gibson, Gordon D. "Double Descent and Its Correlates among the Herero of Ngamiland." *American Anthropologist* 58, no. 1 (1956): 109–139. doi:10.1525/aa.1956.58.1.02a00080.
Hull, Isabel. *Absolute Destruction: Military Culture and the Practices of War in Imperial Germany*. Ithaca, NY: Cornell University Press, 2005.
Krüger, Gesine. *Kriegsbewältigung und Geschichtsbesußtsein: Realität, Deutung und Verarbeitung des deutschen Kolonialkriegs in Namibia 1904 bis 1907*. Göttingen: Vandenhoeck & Ruprecht, 1999.
Krüger, Gesine. "Bestien und Opfer: Frauen im Kolonialkrieg." In *Völkermord in Deutsch-Südwest Afrika: Der Kolonialkrieg (1904–1908) in Namibia und seine Folgen*, edited by Jürgen Zimmerer and Joachim Zeller, 142–159. Berlin: Ch. Links Verlag, 2016.
Kundrus, Birthe. *Moderne Imperialistin Das Kaiserreich im Spiegel seiner Kolonien*. Wien: Böhlau Verlag, 2003.
Madley, Benjamin. "Patterns of Frontier Genocide 1803–1910: The Aboriginal Tasmanians, the Yuki of California, and the Herero of Namibia." *Journal of Genocide Research* 6, no. 2 (2004): 167–192. doi:10.1080/1462352042000225930.
Olusoga, David and Casper W. Erichsen. *The Kaiser's Holocaust: Germany's Forgotten Genocide and the Colonial Roots of Nazism*. London: Faber and Faber, 2010.
Rengurash, Renate. "Is Germany Moving Closer to Paying Reparations for Namibian Genocide?" *Deutsche Welle*, October 8, 2015. http://www.dw.com/en/is-germany-moving-closer-to-paying-repara tions-for-namibian-genoicide/a-18769503
Reuss, Martin. "The Disgrace and Fall of Carl Peters: Morality, Politics, and Staatsräson in the Time of Wilhelm II." *Central European History* 14, no. 2 (June 1981): 110–141. doi:10.1017/S0008938900019609.

Sarkin, Jeremy. *Germany's Genocide of the Herero: Kaiser Wilhelm II, His General, His Settlers, His Soldiers.* Cape Town: UCT Press, 2011.

Schaller, Dominick. "Herero and Nama in German South-West Africa." In *Centuries of Genocide* (4th edition), edited by Samuel Totten and William S. Parsons, 89–116. New York: Routledge, 1997.

Silvester, Jeremy and Jan-Bart Gewald. *Words Cannot Be Found: German Colonial Rule in Namibia, An Annotated Reprint of the 1918 Blue Book.* Leiden: Brill, 2003.

Smith, Helmut Walser. "The Talk of Genocide, the Rhetoric of Miscegenation: Notes on Debates in the German Reichstag Concerning Southwest Africa, 1904–1914." In *The Imagination: German Colonialism and its Legacy*, edited by Sara Friedrichsmeyer et al., 107–123. Ann Arbor, MI: University of Michigan Press, 1996.

Stoecker, Helmuth. *Drang nach Afrika.* Berlin: Akademie Verlag, 1991.

Wallace, Marion. "'A Person Is Never Angry for Nothing,' Women, VD and Windhoek." In *Namibia under South African Rule: Mobility and Containment 1915–1946*, edited by Patricia Hayes, Jeremy Silvester, Marion Wallace, Wolfram Hartmann and James Currey, 77–94. Oxford, UK: James Currey, 1998.

Wildenthal, Lora. *German Women for Empire, 1884–1945.* Durham, NC: Duke University Press, 2001.

Zimmermann, Jürgen. "Rassenkrieg und Völkermord: Der Kolonialkrieg in Deutsch Südwestafrika und die Globalgeschichte des Genozids." In *Genozid und Gedenken: Namibisch-deutsche Geschichte und Gegenwart*, edited by Hennig Melber, 23–48. Frankfurt: Brandes & Apsel, 2005.

29

VIOLENCE, ANXIETIES, AND THE MAKING OF INTERRACIAL DANGERS

Colonial surveillance and interracial sexuality in the Belgian Congo

Amandine Lauro

On February 1, 1911, for the fourth time in a few days, the Belgian Minister of Colonies was about to address the country's Parliament. The previous days had offered one of the rare moments in Belgian imperial history in which colonial issues managed to cause a very public stir[1]: the annual vote of the colony's budget had indeed generated tense debates about the challenges of the country's (young) colonial rule in the Congo. On multiple occasions parliamentarians had explicitly referred to the traumatic shadow of the first colonial regime, when the Belgian Congo was the Congo Free State, a "personal" colony ruled by Belgian King Leopold II. In 1911 this regime was still very recent history; it had only come to a close a few years before, in 1908, when the Belgian state took over the Congo and turned it into a national colony. The extreme violence of the Leopoldian era and the threat that its global denunciations had brought for Belgium's sovereignty still loomed large on every deputy's mind. Not surprisingly, the will to assert the exemplarity of the new colonial regime ran strong through their various interventions, including when addressing interracial liaisons between European colonizers and Congolese women. At the Parliament's rostrum, the Catholic Minister of Colonies, Jules Renkin, declared:

> It is not the role of the State to impose the practice of virtue upon its agents. But I make it a strict obligation to avoid the scandal and to respect the native marriage. I will not allow badly-inspired Whites to give the public the scandalous spectacle of their excesses, nor to display their housewives [*ménagères*] on their veranda in a way that would not be tolerated for a moment in civilized countries. I have said that the Whites did not go to the Congo to dwindle the moral level of the native population, but to raise it up, and I will not admit that native women are treated like lustful cattle. … Native households must be scrupulously respected and those who violate this rule—should the facts be established—will suffer the last rigors of discipline.[2]

This harangue sums up the major concerns at play in broader early twentieth-century attempts to regulate interracial sexual and domestic arrangements in central Africa: interracial relationships were cast as profoundly transgressive from a moral as well as from a racial perspective. Both their nature and their surveillance were not only "matters of intimacy" but also "matters of state."[3] Pronounced anxieties surrounded the visibility of interracial intimacies and the threat they posed for colonial "prestige," raising embarrassing questions about the "civilizing mission" and about the colonial definition of conjugal/sexual norms that underlaid it. Throughout, as historians have shown for the last three decades, concerns about interracial sex were of a deeply political character, resting at the heart of imperial governance. Despite the similarities, the case of the Belgian Congo nevertheless has its own specificities. A colonial state "born of nervousness,"[4] the Belgian Congo was marked by the unrivalled scale of its leaders' anxieties about the securitization of their authority, which translated into an insatiable quest for prestige and bourgeois exemplarity, notably embedded in obsessive discourses on the "model colony." Combined with the unique extent of biopolitical interventions[5] of a colonial power operating in close association with the Catholic Church, this helped create a specific regime of moral surveillance of (interracial) sexual encounters.

Often implicit in colonial official discourses (but no less essential) was the fact that the Belgian colonial state was born of violence. While interracial sexuality had not been a central theme of the global humanitarian campaign against the "Congo atrocities," sexual violence had nevertheless been part of the repertoire of terror and warfare deployed by the Leopoldian regime and its auxiliaries. Evidence and testimonies of sexual violence existed and percolated in pamphlets and reports.[6] They contributed to the fashioning of specific Conradian imaginaries that associated—albeit in somewhat euphemistic terms—violence and white brutality with sexual "excesses" and moral laxity. When denouncing the treatment of Congolese women as "lustful cattle" in front of the Parliament, the Minister of Colonies knew too well that these imaginaries were still part of the everyday reality of life in the Belgian Congo. Just a few weeks before, the Colonial Office had been confronted with a major criminal case involving an agent of the colonial state accused of rape, indecent assault, and arbitrary detention of several Congolese girls and women. The case was particularly sordid, as the corroborating testimonies of the victims had shown: it involved years of abuses shielded in complete impunity. In the colony, some were worried about the public scandal that an official trial would create. But in the metropole the minister thought that an example should be made. Just a few weeks before his intervention in Parliament, the minister wrote to the Governor General in Boma to "insist that everything should be done so that an irrevocable decision can be reached in this case as soon as possible."[7]

Using these two parallel reactions as an entry point, this chapter analyzes the complex conundrum of colonial anxieties and violence in the making of interracial sexual dangers in the Belgian Congo. It chronicles the surveillance of interracial relationships through ambiguous strategies combining legal measures and policing tools (both in the Congo and at the imperial level), and as sexual regulations were transgressed and transformed by various actors. In addition to addressing the specificities of the Belgian empire, this chapter also invites readers to think beyond historiographical oppositions of "state regulation" approaches *versus* "African-centered" perspectives. It shows that colonial legal and judicial interventions related to interracial sexuality operated in close interaction with the experiences, contestations, and (instrumental) investments of Congolese people, evolving along political and coercive lines to shape a distinctive racialized economy of sexuality.

A moral takeover: interracial sexual violence and the legacy of the Congo Free State

The establishment of the Congo Free State (1885–1908) by Leopold II was built on the pretense of a philanthropic mission. From the start, gender and sexuality formed an important part of this argumentation. "Civilizing" also meant delivering Congolese people from their moral wretchedness and conjugal practices that signaled "excessive" sexuality. Behind these grand declarations, however, concrete measures remained virtually non-existent and the state did little more than to cede the initiative to missionaries. The Leopoldian regime had other, more material, priorities. The brutal mode of exploitation of the Congo Free State, based on a forceful extraction of resources and labor, meant that violence was used as a common means of enforcement and repression, including against women. In addition to armed raids led by the *Force Publique* (the colonial army), Congolese women were often used as hostages by Leopoldian auxiliaries to force native men into the forests to collect rubber until they met required quotas of production; chained in the stations, women were frequently subjected to sexual abuses.

The cruelty of colonial auxiliaries often took the central stage in the humanitarian narratives that were part of the global campaign launched at the turn of the century against the "Congo atrocities." But interracial sexual violence was not completely absent from these denunciations, nor from the more diffuse "heart of darkness" imaginaries that informed international outrage. Images of drunk and brutal colonial agents who drowned their bitterness and (racial) isolation in violence and compromising relationships with African women were key in *fin-de-siècle* political and literary representations of the Congo as a site of white degeneration. In some of these narratives, violence against Congolese concubines served as the ultimate sign of the moral and psychological downfall of European colonizers. These narratives were not entirely based on fantasy. Explorers, officers, and other white colonial agents often behaved as "conquistadors."[8] In the 1920s a well-informed colonial underlined that in some regions the prettiest women were fleeing to the bush when Europeans approached a village.[9] It is well known that martial and conquest contexts create environments conducive to the emergence of particular dynamics around sexual violence, in intensifying its brutality, repetitiveness, and permissibility.[10] In colonial central Africa, as in other colonial contexts, racial discourses endorsed the "rapability" of indigenous women.[11] The (concrete) ways in which sexual violence was used as a powerful coercive technique of colonial order have been less examined. Beyond episodes of extreme violence (whether in times of war or in the zones of rubber exploitation), and while impunity was part and parcel of the construction of white male privilege, what is striking in the Congo Free State is maybe less the scope of the abuses *per se* than their absolute nonliability. The criminal case involving an agent of the colonial state accused of rape and arbitrary detention against several Congolese girls and women, mentioned above, provides a telling illustration of this.

The Lioy-Lupis case surfaced in 1910—18 months after the Congo had become Belgian—but the crimes it concerned dated from several years earlier. An Italian trained in agriculture, Pietro Lioy-Lupis had been recruited by the Congo Free State to work as a crop manager in 1905. Soon after his arrival in Sandwe, a small village in eastern Congo, he captured in unclear circumstances five young Congolese girls (only one of them had "reached puberty," as an official report underlined) and built up a fortified property encircled by a stockade to keep them in confinement. Elenga, Sialec, Mayuma, Samba, and Motuma were raped, beaten, and sexually tortured for months. When Lioy-Lupis went back to Europe in 1909 for an in-between-terms period of leave, he even infibulated Motuma to make sure she could not have sexual relations with other men. Once back in the Congo, in October 1909, he was posted to Basoko, a larger village located on the banks of the Congo River and close to Stanleyville (now Kisangani), the capital of the eastern province. He was also promoted, despite a denunciation by a European that left no trace in his career file. Once there he built another enclosed property, called back three of the women he had detained during his previous stay, and compelled another one, named Likisi, to join. Again, all of the women were repeatedly subjected to rape and torture.[12]

As historian Carina Ray has underlined, the "binary opposition between coercion and consent"[13] is not necessarily a useful one to think about interracial sexuality in colonial Africa. The line between the two is not always easy to draw in a context in which multiple unequal power relations impacted and constrained the agency of African women. Even in early colonial Congo, white officers and agents often negotiated their relationships with Congolese women with the male guardians who regulated sexual access to female dependents, especially in the case of (relatively) long-standing relationships. Many of these women were slaves and used as allegiance gifts by their communities. In another criminal case in the early twentieth century involving a Belgian magistrate accused of sexual violence, one of his *ménagères* refused to leave him because, in her own words, "I would be a slave there [in her village]".[14] But in some cases the line between coercion and consent can be easily drawn, as coercion left no space for anything else. In the Lioy-Lupis case it appears that the Italian agent terrorized not only the women but also his subordinates and the villagers. A Congolese husband who refused to send Lioy-Lupis his wife was flogged and imprisoned. Significantly, the legal case against Lioy-Lupis was raised only after a succession of denunciations (from one of the women who had managed to escape; from Congolese workers in the village; and, the determining indictment, from European colleagues who complained about the troubles resulting from his harsh management of Congolese workers and parsimonious distribution of supplies). These complaints found a receptive ear in the person of a recently appointed prosecutor, a man who had started his colonial career coterminous with the takeover of 1908 and who considered the judicial culture of impunity of the Congo Free State a dangerous threat for the maintenance and prestige of Belgian colonial rule.

This case provides but one illustration of the ambiguous meanings of the takeover of 1908 (the *reprise* in French). While the continuity of abuses and of impunity between 1906 and 1910 shows that this institutional rupture did not imply a before/after effect in everyday practices of colonial governance, the willingness of some among the magistracy and the higher levels of the colonial administration to prosecute the case and to ensure an exemplary condemnation cannot be understood without taking into consideration the ambitions of moral/sexual reform that accompanied the takeover of the Congo by Belgium. The "new" colonial authorities were particularly keen to distance themselves, at least discursively, from not only the violent but also "immoral" practices associated with the Congo Free State. They were, in short, eager to promote an exemplary version of colonial rule that prioritized commitment to the "civilizing mission." In this context, Congolese women's status and gender relations appeared more than ever as strategic sites of intervention, and measures to regulate colonized people's conjugal and sexual arrangements were planned. But these ambitions also aimed at raising the respectability of the white community. As in many other colonial contexts,[15] these enterprises were connected: colonial authorities were not only anxious about the threat that concubinage between government officers and African women could represent for white prestige and racial boundaries, but were also concerned about its negative impact on the credibility of European men as agents of the "civilizing mission." This connection appears very clearly in the official set of rules and regulations against interracial concubinage enacted in the 1910s (successively in 1911, 1913, and 1915).[16] While none of them forbade these relationships *per se*, all underlined that interracial concubinage was undermining "civilizing" efforts directed against polygamy and other native conjugal practices, all the more so when European officials blatantly abused their power (when pursuing married women against the will of their husbands, for instance).

With the takeover of the Congo by Belgium, both the visibility of these relationships and the use of violence that they often entailed appeared as features of an era Belgian authorities desperately sought to end. It is important to note that these dimensions proved decisive in the criminal cases reported for follow-up to the Ministry of Colonies. Their prosecution appeared to be less about justice for the victims than about the demonstration of the moralizing ambitions of the new Belgian colonial regime. Lioy-Lupis was, for instance, locked in pre-trial detention—an exceptional procedure for a colonizer in the Congo—on the justification that if "he repeats again his exploits on other black women" it would "give a poor example to the populations we wish to civilize."[17] In analogous cases, concerns were heightened by the publicity that could surround public scandals and trials connected to interracial sexual violence. Official anxieties ran particularly high when the cases risked being exposed in the metropole, as happened in 1913 when a European magistrate was investigated for multiple charges of sexual violence (including against children). The magistrate thought his best defense would be to blame a freemason conspiracy in an open tribune in the Belgian press.[18] But anxieties about reputation and prestige were also very much present in the Congo itself, where the colonial administration feared that interracial sexual violence, and resulting impunity, could be the catalyst for anticolonial violence.

Colonial anxieties and the making of interracial perils

In terms of interracial perils connected to sexuality, the "black peril" scares that plagued other parts of colonial Africa weighted little against anxieties about the prospect of anticolonial violence born of interracial sexual abuses by colonial agents. In the Belgian Congo this "white peril" was a driving force for colonial surveillance of and interventions in interracial relationships, a somewhat paradoxical observation given the peculiar history of violence in the colony. Belgian anxieties were not entirely misplaced in this regard. In the early 1930s the Pende revolt, the largest rural insurgency of the interwar period, while generated by the modes of labor and land and fiscal exploitation in the local palm oil industry, was also galvanized by incidents of abuse and rape of Pende women by some European agents.[19]

On a more individual level, these anxieties played a key role in the initiation of police investigations, official warnings, and even judicial procedures related to interracial relationships. This was especially the case when African people raised formal complaints against Europeans. In 1919 a letter sent to the colonial administration by a Gabonese worker who had settled in the Belgian Congo in 1906 provoked a wave of investigations and interventions. The man had denounced the departure of his wife to become the *ménagère* of a European accountant in Léopoldville (now Kinshasa). It is difficult to determine which aspect of his letter was the most worrying for colonial authorities. Perhaps it was the complainant's statement that he had alerted the French and British consuls, a move that could sharpen the long-running insecurities of Belgian rulers about foreign interference and their already tarnished international reputation. Officials might have also balked at the threatening tone of this letter, which cleverly reminded the colonial administration of its civilizing duties: "It is not reasonable that the Whites take our wives from us ... not admissible, since you are the boss, the family's patriarch." The letter also made thinly veiled threats of retaliation, warning, "Since 1906, I have never been to justice ...

but for the first time I might commit a crime, I already warned all the great leaders of the Colony ... We kill the bee for the honey, for women I will die in the Belgian Congo."[20]

In this case, as in many others, it was less the violated (conjugal) rights of Congolese men that prompted the colonial administration to act than the risk of violence against European agents and the resulting destabilization of colonial rule. But this did not prevent the agency of Congolese to play a significant role in the dynamics of surveillance and regulation that followed. In 1929 an anonymous letter from a group of self-described "Katangese Christians," and addressed to the local bishop, triggered a new ministerial circular condemning relationships between government officers and married African women. The letter complained, "The Whites of this country take away our wives and take them for their women. We ask that you turn to our King Albert to forbid whites from taking black women."[21] Again, the Minister of Colonies made sure to remind his agents that the new measures were justified on the basis that some of the most traumatizing and "bloody episodes" of insurgency in the history of colonial Congo had been caused by "abuses" similar to those "mentioned in the letter"; in the minister's own words, the letter served as a reminder of their "agonizing effect."[22]

These anxieties endured throughout the interwar period and beyond. They must also be understood in light of landmark events that seemed to "confirm" the reality and relevance of colonial concerns. In the early 1920s the famous case of Musafari François, a young Congolese domestic servant who killed a European man for having an affair with his wife, and whose public execution in Elizabethville (now Lubumbashi) in 1922 had a lasting impact on Katangese memories of colonial rule,[23] contributed to colonial authorities' responsiveness to and acute concern with the mobilizing potential of resentment born of interracial sexual affairs. The event itself did not lead to any kind of interdiction—interracial concubinage was still legally tolerated in interwar colonial society—but rather gave rise to increased vigilance if certain social, moral, and political conventions were transgressed, including the visibility of interracial relationships and the abuse of individual power. Cases in which relationships had led to jealous outbursts in public, violence against grumbling husbands or alleged lovers, and blatant sexual exploitation of subordinates' wives were increasingly regarded as threats to the order and stability of the colonial state. A case from 1927 reveals how much this kind of abuse exacerbated colonial authorities' sense of vulnerability. In Budjala, in rural Northern Equateur, a villager whose wife had been appropriated by the local Belgian administrator shouted very publicly "You kill me for my wife," while being brutally flogged. His suspicious death a few days after this episode led the Prosecutor's Office to mount an official inquiry.[24]

It must also be noted that one of the paradoxical effects of colonial authorities' responsiveness is that it could offer some legal recourse to the women who engaged in these relationships. In the interwar period, the monetary and material gains obtained from Congolese women's interracial sexual and domestic labour benefited less their families and more the women themselves, enabling them to accumulate independent wealth and to access new forms of status in the colonial order. Once again, colonial authorities feared scandals and public expressions of grievance. In 1932, Louisa Bonkosi, a woman from northeastern Congo who had settled in Léopoldville after more than ten years spent as the *ménagère* of a Portuguese trader, managed to have her claim for financial compensation heard by a colonial justice and to have her former companion dragged to the capital's Court of First Instance.[25]

With the exception of civil servants, whom administrators could discipline through various sanctions including the revocation of the official's post (the "dignity of private conduct" even became an official criterion for career progression in the 1940s[26]), colonial authorities had limited means for prohibiting interracial relationships. Immigration regulations were among

the famous film *Bongolo et la princesse noire* a few months before, managed to trigger a vast inquiry jointly led by state security, the metropolitan administration, and the colonial police. Lifela's lover had sought information about the possibility of being joined in Belgium by the Congolese actor, whom she was also planning to marry.[39]

Conclusion

Contrary to what historians have shown for other sub-Saharan contexts,[40] anxieties and contests over interracial sex did not infuse Congolese nationalist discourses. The Congolese intelligentsia that was at the forefront of the struggle for independence certainly did use gender and claims to control women's "development" to challenge the moral legitimacy of Belgian colonial rule, but (interracial) sexuality was something else. Sexuality was in fact little discussed as such in public debates among the *Evolués;* maybe in part because the racial assignation of hypersexuality had been so strong in Belgian pater/mater-nalist biopolitics, maybe in part because moral respectability remained a fundamental part of the "cultural embourgeoisement"[41] that defined both the identities and the empowerment strategies of the Congolese elite. In any case, the role played by the episodes of sexual violence in the days that followed the proclamation of independence quickly returned the topic of interracial sexuality to the top of political agendas, even if in a way that did not serve the interests of the new Congolese leaders. In July 1960 the rapes of Belgian women by mutinous Congolese soldiers offered a powerful rationale to Belgian authorities to justify the deployment of metropolitan troops in the former colony, including in front of the international community. Six decades after the campaign against King Leopold's rule in the Congo Free State, (sexual) atrocity narratives about the Congo were back, with global resonances.[42]

As this chapter has demonstrated, expressions of resentment and contestation among colonized people about interracial sexuality regularly surfaced during the colonial period. While interracial concubinage remained an entrenched and little-disputed practice in central Africa until the end of the colonial period (and beyond), coercion and violence provoked criticism and anger that were voiced through various channels, from outbursts of violence to more "formal" contexts (in letters of petition or even in colonial courtrooms). Their perco-lation in the making of colonial anxieties and even of institutional strategies, however limited and ambiguous, testifies to the complex and multiple ways in which the agency of Congolese men and women was part of the conundrum of fear and violence that defined colonial sexual politics and strategies of surveillance, and that created breaches in the foundations of the colonial sexual, gendered, and racialized order.

Notes

1 Vanthemsche, *Belgium and the Congo*, 44–45.
2 *Annales parlementaires de Belgique. Chambre des représentants*, February 1, 1911, 531. See also Vellut, "Matériaux pour une image du blanc dans la société coloniale du Congo Belge," 98.
3 Stoler, "Matters of Intimacy as Matters of State," 893–897.
4 Hunt, *A Nervous State*, 1.
5 See the landmark work of Hunt, *A Colonial Lexicon*.
6 Hunt, "An Acoustic Register." See also Mertens, "Sexual Violence in the Congo Free State"; Bur-roughs, *African Testimony in the Movement for Congo Reform*, 83 & foll.
7 Minister of Colonies to Governor General, November 11, 1910, AA (African Archives, FPS Foreign Affairs, Brussels) GG (Collection Government General of Léopoldville) (4811).
8 Arzel, "Des 'conquistadors' en Afrique centrale."
9 Salkin, *Études africaines*, 89.

10 See notably Smith, *Conquest*; Branche and Virgili, eds., *Rape in Wartime*.
11 On sexual violence and colonial contexts, see Thornberry, *Colonizing Consent*; Anderson and Weis, "The Prosecution of Rape in Wartime."
12 All information related to this case comes from the (incomplete) investigation and judicial archives kept in AA, GG (4811) and from the personal career file of Lioy-Lupis, State Archives of Belgium (SAB), Collection African Archives – Personnel of Africa Department (AA SPA) (1181) 464.
13 Ray, *Crossing the Color Line*, 5.
14 Minutes witness statement of Sulia Mafialala, November 4, 1913, judicial file J. Chaidron, AA, Collection Justice (JUST) (44A).
15 Stoler, "Making Empire Respectable."
16 Lauro, *Coloniaux, ménagères et prostituées*, 124 & foll.
17 State Prosecutor Stanleyville to General Prosecutor Boma, April 1910, AA GG (4811).
18 "La défense d'un magistrat catholique," *La Presse. Journal Quotidien*, September 12, 1913.
19 Vanderstraeten, *La Répression de la révolte des Pende du Kwango en 1931*, 118 & foll.; Henriet, "The Concession Experience Power, Ecology and Labour," 187 & foll.
20 Vincent Onangha to General Commissioner Léopoldville, December 15, 1919, AA GG (20457).
21 Anonymous to Apostolic Vicar Baudouinville (transmitted to the Minister of Colonies), January 1929, AI (Collection Native Affairs) (1395).
22 "Circulaire prescrivant de respecter l'union monogamique des indigènes," February 25, 1929, AA AI (1395).
23 Jewsiewicki, "La Mort de Bwana François à Elisabethville"; Vellut, "Une exécution publique à Elisabethville."
24 Minutes of the questioning led in Budjala, November 22, 1927, AA GG (7793).
25 The case was dealt with between February and June 1927, AA GG (21256).
26 Governor Equatorial Province to all territorial agents, February 26, 1948, AA GG (9122).
27 Ray, "'The White Wife Problem,'" 176.
28 Jackson, "'When in the White Man's Town,'" 195.
29 Levine, *Prostitution, Race and Politics*, 297.
30 Lauro, *Sexe, race et politiques coloniales*.
31 See for instance Chief Territorial Administrator Léopoldville to Urban District Commissionner, October 10, 1944, AA GG (17558).
32 This was also the case for Congolese people, as shown by Gondola, *Villes miroirs*; Martin, *Leisure and Society in Colonial Brazzaville*, 193–194.
33 Stanard, "Belgium, the Congo, and Imperial Immobility."
34 See Ray, "Interracial Sex and the Making of Empire"; Boittin, Firpo and Church, "Hierarchies of Race and Gender."
35 Anxieties about sexual encounters played a significant role in the decision *not* to deploy Congolese troops to the Western Front during the First World War. See i.a. Levine, "Battle Colors"; Lauro, "To Our Colonial Troops," 34–55; Melzer, "Spectacles and Sexualities," 215.
36 Report "Les troupes coloniales en Belgique," September 7, 1930, AA Collection *Force Publique* (FP) (2624).
37 Anonymous to General Van Inthout, August 14, 1958, AA FP (2623).
38 Colonel Darville to General Van Inthout, November 12, 1958, AA FP (2623).
39 See the political correspondence exchanged between November 1953 and February 1954 in AA GG (5950). On Joseph Lifela and his trip to Europe, see Engelen, "Een Congolees aan de Franse Rivièra."
40 Ray, "Decrying White Peril"; Jean-Baptiste, *Conjugal Rights*.
41 Tödt, *"Les Noirs Perfectionnés."* See also Mianda, "Colonialism, Education and Gender Relations in the Belgian Congo."
42 Monaville, "La crise congolaise de juillet 1960."

Bibliography

Anderson, David M. and Julianne Weis. "The Prosecution of Rape in Wartime: Evidence from the Mau Mau Rebellion, Kenya 1952–60." *Law and History Review* 36, no. 2 (2018): 267–294. doi:10.1017/S0738248017000670.

Arzel, Lancelot. "Des 'Conquistadors' En Afrique Centrale : Espaces Naturels, Chasses et Guerres Coloniales Dans l'Etat Indépendant Du Congo (Années 1880 - Années 1900)." Ph.D. diss., Institut d'études politiques, Paris, 2018.

Boittin, Jennifer Anne, Christina Firpo and Emily Musil Church. "Hierarchies of Race and Gender in the French Colonial Empire, 1914–1946." *Historical Reflections/Réflexions Historiques* 37, no. 1 (2011): 60–90. doi:10.3167/hrrh.2011.370104.

Branche, Raphaëlle and Fabrice Virgili. *Rape in Wartime*. New York: Palgrave Macmillan, 2012.

Burroughs, Robert. *African Testimony in the Movement for Congo Reform: The Burden of Proof.* New York: Routledge, 2018.

Engelen, Leen. "Een Congolees aan de Franse Rivièra. Het succesverhaal van Bongolo en de negerprinses (1952)." In *Congo in België. Koloniale cultuur in de metropool*, edited by Vincent Viaene et al., 253–270. Leuven: Leuven University Press, 2009.

Gondola, Didier Charles. *Villes miroirs: migrations et identités urbaines à Brazzaville et Kinshasa, 1930–1970.* Paris: L'Harmattan, 1997.

Henriet, Benoit. "The Concession Experience Power, Ecology and Labour in the Leverville circle (Belgian Congo, 1911–1940)." Ph.D. diss., Université Saint-Louis, 2016.

Hunt, Nancy Rose. *A Colonial Lexicon: Of Birth Ritual, Medicalization, and Mobility in the Congo.* Durham, NC: Duke University Press, 1999.

Hunt, Nancy Rose. "An Acoustic Register, Tenacious Images, and Congolese Scenes of Rape and Repetition." *Cultural Anthropology* 23, no. 2 (2008): 220–253. doi:10.1111/j.1548-1360.2008.00008.x.

Hunt, Nancy Rose. *A Nervous State: Violence, Remedies, and Reverie in Colonial Congo.* Durham, NC: Duke University Press, 2015.

Jackson, Lynette A. "'When in the White Man's Town': Zimbabwean Women Remember Chibeura." In *Women in African Colonial Histories*, edited by Jean Allman et al., 191–215. Bloomington, IN: Indiana University Press, 2002.

Jean-Baptiste, Rachel. *Conjugal Rights: Marriage, Sexuality, and Urban Life in Colonial Libreville, Gabon.* Athens, OH: Ohio University Press, 2014.

Jewsiewicki, Bogumil. "La Mort de Bwana François à Elisabethville: La Mémoire, l'imaginaire et La Connaissance Du Passé." *Annales Aequatoria* 8 (1987): 405–413.

Lauro, Amandine. *Coloniaux, ménagères et prostituées au Congo Belge 1885–1930.* Brussels: Labor, 2005.

Lauro, Amandine. "'To Our Colonial Troops, Greetings from the Far-Away Homeland': Race, Security and (Inter-) Imperial Anxieties in the Discussion on Colonial Troops in World War One Belgium." *Journal of Belgian History*, XLVIII, no. 1/2 (2018): 34–55.

Lauro, Amandine. *Sexe, race et politiques coloniales. Encadrer le mariage et la sexualité au Congo Belge (1908–1945).* Brussels: Editions de l'Université Libre de Bruxelles, 2021.

Levine, Philippa. "Battle Colors: Race, Sex, and Colonial Soldiery in World War I." *Journal of Women's History* 9, no. 4 (1998): 104–130. doi:10.1353/jowh.2010.0213.

Levine, Philippa. *Prostitution, Race and Politics. Policing Venereal Disease in the British Empire.* New York: Routledge, 2003.

Martin, Phyllis M. *Leisure and Society in Colonial Brazzaville.* Cambridge, UK: Cambridge University Press, 2002.

Melzer, Annabelle. "Spectacles and Sexualities. The 'Mise-En-Scène' of the 'Tirailleur Sénégalais' on the Western Front, 1914–1920." In *Borderlines: Genders and Identities in War and Peace, 1870–1930*, edited by Billie Melman, 213–245. New York: Routledge, 2013.

Mertens, Charlotte. "Sexual Violence in the Congo Free State: Archival Traces and Present Reconfigurations." *Australasian Review of African Studies*, 37, no. 1 (2016): 6–20. doi:10.22160/22035184/ARAS-2016-37-1/6-20.

Mianda, Gertrude. "Colonialism, Education and Gender Relations in the Belgian Congo: the Evolué Case." In *Women in African Colonial Histories*, edited by Jean Allman et al., 144–163. Bloomington, IN: Indiana University Press, 2002.

Monaville, Pedro. "La crise congolaise de juillet 1960 et le sexe de la décolonisation." *Sextant* 25 (2008): 87–102.

Ray, Carina E. "'The White Wife Problem': Sex, Race and the Contested Politics of Repatriation to Interwar British West Africa." In *Homes and Homecomings. Gendered Histories of Domesticity and Return*, edited by K.H. Adler and Carrie Hamilton, 174–192. Oxford, UK: Wiley Blackwell, 2010.

Ray, Carina E. "Interracial Sex and the Making of Empire." In *A Companion to Diaspora and Transnationalism*, edited by Ato Quayson et al., 190–211. Oxford, UK: Wiley Blackwell, 2013.

Ray, Carina E. "Decrying White Peril: Interracial Sex and the Rise of Anticolonial Nationalism in the Gold Coast." *The American Historical Review* 119, no. 1 (2014): 78–110. doi:10.1093/ahr/119.1.78.

Ray, Carina E. *Crossing the Color Line: Race, Sex, and the Contested Politics of Colonialism in Ghana*. Athens, OH: Ohio University Press, 2015.

Salkin, Paul. *Études africaines*. Brussels/Paris: Larcier/Challamel, 1920.

Smith, Andrea. *Conquest: Sexual Violence and American Indian Genocide*. Durham, NC: Duke University Press, 2015.

Stanard, Matthew. "Belgium, the Congo, and Imperial Immobility: A Singular Empire and the Historiography of the Single Analytic Field." *French Colonial History* 15 (2014): 87–110.

Stoler, Ann Laura. "Making Empire Respectable: The Politics of Race and Sexual Morality in 20th-Century Colonial Cultures." *American Ethnologist* 16 (1989): 634–660.

Thornberry, Elizabeth. *Colonizing Consent: Rape and Governance in South Africa's Eastern Cape*. Cambridge, UK: Cambridge University Press, 2018. doi:10.1017/9781108659284.

Tödt, Daniel. Les Noirs Perfectionnés: Cultural Embourgeoisement in Belgian Congo during the 1940s and 1950s. Working paper, *Sonderforschungsbereiches* 640, no. 4 (2012).

Vanderstraeten, Louis-François. *La Répression de la révolte des Pende du Kwango en 1931*. Brussels: ARSOM, 2001.

Vanthemsche, Guy. *Belgium and the Congo, 1885–1980*. Cambridge, UK: Cambridge University Press, 2018. doi:10.1017/CBO9781139043038.

Vellut, Jean-Luc. "Matériaux pour une image du blanc dans la société coloniale du Congo Belge." In *Stéréotypes nationaux et préjugés raciaux aux 19éme et 20ème siècles*, edited by Jean Pirotte, 91–116. Leuven: Nauwelaerts, 1982.

Vellut, Jean-Luc. "Une exécution publique à Elisabethville – 2 Septembre 1922. Notes sur la pratique de la peine capitale dans l'histoire du Congo." In *Art Pictural Zaïrois*, edited by Bogumil Jewsiewicki, 171–222. Québec: Septentrion, 1992.

30

LONGING, LOVE, AND LOSS IN TIMES OF WAR

South Asian sepoys on the Western Front

Santanu Das

It is a photograph which does not seem to know whether it belongs to the world of eros, ethnology, or violence, or if it connects all three (Figure 30.1). Semi-naked and wet stand the two South Asian sepoys (from Persian *sipahi*, meaning soldier), interrupted in the middle of their shower—their well-proportioned torsos and limbs uncomfortably stiff, the smooth, wet skin glistening, brows knitted, toes curled—as the camera feels their bodies, framing and fixing them in our gaze. They stand like a pair of polished statues—racialized, eroticized, awkward—in a railway station in France, against a background of uniformed European officers. The photograph, labelled "Indian attending to his ablution," was part of a series of "photographic types" by the French photographer Jean Segaud, who took them in September 1914 as the first contingent of Indian troops arrived in Marseilles and made their way to the Western Front.[1] How do we interpret these brown, semi-naked bodies—are they merely ethnological studies or objects of homoerotic gaze, or are they fantasies of "Oriental" sexuality by a beleaguered white masculinity in times of war?

Segaud's photograph of the sepoys is the fine point where an ethnological photographic project such as *The People of India* (1868–1875) by John William Kaye and John Forbes Watson meets the aestheticism and voyeurism of Edward Degas's toilette series (1886–1890). There is, however, a fundamental difference: the nakedness here is symptomatic not just of colonial power and desire but equally suggestive of wartime vulnerability, somber with our knowledge that the wholeness of form and pristineness of flesh that the photograph so openly fetishizes would soon be mangled. The "violence of representation" here paradoxically resists even as it evokes the imminent and incomparably greater real-life violence that awaits the bodies in the trenches as the two men linger before the camera, their lives momentarily extended, before the other, more fatal, exposure. But what about the experiential world of the men themselves, of their bodies as subjects?

The two Indian soldiers were part of the 1.3 million men from undivided India who were recruited into the British army for World War I.[2] Between 1914 and 1918, in a grotesque reversal of Joseph Conrad's vision, hundreds of thousands of men from South Asia, Africa, and the Caribbean and Pacific islands sailed to the heart of whiteness and beyond to take part in the horror of Western warfare. Four million non-white men were recruited into the

Figure 30.1 "Indian attending to his ablution," Jean Segaud. (Copyright: Musée de l'Armée, Dist. RMN-Grand Palais/image Musée de l'Armée)

armies of Europe and the United States during 1914–1918. Of all the colonies of the French, German, and British empires, undivided India contributed the highest number of men. Between August 1914 and December 1919 it sent overseas for purposes of war 622,224 soldiers and 474,789 non-combatants, who served in places as diverse as the Western Front, East Africa, Mesopotamia, Persia, and Gallipoli.[3] Among these various sites, it was on the Western Front that the activities of the various immigrant groups, both troops and workers, were most zealously monitored and documented, giving us rare insights into the world of interracial contact.

The relationship between non-white troops and European women has garnered the critical attention of scholars working at the intersection of two burgeoning fields: colonial sexuality and First World War studies. Historians of empire such as Ann Laura Stoler have shown how important the colonial context was for imagining the relationship between sex, empire, and European bourgeois identity: sexual contact was where the frontiers between colonizer and colonized, white and non-white were most intimately breached.[4] However, the war presented

340

an exception: rather than the white male going into the colonies and forming liaisons with indigenous women (and occasionally men), we have here an unprecedented situation of hundreds of thousands of non-white men travelling to Europe. Indeed, if World War I is being increasingly reconceptualized as the "global" conflict it was, it was also a turning point in the history of sexuality and empire. A number of scholars, particularly Tyler Stovall and Richard Fogarty, have written powerfully on interracial heterosexual liaisons, with particular reference to French colonial troops.[5] Attention has focused, to use Fogarty's succinct phrase, on "race, sex and imperial anxiety" and has followed three main lines of investigation: documentation of the nature and extent of these liaisons; the ways they were policed by the colonial state; and, above all, the "black body in white imagination."[6] While the censored letters of the non-white troops are being increasingly quoted, the personal and erotic worlds of the non-white men are seldom discussed, with discourses of power and subversion often hijacking a more intimate history of emotions from below.[7]

Taking South Asian sepoys on the Western Front as a case study, this chapter seeks to mark a departure in several ways: first, to reverse the gaze and focus on the sepoy-body and its inner world while factoring in the colonial fantasies swirling around it; second, to take a more capacious view of gender and sexuality by addressing a wider range of intimacies and emotions alongside sexual liaisons, both same-sex and heterosexual; and, third, to use these wartime examples to go beyond a strict Foucauldian paradigm and probe the relation between desire and intimacy in wartime, while being alert to the operations of power. But how do we uncover such worlds, particularly in a context where most of the soldiers did not know how to read or write and did not leave behind the abundance of documents which form the cornerstone of European war memory? In such a scenario it becomes essential to supplement official and state documents with non-conventional sources, including the visual, the aural, and the literary, necessitating a redefinition of the colonial "archive" and an interdisciplinary methodology.[8]

An intriguing, if unusual, entry point is the confiscated trench notebook of Jemadar Mir Mast. A soldier in the British Indian army, he crossed over to the German side on the night of May 2, 1915, and went on to make one of the most extraordinary wartime journeys, first to Istanbul alongside German officials as part of an anti-British *jihadi* mission, and then to Kabul.[9] When I discovered his tatty notebook in the National Archives in Delhi I was thrilled: I expected inflammatory *jihadist* and anti-colonial sentiments. Instead, it appeared that Mir Mast was primarily preoccupied with learning English in the trenches, for there was a list of words in Urdu and their English counterparts. The list was singularly colorful, ranging from the functional ("haversack," "blanket," "please") to the domestic ("hungry," "nephew," "honeymoon") to the demotic: "turnip, carrot, parsnip, potatoes, prick, penus [sic], testacles [sic], harsole [sic], cunt, 'brests' [sic], fuck, flour" (Figure 30.2).[10] It was an insight into what these young men were actually talking about in the trenches; or it may be a basic fact of language learning that we are always interested in concealed body parts. Yet, amidst the carnage of the Western Front, it was also poignant testimony to a young man's appetite for life in its incorrigible plurality, the need for food as well as for bodies to come together. Taking the cue from the notebook, this chapter seeks to investigate the world of desire in all its capaciousness, caprice, and vulnerability with reference to South Asian troops on the Western Front, by realigning it more closely to a range of wartime intimacies beyond the strict categories of gender and sexuality.

In the trenches of the Western Front, mutilation, mortality, and the strain from constant bombardment and loneliness led to searing moments of bodily contact among British soldiers in which different emotions were fused and confused.[11] C.H. Cox, an English private,

Figure 30.2 A page from the trench notebook of Jemadar Mir Mast, National Archives of India, Delhi. Foreign and Political War B (Secret), February 1916. (Private image, taken by author)

remembered how his comrade "laid back in my arms and his last words were for his mother as he died in my arms."[12] How did such moments of intensified male bonding translate across the colonial–racial divide? The letters of the South Asian troops—which were extracted, translated, and copied out by the colonial censors—are curiously silent on this topic. But silence does not mean absence. The army unit diaries can be strangely more helpful: we learn, for example, from the diary of the 47th Sikhs that, after the second battle of Ypres, a distraught sepoy, Mala Singh, ventured into no man's land to carry back a wounded comrade; a sepoy was found performing the duty of a sentry on behalf of a young and terrified boy, on whom he had taken pity; after Lance Naik Buta Sigh was killed, a patrol from his Company (No.2) went out to recover his body.[13] Above all, the photographs of South Asian troops break the silence around touch and intimacy in the colonial context. Consider the classic image of the sepoy supporting his wounded comrade as both hobble toward the nearest casualty station.

But why are such gestures of touch and intimacy, the staple of European war literature, never mentioned in the Indian letters? Perhaps emotional intimacies and bodily intensities between men were already so integral a part of the everyday homosocial continuum in Indian villages that these wartime acts, though more extreme, were not qualitatively different enough to deserve comment; or perhaps these letters—often written by scribes and meant to be read out to big groups—were too public for such private moments; or perhaps these sepoys did not have the language that the public school-educated English officer-poets had to describe their delicate feelings. Curiously, European artists, with access to the Indian camps, often capture this homosocial world, as with the British artist James McBey's enigmatic oil "A Double-Portrait of Punjabis in Campfire" (Figure 30.3), where the two men are huddled together so closely that we do not know where one ends and the other begins; or the French amateur artist Paul Sarrut's intimate sketch of two young sepoys lying together in a moment of Owenesque sensuousness (Figure 30.4). Admittedly these are European representations, but it

Figure 30.3 "Double-portrait of Punjabis at a campfire," James McBey. (Copyright: Imperial War Museum (Art 1595))

343

Figure 30.4 Ink drawing by Paul Sarrut, *British and Indian Troops in Northern France: Seventy War Sketches, 1914–1915* (Arras, FR: Delépine, 1916)

is important to go beyond the color line and an overdetermined framework of power and instead recognize that subaltern intimacies may well pulse under a European artist's brush.

Curiously, it is not from a sepoy writer but a civilian author and university teacher who had never been outside India, Chandradhar Sharma Guleri, that we have the first Indian war story, "Us Ne Kaha Thah" ("By Her Troth"), as early as 1915. A classic trench narrative about Indian sepoy experience—possibly inspired by letters of sepoys, many of whom he would have taught and whose letters he would have read out to their families—it brilliantly conjoins the world of (failed) heterosexual desire with the homosocial intimacy of the trenches. The story centers around the sacrifice of the protagonist, Lehna Singh, who saves the life of the son of his childhood beloved who is now married to another army officer; it climaxes with Singh dying in the arms of his comrade: "Bhaiyya [brother], will you please raise me a little? And place my head on your thigh."[14] Such moments are doubly significant for our purposes. Methodologically, in the absence of testimonies, literature here fills in the gaps of history, dramatizing moments that archival fragments can only hint at. Conceptually, such moments put pressure on and prise open the boundaries between sexuality and intimacy. Indeed, in times of war—as with the examples from the diary of the 47th Sikhs, the photographs, the sketches, and finally this story—the body was more an instrument of pain and vulnerability, and desire has to be nuanced, beyond the homo/hetero dyad or an explicit sexual framework, to a much broader language of non-genital tactile tenderness. Such gestures must be understood in the context of death, as a last stand of life and love against long winter nights, alien lands, and falling shells, opening up a more expansive and diffuse field of desire which impinges on other bodily needs such as reassurance, contact, and support.

At the same time, the erotic pulse was not always wholly absent. A popular song among the Pathan soldiers in the British Indian army was "*Zakhmi Dil*" ("*The Wounded Heart*"), which openly celebrates boy-love: "There's a boy across the river with a bottom like a peach, but, alas, I cannot swim." A sepoy letter, written from France in 1915, ends by saying, "Do not commit sodomy with your messmates."[15] Such warnings were not always heeded. Amar Singh, a Rajput aristocrat serving as an aide-de-camp in France, notes in his diary how he had to adjudicate on a case of alleged sodomy. Interestingly, in both cases, homosexuality is understood as an act rather than an inborn identity, but that does not mean that finer feelings did not exist. Indeed, a couple of the censored letters push the world of wartime camaraderie and casual sex into that of romance and longing. Consider the following letter sent by Dilbar in Lahore on 21 May, 1916, to Abdul Hakim Khan, 19 Lancers, in France:

> Go, my letter, and tell him that when you were leaving me I was weeping and overwhelmed with grief. Tell him that when the rain of his presence falls on me again the dust of separation will be swept away. … In the expectation of a single letter from you he is, as it were, prostrated by sickness.[16]

Or the poem included in a sepoy letter from France to a "friend" in India:

> Since the day you went to the field, Oh heart of my heart,
> From that day I know no ease …
> My soul languishes for communion with you
> And my body is like water.[17]

Both adopt the language of romance: in their self-conscious stylization and excess they resonate with much of the Urdu and Pashto love poetry, often addressed to and exchanged between men. However, such sentiments cannot be confined to the parenthesis of wartime but open up larger histories of male longing and same-sex intimacy in South Asia that scholars such as Ruth Vaneeta and Saleem Kidwai have so painstakingly recovered.[18]

But what about contact across the color line and the feelings of the British officers toward their sepoys? A number of British memoirs gratefully record critical moments of bodily contact when the sepoys had rescued their wounded officers, cradling them in their arms, dragging them to safety under fire, or going to no man's land to recover bodies.[19] A classic example is the trench diary (and a novella based on that diary) by the English officer Roly Grimshaw, of 34th Poona Horse. In the absence of an Indian trench diary, Grimshaw's is possibly the most evocative record of the Indian war experience on the Western Front in the opening months, with his detailed descriptions of Gurkhas, Sikhs, and Pathans "all limping or reeling along like drunken men, some helping an almost foundered comrade."[20] The diary is haunted by memories where violence, touch, and intimacy are compacted: when one of his men, Ashraf Khan, is badly injured and dies, Grimshaw "moved him myself and was astounded at his extraordinary lightness." Later, when a *sowar* (cavalryman) slipped into the mud, he "hauled" him out and "took the poor chap, almost pulseless, to a ruined house a few feet away, stripped him, and four of us massaged him."[21] Many of these moments make their way to his semi-fictionalised novella, *The Experience of Ram Singh,* which veers between trench memoir and imperial romance. Compare the death of Ashraf Khan in the *Diary* with its rewriting in the novella, where he becomes the young Beji Singh:

The killed was Ashraf Khan, one of the nicest looking fellows I have seen. Both his legs were blown off below the knee, and one arm, and half his face. I saw he was a hopeless case and did up the others, two of whom were quite bad. Poor Ashraf Khan, an only son, and his mother a widow. He lived for 40 minutes. I did what I could for him but, as he was unconscious, it was not much use.[22]

Lying in the bottom of the trench was Beji Singh with one leg severed at the knee, the other almost cut away at the fork. The mangled boy was quite conscious ... Smith Sahib bent close over the lad in order to administer a tabloid of morphia. Beji Singh, whose arms were uninjured, brushing aside the proffered drug, seized his Squadron Commander by both hands. Momentarily, he held him in a vice-like grip uttering the words "Sahib, Sahib," then letting go, subsided lifeless.

Covered with blood from the death grip of a young soldier for whom he entertained more than a passing regard, Smith Sahib felt strangely unnerved at the incident.[23]

What does Grimshaw gain by changing the real-life account of being a helpless witness to the fictional death embrace between Smith and Beji in the novella?

The rewriting provides subtle insights into fusion and confusion of racist, imperial hierarchies and interracial homosocial intimacies that structured the British Raj, particularly its army. At a time when some of the sepoys, thrown into the battle, were beginning to recast the British officers as "butchers," Grimshaw not only portrays the latter as the all-caring *pater* but hijacks the sepoy voice itself to wring out ("Sahib, Sahib") at the moment of death, a desperately wishful endorsement of the parental ethos which was supposed to structure the British Indian army. But rather than just an act of "going native" or over-determined by frameworks of power and knowledge, such moments, I would argue, are complex emotional flashpoints and hint at a deeper history of feeling—intensities and intimacies heightened by racial difference and hierarchies in an all-male environment—that the British officers harbored for their men but could not articulate. Such feelings, delicately fringing the text through phrases such as "a young soldier for whom he entertained more than a passing regard" or "one of the nicest looking fellows I have seen" in the diary, could perhaps only be perversely consummated in the death-grip. There might also have been a personal dimension. When Grimshaw was wounded he was carried to safety by an Indian sepoy. Is "Sahib, Sahib," with its combination of trust and forgiveness, a textual rewriting of a desired moment that never happened in real life, a fictional salve for the British officer's own seared conscience when, instead of protecting his men like a "baap" (father), he had in fact led them, like a "butcher," to their deaths?

Far more common—and better documented, because more anxiously monitored—was contact between colonial men and European women.[24] Interracial heterosexual contact was aggressively policed by the colonial governments for it was considered detrimental to the prestige of the Raj; at a more visceral level, it fanned racist fears of miscegenation at a time when the scale of devastation at the Western Front had already rendered white European masculinity fragile. The most famous case was the furore around the publication in the *Daily Mail* on May 24, 1915, of an innocuous photograph of an English nurse with a convalescing Indian sepoy at a hospital in Brighton, where several hospitals for the wounded Indians were situated.[25] The photograph became such a point of controversy that, henceforth, British nurses were either withdrawn from or used only in a supervisory capacity in Indian hospitals, with male attendants catering to the daily physical needs of the Indian patients. The very "scandal" and the policy show how integral the *izzat*, or honour of white women, and policing of touch and proximity across the racial and sexual divide was to the maintenance of the Raj. But such imperial dictate was in sharp contrast to the enthusiasm of the local people of Brighton, particularly its women, who were not immune to the charms of the sepoys; they would crowd around the hospitals and some were seen even promenading with sepoys on the seafront. In a classic intersection of race, class, and gender prejudice, the colonial state fashioned the image of irresponsible and profligate English working-class girls cavorting with sexually depraved sepoys which imperilled, in imperial eyes, the very future of the British Raj.[26] Such was the sexual panic around these encounters that fences were set up around the Brighton Pavilion Hospital and a guard was stationed outside the York Hospital.

However, the most enduring bonds were forged in France, not England, between the homesick sepoys and their aging French "mothers":

> The house in which I was billeted was the house of a well-to-do man, but the only occupant was the lady of advanced years. Her three sons had gone to the war. One had been killed, another had been wounded and was in hospital, and the third was at time in the trenches. ... There are miles of difference between the women of India and the women of this country. During the whole three months I never saw this old lady sitting idle, although she belonged to a high family. Indeed, during the whole three months, she ministered to me to such an extent that I cannot adequately describe her [kindness]. Of her own free will she washed my clothes, arranged my bed, polished my boots for three months. ... When we had to leave that village this old lady wept on my shoulder.

It was not in the world of sexual relations but in these affective dyads between the young sepoys and the elderly, bereaved French mothers that we have some of the strongest examples of colonial intimacy: affection, maternity, bereavement, and loneliness are combined (Figure 30.5).

Figure 30.5 Indian sepoys billeted with a family in France. (Collection Eric Deroo, Paris)

The sexual liaisons in France, by contrast, form a more shadowy area. Our clues are largely the sepoy letters and the increasingly alarmed notes by the colonial censors. There were no organized brothels for the Indian troops, as was the case with French colonial soldiers. Opportunities were, however, not wholly lacking, and sepoy imagination, in any case, ran riot. For many of these men, brought up in patriarchal, gender-segregated, and sexually repressive cultures of north India, the very proximity of European women—the distant and unattainable objects of colonial desire—led to a certain scurrilous interest, resulting in bizarre fantasies and homosocial boasts:

> The ladies are very nice and bestow their favours upon us freely. But contrary to the custom in our country, they do not put their legs over the shoulders when they go with a man. [Balwant Singh, from France, October 24, 1915]
>
> If you want any French women there are plenty here, and they are very good-looking. If you really want any I can send one to you in a parcel. [Umed Sing Bist, from France, November 1915][27]

While misogyny was endemic to World War I army life, the imperial dimension seemed to have added a particularly vicious edge to such imaginings; the pleasure in the above letters is as much in the narrative *jouissance* as in the act itself: "The apples have come into excellent flavours … They are ripe. We wander in the orchards all day."[28] The instrumentality that Fogarty has noted in the case of some of the French colonial soldiers—seeking sex and marriage as a route toward the acquisition of French citizenship, or regarding sexual conquest as a sort of "payback" for European colonization—does not appear in the sepoy letters. But there was no dearth of misogynistic language, refracted through a culturally specific lens; as in the following letter, which conjoins misogyny to caste politics and sexual repression in an abhorrent mirroring of European racism: "There are crowds of 'machines' here also, and the sight of them delights us, but we are ashamed to touch them lest we lose caste."[29]

In spite of official restraints on liaisons across the color line, there were clear examples of sexual contact between the non-white troops and local women in wartime France.[30] Thus, when the Indian cavalry moved in 1915 to a new neighbourhood, some letters of a "violently amatory nature" addressed to them from the French women they had left behind were intercepted and caused widespread anxiety among the colonial officials.[31] However, some of these relationships were serious, and from late 1916 the British authorities would allow the Muslims—though not the Hindus—to marry local women. The best-documented case is that of Mohammed Khan. After the love-match, he wrote the most wonderfully disingenuous letter to his furious, conservative family, bewailing his "misfortune" that the matrimony was forced upon him by nothing short of royal decree, for the girl, in whose house he had billeted, "wrote to the King in London": "But I swear to God that I did not want to marry, but after the King's order I should have got into grave trouble if I had refused."[32] The couple, it transpires, went on to have a boy. Indeed, a romantic liaison happened in my own family. Dr Prasanta Kumar Guha, a great-uncle of mine, went to France as a doctor and got engaged to a local French girl. But being a nationalist, he decided to return to India, putting country before love, though the two continued to correspond in French. When he later got married in Calcutta, the French lady sent bangles as a wedding gift for his Bengali bride![33]

While the archives only provide fragmentary clues, some of these Indo-European wartime encounters in France find their most sustained treatment in Mulk Raj Anand's war novel *Across the Black Waters* (1939). Anand worked for some time as the private secretary to T.S. Eliot and hovered on the fringes of the Bloomsbury group.[34] More importantly, he grew up in Punjab and belonged to the same agricultural–martial community as the sepoys. The novel follows the story of Lalu, a sensitive village youth, and a group of men from his battalion in Punjab who are sent to the Western Front. The novel becomes an exploration of anxious colonial masculinity as these farmer–soldiers land in Marseilles and negotiate Western culture for the first time—including a visit to the pub and brothel—before they are pushed into the trenches. Consider the following two scenes, the first from the brothel, where they are greeted by "laughter and shrieks" of heavily dolled-up women:

> The two other girls also got up and came round Lalu, talking among each other the while, even as they brushed the crumpled shiny satin dresses which they wore.
> "What are these sisters-in-law saying to each other in their own tongue?" said Subah insistent and angry. "And why don't you arrange one for me?"
> "How much money have you got?" asked the Diwan, "for the first money you gave me is finished."
> Subah fumbled in the pockets of his trousers whereupon the fat girl, who was hewn in the image of Madame, jumped on to his lap affecting an air of raped modesty, crying, "Oooi ... Oooo ... la ... la."[35]

and the second, the vague stirrings of romance:

> Hardly had he gone two or three steps when he found that Marie had come and slipped her arm into his.
> The officers and the men of the battalion were walking along the streets and, as Lalu proceeded towards the billets with the girl, he felt embarrassed. ... the sepoys were whistling, hissing and making catcalls.
> But she hung on his arm now with a pride and a childish affection that he knew would certainly be construed officially as a breach of the unwritten law that no sepoy was to be seen on familiar terms with the women in this country. And yet he felt the panic of abandon at the touch of her arm, and the pride of walking along next to her coursed in his veins, blinding him to the military and social prohibitions and weakening him in the defences which he had built up against the mire that had been stirred in India because he had dared to look at the landlord's daughter fondly.[36]

While the passages quoted above may come across as cliched, they are also extended exercises in social realism and resonate with the sentiments of some of the sepoy letters.

Both the scene at the brothel and of the innocent budding romance confront us with the relationship between desire and colonialism at the most intimate recesses of the self. In the first, there is little or no sex but a whole world of colonial anxiety. Monetary bickering, insecure masculinity, and lack of restraint turn the sexual encounter into something utterly degrading: Lalu's uncouth friend Subah tries to grab and kiss the women, and gets slapped in turn, and the whole scene degenerates into "slaps, fisticuffs, kicks." Anand's aim here is to expose Subah but it is also his comment on the double standards of Indian sexual mores: "rigid orthodoxy and custom," he writes, had forced the sepoys to "extremes of asceticism, obscenity and a mawkish sentimentality which found expression in snatches of maudlin songs or abuse."[37] By contrast, the scene with Marie is tender, acute, and convincing. Anand delves into the unwritten tactile codes across the line of color in wartime France, not just to expose racism but to show how such restrictions in turn fuel desire: Lalu's "panic of abandon" is as much a physical sensation as it is a product of racist history, the transgressive thrill of *feeling* a "white" woman on his arm and the "pride" of being *seen* with her. But he does not stop there. Anand now conjoins the hierarchies of empire with those of local feudalism as he tunnels into Lalu's pre-war adolescent years where he, a peasant's son, had rebelled against the sexual conservatism of his village society by having an affair with the landlord's daughter. The moment becomes all the more poignant when we know that it is directly culled from his personal history. Feudal and colonial histories brush against each other in the spark of that bodily contact as Anand goes far beyond a simplistic view of Indian sexuality that has European colonialism as the only point of reference.

It is indeed one of the biggest historical paradoxes that a brutal system that drafted thousands of young men from India into the killing fields of France and Flanders, and monitored their movements and actions, also resulted in the preservation of their voices and experiences, largely absent in peacetime, that helps us to assemble what can be called a more diverse "subaltern archive." Equally importantly, one must know how to approach such an archive and what questions to ask of it: the assumptions, the methodology, and the questions have often, if not always, to be different from those informing European histories of sexuality. Diversification is, after all, not decolonization nor is colonial sexuality a bloodless discursive field. World War I, in both the exceptional richness of its archives and the extreme nature of the circumstances, provides rare glimpses into the shadowy world of sexuality, intimately shaped but never wholly determined by histories of colonialism or warfare—as if race and empire could ever be the sole determinants of human desire—and in all the incorrigible plurality, messiness, and vulnerability of articulate flesh.

Notes

1 The full photographic series is reproduced in Das, *1914–1918*, 45–77.
2 *Statistics of the Military Effort of the British Empire during the Great War, 1914–1920*, 777.
3 Ibid.
4 Stoler, *Carnal Knowledge and Imperial Power.*
5 See Stovall, "The Color Line behind the Lines"; Stovall, "Love, Labor and Race"; Fogarty, *Race and War in France*, 202–229.
6 Smith, "The Black Male Body in White Imagination in the First World War."
7 A partial exception is Fogarty's discussion of French colonial experiences in *Race and War*, 208–210. Also see Das, *Race, Empire and First World War Culture*, which showcases the work of several scholars who seek to recover subaltern histories.
8 For a cultural and literary account of the Indian war experience, see Das, *India, Empire and First World War Culture.*
9 Mast, "Jemadar Mir Mast's Diary."
10 "Jemadar Mir Mast's diary," National Archives of India, Delhi, Foreign and Political, War B (Secret), Feb. 1916, 32–34.
11 For an extended treatment of this argument, see Das, *Touch and Intimacy in First World War Literature*, 111.
12 C.H. Cox, "A Few Experiences of the First World War," Imperial War Museum, 88/11/1.
13 Picton-Phillips, *47th Sikhs: War Records of the Great War, 1914–1918* (Chippenham, 1921), 88, 96, 112.
14 Guleri, "At Her Bidding" ("Us Ne Kaha Thah"), 4, 56.
15 Masters, *Bugles and A Tiger*, 213; Letter from Lal Baz (Afridi) to his brother (Frontier Constabulary, India), September 7, 1915, in Omissi, *Indian Voices of the Great War*, 99.
16 Dilbar, (Pathan), Veterinary College, Lahore, Punjab, to Abdul Hakim Khan, 19 Lancers, France, May 21, 1916, part 5, *Censor of Indian Mails, 1914–1918* (CIM), British Library, London.
17 Risaldar Nadir Ali, (Pathan), 11 Lancers attached 9 Hodson's Horse, France, to Mahomed Amir, Peshawar, NWFP, India, March 7, 1917, Part 2.
18 Vanita and Kidwai, *Same-sex Love in India.*
19 See Das, *India, Empire and First World War Culture*, 221–222.

20 Grimshaw, "Diary of an Indian Cavalry Officer," 54.
21 Ibid., 39, 55.
22 Ibid., 39.
23 Grimshaw, *The Experiences of Ram Singh*, 150.
24 See Omissi, "Europe Through Indian Eyes," 371–396; Visram, *Asians in Britain*; Markovits, "Indian Soldiers' Experience in France," 29–54; Singh, *The Testimonies of Indian Soldiers and the Two World Wars*, 65–127.
25 See Visram, *Asians in Britain*, 185–192.
26 Bardgett, "Indians in Britain during the First World War."
27 Both letters are to be found in Omissi, *Indian Voices*, 113, 114, 123.
28 From Sowar [name withheld], France, October 25, 1915, *CIM*, IOR/L/MIL/5/828/3, 448v.
29 Omissi, *Indian Voices*, 60.
30 Stovall, "Love, Labour and Race"; also see Markovits, "Indian Soldiers' Experience in France," 29–54.
31 Censor's Report, August 21, 1915, *CIM*, IOR L/MIL/5/825/4/703.
32 Excerpted in Omissi, *Indian Voices*, 299.
33 Interview with Indrani Haldar, July 2014, Kolkata.
34 Cowasjee, *So Many Freedoms*.
35 Anand, *Across the Black Waters*, 58.
36 Ibid., 236.
37 Ibid., 238.

Bibliography

Anand, Mulk Raj. *Across the Black Waters*. Delhi: Orient Longman, 1949 [1940].

Bardgett, Suzanne. "Indians in Britain during the First World War." *History Today* 65, no. 3 (March 2015): unpaginated.

Basu, Shrabani. *For King and Another Country: Indian Soldiers on the Western Front, 1914–1918*. London: Bloomsbury, 2014.

Das, Santanu. *Touch and Intimacy in First World War Literature*. Cambridge, UK: Cambridge University Press, 2006.

Das, Santanu, ed. *Race, Empire and First World War Culture*. Cambridge, UK: Cambridge University Press, 2008.

Das, Santanu. *1914–1918: Indians on the Western Front*. Ahmedabad: Mapin, 2015.

Das, Santanu. *India, Empire and First World War Culture*. Cambridge, UK: Cambridge University Press, 2018.

Fogarty, Richard S. *Race and War in France: Colonial Subjects in the French Army, 1914–1918*. Baltimore, MD: Johns Hopkins University Press, 2008.

Grimshaw, Captain Roly. *Indian Cavalry Officer, 1914–1915*. Southborough, UK: Costello, 1986.

Guleri, Chandradhar Sharma. "At Her Bidding ('Us Ne Kaha Thah')." *Indian Literature* (Literary Bi-monthly), XXVII, no. 102 (July–August 1984): 40–50.

Markovits, Claude. "Indian Soldiers' Experience in France." In *The World in World Wars*, edited by Heike Liebau et al., 29–54. Leiden: Brill, 2010.

Mast, Mir. "Jemadar Mir Mast's Diary." *Cultural Exchange in a Time of Global Conflict*. Accessed June 30, 2020. http://sourcebook.cegcproject.eu/items/show/178

Masters, John. *Bugles and A Tiger*. London: Michael Joseph, 1956.

Morton-Jack, George. *The Indian Empire at War: From Jihad to Victory*. Cambridge, UK: Cambridge University Press, 2018.

Omissi, David, ed. *Indian Voices of the Great War: Soldiers' Letters, 1914–1918*. London: Macmillan, 1999.

Omissi, David. "Europe Through Indian Eyes: Indian Soldiers Encounter England and France, 1914–1918." *The English Historical Review* 122, no. 496 (April 2007): 371–396. doi:10.1093/ehr/cem004.

Picton-Phillips, D.B. *47th Sikhs: War Records of the Great War, 1914–1918*. Chippenham, UK: Picton Publishing, 1921.

Singh, Gajendra. *The Testimonies of Indian Soldiers and the Two World Wars: Between Self and Sepoy*. London: Bloomsbury, 2014.

Singha, Radhika. *The Coolie's Great War*. London: Hurst, 2020.

Smith, Richard. "The Black Male Body in White Imagination in the First World War." In *Bodies in Conflict: Corporeality, Materiality and Transformation*, edited by Paul Cornish and Nicholas Saunders, 39–52. London: Routledge, 2013.

Statistics of the Military Effort of the British Empire during the Great War, 1914–1920. London: His Majesty's Stationary Office, 1920.

Stoler, Laura Ann. *Carnal Knowledge and Imperial Power: Race and the Intimate in Colonial Rule.* Berkeley, CA: University of California Press, 2010.

Stovall, Tyler. "The Color Line behind the Lines: Racial Violence in France during the Great War." *The American Historical Review* 103, no. 3 (June 1998): 737–769. https://doi.org/10.1086/ahr/103.3.737

Stovall, Tyler. "Love, Labor and Race: Colonial Men and White Women in France During the Great War." In *French Civilization and Its Discontents*, edited by Tyler Stovall and Georges Van Den Abbeele, 297–323. Lanham, MD: Lexington Books, 2002.

Vanita, Ruth and Saleem Kidwai, eds. *Same-sex Love in India: Readings from Literature and History.* London: Palgrave, 2000.

Visram, Rozina. *Asians in Britain.* London: Pluto Press, 2002.

31

SEXUAL RESTRAINT, SUBSTITUTION, TRANSGRESSION, AND EXTREME VIOLENCE ACROSS THE LATE-COLONIAL DUTCH EAST INDIES AND POSTCOLONIAL INDONESIA

Esther Captain

"We have discovered something we never could have imagined. We have 'faggots' in the camp … This is tempering the mood of the 'real blokes.' It's a shame."[1] These sentences were written by Jack Scholte, a married Dutch man, 30 years of age, living in the Dutch East Indies. He was employed as a police inspector at the Political Intelligence Service of the Dutch colonial regime. In 1942, during World War II, Japan occupied the Dutch East Indies and interned all Europeans in POW or civilian internment camps. Women and men were put in separate camps, with children staying with their mothers. When boys reached the age of 16 (later this age was lowered to 14, 12, and, finally, to 10 years) they were transferred to a men's camp. In his wartime diary, Scholte commented on daily life during internment and among his notes was the discovery of same-sex relationships in the men's camp. It is not clear from the quote whether these men identified as being gay or if they simply pursued eroticism with other men, perhaps for short periods of time. What is clear from the quote, however, is that Scholte was strongly repelled by this "discovery."

In the 1940s, sexuality in the Netherlands and the colonies was usually not openly discussed by Dutch men and women, with homosexuality in particular at the margins of society and discourse. Most diaries are intended for private reflection and therefore this genre of personal writing opens up the possibility of encountering themes that society considers shameful, forbidden, or taboo.[2] Scholte's wartime diary is an illustration of this, with homosexuality featuring as one of the topics in his journal. He wrote the following entry about an adult male that engaged in unspecified sexual acts with a 16-year-old boy: "It is such a shame that it is impossible to do something—but my professional duty screams for the retribution of such a bastard that is leading children into perdition for mischievous self-indulgence."[3] We do not know how Scholte learned of the relationship between the adult male and the boy: did he witness it himself or did he hear about it? A later entry in his diary shows that he again ascribed negative qualities to homosexuality, suggesting that homosexuals were probably responsible for leaving feces in the shared bathroom of the men's camp: "Perhaps it was the horniness and exaggerated carnality of a couple of homosexuals, in other words faggots, that want to express their pleasure this way."[4]

Camp diaries written by internees during the Japanese occupation (1942–1945) of the Dutch East Indies are a genre of their own, as are the camp memoirs that were published after the war. These diaries and memoirs reflect a world into which humans were forced to live during the years of the Japanese occupation based on the following categories of distinction: race, gender, and age. For the Japanese occupier, segregation by race served to remove European influence out of Southeast Asia in order to create a Greater East Asia Co-Prosperity Sphere. Therefore the Japanese army and administration in the Indies literally isolated Europeans (as well as the small mixed Eurasian population group outside the main island of Java) from Indonesian society by putting them into internment camps. European men and women were further separated along gendered lines into men's and women's camps. But age could scramble the gender divide, with young boys under the age of 16 as well as retired men put into women's camps, since they were no longer considered active professionals. Thus race, gender, and age were the leading criteria used by the Japanese rulers to categorize persons in the Dutch East Indies. On Java, where the majority of Eurasians lived, the Japanese expected the Eurasian population group with (albeit partly) Asian descent to blend in with the Indonesians.

It was not that hierarchic categorizations were new in the Indies colonial society: indeed, the Dutch colonizer applied race and gender as dividing principles from the start of their rule, but with Europeans on top of the racial hierarchy. The Japanese occupation of the Dutch East Indies turned the system of colonial hierarchies suddenly and completely upside down by putting Europeans on the lowest societal rank in a racially homogeneous and gender-segregated environment. Camp diaries and memoirs can be considered testimonies of how internees reacted to this reversal. As academics, we are used to applying analytics of race, gender, age, and class for intersectional analyses. While doing this it is crucial not to forget that these categories are related to embodied experiences of human beings, connected to pleasure and pain as well as the (im)possibility of climbing the hierarchical ladder.[5] Sexuality and its regulation guided the everyday practices and overarching ideologies of colonial rule. Research into the creation of colonial societies shows that, in order to create and maintain racial hierarchies, strict control and policing of intimate interactions, relations, sexuality, and reproduction was thought to be paramount.[6] Studies into the connection of homosexuality and imperialism indicate that (European) homosexuality, though disapproved of in the metropole, could still find expression in colonial lands such as the Dutch East Indies.[7] At the same time, we must note that while there were some safe spaces for gay men (and lesbian women) in the Indies and in Indonesian daily life, same-sex desiring individuals were not fully accepted as members of society.[8] Scholte's diary, showing the rejection of homosexual presence and acts, is exemplary of the attitude of Europeans at that time.

In this article I will examine cases of sexual restraint, substitution, transgression, and extreme violence across the spectrum of the Dutch Indies colonial society, the Japanese occupation, and independent Indonesia. This article charts the centrality of sex to the colonial order, its ultimate inversion in the internment period, and, finally, to the violent end of colonial rule. This temporal framework is important, as we cannot understand sex in any one of these contexts without attention to the other. The Japanese occupation and the internment of the European population was the beginning of the end of Dutch colonial rule. Two days after the surrender of the Japanese army, on August 15, 1945, Indonesia proclaimed its sovereignty as an independent nation, only accepted by the Netherlands in December 1949 after four years of aggression, conflict, and war, with outbursts of extreme (sexual) violence on display from both Dutch and Indonesian sides. For each consecutive period of time—the late-colonial Dutch East Indies (1900–1942), the Japanese occupation (1942–1945), and the Indonesian war of independence (1945–1949)—I will analyze sexual politics and practices that oscillate between restraint, substitution, transgression, and (extreme) violence.

Although Europeans had been present in the Indies since the seventeenth century, only from 1900–1942 was a Dutch colonial settler society established. The founding of colonial rule was accompanied by mass violence; more than killing, mass violence "also refers to other forms of coercion and deprivation, such as mass flight, forced resettlement, large-scale deprivation through hunger and epidemics. These are the standard ingredients of Dutch expansionism in the archipelago, from its inception to the end."[9] In view of the mixed-race society that originated from contact between Dutch and Indonesians, in the 1980s historians introduced the concept of the "melting pot" to describe the early colonial era.[10] This seems an adequate description as long as it includes awareness that the Indies was not an idyllic place; relations between the population groups were structurally unequal. Before 1900, fluidity was the norm in the Indies, with European men living together with Indonesian women, starting families, and having Eurasian children. More often than not these relationships were unequal, with Indonesian women living as concubines who could be expelled by their "master" at any time, leaving Eurasian children who were born out of wedlock vulnerable if they were not recognized by their father. Violence was implied throughout the colonial epoch. It included the brutal corporal punishment of enslaved Indonesians at coffee, tea, and cacao plantations as well as in domestic settings, where Indonesian women might also be made to serve as sexual servants.

From 1900, European colonial rulers wanted to modernize the colony. New technological advances such as the creation of the steamship, which made the journey from Europe to Asia much shorter and safer, allowed the introduction of European women to the colony. The ambition of the Dutch colonial government was to establish a separate, white European community in the Indies. Sexual restraint was one of the strategies employed to achieve this supposed modernization of colonial society: European males were expected and encouraged to marry European women and to keep their distance from Indonesian women. Within this modernized racial constellation, Eurasians were present as visible markers of transgression. For Europeans, the biggest fear was to "become Indonesian" (*verindischen*), synonymous with descending to the level of natives. The leading principle for both Europeans and Eurasians was to be as white and European as possible.[11] Achieving "Europeanness" meant being civilized, and the effort to perform European belonging engulfed literally all aspects of life, from physical appearance, hairstyle, food, clothing, and language to choice of friends and friendships, spouses, housing, work, and school. One of the perverse and similarly violent aspects of the colonial system was that all citizens and subjects were to be judged upon these criteria, Indonesian subjects included. As Indonesian subjects could not physically *be* European, the motto was: *act* as European as possible. This also applied to Eurasians who could not easily pass as white because of their outward appearance.[12] Sexual politics were part and parcel of this aspired white European identification: desire in sexual orientation was to be streamlined not only within one's "own" racial group but also according to heteropatriarchal norms. Same-sex desire, relationships, and practices were fiercely rebuked, spurring arrests, prosecutions, imprisonments, dismissals, and several suicides of (suspected) gay European men in the mid-1930s.[13] Same-sex desire among women was virtually unthinkable for European authorities and was therefore invisible to legal or social scrutiny.[14]

Crucial for understanding colonial hierarchies and structures is the insight that neither the colonizer nor the colonized were totally divided in separate spheres, even though the distancing of the groups provided the basis of the colonial system and the ideology that underpinned it. In daily practice the distinction between colonizer and colonized was flexible, and meta-morphosed over time as circumstances themselves changed.[15] Because of the fluidity of boundaries between Europeans and Indonesians, with Eurasians as "trespassers" in between, it was of utmost importance to control the boundaries of belonging.

The need to control one of those boundaries, that of sexuality, can therefore be found in Japanese internment camp diaries, as these writings reflect how internees dealt with the shock of the reversed societal order. One of the ways that Europeans sought to anchor themselves in this otherwise unmooring experience was to stick to the former colonial social order, in which "being civilized" was one of the key elements of being European. There was an "enormous cultural chasm between European virtues, on the one hand, and the supposed lethargy and promiscuity of indigenous society, on the other."[16] Sexual restraint was thus to be performed by the internees as a key element of European identification. Within the context of internment, this resulted for most people in sexual abstention, as spouses were separated from each other. Concerns about how to deal with sexual feelings in the absence of a partner can be found in the early years of the diaries, when circumstances in the camps were not yet too harsh. However, when internment continued and illness and death occurred and continued to increase due to starvation, exhaustion, lack of medicine, neglect, and willful bad treatment by Japanese camp guards, mentions of sexual feelings disappeared from the internee diaries. Jack Scholte wrote he had "no or almost no sexual inclinations anymore" due to "the lack of energy in our food, not being in a civilized (non-vulgar) environment … and not being able to set eyes on feminine beauty."[17]

For now I would like to focus on the earlier period of internment, when entries about sexuality could still be found. As we have seen, Scholte adamantly rejected homosexuality. Diaries of other internees similarly refuse or denounce homosexual acts. For example, Adriaan Kruyt, a married Dutch man, 38 years of age, wrote in his journal: "Requests are being made to drive around the camp boys, if they are playing around in the bathrooms, because of unwanted acts."[18] This may be read as a dismissal of sexual acts in general, as they were performed by underage children ("boys"), and a rejection of homosexual acts in parti-cular. Kruyt's diary shows how interned men were putting homosexuality in the camps in a heteronormative framework, as can be found in an entry where he was writing about adult males chanting the following song: "We are the homosexuals, we don't care about women anymore, we are what the brothels fear." (In Dutch: "*We zijn de homosexuelen, ons kan de vrouwtjes niets meer schelen, wij zijn de schrik voor de bordelen.*") This quote opens up ways for understanding the multiple responses to internment. First, it reaffirms heteronormativity by contextualizing perceived homosexuality in what I would call sexual substitution: the origin of same-sex desire is the lack of women in the segregated internment camps, not a natural desire of men for same-sex companionship—men are thus substitutes for women as the nat-ural objects of desire. Second, it points to all kinds of pursued (or confused) pleasures in camp life. In a context of death, brutality, and uncertainty, some men are seen here to not just be rigorously guarding sexual virtues but to be flouting them openly and in carnivalesque fash-ion. By and large there was a spectrum of responses to deprivation and suffering during internment: one that involved a kind of sexual asceticism, another where all taboos and social norms could be broken (at least temporarily) in the exceptional setting of the camp.

Sexual substitution is also found in the diary of Elisabeth de Jong-Keesing, a married Dutch woman, 31 years of age. She is the only author of the corpus of diaries that I have analyzed who wrote about affective and sexual relations between female internees in the camps. She wrote about "two women who had found each other" and comments: "I just walked into them unsuspectingly. I do not believe it happened a lot. For the one it was out of need for support, for the other it was about protection. It was quite moving even."[19] Interestingly, de Jong-Keesing added a remark in a typed transcript of her diary in 1949, in which she commented that sexual relations between women and girls in the camps did exist but were not explicitly mentioned, nor even remembered, as such:

> I have once found two women in each other's arms; the one I knew was a restless seeker of tenderness, the other was an older helpless idealist: I thought it was not a bad idea for these two and I completely forgot about it immediately afterwards. There are stories about … a number of older women who looked for relief with younger girls. But I do not think it happened often, neither in talks nor in practice—as far as I know. In hindsight, I believe there was more female tenderness, especially among a certain group that I (at least) knew well.

Same-sex desire among women is thus not perceived as a desire on its own, but as substitution for the lack of men as partners and, as such, as a form of "relief." It can be read as an effort to contain the transgression of sexual boundaries by putting forward the suggestion of sexual substitution as a reason for temporary slippage, which ultimately sustains the heteronormative framework of sexuality. But it is also possible, as de Jong-Keesing admits when scrutinizing her own memories, that "female tenderness" occurred not because of a lack of men but that it grew out of autonomous emotions and desires for female relation and partnerships.[20] Should we be looking for the nature of these liaisons, phrased in the words of women themselves and outside European and heteronormative frameworks of interpretation, we may perhaps find that it was easier for a female internee to find a lover or partner in a women's camp, more possible to sustain such a relationship, and less necessary to hide it. Striking in the passage cited is the gendered language that de Jong-Keesing used, highlighting tenderness and emotional depth—ascriptions that in the 1940s more often applied to women than to men. By contrast, according to Adriaan Kruyt's diary, men sang in a bawdy fashion about suddenly becoming homosexuals. These gendered expectations of tenderness for women might have also enabled these kinds of relationships or made them less worthy of comment in women's diaries. The presumed absence of female desire (which made same-sex desire among women practically unthinkable in a wider European society) allowed, however paradoxically, for a more tacit acceptance of closeness, which may have been undetectable or imperceptible for some.

As previously stated, same-sex relationships within colonial society were rebuked, with rationale varying from accusations of being uncivilized to interpretations of homosexuality as a sign of weakness and degeneration. If, at least ideally, Europeans had to conform to a heterosexual identification, it comes as no surprise that (Eur-)Asians were often described as more prone to sexual aberrations, of which homosexuality was one supposed "symptom." Remarkably, the diaries also show a different attitude toward behavior that could be labeled as homosexual. In particular, same-sex acts were not rejected when they concerned the Japanese soldiers who guarded the camps. The diary of Frits Bos, a 27-year-old unmarried Dutch man, shows astonishment at how Japanese soldiers did not share feelings of shame about (seeing) naked human bodies and touching each other: "[They] urinate just like that in a ditch, and in public they loosen the swaddling-bands around their bellies and find it necessary to shake up the released parts; I saw two (Japanese) blokes with their arms around each other's neck, just like that around their other comrades, they also touched each other's genitals."[21] His diary suggests that this encounter with people of Asian descent—who, unlike Indonesians and Eurasians, were perceived as a distant enemy—could also function as a mirror. Bos's diary entry shows incomprehension and astonishment as reactions toward the behavior of Japanese men that he had not encountered before. This reaction may well be explained by the intersection here of sexuality and race. Whereas homosexual behavior was to be rejected when it was related to Europeans, supposedly aberrant sexual behavior was already assumed to be a part of the incomprehensible identity of the Japanese enemy—just as it was for Eurasians and Indonesians that were more familiar to Europeans but whom they considered of a lesser moral standard. Therefore it might have been less urgent to condemn it, quite unlike alleged homosexual acts among European men.

The encounter with the Japanese occupier came in other forms as well, especially in the women's camps. Female internees were controlled by a Japanese camp commander and secured by Japanese, Korean, and even some Indonesian camp guards. Though most female internees tried to avoid interaction with Japanese guards as much as possible, contacts between imprisoned women and Japanese guards did exist and could include sexual encounters. Women might have used these contacts to their "benefit," although this must always be contextualized against the background of war, where ensuring one's survival as well as the survival of one's children or other relations could serve as reason to engage in sexual exchanges. A concept such as "voluntary" or "consensual sex" is thus almost impossible to maintain within the context of confinement and physical and mental deprivation. Internees' diaries mention cases in which women approached Japanese guards for food or other goods, and cases in which they did not reject solicitations from Japanese men. Mary Brückel Beiten, a married Eurasian woman, 38 years of age, wrote disapprovingly of these women: "There are those [women] who lose their prestige because of a cigarette and who engage in more than friendly relationships with the agents."[22] She also writes about a Japanese man who was acquainted with a fellow female internee: "In the camp it is said that he is in love with Mrs. R. After a week, two blocks of gown fabric are brought to her, as well as cigarettes and butter and matches. She accepts everything."[23] Sometimes this mode of survival was accepted by other internees, but most of the time a relationship with a Japanese man was very sensitive as it was considered to be a form of cooperating with the enemy. In a women's camp in Jakarta, a European woman gave birth to the child of a Japanese man. The Japanese camp commander honored the occasion by treating the internees to two pigs to be slaughtered and eaten. Fellow internees, however, disapproved of the birth of the Japanese-European baby, and, despite the hunger in the camp, one woman refused to consume the meat: "For all others, the temptation to finally get some extra food was too strong, so we feasted in honor of the newest slit eye, who was popularly baptized *'foetsie moet-ie.'*"[24] This nickname, which loosely translates into English as "has-to-go," combined with the denigrating epithet "slit eye," clearly shows that mother and baby were scorned because of the transgression of sexual barriers between a European woman and the Japanese enemy.

Another form of transgression was the case of forced prostitution of women of both European and Asian descent by the Japanese army. The euphemism of "comfort women" has long been used to describe women and girls forced to serve in military brothels set up by the Japanese army. In these brothels, women were raped repeatedly on a daily basis and, if they became pregnant, forced to undergo abortions. The fear that women could be violated by the enemy can be considered a universal theme in wartime diaries, regardless of the gender of the author. Diaries within the corpus that I have analyzed confirm this, although I have not found authors who wrote that they themselves had been victims of rape or forced prostitution at the time.

It was decades later, in the 1990s, that a number of women spoke out in public statements and in published memoirs about what had happened to them. Even in the postcolonial era, racial background turned out to be a decisive element in the reception of these voices. In the Netherlands, two Eurasian survivors entered the public realm with their own experiences. Their mixed origins were unnoticed or misconstrued, as the media introduced one of them as the first "Western" victim of the Japanese system of army brothels.[25] Dutch media attention to her story increased, while the stories of Korean, Chinese, Indonesian, Philippine, and also Japanese survivors were still largely ignored. Apparently, interest was heightened by the discovery that European—or in this case Eurasian—women were victims, indicating that sexual violence was "interesting" enough if it also involved the transgression of racial and (former) colonial boundaries.

Other forms of transgression became apparent during the Indonesian Revolution—a period of extreme sexual violence. On August 15, 1945, Japan surrendered to the Allied forces, which formally put an end to World War II. The defeat of Japan, however, was not followed by a period of sustained peace. Two days later, on August 17, 1945, Indonesia proclaimed its independence as a sovereign nation; it was no longer a Dutch colony. For virtually all Dutch men and women, both in the metropole and in the former colony, the proclamation of the Republic of Indonesia came as a surprise. As the Netherlands refused to acknowledge this claim, conflicts and hostilities between the Dutch and Indonesians soon emerged. Every person who could obstruct Indonesia's independence became a target of violence, which included not only the Dutch but also fellow Indonesians who were part of the former colonial government or army. Members of the Chinese population group were also victims. Indonesian freedom fighters especially attacked Eurasian men and women, whose mixed ancestry raised questions about their loyalty. It seems that Eurasians were considered by Indonesian fighters as "'the enemy within', those who might transgress the 'interior frontiers' of the nation-state, who were the same but not quite, potentially more brazen in making claims to an equality of rights with 'true' Europeans, but always suspect patriots of colonial rule."[26] It does explain the particularly excruciating forms of violence against Eurasians, which will be discussed in more detail below.

While violence in itself is disturbing enough, descriptions of the early phase of the Indonesian Revolution (also known in Dutch history as the Bersiap period, which was the Indonesian call to arms and translates as "get ready" to attack) testify to the gruesome character of violence. Typical for the Bersiap period was the use of self-fabricated weapons, such as bamboo spears, bats, clubs, and machetes.[27] Even more unsettling is the observation that extreme sexual violence occurred often during the Bersiap period. Again, stories by eyewitnesses and survivors are scarce on this topic and descriptions often veiled, as we have already seen with the case of rape and forced prostitution. Yet other kinds of sources in military archives, including egodocuments of (former) military men, have offered irrefutable testimony about extensive sexual violence. Before turning toward diaries again, I will use two key historical studies to indicate how historians have written about this epoch. The most recent study, by Rémy Limpach from 2016, is also the most explicit about the nature of violence. Indonesian nationalists are reported to have killed (Indo-)Europeans, Chinese, and Indonesians (the latter suspected of collaboration with the former colonial rulers): "Victims were mostly cuffed and stabbed, while perpetrators also cut off the breasts of women and girls." Other atrocities included "beheadings with Japanese samurai-swords, persons being buried alive and countless cases of rape, also of young girls … even babies with hands and feet cut off, children with cut off noses and ears and castrated boys."[28] The sexual component within these cases of extreme violence is striking and is also found in the following horrific list of tortures: "Among some victims that were still alive, the head was chopped off or the heart was ripped out, while a number of young men inserted spears in the genitals of Dutch women and chopped off the limbs of boys, who were [left] bleeding to death."[29]

An earlier study, by Herman Bussemaker from 2005, wrote about the cruelties as well: "They cut off limbs and breasts, and in some cases chopped their victims into pieces … *Pemoeda* [young Indonesian freedom fighters] … raped a fourteen year old girl and then nailed her to a tree. The husband and baby of a Eurasian couple were killed."[30] More accounts testify to the extreme violence against Eurasians who were reportedly found mutilated: "Especially Eurasian girls and women were terribly mauled before they died … Every day, corpses of women and children were floating in the Tjiliwoeng [a river in the capital city of Jakarta]. … In the Ancol-canal [also in Jakarta], two naked Eurasian girls were floating, nailed on doors."[31] While it is possible to extend this list by citing additional historical works, it is not my intention to create a cabinet of horrors within this article, although the reality was undoubtedly truly shocking and horrifying. By providing these citations it is my goal to try to interpret the interplay between the various elements that are at stake in the display of extreme violence, and sexual violence in particular—and this analysis is not only helpful to better understand these forms of violence during the Bersiap period but also in the colonial era, as violence was endemic and systematic in colonial society too.

Turning back to wartime diaries and memoirs, I found two more or less implicit descriptions of sexual violence. First, there is the diary of L.R. Oldeman, which contained letters to his family in the Netherlands. On March 30, 1946, he wrote in his letter: "…a Eurasian man that escaped the battle in the South of Bandoeng told the most gruesome stories about what had happened there. He estimated the number of murdered, slaughtered persons [as] at least 500. It was a sadistic, completely insane mess."[32] It is important to note that this was not witnessed by Oldeman himself, but is a hearsay account. Second, there is a memoir written in 1948 (which is relatively soon after the Bersiap period, though the memoir itself was published in 1984) by M. Moscou-de Ruyter, a Eurasian woman who experienced the Japanese occupation outside the internment camps. She wrote about a friend who had told her about cruelties that occurred during the Bersiap period: "Mrs. de Neve had heard about a European missionary family, consisting of a husband, wife, grandmother, and three children, who, together with a number of dogs, were all buried alive in a hole. … as were European women after having been violated, slaughtered."[33] Again, we are not dealing with first-hand testimony here, but an indirect testament to the cruel violence. Though these statements are indirect, they are to be considered as reliable testimonies collected by the Governmental Institute for War Studies (*Rijksinstituut voor Oorlogsdocumentatie*) shortly after World War II, which should lead us to treat these cases seriously. Why is it that these accounts of Bersiap violence are by proxy? One reason might be very harsh: that the "true witnesses" who experienced these forms of extreme (sexual) violence did not survive, but perished.[34] Another reason might be that extreme wartime (sexual) violence is deliberately used to denigrate whole communities beyond the immediate victim; in that sense, it can be considered as a "spectacular" form of violence. Above all, it seems, violations of women signaled to male combatants as well as male citizens that they would lose the war since not only women but men, too, were humiliated. They could not protect "their" women against the threat of the enemy. The accounts of Oldeman and Moscou-de Ruyter, which were based on hearsay, may be read as a confirmation of the performance part of this particular kind of violence: one did not necessarily have to experience it in order to relay it, as this was, in part, the point.

Reflecting on sexual violence in a different decolonization context, historian Raphaëlle Branche concluded, "Through the knocked-about, violated, raped woman, military men targeted her family, her village, and every community to which she belonged, including the most important: the … people."[35] As such, sexual violence did not only function to humiliate or shame anti-nationalist male combatants during Indonesian independence. Indeed, sexual violence during the Bersiap period signaled a symbolic and a real break with the colonial period. In the Dutch as in other European empires, the white woman was supposed to be the inviolable object of empire and any threat to white female chastity (or racial purity) could signal wider problems for the empire. The sexual violence of the Bersiap period overturned the expectations of colonial society, where white men often slept with Indonesian women and expected the passivity of Indonesian men. Meanwhile, unions between white women and Indonesian men were practically off limits. The sexual violence that occurred during the Bersiap period thus cannot be understood without attention to the originary violence of colonialism itself, where the bodies of Indonesian subjects were (literally) subjected to a strict system of regulation and prohibition. Not least because of the attention devoted to sexuality by European colonists, sexuality once again featured as a marker of the overturning of the colonial order[36]—as both a symbolic break with the ideologies of colonial rule and as a violent, material rejection of the colonial system meted out upon the bodies of colonizers or those suspected as their collaborators.

While providing this conclusion, it is important to note that sexual violence is not reducible to just one logic. Many wars degraded into ever more radicalized forms of violence as they continued. The Indonesian war of independence was in some respects "new" as it was the first time that Indonesians took up arms to defend their proclaimed sovereignty, but it came after years of tremendous wartime and colonial hardship during the continuum of Dutch and Japanese occupation. Moreover, sexual violence featured broadly in decolonization struggles and Europeans were by no means the only ones victimized; Europeans fully participated in it, too, as research into other decolonization-era struggles, such as in Algeria and Kenya, reveals.[37] Recent scholarship by historians Stef Scagliola and Natalya Vince compared rapes committed by European militaries during the Indonesian war of independence (1945–1949) and the Algerian war of independence (1954–1962).[38] Analyzing soldiers' diaries, spoken testimonies of victims, and court cases, they observed that there has been almost no debate, either in the Netherlands or in Indonesia, about the violation of Indonesian women by Europeans. As has been done in this article, Scagliola and Vince also connect sexual violence of the decolonization era to colonial sexual politics. They argue that both the Dutch and French colonial regimes featured a long history in which the bodies of colonized women were sexually exploited. It thus seems possible to make a link between prevailing European notions about colonized women and the sexual wrongdoings of European men. But Scagliola and Vince also note that, in both conflicts, European forces recruited local men into colonial armies, who likewise participated in the violation of Indonesian and Algerian women. One of the most depraved and unsettling effects of colonialism is that this system functioned by making the local population complicit; for example, as civil servants in the colonial administration and as recruited men in the colonial army. This observation points out that, in these disturbing times, both the colonizer and the colonized could be perpetrators as well as victims, and—even more confusingly—sometimes could be both at once.

In order to better understand the ways in which sexuality has featured in the late-colonial Dutch East Indies and postcolonial Indonesia, the sometimes opaque or hidden and contradictory manifestations of sexuality should be read alongside each other. Varying from sexual restraint, substitution, transgression, and extreme violence, the colonial context with its embedded inequality between Europeans and Indonesians has influenced both colonizer and colonized in sometimes utterly disturbing ways.

Notes

1 I would like to thank Chelsea Schields for her generous support, valuable suggestions, and careful editing of my text. And to Steven du Pui for sharing a family past in Indonesia. Netherlands Institute of War, Holocaust and Genocide Studies (NIOD), Indies Collection (IC): Jack Scholte. Diary entry October 6, 1943. All original diaries are written in Dutch, translations to English are by the author. Underlining in original.

2 While diaries in general can be characterized as a strictly personal expression, the intention of wartime diaries are a notable exception: most of these are explicitly intended for an audience in order to bear witness and to testify. See Captain, "Written with an Eye on History."

3 Jack Scholte. Diary entry, January 2, 1944.

4 Jack Scholte. Diary entry October 26, 1944. Emphasis in original.

5 Bourke, *Pain and the Politics of Sympathy.*

6 McClintock, *Imperial Leather*; Stoler, *Race and the Education of Desire*; Young, *Colonial Desire.*

7 Aldrich, *Colonialism and Homosexuality.*

8 Boelstorff, *Gay Archipelago.*

9 Raben, "Epilogue," 487.

10 Gelman Taylor, *The Social World of Batavia.*

11 Captain, "The Lady and the Gentleman."

12 Captain, "Harmless Identities."

13 Aldrich, *Colonialism and Homosexuality*, 163.

14 Boellstorff, *Gay Archipelago,* 36–37.

15 Captain and Jones, "The Netherlands."

16 Gouda, *Dutch Culture Overseas*, 114.

17 Jack Scholte. Diary entry January 5, 1943.

18 Private property of family of Adrianus Kruyt. Diary entry January 15, 1943.

19 Elisabeth de Jong-Keesing. Diary entry December 12, 1943.

20 Isenia, "Looking for *Kambrada.*"

21 Frits Bos. Diary entry June 4, 1942.

22 Private property of family of Mary Brückel-Beiten. Diary entry August 10, 1944.

23 Ibid. Diary entry December 20, 1944.

24 Luyckx, *Het verbluffende kamp*, 35.

25 O'Herne, *Fifty Years of Silence.*

26 Stoler, *Race and the Education*, 52.

27 Limpach, *Brandende kampongs*, 150. Translation by the author.

28 Ibid., 146.

29 Ibid., 150–151.

30 Bussemaker, *Opstand*, 138. Translation by the author.

31 Ibid., 109.

32 L.R. Oldeman.

33 Moscou-de Ruyter. Also in print as: Moscou-de Ruyter, *Vogelvrij*, 201.

34 Felman and Laub, *Testimony.*

35 Branche, "Sexual Violence."

36 For a similar argument, see Schields, "Eros against Empire."

37 Branche, "Sexual Violence"; Elkins, *Imperial Reckoning.*

38 Scagliola and Vince, "Verkrachting tijdens."

Bibliography

Aldrich, Robert. *Colonialism and Homosexuality.* London and New York: Routledge, 2003.

Boellstorff, Tom. *The Gay Archipelago. Sexuality and Nation in Indonesia.* Princeton, NJ: Princeton University Press, 2003.

Bourke, Joanne. *Pain and the Politics of Sympathy, Historical Reflections 1760s to 1960s.* Utrecht: University of Utrecht, 2003.

Branche, Raphaëlle. "Sexual Violence in the Algerian War." In *Brutality and Desire: War and Sexuality in Europe's Twentieth Century*, edited by Dagmar Herzog, 247–260. New York: Palgrave Macmillan, 2008.

Bussemaker, Herman. *Bersiap! Opstand in het paradijs. De Bersiap-periode op Java en Sumatra 1945–1946.* Zutphen: Walburg Pers, 2005.

Captain, Esther. "'Written with an Eye on History': Wartime Diaries of Internees as Testimonies of Captivity Literature." In *Tydskrif vir Nederlands and Afrikaans* 5, no. 1 (1998): 1–20.

Captain, Esther. "The Lady and the Gentleman. Constructions of European-ness in the Diaries of Civilian Internees in the Dutch East Indies." In *Recalling the Indies. Colonial Culture and Postcolonial Identities*, edited by Joost Coté and Loes Westerbeek, 205–226. Amsterdam: Aksant, 2005.

Captain, Esther. "Harmless Identities. Representations of Racial Consciousness among Three Generations of Indo-Europeans." In *Dutch Racism*, edited by Philomena Essed and Isabel Hoving, 53–69. Amsterdam: Rodopi, 2014.

Captain, Esther and Guno Jones. "The Netherlands: A Small Country with Imperial Ambitions." In *The Age of Empires. Overseas Empires in the Early Modern and Modern World*, edited by Robert Aldridge, 92–111. London: Thames and Hudson, 2007.

Colpani, Gianmaria and Wigbertson Julian Isenia. "Editorial: Imperial Entanglements and Archival Desires." *Tijdschrift voor Genderstudies* 22, no. 2 (2019): 113–124. doi:10.5117/tvgn2019.2.001.colp.

Elkins, Caroline, *Imperial Reckoning. The Untold Story of Britain's Gulug in Kenya.* New York: Henry Holt and Company, 2005.

Felman, Shoshana and Dori Laub. *Testimony. Crisis of Witnessing in Literature, Pyschoanalysis and History.* New York: Routledge, 1992.

Gelman Taylor, Jean. *The Social World of Batavia. European and Eurasian in Dutch Asia.* Madison, WI: University of Wisconsin Press, 1983.

Gouda, Frances. *Dutch Culture Overseas. Colonial Practice in the Netherlands Indies 19001–1942.* Amsterdam: Amsterdam University Press, 1995.

Isenia, Wigbertson Julian. "Looking for *Kambrada*. Sexuality and Social Anxieties in the Dutch Colonial Archive, 1992–1923." *Tijdschrift voor Genderstudies* 22, no. 2 (2019): 113–124. doi:10.5117/tvgn2019.2.002.isen.

Limpach, Rémy. *De brandende kampongs van Generaal Spoor.* Amsterdam: Boom, 2016.

Luyckx, K. *Het verbluffende kamp.* Den Haag: Stok, 1946.

McClintock, Anne. *Imperial Leather. Race, Gender and Sexuality in the Colonial Contest.* New York and London: Routledge, 1995.

Moscou-de Ruyter, M. *Vogelvrij. Het leven buiten de kampen 1942–1945.* Weesp: Fibula-Van Dischoeck, 1984.

Raben, Remco, "Epilogue: On Genocide and Mass Violence in Colonial Indonesia." *Journal of Genocide Research* 14, no. 3/4 (2012): 485–502. doi:10.1080/14623528.2012.719673.

Ruff O'Herne, Jeanne. *Fifty Years of Silence.* New York: Tom Thompson, 1994.

Schields, Chelsea. "Eros against Empire: Visions of Erotic Freedom in Archives of Decolonization." *Tijdschrift voor Genderstudies* 22, no. 2, 2019, 145–162. doi:10.5117/tvgn2019.2.003.schi.

Stef, Scagliola and Natalya Vince. "Verkrachting tijdens de Indonesische en Algerijnse onafhankelijkheidsoorlogen. Motieven, contexten en politiek." *BMGN – Low Countries Historical Review* 135, nr. 2 (2020): 72–92. doi:10.18352/bmgn-lchr.10818/.

Stoler, Ann Laura. *Race and the Education of Desire: Foucault's History of Sexuality and the Colonial Order of Things.* Durham, NC: Duke University Press, 1995.

Wieringa, S.E. "Discursive Contestations Concerning Intersex in Indonesia: Stigma, Rights and Identities." In *Sex and Sexualities in Contemporary Indonesia: Sexual Politics, Health, Diversity and Representations*, edited by L.R. Bennett and S.G. Davies, 169–192. Oxford, UK: Routledge, 2015.

Young, Robert. *Colonial Desire. Hybridity in Theory, Culture and Race.* London and New York: Routledge, 1995.

INDEX

Made in the USA
Middletown, DE
11 October 2023

40602470R00216